THEMATIC CATALOGUE OF THE WORKS OF
CARL PHILIPP EMANUEL BACH

Thematic Catalogue of the Works of Carl Philipp Emanuel Bach

E. EUGENE HELM

Yale University Press
New Haven and London

This publication has been supported by a subvention from the American Musicological Society.

Set in Palatino type by the Hornseth Company. Printed in the United States of America by Thomson-Shore, Inc., Dexter, Michigan.

The paper in this book meets the guidelines for permanence and durability of the Committee on Production Guidelines for Book Longevity of the Council on Library Resources.

Library of Congress Cataloging-in-Publication Data

Helm, E. Eugene.
   Thematic catalogue of the works of Carl Philipp Emanuel Bach.
   Bibliography: p.
   Includes indexes.
   1. Bach, Carl Philipp Emanuel, 1714–1788—Thematic catalogs.
I. Title.
ML134.B08A2 1987   780'.92'4   86-30771
ISBN 0-300-02654-4 (alk. paper)

10 9 8 7 6 5 4 3 2 1

To Sallie

Contents

How to Use This Catalogue: A Typical Item   ix

Preface   xi

General Abbreviations and Library Sigla   xiii

Index of Performance Media   xvi

Index of Genres   xviii

Introduction
Background   xix
Details of the Cataloguing Procedure   xxv

Catalogue

Instrumental
For Keyboard Instrument Alone
Authentic   3
Possibly Authentic   71
Doubtful   74
Spurious   78
Concertos and Sonatinas
Authentic   84
Possibly Authentic   103
Doubtful   105
Spurious   107
Chamber Music with a Leading Keyboard Part
Authentic   109
Possibly Authentic   117
Spurious   118
Solo Sonatas for Wind or String Instruments
Authentic   118
Possibly Authentic   122
Trio Sonatas
Authentic   123
Possibly Authentic   128
Doubtful   129
Other Chamber Music
Authentic   130
Doubtful   139
Spurious   140
Symphonies
Authentic   141
Possibly Authentic   146
Spurious   146

Vocal
For Solo Voice(s) (Songs with Keyboard
Accompaniment, Unless Stated Otherwise)
Authentic   147
Possibly Authentic   174

Major Choral Works   175
Choral Works for Special Occasions
Passions   187
Easter Cantatas   199
Michaelmas Cantatas   202
Christmas Cantatas   204
Other Church Cantatas   205
Inauguration Cantatas   207
Other Congratulatory Cantatas, Part A   218
Other Congratulatory Cantatas, Part B   221
Individual Choruses   223
Chorale Settings   226
Other Individual Movements of Choral Works;
Fragments   227
Doubtful   228
Spurious   229

Theoretical
Authentic   231
Possibly Authentic   232
Spurious   232

Guide to Early Prints Entirely by C. P. E. Bach,
in Order of First Publication   233

Guide to Early Prints Containing Music of
C. P. E. Bach with Music of Other Composers,
in Order of First Publication   235

Works Not Listed in Wotquenne's Thematic
Catalogue (Wotquenne Thématique)
Rachel W. Wade   237

Index of Names of Persons in Special References
Rachel W. Wade   242

Corrections of Work-List in *The New Grove
Dictionary of Music and Musicians* (1980)   247

Concordance of Wotquenne Numbers (W.)
with Item Numbers in This Catalogue (H.)   250

Concordance of Numbers in Kast, *Die Bach-Handschriften* (Wq n.v.) with Item Numbers in This Catalogue (H.)   254

Bibliography   255

How to Use This Catalogue:
A Typical Item[1]

(Numbers in superscript refer to the explanation below.)

138.[2] Sonata.[3] 1759[4] (NV 15).[5] W. 50/3[6]

Mss.: D-brd B, P 790; D-ddr Bds, P 1135 (largely autog. and Michel, containing only rev.: see item 164); B Bc, 5885 (Michel, containing only rev.: see item 164); D-brd Kll, Mb 43[7]

Early prints and lit. about them: See REPRISEN-SONATEN.[8]

Mss. probably copied from an early print: D-brd B, P 773, P 785, BP 143; B Bc, 5874; D-ddr LEm, Poel. Mus. ms. 42; a ms. is in the private collection of E. N. Kulukundis (U.S.).[9]

Mod. edns.: DARBELLAY, HASHIMOTO/REPRISEN, BERG/FACSIMILE[10]

Lit. about this work: BITTER/BRÜDER, I, 74–76; CLERCX, 161; BEURMANN/KLAVIERSONATEN, 111, 114; BARFORD/AFTERTHOUGHTS, 95–96; NEWMAN, 420, 425; RADCLIFFE, 586; SCHULENBERG/INSTRUMENTAL, 6, 24–25[11]

Vnt. of the 3rd mvt.: item 334[12]

See item 24.[12]

Incipits from REPRISEN-SONATEN:[13]

Explanation of the typical item

(See the Bibliography for full listings of the titles abbreviated below. See pp. xxv–xxvii for details of the cataloguing procedure.)

1. Items are arranged by medium of performance (Keyboard Instrument Alone; Concertos, Sonatinas; Chamber Music with a Leading Keyboard Part; and so forth). Within these categories they are subdivided into "Authentic," "Possibly Authentic," "Doubtful," and "Spurious" (see Classifications of Authenticity, pp. xxv–xxvi); and within each subdivision they are arranged chronologically. See the table of contents (pp. vii–viii).

2. Item number in this catalogue. Some numbers are decimalized, and others are marked "Deleted," for the author's convenience in cataloguing and to accommodate future revisions. This has no other significance.

3. Title, subtitle, or first line of text. Where the performance medium is not obvious, it is indicated in square brackets as an addition to the title. For vocal works, the name of the author of the text, if known or if not obvious from the title, appears in parentheses.

4. Date of composition, if not already given after a collective title. "N.d." (no date) means the date is unknown.

5. Source of the date of composition. In the illustration the date comes from NV (NACHLASS-VERZEICHNIS; see General Abbreviations and Library Sigla), page (not item number) xiv.

6. Number in W. (WOTQUENNE/THÉMATIQUE; see General Abbreviations and Library Sigla) if listed there, or reference to number, page, key, and so on in other important listings, if any. A number or letter after a virgule is a subitem in WOTQUENNE/THÉMATIQUE, where it is unnumbered.

7. List of manuscript sources, if any, apparently not copied from an early print and mainly originating before 1800. Some explanation precedes this list in a few cases.

The illustration shows that in D-brd B (the RISM siglum for West Berlin, Staatsbibliothek Stiftung Preussischer Kulturbesitz, Musikabteilung; see General Abbreviations and Library Sigla) the work is contained in a manuscript whose catalogue number there is P 790. In D-ddr Bds (East Berlin, Deutsche Staatsbibliothek, Musikabteilung), revisions of this sonata are to be found in manuscript P 1135; this manuscript has the additional distinction of being largely in the hands of the composer and his chief Hamburg copyist, Michel. It has some connection with item 164 of this catalogue. In B Bc (Brussels, Conservatoire Royal de Musique, Bibliothèque), revisions of this sonata are present in manuscript 5885; this time the copying has been done entirely by Michel, and again there is a connection with item 164. D-brd Kll (Kiel, Schleswig-Holsteinische Landesbibliothek) owns a manuscript copy of this work, catalogued there as Mb 43.

8. List of early prints, if any, and literature about them, if any, along with an occasional descriptive annotation. This information may appear fully here, or, more frequently, a siglum (for example, REPRISEN-SONATEN in the illustration) will refer the reader to the Bibliography in order to avoid excessive repetition and cross-referencing. REPRISEN-SONATEN is a bibliographical entry containing information and references to literature (for example, HAMBURGER CORRESPONDENT, which, in turn, has its own entry in the Bibliography) about various early published collections containing this work, along with a complete list of the C. P. E. Bach works in these collections. "Lit. about" an all-C. P. E. Bach collection deals with the whole collection, but "lit. about" a collection also containing the music of other composers naturally concentrates on only C. P. E. Bach's music in that collection. "Lit." usually means discussion, not merely a listing or a mention. To locate individual exemplars of original prints, either of single works or as part of collections, the reader is referred to RISM, volumes A/I/1 and B II.

9. Manuscripts, if any, probably copied from an early print, as this may be indicated by the title page of a manuscript, a table of contents in a manuscript, a manuscript's resemblance to the format of the print, or the existence, in certain manuscript copies, of all or much of a well-known printed set.

10. Modern editions, if any. As in No. 8 above, a modern edition may be listed fully here, or a siglum (for example, DARBELLAY in the illustration) may refer the reader to the Bibliography, where full publishing information will be found, along with an occasional descriptive annotation.

11. Literature about this individual work, if any, listed in approximately chronological order. This "lit." may overlap that listed in No. 8 above. Again, sigla (for example, BITTER/BRÜDER) refer to the Bibliography.

12. Other information or comments, if any; for example, in the illustration notice is given that item 334 lists a variant of the third movement of this sonata and that there is a connection with item 24.

13. Incipits of all movements (or of the first movement only for some spurious works), listed in order with an indication of their specific source (for example, REPRISEN-SONATEN in the illustration). The main melody is quoted, usually from the opening bars.

14. The name of the instrument or voice whose part is being quoted, if it is not obvious. The name is given exactly as it appears. When provided by the author, it is enclosed in square brackets. A few incipits borrowed from secondary sources do not designate the part being quoted.

Preface

The main purpose of this catalogue is to provide a detailed account of the complete works of Carl Philipp Emanuel Bach (1714–1788), the "Berlin" or "Hamburg" Bach, a composer more widely known before the nineteenth century than any other member of any of the seven generations of this famous family, including his father, Johann Sebastian. I have tried to list all of Emanuel Bach's known works chronologically within categories, with incipits of all movements, and with information about manuscripts, early prints, authenticity, relations among works, and whatever else scholars and prospective editors might find useful.

The complete critical edition begun at the University of Maryland in 1983 is based on this book.

To all the librarians and collectors in Europe and America who have allowed me to use their resources, my sincere thanks. Twelve librarians occupy positions of such central importance to this study, and have been so generous in making their C. P. E. Bach materials available to me over the years, that their help must be acknowledged here by name: Rudolf Elvers and Joachim Jaenecke of the Music Division of the Staatsbibliothek Preussischer Kulturbesitz in West Berlin, and Heinz Ramge, formerly of that division; Wolfgang Goldhan of the Music Division of the Deutsche Staatsbibliothek in East Berlin, and Karl-Heinz Köhler, formerly of that division; Paul Raspé, Andrée Martiny, Julien De Vuyst, and the late Albert Vander Linden of the Brussels Conservatory Library; Bernard Huys of the Music Division of the Bibliothèque Royale in Brussels; Hedwig Mitringer of the Library of the Gesellschaft der Musikfreunde in Vienna; and Franz Grasberger of the Oesterreichische Nationalbibliothek in Vienna.

The fundamental support of the Universities of Iowa and Maryland and their graduate schools, as well as the National Endowment for the Humanities, is here gratefully acknowledged. By keeping me at Maryland, Eugene Troth saved my summers for research. Most of all I thank my wife Sallie, whose help and encouragement have been indispensable and whose forbearance has been endless.

Nearly every page of this catalogue owes something to the present generation of C. P. E. Bach specialists, in two ways: through their reading of the manuscript in various stages of completion and through my extensive use of their own researches. Without the careful criticisms of Gudrun Busch, Rachel Wade, Darrell Berg, Stephen Clark, Jane Stevens, Miriam Terry, Elinor Elder, David Schulenberg, Pamela Fox, and Michelle Fillion, the errors and omissions would have multiplied disastrously. Without their writings on Emanuel Bach—along with those of such scholars as C. H. Bitter, Heinrich Miesner, Ernst Fritz Schmid, Erich Beurmann, Georg von Dadelsen, Paul Kast, Renate Blechschmidt, and Ernst Suchalla—the spadework would have been interminable. Rachel Wade has not only provided the backbone of the concerto section, along with the list of works not in Wotquenne and the index of names, but has also been my chief guide. Her discovery in 1986 of a major body of previously overlooked manuscripts has prevented a glaring lacuna.

The readers of this catalogue who are not C. P. E. Bach specialists have suggested looking at the forest as well as the trees. The observations of James Webster have drastically improved the entire manuscript. William S. Newman, Howard Serwer, Jens Peter Larsen, Alexander Metro, and the late Donald M. McCorkle have caused fundamental changes for the better in organization, cataloguing procedure, format, and language. And in the matter of relating it all to the outside world, my thanks go to Margit Lundstrom McCorkle (especially for aid in finding a publisher), Shelley Davis and Gary Hill (who have shared their library research with me), Cecelia H. Porter, Charles Timbrell, and Cecilia Dunoyer.

A book so full of detail and so wide in coverage is likely still to contain more than the usual number of mistakes and omissions. Information about these will be welcomed and incorporated in most instances, with appropriate credit, in any further editions.

University of Maryland

General Abbreviations
and Library Sigla

See the Bibliography for sigla, names, titles, publishing information, and other material not in this list. Abbreviations for names of libraries are the sigla of RISM (International Inventory of Musical Sources). Capital and lowercase letters designate major and minor keys, respectively.

A	Alto voice
Accomp.	Accompanied recitative
A Gd	Graz, Bibliothek des Bischöflichen Seckauer Ordinariats (Diözese Graz-Seckau)
A M	Melk an der Donau, Benediktiner-Stift Melk
AMZ	Allgemeine musikalische Zeitung (Leipzig, 1798–1849)
Anh.	Anhang
Anon.	Anonymous
Arr.	Arranged, arrangement(s). The composer's own work arranged by him *for a new medium of performance.* Cf. "A.v.," "Rev.," and "Vnt." in this list of abbreviations.
A SL	St. Lambrecht, Benediktiner-Abtei
Autog.	Autograph manuscript
A.v.	Alternate version(s). One or more works or movements *in a different medium of performance,* related to another work by C. P. E. Bach. Unlike the abbreviation "Arr.," "a.v." by itself does not imply authenticity, chronology, or composer-preference. An a.v. may be listed as authentic, possibly authentic, doubtful, or spurious. The chronology of an a.v. may or may not be known; the a.v. is listed in the catalogue accordingly. When it has been discovered that an apparent a.v. is actually the composer's later version, it is of course categorized as "arr." rather than "a.v." Cf. "Arr.," "Rev.," and "Vnt." in this list of abbreviations.
A Wgm	Vienna, Gesellschaft der Musikfreunde, Archiv
A Wn	Vienna, Oesterreichische Nationalbibliothek (formerly K. K. Hofbibliothek), Musiksammlung

A Wst	Vienna, Stadtbibliothek, Musiksammlung
A Z	Zwettl, Zisterzienser-Stift, Bibliothek und Musikarchiv
B	Bass Voice
B Bc	Brussels, Conservatoire Royal de Musique, Bibliothèque
B Br	Brussels, Bibliothèque Royale Albert 1er
Beurm.-Anh.	Works listed in the "Anhang" of BEURMANN/KLAVIERSONATEN (see Bibliography) as previously undiscovered
Bib.	Bibliography of this catalogue
BWV	Item numbers in SCHMIEDER (see Bibliography)
c.	Circa
Cant.	Canto, cantus (soprano voice)
Cemb.	Cembalo
CH BEl	Bern, Schweizerische Landesbibliothek, Musikabteilung
CH Bub	Basel, Öffentliche Bibliothek der Universität Basel, Musiksammlung
CH E	Einsiedeln, Kloster Einsiedeln, Musikbibliothek
CH Zz	Zürich, Zentralbibliothek
Clar.	Clarinet
Clav.	Clavier
CS Bm	Brno, Moravské múzeum-hud. hist. oddělení
CS KRa	Kroměříž, Zamecký hudební archív
CS Pk	Prague, Archív Státní konservatore v Praze
CS Pnm	Prague, Národní múzeum-hud. oddělení
Disc., Disk.	Discant, diskant (soprano voice)
D-brd B	West Berlin, Staatsbibliothek Preussischer Kulturbesitz, Musikabteilung
D-brd Bch	West Berlin, Musikbücherei Charlottenburg
D-brd BFb	Burgsteinfurt, Fürstlich Bentheimsche Bibliothek
D-brd Bhm	West Berlin, Staatliche Hochschule für Musik und darstellende Kunst
D-brd BNba	Bonn, Beethovenarchiv
D-brd BNu	Bonn, Universitätsbibliothek
D-brd DS	Darmstadt, Hessische Landes- und Hochschulbibliothek (formerly Grossherzoglich Hessische Hofmusik-bibliothek; Grossher-

D-brd DS	zoglich Hessische Hof- und Landesbibliothek), Musikabteilung
D-brd Gs	Göttingen, Niedersächsische Staats- und Universitätsbibliothek
D-brd Ha	Hamburg, Staatsarchiv
D-brd Hs	Hamburg, Staats- und Universitätsbibliothek, Musikabteilung
D-brd Hth	Hamburg, Universität Hamburg, Theatersammlung
D-brd HVs	Hannover, Stadtbibliothek, Musikabteilung (Sammlung Kestner)
D-brd KIl	Kiel, Schleswig-Holsteinische Landesbibliothek
D-brd Kl	Kassel, Murhardsche Bibliothek d. Stadt Kassel und Landesbibliothek
D-brd KNu	Cologne, Universitäts- und Stadtbibliothek (with the former Gymnasialbibliothek)
D-brd LB	Langenburg (Württemberg), Fürstlich Hohenlohe-Langenburg'sche Schlossbibliothek
D-brd LÜh	Lübeck, Bibliothek der Hansestadt Lübeck (formerly Stadtbibliothek der Freien und Hansestadt Lübeck), Musikabteilung
D-brd Mbs	Munich, Bayerische Staatsbibliothek (formerly Königliche Hof- und Staatsbibliothek), Musiksammlung
D-brd Ngm	Nürnberg, Germanisches Nationalmuseum, Bibliothek
D-brd Nst	Nürnberg, Stadtbibliothek
D-brd Rtt	Regensburg (Bayern), Fürstlich Thurn und Taxissche Hofbibliothek
D-brd RH	Rheda (Nordrhein-Westfalen), Fürst zu Bentheim-Tecklenburgische Bibliothek (taken over from the Universitätsbibliothek Münster)
D-brd SAAmi	Saarbrücken, Musikwissenschaftliches Institut der Universität des Saarlandes
D-brd Sl	Stuttgart, Württembergische Landesbibliothek (formerly Königliche Hofbibliothek) (Samml. Kraus)
D-ddr ARk	Arnstadt (Thüringen), Kirchenbibliothek
D-ddr Bds	East Berlin, Deutsche Staatsbibliothek (formerly Königliche Bibliothek; Preussische Staatsbibliothek; Oeffentliche Wissenschaftliche Bibliothek), Musikabteilung
D-ddr Dlb	Dresden, Sächsische Landesbibliothek, Musikabteilung (formerly Königliche Oeffentliche Bibliothek)
D-ddr GOl	Gotha (Thüringen), Forschungsbibliothek (formerly Landesbibliothek; Herzogliche Bibliothek)
D-ddr HER	Herrnhut, Archiv der Brüder-Unität
D-ddr LEb	Leipzig, Bach-Archiv
D-ddr LEm	Musikbibliothek der Stadt Leipzig (Musikbibliothek Peters and various collections in the Leipzig Stadtbibliothek)
D-ddr MEIr	Meiningen, Regerarchiv
D-ddr ROu	Rostock, Universitätsbibliothek
D-ddr SWl	Schwerin (Mecklenburg), Mecklenburgische Landesbibliothek (formerly Mecklenburgische Regierungsbibliothek), Musikabteilung
D-ddr WRgm	Weimar, Goethe National-Museum
D-ddr WRgs	Weimar, Goethe-Schiller Archiv
D-ddr WRiv	Weimar, Institut für Volksmusikforschung (formerly Institut für Volksliedforschung)
D-ddr WRtl	Weimar, Thüringische Landesbibliothek (formerly Grossherzogliche Bibliothek), Musiksammlung. Since 1969 this collection has been housed in the Zentralbibliothek der deutschen Klassik, Weimar.
DK As	Århus, Statsbiblioteket
DK Kk	Copenhagen, Det kongelige Bibliotek
DK Kmk	Copenhagen, Det kongelige danske Musikkonservatorium
CPEB	Carl Philipp Emanuel Bach
Ed.	Edited, editor
Edn(s).	Edition(s)
Ex.	Example
Fl.	Flute
F Pc	Paris, Bibliothèque du conservatoire national de musique. In 1964 the most valuable parts, including the CPEB mss., were transferred to the Bibliothèque nationale, Paris.
F Pn	Paris, Bibliothèque nationale
F Sim	Strasbourg, Institut de musicologie de l'Université
GB Lbm	London, British Library (British Museum)
H Bn	Budapest, Országos Széchényi Könyvtár (Széchényi National Library)
Jg.	Jahrgang
JSB	Johann Sebastian Bach
Lit.	Literature about a single work or a collection of works, as listed in both the main text and the Bibliography
Mod. edn(s).	Modern edition(s)
Ms(s).	Manuscript(s)
Mvt(s).	Movement(s)
N.d.	No date
NL DHgm	The Hague, Gemeente Museum
No(s).	Number(s)
NV	NACHLASS-VERZEICHNIS (see Bibliography)
Ob.	Oboe
p.	Page
Pl Kj	Kraków, Biblioteka Jagiellońska
PL Wn	Warsaw, Biblioteka Narodowa
PL WRu	Wrocław (Breslau), Biblioteka Uniwersytecka
PL Wu	Warsaw, Biblioteka Uniwersytecka
Pub(s).	Published, publication(s)
Rev(s).	Revised, revision(s). One or more works or movements *in the same medium of performance*, representing C. P. E. Bach's correction of the musical text, implying a rejection of his original idea (and thus consisting of more

Rev(s).	than just a few different notes here and there). Cf. "A.v.," "Arr.," and "Vnt." in this list of abbreviations.
RISM	Répertoire international des sources musicales (see Bibliography)
S	Soprano voice
SL	Lund, Universitetsbiblioteket
S Skma	Stockholm, Kungliga Musikaliska Akademiens Bibliotek
T, Ten.	Tenor voice
ten.	Tenuto
Tpt.	Trumpet
Trans.	Translator, translated
US AA	Ann Arbor, University of Michigan, Music Library
US BE	Berkeley, University of California, Music Library
US BETm	Bethlehem, Pennsylvania, Archives of the Moravian Church in Bethlehem (Northern Province Archives)
US Bp	Boston, Boston Public Library, Music Department
US CA	Cambridge, Library of Harvard University
US NHu	New Haven, Yale University, The Library of the School of Music
US NYp	New York, New York Public Library at Lincoln Center
USSR KA	Kaliningrad (Königsberg), Oblastnaja biblioteka (see note in item 192)
US Wc	Washington, Library of Congress, Music Division
US WS	Winston-Salem, Moravian Music Archive
Vla.	Viola
Vln.	Violin
Vnt(s).	Variant(s). One or more works *in the same medium of performance*, related to another work by C. P. E. Bach, containing at least one different *passage* rather than merely a few different notes here and there. Unlike the abbreviation "rev.," "vnt." by itself does not imply authenticity, chronology, or composer-preference. A vnt. may be listed as authentic, possibly authentic, doubtful, or spurious. The chronology of a vnt. may or may not be known; the vnt. is listed in the catalogue accordingly. Where it has been discovered that an apparent vnt. is both a later version and the composer's preferred version, it is of course categorized as "rev." rather than "vnt." Cf. "arr.," "a.v.," and "rev." in this list of abbreviations.
W.	Item numbers in WOTQUENNE/THÉMATIQUE (see Bibliography). Numbers after the virgule are subitems unnumbered by Wotquenne.
Wq n.v.	Numbers assigned in KAST (see Bibliography) to works not listed ("nicht verzeichnet") by Wotquenne
=	Is the same composition as

Index of Performance Media
by Item Number

One instrument alone
Keyboard, 1–402
Keyboard, right or left hand alone, 241
Keyboard, bowed, 280
Organ, 53, 84–87, 102, 107, 133–35, 336, 345, 350, 352
Flute, 562
Harp, 386, 563
Glass harmonica, 74, 75

Instrumental duet without continuo
2 keyboards, 610–13
Flute, violin, 598, 640
2 violins, 599
2 clarinets, 636
Glass harmonica, cello, 643

Instrumental trio without continuo
2 violins, viola, 644
2 violins, piano, 646

Instrumental quartet without continuo
3 trumpets, timpani, 621
Oboe, 3 unspecified instruments, 639

Instrumental quintet without continuo
2 horns, 2 clarinets, bassoon, 620
2 horns, 2 oboes, bassoon, 637

Instrumental septet without continuo
2 horns, 2 flutes, 2 clarinets, bassoon, 629–34
2 horns, 2 oboes, 2 clarinets, bassoon, 614–19

One instrument plus continuo
Flute, continuo, 548, 550–56, 560–61, 564, 564.5, 565, 578, 628
Violin, continuo, 578, 579, 628
Oboe, continuo, 549
Cello, continuo, 557
Viola da gamba, continuo, 558, 559

Two instruments plus continuo
Flute, violin, continuo, 567–75, 578, 581, 586, 590.5, 592, 593, 595–97, 600
2 flutes, continuo, 580
2 violins, continuo, 576, 577, 579, 582–85, 587, 590, 591, 592, 605, 607, 609, 627
Violin, viola, continuo, 566
Viola, bass recorder, continuo, 588

Bassoon, bass recorder, continuo, 589

Three instruments plus continuo
Violin, flute, viola, continuo, 641, 642

Four instruments plus continuo
Flute, oboe, violin, viola, continuo, 645
2 clarinets, 2 violins, continuo, 604

Six instruments plus continuo
2 clarinets, 2 horns, 2 violins, continuo, 608
2 clarinets, 2 flutes, 2 violins, continuo, 602, 603
2 horns, 2 flutes, 2 violins, continuo, 623–26

Seven instruments plus continuo
2 horns, 2 flutes, 2 violins, bassoon, continuo, 622

Eight instruments plus continuo
2 clarinets, 2 horns, 2 flutes, 2 violins, continuo, 606

Ten instruments plus continuo
3 trumpets, timpani, 2 flutes, 2 bassoons, 2 violins, continuo, 601

Thirteen instruments plus continuo
3 trumpets, timpani, 2 horns, 2 oboes, 2 flutes, 2 violins, viola, continuo, 638

One instrument plus written-out keyboard part
Keyboard obbligato, flute, 505, 506, 508, 509, 515, 545
Keyboard obbligato, violin, 502–04, 507, 511–14, 535, 536, 542–44
Keyboard obbligato, viola, 541
Keyboard obbligato, viola da gamba, 510
Keyboard obbligato, melody instrument(s), 540

Two instruments plus written-out keyboard part
Keyboard obbligato, violin, cello, 522–34
Keyboard obbligato, violin, bass instrument, 546, 547
Keyboard obbligato, clarinet, bassoon, 516–21

Three instruments plus written-out keyboard part
Keyboard obbligato, flute, viola, bass instrument, 537–39

Orchestra
497, 647–68

Orchestra plus one or two solo instruments
Keyboard, orchestra, 403–07, 409–25, 427–30, 433, 434, 437, 440–44, 446–52, 454–58, 460–65, 467, 469–78, 480–481.5, 483, 484, 484.2–490, 492, 494–96, 498–501

Organ, orchestra, 444, 446
2 keyboards, orchestra, 408, 453, 459, 479
Flute, orchestra, 431, 435, 438, 445, 482, 484.1
Cello, orchestra, 432, 436, 439
Oboe, orchestra, 466, 468
Violin, orchestra, 497
Viola, orchestra, 497
Glass harmonica, orchestra, 491, 493

Vocal soloist(s), keyboard
670–96, 698–721, 724–38, 739.5–760, 763–66, 768–71

Vocal soloist, small instrumental ensemble
Soprano, 2 violins, viola, 859
Soprano, 2 flutes, continuo, 767
Soprano, 2 violins, viola, continuo, 761
Tenor, 2 violins, viola, continuo, 669, 723
Soprano, 2 flutes, 2 violins, viola, continuo, 739

2 vocal soloists, small instrumental ensemble
2 sopranos, continuo, 762

2 sopranos, 2 flutes, continuo, 697

4 vocal soloists, orchestra
699

A cappella chorus
773, 839, 840, 842, 845, 860, 865, 866

Chorus, continuo
774, 780, 781, 825, 826, 843, 844

Chorus, orchestra
827–38, 855, 856, 861

Chorus, vocal soloist(s), orchestra
772, 775–79, 782–805, 807–12, 814–24e, 847, 848, 850, 854,
862–64, 866.5

Miscellaneous
Musical clock, 635
Barrel organ, 635

Index of Genres by Item Number

Allemande, 66, 390

Aria, 125, 390, 669, 685, 761, 767, 770, 818.5, 859, 866.5. *See also* Cantata, choral; Cantata, solo; Magnificat; Oratorio; Passion

Arietta, 371.7, 767

Arioso, 54, 194, 351, 535

Cadenza, 264

Canon, 76, 867

Cantata, choral, 776–79, 803–05, 807–12, 814–24, 850, 854, 855, 859, 863–64, 866.5

Cantata, solo, 688, 697, 723, 735, 739, 739.5

Canzonetta, 275, 770

Character piece, 79–82, 89–98, 109–14, 122–25, 143, 272, 333, 374, 392–392.5

Chorale, 336, 337, 357, 376, 393, 394, 639, 733, 775, 776, 781–83, 785, 787, 789–91, 793, 795–97, 798–805, 807, 810, 812, 814, 815, 821, 822, 842–45, 860. *See also* Part song

Concerto, 190, 242, 383, 384, 403–25, 427–48, 454, 465–79, 481–90, 492, 494–501

Courante, 66, 390

Divertimento, 641, 642, 668

Fantasia, 75, 75.5, 144, 146, 148, 160, 195, 223–25, 234, 277–79, 284, 289, 291, 300, 348, 349, 371.8, 536, 639

Fugue, fughetta, 75.5, 76, 99–102, 285, 349, 350, 360, 371.9–373.5, 377.5, 388–389.6, 867

Gigue, 66, 390, 390.5, 395

Litany, 780

Magnificat, 772

March, 1, 319, 320, 614–19, 621, 635, 637

Mass, 848, 861

Minuet, 1.5, 14, 44, 66, 80, 159, 165, 167, 169, 171, 196, 214, 216, 218, 231, 258, 303–07, 309, 314, 321, 322, 375, 375.5, 390, 397, 398, 399, 600–03, 606, 622–26, 628, 635, 638

Motet, 825, 826, 856, 865, 866

Murky, 81

Oratorio, 775, 777, 779, 822a, 822c, 847, 862

Part song, chorus, 773, 774, 778, 827–41, 855, 857, 858. *See also* Chorale

Partita, 390

Passion, 776, 782–802, 863

Polonaise, 1, 79, 122, 154, 166, 168, 170, 172, 197, 199, 215, 217, 219, 232, 233, 308, 315–18, 323, 340, 353–55, 380, 396, 600, 604, 605, 607–09, 627, 628, 635

Prelude, 107, 357, 371.9, 389.5, 390, 390.5

Program music, 386, 579, 646

Recitative, 818.5, 850, 854. *See also* Cantata, choral; Cantata, solo; Magnificat; Oratorio; Passion

Romance, 226

Rondeau, 89

Rondo, 260–62, 265–68, 271, 272, 274, 276, 283, 288, 290

Sarabande, 66

Serenata, 822b, 822d

Solfeggio, 145, 147, 149, 220–22

Sonata, 2–6, 13, 15–34, 36–43, 46–53, 55–64, 66–68, 70–75, 77, 78, 83–87, 105, 106, 116–21, 126–43, 150–52, 156–58, 161–64, 173–89, 192, 204–13, 240, 243–48, 269, 270, 273, 280–82, 286, 287, 298, 299, 339, 341–47, 358, 359, 362–70, 371.9, 377, 378, 379, 381–83, 385, 387, 502–34, 537–99, 629–34, 636, 640, 643–45. *See also* Trio sonata

Sonatina, 7–12, 292–97, 449–53, 455–64, 480, 480.5, 491, 493

Song, 670–84, 685.5–687, 690–96, 698–721, 724–34, 736–38, 740–60, 762–66, 768–769.5, 771. *See also* Part song

Suite, 66, 390

Symphony, 45, 104, 115, 191, 227, 361, 371, 507, 582, 585, 648–68

Trio, 375.5

Trio sonata, 566–97

Unclassified single movement(s) for instrument(s), 108, 153, 193, 194, 198, 200–03, 228–30, 235–38, 241, 249–57, 301, 302, 310–13, 324–31, 334, 338, 352, 356, 371.5–371.7, 375.5, 391, 400–02, 535, 600, 610–13, 620, 628, 635, 646, 647

Variation, 14, 44, 54, 65, 69, 155, 226, 259, 263, 275, 351, 375, 395, 396, 399, 534, 780, 871

Introduction

BACKGROUND

In writing this catalogue I have searched nearly two hundred libraries in fifteen countries, most of them personally; but in the process I have been guided by many fine scholars. The first of the scholars—the term is appropriate—was Emanuel Bach himself. He began listing his works possibly as early as 1770[1] and was able to provide a summary list quickly in 1773, along with a short autobiographical sketch, when both were requested by the Hamburg publisher J. J. C. Bode as an insertion in the translation of Burney's *Present State of Music in Germany, the Netherlands, and United Provinces* (such insertions were an attempt to counter Burney's unfavorable report on German music).[2] Among the hundreds of letters from Emanuel Bach to J. G. I. Breitkopf of Leipzig, the most important publisher of his works, is a handwritten list of Emanuel's printed compositions made around August of 1786 by Breitkopf, sent to Emanuel for correction, and returned to Breitkopf with Emanuel's disavowal of some titles and addition of others.[3]

In the last few years of his life Emanuel clearly saw the need to pass on to posterity as accurate an idea as possible of what he had created—and almost as important, judging from his letters, what had been falsely ascribed to him. He was also concerned that his heirs reap the greatest possible material benefit from his musical estate. Therefore list-making became a primary concern. As it happened, during 1786–8 a sort of amanuensis for just this purpose

appeared, a man whose avidity to collect every scrap written by or about his favorite composer, in spite of financial sacrifice and family opposition, has had few parallels: J. J. H. Westphal, an obscure organist in the small but musically distinguished town of Schwerin.[4] Emanuel wrote at least twelve letters in 1787–8 (the last known one about a month before his death) to Westphal in response to his requests for compositions, usually by having copies made under his own supervision.[5] These replies are full of assurances that he had composed no more in this or that category, or reminders, on the basis of lists sent by Westphal, that Westphal's collection still had this or that gap. Both musicians were eager collectors of portraits of musicians; in the letters there was much trade in this commodity, and in a letter of August 4, 1787 Emanuel told Westphal that he planned to have a catalogue of his portrait collection printed shortly.[6]

Emanuel admired his correspondent for his order and comprehensiveness, but it is doubtful that he ever realized the intensity of Westphal's collecting-and-cataloguing zeal. For after Emanuel's death Westphal became ever more systematic in acquiring and listing Emanuel's works, largely with the help of the widow and daughter.[7] Two lists—the first begun on the basis of the autobiographical sketch that had appeared in 1773, and the second a chronological rearrangement of the first—are found, among a rich assortment of other information, in a written-out and pasted-up manuscript in Westphal's hand entitled *Gesammlete* [sic] *Nachrichten von dem Leben und den Werken des Herrn Carl Philipp*

---

1. CPEB/1770. Among modern general accounts of Emanuel Bach catalogues and collections, WADE, WADE/AMS, pp. 141-62 of SUCHALLA/ORCHESTERSINFONIEN, and pp. 161-76 of SCHMID/KAMMERMUSIK are the most helpful. (Note: See the Bibliography for explanations of sigla used here and throughout this catalogue.)

2. CPEB/AUTOBIOGRAPHY.

3. CPEB/BREITKOPF.

4. Apparently unrelated to his contemporary the Hamburg publisher J. C. Westphal. See TERRY, M.   J. C. Westphal published the fifth of the *Prussian Sonatas* (item 28 in the present catalogue) as a work of J. S. Bach (see item 25 in the thematic catalogue in BEURMANN/KLAVIERSONATEN)—a mistake that would have been unlikely if there had been more than a tenuous connection between the two Westphals.

5. See TERRY, M., and CPEB/WESTPHAL.

6. Emanuel was probably spurred to publish such a catalogue on his own by E. L. Gerber's notice in CRAMER/MAGAZIN (1.

Jg., 1783, 962ff. and 2. Jg., 1784, 194ff.), in which Gerber suggested that a union catalogue of musicians' portraits be published in CRAMER/MAGAZIN, with Emanuel as the most important contributor: "Meines Wissens besitzt der Hr. Capellmeister Bach die Beträchtlichste Sammlung. Und ich bitte recht sehr, dass Sie uns das Verzeichniss davon in Ihrem Magazine schenken." (Cramer's footnote: "Der Herr Capellmeister Bach hat mir Hoffnung zu diesem Verzeichnisse gemacht, das ich, sobald ich es erhalte, meinen Lesern mittheilen, und dadurch auch Hrn. Gerbers Wunsch erfüllen werde. C. F. C.") In the 1784 issue Gerber announced that he had been successful in compiling a list of 104 portraits, though as yet without Emanuel's participation.

7. The latest date that I have seen mentioned on a Westphal copy of a C. P. E. Bach work is 1803, in the table of contents of manuscript 5899 in the Brussels Conservatory (W. 118; see this catalogue's Concordance of Wotquenne Numbers), where Westphal notes that items 14 and 263 of this catalogue were published in that year; this corresponds to his quotation in the *Gesammlete*

Emanuel Bach . . . nebst einer Sammlung verschiedener Recensionen und Beurteilungen seiner herausgegebenen Werke.[8] But it is Westphal's third list that is most fundamental since it takes the form of a well-ordered thematic catalogue, unsigned by Westphal though unmistakably in his hand and with a title written in an unknown hand (Fétis's?): the *Catalogue thématique des oeuvres de Ch. Ph. Emm. Bach.*[9] Both manuscripts, the *Gesammlete Nachrichten* and the *Catalogue thématique,* are in the Royal Library in Brussels.[10]

In the third month after Emanuel's death, on March 4, 1789, his widow Johanna Maria wrote to thank Breitkopf for his condolences and to answer his inquiry about the possibility of purchasing some of Emanuel's musical estate.[11] She gave a thumbnail list of the types of works she had available or that she could procure from friends who had the pieces but who had given their "solemn promise" not to let them out of their hands; she added that in any event the works could be tracked down because "Herr Westphal" would surely have them listed in his catalogue. She pointed out that many of the works she was offering for sale were completely unknown (she was prompted, no doubt, by Emanuel's astutely having written "ist wenig bekannt" on some of them) and that the unknown works would cost more than the others. She said that a catalogue of her late husband's complete works was in preparation, one not limited to what she had on hand for sale but intended also as a memorial to him.[12] She told Breitkopf that the catalogue would also list Emanuel's collection of pictures and his library of music by J. S. Bach, Emanuel's brothers, and other composers. And she asked Breitkopf whether he might be interested in publishing the catalogue. Finally she urged Breitkopf to bid quickly for whatever items he desired because others were also interested, though she assured him that as her husband's old friend and business associate he would have first choice.

In another six months, on September 5, 1789, Johanna Maria wrote a letter[13] to Sara Levy (née Itzig) of Berlin (great-aunt of Felix Mendelssohn, friend of Emanuel's family before their move from Berlin to Hamburg, pupil of

Wilhelm Friedemann Bach, and collector of an important library of Bach-family music) answering an inquiry similar to the one she had received from Breitkopf. This letter contains a sweeping but fairly inclusive list of Emanuel's compositions based on a list provided by K. B. Wessely, a friend of the Emanuel Bach family and the director of the Royal Theater in Berlin.

The catalogue finally appeared late in 1790. It is a document fundamental to Bach-family research: The *Verzeichniss des musikalischen Nachlasses des verstorbenen Capellmeisters Carl Philipp Emanuel Bach,* published not by Breitkopf but by G. F. Schniebes of Hamburg.[14] It is not the customary auction catalogue but a true monument to Johanna Maria's spouse, just as she wished—though its title page invites the reader to inquire from "die verwittwete Frau Capellmeister Bach" about buying any item listed in it. The treasures this catalogue offered are incalculable. It lists the great majority of Emanuel's works, usually with first-movement incipits and dates of composition (proof that Johanna Maria's main source was a list or lists written by Emanuel, and probably by Westphal and others as well, rather than merely the works themselves since few manuscripts of his works carry dates);[15] more than 150 works by J. S. Bach, including the autograph manuscripts of *The Art of Fugue,* the *Inventions* and *Sinfonias* for keyboard, the *Cello Suites,* the *Christmas Oratorio,* the *Magnificat,* the *St. Matthew Passion,* the *B Minor Mass,* and numerous cantatas; works by Emanuel's brothers Wilhelm Friedemann, Johann Christian, Johann Christoph Friedrich, and Johann Bernhard, as well as Bach-family compositions dating back more than a century (the "Alt-Bachisches Archiv"); an enormous hoard of church and other vocal music by various composers; two clavichords, a harpsichord, a pianoforte, and a "zink" carved from an elephant tusk; no fewer than 377 portraits of past and contemporary "composers, musicians, writers on music, lyrical poets, and various famous connoisseurs of music" (this, of course, is the portrait catalogue Emanuel had planned three years earlier to publish separately); 37 silhouettes of musicians; 104 drawings or paint-

---

Nachrichten (see below) of the 1804 review of item 14 in the *Allgemeine musikalische Zeitung.* Eighteen letters from Emanuel's widow Johanna Maria, written between 1790 and 1794, and nineteen from his daughter Anna Carolina Philippina, written between 1795 and 1804 (the year of Anna Carolina Philippina's death)—all thirty-seven apparently addressed to Westphal—were at last notice in the care of E. F. Schmid's son and widow, 'manfred Schmid and Lotte Schmid, both of Augsburg. See Jacobi's note in CPEB/WESTPHAL, *Journal of the American Musicological Society,* XXVII (Spring, 1974), 125. Darrell Berg has been able to see some of these letters, and she informs me that they contain much information about the disposition of C. P. E. Bach's musical estate through Westphal.

8. WESTPHAL/NACHRICHTEN.

9. WESTPHAL/THÉMATIQUE.

10. Rachel W. Wade establishes the chronology of Westphal's three lists in WADE/AMS. She points out that a copy of the *Catalogue thématique,* with a few explanatory annotations and dated April 1868, is to be found in the Deutsche Staatsbibliothek,

East Berlin, Mus. ms. theor. K 490.

11. CPEB/BREITKOPF. This letter is partially printed in SCHULZE, 449.

12. "Es wird dieser Catalogus eigentlich einen Nachruf aushalten von allen Arbeiten meines seel. Manns, folglich wird darinn aufgenommen werden so wohl was bey mir zu haben ist, als was je von ihm verfertigt worden."

13. BACH/LEVY.

14. NACHLASS-VERZEICHNIS.

15. WADE/JAMS observes that the numbers of this catalogue form part of a good many title pages in Emanuel's hand, often as corrections of earlier numberings. Another indication of the catalogue's multiple authorship: "meines Versuches" on page 10, but "der Selige" on page 54. And the amount of detail in many parts of the catalogue obviously shows the previous existence of a list or lists authored by the composer, as where a sonata's composition and revision dates are both given, for example, even though no title page offers this information.

ings by Emanuel's second son, Johann Sebastian (named after his grandfather), whose promising painter's career had ended with his death in Rome shortly before his thirtieth birthday; and 30 drawings by other artists.

The *Nachlass-Verzeichnis*, to give it its most common short title, differs most strikingly from the Westphal catalogue in its exclusive list of more than 40 large unpublished choral works. Why did the eager disciple Westphal steer clear of these, not only in the *Catalogue thématique* but even—except for a few brief references—in the *Gesammlete Nachrichten*? Probably because Emanuel had said little about them, probably because they resisted cataloguing (and even titling in some cases), owing to their intricate borrowings and interrelationships, and possibly because Westphal did not regard them as highly as he did Emanuel's other works. As Heinrich Miesner was among the first to show (in 1929), the unpublished choral compositions attributed entirely to Emanuel in the *Nachlass-Verzeichnis* are often pastiches of Emanuel's and other composers' music.[16] In the nineteenth and early twentieth centuries such pastiches were looked upon with disfavor; Miesner referred to them as "geflickt." Westphal was certainly aware of their existence by the time of the publication of the *Nachlass-Verzeichnis*, though he apparently remained uninterested in them. The copy of the *Nachlass-Verzeichnis* owned by the Royal Library in Brussels contains notations in Westphal's hand (see also n. 34 below), along with checkmarks next to most of the listings of musical items. The checked items correspond very closely to the items presently owned by the Brussels libraries; there are no checkmarks for the pastiches, and, except for some printed textbooks, no traces of original sources of these works in Brussels.

In the last quarter of the twentieth century we are more willing to seek out whatever is original in such pastiches; we realize now that the eighteenth-century composer's free borrowing from himself and others was the rule, not the exception. Our attitude probably resembles that of Johanna Maria, although we would not go as far as she did in allowing these works to be listed in the *Nachlass-Verzeichnis* as if they were entirely original. Obviously she did not want the portions of these compositions really created by Emanuel, often with great care, to be lost. From the practical standpoint, a good choral work ready for use was a valuable and salable possession, no matter who composed it or what mixture of styles it contained; in the eighteenth century sheer availability outweighed other aspects of a piece of music to a degree that later generations of musicians have found hard to understand. Therefore, apparently, she and Schniebes independently added to Emanuel's own orderly list not only the variously authored lists mentioned above, but also the considerable music in Hamburg church libraries that Emanuel had arranged

under his own name during two decades of incessant performances–ten passion performances within thirteen days in each Easter season, for instance. Emanuel had had at his disposal hundreds of old and excellent sacred choral works by his predecessor Telemann, members of the Bach family, and other composers, and (following a very old Hamburg tradition) he had used these compositions as needed in combination with his own music, though in the surviving parts of the works ascribed to him in the *Nachlass-Verzeichnis* the original far outweighs the borrowed. When the texts of such pastiches were printed for the use of his own congregations, he and his printer did not usually trouble themselves over exact attributions, but he would surely have been embarrassed to see the titles of such works widely published as unequivocally his own. In his cost accounts for these performances he clearly differentiates between "Composition" and "Direction."[17] Because the titles were so published, however, and especially because these works do contain much of his own music—again, much music on which he lavished great care—they are listed in the present catalogue with the authentic portions identified wherever possible. The bulk of these pastiches, mostly in sets of performance parts, went eventually to the library of the Berlin Singakademie, which was destroyed in the Second World War.[18]

If we still had these sets of performance parts we could better understand how, in an era more concerned with practical performance than with niceties of authorship, Johanna Maria might have considered such sets to be essentially integrated works from her husband's pen. Sets of parts are not strong on the attribution of each separate movement; scores are, and so are what can only be called the schematic diagrams that Emanuel left behind. With the scores and diagrams that have come down to us we can often improve on Johanna Maria's blanket attributions. The extant schematic diagrams, usually just a sheet or two, or a few words at the head of a newly composed movement, give us an illuminating glimpse of Emanuel's working life in Hamburg. Far more than mere memoranda to himself, they are instructions for his copyists in the manufacture of performance parts: copy this chorus from there, borrow this recitative and aria from there and transpose them in the process, insert that chorale from that collection after the words such-and-such.

As mentioned above, the *Nachlass-Verzeichnis* goes on to list a large library of music by other composers as part of C. P. E. Bach's musical estate, compositions that helped him fulfill his duties as Hamburg church musician. While the music so attributed presents us with few problems of Emanuel's authorship, some of the surviving portions of it show the same hurried instructions to copyists in Emanuel's handwriting, often involving changes in other

---

16. MIESNER/HAMBURG.

17. RECHNUNGSBUCH.

18. The best assessment of the extant portions of this music is that in CLARK. This assessment will probably lead to a restoration

of many fine choruses, arias, recitatives, chorales, instrumental movements and sections, and other isolated works. See n. 41 regarding a surviving fragment of the Singakademie library. On the general scope of this library, see WELTER.

composers' works. The scores of twenty-eight church cantatas by Georg Benda are a good example: these are in Mus. mss. 1334 and 1335 in the Staatsbibliothek Preussischer Kulturbesitz in West Berlin, copied mostly in the elegant hand of Michel, Emanuel's chief Hamburg copyist. These two manuscripts contain the bookplate of Georg Pölchau (see below), and one of them bears the note "Aus Eman. Bachs Nachlass. Pölchau." They quite possibly constitute the "Jahrgang Kirchenstücke von Georg Benda" listed on page 85 of the *Nachlass-Verzeichnis*. Throughout these scores are Emanuel's rapidly scribbled instructions to his copyist (probably Michel again) on how to extract performance parts: "Die Hoboen blasen den Discant und Alt mit. . . . Statt des folgenden Chorals kommt der Telemañische mit NB gezeichnet, er wird aber einen Ton höher, nehmlich ins A moll transponirt. . . . 2 Flöten blasen blos mit der ersten und zweyten Violin die Rittornelle. . . Dieser Choral bleibt weg, u. komt dafür der Telemañische." Along with such instructions are Emanuel's notes to himself recording the occasions on which this or that cantata was performed. His note in ink: "Am S[onntage] nach dem neuen Jahre." This is followed by his note in pencil: "Ist nach mir gemacht [ink again:], ausser 74 J. [Performed by me each year on this occasion except 1774]."

It may well be, then, that if the sets of parts in the Singakademie library had survived, probably beautifully legible and thoroughly musical, they would have led scholars toward misattributions in the same way that they relaxed Johanna Maria's standards of attribution. It is certain that they would have made more obvious the singular importance of Emanuel's copyists. The chief copyist, whose work would have been prized by any composer in any age, was Michel. His role in transmitting C. P. E. Bach's music is discussed in more detail below.

Other lists were made during and immediately after the composer's lifetime—a good one that comes to mind is that in GERBER[19]—but none has the authority of the ones I have already named. Above all in importance are the Westphal *Catalogue thématique* and the *Nachlass-Verzeichnis*. Among more recent lists, the one in LEDEBUR[20] shows how fundamental the Berlin sources are; the chronological one in C. H. Bitter's pioneer study[21] draws on the *Nachlass-Verzeichnis* while injecting many errors and revealing only an imperfect acquaintance, at best, with the *Catalogue thématique*;[22] Alfred Wotquenne's catalogue,[23] compiled in Brussels, is little more than a copy of the *Catalogue thématique* (containing ten items of music not listed by

Westphal) made, apparently, with hardly a glance at the *Nachlass-Verzeichnis*, although it lists this source (W. 279). Even though the Wotquenne catalogue gives incipits of first movements only (like the *Catalogue thématique* and the *Nachlass-Verzeichnis*) and provides no information about sources, authenticity, modern editions, literature, and so forth, it has become an accepted catalogue of C. P. E. Bach's works. Wotquenne acknowledges Westphal as his source. *Pace* Wotquenne, it seems unfair to Westphal and Johanna Maria, not to mention the composer, that an Alfred-come-lately in the far-off city of Brussels should attach "Wotquenne numbers" to a catalogue essentially written by someone else. Recognizing the wide use of the Wotquenne numbers, however, I have preserved them among other information on each work they apply to and have provided a concordance of this catalogue with Wotquenne's.

So much for catalogues preceding the present one. The question of how a distant Belgian came to publish an obscure Schwerin organist's catalogue of the works of a composer who lived in Berlin and Hamburg takes us to the subject of the locations of the works themselves after Emanuel's death. When Westphal died in 1825,[24] his heirs were at first unsuccessful in selling his library, which had grown to include more than 3,000 compositions and over 600 books on music. After fruitless attempts to interest buyers in Prussia, Hamburg, Austria, Saxony, Mecklenburg, Sweden, and elsewhere, the heirs had the collection auctioned.[25] Most of it was sold some time shortly after 1835 to that admirable figure whose statue stands today in the courtyard of the Brussels Conservatory: F. J. Fétis, who had become the conservatory's director in 1833. Fétis says in the article on Westphal in his *Biographie universelle* that he made the purchase after Westphal's death;[26] he gives 1835 incorrectly as the date of death but helps thereby to date his purchase. By 1840 the Brussels Conservatory's advisory board was considering buying the collection from Fétis[27] but apparently made the actual purchase only from Fétis's estate after his death in 1871.[28] In 1904 the conservatory acquired most of another library rich in the music of Emanuel Bach, that of the nineteenth-century Marburg physician Richard Wagener.[29] As librarian, inspector of studies, and secretary of the conservatory from 1894 to 1918, Wotquenne found a great Emanuel Bach collection close at hand, primarily in fair copies grouped by category, along with Westphal's catalogue—an irresistible combination. The collection has remained in Brussels, divided between the conservatory and the Royal Library, with manu-

19. See Bibliography.

20. See Bibliography.

21. BITTER/BRÜDER.

22. BITTER/BRÜDER refers to Bitter's correspondence with Fétis regarding certain C. P. E. Bach sources in Brussels (I, 18) and offers a summary of the contents of the *Catalogue thématique* (II, 342–44).

23. WOTQUENNE/THÉMATIQUE.

24. Not 1833 or 1835; see TERRY, M.

25. TERRY, M.

26. FÉTIS/BIOGRAPHIE. Fétis describes Westphal's view of C. P. E. Bach as that of "admirateur passioné."

27. According to a letter from the late director of the Brussels Conservatory library, Albert Vander Linden, to Ernst Suchalla; see SUCHALLA/ORCHESTERSINFONIEN, 147–48.

28. TERRY, M., 107.

29. MARTELL, 327.

scripts of music *per se* being concentrated in the conservatory. Among libraries outside Brussels which own small portions of the Westphal collection that somehow escaped Fétis—along with C. P. E. Bach manuscripts from other sources, of course—the library of the Gesellschaft der Musikfreunde and the Österreichische Nationalbibliothek, both in Vienna, are the most important. As one looks through the present catalogue it becomes evident that in one library or another, Westphal's copies—especially his collections-by-genre—are the only sources of many works. Westphal saved many a work from extinction.

Even if we consider the provenance of the Emanuel Bach collection in Brussels, the absence of autographs there is striking: I have found only six (see items 540, 569, 658–61).[30] But seldom have manuscript *copies* of a composer's works boasted a finer pedigree: of the 510 or so C. P. E. Bach compositions in manuscript in the two great Brussels libraries, some 187 are in the hand of Michel, the craftsman-musician mentioned above, Emanuel's tenor soloist and chief copyist in Hamburg; and about 264 are in the hand of Westphal. The Westphal copies are understandably of excellent quality, yet they pale before the astonishingly meticulous Michel copies. Unfortunately, we know little of Michel. Manuscript P 241 in the Music Division of the Staatsbibliothek Preussischer Kulturbesitz in West Berlin, copied by Michel, bears this note in Pölchau's hand:[31]"Von H. Michels Hand. Tenorist beym Bachschen Kirchenchore in Hamburg 1787."[32] Since "H. Michel" is the name frequently superscribed by Emanuel on tenor solos in his church works, the "H." probably stand only for "Herr." Anonymous as he is, Michel deserves our tribute for delivering Emanuel's works to us in such clear and musicianly form. He is the copyist who was kept busiest by Emanuel's promise to Westphal in a letter of January 9, 1787: "If you should need something written by me, I hope you will only let me know. Without the slightest payment for myself, only for the cost of copying, I stand ready to serve you."[33] And Michel probably kept on turning out copies after Emanuel's death. This notice stands at the end of the list of C. P. E. Bach works in the *Nachlass-Verzeichnis* (p. 66): "Whoever would like to own something from among these musical works should tell the widow Frau Capellmeister Bach; she will see that correct and careful copies are made."

Westphal's ambition to collect C. P. E. Bach's works systematically rather than casually probably dates from not long before 1786, if we judge from his correspondence with Emanuel. Emanuel undoubtedly had some copies on hand and ready to be sent to Westphal, but the letters and the music itself indicate that, beginning around 1786–87 and for not many years thereafter, Westphal acquired most of his manuscripts of C. P. E. Bach's music as Michel copies specifically requested of Emanuel, and copied most of the remainder himself. The Brussels collection is thus remarkably homogeneous. The circumstances under which it was created give it a stamp of unusual reliability. Furthermore, this collection obviously represents the composer's latest intentions with regard to many works existing in two or more versions.

To find the bulk of the surviving autographs, copies variously marked by the composer, and copies most intimately associated with him ouside the Westphal connection, we must go back to the *Nachlass-Verzeichnis*. The superb collection of portraits and other pictures was scattered.[34] Fortunately, however, most of the music by Emanuel as well as by the other composers can be traced, thanks to its eventual purchase by Georg Pölchau (1773–1836), extraordinary collector of music and resident of Hamburg from 1799 to 1813.[35] Pölchau augmented his collection of music and related materials of the Bach family after moving from Hamburg to Berlin by buying the library of the early Bach biographer J. N. Forkel in 1819. He traveled throughout Germany and abroad to make other such purchases, and after the death in 1832 of C. F. Zelter, director of the Berlin Singakademie, he acted as Singakademie librarian and helped to put in order yet another great Bach-family collection (of which more below). Pölchau's collection, along with his catalogue of it,[36] was sold in 1841 to the Royal Library in Berlin.[37]

The occasion for the aforementioned letter and list of September 5, 1789, from Johanna Maria to Sara Itzig Levy was, as I have said, Mme. Levy's interest in augmenting her collection of Emanuel's music. The Itzig family, prominent in Berlin banking circles, had collected music of the Bach family for many years. As a descendant of this family, Felix Mendelssohn came by his interest in J. S. Bach naturally. While Zelter was director of the Berlin Singakademie he became acquainted with the Itzigs, probably through

---

30. This paucity of autographs and the absence of the above-mentioned choral works, along with other lacunae, make an exaggeration of Wotquenne's footnote in WOTQUENNE/CONSERVATOIRE, II, 296: "It may be noted that the library of the Brussels Conservatory possesses the complete works of Carl Philipp Emanuel Bach. They were collected by J. H. Westphal, organist. . . . The original manuscript of [Westphal's] precious catalogue is today part of the Fétis library [Royal Library]. . . ." Wotquenne's footnote gives Westphal's catalogue rather more credit than was later given in Wotquenne's own C. P. E. Bach catalogue.

31. See below regarding Pölchau.

32. See also DADELSEN, 24.

33. CPEB/WESTPHAL, printed in BITTER/BRÜDER, I, 305.

34. In the copy of the *Nachlass-Verzeichnis* owned by the Royal Library in Brussels, prices are marked by hand next to all items pertaining to pictures, along with this note in Westphal's hand: "N.B. Die beygeschriebenen Preise sind diejenigen, wofür theils diese Bildnisse verkauft, theils haben verkauft werden sollen. Von der Tochter des seel. Bach habe ich diese Notizen erhalten."

35. The main part of Pölchau's purchase was apparently made at auction in Hamburg on March 4, 1805. A copy of the auction catalogue survives in D-ddr Bds; see AUCTION 1805. Emanuel's daughter, Anna Carolina Philippina, the last surviving member of Emanuel's branch of the Bach family, had died in the previous year.

36. PÖLCHAU.

37. SUCHALLA/ORCHESTERSINFONIEN, 142. In addition to Pölchau, the names of Zelter and C. F. G. Schwenke figure importantly among purchasers of the C. P. E. Bach musical estate. See SCHULZE, 502–04.

K. B. Wessely, the Bach-family friend who had collaborated with Johanna Maria in making the works-list in 1789. It was apparently as a result of this acquaintance that the bulk of the Itzig collection came into the possession of the Singakademie, and it is even possible that Mendelssohn— pupil of Zelter and singer in the Singakademie from the age of ten, director of the Singakademie's famous performance of J. S. Bach's *St. Matthew Passion* in 1829—was instrumental in making the gift. Because of financial need the Singakademie had to sell much of the Itzig collection to the Royal Library in Berlin in 1854.[38] The names Mendelssohn and Bach remained intertwined among C. P. E. Bach sources well into the nineteenth century, as on those manuscripts where Abraham Mendelssohn Bartholdy (1776–1835) crossed out the name "Sara Levy geb. Itzig" and substituted his signature.

One of Emanuel's admirers during his Berlin years under Frederick the Great had been the king's sister Anna Amalia, who named Emanuel her honorary kapellmeister upon his departure from Berlin. Under the guidance of her teacher, J. P. Kirnberger, she assembled a music library of major importance, especially rich in music of Kirnberger's teacher, J. S. Bach, but also strong in works by Emanuel and other Bach-family members. She willed her library[39] to the Joachimsthalsche Gymnasium in Berlin; in 1914 the Gymnasium's collection passed on permanent loan to the Royal Library there. Among other music collections that became part of the library of the Joachimsthalsche Gymnasium and thus went to the Royal Library, that of Friedrich Wilhelm von Thulemeier, willed to the Gymnasium in 1811, contains a number of significant C.P.E. Bach sources.

It is a rich assortment, then, that resides in what we call today the Staatsbibliothek as a somewhat imprecise but still necessary generic term referring to both the Deutsche Staatsbibliothek in East Berlin and the Staatsbibliothek Preussischer Kulturbesitz in West Berlin. These are the institutions holding most of the extant autographs along with many Michel copies. After Emanuel's death this great library acquired many of his compositions from other sources, such as the collections of the Count von Voss-Buch, L. C. Erk, and Franz Hauser.[40] During and immediately after World War II the library's vast holdings were divided for safekeeping between Berlin and some twenty-nine locations in various parts of Germany, the non-Berlin portions eventually being concentrated in Tübingen and Marburg. Such precautions, however, did not prevent the destruction of a good many treasures, including all but a fragment of the Singakademie library.[41]

At the stage during which the core of the Staatsbibliothek's music collection was divided between Tübingen, Marburg, and East Berlin, one of the most important of the recent Bach studies sponsored by the University of Tübingen was published: Paul Kast's *Die Bach-Handschriften der Berliner Staatsbibliothek*,[42] which covers Bach-family manuscripts then housed in these three locations, though not including Staatsbibliothek manuscripts from the old Thulemeier collection (call numbers prefixed by "M.Th.," catalogued in JACOBS), the Amalienbibliothek section of the Staatsbibliothek (call numbers prefixed by "Am.B.," described in BLECHSCHMIDT, mentioned above), the Pretlack collection (call numbers prefixed by "B.P."; see next page), or certain other manuscripts predominantly catalogued as "Mus. ms." rather than with the "P" or "St" (Partitur or Stimmen) prefixes reserved for Bach-family manuscripts.

Recently almost all[43] of the Staatsbibliothek's music collection has been returned to Berlin, though to two libraries: the Deutsche Staatsbibliothek in East Berlin and the Staatsbibliothek Preussischer Kulturbesitz in West Berlin. The Amalienbibliothek is now also divided between these two libraries; Thulemeier manuscripts are housed in the one in East Berlin. Kast's list of Bach-family manuscripts has survived these moves as a vital tool giving catalogue numbers, locations, detailed descriptions of contents, and identification of handwriting.[44]

The latter category of information, all-important to a catalogue of this kind (and indeed the main source of my notes

38. SUCHALLA/ORCHESTERSINFONIEN, 144.

39. A recent catalogue: BLECHSCHMIDT. This catalogue bases its identification of copyists of manuscripts upon researches by Wolfgang Plath at the Johann-Sebastian-Bach Institut in Göttingen.

40. See SASSE, cols. 1733–35; WOLF; SUCHALLA/ORCHESTER-SINFONIEN, 144–45.

41. In 1967 a few surviving Singakademie manuscripts were kept in the apartment of Mathieu Lange, then director of the Singakademie, from whom I procured a microfilm of the Singakademie's only surviving C. P. E. Bach source, albeit an important one: the autograph score of the double concerto for harpsichord, fortepiano, and orchestra, item 479 in the present catalogue. Since 1974 these manuscripts have been on loan to the West-Berlin Staatsbibliothek.

42. KAST.

43. "Almost all," because at this writing a famous group of manuscripts, among the manuscripts sent during the war to Fürstenstein Castle in Silesia and then to the Benedictine monastery at Grüssau (now Krezesow in Poland), now seems to be permanently

located in Cracow at the Biblioteka Jagiellonska, where it has been made available to qualified scholars. It is now definite that new sources of the present catalogue's items 4, 16, 17, 49, 82, 84, 96–98, 106, 152–54, 189, 212, 248, 298, 299, 301, 403, 459, and possibly 635/8 are in the Biblioteka Jagiellonska, as specified in those items. This information comes from Malcolm Frager through Darrell Berg (BERG/NOTES). The thirty-year search for and eventual discovery of the missing manuscripts is summed up in LEWIS. The manuscripts fill some fifty boxes and include important works by the Bach family, Mozart, Beethoven, Schubert, Mendelssohn, Bruckner, and others, along with unique early German works on natural history. The wartime fate of the Staatsbibliothek is described in HILL. See also WHITEHEAD, SMITH 1968, and SMITH 1975.

44. Catalogue numbers marked "Mbg" (Marburg) and "Tb" (Tübingen) in the Kast book are now in West Berlin, and those bearing no mark are in East Berlin. Some manuscripts containing arrangements and alternate versions are assigned Wotquenne numbers by Kast that do not apply to the versions listed in Wotquenne; but this is a flaw that corrects itself.

about copyists), came into the Kast book largely from the work of the Institute of Musicology at the University of Tübingen; much of this work is summed up in an indispensable monograph from that institution, Georg von Dadelsen's *Bemerkungen zur Handschrift Johann Sebastian Bachs, seiner Familie und seines Kreises.*[45] Because of the great importance of the Kast study, a concordance is provided in the back of the present book between my item numbers and the numbers given by Kast to works not listed in the Wotquenne catalogue.

In 1968 an attic-cleaning in the castle of Echzell, Kreis Büdingen in Hesse, resulted in the discovery of a chest packed with music. The music belonged to Franz Freiherr von Pretlack (1709–67), Maria Theresa's ambassador to the Russian court in St. Petersburg, and was passed on to his stepbrother Ludwig Freiherr von Pretlack (1716–81). Consisting of 1,079 works altogether, counting manuscripts and prints, this collection was acquired by the Staatsbibliothek Preussischer Kulturbesitz and catalogued by Joachim Jaenecke of the Staatsbibliothek's music division.[46] It contains hitherto unknown sources of twenty-five C. P. E. Bach compositions (none of which is previously unknown as a composition, however), all in manuscript copies of excellent quality.

Berlin's libraries are the most important repositories of C. P. E. Bach's music, Brussels's are the second most important, and Vienna's (in the Gesellschaft der Musikfreunde and the Österreichische Nationalbibliothek) are third in importance. The Vienna manuscripts are unusually accurate, even when they are not autographs or copies made by Michel or Westphal. A large number of the Gesellschaft's C. P. E. Bach sources belong to its Brahms legacy; many other such sources are part of the precious gift that Anthony van Hoboken made to the Gesellschaft.

As for other collections of this music, it is enough for the present purpose to refer to the RISM abbreviations (General Abbreviations and Library Sigla) of libraries mentioned in this catalogue. The distribution of Emanuel Bach's *published* works was extraordinarily wide in his lifetime, as is attested in many alphabetically arranged lists in his newspaper announcements as well as in the published works themselves; his selling agents, not to mention his subscribers, could be found in such cities, in addition to Berlin and Hamburg, as Braunschweig, Bückeburg, Celle, Copenhagen, Dresden, Eisenach, Göttingen, Gotha, Hannover, Leipzig, London, Ludwigslust, Moscow, Parchim, Petersburg, Prague, Riga, Schleswig, Stettin, Stockholm, Vienna, Warsaw, and Weimar. I have refined these leads primarily through the Eitner *Quellenlexikon*[47] and, thanks to the kind indulgence of F. W. Riedel, through the card files of manuscript and print locations at the RISM office in Kassel. The RISM volume devoted to individual compositions *published* before 1800 has grown out of the card-file stage and into print; its article on Emanuel Bach, by Ernst Suchalla, has provided much useful information.[48]

DETAILS OF THE CATALOGUING PROCEDURE

(See How to Use This Catalogue, at the front of this book, for the basic outline of the cataloguing procedure.)

Classifications of Authenticity

Every work listed in this catalogue is attributed somewhere to Carl Philipp Emanuel Bach. "Attributed to" means that the attribution is written on the music itself, or that it is only in the catalogue of the library or collection holding the work, or that it is merely given in some (any) written source, or any combination of these. This catalogue thus cites every known work for which there is even the slightest reason to suppose that C. P. E. Bach was the composer.

Four classifications of authenticity of these works are adopted here: "authentic," "possibly authentic," "doubtful," and "spurious."

These are the main criteria, obviously not equal in importance, for classifying a work as "authentic": inclusion in NACHLASS-VERZEICHNIS, WESTPHAL/THÉMATIQUE, or other authoritative lists or sources, such as AUCTION 1805, BACH/LEVY, CPEB/AUTOBIOGRAPHY, CPEB/BREITKOPF, CPEB/WESTPHAL, PÖLCHAU, RECHNUNGSBUCH, or WESTPHAL/NACHRICHTEN; the existence of an autograph or a partial autograph, or a copy signed or revised or marked by the composer; the composer's correspondence; and as noted in individual items.

These are the main criteria for the "possibly authentic" classification, even though the work may not be listed in NACHLASS-VERZEICHNIS, WESTPHAL/THÉMATIQUE, or other authoritative lists or sources such as those named above: the existence of a manuscript attributed to C. P. E. Bach and copied by one of his associates (as these associates are identified by the author, WADE, BERG/FACSIMILE, BLECHSCHMIDT, DADELSEN, and KAST); wide dissemination in manuscripts or prints attributed to the composer; association with authenticated works (for example, in part of an otherwise authentic manuscript anthology, or in variants, alternate versions, revisions, or arrangements); biographical facts (as in item 350); printed notices or reviews; style (as in item 348); provenance (especially association with certain sources in Berlin, Hamburg, or Brussels); and as noted in individual items.

Reasons for classifying a work as "doubtful" despite its attribution to C. P. E. Bach: omission from NACHLASS-VERZEICHNIS, WESTPHAL/THÉMATIQUE, and other authoritative lists or sources such as those named above; attributions to other composers in other sources, lists, or catalogues; vagueness of attribution (for example, "Bach"); unproved attributions in now inaccessible sources (as in items 362–67); style (as in item 370); and as noted in individual items.

Reasons for classifying a work as "spurious" despite its attribution somewhere to C. P. E. Bach: omission from NACHLASS-VERZEICHNIS, WESTPHAL/THÉMATIQUE, and

---

45. DADELSEN.
46. JAENECKE. Catalogue numbers prefixed by "B.P."

47. EITNER.
48. SUCHALLA/RISM.

other authoritative lists or sources such as those named above; well-documented attribution of the work to another composer (as in item 376); attributions to other composers in other sources, lists, or catalogues, in combination with evidence that further weakens the C. P. E. Bach connection (as in item 380); the composer's correspondence (as in item 386); style (as in items 392–392.5); and as noted in individual items. (Note that certain items in this category are not "spurious" in the strict sense that authorship by another composer can be documented.)

Title, Subtitle, or First Line of Text

This is usually taken from the source of the incipits (see No. 13 in How to Use This Catalogue, at the front of this book). Occasionally this is shortened when no confusion will result, or is supplied in whole or in part (in square brackets), or is taken from an alternate source such as NACHLASS-VERZEICHNIS. Peculiarities, errors, and inconsistencies in spelling and in the use of accents and diacritical marks (as in item 110) are retained without comment; line-by-line format is not indicated; all titles in the main body of the catalogue are set entirely in lower-case letters, or with only the first letter, proper names, and German nouns capitalized, irrespective of the original usage.

Date and Place of Composition

Items are listed chronologically within each category. For a work composed in one year and revised in another, both dates are listed in the same item, and the item is catalogued in the position corresponding to the earlier of the two dates; but since arrangements, alternate versions, and variants (see General Abbreviations and Library Sigla for the distinctly different meanings of these terms) must often be listed separately, they are often dated separately as well.

About 90 percent of the dates given, including dates of revision, come from NACHLASS-VERZEICHNIS. Other sources of dates are autographs, the composer's correspondence, handwriting of copyists, CPEB/AUTOBIOGRAPHY, WESTPHAL/THÉMATIQUE, WESTPHAL/NACHRICHTEN, notices and reviews in contemporary journals and newspapers, published texts of choral works, publication dates, events in the composer's life, stylistic evidence, and the material in individual items.

Virtually without exception, the dates of the works indicate where they were composed: 1731–34, Leipzig; 1735–38, Frankfurt/Oder; 1739–67, Berlin and Potsdam (a few in Teplitz in 1743 and Zerbst in 1758); 1768–88, Hamburg.

For the sake of simplicity, within a given year the order of items follows the order of WOTQUENNE/THÉMATIQUE wherever possible, rather than the order of NACHLASS-VERZEICHNIS, the order of appearance in original prints, or any other system. All known lists, catalogues, and original prints, except for the original print of item 684 and a few entries in NACHLASS-VERZEICHNIS, are unreliable, when not actually misleading, in determining chronology of composition in more detail than a year-by-year listing. Nowhere in NACHLASS-VERZEICHNIS, for example, is it stated that the numbering of its entries indicates the order

of composition within a given year, nor is there any other reason to suppose that this is the case.

Manuscript Sources

In a very few cases where secondary bibliographical guides to manuscript locations give conflicting library call numbers or omit them, and I have been unable to check them personally, I have given the library's RISM siglum only.

Scores and parts are not particularly segregated in the listings. The bulk of the manuscripts, aside from those of unaccompanied keyboard works, songs, and about three dozen choral works or fragments, consists of sets of parts. The two main Berlin libraries (D-brd B and D-ddr Bds) have a near-monopoly on the manuscript scores; and in these two libraries, the ones richest in C. P. E. Bach's music, scores are designated by "P" (Partitur) and sets of parts by "St" (Stimmen) as prefixes to call numbers, with a few exceptions noted in the listings of this catalogue. In any case it is presumed that readers of this catalogue will want to have all sources of a work.

For a work considered to be spurious and included in another thematic catalogue, only the manuscript carrying the spurious attribution to C. P. E. Bach is listed, along with a reference to the other catalogue.

The handwriting in manuscripts is always that of a copyist unless the manuscript is designated as an autograph—for example, "P 3 (autog.)"—or as a partial autograph, or as a copy signed or revised or marked by the composer (for example, "rev. by CPEB" means the revisions are *in his hand*). A list (by Rachel W. Wade) of autographs appears on p. 242. Copies by Michel and Westphal, second in importance as manuscripts only to those bearing C. P. E. Bach's handwriting (see pp. xxiiff.), are so designated. Copyists of manuscripts in the Berlin Staatsbibliothek (that is, in D-brd B and D-ddr Bds, except for the Staatsbibliothek's Thulemeier, Amalienbibliothek, and Pretlack collections, and certain other manuscripts predominantly catalogued as "Mus. ms.") are identified in KAST; copyists of Amalienbibliothek manuscripts are identified in BLECHSCHMIDT; copyists of concerto manuscripts are identified in WADE; copyists of some solo keyboard manuscripts are identified in the Critical Notes of BERG/FACSIMILE. Identifications of handwriting apply only to the work itself, not necessarily to the entire manuscript; compare manuscript 5634 in items 558 and 559, for instance, or manuscript 5883 in items 211–13 as opposed to items 174–78.

Many manuscripts listed as primary sources should no doubt be demoted to the status of manuscripts probably copied from an early print, as more is learned about them. The more popular a published work or set of works, the more probable it is that a surviving manuscript of it had such an origin—in an age when a manuscript copy could very well cost less than a print—whether this is apparent in the manuscript or not. On the other hand, one can never be sure just what source a manuscript was copied from unless it bears an unequivocal source attribution or is obviously the composer's working draft (that is, not a copy). In applying the criteria given in No. 9 of How to Use directions at the beginning of this catalogue to, say, the DAMENSONATEN (see the Bibliography and the items referred to there), we find that nearly all known manuscripts of these sonatas seem to have originated as copies of the various early prints, although we can never be sure of this. Even in the case of Westphal's monumental manuscript anthologies, organized by genre, that so distinguish the Brussels holdings, his neat tables of contents giving publishing information never flatly declare that any manuscript copy of his *own* comes from a print; perhaps the best example of this is the beautiful manuscript II 4094 in the Royal Library of Brussels, containing the twenty-four sonatas that make up item 62 of the Wotquenne catalogue (see the Concordance of Wotquenne Numbers in the back of the present catalogue). Therefore, again, prospective editors are urged to procure all known sources, printed and in manuscript, and to study the sources as only a specialist can before reaching a decision as to their relative importance. If a manuscript is somehow discovered to be truly a copy of a print, it may still contain important revisions that postdate the printed version of a work. And different exemplars of a single print often vary in important ways.

Early Prints

Both types of early prints, those entirely by C. P. E. Bach and those containing his music along with that of other composers, make up a pair of relatively clear-cut lists (see these in the back matter). For the comprehensiveness and exclusivity of these lists, we are most indebted to NACHLASS-VERZEICHNIS, WESTPHAL/NACHRICHTEN, WESTPHAL/THÉMATIQUE, and C. P. E. Bach's correspondence. These sources show us clearly which early prints were authorized by the composer and which seem to lack such authorization. The latter are pointed out in annotations in the Bibliography or the main text, as indicated on pp. 233 and 235.

Other Information or Comments, If Any

This includes notice of arrangements, alternate versions, revisions, or variants. Again, note in General Abbreviations and Library Sigla the quite different meanings of "arr.," "a.v.," "rev.," and "vnt." Labeling "a.v." and "vnt." has been a straightforward procedure. Whether an "a.v." or a "vnt." is listed separately depends partly on dates of the separate sources (if the dates are known), partly on whether an alternate medium of performance is different enough to change the category of a work, and partly on clarity in cataloguing. But unequivocally identifying one source as the original and another as its "rev." or "arr.," or setting in order more than one revision or arrangement of a work, is not always possible, and may even give casual alterations the false status of discrete variants; nor have I yet been able to determine how little change was needed to warrant the term *erneuert* in NACHLASS-VERZEICHNIS. I disagree with BEURMANN/KLAVIERSONATEN (pp. 104ff. and in Beurmann's works-list), for instance, that the more ornate version of two manuscripts of the same keyboard sonata can always be reliably identified as a revision. In such uncertain cases I have followed the safer course of noting that the work was revised and of listing all sources known to me. When I have been able to find different incipits in different sources of a work, whether the work was previously known to have been changed or not, the different incipits are given, with designations of their sources. To aid in the sorting-out process the *primary* versions of a work are sometimes classified as version 1, version 2, and so forth.

CATALOGUE

Instrumental

FOR KEYBOARD INSTRUMENT ALONE

Note: Aside from the music listed in this section, two categories might be specially pointed out as resembling pure keyboard music very closely, because they were commonly played on keyboard instruments alone in CPEB's time: the music for mechanical instruments (item 635) and the songs (items 670–84, 686, 687, 689–96, 698–721, 724–34, 736–38, 740–60, 762–66, 768, 769, 771).

Authentic

1. [2 Marches, 2 polonaises]. 1730-31 (source of date: DADELSEN/NBA, 70). BWV Anh. 122–25
Ms.: D-brd B, P 225 (autog.)
Mod. edns.: BERG/FACSIMILE; part of various edns. of the *Clavierbüchlein*; in NBA V/4, ed. by G. von Dadelsen (1957), 94–97; and as listed in BWV Anh. 122–25
Lit.: DADELSEN/NBA, 43, 49–50, 68, 70, 87; OTTENBERG, 26, 30, 285, 297
These are the 16th through 19th pieces in P 225, the *Clavierbüchlein* begun by J. S. Bach in 1725 for Anna Magdalena Bach (see item 16). All four pieces are in the very early hand of CPEB. They appear in the order and with the titles and instructions shown in the incipits, obviously intended as a set.
No. 19, the last "Polonoise," appeared as the middle mvt. in a "Sonata per il Cembalo solo di Sig^{re} C. P. E. Bach" in D-brd HS, Cod. ND VI 3191 fol. angeb. Ms. 10, destroyed in World War II, though Rudolf Steglich of Erlangen had a copy in 1957, according to DADELSEN/NBA, 64, 88.
DADELSEN/NBA convincingly argues that CPEB's copying of the four pieces as a set, with "volti" instructions leading from one movement to the next, in addition to the appearance of the final piece in a sonata credited to CPEB elsewhere, is sufficient evidence of CPEB's authorship.

Incipits from NBA V/4:

March

[At end: "Volti Polonoise."]

Polonoise

[At end: "Volti March."]

March

[At end: "Si Volti."]

Polonoise

1.5. Menuet pour le clavecin par C.P.E.B. 1731 (NV 53). W. 111
Mss.: D-brd B, P 563 (Michel); D-ddr Bds, Mus. ms. 30382
Early print: Engraved by CPEB himself
Mod. edn.: BERG/FACSIMILE
Lit.: BITTER/BRÜDER, I, 49–50; VRIESLANDER/BACH, 11; CLERCX, 159–61; NEWMAN, 401; COHEN, 25; OTTENBERG, 29; SCHULENBERG/INSTRUMENTAL, 78
The only exemplar of the engraving that has appeared is that in B Bc, 5866; a 2nd exemplar may be in Dk Kk, mu 6309.1131. In NV, 53, its title is "Menuett mit überschlagenden Händen."

Incipit from 5866:

2. Sonata per il cembalo solo. 1731, rev. 1744 (NV 1). W. 62/1
Mss.: D-brd B, P 677, P 727 (19th-century copy, 1st mvt. only), P 772, P 775, P 790 (2 copies), P 841; D-ddr Bds, P 365; A Wgm, VII 43746
Early print: ALLERLEY, 159. Lit. about ALLERLEY: See this entry in Bib.
Mss. probably copied from the early print: B Br, II 4094 (Westphal); D-ddr LEb, 346
Mod. edns.: FARRENC, BERG/FACSIMILE
Lit. about this work: BERG, 94, 137–8, 186, 200, 203, 211–12; OTTENBERG, 30; SCHULENBERG/INSTRUMENTAL, 13, 99; FOX, 101, 188–92
Some of the original copy in P 772 is struck out, with changes inserted.

Incipits from ALLERLEY:

Presto

3. Sonata per il cembalo solo. 1731, rev. 1744 (NV 1). W. 65/1

Mss.: D-brd B, P 758, P 775; D-ddr Bds, Mus. ms. 7920/1, M.Th. 49; B Bc, 5883 (Michel); A Wgm, VII 43746; US Wc, M23.B13.W.65 (1)

Mod. edn.: BERG/FACSIMILE

Lit.: BEURMANN/KLAVIERSONATEN, 29, 39, 41–42; BERG, 186–87; OTTENBERG, 31; SCHULENBERG/IN-STRUMENTAL, 68–69

Incipits from 5883:

4. Sonata per il cembalo solo. 1732, rev. 1744 (NV 1). W. 65/2

Mss.: D-brd B, P 775 (Michel; title p. and first p. marked by CPEB); B Bc, 5883 (Michel); PL Kj, P 771 (autog.)

Mod. edn.: BERG/FACSIMILE

Lit.: BEURMANN/KLAVIERSONATEN, 14; BERG, 91–94, 139, 186–87

Incipits from P 775:

5. Sonata per il cembalo solo. 1732, rev. 1744 (NV 1). W. 65/3

Mss.: D-brd B, P 772 (rev. by CPEB); D-ddr Bds, P 369, P 371; B Bc, 5883 (Michel)

Mod. edns.: FARRENC, BERG/FACSIMILE

Lit.: GEIRINGER/BACH, 354; BERG, 94, 190; SCHULEN-BERG/INSTRUMENTAL, 49

Incipits from 5883:

6. Sonata [suite] per il cembalo solo. 1733, rev. 1744 (NV 1). W. 65/4

Mss.: D-brd B, P 746 (autog.); D-ddr Bds, P 365, P 371; B Bc, 5883 (Michel); A Wn, 19035 (Michel)

Mod. edn.: BERG/FACSIMILE

Lit.: NEWMAN, 419

Incipits from P 746:

7. Sonatina per il cembalo solo. 1734, rev. 1744 (NV 2). W. 64/1

Mss.: D-brd B, P 775 (Michel), P 1001 (Wq n.v. 31); D-ddr Bds, P 369; B Bc, 5881 (Michel); A Wgm, VII 3872, No. 15 (Michel, marked "Samml. Westphal" in pencil); D-brd Kll, Mb 51:2; US Wc, M23.B13.W.64(1)

Mod. edns. of version 2: A. Kreutz, Mainz: Schott, 1938; BERG/FACSIMILE

Mod. edns. of items 7–12 in version 1: JOHNEN/SONATI-NEN, BERG/FACSIMILE

Lit.: BEURMANN/KLAVIERSONATEN, 21, 39; BERG, 91, 94, 139, 187, 212, 241; OTTENBERG, 32; SCHULENBERG/ INSTRUMENTAL, 96; FOX, 52–55, 99–100, 160; Critical Notes in BERG/FACSIMILE

The 1st mvt. in version 2 is a vnt. of the 1st mvt. in version 1. The 2nd mvt. of version 1 appears as the 2nd mvt. of item 12, version 2. The 2nd mvt. of version 2 appears as the 2nd mvt. of item 12, version 1.

Items 7–12, unpublished in CPEB's lifetime, were obviously intended to be a set; they are numbered, respectively, from 1 to 6 in CPEB's hand in P 775 and grouped the same way by Westphal in 5881. Their collective title as given in W. is not CPEB's but Westphal's.

Note the relations among items 7–12; see also BERG/VARI-ATIONS. Regarding such permutations, see items 216, 869, 875.

See item 344.

Incipits from P 775, 5881, P 369, VII 3872, No. 15, Mb 51 (version 1):

Incipits from P 1001 (version 2):

3rd mvt.: same incipit as for 3rd mvt. in version 1

8. Sonatina per il cembalo solo. 1734, rev. 1744 (NV 2). W. 64/2

Mss.: D-brd B, P 775 (Michel; title p. marked by CPEB); D-ddr Bds, P 369; B Bc, 5881 (Michel); A Wgm, VII 3872, No. 13 (Michel, marked "Samml. Westphal" in pencil)

Mod. edns.: See item 7; BERG/FACSIMILE

Lit.: BEURMANN/KLAVIERSONATEN, 39, 44, 68, 96; BEURMANN/REPRISENSONATEN, 169; BERG, 91, 94; OTTENBERG, 32; FOX, 40–41,82–85, 121; Critical Notes in BERG/FACSIMILE

BEURMANN/KLAVIERSONATEN, 120, gives apparently incorrect source information. See items 7, 10.

Incipits from P 775:

9. Sonatina per il cembalo solo. 1734, rev. 1744 (NV 2). W. 64/3

Mss.: D-brd B, P 775 (Michel; 1st p. marked by CPEB); D-ddr Bds, P 369; B Bc, 5881 (Michel)

Mod. edns.: See item 7; BERG/FACSIMILE

Lit.: BEURMANN/KLAVIERSONATEN, 42, 44, 68; BERG, 94, 139; Critical Notes in BERG/FACSIMILE

Its 2nd mvt. = the 2nd mvt. of item 11, version 2. See item 7.

Incipits from P 775:

10. Sonatina per il cembalo solo. 1734, rev. 1744 (NV 2). W. 64/4

Mss.: D-brd B, P 775 (Michel; 1st p. marked by CPEB); D-ddr

Bds, P 369, P 371; B Bc, 5881 (Michel); A Wgm, VII 3872, No. 6 (Michel, marked "Samml. Westphal" in pencil); US Wc, M23.B13.W.64(4)

Mod. edns.: See item 7; BERG/FACSIMILE

Lit.: BEURMANN/KLAVIERSONATEN, 27; BERG, 94, 166, 186–87; OTTENBERG, 33; Critical Notes in BERG/FACSIMILE

See item 7. I have not been able to see P 371 again, which, according to BERG/NOTES, is a vnt.; it also borrows its 2nd mvt. from item 8.

Incipits from P 775, 5881, P 369, VII 3872, No. 6, M23.B13.W.64(4):

11. Sonatina per il cembalo solo. 1734, rev. 1744 (NV 2). W. 64/5

Mss.: D-brd B, P 775 (2 copies, both by Michel; the 2nd is rev. by CPEB), P 789 (Wq n.v. 32); D-ddr Bds, P 369; B Bc, 5881 (Michel); A Wgm, VII 3872, No. 17 (Michel, marked "Samml. Westphal" in pencil)

Mod. edns.: See item 7; BERG/FACSIMILE

Lit.: BEURMANN/KLAVIERSONATEN, 96, 104; BEURMANN/REPRISENSONATEN, 169; BERG, 139, 240–41; FOX, 68, 83–84, 122; Critical Notes in BERG/FACSIMILE

BEURMANN/KLAVIERSONATEN, 120, gives apparently incorrect source information. See item 7. The 2nd mvt. in version 2 = the 2nd mvt. in item 9.

Incipits from P 775, P 369, 5881, VII 3872, No. 17 (version 1):

Incipits from P 789 (Wq n.v. 32) (version 2):

12. Sonatina per il cembalo solo. 1734, rev. 1744 (NV 3). W. 64/6

Mss.: D-brd B, P 775 (Michel; 1st p. marked by CPEB); D-ddr Bds, P 369, P 371, Mus. ms. 30385; D-brd Kll, Mb 61; B Bc, 5881 (Michel); A Wgm, VII 3872, No. 3 (Michel, marked "Samml. Westphal" in pencil)

Mod. edns.: See item 7; BERG/FACSIMILE

Lit.: BEURMANN/KLAVIERSONATEN, 96–97; BEURMANN/REPRISENSONATEN, 169; BERG, 186–87, 203; Critical Notes in BERG/FACSIMILE

See item 7.

Incipits from P 775, P 369, 5881, VII 3872, No. 3 (version 1):

2nd mvt.: same incipit as for 2nd mvt. of item 7, version 2

Incipits from P 371, Mus. ms. 30385, Mb 61 (version 2):

2nd mvt.: Same incipit as for item 7, version 1
3rd mvt.: Same incipit as for version 1

13. Sonata per il cembalo solo. 1735, rev. 1743 (NV 3). W. 65/5

Mss.: D-brd B, P 772 (rev. by CPEB); D-ddr Bds, P 369; B Bc, 5883 (Michel)

Mod. edn.: BERG/FACSIMILE
Lit.: BEURMANN/KLAVIERSONATEN, 41; BERG, 93–94,
139, 146, 185–87, 191, 241–42; OTTENBERG, 43, 46, 301;
Critical Notes in BERG/FACSIMILE
See items 21, 22.

Incipits from 5883:

14. Menuet mit 3 Veränderungen von Locatelli . . . [21]
Variazioni da C. F. E. Bach. 1735 (NV 3). W. 118/7
Early print: "Menuet de Locatelli avec 21 Variations pour
le Forte-Piano, composées par C. P. E. Bach." Vienne:
chez Jean Traeg [1803] (W. 269). The known lit. gives no
evidence that this (posthumous) print had been au-
thorized by CPEB.
Ms. probably copied from the early print: B Bc, 5899
(Westphal)
Mod. edn.: BERG/FACSIMILE
Lit.: AMZ, VI (1804), 242–44; FISCHER, 192, 199–201, 207–
08, 210–11
The title means that the theme and the 1st 3 variations are
by Locatelli and the remaining variations are by CPEB.

Incipit from 5899:

15. Sonate per il cembalo solo. 1736, rev. 1743 (NV 3). W.
65/6
Mss.: D-brd B, P 772 (Michel, rev. by CPEB), N. Mus. ms.
10067; D-ddr Bds, P 369; B Bc, 5883 (Michel); US Wc,
M23.B13.W.65(6)
Mod. edns.: FARRENC, BERG/FACSIMILE
Lit.: BEURMANN/KLAVIERSONATEN, 39, 104–05; BERG,
94, 213; OTTENBERG, 43, 46, 301; SCHULENBERG/IN-
STRUMENTAL, 59–60; FOX, 165; Critical Notes in BERG/
FACSIMILE
P 772 contains a shorter version of the 3rd mvt., scratched
out and corrected. M23.B13.W.65(6) has as its 3rd mvt.
only the shorter version.

Incipits from 5883:

16. Sonata per il cembalo solo. 1736, rev. 1744 (NV 3). W.
65/7
Mss. ("vnts." classified as those which differ from version
1): D-brd B, P 225 (1st mvt. only, vnt.), P 368 (vnt.), P
775 (1st mvt. only in vnt. form, followed by entire sonata
in the hand of Michel); D-ddr Bds, P 369 (not P 269), P
371 (written-out cadenza in 2nd mvt.); B Bc, 5883; D-ddr
GOl, Mus. 21a, XI; US Wc, M23.B13.W.65(7) (vnt.); PL
Kj, P 771 (autog.)
Mod. edn.: BERG/FACSIMILE
Lit.: BEURMANN/KLAVIERSONATEN, 44, 104; BERG, 94,
139, 191, 196, 203, 241, 359–62; OTTENBERG, 26, 31, 43,
297, 301; SCHULENBERG/INSTRUMENTAL, 24, 122–25
According to BERG/NOTES, a third version in addition to
the two whose incipits are given below, which shares
movements with these two, is contained in P 371 and the
vnt. part of P 775.
P 225 is the *Clavierbüchlein* for Anna Magdalena Bach (actual
title: *A.M.B. 1725*) whose compilation was begun in 1725
by J. S. Bach. The 1st mvt. of the present item appears
in this compilation as the 27th piece, under the title "Solo
per il Cembalo" (BWV Anh. 129), in the "late" hand (after
1733–34, according to KAST) of Anna Magdalena. The
basic melody of this movement is found in Sperontes's
Singende Muse an der Pleisse of 1736 (see BWV Anh. 40)
and in a concerto for 2 keyboards by W. F. Bach (see
FALCK, 62, Anh. 3, and BWV Anh. 188).
See item 1. See also DADELSEN/NBA, 52, 64–65, 70, 96–97.

Incipits from 5883, Michel copy in P 775, P 369 (version 1):

Incipits from M23.B13.W.65(7), P 225, P 368 (version 2):

3rd mvt.: same incipit as for 3rd mvt. of version 1

17. Sonata per il cembalo solo. 1737, rev. 1743 (NV 3). W. 65/8

Mss.: D-brd B, N. Mus. ms. 10067, P 364; D-ddr Bds, P 369, M.Th. 46; B Bc, 5883 (Michel); A Wgm, VII 43747; D-ddr SWl, 859/1; D-brd Mbs, Mus. ms. 1795 (1st mvt. as in version 2, 2nd mvt. as in version 1); PL Kj, P 771 (autog.); US Wc, M23.B13.W. 65(8) (vnt.)

Mod. edn.: BERG/FACSIMILE

Lit.: BEURMANN/KLAVIERSONATEN, 31, 43; BERG, 94, 126–27, 139; OTTENBERG, 43, 301

From BERG/NOTES: Some vnts., differing only slightly from 5883, P 369

Incipits from 5883, P 369 (version 1):

Incipits from M23.B13.W.65(8) (version 2):

3rd mvt.: same incipit as for 3rd mvt. of version 1

18. Sonata per il cembalo solo. 1737, rev. 1743 (NV 4). W. 65/9

Mss.: D-brd B, P 367, P 368, P 370, P 775 (title p. in CPEB's hand); D-ddr Bds, P 369, M.Th. 54; B Bc, 5883 (Michel); A Wgm, VII 43748; US Wc, M23.B13.W.65(9), M23.B13. W.65(9)B. The latter ms. also contains, in a modern hand, notes about vnts.

Early print: HUBERTY

Ms. probably copied from the early print: D-brd B, P 673

Mod. edns.: FRIEDHEIM, BERG/FACSIMILE

Lit.: BEURMANN/KLAVIERSONATEN, 31, 43, 45; BERG, 91, 94, 139, 241; OTTENBERG, 43, 301; SCHULENBERG/INSTRUMENTAL, 24, 30; FOX, 179–81

Incipits from M23.B13.W.65(9), M23.B13.W.65(9)B, P 367, P 368, VII 43748 (version 1):

Incipits from 5883, P 775, P 370, P 369, M.Th. 54 (version 2):

1st mvt.: same incipit as for 1st mvt. of version 1

Incipits from P 673 and the Huberty print (version 3):

1st and 3rd mvts.: same incipits as for 1st and 3rd mvts. of version 1

19. Sonata per il cembalo solo. 1738, rev. 1743 (NV 4). W. 65/10

Mss.: D-brd B, P 367, P 368, P 772 (rev. by CPEB); D-ddr Bds, P 369 (but not also P 370); B Bc, 5883 (Michel, with an extra copy of 2nd mvt. enclosed, in different page format); A Wgm, VII 43749; US Wc, M23.B13.W.65(10), M23.B13.W.65(10)B. The latter ms. also contains, in a modern hand, notes about the two versions.

Early print: HUBERTY

Mod. edn.: BERG/FACSIMILE

Ms. probably copied from the early print: D-brd B, P 673

Lit.: BEURMANN/KLAVIERSONATEN, 72, 104, 111; BERG, 94, 185, 241; OTTENBERG, 43, 301

From BERG/NOTES: The Huberty print and P 673 have a slightly embellished version of the ¾ Andante.

Incipits from 5883, P 772, P 369 (version 1):

Incipits from VII 43749, P 367, P 368, both US Wc mss. (version 2):

1st and 3rd mvts.: same incipits as for 1st and 3rd mvts. of version 1

20. Sonata per il cembalo solo. 1739 (NV 4). W. 62/2

Mss.: D-brd B, P 772 (rev. by CPEB); D-ddr Bds, Mus. ms. 30385; D-brd Kll, Mb 48

Early print: NEBENSTUNDEN, 16

Ms. probably copied from the early print: B Br, II 4094 (Westphal)

Mod. edn.: BERG/FACSIMILE

Lit.: BITTER/BRÜDER, I, 50

From BERG/NOTES: Some slight vnts.

Incipits from P 772:

21. Sonata per il cembalo solo. 1739 (NV 4). W. 65/11, 266

Mss.: D-brd B, P 775 (Michel; 1st p. marked by CPEB); D-ddr Bds, P 369; B Bc, 5883 (Michel, with an additional, different 3rd mvt. inserted); A Wgm, VII 3872, No. 8 (Michel, marked "Samml. Westphal" in pencil), VII 43750

Early print: TROIS SONATES

Mss. probably copied from the early print: D-brd Kll, Mb 52 (2 copies)

Mod. edn.: VRIESLANDER/LEICHTE (incipits a, b, and d apply, respectively, to the 1st, 2nd, and 3rd mvts. of this edn.); FARRENC (using TROIS SONATES as source); BERG/FACSIMILE

Lit.: BEURMANN/KLAVIERSONATEN, 31, 62; BERG, 95, 139, 213, 242–43; SCHULENBERG/INSTRUMENTAL, 55; FOX, 72–73; Critical Notes in BERG/FACSIMILE

From BERG/NOTES: A letter in the E. F. Schmid family's possession (see Introduction, n. 7) from CPEB's widow to Westphal makes it clear that the Allegretto grazioso was sent to Westphal as an alternate 3rd mvt., replacing the Presto.

a. Incipit of 1st mvt. in all sources:

b. Incipit of 2nd mvt. in P 775, 5883, TROIS SONATES, VII 3872, VII 43750:

c. Incipit of 3rd mvt. in P 775, P 369, 5883 insertion, VII 3872, No. 8:

d. Incipit of 3rd mvt. in Mb 52 (both copies), 5883, VII 43750 (the latter transposed from 3rd mvt. of item 13):

e. Incipit of 3rd mvt. in TROIS SONATES (vnt. of incipit c):

22. Sonata per il cembalo solo. 1740 (NV 4). W. 62/3
Mss.: D-brd B, P 368, P 772 (rev. by CPEB), P 774, Mus.
ms. 38049 (3rd mvt. only), BP 143; D-ddr Bds, P 369; A
Wgm, VII 43743
Early print: MARPURG/PRACTISCH, III, 10
Ms. probably copied from the early print: B Br, II 4094
(Westphal)
Mod. edn.: BERG/FACSIMILE
Lit.: BITTER/BRÜDER, I, 50–51; BERG, 139, 146, 191, 241–42

Incipits from P 772, P 369, BP 143:

Incipits from P 368, P 774, VII 43743: as above, except that
the 2nd mvt. is replaced by the 2nd mvt. of item 13 (transposed).

23. Sonata per il cembalo solo. 1740 (NV 4). W. 65/12
Mss.: D-brd B, P 368 (vnt.), P 772 (Michel, rev. by CPEB),
P 786 (rev. by CPEB); B Bc, 5883 (Michel); A Wgm, VII
3872, No. 4 (Michel, marked "Samml. Westphal" in pen-
cil); D-ddr SWl, 859/1; US Wc, M23.B13.W.65(12) (vnt.);
SL, Saml. Miedendorff (vnt.)
Mod. edns.: BERG/EDITIONS, BERG/FACSIMILE
Lit.: BEURMANN/KLAVIERSONATEN, 29, 96, 106; BERG,
84, 241; FOX, 117; Critical Notes in BERG/FACSIMILE
From BERG/NOTES: M23.B13.W.65(12) is somewhat less
elaborate than the other sources.

Incipits from P 772:

Incipits from M23.B13.W.65(12):

24. Sonata. 1740 (NV 4). W. 48/1
Mss.: D-brd B, Mus. ms. 30431 (1st and 3rd mvts. only);
D-ddr SWl, 859/1; F Pc, Ms. 1556 (probably not autog.)
Early print and lit. about it: See PRUSSIAN SONATAS.
Mss. probably copied from the early print: D-brd B, P 773;
A Wgm, VII 41780; US NHu, Mason collection, 5015
Mod. edns.: FARRENC, STEGLICH/PREUSSISCHE, BERG/
FACSIMILE
Lit. about this work: BITTER/BRÜDER, I, 53; SHEDLOCK,
85–86; STEGLICH/HOMILIUS, 109; HADOW, 201–02;
REESER, 37–38; BEURMANN/KLAVIERSONATEN, 40;
GEIRINGER/BACH, 354–55; NEWMAN, 421–22, 428;
BARFORD/KEYBOARD, 59–61; RADCLIFFE, 584;
COHEN, 176; BERG, 146, 188, 213, 241; ROE, 114; OT-
TENBERG, 57, 65–66, 75, 144; SCHULENBERG/INSTRU-
MENTAL, 63–64; FOX, 61–64
Contrary to the impression given by BEURMANN/
KLAVIERSONATEN, D-ddr LEm, Becker III.6.4, III.6.5,
III.6.6, III.6.8, and III.6.9 are not mss. but are the original
prints of PRUSSIAN SONATAS, WÜRTTEMBERG SONA-
TAS, REPRISEN-SONATEN, FORTSETZUNG, ZWEYTE
FORTSETZUNG, KENNER I, and the Hartknoch print of
DAMENSONATEN.

Incipits from PRUSSIAN SONATAS:

25. Sonata. 1740 (NV 4). W. 48/2
Mss.: D-ddr SWl, 859/1; F Pc, Ms. 1556 (probably not autog.)
Early print and lit. about it: See PRUSSIAN SONATAS.
Mss. probably copied from the early print: D-brd B, P 773;
  A Wgm, VII 41780; US NHu, Mason collection, 5015
Mod. edns.: FARRENC, STEGLICH/PREUSSISCHE, MIES,
  BERG/FACSIMILE
Lit. about this work: GEIRINGER/BACH, 355; NEWMAN,
  420; BARFORD/KEYBOARD, 62–64; RADCLIFFE, 584;
  BERG, 139, 242–43; OTTENBERG, 60–61; SCHULEN-
  BERG/INSTRUMENTAL, 128; FOX, 70, 166, 179–81
See item 24.

Incipits from PRUSSIAN SONATAS:

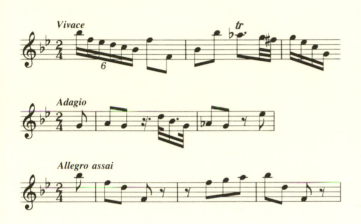

26. Sonata. 1741 (NV 5). W. 48/3
Mss.: D-brd B, P 770 (2nd mvt. only); F Pc, Ms. 1556 (prob-
  ably not autog.)
Early print and lit. about it: See PRUSSIAN SONATAS.
Mss. probably copied from the early print: D-brd B, P 773;
  A Wgm, VII 41780; US NHu, Mason collection, 5015
Mod. edns.: FARRENC, STEGLICH/PREUSSISCHE, BERG/
  FACSIMILE
Lit. about this work: BITTER/BRÜDER, I, 53–54; NEWMAN,
  421, 428; BARFORD/KEYBOARD, 64–66; RADCLIFFE,
  584; BERG, 95, 139, 145–47, 171–72; OTTENBERG, 59, 60,
  302; FOX, 139–40
See item 24.

Incipits from PRUSSIAN SONATAS:

27. Sonata. 1741 (NV 5). W. 48/4
Mss.: F Pc, Ms. 1556 (probably not autog.)
Early print and lit. about it: See PRUSSIAN SONATAS.
Mss. probably copied from the early print: D-brd B, P 773;
  A Wgm, VII 41780; US NHu, Mason collection, 5015
Mod. edns.: FARRENC, STEGLICH/PREUSSISCHE, BERG/
  FACSIMILE
Lit. about this work: STEGLICH/HOMILIUS, 109; SCHMID/
  KAMMERMUSIK, 122; BEURMANN/KLAVIERSONA-
  TEN, 73, 106; BEURMANN/REPRISENSONATEN, 173;
  BARFORD/KEYBOARD, 66–75; BERG, 85, 139, 161–62;
  OTTENBERG, 59, 302; FOX, 115, 118, 179–81
See item 24.

Incipits from PRUSSIAN SONATAS:

28. Sonata. 1741 (NV 5). W. 48/5
Mss.: D-brd B, Mus. ms. 30431 (3rd mvt. only), P 789; A
  Wn, 5018; F Pc, Ms. 1556 (probably not autog.)
Early prints: PRUSSIAN SONATAS; pub. as a sonata of J.
  S. Bach, Hamburg: J. C. Westphal, n.d. Lit. about PRUS-
  SIAN SONATAS: See this entry in Bib.
Mss. probably copied from an early print (PRUSSIAN
  SONATAS): D-brd B, P 773; A Wgm, VII 41780; US NHu,
  Mason collection, 5015 (incomplete)
Mod. edns.: FARRENC, STEGLICH/PREUSSISCHE, BERG/
  FACSIMILE
Lit. about this work: STEGLICH/HOMILIUS, 65–66, 79–80;
  SCHMID/KAMMERMUSIK, 122; BEURMANN/KLA-
  VIERSONATEN, 46; NEWMAN, 421; BARFORD/KEY-
  BOARD, 75–77; BERG, 145, 167–68, 203; FOX, 169–70,
  182–83
The publisher J. C. Westphal was apparently unrelated to
J. J. H. Westphal; see Introduction, n. 4.
See item 24.

Incipits from PRUSSIAN SONATAS:

29. Sonata. 1742 (NV 5). W. 48/6

Ms.: F Pc, Ms. 1556 (probably not autog.)

Early print and lit. about it: See PRUSSIAN SONATAS.

Mss. probably copied from the early print: D-brd B, P 773;
A Wgm, VII 41780

Mod. edns.: FARRENC, RIEMANN, STEGLICH/PREUS-
SISCHE, BERG/FACSIMILE

Lit. about this work: STEGLICH/HOMILIUS, 73–74; BEUR-
MANN/KLAVIERSONATEN, 72; NEWMAN, 420;
COHEN, 168; BERG, 95, 99, 139, 146, 203, 214; SCHULEN-
BERG/INSTRUMENTAL, 69–70; FOX, 87–88, 122, 129–32,
170

See item 24.

Incipits from PRUSSIAN SONATAS:

30. Sonata. 1742 (NV 5). W. 49/1

Mss.: D-brd B, P 773, P 789, P 966; D-ddr Bds, P 365

Early prints and lit. about them: See WÜRTTEMBERG
SONATAS.

Mss. probably copied from the early prints: D-brd B, P 1171;
B Bc, 5873; A Wgm, VII 41780; D-ddr LEm, Poel. Mus.
ms. 49; D-ddr LEb, 341, Gorke 34 and 35; US NHu, Mason
collection, 5010a

Mod. edns.: FARRENC; V. D'Indy, Paris: Senart, 191?;
STEGLICH/WÜRTTEMBERGISCHE; BERG/FACSIMILE

Lit. about this work: SHEDLOCK, 92–93; STEGLICH/
HOMILIUS, 116–19; HADOW, 196–98; NEWMAN, 424;
BARFORD/KEYBOARD, 83–85; COHEN, 66–67; BERG,
187, 200; OTTENBERG, 58, 62–64, 75, 144; SCHULEN-
BERG/INSTRUMENTAL, 6, 64–67; FOX, 161–62, 167, 179–
81

See item 24.

Incipits from WÜRTTEMBERG SONATAS (Haffner edn.):

31. Sonata. 1742 (NV 5). W. 49/2

Mss.: D-brd B, P 773, P 789, P 966; D-ddr Bds, P 365

Early prints and lit. about them: See WÜRTTEMBERG
SONATAS.

Mss. probably copied from the early prints: D-brd B, P 1171;
B Bc, 5873; A Wgm, VII 41780; D-ddr LEm, Poel. Mus.
ms. 49; D-ddr LEb, 341, Gorke 34 and 35; US NHu, Mason
collection, 5010a

Mod. edns.: BÜLOW; FARRENC; V. d'Indy, Paris: Senart,
191?; STEGLICH/WÜRTTEMBERGISCHE; BERG/FAC-
SIMILE

Lit. about this work: SHEDLOCK, 92–93; BEURMANN/
KLAVIERSONATEN, 38–39, 67; NEWMAN, 421, 427;
BARFORD/KEYBOARD, 86–87; BERG, 166–67; ROE, 114;
SCHULENBERG/INSTRUMENTAL, 6, 84–87; FOX, 87–
88, 94, 169

See item 24.

Incipits from WÜRTTEMBERG SONATAS (Haffner edn.):

32. Sonata. 1742 (NV 5). W. 49/4

Mss.: D-brd B, P 773, P 966; D-ddr Bds, P 365; D-brd KIl,
Mb 42

Early prints and lit. about them: See WÜRTTEMBERG
SONATAS.

Mss. probably copied from the early prints: D-brd B, P 1171; B Bc, 5873; A Wgm, VII 41780; D-ddr LEm, Poel. Mus. ms. 49; D-ddr LEb, Gorke 34 and 35; D-brd Gs, Mus. VII 680; US NHu, Mason collection, 5010a; a ms. is in the private collection of E. N. Kulukundis (U.S.).

Mod. edns.: FARRENC, STEGLICH/WÜRTTEMBER-GISCHE, BERG/FACSIMILE

Lit. about this work: STEGLICH/HOMILIUS, 74; BÜCKEN, 165–66; REESER, 39; BEURMANN/KLAVIERSONATEN, 45; NEWMAN, 424; BARFORD/KEYBOARD, 90–91; RADCLIFFE, 585; BERG, 139, 177–78, 242; ROE, 111–14; OTTENBERG, 59, 302; SCHULENBERG/INSTRUMEN-TAL, 6, 63

See item 24.

Incipits from WÜRTTEMBERG SONATAS (Haffner edn.):

32.5. Sonata per il cembalo solo. 1743 (NV 5). W. 65/13
Mss.: D-brd B, P 275, P 359 (mostly autog.), P 368, P 370, P 432, P 775 (title p. marked by CPEB); D-ddr Bds, P 369; B Bc, 5883 (Michel); D-brd KIl, Mb 53:1; A Wgm, VII 43751 (2 copies, both [?] by Michel); US Wc, M23.B13.W.65(13); US NHu, Mason collection, 5016
Mod. edns.: FARRENC, BERG/EDITIONS, BERG/FAC-SIMILE
Lit.: BEURMANN/KLAVIERSONATEN, 46, 55; BERG, 82–83, 96, 139, 188–89, 204
See item 33.

Incipits from 5883:

33. Sonata. 1743 (NV 5). W. 49/3
Mss.: D-brd B, P 773, P 966; D-ddr Bds, P 365; D-brd KIl, Mb 42
Early prints and lit. about them: See WÜRTTEMBERG SONATAS.
Mss. probably copied from the early prints: D-brd B, P 1171; B Bc, 5873; A Wgm, VII 41780; D-ddr LEm, Poel. Mus. ms. 49; D-ddr LEb, 342, Gorke 34 and 35; D-brd Gs, Mus. VII 680; US NHu, Mason collection, 5010a
Mod. edns.: FARRENC, STEGLICH/WÜRTTEMBER-GISCHE, BERG/FACSIMILE
Lit. about this work: BÜCKEN, 164, 166; HADOW, 198–99; NEWMAN, 421; BARFORD/KEYBOARD, 87–90; BERG, 99–100, 129, 146, 170–71, 241; ROE, 114; SCHULENBERG/INSTRUMENTAL, 6, 127; FOX, 139

CPEB/FORKEL, Feb. 10, 1775, speaks of 6 sonatas composed in 1743: "Die 2 Sonaten, welche Ihren Beyfall vorzüglich haben, sind die einzigen von dieser Art, die ich je gemacht habe. Se gehören zu der, aus dem H-moll, die ich Ihnen mitschickte, zu der aus dem B, die Sie nun auch haben, und zu 2en aus der Hafner-Würtembergischen Samm-lung, und sind alle 6 anno 1743, im Töplitzer Bade von mir, der ich darmahls sehr gichtbrüchig war, auf einem Claviacord mit der kurzen Octave verfertiget." But NV, 5, shows only 3 sonatas dating from 1743: items 32.5–34. Possibly item 32 is the one CPEB refers to as being in B♭.
See item 24.

Incipits from WÜRTTEMBERG SONATAS (Haffner edn.):

34. Sonata. 1743 (NV 5). W. 49/5
Mss.: D-brd B, P 773, P 966; US Bp, No. 6 in **M200.9
Early prints and lit. about them: See WÜRTTEMBERG SONATAS.
Mss. probably copied from the early prints: D-brd B, P 1171; B Bc, 5873; A Wgm, VII 41780; D-ddr LEm, Poel. Mus. ms. 49; D-ddr LEb, 343, Gorke 34 and 35; D-brd Gs, Mus. VII 680; USNHu, Mason collection, 5010a
Mod. edns.: FARRENC; V. d'Indy, Paris: Senart, 191?; STEGLICH/WÜRTTEMBERGISCHE, BERG/FACSIMILE
Lit. about this work: STEGLICH/HOMILIUS, 73; HADOW, 201; NEWMAN, 420, 424; BARFORD/KEYBOARD, 91–93;

RADCLIFFE, 585; BERG, 139, 176, 241; OTTENBERG, 59, 302; SCHULENBERG/INSTRUMENTAL, 6, 134; FOX, 70
See items 24, 33.

Incipits from WÜRTTEMBERG SONATAS (Haffner edn.):

35. Deleted

36. Sonata. 1744 (NV 6). W. 49/6
Mss.: D-brd B, P 773, P 966 (3rd mvt. incomplete); D-ddr Bds, P 1135 (largely autog. and Michel, containing only rev.: see item 164); B Bc, 5885 (Michel, containing only rev.: see item 164)
Early prints and lit. about them: See WÜRTTEMBERG SONATAS.
Mss. probably copied from the early prints: D-brd B, P 1171; B Bc, 5873; A Wgm, VII 41780; D-ddr LEm, Poel. Mus. ms. 49; D-ddr LEb, 344, Gorke 34 and 35; D-brd Gs, Mus. VII 680; US NHu, Mason collection, 5010a
Mod. edns.: FARRENC, STEGLICH/WÜRTTEMBER-GISCHE, BERG/EDITIONS, BERG/FACSIMILE
Lit. about this work: STEGLICH/HOMILIUS, 75–79, 97–98, 121; BEURMANN/KLAVIERSONATEN, 58, 72; NEW-MAN, 421; BARFORD/KEYBOARD, 93; BERG, 116, 123, 129, 139, 200, 204; ROE, 114; OTTENBERG, 59, 302; SCHULENBERG/INSTRUMENTAL, 6, 34, 50, 87–90, 99; FOX, 70, 164
See item 24.

Incipits from WÜRTTEMBERG SONATAS (Haffner edn.):

37. Sonata. 1744 (NV 6). W. 52/4
Mss.: D-brd B, P 437; D-ddr GOl, Mus. 21a, XLII; D-brd Gs, Mus. VII 680
Early prints and lit. about them: See ZWEYTE FORTSET-ZUNG.
Ms. probably copied from an early print: D-brd B, BP 143
Mod. edns.: RIEMANN, BERG/EDITIONS, BERG/FAC-SIMILE, HASHIMOTO/ZWEYTE FORTSETZUNG
Lit. about this work: BITTER/BRÜDER, I, 78; BEURMANN/KLAVIERSONATEN, 54; BERG, 97, 154–55, 180, 190
Wotquenne's incipit shows his source (unknown) to be a vnt.
See item 24.

Incipits from ZWEYTE FORTSETZUNG:

38. Sonata per il cembalo solo. 1744 (NV 6). W. 62/4
Mss.: D-brd B, P 774; D-ddr Bds, P 371; D-brd Mbs, Mus. pr. 2747; D-brd KIl, Mb 50; DK Kk, mu 6309.0633
Early print: OEUVRES, III, 4
Ms. probably copied from the early print: B Br, II 4094 (Westphal)
Mod. edns.: FARRENC, BERG/FACSIMILE
Lit.: BITTER/BRÜDER, I, 58–59; BEURMANN/KLAVIER-SONATEN, 33, 56, 58, 61; BERG, 97, 155–56, 175, 179, 241; FOX, 106, 182–83

Incipits from OEUVRES:

39. Sonata per il cembalo solo. 1744 (NV 6). W. 62/5
Mss.: D-brd B, P 364, P 368, P 774; D-ddr Bds, P 371; D-brd
   Mbs, Mus. ms. 1794; A Wgm, H 31221 (VII 43745); F Pn,
   Vm 7, 1955; US Wc, M23.B13.W.62(5)
Early print: OEUVRES, IV, 12
Mss. probably copied from the early print: B Br, II 4094
   (Westphal); D-ddr LEb, 346
Mod. edns.: FARRENC, BERG/FACSIMILE
Lit.: BITTER/BRÜDER, I, 59; BEURMANN/KLAVIER-
   SONATEN, 48, 51–52, 55; BERG, 80–81, 97, 123, 190, 201–
   02

Incipits from OEUVRES:

40. Claviersonate. 1744 (NV 6). W. 62/6
Mss.: D-brd B, P 367, P 368, P 414 (2nd mvt. only); D-ddr
   Bds, P 365; D-brd Kll, Mb 48; D-brd Mbs, Mus. ms. 1795;
   US NHu, Mason collection, 5009
Early print: ALLERLEY, p. 141. Lit. about ALLERLEY: See
   this entry in Bib.
Mss. probably copied from the early print: D-brd B, P 790;
   B Br, II 4094 (Westphal); D-ddr LEb, 346
Mod. edns.: FARRENC, MIES, BERG/EDITIONS, BERG/
   FACSIMILE
Lit. about this work: BITTER/BRÜDER, I, 58, 81–82; BEUR-
   MANN/KLAVIERSONATEN, 40, 45, 48, 54–55, 63; BERG,
   96–97, 123–24, 200; SCHULENBERG/INSTRUMENTAL,
   76–77; FOX, 181–82

Incipits from ALLERLEY:

41. Sonata per il cembalo solo. 1744 (NV 6). W. 62/7
Mss.: D-brd B, P 439, BP 195 (but not also P 349, P 728); A
   Wn, 18677
Early print: COLLECTION II
Ms. probably copied from the early print: B Br, II 4094
   (Westphal)
Mod. edns.: FARRENC, BERG/EDITIONS, BERG/FAC-
   SIMILE
Lit.: BEURMANN/KLAVIERSONATEN, 31, 58, 63, 67;
   BERG, 97, 154; FOX, 163–64
See items 341, 342.

Incipits from COLLECTION II:

42. Sonata per il cembalo solo. 1744 (NV 6). W. 65/14
Mss.: D-brd B, P 364, P 775 (Michel); D-ddr Bds, P 369, P
   371; B Bc, 5883 (Michel); A Wgm, VII 3872, No. 7 (Michel,
   marked "Samml. Westphal" in pencil), VII 43752; D-brd
   Kll, Mb 52, Mb 53; US Wc, M23.B13.W.65(14)
Mod. edns.: VRIESLANDER/LEICHTE, BERG/FACSIMILE
Lit.: BEURMANN/KLAVIERSONATEN, 63; BERG, 97, 190,
   241; SCHULENBERG/INSTRUMENTAL, 49, 100–02

Incipits from 5883:

43. Sonata per il cembalo solo. 1745 (NV 6). W. 65/15
Mss.: D-brd B, P 359 (Michel), P 775 (marked by CPEB);
   D-ddr Bds, P 369; B Bc, 5883 (Michel); A Wgm, VII 3872,

No. 2 (Michel, marked "Samml. Westphal" in pencil), Q 11696 (VII 43753); US Wc, M23.B13.W.65(15)

Mod. edn.: BERG/FACSIMILE

Lit.: BEURMANN/KLAVIERSONATEN, 31, 56, 72; BERG, 97, 140

Incipits from VII 3872, No. 2:

44. Minuetto con v variazioni. 1745 (NV 7). W. 118/3

Mss.: D-brd B, N. Mus. ms. 10067, P 749 (autog.); D-ddr Bds, Mus. ms. 30382; B Bc, 5899 (Westphal); A Wgm, VII 43764; A Wn, 19035 (Michel); SL, Saml. Miedendorff

Mod. edn.: BERG/FACSIMILE

Lit.: FISCHER, 192

Incipit from P 749:

45. Sinfonia per il cembalo solo. 1745 (NV 6). W. 122/1

Mss.: D-ddr Bds, P 369; A Wn, 19035 (Michel)

Early print: HILLER/SINFONIE, III, No. XIII

Mod. edn.: BERG/FACSIMILE

Lit.: HASE, 87

Arr. for unaccompanied harpsichord of a symphony of 1741 (item 648)

Incipits from 19035:

46. Sonata per il cembalo solo. 1746 (NV 7). W. 65/16

Mss.: D-brd B, P 367, P 368, P 775 (Michel, marked by CPEB); D-ddr Bds, P 1131 (autog.); B Bc, 5883 (Michel, with first tempo indication in CPEB's hand); A Wgm, H 31221 (VII 43745); D-brd Kll, Mb 52; D-brd Mbs, Mus. ms. 1794; US Wc, M20. A2. M684, M23.B13.W.65(16)

Mod. edns.: FRIEDHEIM, BERG/FACSIMILE

Lit.: BEURMANN/KLAVIERSONATEN, 32, 34, 51, 53, 62, 64; BERG, 96, 109–10; FOX, 73, 170–72, 210–11

Incipits from P 1131:

[2 mvts. only]

47. Sonata per il cembalo solo. 1746 (NV 7). W. 65/17

Mss.: D-brd B, P 212, P 359 (Michel), P 775 (Michel; 1st p. marked by CPEB); B Bc, 5883 (Michel); A Wgm, VII 3872 (Michel, marked "Samml. Westphal" in pencil), VII 38402; D-brd Kll, Mb 53; a ms. is in the private collection of E. N. Kulukundis (U.S.).

Mod. edns.: FARRENC; in W. S. Newman, ed., *Sons of Bach*, New York: Mercury, 1947; in W. Georgii, ed., *400 Jahre europäischer Klaviermusik*, Cologne: Volk, n.d.; BERG/ EDITIONS; BERG/FACSIMILE

Lit.: HADOW, 198; BEURMANN/KLAVIERSONATEN, 60; NEWMAN, 159, 426–28; BERG, 96–98, 140, 163–64, 169–70; SCHULENBERG/INSTRUMENTAL, 141; FOX, 97–99, 179–81

Incipits from 5883:

48. Sonata per il cembalo solo. 1746 (NV 7). W. 65/18

Mss.: D-brd B, P 775, P 1134 (but not also P 434); B Bc, 5883 (Michel); A Wgm, VII 3872, No. 14 (Michel, marked

"Samml. Westphal" in pencil); D-brd KIl, Mb 53; US Wc,
M23.B13.W.65(18)
Early print: HUBERTY
Ms. probably copied from the early print: D-brd B, P 673
(item 54 substituted for the 2nd and 3rd mvts.)
Mod. edn.: BERG/FACSIMILE
Lit.: BEURMANN/KLAVIERSONATEN, 14; BERG, 97, 140

Incipits from 5883:

49. Sonata per il cembalo solo. 1746 (NV 7). W. 65/19
Mss.: D-ddr Bds, P 369; B Bc, 5883; PL Kj, P 771 (autog.)
Mod. edn.: BERG/FACSIMILE
Lit.: BEURMANN/KLAVIERSONATEN, 96; BERG, 97, 140,
191

Incipits from 5883:

50. Sonata. 1747 (NV 8). W. 52/1
Mss.: D-brd B, P 364; D-brd KIl, Mb 40; D-ddr GOl, Mus.
21a, XXXII (2nd mvt. only, paired with 3rd mvt. of item
119), Mus. 21a, 88 (3rd mvt. only)
Early prints and lit. about them: See ZWEYTE FORTSET-
ZUNG.
Ms. probably copied from the early print: D-brd B, BP 143
Mod. edns.: BERG/EDITIONS, BERG/FACSIMILE,
HASHIMOTO/ZWEYTE FORTSETZUNG

Lit. about this work: BEURMANN/KLAVIERSONATEN, 58;
RADCLIFFE, 588; BERG, 96, 124–25, 146; OTTENBERG,
140
See item 24.

Incipits from ZWEYTE FORTSETZUNG:

51. Sonata per il cembalo solo. 1747 (NV 7). W. 65/20, 266,
268
Mss.: D-brd B, P 359, P 368 (1st mvt. only), P 775 (Michel;
1st p. marked by CPEB), Am.B. 54; B Bc, 5883 (Michel,
with 1st tempo indication in CPEB's hand); D-brd Mbs,
Mus. ms. 1794
Early prints: TROIS SONATES; "Grande Sonate pour le
Clavecin ou Fortepiano, composée par C.Ph.E. Bach.
Oeuvres posthumes No. 1." à Vienne, chez Hoffmeister
et comp. à Leipsic chez Hoffmeister et Kühnel, [c. 1802]
(W. 268). As in the case of TROIS SONATES (see Bib.),
the known lit. gives no evidence that the (posthumous)
Hoffmeister–Kühnel print had been authorized by CPEB.
Mss. probably copied from an early print (TROIS SO-
NATES): D-brd KIl, Mb 52 (3 copies)
Mod. edns.: FARRENC, RIEMANN, BERG/FACSIMILE
Lit.: STEGLICH/HOMILIUS, 62–63, 120–21; BEURMANN/
KLAVIERSONATEN, 65; BERG, 96, 116, 214–15; FOX,
93–94, 192–211

Incipits from 5883:

17

52. Sonata per il cembalo solo. 1747 (NV 8). W. 65/21

Mss.: D/brd B, P 359 (Michel; 4 bars missing in 3rd mvt.), P 772 (rev. by CPEB), P 790; D-ddr Bds, M.Th. 37; B Bc, 5883 (Michel); A Wgm, VII 3872, No. 12 (marked "Samml. Westphal" in pencil); D-brd Kll, Mb 53; US Wc, M23.B13.W.65(21) (4 bars missing in 3rd mvt.), M23.B13.W.65(21)B (with references in a modern hand to vnts. in Berlin sources)

Mod. edn.: BERG/FACSIMILE

Lit.: BERG, 97

Incipits from 5883:

53. Sonata per il cembalo a due tastature. 1747 (NV 8). W. 69

Mss.: D-brd B, P 772 (rev. by CPEB), P 790; D-ddr Bds, P 371, P 1222; A Wgm, VII 43762 (3rd mvt. a vnt.); D-ddr GOl, Mus. 21a 3.70 (3rd mvt. only, vnt.)

Early print and lit. about it: See PRELUDIO.

Mss. probably copied from the early print: D-brd B, P 434 (in c), P 1187

Mod. edns.: LANGLAIS, BRANDTS-BUYS, BERG/EDITIONS, BERG/FACSIMILE

Lit. about this work: BEURMANN/KLAVIERSONATEN, 51; FISCHER, 194, 196, 201; BERG, 97, 219, 222; see also Critical notes in BERG/FACSIMILE.

Incipits from P 772:

54. Arioso con vii variazioni. 1747 (NV 8). W. 118/4

Mss.: D-brd B, Mus. ms. 30433, P 368, P 726, P 734, P 737 (2 copies, one a vnt.), P 747, P 750 (vnt.); D-ddr Bds, Mus. ms. 30382; B Bc, 5899 (Westphal); A Wgm, Q 11711 (VII 14519), VII 43765; A Wn, 19035 (Michel), 5018; US Wc, M23.B13.W.118(4); US NHu, Mason collection, 5009

Early print: HUBERTY

Ms. probably copied from the early print: D-brd B, P 673 (as substitute for 2nd and 3rd mvts. of item 48)

Mod. edns.: VRIESLANDER/KLEINE, BERG/FACSIMILE

Lit.: FISCHER, 192, 196, 200–01, 210–11

Incipit from 19035:

55. Sonata per il cembalo solo. 1748 (NV 8). W. 62/8

Mss.: D-brd B, P 367; D-ddr Bds, Mus. ms. 30448, Mus. ms. 30189, M.Th. 48; A Wgm, SBQ 11711 (VII 14519), VII 43744; D-brd Kll, Mb 48, Mb 50, Mb 85; US AA, M23.B12.S628

Early prints and lit. about them: See HUBERTY, TONSTÜCKE.

Ms. probably copied from TONSTÜCKE: B Br, II 4094 (Westphal)

Ms. probably copied from HUBERTY: D-brd B, P 673. A ms. probably copied from one of the early prints is in the private collection of E. N. Kulukundis (U.S.).

Mod. edns.: FARRENC, BERG/FACSIMILE

Lit. about this work: BEURMANN/KLAVIERSONATEN, 67; BERG, 97, 140, 151–52, 172–73, 200; FOX, 65–66

Incipits from TONSTÜCKE:

56. Sonata per il cembalo solo. 1748 (NV 8). W. 65/22

Mss.: D/brd B, P 368, P 776 (2 copies; 1st a vnt., 2nd has title in CPEB's hand); D-ddr Bds, P 365 (vnt.), Mus. ms. 30385, M.Th. 40; B Bc, 5883 (Westphal); A Wgm, VII 3872, No. 11 (Michel, marked "Samml. Westphal" in pencil), VII 43754; D-brd Kll, Mb 53; SL, Saml. Miedendorff; US

Wc, M23.B13.W.65(22), M23.B13.W.65(22)B (with references in a modern hand to vnts. in Berlin sources)
Early print: HUBERTY
Ms. probably copied from the early print: D-brd B, P 673
Mod. edns.: VRIESLANDER/LEICHTE, BERG/EDITIONS, BERG/FACSIMILE
Lit.: BEURMANN/KLAVIERSONATEN, 34–35, 62; BERG, 97, 204

Incipits from 5883:

57. Sonata per il cembalo solo. 1748 (NV 8). W. 65/23
Mss.: D-brd B, P 366 (Michel; vnts. in 2nd mvt.), P 677, P 772 (partly autog.), P 790; D-ddr Bds, P 371, M.Th. 36, 47 (2nd mvt. only, with vnts.); B Bc, 5883 (Michel); A Wgm, VII 3872, No. 5 (Michel, marked "Samml. Westphal" in pencil), VII 43755; US Wc, M23.B13.W.65(23), M23.B13.W.65(23)B (with references in a modern hand to vnts. in Berlin sources)
Mod. edns.: FRIEDHEIM, BERG/EDITIONS, BERG/FACSIMILE
Lit.: BEURMANN/KLAVIERSONATEN, 30; BERG, 97, 109–10, 140; FOX, 95–97

Incipits from 5883:

58. Sonata per il cembalo solo. 1749 (NV 9). W. 62/9
Mss.: D-brd B, P 716, P 774; D-ddr Bds, M.Th. 36; A Wgm,

H 31221 (VII 43745); D-brd KIl, Mb 48; D-brd Mbs, Mus. pr. 2747
Early print: OEUVRES, I, 14
Ms. probably copied from the early print: B Br, II 4094 (Westphal)
Mod. edns.: FARRENC, BERG/FACSIMILE
Lit.: BEURMANN/KLAVIERSONATEN, 51; BERG, 140

Incipits from OEUVRES:

59. Sonata per il cembalo solo. 1749 (NV 9). W. 62/10
Mss.: D-brd B, P 364, P 367, P 676, P 775 (but not also P 673); US Wc, M20. A2. M68
Early print: MANCHERLEY, 56. Lit. about MANCHERLEY: See this entry in Bib.
Ms. probably copied from the early print: B Br, II 4094 (Westphal)
Mod. edns.: FARRENC, BERG/EDITIONS, BERG/FACSIMILE
Lit. about this work: BEURMANN/KLAVIERSONATEN, 24–27, 51, 62–63, 77, 106; BERG, 81–82, 102–03, 162–63, 200, 363–67; FOX, 66–67, 71, 108, 122

Incipits from MANCHERLEY:

60. Sonata per il cembalo solo. 1749 (NV 9). W. 65/24
Mss.: D-brd B, P 776 (autog.), P 1151; D-ddr Bds, P 369; B Bc, 5883 (Michel)
Mod. edns.: FARRENC, BERG/FACSIMILE

Lit.: BERG, 96; SCHULENBERG/INSTRUMENTAL, 141
P 1151 adds 2 mvts.; see item 371.5.

Incipits from P 776:

61. Sonata per il cembalo solo. 1749 (NV 9). W. 65/25
Mss.: D-brd B, P 359, P 776, P 789 (marked by CPEB), P 845 (1st mvt. only); D-ddr Bds, P 371, M.Th.52; B Bc, 5883 (Michel); A Wgm, VII 3872, No. 9 (Michel, marked "Samml. Westphal" in pencil), Q 11697 (VII 43756); A Wn, 5018; D-brd Kll, Mb 53 (2 copies); US Wc, M23.B13.W.65(25)
Mod. edn.: BERG/FACSIMILE
Lit.: BEURMANN/KLAVIERSONATEN, 34, 47; BERG, 97, 140

Incipits from P 776:

62. Sonata. 1750 (NV 9). W. 51/6
Mss.: D-ddr Bds, P 1135 (largely autog. and Michel, containing only rev.: see item 164); B Bc, 5885 (Michel, containing only rev.: see item 164); D-brd Kll, Mb 45; US Bp, No. 7 in **M200.9
Early prints and lit. about them: See FORTSETZUNG.
Mss. probably copied from an early print: D-brd B, P 674, P 774; D-ddr LEm, Poel. Mus. ms. 42; A Wgm, VII 43739
Mod. edns.: ROSE, HASHIMOTO/FORTSETZUNG, BERG/FACSIMILE
Lit. about this work: BITTER/BRÜDER, I, 77–78
See item 24.

Incipits from FORTSETZUNG:

63. Claviersonate. 1750 (NV 9). W. 62/11
Mss.: D-brd B, P 774 (vnt.); D-ddr Bds, M.Th. 39
Early print: ALLERLEY, 122. Lit. about ALLERLEY: See this entry in Bib.
Ms. probably copied from the early print: B Br, II 4094 (Westphal)
Mod. edns.: H. Albrecht, Lippstadt/London/St. Louis: Kistner & Siegel/Novello/Concordia, 1951; BERG/FACSIMILE
Lit. about this work: BEURMANN/KLAVIERSONATEN, 38, 67; BERG, 140, 178

Incipits from ALLERLEY:

64. Sonata per il cembalo solo. 1750 (NV 9). W. 65/26
Mss.: D-brd B, P 776; D-ddr Bds, P 369, Mus. ms. 30385, M.Th. 51; B Bc, 5883 (Michel); A Wgm, VII 3872, No. 10 (Michel, marked "Samml. Westphal" in pencil), VII 43757; D-brd Kll, Mb 53
Mod. edn.: BERG/FACSIMILE
Lit.: BEURMANN/KLAVIERSONATEN, 30, 56, 67

Incipits from P 776:

65. Allegretto con vi variazioni. 1750 (NV 9). W. 118/5
Mss.: D-brd B, P 359, P 726; B Bc, 5899 (Westphal); A Wn, 19035 (Michel), 5018 (only 5 variations)
Mod. edns.: HERRMANN/LEICHTE, BERG/FACSIMILE
Lit.: FISCHER, 192, 196, 200, 211

Incipit from 5899:

66. Claviersonate [suite]. 1751 (NV 10). W. 62/12
Mss.: D-brd B, P 790; D-ddr Bds, P 371
Early print: ALLERLEY, 92. Lit. about ALLERLEY: See this entry in Bib.
Ms. probably copied from the early print: B Br, II 4094 (Westphal)
Mod. edns.: FARRENC, BERG/EDITIONS
Lit. about this work: NEWMAN, 419

Incipits from ALLERLEY:

67. Sonata per il cembalo solo. 1752 (NV 10). W. 62/13
Ms.: D-brd B, P 295 (3rd mvt. separated from the first two)
Early prints and lit. about them: See MARPURG/RAC-COLTA 1756, 16; HUBERTY.
Ms. probably copied from MARPURG/RACCOLTA 1756: B Br, II 4094 (Westphal). Ms. probably copied from HU-BERTY: D-brd B, P 673
Mod. edn.: BERG/FACSIMILE
Lit. about this work: BITTER/BRÜDER, I, 65; BEURMANN/KLAVIERSONATEN, 67; BERG, 120, 140, 178, 200; SCHULENBERG/INSTRUMENTAL, 128–30

Incipits from MARPURG/RACCOLTA 1756:

68. Sonata per il cembalo solo. 1752 (NV 10). W. 65/27
Mss.: D-brd B, P 776 (rev. by CPEB); D-ddr Bds, P 369, Mus. ms. 30385; B Bc, 5883 (Michel)
Mod. edns.: FARRENC, BERG/FACSIMILE

Incipits from 5883:

69. [24?] Veränderungen über das Lied: Ich schlief, da träumte mir. 1752 (NV 10). W. 118/1
Mss.: D-brd B, Mus. ms. 11631/4 (only 23 variations, entitled "Canzonetta con Variazioni per il Cembalo di Kirnberg e C. P. E. Bach," attributing 8 variations to J. P. Kirnberger

and 15 to CPEB), Mus. ms. 38049 (only 15 variations, "Di Singl. Kirnberg," but with only variations 1–5 marked "K." and some of the others marked "B."), P 433 (only 15 variations), P 731 (only 13 variations), P 732 (only 13 variations), P 733 (only 19 variations), P 736, P 739 (only 15 variations), P 773 (only 17 variations), P 894 (only 13 variations); D-ddr Bds, Mus. ms. 30201 (40 variations: 1–17 attributed to CPEB ["Fine delle Variazioni di Bach"], 18–28 to Kirnberger, 29–40 to F. W. Marpurg), Mus. ms. 30327 (only 19 variations, attributed vaguely to both Kirnberger and CPEB), P 365, Mus. ms. 30382 (the first few variations are attributed to Janitsch [?], the next few to CPEB, the next few to Marpurg, and the last few to Kirnberger); DK As (?); A Wgm, Q 11702 (VII 2149) (only 16 variations), Q 11711 (VII 14519) (only 12 variations), Q 11714 (VII 43763) (only 5 variations); D-brd DS, Mus. ms. 1302 (only 15 variations, and under the title "Was helfen mir tausend Ducaten"); a ms. is in the private collection of E. N. Kulukundis (U.S.).

Early prints: 17 variations in ALLERLEY, 151; 7 variations, after a restatement of the theme, in VIELERLEY, 107; all 24 of these are attributed to CPEB.

Lit. about ALLERLEY and VIELERLEY: See these entries in Bib.

Other early edns., with only 15 variations: "Canzonette with Variations, compos'd by Sigr. Bach. Printed and sold by A. Hummell, in King Street, St. Ann's," and a reissue by Welcker with altered title page: "Canzonette with Variations, 1.ͤ Composed by Sigr. Bach, printed and sold by Welcker in Gerrard Street, St. Ann's Soho" (attributed to Johann Christian Bach in SCHNAPPER). See ROE, 80, 404. The known lit. gives no evidence that either the Hummell or the Welcker print was authorized by CPEB.

Ms. probably copied from ALLERLEY and VIELERLEY (that is, transmitting the same 24 variations and attributing these 24 to CPEB): B Bc, 5899 (Westphal)

Mod. edn.: BERG/FACSIMILE

Lit. about this work: FISCHER, 192–93, 197, 201–02, 204–05, 208, 211–15; see also Critical Notes in BERG/FACSIMILE.

The popularity of the 18th-century pasticcio variation contributes to the vagueness with which variations on this folk melody are attributed. The 24 variations attributed to CPEB in ALLERLEY and VIELERLEY, and in Westphal's copy in B Bc, 5899, might indeed be the ones by CPEB, since NV describes them as appearing in the two prints, although without specifying the number.

Incipit from 5899:

70. Sonata. 1753 (NV 10). W. 63/1
Ms.: D-brd B, P 728
Early prints and lit. about them: See PROBESTÜCKE.
Mss. probably copied from an early print: D-brd B, P 367, P 677; B Bc, 5880; D-ddr LEb, 346

Mod. edns.: DOFLEIN, HOFFMANN-ERBRECHT/PROBE-STÜCKE, BERG/FACSIMILE

Lit. about this work: STEGLICH/HOMILIUS, 81; BEUR-MANN/KLAVIERSONATEN, 34, 56; MÜLLER, 61; NEW-MAN, 421, 424; BARFORD/KEYBOARD, 94; BERG, 102, 192; ELDER, 2–3; OTTENBERG, 112; SCHULENBERG/IN-STRUMENTAL, 7

Items 70–75 are incorrectly listed as works of Johann Christian Bach in TERRY, C. S., 349–50. They are incorrectly reported in BEURMANN/KLAVIERSONATEN to be in D-brd B, P 363.

Incipits from PROBESTÜCKE:

71. Sonata. 1753 (NV 10). W. 63/2
Ms.: D-brd KIl, Mb 51
Early prints and lit. about them: See PROBESTÜCKE.
Mss. probably copied from an early print: D-brd B, P 367, P 677; B Bc, 5880; D-ddr LEb, 346
Mod. edns.: FARRENC, DOFLEIN, HOFFMANN-ER-BRECHT/PROBESTÜCKE, BERG/FACSIMILE
Lit. about this work: BEURMANN/REPRISENSONATEN, 169; BARFORD/KEYBOARD, 94; ELDER, 2–3; SCHU-LENBERG/INSTRUMENTAL, 7; FOX, 161

See item 70.

Incipits from PROBESTÜCKE:

72. Sonata. 1753 (NV 10). W. 63/3
Early prints and lit. about them: See PROBESTÜCKE.

Mss. probably copied from an early print: D-brd B, P 367, P 677; B Bc, 5880; D-ddr LEb, 346

Mod. edns.: FARRENC, DOFLEIN, HOFFMAN-ER-BRECHT/PROBESTÜCKE, BERG/FACSIMILE

Lit. about this work: SCHENKER/BEITRAG, 9; BEURMANN/KLAVIERSONATEN, 60; MÜLLER, 58–59; NEWMAN, 421; BARFORD/KEYBOARD, 94–95; BERG, 178; ELDER, 2–3; OTTENBERG, 110; SCHULENBERG/INSTRUMENTAL, 7

See item 70.

Incipits from PROBESTÜCKE:

Poca allegro ma cantabile

Andante lusingando

Allegro

73. Sonata. 1753 (NV 10). W. 63/4

Ms.: D-ddr GOl, Mus. 21a

Early prints and lit. about them: See PROBESTÜCKE.

Mss. probably copied from an early print: D-brd B, P 677; B Bc, 5880; D-ddr LEb, 346

Mod. edns.: FARRENC, DOFLEIN, HOFFMANN-ER-BRECHT/PROBESTÜCKE, BERG/FACSIMILE

Lit. about this work: STEGLICH/HOMILIUS, 73; REESER, 39; NEWMAN, 420–21; BARFORD/KEYBOARD, 95–97; RADCLIFFE, 586; COHEN, 64–66; BERG, 191; ELDER, 2–3; SCHULENBERG/INSTRUMENTAL, 7, 143

See item 70.

Incipits from PROBESTÜCKE:

Allegretto grazioso
ten.

Largo maestoso

Allegro Siciliano e scherzando

74. Sonata. 1753 (NV 10). W. 63/5

Ms.: CS Pnm, II.B.9 (3rd mvt. only, a.v., with 2nd mvt. of

item 75 to comprise an accompanied sonata for glass harmonica, item 643)

Early prints and lit. about them: See PROBESTÜCKE.

Mss. probably copied from an early print: D-brd B, P 677, P 727 (1st mvt. only); B Bc, 5880; D-ddr LEb, 346

Mod. edns.: FARRENC, CALAND, DOFLEIN, HOFFMANN-ERBRECHT/PROBESTÜCKE, BERG/FACSIMILE

Lit. about this work: BEURMANN/KLAVIERSONATEN, 96, 112; BEURMANN/REPRISENSONATEN, 177; NEWMAN, 421, 428; BARFORD/KEYBOARD, 97–98; RADCLIFFE, 585; BERG, 129–30, 190; ELDER, 2–3; OTTENBERG, 110; SCHULENBERG/INSTRUMENTAL, 7; FOX, 143–44

See item 70.

Incipits from PROBESTÜCKE:

Allegro di molto

Adagio assai mesto e sostenuto

Allegretto arioso ed amoroso

75. Sonata. 1753 (NV 10). W. 63/6

Mss.: D-brd B, N. Mus. ms. 10480 (1st mvt. only; 19th-century copy), P 564 (1st mvt. only, not autog.), P 728 (1st mvt. only), P 790 (1st mvt. only), P 929 (1st mvt. only), P 1003 (1st mvt. only), P 1176 (1st mvt. only); CS Pnm, II.B.9 (2nd mvt. only, a.v. for glass harmonica; see item 74)

Early prints and lit. about them: See PROBESTÜCKE.

Mss. probably copied from an early print: D-brd B, P 677, P 727 (1st mvt. only); B Bc, 5880; D-ddr LEb, 346; US NHu, Mason collection, 4813b; a ms. is in the private collection of E. N. Kulukundis (U.S.).

Mod. edns.: FARRENC, RIEMANN, DOFLEIN, HOFFMANN-ERBRECHT/PROBESTÜCKE, BERG/FACSIMILE

Lit. about this work: Introduction to FORKEL/GESCHICHTE, and CPEB's review of the book in HAMBURGER CORRESPONDENT, 9 Jan. 1788; BITTER/BRÜDER, I, 96–97, 110–112; CHRYSANDER; SCHENKER/BEITRAG, 9; STEGLICH/HOMILIUS, 112–14; VRIESLANDER/BACH, 84, 87–89; ENGELKE, 428–31; SCHERING/REDENDE; SCHMID/KAMMERMUSIK, 48–62; REESER, 38–39; BEURMANN/KLAVIERSONATEN, 60–61; GEIRINGER/BACH, 357; BUSCH, 90–98, 266–70, 276–77; AUERBACH, 68, 90, 93; NEWMAN, 427; BARFORD/KEYBOARD, 19, 31–38, 98–99; HELM/LITERARY; RADCLIFFE, 585–86, 591; SCHLEUNING, introductions in vols. 42–43; COHEN, 28; BERG, 168, 190; ELDER, 2–3, 74–78; ROE, 114; OTTENBERG, 114–19, 181, 217, 316;

SCHULENBERG/INSTRUMENTAL, 7, 18–20; FOX, 58–60; SELINGER-BARBER, 27, 47–48, 56, 60, 66–68, 77–90, 109

The fantasy comprising the 3rd mvt. of this sonata (that is, the last of the 18 PROBESTÜCKE) appeared in CRAMER/FLORA, xii–xiv, 19–27, with two texts set to it by the poet H. W. von Gerstenberg as an experiment (without CPEB's direct participation) in bridging the gap between language and instrumental music (W. 202/M).

See item 70.

Incipits from PROBESTÜCKE:

75.5. Fantasia e fuga a 4. c. 1754 or earlier (source of date: See below). W. 119/7

Mss.: D-brd B, P 362, P 717, P 718, P 721, P 755 (the "Fuga" only), P 766, P 1120; D-ddr Bds, Mus. ms. 30332 (missing); A Wgm, Q 11708 (VII 42122) (the "Fuga" only), Q 11709 (VII 43735) (the "Fuga" only); D-ddr Dlb, 3029.T.16; US Wc, M25.A2B

Early prints: SIX FUGUES (the "Fuga" only); MARPURG/ABHANDLUNG (the "Fuga" only)

Mss. probably copied partly from an early print: D-brd B, P 1147; D-ddr Bds, P 1177, Mus. ms. 30380; B Bc, 5900 (Westphal); US NHu, Mason collection, 5019 (the "Fuga" only); US CA, fMS Mus. 66.2

Mod. edns.: G. Amft, Leipzig: Kahnt, c. 1905; FEDTKE/ORGELWERKE; BERG/FACSIMILE

Lit.: BARFORD/KEYBOARD, 20–21; COHEN, 111; ELDER, 91; SELINGER-BARBER, 66, 69–70, 76, 91–98

See item 349. SELINGER-BARBER, 69–70, notes that the "Fuga" is excerpted as an example in the second part of MARPURG/ABHANDLUNG, published in 1754, and that the last 2 measures of the "Fantasia" are practically identical to the last 2 measures of the 3rd mvt. of item 75 (which is also a fantasia). The beginnings of the two fantasias are also strikingly similar harmonically. This evidence shows that the date of 1755 given in NV, 11, is an error or possibly an indication of the year in which the "Fantasia" and the "Fuga" were combined into a single work. Perhaps by 1754 the "Fantasia" was not complete. CPEB thought of the "6 Clavierfugen" mentioned in item

349 as a group, so the 1755 date in NV might indicate the year in which the entire group was completed.

Incipit from P 717:

76. Duo in contrap[unct] ad 8, 11 & 12 mit Anmerkungen. 1754 or earlier (source of date: 1st pub.). W. 119/1

Ms.: D-ddr Bds, Mus. ms. 30332 (missing)

Early print: MARPURG/ABHANDLUNG (1754)

Ms. probably copied from the early print: B Bc, 5900 (Westphal)

Mod. edn.: BERG/FACSIMILE

Lit.: BARFORD/KEYBOARD, 20–21; COHEN, 111; SELINGER-BARBER, 76

The "Anmerkungen" are probably by Marpurg.

See item 349.

Incipit from 5900:

77. Sonata per il cembalo solo. 1754 (NV 10). W. 62/14

Mss.: D-brd B, P 728, P 1154 (lacking 3rd mvt.); D-ddr Bds, P 365, Mus. ms. 30385, M.Th. 41; D-brd KIl, Mb 49; D-ddr GOl, Mus. 21a 5 72 (has a vnt. 1st mvt.); A Wn, 5018

Early print: MANCHERLEY, 143. Lit. about MANCHERLEY: See this entry in Bib.

Ms. probably copied from the early print: B Br, II 4094 (Westphal)

Mod. edns.: A. Kranz, Wilhelmshaven: O. H. Noetzel Verlag, 1958; BERG/FACSIMILE

Lit. about this work: BEURMANN/KLAVIERSONATEN, 34; BERG, 140, 352–53; SCHULENBERG/INSTRUMENTAL, 7

Incipits from MANCHERLEY:

Incipit of 1st mvt. from 21a 5 72:

78. Sonata per il cembalo solo. 1754 (NV 10). W. 65/28
Mss.: D-brd B, P 359 (Michel), P 364, P 370, P 776; D-ddr
  Bds, P 371; B Bc, 5883 (Michel); A Wgm, VII 43758, H
  31221 (VII 43745); D-brd Kll, Mb 52
Mod. edns.: FARRENC, BERG/EDITIONS, BERG/FAC-
  SIMILE
Lit.: BEURMANN/KLAVIERSONATEN, 51, 53; BERG, 120;
  S. Roe, "J. C. Bach, 1735–1782, Towards a New Biog-
  raphy," *The Musical Times*, 123 (1982), 23–26; ROE, 115,
  157–58

Incipits from 5883:

79. La Borchward. Polonoise. 1754 (NV 11). W. 117/17
Mss.: D-brd B, Mus. ms. 38050 (entitled "La Borchwardt"),
  P 295; D-ddr Dlb, 3029.T.17; US Wc, M23.B13
Early print: MARPURG/RACCOLTA 1756, 45. Lit. about
  MARPURG/RACCOLTA 1756: See this entry in Bib.
Ms. probably copied from the early print: B Bc, 5897 (West-
  phal)
Mod. edn.: BERG/FACSIMILE
Lit. about this work: See Critical Notes in BERG/FACSIMILE

Incipit from 5897:

80. La Pott [= "La Lott"]. Menuet. 1754 (NV 11). W. 117/18
Mss.: D-brd B, Mus. ms. 38050, P 295, P 1154; A Wgm, SBQ
  11713 (VII 43737); D-ddr Dlb, 3029.T.17; US Wc, M23.B13
Early print: MARPURG/RACCOLTA 1756, 46. Lit. about
  MARPURG/RACCOLTA 1756: See this entry in Bib.
Ms. probably copied from the early print: B Bc, 5897 (West-
  phal)
Mod. edn.: BERG/FACSIMILE

Lit. about this work: GEIRINGER/BACH, 360; Critical Notes
  in BERG/FACSIMILE
Arr.: the Tempo di Menuetto of items 453, 480, 480.5

Incipit from 5897:

81. La Boehmer. 1754 (NV 11). W. 117/26
Mss.: D-brd B, Mus. ms. 38050 (entitled "Murky. La
  Böhmer"); D-ddr Bds, Mus. ms. 30235; A Wgm, Q 11701
  (VII 43734) (entitled "Murqui"), SBQ 11713 (VII 43737)
  (entitled "La Mourcqui"); D-ddr Dlb, 3029.T.17; US Wc,
  M20.A2.M684
Early print: MANCHERLEY, 92. Lit. about MANCHERLEY:
  See this entry in Bib.
Ms. probably copied from the early print: B Bc, 5897 (West-
  phal)
Mod. edn.: BERG/FACSIMILE
The last mvt. of Mozart's concerto arrangement K. 40 is
  based on this piece.
Lit. about this work: BITTER/BRÜDER, I, 85–86;
  GEIRINGER/BACH, 360; WADE, 113; DRUMMOND,
  343; OTTENBERG, 261, 328; Critical Notes in BERG/FAC-
  SIMILE

Incipit from 5897:

82. La Gause. 1754 (NV 11). W. 117/37
Mss.: D-brd B, Mus. ms. 38050, P 1154; B Bc, 5897 (West-
  phal); A Wgm, SBQ 11713 (VII 43737); D-ddr Dlb,
  3029.T.17; US Wc, M23.B13; PL Kj, P 745 (autog.)
Mod. edn.: BERG/FACSIMILE
Arr.: the Arioso of items 453, 480, 480.5
See item 96.

Incipit from 5897:

83. Sonata per il cembalo solo. 1755 (NV 11). W. 65/29
Mss.: D-brd B, P 359 (on the first page in an unknown hand:
  "Für Diderot in Paris"), P 776 (Michel); B Bc, 5883 (Michel)
Mod. edns.: BERG/EDITIONS, BERG/FACSIMILE
Lit.: DIDEROT/CPEB; PROD'HOMME; SCHMID/KAM-
  MERMUSIK, 44–46; BEURMANN/KLAVIERSONATEN,
  49–51, 53; NEWMAN, 427

Vnts. of the 3rd mvt.: item 124; see also item 105. Arr. of the 3rd mvt.: item 455

Incipits from P 776:

84. Orgel Sonata. 1755 (sources of date: NV 12, date in CPEB's hand on 1st p. of P 774 source). W. 70/3

Mss.: D-brd B, P 364, P 414, P 762, P 764, P 774 (Michel, marked by CPEB), P 1150; D-ddr Bds, M.Th. 38, P 1223; D-brd Kll, Mb 54 (2 copies); D-ddr GOl; PL Kj, P 771 (autog.)

Early print and lit. about it: See PRELUDIO.

Mss. probably copied from the early print: D-brd B, P 434, P 1187; B Bc, 5879 (Westphal); a ms. of the 1st mvt. only, transposed to D, is in the private collection of E. N. Kulukundis (U.S.).

Mod. edns.: FARRENC, LANGLAIS, BRANDTS-BUYS, FEDTKE/ORGELWERKE, BERG/FACSIMILE

Lit. about this work: BEURMANN/KLAVIERSONATEN, 16; NEWMAN, 89; COHEN, 111; BERG, 102; OTTENBERG, 124

Some of these mss. contain various parts of items 84–87, 107, 133, and 134 as works for "Cembalo" or "Clavier" rather than "Orgel," illustrating the casual interchange between organ (usually without pedal) and stringed keyboard instrument in CPEB's time.

Incipits from 5879:

85. Orgel-Sonata. 1755 (NV 12). W. 70/4
Mss.: D-brd B, P 366, P 761, P 763, P 764, P 1150; D-ddr

Bds, P 1223, M.Th. 53; B Br, Fétis 3918 (marked "ohne Pedal" in CPEB's hand); US Wc, M20.A2.M684

Early print and lit. about it: See PRELUDIO.

Mss. probably copied from the early print: D-brd B, P 434 (in g), P 1187; B Bc, 5879 (Westphal)

Mod. edns.: LANGLAIS, BRANDTS-BUYS, FEDTKE/ORGELWERKE, BERG/FACSIMILE

Lit. about this work: BEURMANN/KLAVIERSONATEN, 16; NEWMAN, 89; COHEN, 111; BERG, 102, 190; OTTENBERG, 124

See item 84.

Incipits from 5879:

86. Orgel-Sonata. 1755 (NV 12). W. 70/5

Mss.: D-brd B, P 764; B Br, Fétis 3918 (marked "ohne Pedal" in CPEB's hand); D-brd Mbs, Mus. ms. 1795; D-brd Kll, Mb 54

Early print and lit. about it: See PRELUDIO.

Mss. probably copied from the early print: D-brd B, P 434, P 1187; B Bc, 5879 (Westphal)

Mod. edns.: LANGLAIS, BRANDTS-BUYS, FEDTKE/ORGELWERKE, BERG/FACSIMILE

Lit. about this work: BEURMANN/KLAVIERSONATEN, 16; NEWMAN, 89; COHEN, 111; BERG, 102; OTTENBERG, 124

See item 84.

Incipits from 5879:

87. Orgel-Sonata. 1755 (NV 11). W. 70/6
Mss.: D-brd B, P 366, P 414, P 760, P 764; D-ddr Bds, Am.B.

479 (4v–9r); A Wgm, VII 38661 (autog.); D-brd KII, Mb 40, Mb 54; D-brd Mbs, Mus. ms. 1795; D-ddr GOl

Early print and lit. about it: See PRELUDIO.

Mss. probably copied from the early print: D-brd B, P 434, P 1187; B Bc, 5879 (Westphal)

Mod. edns.: LANGLAIS, BRANDTS-BUYS, FEDTKE/ ORGELWERKE, BERG/FACSIMILE

Lit. about this work: BEURMANN/KLAVIERSONATEN, 16; NEWMAN, 89; COHEN, 111; BERG, 102, 178; OTTEN-BERG, 124

See item 84.

Incipits from 5879:

88. Deleted

89. La Gleim. Rondeau. 1755 (NV 12). W. 117/19

Mss.: D-brd B, Mus. ms. 38050, P 370, P 793; D-ddr Dlb, 3029.T.17

Early print: MARPURG/RACCOLTA 1756, 34. Lit. about MARPURG/RACCOLTA 1756: See this entry in Bib.

Ms. probably copied from the early print: B Bc, 5897 (West-phal)

Mod. edns.: RIEMANN, BERG/FACSIMILE

Lit. about this work: STEGLICH/HOMILIUS, 90; GEIRINGER/BACH, 342, 360; OTTENBERG, 141; Critical Notes in BERG/FACSIMILE

Incipit from 5897:

90. La Bergius. 1755 (NV 12). W. 117/20

Mss.: D-brd B, Mus. ms. 38050, P 370, P 793; D-ddr Dlb, 3029.T.17

Early print: MARPURG/RACCOLTA 1756, 37. Lit. about MARPURG/RACCOLTA 1756: See this entry in Bib.

Ms. probably copied from the early print: B Bc, 5897 (West-phal)

Mod. edns.: RIEMANN, BERG/FACSIMILE

Lit. about this work: see Critical Notes in BERG/FACSIMILE.

Incipit from 5897:

91. La Prinzette. 1755 (NV 12). W. 117/21

Mss.: D-brd B, Mus. ms. 38050, P 370, P 793, P 818, P 997; D-ddr Bds, Mus. ms. 30193; A Wgm, SBQ 11713 (VII 43737); D-ddr Dlb, 3029.T.17; US Wc, M23.B13; US NHu, Mason collection, 5009

Early print: MARPURG/RACCOLTA 1757, 5. Lit. about MARPURG/RACCOLTA 1757: See this entry in Bib.

Ms. probably copied from the early print: B Bc, 5897 (West-phal)

Mod. edns.: HERRMANN/LEICHTE, BERG/FACSIMILE

Lit. about this work: SCHULENBERG/INSTRUMENTAL, 6; see also Critical Notes in BERG/FACSIMILE.

Incipit from 5897:

92. L'Herrmann. 1755 (NV 12). W. 117/23

Mss.: D-brd B, Mus. ms. 38050, P 370; A Wgm, SBQ 11713 (VII 43737); D-ddr Dlb, 3029.T.17

Early print: MANCHERLEY, 80. Lit. about MANCHERLEY: See this entry in Bib.

Ms. probably copied from the early print: B Bc, 5897 (West-phal)

Mod. edns.: HERRMANN/LEICHTE, BERG/FACSIMILE

Lit. about this work: BITTER/BRÜDER, I, 85; Critical Notes in BERG/FACSIMILE

Incipit from 5897:

93. La Buchholz. 1755 (NV 12). W. 117/24

Mss.: D-brd B, Mus. ms. 38050, P 370, P 793; D-ddr Bds, Mus. ms. 30235; A Wgm, SBQ 11713 (VII 43737), SBQ 11714 (VII 43763); D-ddr Dlb, 3029.T.17

Early print: MANCHERLEY, 82. Lit. about MANCHERLEY: See this entry in Bib.

Ms. probably copied from the early print: B Bc, 5897 (West-phal)

Mod. edn.: BERG/FACSIMILE

Lit. about this work: BITTER/BRÜDER, I, 85; Critical Notes in BERG/FACSIMILE

Incipit from 5897:

94. La Stahl. 1755 (NV 12). W. 117/25
Mss.: D-brd B, Mus. ms. 38050, P 370, P 793, P 991; D-ddr Bds, Mus. ms. 30235; A Wgm, SBQ 11713 (VII 43737); D-ddr Dlb, 3029.T.17
Early print: MANCHERLEY, 95. Lit. about MANCHERLEY: See this entry in Bib.
Ms. probably copied from the early print: B Bc, 5897 (Westphal)
Mod. edns.: RIEMANN, HERRMANN/SONATEN, CALAND–GOEBELS, BERG/FACSIMILE
Lit. about this work: BITTER/BRÜDER, I, 85; MIESNER/STAHL; GEIRINGER/BACH, 360; BARFORD/KEYBOARD, 141

Incipit from 5897:

95. L'Aly Rupalich. 1755 (NV 12). W. 117/27
Mss.: D-brd B, Mus. ms. 38050, P 370, P 793 (entitled "la Bach"); A Wgm, SBQ 11713 (VII 43737); D-ddr Dlb, 3029.T.17
Early print: MANCHERLEY, 130. Lit. about MANCHERLEY: See this entry in Bib.
Ms. probably copied from the early print: B Bc, 5897 (Westphal)
Mod. edns.: RIEMANN, BERG/FACSIMILE
Lit. about this work: BITTER/BRÜDER, I, 85–86; STEGLICH/HOMILIUS, 64

Incipit from 5897:

96. La Philippine. 1755 (NV 11). W. 117/34
Mss.: D-brd B, Mus. ms. 38050; B Bc, 5897 (Westphal); A Wgm, SBQ 11713 (VII 43737); A Wn, 19035 (Michel); D-ddr Dlb, 3029.T.17; PL Kj, P 745 (marked by CPEB)
Mod. edns.: HERRMANN/LEICHTE, BERG/FACSIMILE
SMITH 1968 lists items 96–98, 82, and 301 as being in P 747, among the mss. whose locations at the time of his writing had been uncertain since World War II; but a P 747 not containing these items is presently in D-brd B. Perhaps the ms. meant is P 745, recently relocated in PL Kj.
Arr. of 1st mvt.: item 457

Incipit from 5897:

97. La Gabriel. 1755 (NV 11). W. 117/35
Mss.: D-brd B, Mus. ms. 38050, P 1154; D-ddr Bds, P 365; B Bc, 5897 (Westphal); A Wgm, SBQ 11713 (VII 43737); A Wn, 19035 (Michel); D-ddr Dlb, 3029.T.17; PL Kj, P 745
Mod. edns.: HERRMANN/LEICHTE, BERG/FACSIMILE
See the reference to SMITH 1968 in item 96.

Incipit from 5897:

98. La Caroline. 1755 (NV 11). W. 117/39
Mss.: D-brd B, Mus. ms. 38050, P 1154; D-ddr Bds, P 365; B Bc, 5897 (Westphal); A Wgm, SBQ 11713 (VII 43737); A Wn, 19035 (Michel); D-ddr Dlb, 3029.T.17; D-ddr GOl, Mus. 21a; PL Kj, P 745
Mod. edns.: HERRMANN/LEICHTE, BERG/FACSIMILE
Lit.: BARFORD/KEYBOARD, 141; COHEN, 111
Unrelated to item 143
See the reference to SMITH 1968 in item 96.

Incipit from 5897:

99. Fuga A 2. 1755 (NV 11). W. 119/2
Mss.: D-brd B, P 362, P 717, P 718, P 721, P 755, P 765, P 911, P 1120; D-ddr Bds, Mus. ms. 30332 (missing); A Wgm, Q 11703 (VII 43768); D-ddr Dlb, 3029.T.16
Early prints and lit. about them: See MARPURG/FUGEN, SIX FUGUES.
Mss. probably copied from an early print: D-brd B, P 1147; D-ddr Bds, P 1177; B Bc, 5900 (Westphal); D-ddr Bds, Mus. ms. 30380; US CA, fMS Mus. 66.2
Mod. edns.: in BARFORD/KEYBOARD; BERG/FACSIMILE
Lit. about this work: BITTER/BRÜDER, I, 65; BARFORD/KEYBOARD, 20–21, 133, 137; COHEN, 111; SELINGER-BARBER, 76
See item 349.

Incipit from 5900:

100. Fuga a 3. 1755 (NV 11). W. 119/3

Mss.: D-brd B, P 362, P 717, P 718, P 719, P 720, P 722, P 723, P 755, P 765, P 911, P 1188; D-ddr Bds, Mus. ms. 30448, Mus. ms. 30332 (missing), Mus. ms. 30384; A Wgm, Q 11705 (VII 43769), SBQ 11711 (VII 14519), Q 11704 (VII 42121); D-ddr Dlb, 3029.T.16

Early prints and lit. about them: See TONSTÜCKE, SIX FUGUES.

Mss. probably copied from an early print: D-ddr Bds, P 1177, Mus. ms. 30380; B Bc, 5900 (Westphal); US NHu, Mason collection, 5019; US CA, fMS Mus. 66.2; a ms. is in the private collection of E. N. Kulukundis (U.S.).

Mod. edn.: BERG/FACSIMILE

Lit. about this work: BITTER/BRÜDER, I, 65; BARFORD/ KEYBOARD, 20–21; COHEN, 111; SELINGER-BARBER, 76

See item 349.

Incipit from 5900:

101. Fuga a 3 mit Anmerkungen. 1755 (NV 11). W. 119/4

Mss.: D-brd B, P 362, P 717, P 718, P 724, P 725, P 755, P 765, P 773, P 795, P 911; A Wgm, Q 11706 (VII 43766); D-ddr Dlb, 3029.T.16

Early prints: MARPURG/RACCOLTA 1757, 42; MARPURG/ PRACTISCH, I, ii (it is in the latter edn. that the "Anmerkungen" [by Marpurg] appear); SIX FUGUES. Lit. about MARPURG/RACCOLTA 1757: See this entry in Bib.

Mss. probably copied from an early print: D-ddr Bds, P 1177, Mus. ms. 30380; B Bc, 5900 (Westphal); US NHu, Mason collection, 5019; US CA, fMS Mus. 66.2

Mod. edns.: in BARFORD/KEYBOARD; BERG/FACSIMILE

Lit. about this work: BITTER/BRÜDER, I, 64; BARFORD/ KEYBOARD, 20–21, 133, 135–36; COHEN, 111; OTTEN-BERG, 124, 309; SELINGER-BARBER, 76

See item 349.

Incipit from 5900:

101.5. Fuga a 3. 1755 (NV 11). W. 112/19 (z 119/5)

Mss.: D-brd B, P 362, P 717, P 718, P 721, P 755, P 765, P 911; D-ddr Bds, Mus. ms. 30332 (missing); A Wgm, Q 11707 (VII 43767); A Wn, 18687

Early prints and lit. about them: See VERSCHIEDEN, SIX FUGUES.

Mss. probably copied from an early print: D-ddr Bds, Mus. ms. 30380; B Bc, 5900 (Westphal); US NHu, Mason collection, 5019; US CA, fMS 66.2

Mod. edn.: BERG/FACSIMILE

Lit. about this work: BITTER/BRÜDER, I, 65, 89; BARFORD/ KEYBOARD, 20–21; SELINGER-BARBER, 76

See item 349.

Incipit from VERSCHIEDEN:

102. Fuga a 4 per organo mit Anmerkungen. 1755 (NV 11). W. 119/6

Mss.: D-brd B, P 362, P 717, P 718, P 725, P 755, P 765, P 911; D-ddr Bds, Mus. ms. 30332 (missing); D-ddr Dlb, 3029.T.16

Early prints: MARPURG/PRACTISCH, II, 1 (the "Anmer-kungen" are by Marpurg); SIX FUGUES

Mss. probably copied from an early print: D-ddr Bds, P 1177, Mus. ms. 30380; B Bc, 5900 (Westphal); US NHu, Mason collection, 5019; US CA, fMS Mus. 66.2

Mod. edns.: in BARFORD/KEYBOARD; FEDTKE/ORGEL-WERKE (which incorrectly lists D-brd B, P 677 as a source); BERG/FACSIMILE

Lit.: BITTER/BRÜDER, I, 64; BARFORD/KEYBOARD, 20–21, 133, 136–37; COHEN, 111; SELINGER-BARBER, 76

See item 349.

Incipit from 5900:

103. Deleted

104. Sinfonia per il cembalo solo. Probably 1755 or later (source of date: the symphony of 1755). W. 122/2

Early prints: MARPURG/SINFONIE (not W. 122/1); in "Six Sonatas, for the Piano Forte. Composed by Bach, Wageneil, Benda, Hasse, & Gzaun, Kernberger. London: Printed for Harrison, Cluse & Co. No. 78, Fleet Street," in *The Pianoforte Magazine*, vii/no. 6 (1799) (cited by ROE, 417)

Mod. edn.: BERG/FACSIMILE

Lit.: VRIESLANDER/BACH, 98–99; SCHULENBERG/ IN-STRUMENTAL, 130

A.v. of a symphony of 1755 (item 650). See also ROE, 98–99, 417.

Incipits from MARPURG/SINFONIE:

105. Sonata per il cembalo solo. 1756 (NV 13). W. 62/15

Mss.: D-brd B, P 676; D-ddr Bds, M.Th. 34; D-brd DS, Mus. 53 (see below; D-brd Kll, Mb 39

Early print: MARPURG/RACCOLTA 1757, 39. Lit. about MARPURG/RACCOLTA 1757: See this entry in Bib.

Ms. probably copied from the early print: B Br, II 4094 (Westphal)

Mod. edns.: FARRENC, BERG/FACSIMILE

Lit. about this work: BEURMANN/KLAVIERSONATEN, 56

Mus. 53 appends a 2nd Allegretto, which is the 3rd mvt. of item 83 transposed to D major. See also item 124.

Lit. about this work: BEURMANN/KLAVIERSONATEN, 56

Incipits from MARPURG/RACCOLTA 1757:

106. Sonata per il cembalo solo. 1756 (NV 12). W. 65/30

Mss.: D-brd B, P 359 (Michel), P 364, P 776 (Michel; marked by CPEB), P 789 (rev. by CPEB); D-ddr Bds, M.Th. 35, Mus. ms. 30385; B Bc, 5883 (Michel); PL Kj, P 756 (autog., 3rd mvt. and 3rd-mvt. sketches only). Not in D-brd B, P 570, as reported in BEURMANN/KLAVIERSONATEN, 133

Mod. edns.: BERG/EDITIONS, BERG/FACSIMILE

Lit.: BEURMANN/KLAVIERSONATEN, 26, 109; BERG, 168

Incipits from P 776:

107. Preludio [organ]. 1756 (NV 13). W. 70/7

Mss.: D-brd B, P 767; D-ddr Bds, P 369; B Br, Fétis 3918 (title in CPEB's hand: "Orgelsonate mit dem Pedal"); A Wgm, VII 38661 (autog.); A wn, 19035 (Michel)

Early print and lit. about it: See PRELUDIO.

Mss. probably copied from the early print: D-brd B, P 434; B Bc, 5879 (Westphal)

Mod. edns.: LANGLAIS, BRANDTS-BUYS, FEDTKE/ ORGELWERKE, BERG/FACSIMILE

Lit. about this work: BEURMANN/KLAVIERSONATEN, 16; NEWMAN, 89; COHEN, 111; BERG, 102; OTTENBERG, 124

See item 84.

Incipit from VII 38661:

108. [untitled]. 1756 (NV 13). W. 116/18

Early prints: MARPURG/BRIEFE; KLEINE, III, 2–3

Mod. edn.: BERG/FACSIMILE

Ms. probably copied from one of the early prints: B Bc, 5898 (Westphal)

Incipit from 5898:

109. La complaisante. 1756 (NV 13). W. 117/28

Mss.: D-brd B, Mus. ms. 38050; D-ddr Bds, Mus. ms. 30235; A Wgm, SBQ 11714 (VII 43763); D-ddr Dlb, 3029.T.17

Early print: ALLERLEY, 18. Lit. about ALLERLEY: See this entry in Bib.

Ms. probably copied from the early print: B Bc, 5897 (Westphal)

Mod. edns.: E. Pauer, Leipzig: Breitkopf & Härtel, c. 1880; MIES; BERG/FACSIMILE

Lit. about this work: GEIRINGER/BACH, 360; RADCLIFFE, 592

Arr.: See item 456.

Incipit from 5897:

110. Les langueurs tendres. 1756 (NV 13). W. 117/30

Mss.: D-brd B, Mus. ms. 38050 (entitled "Memoire raisonne"), P 997; D-ddr Bds, Mus. ms. 30235; A Wgm, SBQ 11713 (VII 43737), SBQ 11714 (VII 43763); D-ddr Dlb, 3029.T.17; D-brd DS, Mus. ms. 52 (entitled "la mémoire raisonné")

Early print: ALLERLEY, 39. Lit. about ALLERLEY: See this entry in Bib.

Ms. probably copied from the early print: B Bc, 5897 (Westphal)

Mod. edns.: E. Pauer, Leipzig: Breitkopf & Härtel, c. 1880; in W. Kahl, *Das Charakterstück*, Cologne: Volk, n.d.; MIES; CALAND–GOEBELS; BERG/FACSIMILE

Lit. about this work: BARFORD/KEYBOARD, 142; RADCLIFFE, 592; Critical Notes in BERG/FACSIMILE

Incipit from 5897:

111. L'irresoluë. 1756 (NV 13). W. 117/31

Mss.: D-brd B, Mus. ms. 38050 (entitled "L'Irresolution"); D-ddr Bds, Mus. ms. 30235; D-ddr Dlb, 3029.T.17; D-brd DS, Mus. ms. 52

Early print: ALLERLEY, 43. Lit. about ALLERLEY: See this entry in Bib.

Ms. probably copied from the early print: B Bc, 5897 (Westphal)

Mod. edn.: BERG/FACSIMILE

Lit. about this work: FORKEL/GESCHICHTE, 58; BERG, 217–18, 222

The 3 quarter notes in the ⅜ bar recur "irresolutely" throughout the piece.

Incipit from 5897:

112. La journalière. 1756 (NV 13). W. 117/32

Mss.: D-brd B, Mus. ms. 38050; D-ddr Bds, Mus. ms. 30235; A Wgm, SBQ 11714 (VII 43763); D-ddr Dlb, 3029.T.17

Early print: ALLERLEY, 44. Lit. about ALLERLEY: See this entry in Bib.

Ms. probably copied from the early print: B Bc, 5897 (Westphal)

Mod. edn.: BERG/FACSIMILE

Lit. about this work: GEIRINGER/BACH, 360

Incipit from 5897:

113. La capricieuse. 1756 (NV 13). W. 117/33

Mss.: D-brd B, Mus. ms. 38050 (entitled "Le Caprice"); D-ddr Bds, Mus. ms. 30235; D-ddr Dlb, 3029.T.17; US Wc, M20.A2.M684

Early print: ALLERLEY, 22. Lit. about ALLERLEY: See this entry in Bib.

Mss. probably copied from the early print: B Bc, 5897 (Westphal); A Wgm, VII 43737

Mod. edns.: MIES, BERG/FACSIMILE

Lit. about this work: GEIRINGER/BACH, 360; BERG, 1

Incipit from 5897:

114. La Louise. 1756 (NV 13). W. 117/36

Mss.: D-brd B, Mus. ms. 38050, P 915, P 1154, St 341; B Bc, 5897 (Westphal); A Wgm, SBQ 11713 (VII 43737); A Wn, 19035 (Michel); D-ddr Dlb, 3029.T.17; US Wc, M23.B13

Mod. edn.: BERG/FACSIMILE

Arr. from item 507. A.v.: item 585. Arr.: item 456

Incipit from 5897:

115. Sinfonia per il cembalo solo. Probably 1756 or later (source of date: the symphony of 1756). W. 122/3

Early print: MARPURG/SINFONIE

A.v. of a symphony of 1756 (items 652–653)

Lit.: GEIRINGER/BACH, 367

Incipit of 1st mvt. from WOTQUENNE/THÉMATIQUE:

116. Sonata per il cembalo solo. 1757 (NV 13). W. 62/16

Mss.: D-ddr Bds, P 1135 (largely autog. and Michel, containing only rev.: see item 164), Mus. ms. 30193; B Bc, 5885 (Michel, containing only rev.: see item 164); A Wgm, H 31221 (VII 43745); D-brd Kll, Mb 48; D-ddr LEb, 669; US Wc, M20.A2.M68

Early print: OEUVRES, V, 10

Ms. probably copied from the early print: B Br, II 4094 (Westphal)

Mod. edns.: FARRENC, BERG/EDITIONS, BERG/FACSIMILE

Incipits from OEUVRES:

117. Sonata per il cembalo solo. 1757 (NV 14). W. 62/17
Mss.: D-brd B, P 366; D-ddr Bds, Mus. ms. 30193
Early prints: OEUVRES, XII, 4
Ms. probably copied from the early print: B Br, II 4094
 (Westphal)
Mod. edns.: FARRENC, BERG/FACSIMILE
Lit.: BEURMANN/KLAVIERSONATEN, 30; BEURMANN/
 REPRISENSONATEN, 170; BERG, 174–75, 200

Incipits from OEUVRES:

118. Sonata per il cembalo solo. 1757 (NV 13). W. 62/18
Mss.: D-brd DS, Mus. 51; D-ddr LEb, 669
Early print: MANCHERLEY, 5. Lit. about MANCHERLEY:
 See this entry in Bib.
Ms. probably copied from the early print: B Br, II 4094
 (Westphal)
Mod. edns.: FARRENC, BERG/EDITIONS, BERG/FAC-
 SIMILE
Lit. about this work: BEURMANN/KLAVIERSONATEN,
 33, 35; BERG, 176, 190; SCHULENBERG/INSTRUMEN-
 TAL, 137

Incipits from MANCHERLEY:

119. Sonata per il cembalo solo. 1757 (NV 14). W. 62/19
Mss.: D-brd B, P 677, BP 144; D-ddr Bds, P 365, M.Th. 50;
 D-brd DS, Mus. ms. 54; US Wc, M23.B13.W.62(19)
Early print: MANCHERLEY, 21. Lit. about MANCHERLEY:
 See this entry in Bib.
Ms. probably copied from the early print: B Br, II 4094
Mod. edns.: FARRENC, FRIEDHEIM, BERG/EDITIONS,
 BERG/FACSIMILE
Lit. about this work: BEURMANN/KLAVIERSONATEN,
 31, 64; BERG, 120–21, 164–65, 190; SCHULENBERG/IN-
 STRUMENTAL, 25; FOX, 81, 111
See item 50.

Incipits from MANCHERLEY:

120. Sonata per il cembalo solo. 1757 (NV 14). W. 62/20
Mss.: D-brd B, P 364, P 676, P 728; D-ddr Bds, M.Th. 33a,
 Mus. ms. 30385; A Wgm, VII 18937
Early print: MANCHERLEY, 109. Lit. about MANCHER-
 LEY: See this entry in Bib.
Ms. probably copied from the early print: B Br, II 4094
 (Westphal)
Mod. edn.: BERG/FACSIMILE
Lit. about this work: BEURMANN/KLAVIERSONATEN,
 51, 53; BERG, 125–26, 200
Arr. of 3rd mvt.: item 457

Incipits from MANCHERLEY:

121. Sonata per il cembalo solo. 1757 (NV 13). W. 65/31, 266
Mss.: B Bc, 5883 (Michel, with title in CPEB's hand); A
 Wgm, VII 43759

Early print: TROIS SONATES
Mss. probably copied from the early print: D-brd B, P 1140;
D-brd KIl, Mb 52
Mod. edns.: FARRENC, BERG/EDITIONS, BERG/FAC-
SIMILE
Lit.: HAMBURGER CORRESPONDENT, 1792, No. 90;
BEURMANN/KLAVIERSONATEN, 33, 51, 53, 69; BERG,
202, 368–71; FOX, 89–91

Incipits from 5883:

122. L'Auguste. Polonoise. 1757 (NV 14). W. 117/22
Mss.: D-brd B, Mus. ms. 38050, P 743 (autog.); A Wgm,
SBQ 11713 (VII 43737); D-ddr Dlb, 3029.T.17
Early print: MARPURG/RACCOLTA 1757, 6. Lit. about
MARPURG/RACCOLTA 1757: See this entry in Bib.
Ms. probably copied from the early print: B Bc, 5897 (West-
phal)
Mod. edns.: HERRMANN/LEICHTE, BERG/FACSIMILE
Arr.: 3rd mvt. of item 451

Incipit from P 743:

123. La Xénophon–La Sybille. 1757 (NV 14). W. 117/29
Mss.: D-brd B, Mus. ms. 38050, P 743 (autog.), P 794; D-ddr
Bds, Mus. ms. 30235 (2 copies); A Wgm, SBQ 11714 (VII
43763) ("La Xénophon" only); D-ddr Dlb, 3029.T.17; US
Wc, M20.A2.M684
Early print: ALLERLEY, 10. Lit. about ALLERLEY: See this
entry in Bib.
Ms. probably copied from the early print: B Bc, 5897 (West-
phal)
Mod. edns.: E. Pauer, Leipzig: Breitkopf & Härtel, c. 1880;
K. Nemetz-Fiedler (all under the title "La Sybille"), Vi-
enna: Österreichischer Bundesverlag, 1950; BERG/FAC-
SIMILE
Lit. about this work: RADCLIFFE, 592; OTTENBERG, 141
Arr.: See item 455.

Incipits from P 743:

124. L'Ernestine. 1757 (NV 14). W. 117/38
Mss.: D-brd B, Mus. ms. 38050 (entitled "La Frederique"),
Mus. ms. 38049, P 1154; D-ddr Bds, P 365; B Bc, 5897
(Westphal) (followed in this ms. by a song entitled "L'Er-
nestine," which is item 685.5, unrelated to item 124); A
Wgm, VII 43737; D-ddr Dlb, 3029.T.17
Mod. edn.: BERG/FACSIMILE
Lit.: MIESNER/STAHL, 73
Vnts.: item 83; see also item 105. Arr.: item 455

Incipit from 5897:

125. La Sophie. Aria. 1757 (NV 14). W. 117/40
Mss.: D-brd B, Mus. ms. 38050, P 743 (autog., with text "O
holde Zeit"), P 997; B Bc, 5897 (Westphal) (with same
text); D-ddr Dlb, 3029.T.17
Mod. edn.: BERG/FACSIMILE
Lit.: MIESNER/UMWELT, 136
The sources with text constitute an a.v. (an aria), as noted
in item 685, though NV, 14, lists the work as merely for
keyboard.

Incipit from P 743:

126. Sonata. 1758 (NV 14). W. 50/5
Ms.: D-ddr Bds, P 365
Early prints and lit. about them: See REPRISEN-SONATEN.
Mss. probably copied from an early print: D-brd B, P 773,
P 785, BP 143; B Bc, 5874; D-ddr LEm, Poel. Mus. ms. 42;
a ms. is in the private collection of E. N. Kulukundis
(U.S.).
Mod. edns.: HERRMANN SONATEN, DARBELLAY,
HASHIMOTO/REPRISEN, BERG/FACSIMILE
Lit. about this work: BEURMANN/KLAVIERSONATEN,
34, 113; BEURMANN/REPRISENSONATEN, 171 (where
D-brd B, P 789 is incorrectly listed as a source); BARFORD/
AFTERTHOUGHTS, 97–98; NEWMAN, 424; RAD-
CLIFFE, 586–87, 591; BERG, 192; SCHULENBERG/IN-
STRUMENTAL, 6, 24–25; FOX, 48–52
See item 24.

Incipits from REPRISEN-SONATEN:

127. Sonata. 1758 (NV 14). W. 51/3
Mss.: D-ddr Bds, P 1135 (largely autog. and Michel, contain-
ing only rev.: see item 164); B Bc, 5885 (Michel, containing
only rev.: see item 164); US Bp, No. 7 in **M200.9
Early prints and lit. about them: See FORTSETZUNG.
Mss. probably copied from an early print: D-brd B, P 674,
P 774; D-ddr LEm, Poel. Mus. ms. 42; A Wgm, VII 43739
Mod. edns.: HERRMANN SONATEN, ROSE, HASHI-
MOTO/FORTSETZUNG, BERG/FACSIMILE
Lit. about this work: BUSCH, 296; NEWMAN, 421; RAD-
CLIFFE, 587–88; BERG, 214; FOX, 65
See item 24.

Incipits from FORTSETZUNG:

128. Sonata. 1758 (NV 15). W. 51/4
Mss.: D-brd B, P 364; D-ddr Bds, P 1135 (largely autog. and
Michel, containing only rev.: see item 164); B Bc, 5885
(Michel, containing only rev.: see item 164)
Early prints and lit. about them: See FORTSETZUNG.
Mss. probably copied from an early print: D-brd B, P 674,
BP 143, P 774; D-ddr LEm, Poel. Mus. ms. 42; A Wgm,
VII 43739
Mod. edns.: HERRMANN/SONATEN, ROSE, CALAND–
GOEBELS, HASHIMOTO/FORTSETZUNG, BERG/FAC-
SIMILE
Lit. about this work: BERG, 190
See item 24.

Incipits from FORTSETZUNG:

129. Sonata. 1758 (NV 15). W. 52/6
Early prints and lit. about them: See ZWEYTE FORTSET-
ZUNG.
Ms. probably copied from the early print: D-brd B, BP 143
Mod. edns.: BERG/EDITIONS, BERG/FACSIMILE, HASHI-
MOTO/ZWEYTE FORTSETZUNG
Lit. about this work: BITTER/BRÜDER, I, 78–79; BEUR-
MANN/KLAVIERSONATEN, 27; RADCLIFFE, 588;
BERG, 127–28, 147–48, 152–53, 220–22; SCHULENBERG/
INSTRUMENTAL, 109–14
See item 24.

Incipits from ZWEYTE FORTSETZUNG:

130. Sonata. 1758 (NV 15). W. 55/2
Early print and lit. about it: See KENNER I.
Mss. probably copied from the early print: D-brd B, N. mus.
ms. 10465; B Bc, 5877; D-brd Kll, Mb 41, Mb 45; D-ddr
LEm, Poel. Mus. ms. 40; D-ddr LEb, Gorke 37; US NHu,
Mason collection, 5011
Mod. edns.: BAUMGART, FARRENC, KREBS, SCHEN-
KER/KLAVIERWERKE, BERG/FACSIMILE
Lit. about this work: BITTER/BRÜDER, I, 213; SHEDLOCK,
105–06; SCHENKER/BEITRAG, 14, 18, 24, 27, 32, 46, 52,
72; SCHMID/KAMMERMUSIK, 122–23, Anh. 27 (read W.
55/2); AUERBACH, 68, 85, 90; NEWMAN, 420, 429; BAR-
FORD/KEYBOARD, 108–09; RADCLIFFE, 588–89;
COHEN, 101, 111; BERG, 200; FOX, 162–63
See item 24.

Incipits from KENNER I:

131. Sonata per il cembalo solo. 1758 (NV 14). W. 62/21
Mss.: D-brd B, P 774, P 789 (marked by CPEB); D-ddr Bds,
  Mus. ms. 30193, M.Th. 44; A Wgm, H 31221 (VII 43745);
  US Wc, M20.A2.M68
Early print: OEUVRES, XI, 4
Mss. probably copied from the early print: B Br, II 4094
  (Westphal); D-ddr LEb, Gorke 669
Mod. edns.: FARRENC, BERG/EDITIONS, BERG/FAC-
  SIMILE
Lit.: BEURMANN/KLAVIERSONATEN, 29, 51; BERG, 144,
  191

Incipits from P 789:

132. Sonata per il cembalo solo. 1758 (NV 14). W. 62/22
Mss.: D-brd B, P 370; D-ddr Bds, P 365, M.Th. 45; A Wgm,
  SBQ 11711 (VII 14519); D-brd KII, Mb 49
Early print: COLLECTION I
Ms. probably copied from the early print: B Br, II 4094
  (Westphal)
Mod. edns.: FARRENC, BERG/EDITIONS, BERG/FAC-
  SIMILE
Lit.: BEURMANN/KLAVIERSONATEN, 23, 51

Incipits from COLLECTION I:

133. Orgel-Sonata. 1758 (NV 14). W. 70/1
Mss.: D-brd B, P 789 (cembalo); D-ddr Bds, P 365, M.Th.43,
  Mus. ms. 30193; B Bc, 5879 (Westphal)
Early print: OEUVRES, IX, 4 ("clavessin")
Ms. probably copied from the early print: D-ddr LEb, Gorke
  669
Mod. edns.: FEDTKE/ORGELWERKE (which incorrectly
  names D-ddr Bds, P 369 as a source); BERG/EDITIONS,
  BERG/FACSIMILE
Lit.: BEURMANN/KLAVIERSONATEN, 16; NEWMAN, 89;
  COHEN, 111; BERG, 102; OTTENBERG, 124
Rev.: item 135
See item 84 regarding performance medium. From BERG/
  NOTES: As can be seen in the above list of mss. and in
  the ms. list of item 135, the performance medium an-
  nounced in a title is not a true criterion for distinguishing
  between the original and revised versions of this sonata.

Incipits from 5879:

134. Orgel-Sonata. 1758 (NV 14). W. 70/2
Mss.: D-brd B, P 364 (3rd mvt. only: see item 162), P 370,
  P 774 (Michel, marked by CPEB); A Wgm, VII 42172; a
  ms. (incomplete) is in the private collection of E. N.
  Kulukundis (U.S.).
Early prints and lit. about them: See PRELUDIO, WIN-
  TERSCHMIDT.
Mss. probably copied from an early print (PRELUDIO): D-
  brd B, P 434, P 1187; B Bc, 5879 (Westphal)
Mod. edns.: LANGLAIS, BRANDTS-BUYS, FEDTKE/
  ORGELWERKE, BERG/FACSIMILE
Lit. about this work: BEURMANN/KLAVIERSONATEN, 16;
  NEWMAN, 89; COHEN, 111; BERG, 102; OTTENBERG,
  124
See item 84.

Incipits from PRELUDIO:

135. Sonata per il cembalo. 1758 or later (NV 14). W. 65/32

Mss.: D-brd B, P 774 (organ; Michel, rev. by CPEB, with written-out varied repeats); D-ddr Bds, P 369; B Bc, 5883 (Michel); D-ddr LEm, Becker III 8. 2

Mod. edns.: BERG/EDITIONS, BERG/FACSIMILE

Lit.: BERG, 140; SCHULENBERG/INSTRUMENTAL, 6

Rev. of item 133; in P 774, singled out in CPEB's hand on the cover as "diese Sonate mit dieser Veränderungen." See items 84 and 133 regarding performance medium.

Incipits from 5883:

136. Sonata. 1759 (NV 15). W. 50/1

Mss.: D-brd B, P 790; D-ddr Bds, P 1135 (largely autog. and Michel, containing only rev.: see item 164); B Bc, 5885 (Michel, containing only rev.: see item 164); US Wc, M23.B13

Early prints and lit. about them: See REPRISEN-SONATEN.

Mss. probably copied from an early print: D-brd B, P 773, P 785, BP 143; B Bc, 5874; D-ddr LEm, Poel. Mus. ms. 42; a ms. is in the private collection of E. N. Kulukundis (U.S.).

Mod. edns.: in H. Fischer, *Die Sonate*, Berlin: Vieweg, 1937; DARBELLAY, HASHIMOTO/REPRISEN, BERG/FACSIMILE

Lit. about this work: BEURMANN/KLAVIERSONATEN, 57, 111; RADCLIFFE, 586; BERG, 118, 178; OTTENBERG, 140; SCHULENBERG/INSTRUMENTAL, 6, 24–25

See item 24.

Incipits from REPRISEN-SONATEN:

137. Sonata. 1759 (NV 15). W. 50/2

Mss.: D-ddr Bds, P 1135 (largely autog. and Michel, containing only rev.: see item 164); B Bc, 5885 (Michel, containing only rev.: see item 164); D-brd KIl, Mb 43; US Wc, M23.B13 (1st mvt. only)

Early prints and lit. about them: See REPRISEN-SONATEN.

Mss. probably copied from an early print: D-brd B, P 773, P 785, BP 143; B Bc, 5874; D-ddr LEm, Poel. Mus. ms. 42; a ms. is in the private collection of E. N. Kulukundis (U.S.).

Mod. edns.: DARBELLAY, HASHIMOTO/REPRISEN, BERG/FACSIMILE

Lit. about this work: CLERCX, 161; BEURMANN/KLAVIER-SONATEN, 107, 110; BEURMANN/REPRISENSONA-TEN, 174, 176; BARFORD/AFTERTHOUGHTS, 95; SCHULENBERG/INSTRUMENTAL, 6, 24–25

See item 24.

Incipits from REPRISEN-SONATEN:

138. Sonata. 1759 (NV 15). W. 50/3

Mss.: D-brd B, P 790; D-ddr Bds, P 1135 (largely autog. and Michel, containing only rev.: see item 164); B Bc, 5885 (Michel, containing only rev.: see item 164); D-brd KIl, Mb 43

Early prints and lit. about them: See REPRISEN-SONATEN.

Mss. probably copied from an early print: D-brd B, P 773, P 785, BP 143; B Bc, 5874; D-ddr LEm, Poel. Mus. ms. 42; a ms. is in the private collection of E. N. Kulukundis (U.S.).

Mod. edns.: DARBELLAY, HASHIMOTO/REPRISEN, BERG/FACSIMILE

Lit. about this work: BITTER/BRÜDER, I, 74–76, CLERCX, 161; BEURMANN/KLAVIERSONATEN, 111, 114; BAR-FORD/AFTERTHOUGHTS, 95–96; NEWMAN, 420, 425; RADCLIFFE, 586; SCHULENBERG/INSTRUMENTAL, 6, 24–25

Vnt. of the 3rd mvt.: item 334

See item 24.

Incipits from REPRISEN-SONATEN:

139. Sonata. 1759 (NV 15). W. 50/4
Ms.: D-brd B, KIl, Mb 43
Early prints and lit. about them: See REPRISEN-SONATEN.
Mss. probably copied from the early print: D-brd B, P 773,
   P 785, BP 143; D-ddr LEm, Poel. Mus. ms. 42; a ms. is in
   the private collection of E. N. Kulukundis (U.S.).
Mod. edns.: DARBELLAY, HASHIMOTO/REPRISEN,
   BERG/FACSIMILE
Lit. about this work: HADOW, 77–78; BEURMANN/
   KLAVIERSONATEN, 111; BARFORD/AFTER-
   THOUGHTS, 96–97; NEWMAN, 427; RADCLIFFE, 586;
   SCHULENBERG/INSTRUMENTAL, 6, 24–25
See item 24.

Incipits from REPRISEN-SONATEN:

140. Sonata. 1759 (NV 15). W. 50/6
Early prints and lit. about them: See REPRISEN-SONATEN.
Mss. probably copied from an early print: D-brd B, P 773,
   P 785; a ms. is in the private collection of E. N. Kulukundis
   (U.S.).
Mod. edns.: DARBELLAY, HASHIMOTO/REPRISEN,
   BERG/FACSIMILE
Lit. about this work: BITTER/BRÜDER, I, 76; NEWMAN,
   78, 419, 424; SCHULENBERG/INSTRUMENTAL, 6, 24–25
See item 24.

Incipit from REPRISEN-SONATEN:

[1 mvt. only]

141. Sonata. 1759 (NV 15). W. 51/5
Mss.: D-brd B, P 364; D-ddr Bds, P 1135 (largely autog. and
   Michel, containing only rev.: see item 164); B Bc, 5885
   (Michel, containing only rev.: see item 164)
Early prints and lit. about them: See FORTSETZUNG.
Mss. probably copied from an early print: D-brd B, P 674,
   BP 143, P 774; D-ddr LEm, Poel. Mus. ms. 42; A Wgm,
   VII 43739
Mod. edns.: ROSE, CALAND–GOEBELS, HASHIMOTO/
   FORTSETZUNG, BERG/FACSIMILE
Lit. about this work: BEURMANN/KLAVIERSONATEN, 56;
   RADCLIFFE, 587; BERG, 200
See item 24.

Incipits from FORTSETZUNG:

142. Sonata. 1759 (NV 15). W. 52/2
Early prints and lit. about them: See ZWEYTE FORTSET-
   ZUNG.
Ms. probably copied from the early print: D-brd B, BP 143
Mod. edns.: CALAND, FRIEDHEIM, BERG/FACSIMILE,
   HASHIMOTO/ZWEYTE FORTSETZUNG
Lit. about this work: BEURMANN/KLAVIERSONATEN,
   31, 47, 56; RADCLIFFE, 588; BERG, 200
See item 24.

Incipits from ZWEYTE FORTSETZUNG:

143. Sonata per il cembalo. 1759 (NV 15). W. 65/33

Mss.: D-ddr WRgs (autog., 2nd and 3rd mvts. respectively entitled "La Guillelmine" and "La Coorl"; my thanks to Hans-Günter Ottenberg for notice of this ms., which authenticates the nicknames); D-brd B, Mus. ms. 38050 (2nd and 3rd mvts. only, respectively entitled "La Guilielmine" and "La Coorl"), P 359, P 776 (title p. marked by CPEB); D-ddr Bds, Mus. ms. 30385 (2nd mvt. entitled "La Guillelmine," 3rd mvt. "La Coorl"); B Bc, 5883 (Michel); A Wgm, VII 43760; D-brd KIl, Mb 50 (3rd mvt. entitled "La Caroline," unrelated to item 98), Mb 52, Mb 53; D-brd KNu, Bücken-Nachlass cat. p. 163 (2nd and 3rd mvts. only, respectively entitled "La Guillelmine" and "La Caroline," the latter being unrelated to item 98); US Wc, M20.A2.M68, M23.B13.W.65(33)

Mod. edns.: VRIESLANDER/LEICHTE, BERG/FACSIMILE

Lit.: CLERCX, 162; BEURMANN/KLAVIERSONATEN, 34; BERG, 140, 192

Incipits from 5883:

144. Fantasia. 1759 (NV 16). W. 112/2 (= 117/8)

Early print and lit. about it: See VERSCHIEDEN.

Mss. probably copied from the early print: B Bc, 5897 (Westphal); A Wn, 18687

Mod. edn.: VRIESLANDER/KLEINE, BERG/FACSIMILE

Lit. about this work: ELDER, 87ff.; SELINGER-BARBER, 61–66

Incipit from VERSCHIEDEN:

145. Solfeggio. 1759 (NV 16). W. 112/4 (= 117/5)

Early print and lit. about it: See VERSCHIEDEN.

Mss. probably copied from the early print: B Bc, 5897 (Westphal); A Wn, 18687

Mod. edns.: HERRMANN/LEICHTE, BERG/FACSIMILE

Incipit from VERSCHIEDEN:

146. Fantasia. 1759 (NV 16). W. 112/8 (= 117/9)

Ms.: D-brd B, P 704

Early print and lit. about it: See VERSCHIEDEN.

Mss. probably copied from the early print: B Bc, 5897 (Westphal); A Wn, 18687

Mod. edns.: VRIESLANDER/KLEINE, BERG/FACSIMILE

Lit. about this work: ELDER, 87ff.; SELINGER-BARBER, 61–66

Incipit from VERSCHIEDEN:

147. Solfeggio. 1759 (NV 16). W. 112/10 (= 117/6)

Ms.: D-brd B, P 704

Early print and lit. about it: See VERSCHIEDEN.

Mss. probably copied from the early print: B Bc, 5897 (Westphal); A Wn, 18687

Mod. edns.: HERRMANN/LEICHTE, BERG/FACSIMILE

Incipit from VERSCHIEDEN:

148. Fantasia. 1759 (NV 16). W. 112/15 (= 117/10)

Mss.: D-brd B, P 509, P 704, P 740

Early print and lit. about it: See VERSCHIEDEN.

Mss. probably copied from the early print: B Bc, 5897 (Westphal); A Wn, 18687

Mod. edns.: VRIESLANDER/KLEINE, BERG/FACSIMILE

Lit. about this work: ELDER, 87ff.; SELINGER–BARBER, 77–90

Incipit from VERSCHIEDEN:

149. Solfeggio. 1759 (NV 16). W. 112/18 (= 117/7)

Early print and lit. about it: See VERSCHIEDEN.

Mss. probably copied from the early print: B Bc, 5897 (Westphal); A Wn, 18687

Mod. edns.: VRIESLANDER/KLEINE, BERG/FACSIMILE

Incipit from VERSCHIEDEN:

150. Sonata. 1760 (NV 16). W. 51/1
Ms.: D-brd B, P 364 (but not also P 367)
Early prints and lit. about them: See FORTSETZUNG.
Mss. probably copied from an early print: D-brd B, P 674,
    BP 143, P 774; D-ddr LEm, Poel. Mus. ms. 42; A Wgm,
    VII 43739
Mod. edns.: ROSE, BERG/EDITIONS, HASHIMOTO/
    FORTSETZUNG, BERG/FACSIMILE
Lit. about this work: BITTER/BRÜDER, I, 74–75; BEUR-
    MANN/KLAVIERSONATEN, 73, 103; BERG, 103–04, 196,
    200; OTTENBERG, 140; SCHULENBERG/INSTRUMEN-
    TAL, 44–47, 102; FOX, 24–30
Rev.: items 156, 157
See item 24.

Incipits from FORTSETZUNG:

151. Sonata. 1760 (NV 16). W. 51/2
Mss.: D-ddr Bds, P 365, P 1135 (largely autog. and Michel,
    containing only rev.: see item 164); B Bc, 5885 (Michel,
    containing only rev.: see item 164); D-brd Kll, Mb 40;
    D-ddr GOl, Ms. Mus. 21a, No. XXI (vnt.); F Pc, Ms. 1562
    (probably not autog.; fragments of 2nd and 3rd mvts.;
    reproduced as the frontispiece of BARFORD/KEY-
    BOARD)
Early prints and lit. about them: See FORTSETZUNG.
Mss. probably copied from an early print: D-brd B, P 674,
    BP 143, P 774; D-ddr LEm, Poel. Mus. ms. 42; A Wgm,
    VII 43739
Mod. edns.: CALAND, ROSE, HASHIMOTO/FORTSET-
    ZUNG, BERG/FACSIMILE
Lit. about this work: RADCLIFFE, 587; BERG, 200;
    SCHULENBERG/INSTRUMENTAL, 140
See item 24.

Incipits from FORTSETZUNG:

152. Sonata per il cembalo. 1760 (NV 16). W. 65/34
Mss.: D-brd B, P 359 (Michel?); B Bc, 5883 (Michel); PL Kj,
    P 771 autog.)
Mod. edn.: BERG/FACSIMILE
Lit.: BEURMANN/KLAVIERSONATEN, 51, 110; BEUR-
    MANN/REPRISENSONATEN, 169; BERG, 200

Incipits from 5883:

153. Fürs Clavier. 1760 (NV 16). W. 116/21
Mss.: D-brd B, P 742 (autog.; before erasure the heading
    was "für eine Spieluhr"); PL Kj, P 741 (autog.); B Bc, 5898
    (Westphal); A Wn, 19035 (Michel)
Mod. edns.: HERRMANN/SONATEN, BERG/FACSIMILE
Lit.: WADE, 3
See item 635 regarding pieces for mechanical instruments.

Incipit from P 742:

154. Polonoise. 1760 (NV 16). W. 116/22
Mss.: D-brd B, P 742 (autog.); PL Kj, P 741 (autog.); B Bc,
    5898 (Westphal); A Wn, 19035 (Michel)
Vnt.: item 168
Mod. edn.: BERG/FACSIMILE
Lit.: WADE, 3

Incipit from P 742:

155. Clavierstück mit [22] Veränderungen. 1760 (NV 16). W. 118/2

Mss.: D-brd B, Mus. ms. 38049 (only 10 variations; "Arietta con variationes di Bach"), P 367 (only 10 variations), P 735; D-ddr Bds, Mus. ms. 30382; A Wn, 19035 (Michel; only 8 variations)

Early prints: Variations 1–17 appear in ALLERLEY, 190; variations 18–22, after a restatement of the theme, in VIELERLEY, 113. Lit. about ALLERLEY and VIELERLEY: See these entries in Bib.

Mod. edn.: BERG/FACSIMILE

Ms. probably copied from these two early prints: B Bc, 5899 (Westphal)

Lit. about this work: FISCHER, 192–93, 196, 201–02, 204–05, 213–15; WADE, 12; see also Critical Notes in BERG/FACSIMILE.

A pasticcio variation. Westphal identifies these composers in 5899: theme ("Ariette"), [J. F.] Agricola; variation 1, [J. A.?] Steffan; 2, anon.; 3–4, Steffan; 5, anon.; 6, Steffan; 7–11, anon.; 12, C. F. C. Fasch; 13–14, CPEB; 15–16, Fasch; 17–22, CPEB. NV, 16, says that "Die Ariette selbst, mit ihren italienischen Veränderungen ist, wo es nöthig war, verdeutschet" [meaning, presumably, notated according to German convention].

Incipit from 5899:

156. Sonata per il cembalo solo. 1760 or later (NV 16). W. 65/35

Mss.: D-brd B, P 776 (title p. by CPEB); B Bc, 5883 (Michel)

Mod. edns.: BERG/EDITIONS, BERG/FACSIMILE

Lit.: BEURMANN/KLAVIERSONATEN, 103; BERG, 103–04, 196; SCHULENBERG/INSTRUMENTAL, 24, 45–47; FOX, 24–30

Rev. of item 150 (see item 157). On the title p. of the 5883 copy: "Die erste Sonate aus der Fortsetzung der Reprisen-Sonaten Zweymahl durchaus verändert von C. P. E. Bach." NV, 16, referring to item 150: "Diese Sonate ist nachhero 2 mal durchaus verändert."

Incipits from 5883:

157. Sonata per il cembalo solo. 1760 or later (NV 16). W. 65/36

Mss.: D-brd B, P 776 (Michel); B Bc, 5883 (Michel)

Mod. edns.: BERG/EDITIONS, BERG/FACSIMILE

Lit.: BERG, 103–04, 196; SCHULENBERG/INSTRUMENTAL, 24, 45–47; FOX, 24–30

A 2nd rev. of item 150 (see item 156). On the title p. of the 5883 copy: "2t^e Veränderungen der erste Sonate aus der Fortsetzung der Reprisen Sonaten von C. P. E. Bach."

Incipits from 5883:

158. Sonata. 1761 (NV 16). W. 52/3

Mss.: D-ddr Bds, P 1135 (largely autog. and Michel, containing only rev.: see item 164); B Bc, 5885 (Michel, containing only rev.: see item 164); D-brd KIl, Mb 40; US AA, M25.B116.A4.17-- (2nd mvt. only)

Early prints and lit. about them: See ZWEYTE FORSETZUNG.

Ms. probably copied from the early print: D-ddr Bds, BP 143

Mod. edns.: HERRMANN/SONATEN, BERG/FACSIMILE, HASHIMOTO/ZWEYTE FORSETZUNG

Lit. about this work: BEURMANN/KLAVIERSONATEN, 24, 53; COHEN, 143; BERG, 113–14

See item 24.

Incipits from ZWEYTE FORSETZUNG:

159. Menuet I–II. Probably 1762 or earlier (source of date: 1st pub. in item 601 version). W. 116/15

Ms.: B Bc, 5898 (Westphal)

Mod. edn.: BERG/FACSIMILE

A.v.: item 601

Incipits from 5898:

160. Fantasia. 1762 or earlier (source of date: pub. date of item 870). W. 117/14
Mss.: D-brd B, P 435, P 793
Mod. edn.: BERG/FACSIMILE
Lit.: COHEN, 28; ELDER, 72–73; SCHULENBERG/INSTRU-MENTAL, 21; SELINGER–BARBER, 48, 77–90
Used as an example in Part II of the *Versuch* (item 870)
Ms. probably copied from the printed *Versuch:* B Bc, 5897 (Westphal)

Incipit from the *Versuch:*

161. Sonata. 1762 (NV 17). W. 52/5
Ms.: US Bp, No. 8 in **M200.9
Early prints and lit. about them: See ZWEYTE FORTSET-ZUNG.
Ms. probably copied from the early print: D-brd B, BP 143
Mod. edns.: BERG/FACSIMILE, HASHIMOTO/ZWEYTE FORTSETZUNG
Lit. about this work: BEURMANN/KLAVIERSONATEN, 23, 32; RADCLIFFE, 588; BERG, 190
See item 24.

Incipits from ZWEYTE FORTSETZUNG:

162. Sonata. 1762 (NV 17). W. 53/1
Mss.: D-brd B, P 364 (3rd mvt. of item 134 substituted for its 3rd mvt.); D-ddr Bds, P 1135 (largely autog. and Michel, containing only rev.: see item 164); B Bc, 5885 (Michel, containing only rev.: see item 164). Not in D-brd B, P 433, as reported in BEURMANN/KLAVIERSONATEN, 138.

Early prints and lit. about them: See LEICHTE.
Mss. probably copied from an early print: D-brd B, P 675; D-ddr Bds, Mus. ms. 30201 (3rd mvt. only), Mus. ms. 30235 (2nd mvt. only), Mus. ms. 30385; D-ddr LEm, Poel. Mus. ms. 48; A Wgm, VII 8811
Mod. edns.: J. Zürcher, Mainz: Schott, 1964; BERG/FAC-SIMILE
Lit. about this work: BEURMANN/REPRISENSONATEN, 173–74; BERG, 140; OTTENBERG, 142
A.v.: item 635/30

Incipits from LEICHTE:

163. Sonata. 1762 (NV 17). W. 53/5
Mss.: D-ddr Bds, P 1135 (largely autog. and Michel, containing only rev.: see item 164); B Bc, 5885 (Michel, containing only rev.: see item 164)
Early prints and lit. about them: See LEICHTE.
Mss. probably copied from an early print: D-brd B, P 675; D-ddr Bds, Mus. ms. 30385; D-ddr LEm, Poel. Mus. ms. 48; A Wgm, VII 8811
Mod. edns.: J. Zürcher, Mainz: Schott, 1964; BERG/FAC-SIMILE
Lit. about this work: BEURMANN/KLAVIERSONATEN, 106; BERG, 140, 165

Incipits from LEICHTE:

164. Veränderungen und Auszierungen über einige meiner Sonaten. Completed 1762 or later (source of date: latest works affected [items 162, 163] date from 1762). W. 68

Mss.: D-ddr Bds, P 1135 (largely autog. and Michel); B Bc, 5885 (Michel)
Mod. edn.: BERG/FACSIMILE
Lit.: WADE, 97; SCHULENBERG/INSTRUMENTAL, 24
Both mss. contain the composer's changes in items 36, 62, 116, 127, 128, 136–38, 141, 151, 158, 162, 163.

165. Minuetto I–II. Between 1762 and 1765 (NV 17). W. 112/3 (=116/9)
Early print and lit. about it: See VERSCHIEDEN.
Mss. probably copied from the early print: D-brd B, P 676; B Bc, 5898 (Westphal)
Mod. edns.: HERRMANN/LEICHTE, BERG/FACSIMILE
A.v.: item 602

Incipits from VERSCHIEDEN:

[Minuetto I is repeated after Minuetto II.]

166. Alla polacca. Between 1762 and 1765 (NV 17). W. 112/5 (= 116/10)
Early print and lit. about it: See VERSCHIEDEN.
Mss. probably copied from the early print: D-brd B, P 676; B Bc, 5898 (Westphal)
Mod. edns.: VRIESLANDER/KLEINE; W. Rehberg, Mainz: Schott, n.d.; BERG/FACSIMILE
A.v.: item 605

Incipit from VERSCHIEDEN:

167. Minuetto I–II. Between 1762 and 1765 (NV 17). W. 112/9 (= 116/11)
Early print and lit. about it: See VERSCHIEDEN.
Mss. probably copied from the early print: D-brd B, P 676; B Bc, 5898 (Westphal)
Mod. edn.: BERG/FACSIMILE
A.v.: item 603

Incipits from VERSCHIEDEN:

[Minuetto I is repeated after Minuetto II.]

168. Alla polacca. Between 1762 and 1765 (NV 17). W. 112/11 (= 116/12)
Early print and lit. about it: See VERSCHIEDEN.
Mss. probably copied from the early print: D-brd B, P 676; B Bc, 5898 (Westphal)
Mod. edns.: VRIESLANDER/KLEINE, BERG/FACSIMILE
Vnt.: item 154

Incipit from VERSCHIEDEN:

169. Minuetto I–II. Between 1762 and 1765 (NV 17). W. 112/16 (= 116/13)
Early print and lit. about it: See VERSCHIEDEN.
Mss. probably copied from the early print: D-brd B, P 676; B Bc, 5898 (Westphal)
Mod. edns.: HERRMANN/LEICHTE, BERG/FACSIMILE

Incipits from VERSCHIEDEN:

[Minuetto I is repeated after Minuetto II.]

170. Alla polacca. Between 1762 and 1765 (NV 17). W. 112/17 (= 116/14)
Early print and lit. about it: See VERSCHIEDEN.
Mss. probably copied from the early print: D-brd B, P 676; B Bc, 5898 (Westphal)
Mod. edns.: VRIESLANDER/KLEINE, BERG/FACSIMILE
A.v.: item 604

Incipit from VERSCHIEDEN:

171. Menuet I–II. 1763 or earlier (source of date: 1st pub.).
W. 116/1

Ms.: D-brd B, Mus. ms. 38050 (autog.)

Early print: MANCHERLEY, 174 (1763). Lit. about MAN-
CHERLEY: See this entry in Bib.

Ms. probably copied from the early print: B Bc, 5898 (Westphal)

Mod. edns.: A. Kranz, Wilhelmshaven: O. Noetzel Verlag,
1958; BERG/FACSIMILE

A vnt. of Menuet I is in D-brd B, P 672 (Michel, Wq n.v.
53, the 3rd incipit given here). The pocket-size P 672,
containing little keyboard pieces by various members of
the Bach family and J. C. Altnikol, is possibly the "kleines
Büchlein" listed in NV, 66. See item 340 and JONES/NBA,
35.

Incipits from MANCHERLEY:

[Menuet I is repeated after Menuet II.]

Incipit from P 672:

172. Polonoise. 1763 or earlier (source of date: 1st pub.).
W. 116/2

Ms.: D-brd B, Mus. ms. 38050 (autog.)

Early print: MANCHERLEY, 188 (1763). Lit. about MAN-
CHERLEY: See this entry in Bib.

Ms. probably copied from the early print: B Bc, 5898 (Westphal)

Mod. edns.: A. Kranz, Wilhelmshaven: O. Noetzel Verlag,
1958; BERG/FACSIMILE

Incipit from from MANCHERLEY:

173. Sonata. 1763 (NV 17). W. 57/6

Mss.: D-brd B, P 774, P 993, P 1187 (1st mvt. only). Not in
D-brd B, P 1178, as reported in BEURMANN/KLAVIER-
SONATEN, 138

Early prints: KENNER III; "Sonate für Piano Forte," Berlin:
Lischke, n.d. Lit. about KENNER III: See this entry in

Bib. The known lit. gives no evidence that the Lischke
print was authorized by CPEB.

Ms. probably copied from an early print (KENNER III): D-
brd B, P 433; D-ddr LEm, Poel. Mus. ms. 40; D-ddr LEb, 33

Mod. edns.: BAUMGART, KREBS, BÜLOW, FARRENC,
RIEMANN, SCHENKER/KLAVIERWERKE, BERG/FAC-
SIMILE

Lit. about this work: FORKEL/ALMANACH, III (1784), 22–
38, 636; BITTER/BRÜDER, I, 217–20; SCHENKER/BEI-
TRAG, 18–19, 23–24, 27, 54; BEURMANN/KLAVIER-
SONATEN, 62, 66, 76, 159–64; NEWMAN, 421; BAR-
FORD/KEYBOARD, 117–18; RADCLIFFE, 289; BERG, 57,
77–78, 150–51; OTTENBERG, 264–65; SCHULENBERG/
INSTRUMENTAL, 94–95, 114–17, 123, 126–27, 138–40,
162; FOX, 85, 176–77

Incipits from KENNER III:

174. Sonata per il cembalo. 1763 (NV 17). W. 65/37

Mss.: D-brd B, P 359 (Michel?); B Bc, 5883 (Michel)

Mod. edns.: FARRENC, BERG/EDITIONS, BERG/FAC-
SIMILE

Lit.: BEURMANN/KLAVIERSONATEN, 65; BERG, 79–80,
190

Incipits from 5883:

175. Sonata per il cembalo. 1763 (NV 17). W. 65/38

Mss.: D-brd B, P 776 (Michel; title p. marked by CPEB); B
Bc, 5883 (Michel)

Mod. edn.: BERG/FACSIMILE
Lit.: BEURMANN/KLAVIERSONATEN, 30, 267

Incipits from P 776:

176. Sonata per il cembalo. 1763 (NV 17). W. 65/39
Mss.: D-brd B, P 359 (Michel, signed and marked by CPEB),
    P 772 (rev. by CPEB); B Bc, 5883 (Michel)
Mod. edns.: FARRENC, BERG/FACSIMILE
Lit.: BERG, 190

Incipits from P 772:

177. Sonata per il cembalo. 1763 (NV 18). W. 65/40
Mss.: D-brd B, P 776 (Michel; title p. in CPEB's hand), P
    1132 (autog.); B Bc, 5883 (Michel)
Mod. edns.: FARRENC, BERG/EDITIONS, BERG/FAC-
    SIMILE
Lit.: BERG, 148–49, 154, 188, 355–58; FOX, 123

Incipits from P 776:

178. Sonata per il cembalo. 1763 (NV 18). W. 65/41
Mss.: D-brd B, P 359 (Michel), P 776 (Michel); B Bc, 5883
    (Michel)
Mod. edns.: FARRENC, BERG/EDITIONS, BERG/FAC-
    SIMILE
Lit.: BEURMANN/KLAVIERSONATEN, 35; BERG, 200

Incipits from 5883:

179. Sonata per il cembalo. 1763 (NV 17). W. 112/7
Mss.: D-brd B, P 728, BP 143
Early print and lit. about it: See VERSCHIEDEN.
Mss. probably copied from the early print: D-ddr Bds, Mus.
    ms. 30195 (2nd mvt. only); B Br, II 4094 (Westphal)
Mod. edns.: FARRENC, BERG/FACSIMILE
Lit. about this work: BEURMANN/KLAVIERSONATEN, 27;
    BERG, 190
Mus. ms. 30195 pairs the 2nd mvt., retitled "Praeludium,"
    with a spurious "Fuga" (item 389.5).

Incipits from VERSCHIEDEN:

180. Sonata. 1764 (NV 18). W. 53/2
Early prints and lit. about them: See LEICHTE.
Mss. probably copied from an early print: D-brd B, P 675;
    D-ddr Bds, Mus. ms. 30385; A Wgm, VII 8811; D-ddr
    LEm, Poel. Mus. ms. 48
Mod. edn.: BERG/FACSIMILE
Lit. about this work: SHEDLOCK, 101; BEURMANN/
    KLAVIERSONATEN, 73; BERG, 156–57, 190, 200

Incipits from LEICHTE:

Allegretto grazioso

Larghetto

Allegro ma non presto

181. Sonata. 1764 (NV 18). W. 53/3
Early prints and lit. about them: See LEICHTE.
Mss. probably copied from an early print: D-brd B, P 675;
D-ddr Bds, Mus. ms. 30385; D-ddr LEm, Poel. Mus. ms.
48; A Wgm, VII 8811
Mod. edn.: BERG/FACSIMILE

Incipits from LEICHTE:

Allegro

Poco andante

Allegro assai

182. Sonata. 1764 (NV 18). W. 53/4
Ms.: D-ddr Bds, P 365
Early prints and lit. about them: See LEICHTE.
Mss. probably copied from an early print: D-brd B, P 675;
D-ddr Bds, Mus. ms. 30201 (3rd mvt. only); Mus. ms.
30385; D-ddr LEm, Poel. Mus. ms. 48; A Wgm, VII 8811
Mod. edns.: FRIEDHEIM, BERG/FACSIMILE

Incipits from LEICHTE:

Allegro
ten.   ten.

Largo e tenero

Presto

183. Sonata. 1764 (NV 18). W. 53/6
Mss.: D-brd B, P 364
Early prints and lit. about them: See LEICHTE.
Mss. probably copied from an early print: D-brd B, P 675;
D-ddr LEm, Poel. Mus. ms. 48; A Wgm, VII 8811
Mod. edns.: J. Zürcher, Mainz: Schott, 1964; BERG/FAC-
SIMILE
Lit. about this work: SHEDLOCK, 100; BEURMANN/
KLAVIERSONATEN, 75; NEWMAN, 385; RADCLIFFE,
588; OTTENBERG, 137–40

Incipits from LEICHTE:

Allegro di molto

Andantino

Presto

184. Sonata. 1765 (NV 18). W. 54/3
Early prints and lit. about them: See DAMENSONATEN.
Mss. probably copied from an early print: D-brd B, P 432,
P 774; D-ddr LEb, 348; US AA, M23.B12.S543.17--; a ms.
is in the private collection of E. N. Kulukundis (U.S.).
Mod. edns.: JOHNEN/SONATEN, BERG/FACSIMILE
Lit. about this work: BEURMANN/KLAVIERSONATEN, 40;
BERG, 194–95, 200
See item 24.

Incipits from DAMENSONATEN:

Allegro ma non troppo

Larghetto

Prestissimo

185. Sonata. 1765 (NV 19). W. 54/5
Early prints and lit. about them: See DAMENSONATEN.
Mss. probably copied from an early print: D-brd B, P 432, P 774; D-ddr LEb, 347; US AA, M23.B12.S545.17--; a ms. is in the private collection of E. N. Kulukundis (U.S.).
Mod. edns.: JOHNEN/SONATEN, BERG/FACSIMILE
Lit. about this work: BEURMANN/REPRISENSONATEN, 169
See item 24.

Incipits from DAMENSONATEN:

186. Sonata. 1765 (NV 19). W. 55/4
Early prints: KENNER I; "A Favorite Sonata for the Harpsichord or Piano-forte . . . ," London: Corri, n.d. Lit. about KENNER I: See this entry in Bib. The known lit. gives no evidence that the Corri print was authorized by CPEB.
Mss. probably copied from an early print (KENNER I): D-brd B, N. Mus. ms. 10465; B Bc, 5877; D-brd KIl, Mb 41; D-ddr LEm, Poel. Mus. ms. 40; D-ddr LEb, 351, Gorke 37; D-ddr ROu; US NHu, Mason collection, 5011
Mod. edns.: BAUMGART, KREBS, BÜLOW, FARRENC, SCHENKER/KLAVIERWERKE, BERG/FACSIMILE
Lit. about this work: BITTER/BRÜDER, I, 213; SCHENKER/BEITRAG, 11–12, 14, 17, 21, 23–24, 27, 32, 38; BEURMANN/KLAVIERSONATEN, 51, 77; MÜLLER, 64, 66; NEWMAN, 421, 427; BARFORD/KEYBOARD, 110–12; RADCLIFFE, 589; BERG, 200; SCHULENBERG/INSTRUMENTAL, 103–05, 131, 140; FOX, 39, 181–82, 236–46
See item 24.

Incipits from KENNER I:

187. Sonata. 1765 (NV 19). W. 55/6
Early print and lit. about it: See KENNER I.
Mss. probably copied from the early print: D-brd B, N. Mus. ms. 10465; B Bc, 5877; D-brd KIl, Mb 41; D-ddr LEm, Poel. Mus. ms. 40; D-ddr LEb, Gorke 37; D-ddr ROu; US NHu, Mason collection, 5011
Mod. edns.: BAUMGART, KREBS, BÜLOW, FARRENC, SCHENKER/KLAVIERWERKE, BERG/FACSIMILE
Lit. about this work: BITTER/BRÜDER, I, 213; SCHENKER/BEITRAG, 19, 21, 27, 56; BEURMANN/KLAVIERSONATEN, 62, 68; MÜLLER, 62–63; NEWMAN, 421, 427–28; BARFORD/KEYBOARD, 112–14; RADCLIFFE, 589, 592; BERG, 187–88, 200–01; SCHULENBERG/INSTRUMENTAL, 34; FOX, 42, 95, 102, 123, 172–74, 229–46
See item 24.

Incipits from KENNER I:

188. Sonata. 1765 (NV 19). W. 58/4
Ms.: A ms. described as an autograph of KENNER IV in its entirety is in the possession of Mme Jacqueline Roskam of Liège. A microfilm copy of this ms. is in B Br, 7C/715/MUS; if one judges from this copy, the ms. may indeed be an autograph. The provenance of the ms. is apparently that of the CPEB household, as it bears the familiar numbering and title style of NV on each piece. My thanks to Richard Kramer for telling me of this ms.
Early print and lit. about it: See KENNER IV.
Mss. probably copied from the early print: D-ddr LEm, Poel. Mus. ms. 40; US NHu, Mason collection, 5012
Mod. edns.: SCHENKER/KLAVIERWERKE (incomplete), BAUMGART, KREBS, CALAND (2nd mvt. only), BERG/FACSIMILE
Lit. about this work: BITTER/BRÜDER, I, 224; SCHENKER/BEITRAG, 19; BEURMANN/KLAVIERSONATEN, 56; MÜLLER, 57, 67; BARFORD/KEYBOARD, 118–19; RADCLIFFE, 589; FOX, 127, 168

Incipits from KENNER IV:

189. Sonata per il cembalo. 1765 (NV 19). W. 65/42
Mss.: B Bc, 5883 (Michel); A Wgm, Q 11698 (VII 3444); F
  Pc, Ms. 12 (autog.); PL Kj, P 771 (autog.)
Mod. edns.: FARRENC, BERG/EDITIONS, BERG/FAC-
  SIMILE
Lit.: FOX, 75–76

Incipits from 5883:

190. Concerto per il cembalo solo. 1765 (NV 18). W. 112/1
Mss.: D-brd B, P 1130 (autog., in D, fragment, arr. for
  strings, apparently as added introduction to a cantata,
  entitled in J. S. Bach's hand "Dominica 6 post Trinit.,
  Concerto a 4 Voci e 4 Stromenti"; see item 820, then items
  693, 842), BP 143; D-brd DS, Mus. ms. 1306
Early prints: VERSCHIEDEN; "A Favourite Concerto for the
  Harpsichord, or Piano Forte," London: Longman, Lukey
  & Co., [c. 1770]. Lit. about VERSCHIEDEN: See this entry
  in Bib. The known lit. gives no evidence that the
  Longman, Lukey & Co. print was authorized by CPEB.
Mod. edns.: E. Pauer, Leipzig: Breitkopf & Härtel, [c. 1885];
  W. Danckert, Kassel: Bärenreiter, 1930 (for "Cem-
  balochord" and "Kielflügel"); BERG/FACSIMILE
Lit. about this work: BITTER/BRÜDER, I, 88; VRIESLAN-
  DER/BACH, 94–95; BÜCKEN, 168; GEIRINGER/BACH,
  358; WADE, 51; OTTENBERG, 142
I have not found an a.v. or arr. as a concerto for keyboard
  and orchestra.

Incipits from VERSCHIEDEN:

191. Sinfonia per il cembalo solo. 1765 (NV 15). W. 112/13
(z122/4)
Early print and lit. about it: See VERSCHIEDEN.
Mod. edn.: BERG/FACSIMILE
Lit. about this work: BITTER/BRÜDER, I, 89; VRIESLAN-
  DER/BACH, 98–99; SCHULENBERG/INSTRUMENTAL,
  67–68
Arr. for unaccompanied keyboard of a symphony of 1758
  (item 655)

Incipits from VERSCHIEDEN:

192. Sonata per il cembalo solo. 1765–66 (NV 19). W. 65/43
Mss.: D-brd B, P 359 (Michel), P 772 (rev. by CPEB?); B Bc,
  5883 (Michel); USSR KA, Rf b 3, Bd. I (unverified; a version
  in G, says BEURMANN/KLAVIERSONATEN, 141)
Mod. edns.: FARRENC, BERG/FACSIMILE
Lit.: BEURMANN/REPRISENSONATEN, 169
Regarding USSR KA: According to a letter of 10 Jan. 1975
  received by Rachel W. Wade from S. V. Zhitomirskaia,
  head of the Manuscript Department, Gosudarstvennaja
  biblioteka SSR im V. I. Lenina, Moscow, the location of
  the mss. formerly in Königsberg (now Kaliningrad) is
  uncertain, and it can be assumed that they were burned
  during World War II. My thanks to Dr. Wade for this
  information, which, in view of the resurrection of many
  mss. assumed to be lost in the war, should not be taken
  as the final word. MÜLLER/SCHÄTZE is a detailed and
  tantalizing catalogue of music in the old Königsberg library.

Incipits from P 772:

193. [untitled]. 1765 or 1766 (NV 18–19). W. 113/1
Early prints and lit. about them: See KURZE I.
Mss. probably copied from an early print: D-brd B, P 367,
  P 676, P 728, P 773; B Bc, 5867
Mod. edns.: VRIESLANDER/KURZE; in H. Schenker, *Der Tonwille,* Vienna, 1923; W. Rehberg, Mainz: Schott, n.d.;
  JONAS; BERG/FACSIMILE
Lit. about this work: MÜLLER, 65–66, OTTENBERG, 140

Incipit from KURZE I:

194. Arioso. 1765 or 1766 (NV 18–19). W. 113/2
Early prints and lit. about them: See KURZE I.
Mss. probably copied from an early print: D-brd B, P 367,
  P 676, P 773; B Bc, 5867
Mod. edns.: VRIESLANDER/KURZE, JONAS, BERG/FAC-
  SIMILE

Incipit from KURZE I:

195. Fantasia. 1765 or 1766 (NV 18–19). W. 113/3 (= 117/15)
Early prints and lit. about them: See KURZE I.
Mss. probably copied from an early print: D-brd B, P 367,
  P 676, P 728, P 773, P 793; B Bc, 5867, 5897 (Westphal)
Mod. edns.: VRIESLANDER/KURZE, JONAS, BERG/FAC-
  SIMILE
Lit. about this work: ELDER, 88ff.; SELINGER-BARBER,
  61–66

Incipit from KURZE I:

196. Minuetto I–II. 1765 or 1766 (NV 18–19). W. 113/4
Early prints and lit. about them: See KURZE I.
Mss. probably copied from an early print: D-brd B, P 367,
  P 676, P 773; B Bc, 5867

Mod. edns.: VRIESLANDER/KURZE, JONAS, BERG/FAC-
  SIMILE
Lit. about this work: MÜLLER, 64

Incipits from KURZE I:

[Minuetto I is repeated after Minuetto II.]

197. Alla polacca. 1765 or 1766 (NV 18–19). ·W. 113/5
Early prints and lit. about them: See KURZE I.
Mss. probably copied from an early print: D-brd B, P 676;
  B Bc, 5867
Mod. edns.: VRIESLANDER/KURZE, JONAS, BERG/FAC-
  SIMILE

Incipit from KURZE I:

198. [untitled]. 1765 or 1766 (NV 18–19). W. 113/6
Early prints and lit. about them: See KURZE I.
Mss. probably copied from an early print: D-brd B, P 676,
  P 728, P 773; B Bc, 5867
Mod. edns.: VRIESLANDER/KURZE, JONAS, BERG/FAC-
  SIMILE

Incipit from KURZE I:

199. Alla polacca. 1765 or 1766 (NV 18–19). W. 113/7
Early prints and lit. about them: See KURZE I.
Mss. probably copied from an early print: D-brd B, P 676;
  B Bc, 5867
Mod. edns.: VRIESLANDER/KURZE, JONAS, BERG/FAC-
  SIMILE

Incipit from KURZE I:

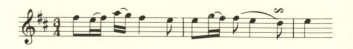

200. [untitled]. 1765 or 1766 (NV 18–19). W. 113/8
Early prints and lit. about them: See KURZE I.
Mss. probably copied from an early print: D-brd B, P 676;
B Bc, 5867
Mod. edns.: VRIESLANDER/KURZE, JONAS, BERG/FAC-
SIMILE

Incipit from KURZE I:

201. [untitled]. 1765 or 1766 (NV 18–19). W. 113/9
Early prints and lit. about them: See KURZE I.
Mss. Probably copied from an early print: D-brd B, P 676;
B Bc, 5867
Mod. edns.: VRIESLANDER/KURZE, JONAS, BERG/FAC-
SIMILE
Lit. about this work: BARFORD/KEYBOARD, 138–39

Incipit from KURZE I:

202. [untitled]. 1765 or 1766 (NV 18–19). W. 113/10
Early prints and lit. about them: See KURZE I.
Mss. probably copied from an early print: D-brd B, P 676;
B Bc, 5867
Mod. edns.: VRIESLANDER/KURZE, JONAS, BERG/FAC-
SIMILE

Incipit from KURZE I:

203. [untitled]. 1765 or 1766 (NV 18–19). W. 113/11
Early prints and lit. about them: See KURZE I.
Mss. probably copied from an early print: D-brd B, P 676;
B Bc, 5867
Mod. edns.: VRIESLANDER/KURZE, JONAS; W. Rehberg,
Mainz: Schott, n.d.; BERG/FACSIMILE

Incipit from KURZE I:

204. Sonata. 1766 (NV 20). W. 54/1
Early prints and lit. about them: See DAMENSONATEN.
Mss. probably copied from an early print: D-brd B, P 432,

P 774; D-ddr LEb, 350; US AA, M23.B12.S541.17--; a ms.
is in the private collection of E. N. Kulukundis (U.S.).
Mod. edns.: JOHNEN/SONATEN, BERG/FACSIMILE
Lit. about this work: BERG, 112
See item 24.

Incipits from DAMENSONATEN:

205. Sonata. 1766 (NV 20). W. 54/2
Early prints and lit. about them: See DAMENSONATEN.
Mss. probably copied from an early print: D-brd B, P 432,
P 774 (not 744); D-ddr LEb, 349; US AA, M23.B12.S542.17--
a ms. is in the private collection of E. N. Kulukundis
(U.S.).
Mod. edns.: JOHNEN/SONATEN, BERG/FACSIMILE
Lit. about this work: BEURMANN/KLAVIERSONATEN,
27, 70
See item 24.

Incipits from DAMENSONATEN:

206. Sonata. 1766 (NV 20). W. 54/4
Ms.: A Wgm, Q 11692 (VII 43740)
Early prints and lit. about them: See DAMENSONATEN.
Mss. probably copied from an early print: D-brd B, P 432,
P 774; US AA, M23.B12.S544.17--; a ms. is in the private
collection of E. N. Kulukundis (U.S.).
Mod. edns.: JOHNEN/SONATEN, BERG/FACSIMILE
Lit. about this work: BEURMANN/KLAVIERSONATEN, 85,
97, 109, 112, 114; BERG, 191; FOX, 69
See item 24.

Incipits from DAMENSONATEN:

Incipits from KENNER III:

207. Sonata. 1766 (NV 20). W. 54/6
Early prints and lit. about them: See DAMENSONATEN.
Mss. probably copied from an early print: D-brd B, P 432,
    P 774; D-ddr LEb, 349; US AA, M23.B12.S546; a ms. is in
    the private collection of E. N. Kulukundis (U.S.).
Mod. edns.: JOHNEN/SONATEN, BERG/FACSIMILE
Lit. about this work: RADCLIFFE, 588; BERG, 168
See item 24.

Incipits from DAMENSONATEN:

208. Sonata. 1766 (NV 21). W. 57/4
Early print and lit. about it: See KENNER III.
Mss. probably copied from the early print: D-brd B, P 433;
    D-ddr LEm, Poel. Mus. ms. 40
Mod. edns.: BAUMGART, KREBS, BÜLOW, FARRENC,
    SCHENKER/KLAVIERWERKE; 2nd mvt. in Riemann and
    Schering, *Musikgeschichte in Beispielen,* 4th edn. (Leipzig,
    1929); BERG/FACSIMILE
Lit. about this work: BITTER/BRÜDER, I, 220; SCHENKER/
    BEITRAG, 11–12, 17, 23, 27, 32, 46, 48, 51, 56; STEGLICH/
    HOMILIUS, 63; BEURMANN/KLAVIERSONATEN, 75;
    NEWMAN, 421; MÜLLER, 58; BARFORD/KEYBOARD,
    116; RADCLIFFE, 589; COHEN, 90; FOX, 124, 137–39

209. Una sonata per il cembalo solo. 1766 (NV 20). W. 60
Ms.: D-ddr Bds, P 369
Early print: Lipsia e Dresda: Breitkopf, 1785
Mod. edn.: BERG/FACSIMILE
Lit.: CPEB/BREITKOPF, 23 Sept., 19 Oct. 1784; HASE, 101–
    02; BERG, 120, 178, 200; see also Critical Notes in BERG/
    FACSIMILE.

Incipits from the early print:

210. Clavier-Sonate. 1766 (NV 20). W. 62/23
Ms.: D-brd B, P 775
Early print: VIELERLEY, 81. Lit. about VIELERLEY: See this
    entry in Bib.
Ms. probably copied from the early print: B Br, II 4094
    (Westphal)
Mod. edn.: BERG/FACSIMILE
Lit. about this work: AUERBACH, 86–87; BERG, 117, 169,
    190, 200

Incipits from VIELERLEY:

211. Sonata per il cembalo solo. 1766 (NV 20). W. 65/44

Mss.: D-brd B, P 359 (Michel), P 776 (Michel. rev. by CPEB), P 1133 (autog.); D-ddr Bds, P 369; B Bc, 5883; PL Kj, P 258b (autog.)

Mod. edns.: FARRENC, BERG/EDITIONS, BERG/FACSIMILE

Lit.: BEURMANN/KLAVIERSONATEN, 29, 112; NEWMAN, 419; BERG, 112

Rev. of 2nd mvt.: 2nd mvt. of item 282. From BERG/NOTES: P 1133 is the only source (probably the earliest) containing all 3 mvts.: its 1st mvt. has no varied reprises. The mss. in D-brd B, D-ddr Bds, and B Bc contain only 2 mvts., omitting the Larghetto; their 1st mvt. has written-out varied reprises, and their last mvt. contains a few embellishments not found in the last mvt. in P 1133. P 258b has only the varied reprises for the 1st mvts., plus a transition to the 3rd mvt.

Incipits from P 1133:

212. Sonata per il cembalo solo. 1766 (NV 20). W. 65/45

Mss.: D-brd B, P 359 (Michel); D-ddr Bds, P 369; B Bc, 5883; PL Kj, P 771 (autog. and Michel, with alternate 3rd mvt., along with a note in an unknown hand discussing this substitution)

Mod. edns.: FARRENC, BERG/FACSIMILE

Lit.: BERG, 154

Incipits from 5883:

Incipit of the alternate 3rd mvt. in P 771, from BERG/NOTES:

213. Sonata per il cembalo solo. 1766 (NV 20). W. 65/46

Mss.: D-brd B, P 359 (Michel), P 364 (autog., the only source without written-out varied reprises), P 776 (2 copies, the first by Michel); D-ddr Bds, P 369; B Bc, 5883; PL Kj, P 258b (autog.), containing only the varied reprises for the two outer mvts.

Mod. edns.: FARRENC, BERG/FACSIMILE

Lit.: BEURMANN/KLAVIERSONATEN, 30, 109; BEURMANN/REPRISENSONATEN, 169, 175; BERG, 120, 192; FOX, 167–68

Incipits from P 776:

214. Zwo abwechselnde Menuetten. 1766 (NV 21). W. 116/3

Early print: VIELERLEY, 112. Lit. about VIELERLEY: See this entry in Bib.

Ms. probably copied from the early print: B Bc, 5898 (Westphal)

Mod. edns.: VRIESLANDER/KLEINE, BERG/FACSIMILE

Lit. about this work: HILLER/NACHRICHTEN, 4 (1770), 314; see also Critical Notes in BERG/FACSIMILE.

A.v.: item 606

Incipits from VIELERLEY:

[Menuet I is repeated after Menuet II.]

215. Alla polacca. 1766 (NV 21). W. 116/4
Ms.: D-brd B, P 370
Early print: VIELERLEY, 39. Lit. about VIELERLEY: See this
  entry in Bib.
Ms. probably copied from the early print: B Bc, 5898 (West-
  phal)
Mod. edns.: VRIESLANDER/KLEINE, BERG/FACSIMILE
Lit. about this work: HILLER/NACHRICHTEN, 4 (1770),
  158; see also Critical Notes in BERG/FACSIMILE.
A.v.: item 609

Incipit from VIELERLEY:

216. Zwo abwechselnde Menuetten. 1766 (NV 21). W. 116/5
Early print: VIELERLEY, 48. Lit. about VIELERLEY: See this
  entry in Bib.
Mss. probably copied from the early print: B Bc, 5898
  (Westphal); a ms. is in the private collection of E. N.
  Kulukundis (U.S.).
Mod. edns.: VRIESLANDER/KLEINE, BERG/FACSIMILE
Lit. about this work: HILLER/NACHRICHTEN, 4 (1770),
  118, 180–81; AMZ, VIII (1805–06), 496; see also Critical
  Notes in BERG/FACSIMILE.

The first minuet of the pair can be played forward or back-
ward, and its first half is the retrograde of its second half.
On p. 20 of VIELERLEY, the first fourth of this minuet
is followed by its third fourth and breaks off inconclu-
sively. Apparently the reader is supposed to discover for
himself that combining the second fourth with the fourth
fourth will produce the retrograde of the first and third
fourths. Regarding such permutations, see items 7–12,
869, 875.

Incipits from VIELERLEY:

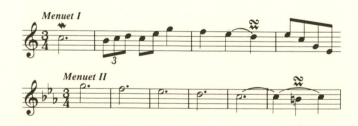

[Menuet I is repeated after Menuet II.]

217. Alla polacca. 1766 (NV 21). W. 116/6
Mss.: D-brd B, P 370; US NHu, Mason collection, 5006
Early print: VIELERLEY, 66. Lit. about VIELERLEY: See this
  entry in Bib.
Ms. probably copied from the early print: B Bc, 5898 (West-
  phal)
Mod. edn.: BERG/FACSIMILE

Lit. about this work: HILLER/NACHRICHTEN, 4 (1770),
  182; see also Critical Notes in BERG/FACSIMILE.
A.v.: item 608

Incipit from VIELERLEY:

218. Zwo abwechselnde Menuetten. 1766 (NV 21). W. 116/7
Early print: VIELERLEY, 72. Lit. about VIELERLEY: See this
  entry in Bib.
Ms. probably copied from the early print: B Bc, 5898 (West-
  phal)
Mod. edns.: VRIESLANDER/KLEINE, BERG/FACSIMILE
Lit. about this work: HILLER/NACHRICHTEN, 4 (1770),
  182; see also Critical Notes in BERG/FACSIMILE.

Incipits from VIELERLEY:

[Menuet I is repeated after Menuet II.]

219. Alla polacca. 1766 (NV 21). W. 116/8
Early print: VIELERLEY, 197. Lit. about VIELERLEY: See
  this entry in Bib.
Mss. probably copied from the early print: B Bc, 5898 (West-
  phal); D-brd B, Mus. ms. 30327
Mod. edn.: BERG/FACSIMILE
Lit. about this work: See Critical Notes in BERG/FAC-
  SIMILE.
A.v.: item 607

Incipit from VIELERLEY:

220. Solfeggio [not "Solfeggietto"]. 1766 (NV 21). W. 117/2
Mss.: D-brd B, N. Mus. ms. 10480 (19th-century copy), P
  509, P 784, Mus. ms. 30194; D-ddr Bds, P 371; A Wn,
  18687; D-ddr SWl; US NHu, Mason collection, 5006
Early prints: VIELERLEY, 19; "Solfeggio für's Forte-
  Piano," Berlin: Christiani, n.d. (W. 271); "Solfeggio für's Forte-
  Piano," Stockholm: Müller, n.d. Lit. about VIELERLEY:

See this entry in Bib. The known lit. gives no evidence that either the Christiani or the Müller print was authorized by CPEB.

Ms. probably copied from an early print (VIELERLEY): B Bc, 5897 (Westphal)

Mod. edns.: RIEMANN; VRIESLANDER/KLEINE; W. Rehberg, Mainz: Schott, n.d.; BERG/FACSIMILE. Arranged for left hand alone by A. R. Parsons, New York: G. Schirmer, 1885. Among the other modern treatments of this little piece are arrangements for harp, accordion, viola and piano, 2 pianos, Spanish guitar, symphonic band, and the Swingle Singers.

Lit. about this work: HILLER/NACHRICHTEN, 4 (1770), 118; GEIRINGER/BACH, 359; NEWMAN, 373; see also Critical Notes in BERG/FACSIMILE.

Incipit from VIELERLEY:

221. Solfeggio. 1766 (NV 21). W. 117/3

Early print: VIELERLEY, 156. Lit. about VIELERLEY: See this entry in Bib.

Ms. probably copied from the early print: B Bc, 5897 (Westphal)

Mod. edns.: VRIESLANDER/KLEINE, BERG/FACSIMILE

Lit. about this work: HILLER/NACHRICHTEN, 4 (1770), 345

Incipit from VIELERLEY:

222. Solfeggio. 1766 (NV 21). W. 117/4

Mss.: D-brd B, P 370, P 739; A Wn, 18687

Early print: VIELERLEY, 78. Lit. about VIELERLEY: See this entry in Bib.

Ms. probably copied from the early print: B Bc, 5897 (Westphal)

Mod. edns.: VRIESLANDER/KLEINE, BERG/FACSIMILE

Lit. about this work: HILLER/NACHRICHTEN, 4 (1770), 234; see also Critical Notes in BERG/FACSIMILE.

Read "3 Solfeggien" instead of "2 Solfeggien" in No. 160 on p. 21 of NV. The error was probably made because this solfeggio is omitted from the table of contents of VIELERLEY.

Incipit from VIELERLEY:

223. Fantasia. 1766 (NV 21). W. 117/11

Ms.: A Wn, 18687

Early print: VIELERLEY, 80. Lit. about VIELERLEY: See this entry in Bib.

Mss. probably copied from the early print: B Bc, 5897 (Westphal); D-brd B, Mus. ms. 30327

Mod. edns.: VRIESLANDER/KLEINE, BERG/FACSIMILE

Lit. about this work: HILLER/NACHRICHTEN, 4 (1770), 234; ELDER, 87ff.; SELINGER–BARBER, 61–66; see also Critical Notes in BERG/FACSIMILE.

Incipit from VIELERLEY:

224. Fantasia. 1766 (NV 21). W. 117/12

Ms.: A Wn, 18687

Early print: VIELERLEY, 80. Lit. about VIELERLEY: See this entry in Bib.

Mss. probably copied from the early print: B Bc, 5897 (Westphal); D-brd B, Mus. ms. 30327

Mod. edns.: VRIESLANDER/KLEINE, BERG/FACSIMILE

Lit. about this work: HILLER/NACHRICHTEN, 4 (1770), 234; ELDER, 87ff.; SELINGER–BARBER, 61–66; see also Critical Notes in BERG/FACSIMILE.

Incipit from VIELERLEY:

225. Fantasia. 1766 (NV 21). W. 117/13

Mss.: D-brd B, P 370, P 435; D-ddr Bds, P 365; A Wn, 18687

Early print: VIELERLEY, 13. Lit. about VIELERLEY: See this entry in Bib.

Mss. probably copied from the early print: B Bc, 5897 (Westphal); a ms. is in the private collection of E. N. Kulukundis (U.S.).

Mod. edns.: SCHLEUNING, vol. 43, p. 27; BERG/FACSIMILE

Lit. about this work: HILLER/NACHRICHTEN, 4 (1770), 56; ELDER, 87ff.; SELINGER–BARBER, 77–90; see also Critical Notes in BERG/FACSIMILE.

Incipit from VIELERLEY:

226. Romance, avec xii variations. 1766 (NV 19). W. 118/6
Mss.: D-brd B, P 744 (autog.); B Bc, 5899 (Westphal)
Mod. edn.: BERG/FACSIMILE
Lit.: FISCHER, 192, 197, 201–03, 205, 211, 213–15

Incipit from P 744:

Co- lin   à peine à seize ans ai - mait dé -ja

227. Sinfonie. 1766 (NV 15). W. 122/5
Mss.: D-brd B, P 432, P 999 (Michel)
Early print: VIELERLEY, 147. Lit. about VIELERLEY: See
  this entry in Bib.
Mod. edn.: BERG/FACSIMILE
Lit. about this work: HILLER/NACHRICHTEN, 4 (1770), 314
Arr. for unaccompanied keyboard of a symphony of 1762
  (item 656)

Incipits from VIELERLEY:

228. [untitled]. 1767 (NV 21). W. 114/1
Early prints and lit. about them: See KURZE II.
Mss. probably copied from an early print: D-brd B, P 676,
  P 740; B Bc, 5868
Mod. edns.: VRIESLANDER/KURZE, JONAS, BERG/FAC-
  SIMILE
Lit.: OTTENBERG, 140

Incipit from KURZE II:

229. [untitled]. 1767 (NV 21). W. 114/2
Early prints and lit. about them: See KURZE II.
Mss. probably copied from an early print: D-brd B, P 676,
  P 740; B Bc, 5868; D-ddr Bds, Mus. ms. 30169
Mod. edns.: VRIESLANDER/KURZE, JONAS, BERG/FAC-
  SIMILE

Incipit from KURZE II:

230. [untitled]. 1767 (NV 21). W. 114/3
Early prints and lit. about them: See KURZE II.
Mss. probably copied from an early print: D-brd B, P 676,
  P 740; B Bc, 5868; D-ddr Bds, Mus. ms. 30169
Mod. edns.: VRIESLANDER/KURZE; JONAS; W. Rehberg,
  Mainz: Schott, n.d.; BERG/FACSIMILE

Incipit from KURZE II:

231. Minuetto I–II. 1767 (NV 21). W. 114/4
Early prints and lit. about them: See KURZE II.
Mss. probably copied from an early print: D-brd B, P 676,
  P 740; B Bc, 5868; D-ddr Bds, Mus. ms. 30169
Mod. edns.: VRIESLANDER/KURZE, JONAS, BERG/FAC-
  SIMILE

Incipits from KURZE II:

[Minuetto I is repeated after Minuetto II.]

232. Alla polacca. 1767 (NV 21). W. 114/5
Early prints and lit. about them: See KURZE II.
Mss. probably copied from an early print: D-brd B, P 676,
  P 740; B Bc, 5868; D-ddr Bds, Mus. ms. 30169
Mod. edns.: VRIESLANDER/KURZE, JONAS, BERG/FAC-
  SIMILE

Incipit from KURZE II:

233. Alla polacca. 1767 (NV 21). W. 114/6
Early prints and lit. about them: See KURZE II.
Mss. probably copied from an early print: D-brd B, P 676,
  P 740; B Bc, 5868

Mod. edns.: VRIESLANDER/KURZE, JONAS, BERG/FAC-
SIMILE

Incipit from KURZE II:

234. Fantasia. 1767 (NV 21). W. 114/7 (= 117/16)
Ms.: D-brd B, P 793
Early prints and lit. about them: See KURZE II.
Mss. probably copied from an early print: D-brd B, P 676,
P 740; B Bc, 5868, 5897 (Westphal); A Wgm, VII 33637
Mod. edns.: RIEMANN; VRIESLANDER/KURZE; JONAS;
SCHLEUNING, vol. 42; BERG/FACSIMILE
Lit. about this work: SELINGER–BARBER, 77–90

Incipit from KURZE II:

235. [untitled]. 1767 (NV 21). W. 114/8
Early prints and lit. about them: See KURZE II.
Mss. probably copied from an early print: D-brd B, P 676,
P 740; B Bc, 5868
Mod. edns.: VRIESLANDER/KURZE, JONAS, BERG/FAC-
SIMILE

Incipit from KURZE II:

236. [untitled]. 1767 (NV 21). W. 114/9
Early prints and lit. about them: See KURZE II.
Mss. probably copied from an early print: D-brd B, P 676,
P 740; B Bc, 5868
Mod. edns.: VRIESLANDER/KURZE, JONAS, BERG/FAC-
SIMILE

Incipit from KURZE II:

237. [untitled]. 1767 (NV 21). W. 114/10
Early prints and lit. about them: See KURZE II.
Mss. probably copied from an early print: D-brd B, P 676,
P 740; B Bc, 5868
Mod. edns.: VRIESLANDER/KURZE, JONAS, BERG/FAC-
SIMILE

Incipit from KURZE II:

238. [untitled]. 1767 (NV 21). W. 114/11
Early prints and lit. about them: See KURZE II.
Mss. probably copied from an early print: D-brd B, P 676,
P 740; B Bc 5868
Mod. edns.: VRIESLANDER/KURZE, JONAS, BERG/FAC-
SIMILE

Incipit from KURZE II:

239. Deleted

240. Clavier-Sonate mit veränderten Reprisen. 1769 (NV
21). W. 62/24
Mss.: D-brd B, P 370, P 607; F Pc, Ms. 1566.3
Early print: VIELERLEY, 2. Lit. about VIELERLEY: See this
entry in Bib.
Ms. probably copied from the early print: B Br, II 4094
(Westphal)
Mod. edns.: BERG/EDITIONS, BERG/FACSIMILE
Lit. about this work: BEURMANN/KLAVIERSONATEN,
35, 57, 113, 115–16; GEIRINGER/BACH, 358; BEUR-
MANN/REPRISENSONATEN, 169; see also Critical Notes
in BERG/FACSIMILE.

Incipits from VIELERLEY:

241. Clavierstück für die rechte oder linke Hand allein. 1770
or earlier (source of date: 1st pub.). W. 117/1
Early print: VIELERLEY, 203 (1770). Lit. about VIELERLEY:
See this entry in Bib.
Ms. probably copied from the early print: B Bc, 5897 (West-
phal)
Mod. edns.: VRIESLANDER/KLEINE, BERG/FACSIMILE

Incipit from VIELERLEY:

242. Concerto per il cembalo solo. 1770 (NV 21)
Mss.: D-brd B, P 713 (autog.); D-ddr Bds, P 369; B Bc, 5887 (see item 470)
Mod. edn.: BERG/FACSIMILE
A.v. for unaccompanied keyboard of a concerto for harpsichord and orchestra of 1770 (item 470). Both versions are mentioned in the NV listing.
Lit.: WADE, 6, 41, 76–77, 112–13

Incipits from P 713:

243. Sonata. 1772 (NV 22). W. 55/5
Early print and lit. about it: See KENNER I.
Mss. probably copied from the early print: D-brd B, N. Mus. ms. 10465; B Bc, 5877; D-brd Kll, Mb 41; D-ddr ROu (incomplete); US NHu, Mason collection, 5011
Mod. edns.: BAUMGART, KREBS, SCHENKER/KLAVIER-WERKE, BERG/FACSIMILE
Lit. about this work: BITTER/BRÜDER, I, 213; SHEDLOCK, 103–04; SCHENKER/BEITRAG, 11, 13, 17, 32, 52; VRIES-LANDER/BACH, 64; MÜLLER, 61–62; NEWMAN, 420–21; BARFORD/KEYBOARD, 112; RADCLIFFE, 589–90, 593; BERG, 121, 147; SCHULENBERG/INSTRUMENTAL, 164; FOX, 103, 133–136, 217–24
See item 24.

Incipits from KENNER I:

244. Sonata. 1773 (NV 22). W. 55/1
Early print and lit. about it: See KENNER I.
Mss. probably copied from the early print: D-brd B, N. Mus. ms. 10465; B Bc, 5877; D-ddr LEm, Poel. Mus. ms. 40; D-ddr LEb, Gorke 37; D-ddr ROu; US NHu, Mason collection, 5011
Mod. edns.: BAUMGART, KREBS, FARRENC, SCHEN-KER/KLAVIERWERKE, BERG/FACSIMILE
Lit. about this work: BITTER/BRÜDER, I, 78, 212–13; SCHENKER/BEITRAG, 13–14, 16–17, 22–23, 27, 48, 57; BEURMANN/KLAVIERSONATEN, 27; MÜLLER, 63; BARFORD/KEYBOARD, 106–07; BERG, 106, 190, 424; OTTENBERG, 171–72, 187–88, 220, 226–28; SCHULENBERG/INSTRUMENTAL, 49; FOX, 115–16
See item 24.

Incipits from KENNER I:

245. Sonata. 1774 (NV 22). W. 55/3
Early print and lit. about it: See KENNER I.
Mss. probably copied from the early print: D-brd B, N. Mus. ms. 10465; B Bc, 5877; D-brd Kll, Mb 41, Mb 48; D-ddr LEm, Poel. Mus. ms. 40; D-ddr LEb, Gorke 37; D-ddr ROu; US NHu, Mason collection, 5011
Mod. edns.: BAUMGART, KREBS, SCHENKER/KLAVIER-WERKE (incomplete); H. Lamann, Berlin: Kaunt Verlag, n.d.; BERG/FACSIMILE
Lit. about this work: BITTER/BRÜDER, I, 213; SCHENKER/BEITRAG, 19; AUERBACH, 90; MÜLLER, 57–59, 63, 65; NEWMAN, 419–21; BARFORD/KEYBOARD, 109–10; RADCLIFFE, 589–91; COHEN, 12–13; BERG, 110, 160–61; FOX, 37–39, 64–65, 103, 133–36, 147–55
See item 24.

Incipits from KENNER I:

246. Sonata. 1774 (NV 22). W. 56/2
Early print and lit. about it: See KENNER II.
Mss. probably copied from the early print: D-brd B, P 1170;
   D-brd KIl, Mb 41; D-ddr LEm, Poel. Mus. ms. 40; D-ddr
   LEb, 345, 353; A Wgm, VII 26001
Mod. edns.: BAUMGART, KREBS, FARRENC, SCHEN-
   KER/KLAVIERWERKE, BERG/FACSIMILE
Lit. about this work: BITTER/BRÜDER, I, 215; SCHENKER/
   BEITRAG, 11–13, 17, 23, 27, 32, 38, 48; STEGLICH/
   HOMILIUS, 115; BARFORD/KEYBOARD, 114–15;
   COHEN, 90, 176; BERG, 110, 130–32, 144; FOX, 124, 141–
   42

Incipits from KENNER II:

247. Sonata. 1774 (NV 22). W. 57/2
Early print and lit. about it: See KENNER III.
Mss. probably copied from the early print: D-brd B, P 433;
   D-ddr LEm, Poel. Mus. ms. 40
Mod. edns.: BÜLOW, BAUMGART, FARRENC, KREBS,
   SCHENKER/KLAVIERWERKE, BERG/FACSIMILE
Lit. about this work: BITTER/BRÜDER, I, 220; SCHENKER/
   BEITRAG, 11, 14, 17, 23, 48, 54; MÜLLER, 62; NEWMAN,
   420, 424, 427; BARFORD/KEYBOARD, 116; RADCLIFFE,
   590; BERG, 200; FOX, 74–75, 104, 116–17, 181–82

Incipits from KENNER III:

248. Sonata per il cembalo solo. 1775 (NV 22). W. 65/47
Mss.: D-brd B, P 359 (Michel); D-ddr Bds, P 369; B Bc, 5883;
   PL Kj, P 771 (autog.)
Mod. edns.: BERG/EDITIONS, BERG/FACSIMILE
Lit.: BEURMANN/KLAVIERSONATEN, 62, 77, 85; NEW-
   MAN, 426; BERG, 110, 129, 141–42, 347–51; SCHULEN-
   BERG/INSTRUMENTAL, 35, 78–79; FOX, 109

Incipits from 5883:

[2 mvts. only]

249. [untitled]. 1775 (NV 22). W. 116/23
Mss.: D-brd B, P 748 (CPEB and Michel); B Bc, 5898
   (Westphal)
Mod. edn.: BERG/FACSIMILE
Items 249–54 make up, in numerical order, a set collectively
   entitled *Sechs leichte Clavier-Stückgen* in P 748 and grouped
   the same way in 5898. These are the *Sechs leichte kleine
   Clavierstücke* listed on p. 22 of NV with the incipit of only
   item 249. A.v. of item 249: item 493. Arr. of item 249:
   item 534. Vnt. of item 249: item 259

Incipit from P 748:

250. [untitled]. 1775 (NV 22). W. 116/24
See item 249.
Mod. edn.: BERG/FACSIMILE
A.v.: items, 611, 620/2

Incipit from P 748:

251. [untitled]. 1775 (NV 22). W. 116/25
See item 249.
Mod. edn.: BERG/FACSIMILE
A.v.: items 521, 610, 635/2
Lit.: SCHULENBERG/INSTRUMENTAL, 87–89

Incipit from P 748:

252. [untitled]. 1775 (NV 22). W. 116/26
See item 249.
Mod. edn.: BERG/FACSIMILE
A.v.: item 616. Vnt.: item 256

Incipit from P 748:

253. [untitled]. 1775 (NV 22). W. 116/27
See item 249.
Mod. edn.: BERG/FACSIMILE

Incipit from P 748:

254. [untitled]. 1775 (NV 22). W. 116/28
See item 249.
Mod. edn.: BERG/FACSIMILE
A.v.: items 518, 613, 614. Vnt.: item 255

Incipit from P 748:

255. [untitled]. Probably 1775 (source of date: see below)
Mod. edn.: BERG/FACSIMILE
In the partly autog. ms. mentioned in item 249. Vnt. of item 254, which is in the same ms. A.v.: items 613, 614

Incipit from P 748:

256. [untitled]. Probably 1775 (source of date: see below).
Wq n.v. 37
Mod. edn.: BERG/FACSIMILE

In the partly autog. ms. mentioned in item 249. Vnt. of item 252, which is in the same ms. A.v.: item 616

Incipit from P 748:

257. [untitled]. Probably 1775 (source of date: see below).
Wq n.v. 38
Mod. edn.: BERG/FACSIMILE
In the partly autog. ms. mentioned in item 249. A.v.: item 635/24

Incipit from P 748:

258. Menuet. Probably 1775 (source of date: see below). Wq n.v. 39
Mod. edn.: BERG/FACSIMILE
In the partly autog. ms. mentioned in item 249. A.v.: items 625, 635/12. Vnt.: item 306

Incipit from P 748:

259. Variationes mit veränderten Reprisen . . . 1777 or later (sources of date: date of item 534; NV 53). W. 118/10
Mss.: D-brd B, P 1000; B Bc, 5899 (Westphal)
Mod. edn.: BERG/FACSIMILE
Lit.: FISCHER, 193; SCHULENBERG/INSTRUMENTAL, 23–24
Variations on the theme of item 534, and so described in NV, 53. Item 534 itself is a set of variations on item 249, with each variation repeated; in item 259 the repeats are written out and varied. Ms. 5896 in B Bc contains these repeats only in their varied forms—that is, every other variation in item 259 and none of the variations in item 534. Another kind of selectivity is apparent in item 493.
See item 344.

Incipit from 5899:

260. Rondo. 1778 (NV 22). W. 56/1
Mss.: D-brd B, P 212, St 236 (fragment, autog.)
Early print and lit. about it: See KENNER II.

Mss. probably copied from the early print: D-brd B, P 937,
P 1170; D-brd Kll, Mb 47; A Wgm, VII 26001
Mod. edns.: BAUMGART, KREBS, BERG/FACSIMILE
Lit. about this work: SHEDLOCK, 107; STEGLICH/HOMI-
LIUS, 67, 83; VRIESLANDER/BACH, 63; SCHMID/KAM-
MERMUSIK, 166; MÜLLER, 61; BARFORD/KEYBOARD,
127; OTTENBERG, 171–72, 187–88, 220–21, 226–28
See item 870.

Incipit from KENNER II:

261. Rondo. 1778 (NV 23). W. 56/3
Ms.: D-brd B, P 212
Early print and lit. about it: See KENNER II.
Mss. probably copied from the early print: D-brd B, P 937,
P 1170; D-brd Kll, Mb 47; A Wgm, VII 26001
Mod. edns.: BAUMGART, KREBS, CALAND–GOEBELS,
BERG/FACSIMILE
Lit. about this work: BITTER/BRÜDER, I, 215; BÜCKEN,
166; BARFORD/KEYBOARD, 123

Incipit from KENNER II:

262. Rondo. 1778 (NV 23). W. 56/5
Early print and lit. about it: See KENNER II.
Mss. probably copied from the early print: D-brd B, P 937,
P 1170; D-brd Kll, Mb 47; A Wgm, VII 26001
Mod. edns.: BAUMGART, KREBS, BERG/FACSIMILE
Lit. about this work: BITTER/BRÜDER, I, 216; STEGLICH/
HOMILIUS, 82, 98–99; AUERBACH, 90; MÜLLER, 62;
BARFORD/KEYBOARD, 123–27; COHEN, 73–74, 101;
OTTENBERG, 229; SCHULENBERG/INSTRUMENTAL,
39–40

Incipit from KENNER II:

263. 12 Variationes über die folie d'Espagne. 1778 (NV 22).
W. 118/9
Mss.: D-brd B, P 359 (Michel), P 729 (begins with 1st variation)
Early print: Vienne: Traeg, 1803 (W. 270). The known lit.
gives no evidence that this (posthumous) print had been
authorized by CPEB.

Ms. probably copied from the early print: B Bc, 5899 (Westphal)
Mod. edns.: HERRMANN/SONATEN; H. Ruf, Frankfurt
am Main: Deutscher Ricordi, 1955; BERG/FACSIMILE
Lit.: AMZ, VI (1803–04), 242–44; FISCHER, 193, 197–98, 206–
207, 209, 215, 218; BARFORD/KEYBOARD, 141–42;
COHEN, 184

Incipit from 5899:

264. Cadenzen. 1778 or later (source of date: latest work
affected, item 478, dates from 1778). W. 120
Ms.: B Bc, 5871 (Michel)
Lit.: KNÖDT; WADE, 148, 257; DRUMMOND, 317–18
75 (not 80) cadenzas, elaborations, and improvisatory ideas.
About half the cadenzas utilize themes from their movements. Of the 75, 17 are designed to be added to any
suitable movement in a given key; the remainder are intended for specific works. There are no duplicates, although a given movement might be assigned more than
one cadenza. The 75 are not numbered consecutively but
are assigned numbers corresponding to the numbers in
NV (for example, "Cadenz zum ersten Allegro des Concerts No. 51").

[1] Allegretto of item 478
[2] Allegro di molto of item 429
[3] Prestissimo of item 429
[4] Largo of item 428
[5] Adagio ma non troppo of item 423
[6] Largo of item 428
[7] An adagio in f
[8] An adagio in f
[9] Allegro di molto of item 444
[10] Largo of item 444
[11] Presto of item 444
[12] Siciliana of item 433
[13] Allegro di molto of item 444
[14] Largo of item 428
[15] Allegro di molto of item 414
[16] Adagio non molto of item 414
[17] Largo of item 428
[18] Allegro assai of item 432
[19] Andante of item 432
[20] "Einfall" (a short idea in B♭
[21] 1st mvt. of item 420
[22] Un poco adagio of item 420
[23] Adagio of item 436
[24] Allegro di molto of item 429
[25] Allegro di molto of item 444
[26] Poco adagio of item 417
[27] Allegro of item 417
[28] Prestissimo of item 429
[29] Largo of item 444

[30] Presto of item 444
[31] Largo mesto of item 439
[32] Allegro di molto of item 440
[33] Un poco andante of item 416
[34] Adagio non molto of item 407
[35] Allegro of item 447
[36] Poco adagio of item 447
[37] Allegro assai of item 447
[38] Allegro of item 424
[39] Adagio of item 424
[40] Adagio of item 418
[41] An adagio in c
[42] An adagio in a
[43] An adagio in c
[44] An adagio in C
[45] Allegro di molto of item 441
[46] Poco andante of item 427
[47] Allegro assai of item 427
[48] Allegro di molto of item 429
[49] Prestissimo of item 429
[50] Un poco andante of item 442
[51] A movement in D
[52] A movement in G
[53] Largo of item 469
[54] Largo of item 408
[55] An adagio "order vielmehr Andante" in E
[56] An allegro in A
[57] An allegro in Bb
[58] An adagio in Eb
[59] Largo-Prestissimo of item 469
[60] Allegro di molto of item 414
[61] Largo of item 408
[62] Adagio non molto of item 414
[63] Siciliana of item 433
[64] Un poco andante of item 442
[65] Adagio of item 440
[66] An adagio in Eb
[67] Poco adagio of item 417
[68] Allegro of item 417
[69] An allegro in Bb
[70] Largo of item 413
[71] Allegro di molto of item 444
[72] An andante in ¾ meter and in C
[73] An andante in C
[74] Largo of item 409
[75] Andante ed arioso of item 449

265. Rondo. 1779 (NV 23). W. 57/1
Early print and lit. about it: See KENNER III.
Mss. probably copied from the early print: D-brd B, P 433, P 937
Mod. edns.: BAUMGART, KREBS, RIEMANN, BERG/FAC-SIMILE
Lit. about this work: BITTER/BRÜDER, I, 220; STEGLICH/HOMILIUS, 85; HADOW, 204–05; CLERCX, 164–66; BARFORD/KEYBOARD, 127–29; COLE, 389; OTTENBERG, 171–72, 187–88, 220–21, 226–28

Incipit from KENNER III:

266. Rondo. 1779 (NV 23). W. 57/5
Early print and lit. about it: See KENNER III.
Ms. copied from the early print: D-brd B, P 433
Mod. edns.: BAUMGART, KREBS, BERG/FACSIMILE
Lit. about this work: BITTER/BRÜDER, I, 220–21

Incipit from KENNER III:

267. Rondo. 1779 (NV 23). W. 58/5
Mss.: D-brd B, P 212, P 937; D-brd Kl, Ms. Eschstruth 2° Mus. 440 (autog., 1st 134 bars only; my thanks to Miriam Terry for telling me of this source); see item 188
Early print and lit. about it: See KENNER IV.
Ms. probably copied from the early print: US NHu, Mason collection, 5012
Mod. edns.: BAUMGART, FARRENC, KREBS; V. d'Indy, Paris: Senart, [191?]; BERG/FACSIMILE
Lit. about this work: CPEB/BREITKOPF, 23 July 1783; BITTER/BRÜDER, I, 224–25; STEGLICH/HOMILIUS, 68–69, 82, 85–88; CLERCX, 149–50; BARFORD/KEYBOARD, 130; COLE, 391–92

Incipit from KENNER IV:

268. Rondo. 1779 (NV 23). W. 59/2
Early print and lit. about it: See KENNER V.
Mod. edns.: BAUMGART, KREBS, SCHENKER/KLAVIER-WERKE, BERG/FACSIMILE
Ms. probably copied from the early print: US NHu, Mason collection, 5013
Lit. about this work: SCHENKER/BEITRAG, 20, 23; CLERCX, 150; MÜLLER, 64–65; SCHULENBERG/INSTRUMENTAL, 147–53

Incipit from KENNER V:

269. Sonata. 1780 (NV 23). W. 56/4
Ms.: D-brd B, St 236 (fragment, autog.)
Early print and lit. about it: See KENNER II.
Mss. probably copied from the early print: D-brd B, P 1170;
   D-brd KIl, Mb 41, Mb 46; D-ddr LEm, Poel. Mus. ms. 40;
   D-ddr LEb, 345, 353; A Wgm, VII 26001
Mod. edns.: BAUMGART, FARRENC, KREBS, BERG/FAC-
   SIMILE
Lit. about this work: BITTER/BRÜDER, I, 215; STEGLICH/
   HOMILIUS, 115; BEURMANN/KLAVIERSONATEN, 86,
   111, AUERBACH, 88; NEWMAN, 419; BARFORD/
   KEYBOARD, 115; RADCLIFFE, 590; BERG, 106–08, 112,
   140, 192; SCHULENBERG/INSTRUMENTAL, 142; FOX,
   118–19, 124

Incipits from KENNER II:

[2 mvts. only]

270. Sonata. 1780 (NV 23). W. 56/6
Early print and lit. about it: See KENNER II.
Mss. probably copied from the early print: D-brd B, P 1170;
   D-brd KIl, Mb 41, Mb 46; D-ddr LEm, Poel. Mus. ms. 40;
   D-ddr LEb, 345, 353; A Wgm, VII 26001
Mod. edns.: BAUMGART, KREBS; A. Baresel, Leipzig: Zim-
   mermann-Verlag, 1935; BERG/FACSIMILE
Lit. about this work: BITTER/BRÜDER, I, 215; STEGLICH/
   HOMILIUS, 96; BEURMANN/KLAVIERSONATEN, 86;
   NEWMAN, 421; BARFORD/KEYBOARD, 115–16; BERG,
   112–13

Incipit from KENNER II:

[1 mvt. only]

271. Rondo. 1780 (NV 23). W. 57/3
Early print and lit. about it: See KENNER III.
Mss. probably copied from the early print: D-brd B, P 433,
   P 937
Mod. edns.: BAUMGART, KREBS, BERG/FACSIMILE
Lit. about this work: BITTER/BRÜDER, I, 220; STEGLICH/
   HOMILIUS, 115; CLERCX, 148; MÜLLER, 62

Incipit from KENNER III:

272. Abschied von meinem Silbermannischen Claviere, in
einem Rondo. 1781 (NV 23). W. 66
Mss.: D-brd B, P 359 (Michel), P 738 (Michel); D-ddr Bds,
   P 369; B Bc, 5894 (Michel); A Wgm, Q 11699 (VII 43761),
   Q 11700 (also numbered VII 43761); A Wn, 19035 (Michel);
   US AA, M24.B114.A2.1781a. A ms. apparently in Mitau,
   in the USSR (autog.?), is presently inaccessible.
Mod. edns.: Anon. [ed. by O. Vrieslander from a ms. found
   in Mitau in 1916? See VRIESLANDER/BACH, 95–96, 174],
   Mitau: Steffenhagen, 1916; A. Kreutz, Mainz: Schott, 1958
   (based on the "Mitau" ms. and containing an edn. of
   Grotthus's "Antwortrondo," "Freude über den
   Empfang . . . ," taken from this same ms.); in W. Kahl,
   Das Charakterstück, Cologne: Volk, n.d.; BERG/FAC-
   SIMILE
Other lit.: GEIRINGER/BACH, 360; BUSCH, 276; AUER-
   BACH, 68, 90, 93; NEWMAN, 650; BARFORD/KEY-
   BOARD, 132; RADCLIFFE, 592; COHEN, 111; OTTEN-
   BERG, 231–32
Sent by CPEB to his pupil D. E. von Grotthus on the occasion
   of his transfer of a favorite clavichord to Grotthus (as a
   wedding gift? See item 824a)

Incipit from 5894:

273. Sonata. 1781 (NV 24). W. 58/2
Ms.: See item 188. Not in D-ddr Bds, P 365, as reported in
   BEURMANN/KLAVIERSONATEN, 144
Early print and lit. about it: See KENNER IV.
Mss. probably copied from the early print: D-ddr LEm, Poel.
   Mus. ms. 40; US NHu, Mason collection, 5012
Mod. edns.: BAUMGART, KREBS, BERG/FACSIMILE
Lit. about this work: STEGLICH/HOMILIUS, 115, 124–25;
   REESER, 36–37; BEURMANN/KLAVIERSONATEN, 85–
   86, 107; BEURMANN/REPRISENSONATEN, 174; MÜL-
   LER, 60, 66; NEWMAN, 419–20, 429; BARFORD/
   KEYBOARD, 118; RADCLIFFE, 590; BERG, 59, 107, 132–
   33, 140, 143–44; SCHULENBERG/INSTRUMENTAL, 143–
   44; FOX, 176–77

Incipits from KENNER IV:

274. Rondo. 1781 (NV 23). W. 58/3
Mss.: D-brd B, P 796; see item 188.
Early print and lit. about it: See KENNER IV.
Ms. probably copied from the early print: US NHu, Mason collection, 5012
Mod. edns.: BAUMGART, FARRENC, KREBS, CALAND–GOEBELS; V. d'Indy, Paris: Senart, [191?]; BERG/FACSIMILE
Lit. about this work: CLERCX, 149; BARFORD/KEYBOARD, 129–30; SCHULENBERG/INSTRUMENTAL, 144

Incipit from KENNER IV:

275. Canzonetta der Herzogin von Gotha, mit 6 Veränderungen. 1781 (NV 24). W. 118/8
Mss.: D-brd B, P 359 (Michel), P 730 (autog.)
Early print: Part of a set of pasticcio variations published as "Canzonette fürs Clavier von einer Liebhaberin der Musik, mit Veränderungen von verschiedenen Tonkünstlern" (Gotha, 1781). The other variations were composed by G. Benda, C. F. Cramer, Golde, Scheidler, Scherlitz, and A. Schweitzer.
Ms. probably copied from the early print: B Bc, 5899 (Westphal)
Mod. edn.: BERG/FACSIMILE
Lit.: FISCHER, 194, 198, 209, 214–15
The "Herzogin von Gotha" who composed the Canzonetta appears to have been Luise Dorothea (1710–67), according to Heinrich Miesner, "Graf v. Keyserlingk und Minister v. Happe, zwei Gönner der Familie Bach," *Bach-Jahrbuch*, 31 (1934), 111–12.

Incipit from P 730:

276. Rondo. 1782 (NV 24). W. 58/1
Mss.: D-brd B, P 212, P 937; D-ddr Bds, P 365; DK Kk, mu 6309.0433; see item 188.
Early print and lit. about it: See KENNER IV.
Ms. probably copied from the early print: US NHu, Mason collection, 5012

Mod. edns.: BAUMGART, FARRENC, KREBS, CALAND–GOEBELS, BERG/FACSIMILE
Lit. about this work: BITTER/BRÜDER, I, 224; STEGLICH/HOMILIUS, 72, 98–100; CLERCX, 149; BARFORD/KEYBOARD, 129; OTTENBERG, 171–72, 187–88, 221, 226–28

Incipit from KENNER IV:

277. Fantasia. 1782 (NV 24). W. 58/6
Mss.: See item 188; a ms. is in the private collection of E. N. Kulukundis (U.S.).
Early print and lit. about it: See KENNER IV.
Ms. probably copied from the early print: US NHu, Mason collection, 5012
Mod. edns.: BAUMGART, KREBS, GÁT, BERG/FACSIMILE
Lit. about this work: CPEB/FORKEL, 10 Feb. 1775; CPEB/BREITKOPF, 23 July 1783; BITTER/BRÜDER, I, 224; BARFORD/KEYBOARD, 45–49; ELDER; OTTENBERG, 234; SCHULENBERG/INSTRUMENTAL, 38–39, 143; SELINGER/BARBER, 60, 77–90
See item 870.

Incipit from KENNER IV:

278. Fantasia. 1782 (NV 24). W. 58/7
Mss.: D-brd B, P 212; see item 188; a ms. is in the private collection of E. N. Kulukundis (U.S.).
Early print and lit. about it: See KENNER IV.
Ms. probably copied from the early print: US NHu, Mason collection, 5012
Mod. edns.: BAUMGART, KREBS, CALAND, GÁT, BERG/FACSIMILE
Lit. about this work: CPEB/FORKEL, 10 Feb. 1775; CPEB/BREITKOPF, 2 Jan. 1782; 26 Apr., 25 June 1783; BITTER/BRÜDER, I, 222–24; HADOW, 72–73; RADCLIFFE, 591; SCHLEUNING, introductions in vols. 42–43; ELDER; OTTENBERG, 11, 234; SCHULENBERG/INSTRUMENTAL, 143; SELINGER-BARBER, 60, 77–90
See item 870.

Incipit from KENNER IV:

279. Fantasia. 1782 (NV 24). W. 59/5
Early print and lit. about it: See KENNER V.
Ms. probably copied from the early print: US NHu, Mason
collection, 5013
Mod. edns.: BAUMGART, KREBS, BERG/FACSIMILE
Lit. about this work: CPEB/FORKEL, 10 Feb. 1775; MÜLLER,
58–60; RADCLIFFE, 591; ELDER; SELINGER/BARBER,
77–90
See item 870.

Incipit from KENNER V:

280. Sonata fürs Bogen-Clavier. 1783 (NV 24). W. 65/48
Mss.: D-brd B, P 359 (Michel), P 776 (Michel); D-ddr Bds,
P 369; B Bc, 5883 (Michel); A Wn, S.A.67.A.12 (Michel)
Mod. edns. (for standard keyboard instruments): FAR-
RENC, HERRMANN/SONATEN, BERG/EDITIONS,
BERG/FACSIMILE
Also designated for bowed keyboard in NV. Concerning
the bowed clavier and its inventor Hohlfeld, see
MIESNER/UMWELT, 142–43; the introduction to part II
of the *Versuch* (item 870), p. 172 in the Mitchell translation,
along with Mitchell's footnote; and item 719. Other lit.:
BEURMANN/KLAVIERSONATEN, 84–85; COHEN, 99;
BERG, 196–98

Incipits from P 776:

281. Sonata. 1784 (NV 24). W. 59/1
Ms.: D-brd B, P 898
Early print and lit. about it: See KENNER V.
Mss. probably copied from the early print: D-ddr LEm, Poel.
Mus. ms. 40; US NHu, Mason collection, 5013
Mod. edns.: BAUMGART, KREBS, BERG/FACSIMILE
Lit. about this work: BEURMANN/KLAVIERSONATEN,
35, 86; NEWMAN, 420; BARFORD/KEYBOARD, 119;
RADCLIFFE, 590; BERG, 106, 110, 142–43; OTTENBERG,
171–72, 187–88, 221, 226–28, 230; SCHULENBERG/IN-
STRUMENTAL, 32–33; FOX, 125, 142–43, 247–57

Incipits from KENNER V:

282. Sonata. 1784 (NV 24). W. 59/3
Early print and lit. about it: See KENNER V.
Ms. probably copied from the early print: US NHu, Mason
collection, 5013
Mod. edns.: BAUMGART, FARRENC, KREBS, SCHEN-
KER/KLAVIERWERKE (incomplete), BERG/FACSIMILE
Lit. about this work: SCHENKER/BEITRAG, 20; VRIESLAN-
DER/BACH, 64–65; BÜCKEN, 165; REESER, 40–41; BEUR-
MANN/KLAVIERSONATEN, 27, 62; NEWMAN, 420,
429; BARFORD/KEYBOARD, 120; RADCLIFFE, 590–91;
BERG, 187–88; SCHULENBERG/INSTRUMENTAL, 57–
59; FOX, 104–05, 120, 166
2nd mvt. is a rev. of 2nd mvt. of item 211.

Incipits from KENNER V:

283. Rondo. 1784 (NV 25). W. 59/4
Ms.: D-brd B, P 212
Early prints and lit. about them: See KENNER V, TROIS
RONDEAUX
Ms. probably copied from the early print: US NHu, Mason
collection, 5013
Mod. edns.: BAUMGART, FARRENC, KREBS, CALAND,
BERG/FACSIMILE
Lit. about this work: BITTER/BRÜDER, I, 226–27; CLERCX,
150; BARFORD/KEYBOARD, 130–31; RADCLIFFE, 591;
COHEN, 71–72

Incipit from KENNER V:

284. Fantasia. 1784 (NV 24). W. 59/6
Early print and lit. about it: See KENNER V.
Ms. probably copied from the early print: US NHu, Mason
  collection, 5013
Mod. edns.: BAUMGART, KREBS, CALAND, GÁT; V.
  d'Indy, Paris: Senart, [191?]; BERG/FACSIMILE
Lit. about this work: CPEB/FORKEL, 10 Feb. 1775; ELDER;
  SCHULENBERG/INSTRUMENTAL, 147, 153–61; SELIN-
  GER/BARBER, 77–90
See item 870.

Incipit from KENNER V:

285. [untitled fughetta on the name "C. Filippo E. Bach"
  (C-F-E-B-A-C-H)]. 1784 (source of date: See below).
Ms.: B Bc, 5895 (Westphal, taken from CPEB/28 APR. 1784;
  5895 is listed in its entirety as item 867)
See also items 371.9, 373, 389.6, 484.6, 659, 733/41, 867.

Incipit from 5895:

286. Sonata. 1785 (NV 25). W. 61/2
Early print and lit. about it: See KENNER VI.
Ms. probably copied from the early print: D-ddr LEm, Poel.
  Mus. ms. 40
Mod. edns.: BAUMGART, KREBS, BERG/FACSIMILE
Lit. about this work: AUERBACH, 86; NEWMAN, 421; BAR-
  FORD/KEYBOARD, 120–21; RADCLIFFE, 591; BERG,
  106, 190; FOX, 104–05, 109–10, 112–13

Incipits from KENNER VI:

287. Sonata. 1785 (NV 25). W. 61/5
Early print and lit. about it: See KENNER VI.
Ms. probably copied from the early print: D-ddr LEm, Poel.
  Mus. ms. 40
Mod. edns.: BAUMGART, KREBS, BERG/FACSIMILE
Lit. about this work: SHEDLOCK, 104–05; MÜLLER, 61;
  NEWMAN, 426; BERG, 192; SCHULENBERG/INSTRU-
  MENTAL, 32–33; FOX, 85–86, 176–77

Incipits from KENNER VI:

288. Rondo. 1786 (NV 25). W. 61/1
Early prints and lit. about them: See KENNER VI, TROIS
  RONDEAUX.
Mod. edns.: BAUMGART, KREBS, HERRMANN/SONA-
  TEN, BERG/FACSIMILE
Lit. about this work: BITTER/BRÜDER, I, 228–29; BAR-
  FORD/KEYBOARD, 123, 131; COHEN, 90; OTTENBERG,
  171–72, 187–88, 221, 226–30

Incipit from KENNER VI:

289. Fantasia. 1786 (NV 25). W. 61/3
Ms.: US Wc, ML96.B18 (autog.)
Early print and lit. about it: See KENNER VI.
Mod. edns.: BAUMGART, KREBS, BERG/FACSIMILE
Lit. about this work: CPEB/FORKEL, 10 Feb. 1775; MÜLLER,
  60–61; ELDER; SELINGER/BARBER, 77–90
See item 870.

Incipit from KENNER VI:

290. Rondo. 1785 (NV 25). W. 61/4
Ms.: in Fulda, Schloss Fasanerie, ex. Sammlung Heyer
  (autog.?). I am indebted to Margit McCorkle for informing
  me of this ms.

Early prints and lit. about them: See KENNER VI, TROIS RONDEAUX.

Mod. edns.: BAUMGART, KREBS, BERG/FACSIMILE

Incipit from KENNER VI:

291. Fantasia. 1786 (NV 25). W. 61/6

Early print and lit. about it: See KENNER VI.

Ms. probably copied from the early print: D-ddr LEm, Poel. Mus. ms. 40

Mod. edns.: BAUMGART, KREBS, RIEMANN, GÁT; ed. as one of the *Ausgewählte Werke aus dem Concert-Programm von Eugen d'Albert's Klavierabenden . . .*, Leipzig: Forberg, 1908; J. Friskin, New York: J. Fischer, 1954; BERG/FACSIMILE

Lit. about this work: CPEB/FORKEL, 10 Feb. 1775; BITTER/ BRÜDER, I, 229–30; STEGLICH/HOMILIUS, 128–29; BEURMANN/KLAVIERSONATEN, 74; RADCLIFFE, 591; ELDER; OTTENBERG, 222–26; SELINGER–BARBER, 77–90

See item 870.

Incipit from KENNER VI:

292. Sonatina. 1786 (NV 25). W. 63/7

Ms.: D-brd B, P 775 (Michel) (but not also P 439)

Early print and lit. about it: See SECHS NEUEN.

Mod. edns.: VRIESLANDER/KLEINE; HOFFMANN-ER-BRECHT/PROBESTÜCKE; in W. Rehberg, ed., *Die Söhne Bach*, Mainz: Schott, n.d.; BERG/FACSIMILE

Lit. about this work: ELDER, 12–15

The 6 mvts. comprising SECHS NEUEN, items 292–97, make up the 2 (3-mvt.) "sonatas" puzzlingly listed on p. 25 of NV as having been printed in 1786 by Schwickert. Apparently items 292–97 were conceived as "Sechs Probestücke in Zwei Sonaten" (to take the liberty of paraphrasing the collective title of items 70–75) but were given a different title to promote sales of the 1787 *Versuch;* the superior salability of these single mvts. is the subject of a letter written by CPEB to Schwickert in 1786 (see PLAMENAC, 566–68). Supporting the conclusion that CPEB seems to have thought privately of SECHS NEUEN as 2 works rather than 6 are the above-listed mss., which combine the supposedly discrete mvts. of items 292–94 (in P 439, P 775, 5880) and items 295–97 (in P 775, 5880), respectively, into two 3-mvt. sonatas, without regard for the unusual, though not rare, key relations that result.

Incipit from SECHS NEUEN:

293. Sonatina. 1786 (NV 25). W. 63/8

Ms.: D-brd B, P 775 (Michel) (but not also P 439)

Early print and lit. about it: See SECHS NEUEN.

Ms. probably copied from the early print: B Bc, 5880 (Westphal)

Mod. edns.: CALAND, VRIESLANDER/KLEINE, HOFFMANN-ERBRECHT/PROBESTÜCKE, BERG/FAC-SIMILE

Lit. about this work: RADCLIFFE, 592; ELDER, 12–15

See item 292.

Incipit from SECHS NEUEN:

294. Sonatina. 1786 (NV 25). W. 63/9

Ms.: D-brd B, P 775 (Michel) (but not also P 439)

Early print and lit. about it: See SECHS NEUEN.

Ms. probably copied from the early print: B Bc, 5880 (Westphal)

Mod. edns.: VRIESLANDER/KLEINE, HOFFMANN-ER-BRECHT/PROBESTÜCKE, BERG/FACSIMILE

Lit. about this work: ELDER, 12–15

See item 292.

Incipit from SECHS NEUEN:

295. Sonatina. 1786 (NV 25). W. 63/10

Ms.: D-brd B, P 775 (Michel)

Early print and lit. about it: See SECHS NEUEN.

Ms. probably copied from the early print: B Bc, 5880

Mod. edns.: VRIESLANDER/KLEINE, HOFFMANN-ER-BRECHT/PROBESTÜCKE, BERG/FACSIMILE

Lit. about this work: ELDER, 12–15

See item 292.

Incipit from SECHS NEUEN:

296. Sonatina. 1786 (NV 25). W. 63/11

Ms.: D-brd B, P 775 (Michel)

Early print and lit. about it: See SECHS NEUEN.

Ms. probably copied from the early print: B Bc, 5880
Mod. edns.: VRIESLANDER/KLEINE, CALAND, HOFFMANN-ERBRECHT/PROBESTÜCKE, BERG/FAC-SIMILE
Lit. about this work: ELDER, 12–15
See item 292.

Incipit from SECHS NEUEN:

297. Sonatina. 1786 (NV 25). W. 63/12
Ms.: D-brd B, P 775 (Michel)
Early print and lit. about it: See SECHS NEUEN.
Ms. probably copied from the early print: B Bc, 5880
Mod. edns.: VRIESLANDER/KLEINE, HOFFMANN-ER-BRECHT/PROBESTÜCKE, BERG/FACSIMILE
Lit. about this work: ELDER, 12–15
See item 292.

Incipit from SECHS NEUEN:

298. Sonata per il cembalo solo. 1786 (NV 25). W. 65/49
Mss.: D-brd B, P 359 (Michel); D-ddr Bds, P 369; B Bc, 5883; PL Kj, P 771 (autog.)
Mod. edns.: FARRENC, BERG/FACSIMILE
Lit.: BEURMANN/REPRISENSONATEN, 169; BERG, 178; FOX, 68

Incipits from 5883:

299. Sonata per il cembalo solo. 1786 (NV 25). W. 65/50
Mss.: D-brd B, P 359 (Michel); D-ddr Bds, P 369; B Bc, 5883 (Michel); PL Kj, P 771 (autog.)
Mod. edn.: BERG/FACSIMILE
Lit.: BEURMANN/KLAVIERSONATEN, 97; BEURMANN/REPRISENSONATEN, 169
A.v.: items 517, 520. The 1st mvt. is an arr. of item 633; the 2nd mvt. is an arr. of item 630.

Incipits from 5883:

300. Freie Fantasie fürs Clavier. 1787 (NV 26). W. 67
Mss.: D-brd B, P 359 (autog.); D-ddr Bds, P 369; B Bc, 5884 (Michel), 5895 (mostly Michel; sketches); H Bn
Mod. edn.: BERG/FACSIMILE
Lit.: BARFORD/FANTASIA; NEWMAN, 423; BARFORD/KEYBOARD, 20; SCHLEUNING, introductions in vols. 42, 43; COHEN, 176, 187–238; BERG, 228; WADE, 53; ELDER, 92–95; H. Poos, "Harmoniestruktur und Hermeneutik in C.Ph.E. Bachs Fis-Moll Fantasie," *Bericht über den internationalen musikwissenschaftlichen Kongress Berlin 1974*, ed. H. Kühn and Peter Nitsche (Kassel, 1980), 319–23; SELINGER-BARBER, 77–90
Arr.: item 536

Incipit from P 359:

301. [untitled]. n.d. W. 116/19
Mss.: D-brd B, Mus. ms. 38050; B Bc, 5898 (Westphal); A Wn, 19035 (Michel); PL Kj, P 745 (marked by CPEB)
Mod. edn.: BERG/FACSIMILE
See the reference to SMITH 1968 in item 96.

Incipit from 5898:

302. [untitled]. n.d. W. 116/20
Mss.: D-brd B, Mus. ms. 38050; B Bc, 5898 (Westphal); A Wn, 19035 (Michel); PL Kj, P 745 (marked by CPEB)
Mod edn: BERG/FACSIMILE

Incipit from 5898:

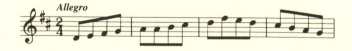

303. Minuett-trio. n.d. W. 116/29
Ms.: B Bc, 5898 (Westphal)
Mod. edn.: BERG/FACSIMILE
A.v.: item 622

Incipits from 5898:

[The Minuett is repeated after the Trio.]

304. Minuetto I–II. n.d. W. 116/30
Ms.: B Bc, 5898 (Westphal)
Mod. edn.: BERG/FACSIMILE
A.v.: item 623

Incipits from 5898:

[Minuetto I is repeated after Minuetto II.]

305. Minuetto I–II. n.d. W. 116/31
Ms.: B Bc, 5898 (Westphal)
Mod. edn.: BERG/FACSIMILE
A.v.: items 624, 635/9

Incipits from 5898:

[Minuetto I is repeated after Minuetto II.]

306. Minuetto I–II. n.d. W. 116/32
Ms.: B Bc, 5898 (Westphal)
Mod. edn.: BERG/FACSIMILE
A.v.: items 625, 635/12. Vnt.: item 258

Incipits from 5898:

[Minuetto I is repeated after Minuetto II.]

307. Menuett I, Menuett II. n.d. W. 116/33
Ms.: B Bc, 5898 (Westphal)
Mod. edn.: BERG/FACSIMILE
A.v.: item 626

Incipits from 5898:

[Menuett I is repeated after Menuett II.]

308. Polonoise. n.d. W. 116/34
Ms.: B Bc, 5898 (Westphal)
Mod. edn.: BERG/FACSIMILE
A.v.: item 627

Incipit from 5898:

309. Minuetto I–II. n.d. W. 116/35
Ms.: B Bc, 5898 (Westphal)
Mod. edn.: BERG/FACSIMILE
A.v.: item 638

Incipits from 5898:

[Minuetto I is repeated after Minuetto II.]

310. [untitled]. n.d. W. 116/36
Ms.: B Bc, 5898 (Westphal)
Mod. edns.: HERRMANN/LEICHTE, BERG/FACSIMILE
A.v.: item 635/5

Incipit from 5898:

311. [untitled]. n.d. W. 116/37
Ms.: B Bc, 5898 (Westphal)
Mod. edns.: HERRMANN/SONATEN, BERG/FACSIMILE
A.v.: item 635/6

Incipit from 5898:

312. [untitled]. n.d. W. 116/38
Ms.: B Bc, 5898 (Westphal)
Mod. edn.: BERG/FACSIMILE
A.v.: item 635/8

Incipit from 5898:

313. [untitled]. n.d. W. 116/39
Ms.: B Bc, 5898 (Westphal)
Mod. edn.: BERG/FACSIMILE
A.v.: item 635/7

Incipit from 5898:

314. Menuett. n.d. W. 116/40
Ms.: B Bc, 5898 (Westphal)
Mod. edn.: BERG/FACSIMILE
A.v.: item 635/11

Incipit from 5898:

315. Polonoise. n.d. W. 116/41
Ms.: B Bc, 5898 (Westphal)
Mod. edn.: BERG/FACSIMILE
A.v.: item 635/13

Incipit from 5898:

316. Polonoise. n.d. W. 116/42
Ms.: B Bc, 5898 (Westphal)
Mod. edn.: BERG/FACSIMILE
A.v.: item 635/14

Incipit from 5898:

317. Polonoise. n.d. W. 116/43
Ms.: B Bc, 5898 (Westphal)
Mod. edn.: BERG/FACSIMILE
A.v.: item 635/15

Incipit from 5898:

318. Polonoise. n.d. W. 116/44
Ms.: B Bc, 5898 (Westphal)
Mod. edn.: BERG/FACSIMILE
A.v.: item 635/16

Incipit from 5898:

319. Marsch. n.d. W. 116/45
Ms.: B Bc, 5898 (Westphal)
Mod. edn.: BERG/FACSIMILE
A.v.: items 635/17, 637/1

Incipit from 5898:

320. Marsch. n.d. W. 116/46
Ms.: B Bc, 5898 (Westphal)
Mod. edns.: HERRMANN/LEICHTE, BERG/FACSIMILE
A.v.: items 635/18, 637/2

Incipit from 5898:

321. Menuet. n.d. W. 116/47
Ms.: B Bc, 5898 (Westphal)
Mod. edn.: BERG/FACSIMILE
A.v.: item 635/19

Incipit from 5898:

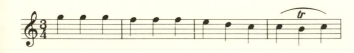

322. Menuet. n.d. W. 116/48
Ms.: B Bc, 5898 (Westphal)
Mod. edn.: BERG/FACSIMILE
A.v.: item 635/20

Incipit from 5898:

323. Polonoise. n.d. W. 116/49
Ms.: B Bc, 5898 (Westphal)
Mod. edn.: BERG/FACSIMILE
A.v.: item 635/21

Incipit from 5898:

324. [untitled]. n.d. W. 116/50
Ms.: B Bc, 5898 (Westphal)
Mod. edn.: BERG/FACSIMILE
A.v.: items 612, 620/1, 635/28

Incipit from 5898:

325. [untitled]. n.d. W. 116/51
Ms.: B Bc, 5898 (Westphal)
Mod. edns.: HERRMANN/LEICHTE, BERG/FACSIMILE
A.v.: item 635/29

Incipit from 5898:

326. [untitled]. n.d. W. 116/52
Ms.: B Bc, 5898 (Westphal)
Mod. edn.: BERG/FACSIMILE
A.v.: item 632

Incipit from 5898:

327. [untitled]. n.d. W. 116/53
Ms.: B Bc, 5898 (Westphal)
Mod. edn.: BERG/FACSIMILE
A.v.: item 615

Incipit from 5898:

328. [untitled]. n.d. W. 116/54
Ms.: B Bc, 5898 (Westphal)
Mod. edn.: BERG/FACSIMILE
A.v.: item 617

Incipit from 5898:

329. [untitled]. n.d. W. 116/55
Ms.: B Bc, 5898 (Westphal)
Mod. edn.: BERG/FACSIMILE
A.v.: item 618

Incipit from 5898:

330. [untitled]. n.d. W. 116/56
Ms.: B Bc, 5898 (Westphal)
Mod. edn.: BERG/FACSIMILE
A.v.: item 619

Incipit from 5898:

331. [untitled]. n.d. W. 116/57
Ms.: B Bc, 5898 (Westphal)
Mod. edn.: BERG/FACSIMILE
A.v.: item 634

Incipit from 5898:

332. Deleted

333. La Juliane. n.d.
Ms.: A Wn, 15961 (signed by CPEB)

Incipit from 15961:

334. [untitled]. n.d.
Ms.: D-ddr LEm, Ms. R 12
Vnt. of the 3rd mvt. of item 138. Nearly all of the ornamented
    top line is in the hand of CPEB, and Jürgen Jürgensen
    copied the rest, according to Peter Krause, *Handschriften
    der Werke Johann Sebastian Bachs in der Musikbibliothek der
    Stadt Leipzig* (Bibliographische Veröffentlichungen der
    Musikbibliothek der Stadt Leipzig, 1964), 46–48. This vnt.
    was written after item 138, judging from the characteristic
    tremor of CPEB's handwriting.

Incipit from Ms. R 12:

335. Deleted

336. 5 Choräle mit ausgesetzten Mittelstimmen. n.d. NV,
64 (not by title); Wq n.v. 21, 20 (the 4th and 5th chorales);
W., footnote on p. 96
Mss.: D-brd B, P 788 (Michel?; Wq n.v. 21, 20 only); D-ddr
    Bds, Gr 924 (M 1893.5) (?); B Bc, 16.083 (Westphal; source
    of the collective title)
Textless, scored for keyboard, or organ with pedals

Incipits from 16.083:

337. Choral [Wo Gott zum Haus nicht gibt]. n.d. Wq n.v. 18
Ms.: D-ddr Bds, P 339 (autog.)
4 textless parts in open score, with continuo. Since the rest
    of P 339 consists almost entirely of items 800, 802, and

807, this chorale probably belongs to one of those choral works.

Incipit from P 339:

Possibly Authentic

338. [untitled]. 1755 or earlier (source of date: 1st pub.). W. 116/16–17; NV, 11 (?)
Early print: MARPURG/ANLEITUNG
Ms. probably copied from the early print: B Bc, 5898 (Westphal)
Mod. edns.: HERRMANN/SONATEN, BERG/FACSIMILE
Marpurg prints the 2 mvts. without a composer's name, suggesting that he is the composer; but Westphal includes them in 5898 as successive items among works known to be by CPEB, and they are possibly the "zwey Allegro" dated 1755 on p. 11 of NV.

Incipits from 5898:

339. Sonata per il cembalo solo. 1762 or earlier (source of date: 1st pub.). Wq n.v. 27; Beurm.-Anh. 7
Ms.: D-brd B, P 364
Early print (as an anon. work): MANCHERLEY, 83 (1762)
"Di C. F. E. Bach," says the title p. in the hand of the anonymous copyist, although this attribution is crossed out in apparently the same ink. P 364 is a 221-p. ms. in the hands of several anonymous copyists, two of whom are known to have copied genuine C. P. E. Bach works. CPEB is well represented in ALLERLEY and MANCHERLEY and was the editor of VIELERLEY, the third in this group of popular collections. He was certainly not above selling a sonata to the editor of MANCHERLEY on the condition that its composer not be named. Lit. about these collections: See these entries in Bib. and the general description of the three under ALLERLEY in Bib.

Incipits from MANCHERLEY:

340. Polonoise. Probably 1768 or later (source of date: Michel was CPEB's main Hamburg copyist). Wq n.v. 54
Ms.: D-brd B, P 672 ("di C. P. E. Bach"; Michel)
See item 171.

Incipit from P 672:

341. Sonata. n.d. Wq n.v. 23; Beurm.-Anh. 1
Mss.: D-brd B, P 439; A Wn, 5669, 18677
A Wn, 18677, entitled "Sonates per il Clavi Cembalo Del Sigl. C. P. E. Bach," is made up of items 341, 342, and 41. A Wn, 5669, with an overall title of "XII. Polonoisen von W. F. Bach," contains, on pp. LXII–LXXX, items 341 and 342 (but with the 2nd mvt. of item 342 borrowed from item 41), each attributed to CPEB on its own title p. D-brd B, P 439, entitled "4 Sonates per il Clavi Cembalo. No. 4.5.6.7. Del Sig. C. P. E. Bach," and signed by the owner, Aloys Fuchs (1799–1853), is made up of items 341, 342, 368 and 41. Thus all 3 mss. are of Viennese provenance. (Much of Fuchs's library went to the Deutsche Staatsbibliothek in Berlin.) Items 341 and 342 are represented in all 3 mss., item 368 in two; all 3 mss. contain genuine CPEB works. The authorship of item 368 (q.v.) is cast into doubt by its attribution to Johann Ernst Bach in OEUVRES, but no such conflicting attribution has been found for items 341 and 342.

Incipits from P 439:

342. Sonata. n.d. Wq n.v. 24; Beurm.-Anh. 3
Mss.: D-brd B, P 439; A Wn, 5669 (but with a 2nd mvt. borrowed from that of item 41), 18677
See item 341.

Incipits from P 439:

Incipits from P 1002:

343. Sonata per il cembalo solo. n.d. Wq n.v. 25; Beurm.-Anh. 5

Mss.: D-brd B, P 364; D-ddr Bds, P 371; USSR KA, Ms. Rf b 3, Bd. I (unverified)

Regarding P 364, see item 339. In P 364 this sonata is not attributed, although a later hand has written "del Sigl Bach" in pencil. P 371 is a 150-p. ms. in the hands of several anonymous copyists; nearly all these, including the copyist of item 343 in this ms., are known to have copied genuine CPEB works. P 371 consists of 15 keyboard works; item 343, not attributed in this ms., is the only one of these whose authenticity is unproved. Regarding USSR KA, see item 192.

Incipits from P 371:

344. Sonata. Cembalo solo. n.d. Wq n.v. 26; Beurm.-Anh. 6

Ms.: D-brd B, P 1002 ("di C. P. E. Bach")

Mod. edn: A. Kreutz, Mainz: Schott, 1938

P1000/1001/1002 are 3 mss. in one bundle, 20, 10, and 10 pp., respectively, in 2 unknown hands (one of which closely resembles that of an anonymous copyist known to have copied genuine CPEB works), consisting, respectively, of item 259, part of item 7, and item 344. The bundle was owned by Sara Levy (1761–1854) and Abraham Mendelssohn Bartholdy (1776–1835); see Introduction, pp. xx, xxiii–xxiv.

345. Solo. n.d. Wq n.v. 28; Beurm.-Anh. 9

Ms.: D-brd B, P370

P 370, entitled "C. Ph. E. Bach/Sonates et petites pièces pour le Clavecin (Organo)," is a 100-p. ms. in a single anonymous hand known to be that of many Amalienbibliothek mss., consisting of 19 keyboard works, of which 17 are authentic compositions of CPEB and one is an authentic work of Johann Christian Bach (see KAST). Item 345, not attributed in the ms., is the only piece in the ms. whose authorship is unproved.

Incipits from P 370:

346. Sonata per il chembalo solo. n.d.

Ms.: D-ddr GOl, Ms. Mus. 21a, No. XIII, "del Sigl. C. P. E. Bach"

Despite the spelling of the title and the provenance of the ms. (see item 378), This is a substantial work whose style is quite close to that of CPEB.

Incipits from Ms. Mus. 21a, No. XIII:

Presto

347. Sonata per il cembalo solo. n.d.
Ms.: D-ddr GOl, Ms. Mus. 21a, No. 62, "de Sigl. Carolo
   Filippo Emanuele Bach"
Despite the unreliability of attribution in Ms. Mus. 21a (see
   item 378), this item, like item 346, is a substantial work
   whose style is quite close to that of CPEB.

Incipits from Ms. Mus. 21a, No. 62:

Allegro moderato

Adagio

Vivace   *tr*

348. Fantasia. n.d.
Ms.: D-ddr Bds, Mus. ms. autogr. Nichelmann 1 N (formerly
   Mus. ms. 103) (in the hand of CPEB, not Nichelmann)
Lit.: SCHULZE/SCHRIEBER, 107; SELINGER-BARBER, 56–
   58, 77–90, 98–107, 134–41
Not attributed in this ms., which is a collection of keyboard
   works by C. Nichelmann. Apparently the insertion of a
   CPEB autograph into a collection otherwise in the hand
   of Nichelmann, CPEB's colleague and pupil at the Berlin
   court, was undetected by the library cataloguer. I am
   assured by Douglas A. Lee (see LEE in the Bib.) that
   Nichelmann's handwriting is in no way similar to CPEB's.
   The peculiar and inexplicable fate of the ms. is evidence
   against CPEB's authorship (he would not wish to bury
   his own work, even if he meant it only as an example for
   his pupil), as is CPEB's lifelong copying of the works of
   other composers (for example, compositions by the members of his own family, as illustrated throughout KAST).
   On the other hand, the style is very much like that of
   CPEB's authentic fantasias: dynamic fussiness, rehar-
   monizations of repeated notes, absence of barlines, arpeg-
   giations flung across the entire range of the instrument.
   Nichelmann may be the one responsible for placing
   among his own works an unsigned gift from his teacher
   (I have not been able to study the physical structure of
   Mus. ms. autogr. Nichelmann 1 N). My thanks to Douglas
   Lee for bringing this fine fantasia to my attention; he is
   presently making an edn. of it. SELINGER-BARBER, 57,
   suggests a date of 1745 or earlier for the ms., based
   on paleographic information supplied by Yoshitake
   Kobayashi. Regarding Nichelmann's position as CPEB's
   pupil, see the original document quoted in MIESNER/
   UMWELT, 139.

Incipit from Mus. ms. autogr. Nichelmann 1 N:

349. Fantasia e fuga. n.d.
Ms.: B Bc, 5896 (Westphal)
Not only copied but also signed on the cover by Westphal-
   as-copyist. On the other hand, CPEB/WESTPHAL, 25 Oct.
   1787 (printed in BITTER/BRÜDER, II, 306): "Ausser den
   6 Clavierfugen, die Sie schon haben, habe ich Keine mehr
   gemacht. . . ." The "6" are in all probability items 75.5,
   99–101, 101.5, 102; this is attested by Westphal's careful
   documentation of the "6" (along with the "Duo in Contrap.," item 76) in his own copy of items 75.5, 76, 99–101,
   101.5, 102 in B Bc, 5900.
Lit. (including a persuasive argument against CPEB's authorship): SELINGER-BARBER, 58–60, 67–68, 71–76

Incipits from 5896:

Allegro moderato e Andante

Moderato non molto

350. Fuga per il organo. n.d. Wq n.v. 35
Ms.: D-brd B, P 367 (consisting almost entirely of genuine
   works composed before 1767, that is, while CPEB might
   still have been interested in fugues; but see item 349)
P 367 is a 146-p. ms. consisting of 20 works, all but 2 of
   which (item 350 and a vnt. of No. 16 of item 776) are
   known to be authentic keyboard compositions of CPEB.
   It is in the hands of J. S. Borsch (c. 1744–1804); J. G.
   Müthel (1728–1788), a Bach-family acquaintance whose
   works imitated CPEB's *empfindsamer Stil*; and anonymous
   18th-century copyists. The attribution of this fugue in P 367
   reads, "di C. Ph. E. Bach"; a later hand has written "(oder
   vielleicht von J. S. Bach?)."

Incipit from P 367:

351. Arioso con variazioni. n.d.
Mss.: D-ddr Bds, M.Th. 42 ("dell' Sigl. Bach"; a later hand
   has added "C. Ph. E. Bach"); D-brd KIl, Mb 62:1 ("di

Bach"); D-brd Mbs, Mus. ms. 1797; D-ddr GOl, Ms. Mus. 21a, No. 6 73 (entitled "Sonata"). Regarding the reliability of attribution in Ms. Mus. 21a, see item 378.

ROE, 33, believes on stylistic grounds that this work is more likely to be by Emanuel than by Christian Bach. See also ROE, 403.

Incipit from Mb 62: 1:

352. Adagio per il organo a 2 clavire e pedal. n.d. Wq n.v. 66
Mss.: D-brd B, P 1151 ("di Sigl. C. P. E. Bach"); D-ddr Bds, Am.B. 505 ("da Bach")
Mod. edn.: FEDTKE/ORGELWERKE
P 1151 is a 12-p. ms. in the hand of an anonymous copyist known to have copied genuine CPEB works; it consists of this work, item 60, and item 371.1. Regarding mss. in Am.B., see the Introduction, p. xxvi.

Incipit from P 1151:

353. Polonoise. n.d. Wq n.v. 50
Ms.: D-brd B, P 728
This work and item 354 are vnts. of each other. Contrary to Kast's notation, neither is related to item 217 past the first few bars. P 728, bearing the overall title "C. P. E. Bach u. Andere/Claverstücke," is a 32-p. ms. of keyboard music (with one vocal piece) in the hands of several anonymous copyists, 4 of whom were active in the 18th century. It consists of 14 works: 8 known to be by CPEB and one attributed to Kirnberger, along with the unattributed items 353–56, 770. Items 353 and 354 resemble many genuine CPEB works in their exercise of the principles of variant version and varied reprise.

Incipit from P 728:

354. Polonoise. n.d. Wq n.v. 51
Ms.: D-brd B, P 728
See the note in item 353.

Incipit from P 728:

355. Polonoise. n.d. Wq n.v. 52
Ms.: D-brd B, P 728
See item 353.

Incipit from P 728:

356. [untitled]. n.d. Wq n.v. 55
Ms.: D-brd B, P 728
See item 353.

Incipit from P 728:

357. [Choral-Vorspiel]. n.d.
Early print: *Choral-Vorspiele für die Orgel und das Klavier. Gesammlet und herausgegeben von Johann Christoph Kühnau,* Berlin: im Verlag des Autors, n.d.
The chorale prelude attributed to CPEB is No. 9, on p. 19, where it appears without a title and with the attribution printed over the top staff, "Von C. Ph. E. Bach." C. P. E. Bach composed a setting of this melody, "Gott, deine Güte," for solo voice (item 686/9) and, in addition, an arrangement for soprano, alto, and continuo (item 826/3).

Incipit from "Choral-Vorspiele":

Doubtful

358. [Sonata for keyboard]. 1732 (source of date: BITTER/ BRÜDER)
Listed in BITTER/BRÜDER, II, 325; ¼ meter, key of C. I have not been able to find such a work.

359. Garten-Sonata. 1762 or earlier (source of date: 1st pub.)
Ms.: D-ddr GOl, Ms. Mus. 21a, attributed to "Carl Fridr. Emanuel Bach"
Early print (as an anon. work): MANCHERLEY, 125 (1762)
Regarding the reliability of attribution in Ms. Mus. 21a, see item 378. See also the discussion of ALLERLEY, MAN-CHERLEY, and VIELERLEY in the Bib.

Incipits from MANCHERLEY:

360. Fuga. 1764? (source of date: see below). Wq n.v. 34
Ms.: D-brd B, P 918
The title p. reads, "Fuga in B Dur a due voci di Bach." Below
this, another hand has added "(Carl Ph. Em.)." P 918
consists only of this work. Contrary to Kast's notation,
this piece is not listed in NV. A note on the last p. reads:
"1830 copirt durch Scheffler für [A.] E. Grell nach einem
Exemplar bezeichnet: 1764." See item 349.

Incipit from P 918:

361. A favourite overture of Sig. Bach of Berlin [for unac-
companied piano]. c. 1785 (source of date: GB Lbm
catalogue). TERRY, C. S., 277
Early prints: the above title, London: Bland, [c. 1785]; "Bach
of Berlin Symphonie," *The Piano-Forte Magazine*, II, No. 5
(London, 1797), 41
Lit.: ROE, 103, 451
Arrangement for piano of a symphony attributed to Johann
Christian Bach in a ms. in CH E, M. 678, 22

Incipit from *The Piano-Forte Magazine*, 1st mvt.:

362. Sonata. n.d. Beurm.-Anh. 2
Ms.: USSR KA, MS. Rf b 55 (unverified)
Rf b 55 is inaccessible (see item 192). Since items 362–67 are
merely listed in BEURMANN/KLAVIERSONATEN with
little evidence as to their possible authenticity, and since
they are now inaccessible, they must be categorized as
of doubtful authenticity. Further cause for doubt exists
for item 363 (q.v.).

Incipits from Beurm.-Anh. 2:

363. Sonata. n.d. Beurm.-Anh. 8; FALCK, 3
Ms.: USSR KA, Rf b 3, Bd. II (unverified)
Lit.: BERG, 244–48
This sonata has the same 2nd mvt. (transposed) as a sonata
in D-brd B, P 368, uncertainly attributed by Falck to W.
F. Bach.
Rf b 3 is inaccessible (see item 192). See also item 362.

Incipits from Beurm.-Anh. 8:

364. Sonata. n.d. Beurm.-Anh. 11
Ms.: USSR KA, Ms. Rf b 55 (unverified)
Rf b 55 is inaccessible (see item 192). See also item 362.

Incipits from Beurm.-Anh. 11:

365. Sonata. n.d. Beurm.-Anh. 12
Ms.: USSR KA, Ms. Rf b 55 (unverified)
Rf b 55 is inaccessible (see item 192). See also item 362.

Incipits from Beurm.-Anh. 12:

366. Sonata. n.d. Beurm.-Anh. 13
Ms.: USSR KA, Ms. Rf b 3, Bd. II (unverified)
Rf b 3 is inaccessible (see item 192). See also item 362.

Incipits from Beurm.-Anh. 13:

367. Sonata. n.d. Beurm.-Anh. 15
Ms.: USSR KA, Ms. Rf b 55 (unverified)
Rf b 55 is inaccessible (see item 192). See also item 362.

Incipits from Beurm.-Anh. 15:

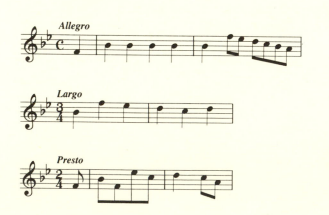

368. Sonata. n.d. Wq n.v. 29; Beurm.-Anh. 10
Mss.: D-brd B, P 439; A Wn, 18677
Early print: OEUVRES, V, 14, where it is attributed to
   Johann Ernst Bach
Lit.: BERG, 244–48
See item 341.

Incipits from P 439:

369. Sonata. n.d.
Ms.: US Bp, one of two sonatas in No. 8 of **M200.9
**M200.9 also contains copies of items 34 and 127; but the
   odd key relations between movements in this work might
   indicate that it is an anonymous pastiche.

Incipits from **M200.9:

370. Sonata [Suite] a clavicembalo solo. n.d.
Ms.: D-brd KII, Mb 62:2 (Hortschansky cat. no. 814, where
   the key is incorrectly given as g)
Lit. (with evidence against CPEB's authorship): SELINGER-
   BARBER, 58–60, 67–68, 71–72, 74–76
A substantial work, in a style and genre much more favored
   by JSB than by CPEB

Incipits from Mb 62:2:

Tempo di Minuetto

371. Sinfonia per il clavicembalo. n.d.
Ms.: D-ddr LEm, Poel. Mus. ms. 50
On the cover: "Possessor [K. H. L.] Poelitz 1786." Since
    Poelitz was born in 1772, the date could be that of either
    composition or acquisition. The melodic and harmonic
    predictability of this "sinfonia," and its squareness and
    symmetry of phrase structure, are at odds with CPEB's
    idea of "symphonic" style, even when that style is trans-
    ferred to the medium of the keyboard (cf. items 45, 104,
    115, 191, 227).

Incipits from Poel. Mus. ms. 50:

371.5. Andante, Allabreve. n.d.
Ms.: D-brd B, P 1151
The Andante is inserted without individual attribution be-
    tween the 1st and 2nd mvts. of item 60; the Allabreve is
    at the end of that item, again without individual attribu-
    tion. See item 352.

Incipits from P 1151:

371.6. Andante. n.d.
Ms.: D-brd B, Mus. ms. 30431
The ms. is characterized by its selection of single mvts. from
    multi-mvt. works. This item is attributed to "Bach."

Incipit from Mus. ms. 30431:

371.7. Arietta con variationes. n.d.
Ms.: D-brd B, Mus. ms. 38049 ("di Bach")
The same ms. contains other sets of variations, including
    items 155 (also entitled "Arietta con variationes di Bach")
    and 69.

Incipit from Mus. ms. 38049:

371.8. Fantasia. n.d.
Ms.: US NHu, Mason collection, 4679a
Foreign in provenance and style

Incipit from 4679a:

371.9. Sonata di Preludio e Fuga [on B-A-C-H]. n.d.
Ms.: US NHu, Mason collection, 4858b
See item 349. See also items 285, 373, 389.6, 484.6, 659,
    733/41, 867.

Incipits from 4858b:

372. Fuga. n.d.
Ms.: D-ddr Bds, Mus. O. 13457 (presently unavailable)
Ed. as CPEB's in FEDTKE/ORGELWERKE, and also by O.
    Gaus in *Orgelkompositionen aus alter und neuer Zeit*, I, Re-
    gensburg, 1910; but see item 349.

Incipit from FEDTKE/ORGELWERKE:

373. Fuga (sopra il nome de Bach). n.d. BWV Anh. 108
Mss.: D-brd B, P 721; A Wgm, Q 11710 (VII 43736); A Wn, 18687; US, NHu, Mason Collection, 4918, 5018
P 719/720/721, consisting of 4 authentic CPEB fugues (items 75.5, 99, 100, 101.5) and item 373, was partly owned and partly copied by Josef Fischhof (1804–57). The A Wgm ms., part of the Hoboken legacy to that library, is entitled "Fuga C Dur (B-A-C-H)"; over this title another hand has written "Ph. E. Bach." The A Wn ms. is entitled "Fuga"; over this a later hand has written "Sopra il nome di Bach," and under it the same hand has written "Del Sigl. Carlo Fil. Eman. Bach." Item 373 is one of the five fugues on "B-A-C-H" that SCHMIEDER lists as dubious among J. S. Bach's works. SIMON/B-A-C-H says there is no ground for doubting that this fugue is by CPEB; but see item 349. See also items 285, 371.9, 389.6, 484.6, 659, 733/41, 867.

Incipit from Q 11710 (VII 43736):

373.5. Fugetta ex D moll, Fugetta in D moll, Fugetta in D dur. n.d. BWV Anh. 100, Anh, 98, Anh. 96
Ms.: D-brd B, P 751/752/753
Each of the fughettas has its own title p. with attributions to CPEB, numbered "N^ro 1 . . . N^ro 2 . . . N^ro 3." SCHMIEDER lists them as doubtful among JSB's works. See item 349.

Incipits from P 751/752/753:

374. La Walhauer. n.d.
Ms.: D-ddr GOl, Ms. Mus. 21a
This type of character piece is a genre unusually favored by CPEB; but arguing against his authorship is the general unreliability of attribution in Ms. Mus. 21a (see item 378), as well as the musical style. The syncope that opens the piece is heard throughout; this high-Classic melodic mannerism is almost never heard in the works of CPEB.

Incipit from Ms. Mus. 21a:

375. Menuetto mit v Variazionen. n.d.
Ms.: D-brd Kll, Mb 62:3
Attributed to CPEB on the cover, only to "Bach" (in a different hand) on the first p.

Incipit from Mb 62:3:

375.5. Menuetto, Trio, Menuetto [with 7 variations]. n.d.
Ms.: D-ddr Bds, Mus. ms. 30327
Mus. ms. 30327 is a collection of minuets, polaccas, and other miniatures entitled "Clavier Stücke./Rosina Elisabeth von Münch./1777." The first Menuetto is paired with the Trio ("Trio" is an uncharacteristic name for the 2nd of CPEB's coupled minuets); the second Menuetto, with 7 variations, comes some pages later. All three of these mvts. are in the style of Kirnberger, although the same ms. is a source of items 219, 223, and 224.

Incipits from Mus. ms. 30327:

Spurious

376. Ach Gott und Herr. c. 1732 (source of date: date of the J. S. Bach cantata). Wq n.v. 14; BWV 48
Ms.: D-brd B, P 349 (autog.)
Lit.: MIESNER/HAMBURG, 109–10; VRIESLANDER/ BACH, 128–29, uses this chorale as illustration of CPEB's drastic divergence from his father's chorale style.
Textless chorale, scored for keyboard. Though this copy is in CPEB's hand, the setting is that of the chorale "Solls ja so sein" from *Cantata 48* (BWV 48) by J. S. Bach.

Incipit from P 349:

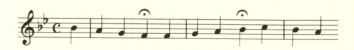

377. [Sonata in a minor]. c. 1735 or c. 1747 (source of dates: dates of original and revised versions of item 572)
Ms.: B Bc, 27, 134

According to ROE, 68, 485, B. A. Mekota, in *The Solo and Ensemble Keyboard Works of Johann Christian Bach* (Ph.D. dissertation, University of Michigan, 1969), 49, identifies this "sonata" as an arrangement of the lower two parts of item 572. The incipit is not given.

377.5. Contrapunctus. 4 Fugen. c. 1745–50 (source of date: WOLFF). BWV 1080
Ms.: US NHu, Mason collection, 4858a
A copy of Contrapunctus 1–4 of JSB's *Kunst der Fuge*

378. VI Sonate. 1757 or earlier (source of date: pub. date)
Ms.: D-ddr GOl, Ms. Mus. 21a, entitled "VI Sonate von P. E. Bach"
A copy of G. Benda's *Sei Sonate per il Cembalo*, Berlin: [G. L.] Winter, 1757. D-ddr GOl, Ms. Mus. 21a, a large ms. of keyboard music in upright format and apparently in a single (unknown) hand, contains only a few accurate attributions; most of its attributions seem to have been assigned almost randomly. No fewer than 14 works attributed to CPEB in this ms. are doubtful or spurious (items 378, 359, 374, 380, 382, 383, 385).

Incipits from Ms. Mus. 21a, 1st mvts.:

Sonata I

Sonata II

Sonata III

Sonata IV

Sonata V

Sonata VI

379. Sonata. c. 1763 (source of date: ROE). Wq n.v. 30; accompanied version listed in TERRY, C. S., 313
Ms.: D-brd B, P 364
Lit.: BERG, 244–48
Not attributed on the ms. ROE, 21–22, 77, notes that this is the keyboard part only of Johann Christian Bach's Sonata for Harpsichord, Violin and Cello, Op. II/1. Regarding P 364, see item 339.

Incipit from P 364, 1st mvt.:

380. Polonoise. c. 1765 (source of date: FALCK). FALCK, p. 4
Ms.: D-ddr GOl, Ms. Mus. 21a
By W. F. Bach, according to FALCK
Regarding the reliability of attribution in Ms. Mus. 21a, see item 378.

Incipit from Ms. Mus. 21a:

381. Clavier-Sonate. 1770 or earlier (source of date: pub. date). KAST, "J. C. F. Bach 18"; SCHÜNEMANN, xiii
Mss.: D-brd B, P 364 ("Del Sigl. Bach"); P 370 ("Dall' Sigr. Bach")
Early print: VIELERLEY, 164, where it is labeled (by CPEB, the editor) as a work of J. C. F. Bach. Lit. about VIELERLEY: See this entry in Bib.
Regarding P 364, see item 339; regarding P 370, see item 345.

Incipit from VIELERLEY, 1st mvt.:

382. 5., 4., 6. Sonate . . . . c. 1770 (source of date: pub. date). TERRY, C. S., 338–39
Ms.: D-ddr GOl, Ms. Mus. 21a
TERRY, C. S. lists nos. "5" and "6" as the 5th and 6th sonatas in a published set by Johann Christian Bach. No. "4" is by CPEB (item 73).
Regarding the reliability of attribution in Ms. Mus. 21a, see item 378.

Incipits from Ms. Mus. 21a, 1st mvts.:

Sonate 5

Sonate 6

383. Sonata. Concerto. c. 1771 (source of date: pub. date). TERRY, C. S., 297

Ms.: D-ddr GOl, Ms. Mus. 21a

An arrangement for unaccompanied keyboard of a published concerto by Johann Christian Bach (see WADE, 15, 100, 272–73). See also items 384, 490. In view of the unreliability of attribution in Ms. Mus. 21a (see item 378) and the publication date of the J. C. Bach concerto, it hardly seems likely that this is an arrangement by CPEB of his brother's composition.

Incipits from Ms. Mus. 21a, 1st and 2nd mvts.:

384. A favourite concerto for the harpsicord or piano forte [unaccompanied]. c. 1771? (source of date: pub. date of source of item 383). TERRY, C. S., 297

Early print: The above title, "Printed for C. and S. Thompson," London, [c. 1775]

By Johann Christian Bach. Vnt. of item 383, a.v. of item 490. See WADE, 15, 100, 272–73.

Same incipits as for item 383

385. Due sonate per il cembalo solo del sigl. Daniele Turck, la troisi- la quartiem mons. P. E. Bach. 1776 or earlier (date of the two attributed to CPEB. Source of date: pub. date)

Ms.: D-ddr Gol, Ms. Mus. 21a

Despite the (confusing) title, the 2 sonatas attributed to CPEB are also attributed to Türk as the 2nd and 3rd of *Sechs Sonaten für das Clavier*, Leipzig: Breitkopf, 1776.

Regarding the reliability of attribution in Ms. Mus. 21a, see item 378.

Incipits of the 2 attributed to CPEB, from Ms. Mus. 21a, 1st mvts.:

Sonata III

Sonata IV

386. La Bataille de Bergen, sonate pour le piano-forte ou harpe, composée par C. E. Bach. c. 1778 (source of date: the advertisement in HAMBURGER CORRESPONDENT). W. 272; TERRY, C. S., 343–44

Mss.: B Bc, 13.549; S Skma, Falléns saml. (entitled "Allegro de Bataille" by "Bach," in a collection of *Sonates pour le Clavecin Seul*); US Wc, M23.B13 (as Bataille de Rosbach" by "Bach"). One ms. source in GB Lbm attributes it to Johann Christian Bach, another there to "Graun."

Early prints, varying slightly: Worms: Kreitner, n.d.; Mannheim: Götz, n.d.; Paris: Huberty, n.d.; London: Jackson and Smith, 1782 (as "Sonata pour le Clavecin ou Forte Piano, qui Represente La Bataille de Rosbach," by "Mr. Bach")

Lit.: SHEDLOCK, 239; NEWMAN, 704; ROE, 98–99, 418

An advertisement in HAMBURGER CORRESPONDENT, 12 Dec. 1778, states that this work is by one C. E. Bach; it emphasizes in boldface type that the composer is "not the Hamburger." CPEB/WESTPHAL, in a probable reference to this piece: "The *Bataille* you mention is not by me. Such-like is not my style."

Incipits from 13.549:

387. Sonata. n.d. TERRY, C. S., 358; Beurm.-Anh. 14

Mss.: USSR KA, ms. Rf b 3, Bd. I (unverified); D-ddr Bds, Mus. ms. 30385

Rf b 3 is inaccessible (see item 192).

Not only the listing in TERRY, C. S. indicates the authorship of Johann Christian Bach, but BERG/JAMS, 298, points out that the copyist of 30385 also copied "da me J. C. Bach" onto the first page of the sonata.

Incipits from Beurm.-Anh. 14:

Allegretto

388. Fuga. n.d. BWV Anh. 90
Mss.: D-brd B, P 644, P 804; F Pc, D 567
P 644, copied and owned by F. A. Grasnick (d. 1877), contains only this work, "di Bach." P 804, copied in the 1st half of the 18th century (much of it by 1725) mostly by J. P. Kellner (1705–72), consists almost entirely of genuine JSB works and attributes this work "di Bach." F Pc, D 567, is entitled "Fuga in c di Bach. Scrips. Joh. Riegel"; a later hand has added, in pencil, "C.Ph." before "Bach." SCHMIEDER lists this work as dubious among JSB's works. Date, attributions, provenance, and CPEB's own statement (see item 349) all indicate that the added-on F Pc attribution is spurious.

Incipit from D 567:

389. Fuga. n.d. BWV 575
Listed by SCHMIEDER as genuine among J. S. Bach's works but edited as a work of CPEB by O. Beringer in *Two Fugues . . . by Philipp Emanuel Bach . . . . [and] W. Friedemann Bach,* London: Bosworth, 1899
See item 349.

Incipit from the Beringer edn.:

389.5. Fuga, Praeludium. n.d. (The Fuga is BWV Anh. 88, transposed.)
Ms.: D-ddr Bds, Mus. ms. 30195
This "Fuga" and "Praeludium" follow a "Praeludium" that is the retitled 2nd mvt. of item 179. Mus. ms. 30195 is an anthology of organ music whose copyists' attributions occasionally conflict: The retitled 2nd mvt. of item 179 is attributed "Von C. P. E. Bach" in a hand different from that of the copyist; the "Fuga," listed by SCHMIEDER as doubtful among JSB's works, is attributed by the copyist, at the end, "von Kirnberger"; the "Praeludium" that follows is attributed by the copyist "von C. P. E. Bach," but the apparently same copyist crossed this out and substituted "von Reichardt." My thanks to Rachel Wade for pointing out that this second "Praeludium" is correctly identified in Hanns Dennerlein's *Johann Friedrich Reichardt* (Münster, 1930) as slow mvt. of the fourth of Reichardt's six "Prussian" sonatas. And the fugue is branded as spurious by the plodding quality of its theme, combined with CPEB's statement limiting the number of fugues that should be attributed to him (see item 349).

Incipits of the "Fuga" and second "Praeludium" from Mus. ms. 30195:

389.6. [Two Fugue expositions on B-A-C-H]. n.d.
Ms.: D-brd B, P 774
P 774 leaves a few blank staves on the last page. On these staves a later, amateurish hand has added what looks like a composition lesson in the form of two fugue expositions on the notes B-A-C-H. The appearance of this subject is self-consciously pointed out at various places with "t"; at the bottom of the page is the gratuitous note that if CPEB's full name is spelled "In Italieno," the notes C-F-E might be added to the subject. This is obviously a spurious addition to a ms. of otherwise distinguished provenance.
See item 349. See also items 285, 371.9, 373, 484.6, 659, 733/41, 867.

390. Parthia. n.d. Wq n.v. 41
Ms.: D-brd B, P 843/844
The title p. bears the names of "Carlo," "Sebastian," and "Ph.E." Bach, with all three names scratched out. At the bottom of the title p. is this note in pencil: "C.Ph.E. Jugendarbeit. Vide [illegible]." P 843/844, copied in an anonymous and amateurish hand around 1800, consists only of items 390 and 391. The uncertain provenance of the ms. and the weakness of the music indicate that both works are spurious.

Incipits from P 843:

390.5. Gigue. n.d.
Ms.: D-brd B, N. Mus. ms. 10480

The ms., a 19th-century copy entitled "Preludii fürs Piano-Forte von Philip Emanuel Bach," consists of two works standardized by 19th-century pianists—the 1st mvt. of item 75, item 220 (the so-called "Solfeggietto"), and BWV 846 (JSB's C major prelude from Book I of *The Well-Tempered Clavier*)—plus this "Gigue" that has no known connection with CPEB.

Incipit from N. Mus. ms. 10480:

391. And.te ed allegro. n.d. Wq n.v. 42, 43
Ms.: D-brd B, P 844

Attributed only to "Bach" on the title p. "Allegro" is changed to "Presto" at the beginning of the 2nd mvt.
See item 390.

Incipits from P 844:

392. Le travagant. n.d. Wq n.v. 56
Ms.: D-brd B, P 754

Items 392–392.5 make up, in numerical order, the "VI Petites Pièces Arrangée pour le piano forte/Par Mons. Emanuel Bach./a Hambourg," constituting P 754. I am grateful to Miriam Terry for persuading me that the triviality of this set (not to mention the spelling of its title) brands it as spurious, despite CPEB's association with this type of character piece during part of his career.

Incipit of "Le Travagant" from P 754:

392.1. Le caressant ou affectueux–Le contente. n.d. Wq n.v. 57
See item 392.

Incipits from P 754:

392.2. Le petit maître. n.d. Wq n.v. 58
See item 392.

Incipits from P 754:

392.3. Le flegmatique–en colère. n.d. Wq n.v. 59
See item 392.

Incipits from P 754:

392.4. Le moribant. n.d. Wq n.v. 60
See item 392.

Incipits from P 754:

392.5. Il est vive. n.d. Wq n.v. 61
See item 392.

Incipit from P 754:

393. Allein Gott in der Höh sey Ehr. n.d. Wq n.v. 15
Ms.: D-brd B, P 766
Textless chorale, scored for keyboard (melody and figured bass, with the harmony filled in with dots). P 766, containing only items 75.5, 393, 394, is apparently in the hand of F. A. Grasnick (d. 1877).

Incipit from P 766:

394. Vater unser im Himmelreich. n.d. Wq n.v. 17
Ms.: D-brd B, P 766
The comment in item 393 applies also to this chorale.

Incipit from P 766:

395. Giga con variazioni. n.d.
Ms.: US Wc, M23.B13
M23.B13, consisting of items 395–97, bears the overall title "Sonati per il Cembalo con Variazioni." A later hand has added above this title, "Bach (C. Ph. E.)." The triviality of these works and the equivocal attribution rule out the possibility that CPEB is the composer.

Incipit from M23.B13:

396. Alla pol[acca] con variatio. n.d.
Ms.: US Wc, M23.B13
See item 395.

Incipit from M23.B13:

397. Minuetto [I–II]. n.d.
Ms.: US Wc, M23.B13
See item 395.

Incipits from M23.B13:

[The 2nd Minuetto is repeated after the 1st.]

398. Menueten zum tantzen: Menuet 1. n.d. Wq n.v. 49
Ms.: D-brd B, P 726
Fragment; upper part only, doubled by violin. P 726 contains items 54, 65, and 398 in the hand of an anonymous copyist of the 2nd half of the 18th century. This unattributed fragment appears on the last page after the words "Il Fine."

Incipit from P 726:

399. Tempo di men[uetto]-variation. n.d. Wq n.v. 45
Ms.: D-brd B, P 1154
Early print: Identified as a work of J. P. Kirnberger, after Tartini, in Kirnberger's *Vermischte Musikalien*, Berlin, 1769, 3–4. My thanks for this information to Ruth Engelhardt of Frankfurt am Main, who left a note dated 1974 in P 1154. P 1154, in the hands of 2 anonymous copyists of the 2nd half of the 18th century, consists of 11 keyboard works (7 known to be by CPEB, 2 [including item 399] known to be by Kirnberger [see KAST] and items 400, 401), along with one lied possibly by CPEB (item 768).

Incipits from P 1154:

400. [untitled]. n.d. Wq n.v. 46
Ms.: D-brd B, P 1154 (not attributed on the ms.)
By Kirnberger? See the note in item 399. Items 400 and 401 have the character of exercises: thinly harmonized scale passages marked (in item 401) with fingerings (originally intended as examples for Kirnberger's *Clavierübungen mit der [C. P. E.] Bachischen Applicatur?* See item 402). Items 400 and 401 are foreign to CPEB's style, even the style of his didactic works.

Incipit from P 1154:

401. [untitled]. n.d. Wq n.v. 47
Ms.: D-brd B, P 1154 (not attributed on the ms.)
By Kirnberger? See notes in items 399, 400.

Incipit from P 1154:

402. [untitled]. n.d. Wq n.v. 48
Ms.: D-brd B, P 704
Fragment, not attributed on the ms.; P 704 consists of items 147, 146, 148, and then this fragment. First 5 measures of Variatio IV from J. P. Kirnberger's *Clavierübungen mit der [C. P. E.] Bachischen Applicatur . . .*, 4 vols. (Berlin, 1762–66), II, 8. I am indebted to Ruth Engelhardt of Frankfurt am Main for this information, which she left in a note dated 1973 in P 704.

Incipit from P 704:

CONCERTOS AND SONATINAS

Authentic

(Note: The sonatinas in this section, beginning with item 449, might be categorized as miniature concertos, despite their frequent inflation through repetition, because their keyboard parts are *concertato*. These experimental works also resemble the sonata in their use of diminutive binary and sonata forms (hence the term *sonatina*); the suite, in their general adherence to a single key throughout, with fluctuations between major and minor modes; and the Viennese divertimento, in consisting of from two to ten sections or movements that are light or even trivial in musical content.)

403. Concerto per il cembalo concertato accompagnato da due violini, violetta e basso. 1733, rev. 1744 (NV 26). W. 1
Mss.: D-brd B, P 235, P 438 (both of which incorrectly attribute the work to J. S. Bach: see BWV Anh. 189), P 239; B Bc, 5887 (Michel); A Wgm, H 31198 (VII 23442); D-ddr LEm, Poel. Mus. ms. 41; CS KRa, II F 4 (?); PL Kj, St 495 (partial autog.)
Lit.: ULDALL, 27, 55; HAAG, 41–48, 60–61; CRICKMORE, 229; SUCHALLA/ORCHESTERSINFONIEN, 168–69; WADE, 3, 30, 34–36, 42, 88–89, 93, 95, 149, 235; DRUMMOND, 290, 328–29

Incipits from P 239:

2nd-mvt. incipit from P 235, 5887:

404. Concerto per il cembalo concertato accompagnato da due violini, violetta e basso. 1734, rev. 1743 (NV 26). W. 2
Mss.: D-brd B, P 354 (autog.), St 203; B Bc, 5887 (Westphal); D-ddr Dlb, 3029.O.4; D-ddr GOl, Ms. Mus. 5; US Wc, M1010.A2B13.W2
Early print: "Concerto pour le clavecin . . . Oeuvre 2," Paris: Huberty, n.d. The known lit. gives no evidence that this print was authorized by CPEB.
Lit.: ULDALL, 27; HAAG, 48–55, 60–61; CRICKMORE, 229; SUCHALLA/ORCHESTERSINFONIEN, 169–70; WADE, 25, 38, 45, 48–49, 55, 57–58, 86, 90, 95, 128, 131, 149, 235; DRUMMOND, 290, 306, 328–29; SCHULZE/WADE

Incipits from M1010.A2B13.W.2:

405. Concerto per il cembalo concertato accompagnato da due violini, violetta e basso. 1737, rev. 1745 (NV 26). W. 3
Mss.: D-brd B, P 708, St 214, St 496, St 497; D-ddr Bds, P 352 (autog.); B Bc, 5887 (Michel); US Wc, M1010.A2B13. W.3

Lit.: ULDALL, 28; HAAG, 55–61; CRICKMORE, 229; SUCHALLA/ORCHESTERSINFONIEN, 170; WADE, 20, 91, 140, 149, 235–36; DRUMMOND, 329; OTTENBERG, 43–46, 301; SCHULZE/WADE

Incipits from P 352:

406. Concerto per il cembalo concertato accompagnato da due violini, violetta e basso. 1738 (NV 26). W. 4
Mss.: D-brd B, St 498, St 618 (marked by CPEB); D-ddr Bds, M.Th. 18; B Bc, 5887 (keyboard part copied by Michel); D-ddr Dlb, 3029.0.5; D-ddr WRtl; D-ddr MEIr, Bl 14; US Wc, M1010.A2B13.W.4
Lit.: ULDALL, 28; HAAG, 65–69, 103–05; STEVENS, 23, 33–50, 66, 77, 116, 141–42, 145, 151, 164–66, 192; SUCHALLA/ORCHESTERSINFONIEN, 171; WADE, 48–49, 52, 86, 91–93, 133, 140, 149, 236; DRUMMOND, 329; SCHULZE/WADE

Incipits from M1010.A2B13.W.4:

407. Concerto per il cembalo concertato accompagnato da due violini, violetta e basso. 1739, rev. 1762 (NV 27). W. 5
Mss.: D-brd B, P 295 (3rd mvt. only, arranged for unaccompanied keyboard; Wq n.v. 40), St 197, St 523 (partly Michel; includes a written-out cadenza for the 2nd mvt.), Am.B. 99; D-ddr Bds, M.Th. 10; B Bc, 5887; D-brd DS, Mus. ms. 970; D-ddr Dlb, 3029.0.6; D-ddr WRtl, Mus. IV c:8; US Wc, M1010.A2B13.W.5 (with an added part for violone); US BE, Ms. 727 (see item 481.5)

Lit.: ULDALL, 28–29; HAAG, 70–73, 103–05; STEVENS, 50, 66, 116, 141–42, 145, 151, 167; SUCHALLA/ORCHESTERSINFONIEN, 171–72; WADE, 18, 38, 41, 47–48, 92–95, 98, 112, 128, 130–131, 149, 236–37, 309, 333; ; DRUMMOND, 290, 329; SCHULZE/WADE
Cadenza(s): See item 264.

Incipits from M1010.A2B13.W.5:

408. Concerto doppio a due cembali concertati accompagnati da due corni, due violini, violetta e basso. 1740 (NV 27). W. 46
Mss.: D-brd B, St 209 (marked by CPEB), St 362 (partly autog.), Am.B. 100; D-ddr Bds, P 352 (autog.), M.Th. 16; B Bc, 5889 (Michel); US Wc, M1010.A2B13.W.46; US AA, Music Microfilm Archive No. 67 (copy of a ms. once owned by A. E. Grell (1800–86); in the G. B. Weston collection, Cambridge, Mass., at the time of filming); US CA, fMS Mus. 66 (the Grell ms., donated by Weston in the mid-20th century to US CA)

Mod. edn. for the full instrumentation and in a 2-keyboard arrangement, both with additions to the harmony: H. Schwartz, Leipzig: Steingräber, [c. 1916]
Lit.: ULDALL, 52; SUCHALLA/ORCHESTERSINFONIEN, 218–19; WADE, 20, 27, 31, 41, 54, 75–76, 100, 102, 149, 237–38, 334; DRUMMOND, 290–91, 294; SCHULZE/WADE
A.v.: P 352 and St 209 are without horns.
Cadenza(s): See item 264.

Incipits from P 352:

409. Concerto per il cembalo concertato accompagnato da due violini, violetta e basso. 1740 (NV 27). W. 6

Mss.: D-brd B, P 712, St 217 (Michel?), St 532, St 533, Am.B. 99 (autog.); D-ddr Bds, M.Th.19; B Bc, 5887 (Michel); GB Lbm, Add. 31679; US Wc, M1010.A2B13.W.6 (with an added part for violone); US BE, ms. 728

Mod. edn.: F. Oberdörffer, Kassel: Bärenreiter, 1952

Lit.: ULDALL, 29–30; HAAG, 73–79, 103–05; CRICKMORE, 231; STEVENS, 31, 142–45, 208–09; SUCHALLA/ ORCHESTERSINFONIEN, 172–73; WADE, 31, 38, 41, 47, 128, 136, 149, 238, 335; DRUMMOND, 303–06, 313–14

See item 483.

Cadenza(s): See item 264.

Incipits from M1010.A2B13.W.6:

410. Concerto per il cembalo concertato accompagnato da due violini, violetta e basso. 1740 (NV 27). W. 7

Mss.: D-brd B, St 219, St 515 (marked by CPEB); D-ddr Bds, P 352 (autog.); B Bc, 5887 (Michel); US Wc, M1010.A2B13. W.7

Lit.: ULDALL, 30–31; HAAG, 79–81, 103–05; STEVENS, 31, 50–56, 58–59, 61–67, 69, 71, 95–96, 144–45; SUCHALLA/ ORCHESTERSINFONIEN, 173–74; WADE, 20, 31, 69–70, 78–79, 89, 100, 140, 149, 238–39; SCHULZE/WADE

Incipits from P 352:

411. Concerto per il cembalo concertato accompagnato da due violini, violetta e basso. 1741 (NV 27). W. 8

Mss.: D-brd B, St 218; D-ddr Bds, P 352 (autog.); B Bc, 5887; US Wc, M1010.A2B13.W.8; D-brd BFb, Bach 20; D-ddr WRtl; US BE, Ms. 729; a ms. is in the private collection of E. N. Kulukundis (U.S.).

Lit.: ULDALL, 30–31; HAAG, 81–84, 103–05; STEVENS, 24, 40–42, 56–66, 69, 71, 95–96, 106–07, 142, 144; SUCHALLA/ ORCHESTERSINFONIEN, 174–75; WADE, 31, 45, 53, 128, 131, 134, 140, 146, 149, 239; DRUMMOND, 290; SCHULZE/WADE; SCHULENBERG/INSTRUMENTAL, 134–35

Incipits from P 352:

412. Concerto per il cembalo concertato accompagnato da due violini, violetta e basso. 1742 (NV 28). W. 9

Mss.: D-ddr Bds, P 352 (autog.); B Bc, 5887 (with the two violin parts occasionally interchanged); D-ddr GOl, Ms. Mus. 5; PL Wu, Mf 1700; US Wc, M1010.A2B13.W.9 (a.v.: "Cembalo o Organo Concertato," with an added part for violone)

Lit.: ULDALL, 31; HAAG, 84–87, 103–05; STEVENS, 31, 66–67, 70, 72, 106–07, 115, 127, 144; SUCHALLA/OR-CHESTERSINFONIEN, 174–76; WADE, 47, 52, 140, 149, 239–40; SCHULZE/WADE

Incipits from P 352:

413. Concerto per il cembalo concertato accompagnato da due violini, violetta e basso. 1742 (NV 28). W. 10

Mss.: B Bc, 5887 (Michel); D-ddr LEb, Gorke 354 (cembalo part only)

Lit.: ULDALL, 31; HAAG, 87–91, 103–05; STEVENS, 66–67, 70, 72, 106–07, 115, 137–39, 145–49, 158–60; SUCHALLA/ ORCHESTERSINFONIEN, 176–77; WADE, 52–53, 128, 149, 240, 334; DRUMMOND, 290
Cadenza(s): See item 264.

Incipits from 5887:

414. Concerto per il cembalo concertato accompagnato da due violini, violetta e basso. 1743 (NV 28). W. 11
Mss.: D-brd B, P 354 (autog.), St 202; B Bc, 12.217 (in J. C. F. Bach's hand, says a note on the wrapper); D-ddr GOl, Ms. Mus. 5; D-ddr Dlb, 2.0.3,4; F Pc, Ms. 1552 a–e (not autog.); PL Wu, 8172; Dk Kmk, R 443; US AA, M1105.B116.C7.17--a; US BE, Ms. 730 (lacking cembalo part)
Early prints: "Concerto per il Cembalo concertato accompagnato da 2 Violini, Violetta e Basso. composto da Carlo Filippo Emanuele Bach, Musico di Camera di S.M. il Rè de Prussia, Alle Spese di Balthas. Schmid. Norimb. [1745]"; CONCERTOS I
Lit.: BITTER/BRÜDER, I, 58; ULDALL, 31; HAAG, 91–93, 103–05; CRICKMORE, 232; STEVENS, 66–67; SUCHALLA/ORCHESTERSINFONIEN, 177–78; WADE, 20, 32, 45–47, 52–53, 55–56, 58, 69–70, 149, 240–41, 332, 334; DRUMMOND, 312–13
Cadenza(s): See item 264.

Incipits from the Schmid print:

415. Concerto per il cembalo concertato accompagnato da due violini, violetta e basso. 1744 (NV 28). W. 12
Mss.: D-brd B, St 210, St 361, St 541; D-ddr Bds, P 352 (autog.); B Bc, 5887; F Pc, Ms. 1553 a–e (not autog.); US Wc, M1010.A2B13.W.12; US BE, Ms. 731
Lit.: ULDALL, 31–32; HAAG, 94–98, 103–05; STEVENS, 31, 66–72; SUCHALLA/ORCHESTERSINFONIEN, 179; WADE, 45–47, 70, 78, 89, 128, 131, 140, 149, 241; DRUMMOND, 290; SCHULZE/WADE

Incipits from P 352:

416. Concerto per il cembalo concertato accompagnato da due violini, violetta e basso. 1744 (NV 28). W. 13
Mss.: D-brd B, St 200; B Bc, 5887 (Michel); US Wc, M1010.A2B13.W.13 (with "2 Bassi Rippieni")
Lit.: ULDALL, 32; HAAG, 98–101, 103–05, 115–16; STEVENS, 23–32, 66, 77–78, 139–40, 168–72, 174; SUCHALLA/ ORCHESTERSINFONIEN, 179–80; WADE, 47, 149, 241, 333–34
No a.v. or arr. of this work as a flute concerto has yet been identified, although SCHMID/MGG, col. 932, lists such a version.
Cadenza(s): See item 264.

Incipits from M1010.A2B13.W.13:

417. Concerto per il cembalo concertato accompagnato da due violini, violetta e basso. 1744 (NV 28). W. 14
Mss.: D-brd B, St 207 (the Winter print with added ms.),

St 365 (the Winter print with added ms.), St 516, St 517 (including 2 written-out cadenzas for the 1st mvt. and 2 for the 2nd mvt.), St 627, Am.B. 93, BP 146; Dk Kmk, R. 444 (lent to DK Kk); F Pc, Ms. 1550 a–c (not autog.)

Early prints: "Concerto III per il Cembalo concertato, accompagnato da II. Violini, Violetta e Basso, composto da Carlo Filippo Emanuele Bach. In Berlino alle spese di G. L. Winter. MDCCLX"; CONCERTOS I

Lit.: VRIESLANDER/BACH, 93–94; ULDALL, 32–33; HAAG, 101–05; CRICKMORE, 230–31; STEVENS, 127; SUCHALLA/ORCHESTERSINFONIEN, 180–81; WADE, 20, 30, 34, 38, 41, 45–46, 53, 55–56, 58, 131, 149, 241–42, 332, 334; DRUMMOND, 307, 311–12, 317; OTTENBERG, 67, 69–70; SCHULENBERG/INSTRUMENTAL, 43–44, 72–74

A.v.: St 517 includes parts for 2 horns.

Cadenza(s): See item 264.

On p. 369 of CPEB/AUTOBIOGRAPHY in the Newman translation there is reference to a "flute" concerto in E major published by Winter in 1760; this is corrected to mean a cembalo concerto, W. 14, in the correction sheet supplied with CPEB/AUTOBIOGRAPHY in Newman's annotated facsimile edition.

Incipits from the Winter print:

418. Concerto per il cembalo concertato accompagnato da due violini, violetta e basso. 1745 (NV 29). W. 15

Mss.: D-ddr Bds, P 352 (autog.); B Bc, 26.646 (incomplete); US Wc, M1010.A2B13.W.15 (vnt., with an added part for violone)

Lit.: ULDALL, 33–34; HAAG, 106–09, 146–47; STEVENS, 31, 66–67, 172–74; SUCHALLA/ORCHESTERSINFONIEN, 181–82; WADE, 17, 71, 73–74, 76, 93, 149, 242, 333; SCHULZE/WADE

Cadenza(s): See item 264.

Incipits from P 352:

419. Concerto per il cembalo concertato accompagnato da due violine, violetta e basso. 1745 (rev. of a 1738 version?) (NV 29). W. 16

Mss.: D-brd B, St 360, St 499 (including a written-out cadenza for the 2nd mvt.); B Bc, 5887 (Michel); US BE, Ms. 732

Lit.: ULDALL, 34; HAAG, 109–12, 146–47; STEVENS, 20, 70–71, 127; SUCHALLA/ORCHESTERSINFONIEN, 182–83; WADE, 16, 51–52, 128, 146, 148–49, 242; DRUMMOND, 290

Vnts.: 5887 is an ornamented version of St 360 and St 499. Ms. 732 is inscribed with two dates, 1738 and 1745, with the former crossed out and followed by a question mark; this is a vnt., apparently the original version, according to BUCK; but see WADE/JAMS.

Incipits from St 499:

420. Concerto per il cembalo concertato accompagnato da due violini, violetta e basso. 1745 (NV 29). W. 17

Mss.: D-brd B, P 714, St 542, St 543, St 544, St 545 (cembalo part only); D-ddr Bds, P 352 (autog.), M.Th. 12; B Bc, 5887; F Pc, Ms. 1551 a–e (not autog.?); D-ddr SWl, 859/4; US Wc, M1010.A2B13.W.17

Lit.: ULDALL, 34; HAAG, 112–16, 146–47; CRICKMORE, 232–33; STEVENS, 70–71; SUCHALLA/ORCHESTERSINFONIEN, 183–84; WADE, 20–21, 45–47, 49, 70–71, 128, 140, 149, 242–43, 332; DRUMMOND, 290; SCHULZE/WADE; SCHULENBERG/INSTRUMENTAL, 35–37, 131

Cadenza(s): See item 264.

Incipits from P 352:

421. Concerto per il cembalo concertato accompagnato da due violini, violetta e basso. 1745 (NV 29). W. 18

Mss.: D-brd B, St 199, St 271, St 366, St 508, St 576, BP 145; D-ddr Bds, P 352 (autog.), M.Th. 20; D-ddr GOl, Ms. Mus. 4/1; B Bc, 5887; DK Kmk, R 401; US Wc, M1010.A2B13.W.18; US BE, Ms. 733

Early print: CONCERTOS II

Mod. edn.: H. Riemann, Leipzig: Steingräber, 188? (arranged for 2 keyboards)

Lit.: ULDALL, 34; HAAG, 116–18, 146–47; STEVENS, 20, 31, 70–71; SUCHALLA/ORCHESTERSINFONIEN, 184–85; WADE, 18, 20–21, 53, 55, 58, 66–67, 73, 128, 131, 146, 149, 243–44; DRUMMOND, 290; SCHULZE/WADE

See item 483.

Incipits from P 352:

422. Concerto per il cembalo concertato accompagnato da due violini, violetta e basso. 1746 (NV 29). W. 19

Mss.: D-brd B, St 220, St 512, St 513 (partly Michel), St 514, St 628, Am.B. 97; D-ddr Bds, P 352 (autog.); D-ddr GOl (attributed to "Gius. Fr. Bach"); B Bc, 5887; A Wgm, Q 11689 (VII 18933); US Wc, M1010.A2B13.W.19 (with an added part for violone)

Lit.: ULDALL, 34–35; HAAG, 118–21, 146–47; STEVENS, 71, 149–50; SUCHALLA/ORCHESTERSINFONIEN, 185–86; WADE, 16, 18, 31, 38, 42, 47, 54, 89, 128, 131, 134, 149, 244; DRUMMOND, 290; SCHULZE/WADE

Incipits from P 352:

423. Concerto per il cembalo concertato accompagnato da due violini, violetta e basso. 1746 (NV 29). W. 20

Mss.: D-brd B, P 354 (autog.), St 193, St 493 (partly autog.), Am.B. 96; B Bc, 5887 (Michel); US Wc, M1010.A2B13.W. 20; a ms. is in the private collection of E. N. Kulukundis (U.S.).

Lit.: ULDALL, 35; HAAG, 122–24, 146–47; STEVENS, 24, 86–98, 124, 148, 160–61, 181–82, 192; SUCHALLA/ORCHESTERSINFONIEN, 186; WADE, 27, 38, 128, 131, 139–40, 149, 245, 331; DRUMMOND, 290

Cadenza(s): See item 264.

Incipits from P 354:

424. Concerto per il cembalo concertato accompagnato da due violini, violetta e basso. 1747, rev. 1775 (NV 30). W. 21

Mss.: B Bc, 5887 (Michel); US Wc, M1010.A2B13.W.21 (with an extra part for violone)

Lit.: HAAG, 124–27, 146–47; SUCHALLA/ORCHESTERSINFONIEN, 187; WADE, 47, 95, 149, 245, 333

Cadenza(s): See item 264.

Incipits from 5887:

425. Concerto per il cembalo concertato accompagnato da due violini, violetta e basso. 1747 (NV 30). W. 22
Ms.: B Bc, 5887 (Michel)
Lit.: HAAG, 127–31, 146–47; STEVENS, 20, 106–07; SUCHALLA/ORCHESTERSINFONIEN, 187–88; WADE, 110–11, 149, 245, 310; DRUMMOND, 293
A.v.: item 484.1

Incipits from 5887:

426. Deleted

427. Concerto per il cembalo concertato accompagnato da due violini, violetta e basso. 1748 (NV 30). W. 23
Mss.: D-brd B, P 354 (autog.), P 715; B Bc, 5887 (Michel); US Wc, M1010.A2B13.W.23
Mod. edns.: A. Schering and H. J. Moser in *Denkmäler deutscher Tonkunst*, XXIX–XXX (Leipzig, 1904–08, reprinted Wiesbaden, 1958); B. Hinze-Reinhold, Leipzig: Steingräber, 1909–13, reprinted 1964, for the full instrumentation and in a 2-keyboard arrangement; K. Straube, Leipzig: Breitkopf & Härtel, 1926; G. Wertheim, Leipzig: Breitkopf & Härtel, 1956; G. Darvas, Budapest: Editio Musica, 1968, for the full instrumentation and in a 2-keyboard arrangement
Lit.: BÜCKEN, 168; GEIRINGER/BACH, 365; HAAG, 131–34, 146–47; CRICKMORE, 229; STEVENS, 23, 72–86, 89–93, 95–99, 106, 141, 150–51, 161–62, 176, 184–85, 190, 192; SUCHALLA/ORCHESTERSINFONIEN, 188–89; WELLESZ–STERNFELD/CONCERTO, 453–54; WADE, 80, 98–99, 149, 245–46, 333; DRUMMOND, 304, 312, 314–17, 332–33, 337; OTTENBERG, 70–72; SCHULENBERG/INSTRUMENTAL, 6, 50–52, 130, 132–33, 141, 144–45, 163
Cadenza(s): See item 264.

Incipits from P 354:

428. Concerto per il cembalo concertato accompagnato da due violini, violetta e basso. 1748 (rev. of an earlier version?) (NV 30). W. 24
Mss.: D-brd B, P 709, St 208, St 363, St 504 (cembalo part only), St 505 (with a written-out cadenza for the 2nd mvt.), Am.B. 94; D-ddr Bds, M.Th. 13; B Bc, 5887; DK Kmk, R. 402; D-ddr WRtl, Mus IV c:9; US Wc, M1010.A2B13.W.24 (with an extra part for violone); US BE, Ms. 734 (viola and bass parts only, apparently from an earlier a.v.; see BUCK)
Early print: CONCERTOS II
Lit.: ULDALL, 36; HAAG, 134–36, 146–47; STEVENS, 106; SUCHALLA/ORCHESTERSINFONIEN, 189–90; WADE, 14, 20, 51, 53, 55, 58, 97, 101, 128, 131, 246, 331–32; DRUMMOND, 290
Cadenza(s): See item 264.
WADE/JAMS says that these sources present four different versions of the work: version A, St 208, St 505, P 709, Mus IV c:9; version B, 5887, St 363, Am.B. 94; version C, St 504, M1010.A2B13.W.24; version D, CONCERTOS II.

Incipits from M1010.A2B13.W.24:

429. Concerto per il cembalo concertato accompagnato da due violini, violetta e basso. 1749 (NV 30). W. 25
Mss.: D-brd B, P 355 (autog.), St 531, BP 149; D-ddr Bds, M.Th. 15; B Bc, 14.885 (2nd mvt. only, vnt.); F Pc, Ms. 1549 a–e (not autog.); D-ddr LEb, Gorke 38; D-ddr GOl, Ms. Mus. 4/2; D-ddr SWl, Mus. 847; DK Kmk, R.421; S L, Samml. Kraus 188; D-ddr Dlb, 3029.0.9, 3029.0.10 (a.v. for 2 unaccompanied keyboards); an exemplar of the Schmid print in GB Lbm contains a ms. copy of the 2nd mvt. in vnt. form.
Early prints: "Concerto per il Cembalo concertato, accom-

pagnato da II. Violini, Violetta, Basso composto da Carlo Filippo Emanuele Bach, Musico di Camera di S. M. il RE di Prussia. Alle spese della Vedova di Balth. Schmid. Norimb [1752]"; CONCERTOS I

Lit.: BITTER/BRÜDER, I, 58; ULDALL, 36–37; HAAG, 136–38, 146–47; CRICKMORE, 232, 238; STEVENS, 108, 216; SUCHALLA/ORCHESTERSINFONIEN, 190–92; WADE, 13–14, 18, 46–47, 49, 52–53, 55–56, 58, 80–82, 149, 247, 312, 331–33; DRUMMOND, 316, 319–20, 334

Cadenza(s): See item 264.

Incipits from P 355:

430. Concerto per il cembalo concertato accompagnato da due violini, violetta e basso. 1750 (NV 31). W. 26

Mss.: D-brd B, BP 150; D-ddr Bds, Mb 802 (missing); B Bc, 5887 (Michel); US Wc, M1010.A2B13.W.26; a ms. is in the private collection of E. N. Kulukundis (U.S.).

Mod. edn. for the full instrumentation and in a 2-keyboard arrangement: G. Amft, Leipzig: Kahnt, 1905

Lit.: ULDALL, 37; HAAG, 138–44, 146–47; STEVENS, 128, 162–63; SUCHALLA/ORCHESTERSINFONIEN, 192–93; WELLESZ–STERNFELD/CONCERTO, 453–54; WADE, 14, 101, 108, 128, 139–40, 149, 248; DRUMMOND, 290, 293, 335; SCHULENBERG/INSTRUMENTAL, 47

A.v.: items 431, 432

Incipits from 5887:

431. Concerto a flauto traverso concertato accompagnato da due violini, violetta e basso. Probably c. 1750 (source of date: date of item 430). W. 166

Ms.: B Bc, 5516 (Michel)

Mod. edns.: F. Grützmacher, Leipzig: Breitkopf & Härtel, 1893 (orchestral parts reduced for keyboard); G. Amft, Leipzig: Kahnt, 1905 (orchestral parts reduced for keyboard)

Lit.: HAAG, 138–44, 146–47; STEVENS, 128; SUCHALLA/ORCHESTERSINFONIEN, 239: WADE, 150

A.v.: items 430, 432

Incipits from 5516: Same as for item 430

432. Concerto a violoncello concertato accompagnato da due violini, violetta e basso. Probably c. 1750 (source of date: date of item 430). W. 170

Mss.: D-brd B, P 355 (autog.); B Bc, 5633 (Michel)

Mod. edns.: F. Grützmacher, Leipzig: Breitkopf & Härtel, 1893 (orchestral parts reduced for keyboard); R. Boulay, Paris: Luduc, 1965 (arranged for viola and piano). Since the 3 versions are alike in their orchestral parts—not always the case with such a.v.—a single edn. offering the option of having the harpsichord, flute, or cello as soloist was made by W. Altmann, London: Eulenburg, 1938, reprinted 1954.

Lit.: ULDALL, 57; HAAG, 138–44, 146–47; STEVENS, 128; SUCHALLA/ORCHESTERSINFONIEN, 242–43; WADE, 108, 332

A.v.: items 430, 431. Cadenza(s): See item 264.

Incipits from P 355: same as for item 430

433. Concerto per il cembalo concertato accompagnato da due violini, viola e basso, con due trombe o corni, tympani, due oboi e due flauti ad libitum. 1750 (NV 31). W. 27

Mss.: D-brd B, P 355 (autog., for cembalo and strings only); B Bc, 5887 (Michel); GB Lbm, Add. 29907 (for cembalo and strings only); US Wc, M1010.A2B13.W.27 (with 2 bass parts, and lacking timpani part)

Mod. edn. for the full instrumentation: E. N. Kulukundis, Madison, Wisc.: A-R Editions, 1970

Lit.: ULDALL, 37; HAAG, 144–47; CRICKMORE, 232; STEVENS, 108, 135, 174–76; SUCHALLA/ORCHESTERSINFONIEN, 193; WADE, 47, 79–80, 99–101, 128, 148, 248, 332, 334; DRUMMOND, 290, 294–95, 302–03

Cadenza(s): See item 264.

NV, p. 31, gives the basic instrumentation as strings with a pair of horns, with the ad lib. addition consisting of 3 trumpets, timpani, 2 oboes, 2 flutes.

Incipits from 5887:

434. Concerto per il cembalo concertato accompagnato da due violini, violetta e basso. 1751 (NV 31). W. 28

Mss.: D-brd B, St 221 (with a written-out cadenza for the 2nd mvt.); D-ddr Bds, M.Th. 21; B Bc, 5887 (Michel, cembalo part only); Dk Kmk, R. 403; a ms. is in the private collection of E. N. Kulukundis (U.S.).

Lit.: ULDALL, 38; HAAG, 149–51, 187–88; STEVENS, 108, 128, 208–09, 216; SUCHALLA/ORCHESTERSINFONIEN, 194–95; WADE, 53, 128, 131, 139–40, 149–50, 248; DRUMMOND, 290, 293; SCHULENBERG/INSTRUMENTAL, 47

A.v.: items 435–36

Incipits from St 221:

435. Concerto a flauto traverso concertato accompagnato da due violini, violetta e basso. Probably c. 1751 (source of date: date of item 434). W. 167

Ms.: B Bc, 5516 (Michel)

Mod. edn.: D. Lasocki, London: Musica Rara, 1975

Lit.: STEVENS, 128; SUCHALLA/ORCHESTERSINFO-NIEN, 240; WADE, 150

A.v.: items 434, 436. Though the incipits in items 434–36 are identical, the orchestral parts differ.

Not the "flute" concerto in B♭ reported in the Newman commentary on CPEB/AUTOBIOGRAPHY (p. 368 in *The Musical Quarterly*) to have been pub. in 1752 by Schmid, since not a single exemplar of such a print has yet been identified. CPEB was referring here to the harpsichord concerto in the same key that Schmid published in the same year (item 429).

Incipits from 5516: same as for item 434

92

436. Concerto a violoncello concertato accompagnato da due violini, violetta e basso. Probably c. 1751 (source of date: date of item 434). W. 171

Ms.: B Bc, 5633 (Michel)

Mod. edns.: P. Klengel and W. Schulz, Leipzig: Breitkopf & Härtel, 1930 (orchestral parts reduced for keyboard); W. Schulz, Leipzig: Breitkopf & Härtel, 1939

Lit.: STEVENS, 128; SUCHALLA/ORCHESTERSINFO-NIEN, 243–44; WELLESZ–STERNFELD/CONCERTO, 454; WADE, 150, 332; DRUMMOND, 304, 334–35

A.v.: items 434, 435

Cadenza(s) See item 264.

Incipits from 5633: same as for item 434

437. Concerto per il cembalo concertato accompagnato da due violini, violetta e basso. 1753 (NV 31). W. 29

Mss.: B Bc, 5887 (Michel); US Wc, M1010.A2B13.W.29

Lit.: ULDALL, 38; HAAG, 151–53, 187–88; STEVENS, 109, 113–116, 128; SUCHALLA/ORCHESTERSINFONIEN, 195; WADE, 31, 54, 103, 108, 128, 149, 248; DRUMMOND, 290, 293, 304, 316; ROE, 118, 120, 124; SCHULENBERG/INSTRUMENTAL, 47, 131–32

A.v.: items 438, 439

Incipits from M1010.A2B13.W.29:

438. Concerto a flauto traverso concertato accompagnato da due violini, violetta e basso. Probably c. 1753 (source of date: date of item 437). W. 168

Ms.: B Bc, 5515 (Michel)

Mod. edns.: G. Piccioli, New York: International, 1954 (arranged for flute and piano); H. M. Kneihs, London: Eulenburg, 1967

Lit.: STEVENS, 128; SUCHALLA/ORCHESTERSINFO-NIEN, 241; WADE, 150

A.v.: items 437, 439

Incipits from 5515: same as for item 437

439. Concerto a violoncello concertato accompagnato da due violini, violetta e basso. Probably c. 1753 (source of date: date of item 437). W. 172

Ms.: B Bc, 5633 (Michel)

Mod. edns., all arranged for cello and piano: F. Pollain, Paris: Senart, 1924 (heavily overedited, and with anachronistic cadenzas added by the editor); G. Cassado, New York: International, 1949; H. M. Kneihs, London: Eulenburg, 1968

Lit.: STEVENS, 128; SUCHALLA/ORCHESTERSINFONIEN, 245; WADE, 150, 333

A.v.: items 437, 438

Cadenza(s): See item 264.

Incipits from 5633: same as for item 437

440. Concerto per il cembalo concertato accompagnato da due violini, violetta e basso. 1753 (NV 32). W. 30

Mss.: D-brd B, P 354 (autog.), St 510 (on the cover in CPEB's hand: "ist wenig bekannt"), St 511 (cembalo part only); B Bc, 5887

Lit.: ULDALL, 38; HAAG, 153–57, 187–88; STEVENS, 116–19, 187–89, 194–98, 204–08, 213–14, 242; SUCHALLA/ORCHESTERSINFONIEN, 196; WADE, 127, 149, 248–49, 333–34; DRUMMOND, 321–22

Cadenza(s): See item 264.

Incipits from P 354:

441. Concerto per il cembalo concertato accompagnato da due violini, violetta e basso. 1753 (NV 32). W. 31

Mss.: D-brd B, P 711 (autog., containing only written-out ornamentations of the 2nd mvt.), St 524 (partly autog., containing the 2nd mvt., then the entire concerto); D-ddr Bds, P 352 (autog.); B Bc, 5887 (Michel); a ms. is in the private collection of E. N. Kulukundis (U.S.).

Mod. edn.: G. Balla, Kassel: Bärenreiter, 1976

Lit.: ULDALL, 38–39; HAAG, 157–61, 187–88; CRICKMORE, 229, 232; STEVENS, 24, 125, 189–90, 202–04, 213, 215–25, 242; SUCHALLA/ORCHESTERSINFONIEN, 196–97; WADE, 27, 96–97, 100, 127, 139–40, 149, 249, 333; DRUMMOND, 321, 331; OTTENBERG, 72, 266; SCHULZE/WADE; SCHULENBERG/INSTRUMENTAL, 24–25, 51–55

Cadenza(s): See item 264.

Incipits from P 352:

442. Concerto per il cembalo concertato accompagnato da due violini, violetta e basso. 1754 (NV 32). W. 32

Mss.: D-brd B, St 216, St 534 (partly autog.), St 535, St 536, St 619, Am.B. 95, BP 148 (lacking 1st violin part); D-ddr Bds, P 352 (autog.), M.Th. 14; B Bc, 5887 (Westphal?); D-brd Bhm; D-brd Hs; D-brd DS, Mus. ms. 522 (title p. in CPEB's hand); DK Kk, mu 6309.1730; US Wc, M1010.A2B13.W.32; US BE, Ms. 735; US NHu, Mason collection, 5017 (first p. of cembalo part only)

Lit.: ULDALL, 39; HAAG, 161–63, 187–88; STEVENS, 120–25, 154, 198–201; SUCHALLA/ORCHESTERSINFONIEN, 197–98; WADE, 19–21, 27, 30–31, 39, 41, 45, 47–48, 53–54, 74–75, 97, 131, 140, 149, 249–50, 333–34; DRUMMOND, 290, 334; SCHULZE/WADE

A.v.: Wotquenne's title, listing 2 flutes among the instrumentation, applies only to St 534 and 5887.

See item 483.

Cadenza(s): See item 264.

Incipits from P 352:

443. Concerto per il cembalo concertato accompagnato da due violini, violetta e basso. 1755 (NV 32). W. 33

Mss.: D-brd B, St 211, St 538 (marked by CPEB), St 539 (marked by CPEB); D-ddr Bds, P 354 (autog., incomplete); B Bc, 5888 (Westphal); D-ddr WRtl; DK Kk, mu 6309.1731; GB Lbm, Add. 29907

Mod. edn.: F. Oberdörffer, Kassel: Bärenreiter, 1952

Lit.: ULDALL, 39–41; HAAG, 163–66, 187–88; STEVENS, 154–58, 176, 184–87, 192–94, 200; SUCHALLA/ORCHESTERSINFONIEN, 198–99; WADE, 20, 128, 149, 250–51; DRUMMOND, 290

See item 483.

Incipits from St 538:

444. Concerto per l'organo overo il cembalo concertato accompagnato da due violini, violetta e basso. 1755 (NV 32). W. 34

Mss.: D-brd B, P 354 (autog., entitled "Concerto per il Organo"), P 769 (partly autog.; see note in item 445), P 1211 (cembalo part only), N. Mus. ms. 42 (autog. title p. on wrapper; includes 5 cadenzas for 1st mvt., 2 cadenzas for 2nd mvt., 2 "Fermate" for 3rd mvt., all in Michel's [?] hand; owner and main copyist was J. H. Grave), St 213, St 359, St 501, St 502, BP 147; D-ddr Bds, St 500 (partly autog., with rev. in CPEB's hand), M.Th. 17 (lacking bass part); B Bc, 5887; D-ddr GÖl, Ms. Mus. 5; US Wc, M1010.A2B13.W.34

Early print: CONCERTOS II

Mod. edn. (as organ, harpsichord, or piano concerto): H. Winter, Hamburg: Sikorski, 1964

Lit.: ULDALL, 41–42; HAAG, 166–70, 187–88; STEVENS, 128, 165–67, 208–09; SUCHALLA/ORCHESTERSINFONIEN, 199–200; COHEN, 111; WADE, 20–21, 31, 47, 55, 58, 70, 104–05, 107, 128, 131–32, 149, 251, 332–33, 335; DRUMMOND, 290–91, 293, 316; OTTENBERG, 124

A.v.: item 445. In P 1211, St 213, St 501, St 500, and Ms. Mus. 5 the work is termed simply a harpsichord concerto. NV, p. 32, lists the organ first in the title.

Cadenza(s): See item 264.

Incipits from 5887:

445. Concerto a flauto traverso concertato accompagnato da due violini, violetta e basso. 1755 or later (source of date: date of item 444). W. 169

Mss.: D-brd B, P 769 (partly autog.); B Bc, 5515 (Michel)

Mod. edn.: D. Lasocki, London: Musica Rara, 1973

Lit.: SUCHALLA/ORCHESTERSINFONIEN, 241–42; WADE, 103–10

A.v. of item 444, whose listing in NV, 32, notes that it "ist auch für die Flöte gesetzt." Westphal's catalogue adds, "jedoch etwas verändert" (meaning that the orchestral parts are also changed). These statements seem to indicate that item 444 is the original version. ULDALL, 56, and Lasocki incorrectly describe P 769 as an "autograph"; only the solo flute part and a few corrections are in CPEB's hand. P 769 was at first a complete score, in an anonymous hand, of the item 444 version of this concerto but with a blank staff provided for a solo flute part. CPEB wrote the solo flute part into this blank staff as an optional substitute for the keyboard part, which obviously shows that the keyboard version did indeed come first. ULDALL's description (p. 56) of a "durchgestrichen" keyboard part is incorrect.

Incipits from P 769: same as for item 444

446. Concerto per l'organo overo il cembalo concertato accompagnato da due corni, due violini, violetta e basso. 1759 (NV 33). W. 35

Mss.: D-brd B, P 710, St 206, St 518, St 519 (marked by CPEB), St 520, St 581 (with a written-out cadenza); D-ddr Bds, P 356 (partly autog.); B Bc, 5887, 12217; D-ddr WRtl; GB Lbm, Add. 29907; US Wc, M1010.A2B13.W.35

Mod. edn. (as organ, harpsichord, or piano concerto, for the full instrumentation): H. Winter, Hamburg: Sikorski, 1964

Lit.: ULDALL, 41–44; HAAG, 170–74, 187–88; STEVENS, 34, 182–83, 210–13; SUCHALLA/ORCHESTERSINFONIEN, 200–01; COHEN, 111; WADE, 27, 32, 38, 45, 54, 128, 131–32, 149, 252; DRUMMOND, 290–91, 294–95, 307–10, 313, 331–32; OTTENBERG, 124

A.v.: M1010.A2B13.W.35 is without horn parts; in P 356 the horn parts are the only parts in the hand of CPEB.

In P 710, St 519, St 520, P 356, Add. 29907, and M1010.A2B13.W.35 the work is termed simply a harpsichord concerto; in St 581 it is termed simply an organ concerto. NV, 33, lists the organ first in the title.

Incipits from P 356:

447. Concerto per il cembalo concertato accompagnato da due violini, violetta e basso. 1762 (NV 33). W. 36

Mss.: D-brd B, St 530 (partly Michel, with "ist wenig bekannt" in CPEB's hand on the cover); D-ddr Bds, P 356 (autog.); B Bc, 5887 (Michel)

Lit.: ULDALL, 44; HAAG, 174–75, 187–88; SUCHALLA/ORCHESTERSINFONIEN, 202; WADE, 27, 66, 127, 149, 252–53, 333

Cadenza(s): See item 264.

Incipits from P 356:

448. Concerto per il cembalo concertato accompagnato da due corni, due violini, violetta e basso. 1762 (NV 33). W. 37

Mss.: D-brd B, St 198 (Michel?), St 526 (partly Michel, marked by CPEB, with "ist wenig bekannt" in CPEB's hand on the cover); D-ddr Bds, P 356 (a.v., autog., with the horn parts added separately, at the end of an otherwise complete score); B Bc, 5887 (Michel)

Lit.: ULDALL, 44–45; HAAG, 175–78, 187–88; SUCHALLA/ORCHESTERSINFONIEN, 203; WADE, 97, 127, 131, 149, 253; DRUMMOND, 294–95

Incipits from P 356:

449. Sonatina . . . a cembalo concertato, 2 corni, 2 flauti, 2 violini, viola e basso. 1762 (NV 46). W. 96

Mss.: D-brd B, P 1128 (autog.), St 506 (mostly autog.), St 507 (only viola and bass parts); D-ddr Bds, M.Th. 28; B Bc, 6352 (Michel)

Lit.: ULDALL, 59–61, 66; SCHMID/KAMMERMUSIK, 151–52, 164; NEWMAN, 419; STEVENS, 226–33; SUCHALLA/ORCHESTERSINFONIEN, 220–21; WADE, 4, 335; DRUMMOND, 326–27; SCHULENBERG/INSTRUMENTAL, 6

A.v., vnt.: D-ddr LEm, PM 5216 (without horn parts, varied, and condensed through elimination of the written-out varied repeats); see item 480.

Cadenza(s): See item 264.

Incipits from 6352:

[The Andante ed arioso is repeated here in variant form.]

[The Andante ed arioso is repeated here in yet another variant form.]

450. Sonatina . . . a cembalo conc., 2 corni, 2 flauti, 2 violini, viola e basso. 1762 (NV 46). W. 97

Ms.: B Bc, 6352 (Michel)

Lit.: ULDALL, 59–66; SCHMID/KAMMERMUSIK, 152, 165; NEWMAN, 419; STEVENS, 226–33; SUCHALLA/ORCHESTERSINFONIEN, 221–22; WADE, 4; DRUMMOND, 326–27; SCHULENBERG/INSTRUMENTAL, 6

The Andantino, Presto, and Tempo di Minuetto are arr. of item 600, Nos. 11, 4, and 1, respectively.

Incipits from 6352:

[The Andantino, then the Presto, then the Andantino again, are repeated here, each time in a fresh variant form.]

[The Tempo di Minuetto is repeated here in variant form.]

[The Tempo di Minuetto is repeated here in yet another variant form.]

451. Sonatina . . . a cembalo oblig., 2 corni, 2 flauti, 2 violini, viola e basso. 1762 (NV 46). W. 98

Mss.: D-brd B, St 222; B Bc, 6352 (Michel; lacking the bass part); D-ddr SWl, 846 (entitled "Concertino")

Lit.: ULDALL, 59–62, 66; SCHMID/KAMMERMUSIK, 152, 165; NEWMAN, 419; STEVENS, 226–33; SUCHALLA/ORCHESTERSINFONIEN, 222–23; WADE, 4; DRUMMOND, 326–27; SCHULENBERG/INSTRUMENTAL, 6

The 3rd mvt. is an arr. of item 122.

Incipits from 6352:

452. Sonatina . . . a cembalo conc., 2 corni, 2 flauti, 2 violini, viola e basso. 1762 (NV 46). W. 99

Mss.: B Bc, 6352 (Michel); D-ddr SWl, 845 (entitled "Concertino")

Lit.: ULDALL, 59–60, 66; SCHMID/KAMMERMUSIK, 152, 165; NEWMAN, 419; STEVENS, 226–33; SUCHALLA/ORCHESTERSINFONIEN, 223–24; WADE, 4; DRUMMOND, 326–27; SCHULENBERG/INSTRUMENTAL, 6

Incipits from 6352:

453. Sonatina . . . con 18 stromenti . . . a 2 cembali concertati, 3 trombe, tympani, 2 corni, 2 flauti, 2 oboi, 2 violini, viola, violoncello, bassono e violono. 1762 (NV 46). W. 109

Mss.: D-brd B, P 355 (partly autog.), St 259 (partly CPEB and Michel, with a 10-bar written-out cadenza for both harpsichords in CPEB's hand, connecting the Allegro and the 2nd statement of the Tempo di Minuetto without pause); B Bc, 6352 (Michel)

Lit.: ULDALL, 59–60, 63–64, 66; SCHMID/KAMMERMUSIK, 154, 166; NEWMAN, 419; STEVENS, 226–33; SUCHALLA/ORCHESTERSINFONIEN, 235–36; WADE, 28; DRUMMOND, 326–27; SCHULENBERG/INSTRUMENTAL, 6

The Arioso is an arr. of item 82 and an a.v. from items 480 and 480.5. The tempo di Minuetto is an arr. of item 80 and an a.v. from items 480 and 480.5.

Incipits from P 355:

[The Presto and then the Arioso are repeated here, both in variant form.]

[The Tempo di Minuetto is repeated here in variant form.]

454. Concerto a cemb. conc., 2 flauti ad libitum, 2 violini, violetta e basso. 1763 (NV 33). W. 38

Mss.: D-brd B, St 540 (partly autog.; on the cover in CPEB's hand: "ist nicht sonderlich bekannt"); D-ddr Bds, P 356 (autog.); B Bc, 5887 (Michel)

Lit.: ULDALL, 45; HAAG, 178–81, 187–88; SUCHALLA/ORCHESTERSINFONIEN, 203–04; WADE, 149, 253; DRUMMOND, 294

Incipits from St 540:

455. Sonatina . . . a cembalo conc., 2 corni, 2 flauti, 2 violini, viola e basso. 1763 (NV 47). W. 100

Mss.: B Bc, 6352 (Michel); PL Kj, St 258b (partial autog., keyboard part only)

Lit.: ULDALL, 59–60, 62, 66; SCHMID/KAMMERMUSIK, 165; NEWMAN, 419; STEVENS, 226–33; SUCHALLA/ORCHESTERSINFONIEN, 224; WADE, 4; DRUMMOND, 326–27; SCHULENBERG/INSTRUMENTAL, 6

The 1st mvt. is an arr. of the 1st mvt. of item 123. The 2nd mvt. is an arr. of items 83 (3rd mvt.) and 124.

Incipits from 6352:

[2 mvts. only]

456. Sonatina . . . a cembalo concert., 2 corni, 2 flauti, 2 violini, viola e basso. 1763 (NV 47). W. 102

Ms.: B Bc, 6352 (Michel)

Lit.: ULDALL, 59–60, 66; SCHMID/KAMMERMUSIK, 152, 165; NEWMAN, 419; STEVENS, 226–33; SUCHALLA/ORCHESTERSINFONIEN, 226; WADE, 4; DRUMMOND, 326–27; SCHULENBERG/INSTRUMENTAL, 6

The Allegretto grazioso and Presto are arr. of items 109 and 600/7, respectively; the Allegretto is an arr. of item 114.

Incipits from 6352:

[The Allegretto grazioso and Presto are repeated literally here, followed by a varied repeat of the Allegretto grazioso.]

457. Sonatina . . . a cembalo concert., 2 corni, 2 flauti, 2 violini, viola e basso. 1763 (NV 47). W. 103

Ms.: B Bc, 6352 (Michel)

Lit.: ULDALL, 59–60, 66; SCHMID/KAMMERMUSIK, 165; NEWMAN, 419; STEVENS, 226–33; SUCHALLA/ORCHESTERSINFONIEN, 227; WADE, 4; DRUMMOND, 326–27; SCHULENBERG/INSTRUMENTAL, 6

The 3rd mvt. is an arr. of the 3rd mvt. of item 120; the 1st mvt. is an arr. of the 1st mvt. of item 96.

Incipits from 6352:

[The Arioso is repeated here.]

458. Sonatina I. a cembalo concertato, II. Flauti traversi, II. Violini, violetta e basso da Carlo Filippo Emanuele Bach. 1763 (NV 47). W. 106

Mss.: D-brd B, St 258a (autog., cembalo part only); D-ddr Bds, M.Th. 24

Early print: the above title, "In Berlino, 1764. Alle spese di Giorgio Ludovico Winter"

Mod. edn.: H. von Dameck, Berlin: Bote & Bock, 1961

Lit.: HILLER/NACHRICHTEN, 1766, 35–36; BITTER/ BRÜDER, I, 87–88; ULDALL, 59–60, 66; SCHMID/KAMMERMUSIK, 151–52, facing 152, 154, 165–66, Anh. 71; NEWMAN, 419; STEVENS, 226–33; SUCHALLA/ORCHESTERSINFONIEN, 229–30; DRUMMOND, 326–27; SCHULENBERG/INSTRUMENTAL, 6

Where the print contains simple repeats of sections, St 258a presents written-out variations of these repeats for the cembalist. On the other hand, the tutti cembalo parts are only figured bass in St 258a but are fully realized in the print.

Rev.: Item 460 (St 258a may be used with either version)

Incipits from the Winter print:

459. Sonatina . . . a 10. 2 cembali conc., 2 corni . . ., 2 flauti, 2 violini, viola e basso. 1763 (NV 47). W. 110

Mss.: B Bc, 6532 (Michel); D-ddr SWl, 859/5 (a.v. for "Piano Forte, Cembalo, due Flauti, due Violini, Viola e Basso"); D-ddr LEm, PM 5216 (a.v. for "Piano forte, Flauto Primo, Flauto Seconto, Violino Primo, Violino Seconto, Viola e Basso"; see item 480); PL Kj, P 1129 (autog.)

Lit.: ULDALL, 59–60, 64–66; SCHMID/KAMMERMUSIK, 166; NEWMAN, 419; STEVENS, 226–33; SUCHALLA/ORCHESTERSINFONIEN, 236–37; DRUMMOND, 326–27; SCHULENBERG/INSTRUMENTAL, 6

Incipits from 6532:

460. Sonatina . . . a cembalo conc., 2 corni, 2 flauti, 2 violini, viola e basso. 1763 or later (NV 47–48). W. 101

Mss.: D-brd B, St 258a (autog., cembalo part only; see item 458); B Bc, 6352 (lacking the 1st flute part)

Lit.: ULDALL, 59–60, 62, 66; SCHMID/KAMMERMUSIK, 151–52, 165–66, Anh. 71; STEVENS, 226–33; SUCHALLA/ ORCHESTERSINFONIEN, 225; WADE, 4; DRUMMOND, 326–27; SCHULENBERG/INSTRUMENTAL, 6

Rev. of item 458. WOTQUENNE/THÉMATIQUE incorrectly implies that this version is the original. NV, 48, states that items 458, 461, and 462 were "gedruckt, aber nachhero ganz verändert." 6352 is like St 258a in giving the cembalist the same written-out varied repeats and figured-bass tuttis.

Incipits from 6352: same as for item 458

461. Sonatina II. a cembalo concertato, II. Flauti traversi, II. Violini, violetta e basso da Carlo Filippo Emanuele Bach. 1764 (NV 48). W. 107

Ms.: D-brd B, St 546

Early print: the above title, "In Berlino, 1764. Alle spese di Giorgio Ludovico Winter" (title plate reused with slight alteration from his printing of item 458 without changing the 1764 date? In CPEB/AUTOBIOGRAPHY, p. 370 of the Newman translation, as well as in CPEB/BREITKOPF, around Aug. 1786 [see p. xix], CPEB says that the printing took place in 1765.)

Mod. edn.: F. Oberdörffer, Kassel: Bärenreiter, 1951

Lit.: HILLER/NACHRICHTEN, 1766, 35–36; BITTER/ BRÜDER, I, 87–88; SCHMID/KAMMERMUSIK, 151–52, 154, 165–66; ULDALL, 59–60, 66; NEWMAN, 419; STEVENS, 226–33, 240; SUCHALLA/ORCHESTERSINFONIEN, 231–32; DRUMMOND, 326–27; SCHULENBERG/INSTRUMENTAL, 6

Rev.: item 463. The item 461 version of this sonatina provides a fully written-out cembalo part in the tuttis, whereas item 463, the rev., contains only figured bass at these places.

Incipits from the Winter print:

462. Sonatina III. a cembalo concertato, II. flauti traversi, II. violini, violetta e basso da Carlo Filippo Emanuele Bach. 1764 or 1765 (NV 48). W. 108

Early print: the above title, "In Berlino, 1766. Alle spese di Georgio Ludovico Winter"

Mod. edn.: F. Oberdörffer, Kassel: Bärenreiter, 1951

Lit.: HILLER/NACHRICHTEN, 1766, 35–36; BITTER/ BRÜDER, I, 87–88; ULDALL, 59–60, 66; SCHMID/KAM-MERMUSIK, 151–52, 154, 165–66; NEWMAN, 419; STE-VENS, 226–33; SUCHALLA/ORCHESTERSINFONIEN, 233–34; DRUMMOND, 326–27; SCHULENBERG/IN-STRUMENTAL, 6

Rev.: item 464. The 1st mvts. are vnts. of each other. The item 462 version of this sonatina provides a fully written-out cembalo part in the tuttis, whereas item 464, the rev., contains only figured bass at these places. On the other hand, the 2nd mvt. in item 464 contains written-out varied repeats, whereas these sections are literal repeats in the print.

Incipits from the Winter print:

463. Sonatina a cembalo obligato, 2 flauti, 2 corni, 2 violini, viola e basso. 1764 or later (NV 48). W. 104

Ms.: B Bc, 6352 (Michel)

Lit.: ULDALL, 59–60, 62, 66; SCHMID/KAMMERMUSIK, 151–52, 165–66; STEVENS, 226–33; SUCHALLA/OR-CHESTERSINFONIEN, 227–28; WADE, 4; DRUM-MOND, 326–27; SCHULENBERG/INSTRUMENTAL, 6

Rev. of item 461. WOTQUENNE/THÉMATIQUE incorrectly implies that this version is the original; see the reference to NV in item 460.

Incipits from 6352: same as for item 461

464. Sonatina a cembalo conc., 2 corni, 2 flauti, 2 violini, viola e basso. 1764 or later (NV 48). W. 105

Ms.: B Bc, 6352 (Michel)

Lit.: ULDALL, 59–60, 66; SCHMID/KAMMERMUSIK, 151–

52, 165–66; STEVENS, 226–33; SUCHALLA/ORCHES-TERSINFONIEN, 228–29; DRUMMOND, 326–27; SCHULENBERG/INSTRUMENTAL, 6

Rev. of item 462. The 1st mvts. are vnts. of each other. WOTQUENNE/THÉMATIQUE incorrectly implies that this version is the original; see the reference to NV in item 460.

Incipit of 1st mvt. from 6352:

Incipits of 2nd and 3rd mvts. from 6352: same as for item 462

465. Concerto per il cembalo concertato, violino primo, violino secondo, viola e basso. 1765 (NV 33). W. 39

Mss.: D-brd B, St 528, St 529 (autog.); B Bc, 5887 (Michel); US Wc, M1010.A2B13.W.39; US BE, Ms. 736 (lacking cembalo part)

Lit.: HAAG, 181–83, 187–88; STEVENS, 127–29; SUCHAL-LA/ORCHESTERSINFONIEN, 204–05; WADE, 106–10, 149, 253; DRUMMOND, 293

A.v.: item 466

Incipits from St 529:

466. Concerto a oboe concertato accompagnato da due violini, violetta e basso. Probably c. 1765 (source of date: date of item 465). W. 164

Mss.: D-ddr Bds, P 356 (autog.); B Bc, 5520 (Michel)

Mod. edns. (both for the full instrumentation as well as with orchestral parts reduced for keyboard): R. Lausch-mann, New York: Peters, 1952; O. Kaul, Munich: Leuck-art, 1943, reprinted 1954

Lit.: ULDALL, 56–57, 59; SUCHALLA/ORCHESTERSINFO-NIEN, 237–38; WADE, 106–08

A.v. of item 465, probably the original, if one judges from the oboe-like melodic style and the careful autograph score in P 356 (title and note on the cover, in CPEB's hand: "Ein Hobo Concert von C. P. E. Bach. ist wenig bekannt")

Incipits from P 356: same as for item 465

467. Concerto a cembalo conc., violino primo, violino secondo, viola e basso. 1765 (NV 34). W. 40
Ms.: B Bc, 5887 (Michel)
Lit.: HAAG, 183–88; STEVENS, 127–29; SUCHALLA/ORCHESTERSINFONIEN, 205–06; WADE, 106, 108, 110, 149, 254; DRUMMOND, 293
A.v.: item 468

Incipits from 5887:

468. Concerto a oboe concertato accompagnato da due violini, violetta e basso. Probably c. 1765 (source of date: date of item 467). W. 165
Mss.: D-ddr Bds, P 356 (autog.); B Bc, 5519 (Michel)
Mod. edns.: H. Töttcher and K. Grebe, Hamburg: Sikorski, 1959; anon., Hamburg: Lichnowski, [1954] (orchestral parts reduced for keyboard); A. Fodor, Zurich: Eulenburg, 1980
Lit.: ULDALL, 57–59; SUCHALLA/ORCHESTERSINFONIEN, 238; WADE, 106, 108; DRUMMOND, 306–07, 335
A.v. of item 467, probably the original, if one judges from the criteria mentioned in item 466 (the same title and note in CPEB's hand are on the cover, probably written at the same time as the cover for item 466)

Incipits from P 356: same as for item 467

469. Concerto a cembalo conc., 2 corni, 2 flauti, 2 violini, 2 viole e basso. 1769 (NV 34). W. 41
Mss.: D-brd B, P 353 (partly autog.); B Bc, 5887 (Michel)
Lit.: ULDALL, 46–48; HAAG, 191–96, 224–25; STEVENS, 111, 236–50, 268, 271, 279; SUCHALLA/ORCHESTERSINFONIEN, 206–07; WELLESZ–STERNFELD/CONCERTO, 453; WADE, 27, 100, 149, 254, 334; DRUMMOND, 296, 320–21, 323–28
Cadenza(s): See item 264.

Incipits from P 353:

470. Concerto per il cembalo concertato accompagnato da due corni, due violini, violetta e basso. 1770 (NV 34). W. 42
Mss.: D-brd B, St 212; B Bc, 5887 (Michel; this ms. also includes the a.v.)
Lit.: ULDALL, 47; HAAG, 196–99, 224–25; STEVENS, 111, 238, 250; SUCHALLA/ORCHESTERSINFONIEN, 207–08; WADE, 6, 41, 76–77, 112–13, 131, 149, 254; DRUMMOND, 320–21, 323–28
A.v.: item 242

Incipits from 5887:

471. Concerto [for harpsichord, 2 violins, viola, 2 horns, 2 flutes, bass]. 1771 (NV 34). W. 43/1
Mss.: D-brd B, St 537, St 575, St 619; D-ddr GOl, Mus. pag. 4/13; CS Pnm, XVII F 20 (cembalo part only); F Pc, Ms. 1555 a–g (not autog.; without flute parts)
Early print and lit. about it.: See SEI CONCERTI.
Mss. probably copied from the early print: B Bc, 5893; A Wgm, Q 16185 (VII 3871) (lacking violin and viola parts); D-ddr Dlb, 3029.0.3
Mod. edn.: CRANZ
Lit. about this work: ULDALL, 49–51; GEIRINGER/BACH, 366; HAAG, 201–05, 224–25; CRICKMORE, 236; STEVENS, 238, 268–69; SUCHALLA/ORCHESTERSINFONIEN, 210–11; WADE, 19–21, 46, 50, 149, 254; DRUMMOND, 290, 304, 318–22, 320–28, 340, 343
See item 483.

Incipits for SEI CONCERTI:

Incipits from SEI CONCERTI:

472. Concerto [for harpsichord, 2 violins, viola, 2 horns, 2 flutes, bass]. 1771 (NV 34). W. 43/2

Mss.: D-brd B, St 201, St 509; D-ddr GOl, Mus. pag. 4/11

Early print and lit. about it: See SEI CONCERTI.

Mss. probably copied from the early print: B Bc, 5893; A Wgm, Q 16185 (VII 3871); D-ddr Dlb, 3029.0.3

Mod. edns.: CRANZ; H. Riemann, Leipzig: Steingräber, 188? (arranged for 2 keyboards alone); L. Landshoff, Berlin: Adler, 1932, reprinted New York: Peters, 1967

Lit. about this work: ULDALL, 48–49; HAAG, 205–09, 224–25; CRICKMORE, 233–34; STEVENS, 237, 252–53, 258–59, 262; SUCHALLA/ORCHESTERSINFONIEN, 211–12; WELLESZ–STERNFELD/CONCERTO, 455; WADE, 12, 20, 140, 149, 255; DRUMMOND, 290, 296, 318, 320–28, 340

See item 483.

Incipits from SEI CONCERTI:

473. Concerto [for harpsichord, 2 violins, viola, 2 flutes, bass]. 1771 (NV 34). W. 43/3

Mss.: D-brd B, St 205, St 521; A Wgm, Q 16202 (VII 43731); D-ddr GOl, Mus. pag. 4/12; D-ddr SWl, 859/2

Early print and lit. about it: See SEI CONCERTI.

Mss. probably copied from the early print: B Bc, 5893; A Wgm, Q 16185 (VII 3871); D-ddr Dlb, 3029.0.3

Mod. edns.: CRANZ; H. Riemann, Leipzig: Steingräber, 188? (arranged for 2 keyboards alone)

Lit. about this work: ULDALL, 50; HAAG, 209–10, 224–25, 237; CRICKMORE, 235–36; STEVENS, 253, 264–68; SUCHALLA/ORCHESTERSINFONIEN, 212–13; WADE, 20, 49, 140, 255; DRUMMOND, 290, 296, 298, 318, 320–28, 334, 340

See item 483.

474. Concerto [for harpsichord, 2 violins, viola, 2 horns, 2 flutes, bass]. 1771 (NV 35). W. 43/4

Mss.: D-brd B, St 196, St 527; D-ddr GOl, Mus. pag. 4/14; D-ddr SWl, 859/3; US NYp, MW

Early print and lit. about it: See SEI CONCERTI.

Mss. probably copied from the early print: B Bc, 5893; A Wgm, Q 16185 (VII 3871); D-ddr Dlb, 3029.0.3

Mod. edns.: CRANZ; H. Riemann, Leipzig: Steingräber, 188? (arranged for 2 keyboards alone)

Lit. about this work: BÜCKEN, 168; ULDALL, 15, 49–50; GEIRINGER/BACH, 366; HAAG, 210–14, 224–25; CRICKMORE, 234–36; STEVENS, 236, 262–63; SUCHALLA/ORCHESTERSINFONIEN, 213–14; WADE, 20, 49–50, 140, 149, 255–56; DRUMMOND, 290, 296, 318, 320–28, 340; SCHULENBERG/INSTRUMENTAL, 90–91

See item 483.

Incipits from SEI CONCERTI:

475. Concerto [for harpsichord, 2 violins, viola, 2 horns, 2 flutes, bass]. 1771 (NV 35). W. 43/5

Mss.: D-brd B, St 215, St 503; D-ddr Dlb, 3029.0.3

Early print and lit. about it: See SEI CONCERTI.

Mss. probably copied from the early print: B Bc, 5893; A Wgm, Q 16185 (VII 3871); D-ddr Dlb, 3029.0.3

Mod. edns.: CRANZ; H. Riemann, Leipzig: Steingräber, 188? (arranged for 2 keyboards alone)

Lit. about this work: ULDALL, 48; GEIRINGER/BACH, 366; HAAG, 214–16, 224–25; CRICKMORE, 235; STEVENS, 237, 252, 259–64, 268; SUCHALLA/ORCHESTERSINFONIEN, 215–16; WELLESZ–STERNFELD/CONCERTO, 453; WADE, 20, 50, 149, 256; DRUMMOND, 290, 296, 318, 320–28, 340; SCHULENBERG/INSTRUMENTAL, 108–09

See item 483.

Incipits from SEI CONCERTI:

[2 mvts. only]

476. Concerto [for harpsichord, 2 violins, viola, 2 horns, 2 flutes, bass]. 1771 (NV 35). W. 43/6

Mss.: D-brd B, St 194, St 494; A Wgm, Q 16201 (VII 1407); F Pc, Ms. 1554 a–e (not autog.); D-ddr GOl, Ms. Mus. 5; D-brd LB, gelbe Mappe IX/10 ("Autograph? ca. 1783," say the RISM card files; not verified)

Early print and lit. about it: See SEI CONCERTI.

Mss. probably copied from the early print: B Bc, 5893; A Wgm, Q 16185 (VII 3871); D-ddr Dlb, 3029.0.3

Mod. edn.: CRANZ

Lit. about this work: ULDALL, 49; HAAG, 216–19, 224–25; STEVENS, 237, 253–57; SUCHALLA/ORCHESTERSINFONIEN, 216–17; WADE, 20, 46–47, 53, 148–49, 256–57; DRUMMOND, 290, 296, 318, 320–28, 340; SCHULENBERG/INSTRUMENTAL, 93–94

Incipits from SEI CONCERTI:

477. Concerto per il cembalo concertato accompagnato da due corni, due violini, violetta e basso. 1778 (NV 35). W. 44

Mss.: D-brd B, P 353 (autog.); B Bc, 5887 (Michel)

Lit.: ULDALL, 51; HAAG, 219–21, 224–25; STEVENS, 237, 271–77; SUCHALLA/ORCHESTERSINFONIEN, 217; WADE, 71–72, 257; DRUMMOND, 320–28; SCHULENBERG/INSTRUMENTAL, 138

Incipits from P 353:

478. Concerto per il cembalo concertato accompagnato da due corni, due violini, violetta e basso. 1778 (NV 35). W. 45

Mss.: D-brd B, P 353 (autog.); B Bc, 5887 (Michel)

Lit.: ULDALL, 51–52; HAAG, 221–25; STEVENS, 237, 271–73; SUCHALLA/ORCHESTERSINFONIEN, 218; WADE, 73, 97–98, 100, 149, 257, 331; DRUMMOND, 320–28; SCHULENBERG/INSTRUMENTAL, 118–20, 138

Cadenza(s): See item 264.

Incipits from P 353:

479. Concerto doppio a cembalo concertato, fortepiano concertato, accompagnati da due corni, due flauti, due violini, violetta e basso. 1788 (NV 35). W. 47

Mss.: D-brd B, N. Mus. SA 4 (autog. score on loan there since 1974, along with a few other mss. surviving from the Berlin Singakademie library; see p. xxiv); B Bc, 5890; H Bn, Ms. mus. IV 694

Mod. edns.: H. Schwartz, Leipzig: Steingräber, [c. 1914] (arranged for two keyboards alone, with additions to the harmony); E. R. Jacobi, Kassel: Bärenreiter, 1958 (supplementary commentary in JACOBI/CONCERTO); G. Darvas, London: Eulenburg, [1969] (in the original instrumentation and for 3 pianos)

Other lit.: ULDALL, 52–54; GEIRINGER/BACH, 367; CRICKMORE, 230; STEVENS, 236–37, 271–72, 275–82; SUCHALLA/ORCHESTERSINFONIEN, 219–20; WADE, 41, 44, 53–54, 149, 257; DRUMMOND, 291–92, 296, 320–28, 330, 342; OTTENBERG, 243; SCHULENBERG/IN-STRUMENTAL, 31–32, 42–43, 74–75

Incipits from the autog.:

Possibly Authentic

480. Sonatina III, cembalo concertato, violino primo, violino secondo, due flauti, violetta e basso. Probably c. 1762 (source of date: the ingredients from item 453, dated 1762, are the latest.)

Ms.: D-ddr LEm, PM 5216, collectively entitled *Tre Sonatine*. The other 2 sonatinas are items 449 and 459.

The Arioso is an arr. of item 82 and an a.v. from items 453, 480.5. The Andantinos are arr. from item 600/12 and are a.v. of the Andantino of item 480.5. The Tempo di Minuetto is an arr. of item 80 and an a.v. from items 453, 480.5.

Even when the music in one version or another is authentic, many of the arrangements of this music that seem to be invited by the nature of the "sonatina" genre (see the note on p. 84) were obviously not sanctioned by the composer.

Incipits from PM 5216:

[The Arioso is repeated here.]

[The Arioso is repeated again here.]

480.5. Sonatina a [cembalo concertato,] 2 flauti, 2 violini, viola e basso. Probably c. 1762 (source of date: same as for item 480)

Ms.: D-brd B, St 577

Lit.: SCHMID/KAMMERMUSIK, 154; SUCHALLA/OR-CHESTERSINFONIEN, 278–79

The Arioso is an arr. of item 82 and an a.v. from items 453, 480. The Andantinos are arr. of item 600/12 and a.v. from item 480. The Tempo di Minuetto is an arr. of item 80 and an a.v. from items 453, 480. The Allegretto is an arr. of item 600/9.

See the note about authenticity in the "sonatina" genre in item 480. St 577 is written in a hand resembling that of S. Hering, who worked as CPEB's assistant (see WADE, 40).

Incipits from St 577:

[The Arioso is repeated here, followed by a varied repeat of Andantino 1 (entitled "Andantino 2"), followed by another repetition of the Arioso.]

[The Tempo di Minuetto is repeated here.]

481. Concerto cembalo, violino primo, violino secondo, viola e basso. n.d. WADE, Appendix B, item X12
Ms.: US Wc, M1010.A2B13.LC1. See item 481.5. See also WADE, 18, 286–87.
Lit.: SCHULZE/WADE

Incipits from M1010.A2B13.LC1:

481.5. Concerto cembalo, violino primo, violino secondo, viola e basso. n.d. WADE, Appendix B, item X19
Ms.: US Wc, M1010.A2B13.LC2 (attributed only to "Bach"). Same copyist, and same (owner's?) name (illegible; probably A. E. Grell, 1800–1886) on the cover, as for item 481 and the US BE source of item 408. See WADE, 18, 297–98; SCHULZE/ WADE.

Incipits from M1010.A2B13.LC2:

482. [11 flute concertos]. n.d.
Mss.: Formerly in the library of the Berlin Singakademie, of questionable authorship, now lost or destroyed, according to SCHMID/MGG, col. 933. See also WADE, 270–71. WELTER quotes a puzzling entry in a surviving catalogue compiled during C. F. Zelter's tenure as Singakademie director: "11 Conc. flauto traverso solo e basso."

483. [Concertos for harpsichord and orchestra]
In LANDOWSKA, p. 305, Wanda Landowska writes: "I had the privilege of acquiring at the sale of the celebrated collector Prieger, in Bonn, July 15, 1924 [see PRIEGER in Bib.], the separate parts of several of Karl Philipp Emanuel Bach's concertos copied by Ernst Ludwig Gerber [see the BÜCKEN quotation in item 490], the justly famous author of the *Lexicon der Tonkünstler* (1790). His father, Heinrich Nicolaus, was one of Johann Sebastian Bach's pupils . . . . [T]hese manuscripts are of great value, and it is from them, together with a confrontation of Karl Philipp Emanuel's original autograph, that I have reconstituted the full scores."

Restout's editorial note on the same page: "These manuscripts, as well as Landowska's reconstituted scores, were part of her library seized by the Nazis in 1940. . . . Early in 1943 Wanda Landowska was asked to identify manuscript copies of several of Karl Philipp Emanuel Bach's concertos, then in the possession of the late Adolf Koldofsky of Toronto, Ontario."

In her editorial introduction to LANDOWSKA, p. 21, Restout writes: ". . . Wanda Landowska was planning a new book. . . . But before the book could materialize . . . tragedy struck—the second World War. St.-Leu [Landowska's residence] had to be abandoned with all its treasures. In our hasty departure we could only attempt to save what three small boxes would hold. In them went a few indispensable books and music scores and some notebooks. Landowska wanted to take along a collection of priceless manuscripts of Karl Philipp Emanuel Bach's concertos. I insisted instead upon filling the space with the notes from the master classes. She protested. Despite my deep respect for Wanda Landowska, I threw in the notes and left the Karl Philipp Emanuel manuscripts. I was later to hear about that in no uncertain terms, but I never felt sorry for my disobedience. Other manuscripts of Karl Philipp Emanuel Bach's concertos existed in libraries and could be photostated. Of the notes, there was no other copy in existence; they represented fourteen years of Landowska's teaching."

"After spending eighteen months in the south of France . . . Landowska was told that St-Leu had been thoroughly looted by the Nazis."

One wonders about the relation between Landowska's mss. and the group of concerto mss., apparently not copied by Gerber, purchased in 1966 by US BEu (see BUCK, 127) from Koldofsky's widow, Gwendolin Koldofsky, and duly noted in the present catalogue. Restout's unpleasant implication is belied through a lack of connection between Gerber and the US BEu mss. and through a lack of correspondence of dates: In a letter of 25 April 1975 to Rachel Wade (see WADE, 51, 138), Vincent Duckles, head of US BEu, stated that the acquisition consisted of ten manuscript copies of concertos procured from Gwendolin Koldofsky, whose husband had bought them from a Canadian bookseller in the 1930s.

As for the mss. copied by Gerber, entries 192–94 of the Prieger auction catalogue (see PRIEGER in Bib.) list 10 harpsichord concertos in Gerber's hand: Prieger 192, items 409, 421, 442, and 443 of the present catalogue; Prieger 193, almost certainly item 490; Prieger 194, items 471–75. Items 409, 421, and 442 are represented by mss.

in US Wc; despite the general importance of Prieger mss. in US Wc, these three mss. are in different hands and do not bear Gerber's owner's mark. The other ms. sources of these three items do not, to my knowledge, include Gerber copies. Item 443 lists no ms. copied by Gerber. Item 490 shows that in all probability Ernst Bücken also attended the auction in Bonn on 15 July 1924 and purchased at least this (misattributed) work. Items 471–75, again, include no ms. in Gerber's hand that I know of, and in any case are represented by an important early print (SEI CONCERTI), which makes ms. copies of these works generally less valuable.

Landowska's "several concertos," then, were probably the four listed as Prieger 192: items 409, 421, 422 and 443 in the present catalogue. Yet on the chance that she was allowed to buy choice items not listed in the Prieger auction catalogue—a common procedure—this entry in the present catalogue is placed among concertos "possibly by" CPEB, with cross-references to other sections.

Doubtful

484. Cembalo [con]certato, due violini, viola e cont. c. 1732–34 (source of date: FISCHER/NBA, 36–37). BWV 1052a; WADE, Appendix B, item X30

Ms.: D-brd B, St 350 (autog., but not identified by CPEB as his work)

Lit.: OTTENBERG, 26, 297–98; H. J. Schulze, editorial commentary in his edn. of JSB's *Konzert D-Moll für Cembalo und Streichorchester BWV 1052* (Leipzig: Peters, 1974), iii–xi; A. Glöckner, "Neuerkenntnisse zu Johann Sebastian Bachs Auffürungskalender zwischen 1729 und 1735," *Bach-Jahrbuch*, 67 (1981), 43–75.

According to SIEGELE, especially 142–43, FISCHER/NBA, 36–37, and BREIG, especially 23ff., CPEB made this arrangement, amounting partly to recomposition, of JSB's lost violin concerto in D minor. But WADE, 114–17, points out that the separate title p. of St 350, in the hand of Pölchau, reads, ". . . von Johann Sebastian Bach. von der hand seines Söhnes Carl Phil. Eman. Bach." This inscription, says WADE, has been overlooked by many recent scholars, probably because it is written on blue paper and is invisible on microfilm. WADE further observes that St 350 bears little evidence of CPEB's compositional activity—evidence that is abundant in other concerto autographs — and that its peculiar notation and gathering structure seem to be for the sake of the performer, as would apply to a transcription but not a recomposition.

Incipits from BWV 1052a:

484.1. Concerto per il flauto traverso con due violini, viola e basso. Probably c. 1747 (source of date: date of item 425). WADE, Appendix B, item X28

Mss.: D-brd B, P 768, Am.B. 101 ("F. Benda" crossed out on title p., "C. F. E. Bach" substituted)

Mod. edn.: K. Redel, Munich: Leuckart, 1960

Lit.: ULDALL, 57–58; WADE, 110–11, 130, 310–11; SCHULENBERG/INSTRUMENTAL, 41

A.v. of item 425. SUCHALLA/ORCHESTERSINFONIEN, 188, 280, apparently bases part of his doubt about the authenticity of this version upon D-brd B, P 768, a poor 19th-century copy. But Am.B. 101 (which he incorrectly lists as a source of item 425) is an 18th-century copy of excellent quality and likely provenance. My thanks to Rachel Wade for deciphering the nearly illegible name of Benda on the title p. of Am.B. 101, which casts an ineradicable shadow of doubt on the authenticity of this a.v.

Incipits from Am.B. 101: same as for item 425

484.2. Concert für clavier . . . [harpsichord, 2 violins, viola, bass]. Probably c. 1753 (source of date: period of Johann Christian Bach's study with CPEB). TERRY, C. S., 9, 301; WADE, Appendix B, item X7

Mss.: D-brd B, P 680 (attributed to Wilhelm Friedemann Bach); St 482 (on cover, in the hand of Nichelmann: ". . . dal Sgr. *J. C. Bach* detto il Milanese/riveduto dal Sgr. C. F. E. Bach"; yet attributed to CPEB on the title p. of the cembalo part); St 483 (title p.: "Del Sigr. C. F. E. Bach," then, in a different hand, "von Joh. Cretien bearb. in Berlin unter E. Aufsicht"; this ms. belonged to J. H. Grave, lawyer and friend of CPEB); D-ddr LEb, Gorke 40 (copied by J. C. Altnickol and with title-p. inscription "Concerto da J. C. Bach" in the hand of Johann Christian Bach, according to Hans-Joachim Schulze [see WADE, 16, 124]).

Mod. edns.: Ed. as a work of CPEB by W. Szarvady, Leipzig: Breitkopf & Härtel, late 19th or early 20th century, and as a work of Wilhelm Friedemann Bach by W. Smigelski, Hamburg: Hans Sikorski, [c. 1959]

Lit.: CRICKMORE, 233; WADE, 15–17, 128, 274–76; Jane R. Stevens, "Concerto No. 6 in F Minor: By Johann Christian Bach?" *R.M.A. Research Chronicle*, XXI (1988), 53–56 (with new evidence favoring J.C. Bach's authorship).

According to ULDALL, p. 66, the Singakademie held a ms. copy (D II 1472 z) of this work, now lost.

Probably composed by Johann Christian Bach and revised by CPEB

Incipit from the Szarvady edn., 1st mvt.:

484.3. Concerto . . . cembalo obligato, violino primo, violino secondo, viola e violono. n.d. Wq n.v. 68; WADE, Appendix B, item X11
Ms.: D-brd B, St 522
A mid-century work by a minor Berlin composer? See UL-DALL, 67; WADE, 17–18, 284–85. St 522 was owned and partly copied by J. E. Oppel (2nd half of the 18th century).

Incipits from St 522:

484.4. Concerto a cembalo concertato, 2 violini, viola, basso. n.d. Wq n.v. 67; WADE, Appendix B, item X23
Ms.: D-brd B, St 619 (which does not attribute this work, but also contains 2 genuine concertos, items 442 and 471)
Lit: WADE, 19–21, 304
WADE shows that item 484.4 belonged to the collection of Otto Karl Friedrich von Voss and was placed with items 442 and 471 as a consequence of Voss's numbering system, not necessarily because it is a CPEB work.

Incipits from St 619:

484.5. Concerto . . . [harpsichord, 2 horns, 2 flutes, 2 oboes, 2 violins, viola, bass]. n.d. WADE, Appendix B, item X18
Mss.: CS Bm, II G 1 ("del Sig. Bach"); D-brd DS, Mus. ms. 56 (attributed to "Carlo Bach")
The provenance and attribution of II G 1 are uncertain, as is the attribution in Mus. ms. 56. See WADE, 123–24, 296.

Incipit from II G 1, 1st mvt.:

484.6. Concerto a 5 pp: cembalo concertato, violino primo, violino secondo, viola e basso. n.d. KAST, Bach-Incerta 35; WADE, Appendix B, item X20
Mss.: D-brd B, St 144 ("Del Sigre J. S. Bach"); D-ddr Dlb, 3374/0/9 (formerly Ce VIa) (attributed to Johann Christian Bach)
The final mvt. is a fugue on B-A-C-H (see also items 285, 371.9, 373, 389.6, 659, 733/41, 867).
It is not clear why KAST classifies St 144 as "Bach-Incerta." WADE, 18–20, 299–300, reports E. N. Kulukundis's evidence that this concerto may be by Johann Michael Bach; the main part of this evidence is a print published by Hummel (RISM, AI, 1, pp. 181–82). H.-J. Schulze referred to this concerto as by Johann Michael Bach in "Die Bach-Überlieferung—Plädoyer für ein notwendiges Buch," *Beiträge zur Musikwissenschaft*, 17 (1975), pp. 55, 57, and mentioned that WESTPHAL/NACHRICHTEN lists this concerto as a composition of JSB.

Incipit from St 144, 1st mvt.:

484.7. Concerto per il clavicembalo con due violini, violetta, e basso. n.d. WADE, Appendix B, item X13
Ms.: In the private collection of E. N. Kulukundis (U.S.)
A two-movement work whose 2nd mvt. is a rondo, so entitled; this, says WADE, 288, is sufficient reason for doubting its authenticity, since in a letter to [Advocaten] Grave of April 28, 1784, CPEB wrote that he had not yet used a rondo in a concerto. CPEB's only authenticated concerto after 1778 is item 479, composed in 1788; it does not include a rondo.

Incipit of the 1st mvt. from WADE, 288:

484.8. Concerto per il cembalo. n.d. KAST, Bach-Incerta 36; WADE, Appendix B, item X21
Ms.: D-brd B, St 616 ("di Bach")
St 616 is in the hand of an anonymous 18th-century copyist. It is quite unlikely to be by CPEB, says WADE, 19, 301, in observing the carelessness and haste with which the ms. was copied.

Incipit from St. 616, 1st mvt.:

484.9. Ex c. moll cembalo certato. violin: 1, violin: 2, viola e basso. n.d. WADE, Appendix B, item X24
Ms.: D-ddr GO1, Mus. pag. 4/3 ("del Sign. Bach")
There is no evidence that this work was composed by CPEB, says WADE, 18, 305, citing the general ambiguity and carelessness of "Bach" attributions in the mss. of D-ddr GO1.

Incipit from Mus. pag. 4/3, 1st mvt.:

485. Concerto . . . [harpsichord, 2 violins, viola, bass]. n.d. WADE, Appendix B, item X10
Ms.: CS Bm, II G 2 ("Del Sig. Emen. Pach")
Provenance and style very unlikely. See WADE, 123–24, 283.

Incipit from II G 2, 1st mvt.:

486. Concerto . . . [harpsichord, 2 violins, viola, bass]. n.d. WADE, Appendix B, item X17
Ms.: CS Bm, II F 3 ("Del Sig. Bach")
Provenance and style very unlikely. See WADE, 123–24, 295.

Incipit from II F 3, 1st mvt.:

Spurious

487. Concerto cembalo concertato, violino 1ᵐᵒ, violino 2ᵈᵒ, viola, basso. c. 1759 (source of date: LEE). Wq n.v. 33; WADE, Appendix B, item X1
Ms.: D-brd B, P 926 (a set of parts despite the "P"). The name "Nichelmann" is scratched out on the title p. and that of CPEB substituted.
By C. Nichelmann. Properly identified in A Wgm, VII 36258; D-ddr Bds, M.Th. 170; B Bc, 6154. See Concertos VII and XIV in LEE; SUCHALLA/ORCHESTERSINFONIEN, 281–82; WADE, 14, 137, 262–64.

Incipit from P 926, 1st mvt.:

488. Concerto . . . [harpsichord, 2 violins, bass]. 1763 or earlier (source of date: pub. date). TERRY, C. S., 292; WADE, Appendix B, item X14
Ms.: CS Bm, II F 2 ("Del Sigre Bach")
Early print: See TERRY, C. S., 292.
By Johann Christian Bach. See WADE, 289–90.

Incipit from II F 2, 1st mvt.:

489. Concerto . . . [harpsichord, 2 violins, bass]. 1763 or earlier (source of date: pub. date). TERRY, C. S., 292; WADE, Appendix B, item X15
Ms.: CS Bm, II F 5
Early print: See TERRY, C. S., 292.
By Johann Christian Bach. See WADE, 123–24, 291–93.

Incipit from II F 5, 1st mvt.:

490. [Concerto for harpsichord and orchestra]. 1768 or earlier (source of date: See below). WADE, Appendix B, item X6
Mentioned in BÜCKEN, 168–69, as part of his private collection. Bücken quotes the beginning of the slow mvt., describing his copy as an "Abschrift E.L. Gerbers vom 17. Mai 1768 als Werk Ph.E. Bach bezeugtes, bisher unbekanntes Cembalokonzert in A-dur."
A.v. of items 383, 384, which are by Johann Christian Bach. WADE, 15, 100, 272–73, reports seeing a film copy of the Gerber–Bücken ms. in A Wn, PhA 73, and identifies it with items 383 and 384. In all probability, Bücken purchased this ms., incorrectly represented as genuine, at the auction of the Prieger collection in Bonn on 15 July 1924. A concerto ms. is described in entry 193 of the auction catalogue (see PRIEGER in Bib.) in words similar to those of Bücken: "Abschrift der Stimmen von E.L. Gerber, Leipzig im Mai 1768." The Prieger entry also mentions, without call no., another ms. of the Prieger-owned work in D-ddr Bds, M.Th., attributed only to "Bach."
Wanda Landowska attended the same auction and was somewhat more fortunate in her purchases; see item 483.

Incipit of slow mvt., as quoted by Bücken:

491. Sonatina a harmonica [glass harmonica], 2 violini e violoncello. 1775 or later (sources of date: dates of items 522, 524)
Ms.: CS Pnm, II B 11
Foreign in provenance and medium of performance. Arranges 2nd mvt. of item 522 as its 1st mvt., and 2nd and 3rd mvts. of item 524 as its 2nd and 3rd mvts.
See the note about authenticity in the "sonatina" genre in item 480.

Incipit from II B 11, 1st mvt.:

492. Concerto per il clavi cembalo, violino primo, violino secondo, viola e basso. 1777 or earlier (source of date: pub. date). TERRY, C. S., 295; WADE, Appendix B, item X4
Ms.: CS Bm, II F 6 ("Del Sig. Carlo Pach")
Early print: See TERRY, C. S., 295.
By Johann Christian Bach. See WADE, 123, 269.

Incipit from II F 6, 1st mvt.:

493. Sonatina a harmonica [glass harmonica], 2 violini, viola e basso. 1777 or later (source of date: date of item 259)
Ms.: CS Pnm, II B 10
Foreign in provenance and medium of performance. Consists entirely of variations selected and arranged from item 259. The more technical variations are omitted. See item 249.
See the note about authenticity in the "sonatina" genre in item 480.

Incipit from II B 10, 1st mvt.:

494. Concerto . . . [harpsichord, 2 violins, viola, bass]. 1780 or earlier? (source of date: pub. date). TERRY, C. S., 294; WADE, Appendix B, item X3
Ms.: D-ddr GOl, Ms. Mus. 5
Early print: See TERRY, C. S., 294.
By Johann Christian Bach. See WADE, 15, 267–68.

Incipit from Ms. Mus. 5, 1st mvt.:

495. Concerto per il cembalo concert. con due violini e basso del Sigr. Bach. 1780 or earlier? (source of date: pub. date). TERRY, C. S., 293; WADE, Appendix B, item X25
Ms.: D-ddr GOl, Mus. pag. 4/4 ("Del Sigr. Bach")
Early print: See TERRY, C. S., 293.
By Johann Christian Bach. See WADE, 18, 306–07.

Incipit from Mus. pag. 4/4, 1st mvt.:

496. Concerto di cembalo . . . accompagnato di due violini e vioncello. 1780 or earlier (source of date: pub. date). TERRY, C. S., 294; WADE, Appendix B, item X16
Ms.: D-ddr WRtl, mus. LV c: 16
Early print: See TERRY, C. S., 294.
By Johann Christian Bach. See WADE, 294.

Incipit from Mus. IV c: 16, 1st mvt.:

497. Concerto for violin or viola with piano or orchestra accompaniment [also arranged as a concerto for orchestra, concerto for 4 viols, etc.]. c. 1905. WADE, Appendix B, item X9
A deliberate falsification by Henri Casadesus, according to his widow and his brother Marius, as reported by Walter Lebermann, "Apokryph, Plagiat, Korruptel oder Falsifikat?" *Die Musikforschung*, 20 (1967), 422, 425. The work first appeared at the start of this century as a concerto "for Four Viols Concertante" in the concerts of the Paris Société nouvelle des Instruments anciens, and has been continued through a well-known arrangement commissioned from Maximilian Steinberg by Serge Koussevitzky in 1909 (*Concerto instrumenté pour petit orchestre*, Paris: Edition russe de musique, [1912], reprinted New York: Broude, n.d.), recordings, and performances in various versions up to the present. An attractive composition in its own right, it has, ironically, become one of the best-known works attributed to CPEB. See CUDWORTH; SERBIN; WADE, 21, 279–82. See also item 647.

Incipit from the Steinberg arrangement, 1st mvt.:

498. Concerto . . . [harpsichord, 2 violins, viola, bass]. n.d.
Wq n.v. 36; WADE, Appendix B, item X2
Ms.: D-brd B, P 295 (incomplete)
By C. Nichelmann. Attributed to him in D-ddr Bds, Am.B.

521 (in his own hand); D-brd B, Mus. ms. 16165/7. See Concerto X in LEE; ULDALL, 67; SUCHALLA/ORCHES-TERSINFONIEN, 282–83; WADE, 14, 265–66.

Incipit from P 295, 1st mvt.:

499. Concerto . . . [harpsichord, 2 violins, viola, bass]. n.d. WADE, Appendix B, item X8
Ms.: D-ddr GOl, Ms. Mus. 5 (cembalo part only)
By G. Benda; see ULDALL, 83. Attributed to Benda in D-brd B, Mus. ms. 1364. WADE, 17, 278, notes that this concerto is listed in BREITKOPF alphabetically—that is, right after the CPEB listings—which may have caused the misattribution.

Incipit from Ms. Mus. 5, 1st mvt.:

500. [Harpsichord concerto]. n.d. Kast, Bach-Incerta 37; WADE, Appendix B, item X22
Mss.: D-brd B, St 624 (no title p., no attribution), Mus. ms. 20776, Mus. ms. 20665
By Johann Gabriel Seifert. St 624 is the cembalo part only, accompanied by this note: "Re: Bach St 624. This cembalo part belongs to Seifert Mus. ms. 20665. J.K. Wolf. Feb. 4, 1965." The other two mss. attribute the work to Seifert. ULDALL, 80–82, discusses this concerto as one by Seifert, with no mention of an attribution problem. My thanks to Rachel Wade for this information.
Other lit.: WADE, 19, 302–03

Incipit from St 624, 1st mvt.:

501. [Harpsichord concerto]. n.d. WADE, Appendix B, item X26
Mss.: Ch Bub, Sammlung Geigy-Hagenbach 1627 (no title p., and consisting of only a portion of the 1st violin part; contains an elaborate attestation by one Hermann Naegeli that the work is by J. S. Bach, says WADE, 308–09); Ch Zz, AMC XIV 490; D-brd B, Mus. ms. 21917/5
By Johann Nikolaus Tischer. BREITKOPF lists a keyboard concerto with this incipit as by "Giov. Tischer." ULDALL, 94, discusses this work as Tischer's without any mention of attribution. This information is from WADE, 308–09.

Incipit from the fragment in Ch Bub:

CHAMBER MUSIC WITH A LEADING KEYBOARD PART

Authentic

502. Sonata a cembalo conc. e violino. 1731, rev. 1746 (NV 36). W. 71
Mss.: D-brd B, St 262, St 562; B Bc, 6354 (missing); A Wgm, XI 36264 (marked by CPEB)
Mod. edns.: E. F. Schmid, Karlsbad: Hohler, 1932; H. Ruf, Frankfurt am Main: Deutscher Ricordi, 1954
Lit.: SCHMID/KAMMERMUSIK, 123–26, 131–32, 161, Anh. 40–41; GEIRINGER/CHAMBER, 535; BERG, 189

Incipits from XI 36264:

503. Sonata . . . a cembalo obligato e violino concertato. 1731, rev. 1747 (NV 36). W. 72
Mss.: D-brd B, St 261, St 563; B Bc, 6354 (missing); A Wgm, XI 36308 (title p. marked by CPEB)
Mod. edn.: H. Ruf and P. Hoffmann, Frankfurt am Main: Deutscher Ricordi, 1954
Lit.: SCHMID/KAMMERMUSIK, 125–26, 132, 161; BERG, 189
A.v.: item 596

Incipits from St 261:

504. Sonata per il cembalo obligato con violino. 1745 (NV 37). W. 73

Mss.: D-brd B, St 240 I (a.v. for harpsichord and flute), St 240 II (a.v. for harpsichord and violin or flute; harpsichord right-hand part exchanged with violin/flute part); D-ddr SWl, 848; B Bc, 6354 (Michel); US AA, M322.B12.T49.17--

Mod. edn.: H. Ruf, Frankfurt am Main: Deutscher Ricordi, 1957 (based partly on item 573, resulting in interchange of parts)

Lit.: SCHMID/KAMMERMUSIK, 161

A.v.: item 573. The listing in NV, 37 is for "Flöte oder Clavier, Violine und Bass."

Incipits from 848:

505. Sonata a cembalo obligato e flauto. Probably 1747 or later (source of date: date of item 575). W. 83

Ms.: B Bc, 6354 (Michel, with title p. in CPEB's hand)

Mod. edns.: G. Scheck and H. Ruf, Frankfurt am Main: Deutscher Ricordi, 1954; WALTHER/SONATEN

Lit.: SCHMID/KAMMERMUSIK, 162

The a.v. as a trio sonata (item 575) is dated 1747 in NV, 38; the item 505 version is not listed in NV.

Incipits from 6354:

506. Trio fürs clavier und . . . flöte. Probably 1749 or later (NV 38). W. 84

Mss.: D-brd B, P 357 (autog.), St 478; A Wgm, XI 36267 (for the indicated instrumentation despite the wrapper, marked by CPEB ". . . a 2 Flauti Traversi e Basso")

Mod. edn.: WALTHER/SONATEN

Lit.: SCHMID/KAMMERMUSIK, 124 (read W. 84 instead of W. 162), 162

The a.v. as a trio sonata (item 580) is dated 1749 in NV, 38, with the note that the trio sonata "ist auch für die Flöte und Clavier gesetzt."

Incipits from P 357:

507. Sonata o vero sinfonia a cemb. oblig., 1 violino. 1754 (NV 39). W. 74

Mss.: D-brd B, St 560 (Michel); A Wgm, XI 36265 (title on wrapper is in CPEB's hand); A Wn, 16786 (Michel)

Lit.: SCHMID/KAMMERMUSIK, 123–26, 135, 161, Anh. 27–28; GEIRINGER/BACH, 362

An a.v. in trio-sonata instrumentation (item 585) is as well known as this version. Item 114 is an arr. of the 3rd mvt. of item 507. Item 507 is listed as falsely ascribed to J. S. Bach in SCHMIEDER, BWV-Anh. 185; but only D-brd B, St 341 (an a.v. in trio-sonata instrumentation; see item 585) is attributed to him.

Incipits from XI 36265:

508. Sonata a flauto e cembalo. 1754 (NV 38). W. 85

Mss.: B Br; A Wgm, XI 36262 (Michel; title p. in CPEB's

hand; a modern ms. copy is shelved under the same call no.)

Mod. edns.: G. Scheck and H. Ruf, Frankfurt am Main: Deutscher Ricordi, 1955; WALTHER/SONATEN

Lit.: SCHMID/KAMMERMUSIK, 162

A.v.: items 581, 583

Incipits from XI 36262:

509. Sonata a cembalo obligato e flauto. 1755 (NV 39). W. 86

Mss.: D-brd B, St 574 (Michel); B Bc, 6354 (Michel)

Mod. edn.: WALTHER/SONATEN

Lit.: SCHMID/KAMMERMUSIK, 163

A.v.: item 586

Incipits from 6354:

510. Sonata a cembalo e viola da gamba. 1759 (NV 40). W. 88

Mss.: D-brd B, P 357 (autog.); D-ddr Bds, Nachlass Klingenberg 5 (modern copy); B Bc, 5635 (Michel; vnt. playable on modern viola); A Wgm, XI 36270 (title p. marked by CPEB); A Wn, 16786 (Michel)

Mod. edns.: F. Grützmacher, Leipzig: Peters, 1881, reprinted 1928 (arranged for cello and piano); W. Primrose, New York: International, 1955 (arranged for viola and piano)

Lit.: BITTER/BRÜDER, I, 90; SCHMID/KAMMERMUSIK, 122, 125–26, 163; SCHULENBERG/INSTRUMENTAL, 7

Incipits from P 357:

511. Sonata a cembalo e violino. 1763 (NV 40). W. 75

Mss.: D-brd B, P 357 (autog.); B Bc, 6354; A Wgm, XI 36268 (title p. in CPEB's hand); A Wn, 16786 (Michel); US AA, M219.B114.S75.17--

Lit.: SCHMID/KAMMERMUSIK, 123, 125–26, 161; SCHULENBERG/ INSTRUMENTAL, 74–75

Incipits from P 357:

512. Sonata a cembalo e violino. 1763 (NV 40). W. 76

Mss.: D-brd B, P 357 (autog.); B Bc, 6354 (missing); A Wgm, XI 36263 (2 copies, both by Michel: one marked by CPEB, the other marred by modern pencil markings in the cembalo part); A Wn, 16786 (Michel); US AA, M219.B114.S76.17--

Mod. edns.: [J. Brahms,] Leipzig: Rieter-Biedermann, 1864; H. Sitt, New York: Peters, n.d.; H. Ruf, Mainz: Schott, 1965

Lit.: BITTER/BRÜDER, I, 90; SCHMID/KAMMERMUSIK, 72, facing 96, 115, 123, 125–26, 161, Anh, 24; OTTENBERG, 274–75; SCHULENBERG/INSTRUMENTAL, 79–82

Incipits from P 357:

Allegretto siciliano
Vln.

513. Sonata a cembalo conc. e violino. 1763 (NV 40). W. 77
Mss.: D-brd B, P 357 (autog.); B Bc, 6354 (missing); A Wgm, XI 36309 (2 copies; title p. of one marked by CPEB); A Wn, 16786 (Michel)
Mod. edns.: L. Landshoff, Leipzig: Peters, n.d.; H. Ruf, Frankfurt am Main: Deutscher Ricordi, [1956]
Lit.: SCHMID/KAMMERMUSIK, 123, 125–26, 161

Incipits from P 357:

Allegro di molto
Vln.

Largo
Cemb.

Presto
Cemb.

514. Sonata a cembalo e violino. 1763 (NV 40). W. 78
Mss.: D-brd B, P 357 (autog.), P 742 (autog. of sketches for the 1st 2 mvts.; not sketches for a vocal work, contrary to KAST), St 564 (Michel); A Wgm, XI 31767 (Michel; marred by modern pencil markings; a modern copy is shelved under the same number); A Wn, 16786 (Michel); US AA, M219.B114.S78.17--
Mod. edns.: [J. Brahms,] Leipzig: Rieter-Biedermann, 1864; H. Sitt, New York: Peters, n.d. (includes an incorrect dal segno repetition in the 1st mvt.)
Lit.: BITTER/BRÜDER, I, 90; SCHMID/KAMMERMUSIK, 72, 115, 123, 125–26, 130–31, 162, Anh. 25, 37–39; OTTENBERG, 274–75

Incipits from P 357:

Allegro moderato
Vln.

Adagio
Cemb.

Presto
Vln.

515. Trio a cembalo e flauto. 1766 (NV 41). W. 87
Mss.: D-brd B, St 565 (partly Michel), P 742 (sketches); B Bc, 6354 (Michel); A Wn, 16786 (Michel); F Pc, Bach Ms. 3, 6 (partial autog.)
Mod. edns.: A. van Leeuwen, Leipzig: Zimmermann, [1923]; G. Scheck and H. Ruf, Frankfurt am Main: Deutscher Ricordi, 1955; J.-P. Rampal, New York: International, 1955
Lit.: SCHMID/KAMMERMUSIK, 123, 125, 163; WADE, 3, 111

Incipits from 16786:

Allegretto
Cemb.

Andantino
Fl.

Cemb.

516. Sonata [harpsichord, clarinet, bassoon]. After 1767 (NV 52). W. 92/1
Ms.: B Bc, 6359, containing, in numerical order, items 516–21, which make up the *Sei Sonate per il Cembalo obligato con accompagnate Un B Clarinett, Un Fagott,* 6 single mvts. altogether, listed on p. 52 of NV without date as having been composed in Hamburg
Mod. edns. of item 516: OBERDÖRFFER/SONATEN, BALASSA, SIMON/SONATAS
A.v. of item 516: item 629
Lit. on the set: SCHMID/KAMMERMUSIK, 139–40; GEIRINGER/BACH, 364; WADE, 54

Incipit of item 516 from 6359:

Allegretto
Cemb.

517. Sonata [harpsichord, clarinet, bassoon]. After 1767 (NV 52). W. 92/2
See item 516.
Mod. edns.: OBERDÖRFFER/SONATEN, BALASSA, SIMON/SONATAS
Lit.: SCHMID/KAMMERMUSIK, 148, Anh. 68–70
A.v.: items 299, 633

Incipit from 6359:

Allegro di molto
Cemb.

518. Sonata [harpsichord, clarinet, bassoon]. After 1767 (NV 52). W. 92/3
See item 516.
Mod. edns.: OBERDÖRFFER/SONATEN, BALASSA, SIMON/SONATAS
A.v.: items 254, 255, 613, 614

Incipit from 6359:

519. Sonata [harpsichord, clarinet, bassoon]. After 1767 (NV 52). W. 92/4
See item 516.
Mod. edns.: OBERDÖRFFER/SONATEN, BALASSA, SIMON/SONATAS
A.v.: item 631

Incipit from 6359:

520. Sonata [harpsichord, clarinet, bassoon]. After 1767 (NV 52). W. 92/5
See item 516.
Mod. edns.: OBERDÖRFFER/SONATEN, BALASSA, SIMON/SONATAS
Lit.: SCHMID/KAMMERMUSIK, 148
A.v.: items 299, 630

Incipit from 6359:

521. Sonata [harpsichord, clarinet, bassoon]. After 1767 (NV 52). W. 92/6
See item 516.
Mod. edns.: OBERDÖRFFER/SONATEN, BALASSA, SIMON/SONATAS
A.v.: items 251, 610, 635/2

Incipit from 6359:

522. Sonata [keyboard, violin, cello]. 1775 (NV 41). W. 90/1
Mss.: D-brd B, P 358 (autog.), St 567, St 629
Early print and lit. about it: See ACCOMPANIED SONATAS I.

Lit. about this work: SCHMID/KAMMERMUSIK, 139–40, 143–44; OTTENBERG, 187–88; SCHULENBERG/INSTRU-MENTAL, 40–41
See item 491.

Incipits from ACCOMPANIED SONATAS I:

523. Sonata [keyboard, violin, cello]. 1775 (NV 41). W. 90/2
Ms.: D-brd B, P 358 (autog.)
Early print and lit. about it: See ACCOMPANIED SONATAS I.
Lit. about this work: FORKEL/BIBLIOTHEK, II, 281–93; KOLLMANN, 6; BITTER/BRÜDER, I, 209–10; STEG-LICH/HOMILIUS, 70–72, 86–87; SCHMID/KAMMER-MUSIK, 139–41, 143–44, Anh. 54–57, 63–64; COLE, 390–93; OTTENBERG, 175–77

Incipits from ACCOMPANIED SONATAS I:

524. Sonata [keyboard, violin, cello]. 1775 (NV 41). W. 90/3
Mss.: D-brd B, P 358 (autog.), St 566
Early print and lit. about it: See ACCOMPANIED SONATAS I.
Mod. edn.: F. Oberdörffer, Kassel: Bärenreiter, [1949], re-printed 1965
Lit. about this work: SCHMID/KAMMERMUSIK, 139–40; SCHULENBERG/INSTRUMENTAL, 48–49
See item 491.

Incipits from ACCOMPANIED SONATAS I:

Incipits from P 358:

525. Sonata [keyboard, violin, cello]. 1775 or 1776 (source of date: see below). W. 89/1

Ms.: D-brd B, P 358 (autog.)

Early prints and lit. about them: See ACCOMPANIED SONATAS II.

Ms. probably copied from an early print: B Bc, 6357

Mod. edn.: SCHMID/TRIOS

Lit. about this work: SCHMID/KAMMERMUSIK, 139–40, 147–48

NV, 42, gives 1778 as the date of composition of all 6 sonatas comprising items 525–30 as a set, not taking the Bremner print of ACCOMPANIED SONATAS II into account. A notation in WESTPHAL/NACHRICHTEN supports the 1776 date. CPEB corresponded with Forkel about such works in late 1775 (see CPEB/FORKEL in BITTER/BRÜDER, I, 209).

Incipits from P 358:

526. Sonata [keyboard, violin, cello]. 1775 or 1776 (source of date: see item 525). W. 89/2

Ms.: D-brd B, P 358 (autog.)

Early prints and lit. about them: See ACCOMPANIED SONATAS II.

Ms. probably copied from an early print: B Bc, 6357

Mod. edns.: SCHMID/TRIOS; ed. K. Geiringer in *Music of the Bach Family: an Anthology,* Cambridge: Harvard University Press, 1955 (1st and 2nd mvts. only)

Lit. about this work: SCHMID/KAMMERMUSIK, 139–40, 147–48

527. Sonata [keyboard, violin, cello]. 1775 or 1776 (source of date: see item 525). W. 89/3

Ms.: D-brd B, P 358 (autog.)

Early prints and lit. about them: See ACCOMPANIED SONATAS II.

Ms. probably copied from an early print: B Bc, 6357

Mod. edns.: H. Fischer and F. Oberdörffer, Berlin: Vieweg, 1936, reprinted as part of *Deutsche Klaviermusik des 17. und 18. Jahrhunderts,* 2nd edn., Berlin: Vieweg, 1960; SCHMID/TRIOS

Lit. about this work: SCHMID/KAMMERMUSIK, 139–40, 143–45

Incipits from P 358:

528. Sonata [keyboard, violin, cello]. 1775 or 1776 (source of date: see item 525). W. 89/4

Ms.: D-brd B, P 358 (autog.)

Early prints and lit. about them: See ACCOMPANIED SONATAS II.

Ms. probably copied from an early print: B Bc, 6357

Mod. edn.: SCHMID/TRIOS

Lit. about this work: SCHMID/KAMMERMUSIK, 139–40

Incipits from P 358:

529. Sonata [keyboard, violin, cello]. 1775 or 1776 (source of date: see item 525). W. 89/5

Ms.: D-brd B, P 358 (autog.)

Early prints and lit. about them: See ACCOMPANIED SONATAS II.

Ms. probably copied from an early print: B Bc, 6357

Mod. edns.: H. Fischer and F. Oberdörffer, Berlin: Vieweg, 1936, reprinted as part of *Deutsche Klaviermusik des 17. und 18. Jahrhunderts,* 2nd edn., Berlin: Vieweg, 1960; SCHMID/TRIOS

Lit. about this work: SCHMID/KAMMERMUSIK, 139–40, 143–45, Anh. 64

Incipits from P 358:

530. Sonata [keyboard, violin, cello]. 1775 or 1776 (source of date: see item 525). W. 89/6

Ms.: D-brd B, P 358 (autog.)

Early prints and lit. about them: See ACCOMPANIED SONATAS II.

Ms. probably copied from an early print: B Bc, 6357

Mod. edn.: SCHMID/TRIOS

Lit. about this work: SCHMID/KAMMERMUSIK, 139–40

Incipits from P 358:

531. Sonata [keyboard, violin, cello]. 1777 (NV 41). W. 91/1

Ms.: D-brd B, P 360 (autog.)

Early print and lit. about it: See ACCOMPANIED SONATAS III.

Ms. probably copied from the early print: D-brd B, P 912

Lit. about this work: SCHMID/KAMMERMUSIK, 139–40, 143; SCHULENBERG/INSTRUMENTAL, 142–43

Incipits from ACCOMPANIED SONATAS III:

532. Sonata [keyboard, violin, cello]. 1777 (NV 41). W. 91/2

Ms.: D-brd B, P 360 (autog.)

Early print and lit. about it: See ACCOMPANIED SONATAS III.

Ms. probably copied from the early print: D-brd B, P 912

Lit. about this work: FORKEL/BIBLIOTHEK, II, 28; STEGLICH/HOMILIUS, 87, 91–94; SCHMID/KAMMERMUSIK, 139–40, 143–46; GEIRINGER/BACH, 363

Incipits from ACCOMPANIED SONATAS III:

533. Sonata [keyboard, violin, cello]. 1777 (NV 41). W. 91/3

Ms.: D-brd B, P 360 (autog.)

Early print and lit. about it: See ACCOMPANIED SONATAS III.

Ms. probably copied from the early print: D-brd B, P 912

Lit. about this work: STEGLICH/HOMILIUS, 129–30; SCHMID/KAMMERMUSIK, 139–40; GEIRINGER/BACH, 363

Incipits from ACCOMPANIED SONATAS III:

534. Sonata [keyboard, violin, cello]. 1777 (NV 42). W. 91/4
Mss.: D-brd B, P 358 (Michel and CPEB), P 360 (autog.)
Early print and lit. about it: See ACCOMPANIED
   SONATAS III.
Ms. probably copied from the early print: D-brd B, P 912
Mod. edn.: H. Fischer and F. Oberdörffer, Berlin: Vieweg,
   1936, reprinted as part of *Deutsche Klaviermusik des 17. und
   18. Jahrhunderts,* 2nd edn., Berlin: Vieweg, 1960
Lit. about this work: SCHMID/KAMMERMUSIK, 139–40,
   facing 144, 148; FISCHER, 193, 205–06, 209, 214–16, 218;
   WADE, 3
This single-mvt. "sonata" is a set of variations on item 249;
   it became in turn the subject of other approaches to vari-
   ation form (see item 259).

Incipit from ACCOMPANIED SONATAS III:

[1 mvt. only]

535. Arioso per il cembalo e violino. 1781 (NV 42). W. 79
(= Wq n.v. 70)
Mss.: D-brd B, N. Mus. ms. 10322 (Michel), St 573 (Michel);
   B Bc, 6354 (missing); A Wgm, XI 36269 (score copied by
   Michel, parts autog.); A Wn, 16786 (Michel); D-ddr LEm,
   Becker III 8.2
Mod. edn.: H. Ruf, Frankfurt am Main: Deutscher Ricordi,
   1954
Lit.: SCHMID/KAMMERMUSIK, 139–40, 148, 162;
   FISCHER, 194, 198, 205, 209, 216–18; GEIRINGER/BACH,
   362; SCHULENBERG/INSTRUMENTAL, 141

Incipit from 36269:

536. Clavier-fantasie mit Begleitung einer Violine, "C. P.
E. Bachs Empfindungen." 1787 (NV 42). W. 80
Mss.: D-brd B, P 361 (autog.); B Bc, 6354 (missing), 5895
   (mostly Michel; sketches); A Wgm, XI 36266 (Michel; title
   p. marked by CPEB); F Sim; H Bn
Mod. edn.: A. Schering, Leipzig: Kahnt, 1938
Lit.: SCHMID/KAMMERMUSIK, 65, 139–40, 148–50, 162;
   REESER, 30–31; GEIRINGER/BACH, 362–63; BUSCH,
   276, 369–70; NEWMAN, 423; BERG, 228; ELDER, 92–95;
   OTTENBERG, 243
Arr. of item 300, with new music added (". . . zu einem
   Trio [that is, for keyboard and violin] gearbeitet," says
   NV, 42).
See item 867.

Incipit from P 361:

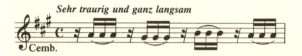

537. Quartetto fürs Clavier, Flöte, Bratsche und Bass. 1788
(NV 51). W. 93
Mss.: B Bc, 6358 (Michel; "Quartetto I"); H Bn
Mod. edns.: E. F. Schmid, Kassel: Bärenreiter, 1952; G. Pic-
   cioli, New York: International, [1955]
Lit.: SCHMID/KAMMERMUSIK, 142–43, 146–47, 164, Anh.
   57–61, 65–66; GEIRINGER/BACH, 362–63; BERG, 1;
   WADE, 54; OTTENBERG, 88, 243, 248–49; SCHULEN-
   BERG/INSTRUMENTAL, 7
Also termed a quartet in NV, 51–52. An autog. ms. formerly
   in the library of the Berlin Singakademie bore marks of
   articulation for cello in the bass line of the keyboard part,
   according to SCHMID/KAMMERMUSIK, 139. In 1788 a
   separate "bass" part and a completely written-out
   keyboard part would probably have been the reason for
   classifying the work as a quartet rather than as a trio
   sonata.

Incipits from 6358:

538. Quartetto fürs Clavier, Flöte, Bratsche und Bass. 1788
(NV 52). W. 94
Mss.: B Bc, 6358 (Michel; "Quartetto II"); H Bn

Mod. edns.: E. F. Schmid, Kassel: Bärenreiter, 1952; G. Piccioli, New York: International, [1955]
Lit.: SCHMID/KAMMERMUSIK, 65, 140, 143, 147, 164, Anh. 53–54, 61, 66–68; GEIRINGER/BACH, 362–63; BERG, 1; WADE, 53; OTTENBERG, 88, 243, 248; SCHULENBERG/INSTRUMENTAL, 7
The note in item 537 applies also to this work.

Incipits from 6358:

539. Quartetto fürs Clavier, Flöte, Bratsche und Bass. 1788 (NV 52). W. 95
Ms.: B Bc, 6358 (Michel; "Quartetto III")
Mod. edns.: E. F. Schmid, Münster: Bisping, 1930; idem, Kassel: Bärenreiter, 1952; G. Piccioli, New York: International, [1955]
Lit.: SCHMID/KAMMERMUSIK, 143, 164, Anh. 62–63; GEIRINGER/BACH, 362–63; BERG, 1; OTTENBERG, 88, 243, 248, 250; SCHULENBERG/INSTRUMENTAL, 7
The note in item 537 applies also to this work.

Incipits from 6358:

[2 mvts. only]

540. [Sonata fragment for keyboard and melody instrument(s)]. n.d.
Ms.: B Bc, 27.914 (autog., keyboard part only)
See SCHMID/KAMMERMUSIK, 176.

Incipit from 27.914:

541. [Sonata for keyboard and viola]. n.d.
Key of F. A modern copy in score is listed as entry No. 186 in PRIEGER; it is now presumably in an unknown private collection.
See SCHMID/KAMMERMUSIK, 176.

Incipits not available

Possibly Authentic

542. Sonata per il cembalo e violino. Probably c. 1731 or 1747 (source of dates: dates of item 570)
Ms.: D-brd B, St 571 ("Dal Sigr. C. P. E. Bach")
A.v. of item 570. The title page bears the name of the owner, [J. H.] Grave (fl. 1750–1800), who owned many other Bach-family mss. See KAST, 135.

Incipits from St 571:

542.5. Sonata, cembalo obligato con violino. c. 1734 or earlier (source of date: MARSHALL, 473). BWV 1020
Mss.: A Wgm, XI 36271 (Michel); D-brd B, P 471 (attributed to J. S. Bach), P 1059 (attributed to "Bach")
Mod. edn.: DÜRR
Also credited to CPEB in BREITKOPF, 12. Listed in SCHMIEDER as doubtful among J. S. Bach's works. In CPEB/FORKEL, 26 Aug. 1774 (printed in BITTER/BRÜDER, I, 338), CPEB writes that the ms. copies sold under his name by Breitkopf "sind theils nicht von mir, wenigstens sind sie alt und falsch geschrieben."
But MARSHALL makes a case for CPEB's composition of this work on the model of a sonata by J. S. Bach, BWV 1031 (item 545 in the present catalogue). And KOBAYASHI, 52–53, offers three main arguments in favor of CPEB's authorship: (1) The Michel copy is attributed to CPEB in Michel's hand (regarding Michel, see p. xxiii). (2) P 1059, from the estate of the Thomascantor J. G. Schicht and attributed only to "Bach," was, according to DÜRR, the source of P 471; the attribution on P 471 to J. S. Bach is therefore without foundation. (3) Schicht's musical estate was kept together by the Breitkopf firm and was apparently the source of this work as advertised under CPEB's name by Breitkopf.

Incipits from XI 36271:

543. Trio a cembalo obligato e violino. Probably c. 1755 (source of date: date of items 587, 588)

Mss.: D-brd B, St 244 ("Dell Sigl. Bach"; a.v. for harpsichord and flute; parts reversed), St 253; US Wc, M412.A2B13

A.v. of items 587–89. Parts are also provided in all 3 mss. for performance as a trio sonata (that is, in the item 587 version). St 253 also contains an a.v. of items 543 and 587 for two keyboards.

Incipits from M12.A2B13:

544. Sonata ex E♯ a cembalo e violino. n.d.

Ms.: D-brd DS, Mus. ms. 523 ("dell Sigr. Bach")

Owner's name illegible on title p. A substantial work in a style like that of CPEB, yet unmentioned in any catalogue or other source known to me

Incipits from Mus. ms. 523:

Spurious

545. Es d[ur] Trio fürs obligate Clavier u. die Flöte. Mid-18th century (source of date: DÜRR). BWV 1031

Mss.: D-brd B, P 649 (title p. in CPEB's hand, attributing the work to J. S. Bach; source of the title given here), P 1056 (also attributing the work to J. S. Bach; once in the possession of C. F. Penzel, "one of the most important and reliable transmitters and copyists of Sebastian Bach's music," says MARSHALL, 467)

Mod. edn.: DÜRR

MARSHALL, based on the facts about P 649 and P 1056 noted above, and reminding us that this work's galant style is occasionally present in other J. S. Bach works of the period, argues convincingly for restoring this work "to the [J. S.] Bach canon" despite recent supposition, based on its galant style, that it is CPEB's.

See item 542.5.

Incipit from BWV 1031:

546. Sonate pour le clavecin, le violon et la basse. c. 1775 (source of date: date of pub.). TERRY, C. S., 322

Mss.: D-brd RH, ms. 865; D-brd DO, Mus. ms. 153 (slightly varied)

By Johann Christian Bach; see the list of prints in TERRY, C. S., 322–23.

Incipit from ms. 865, 1st mvt.:

547. Sonate pour le clavecin, le violon et la basse. c. 1775 (source of date: date of pub.). TERRY, C. S., 322

Ms.: D-brd RH, ms. 865

By Johann Christian Bach; see the list of prints in TERRY, C. S., 322–23.

Incipit from ms. 865, 1st mvt.:

SOLO SONATAS FOR WIND OR STRING INSTRUMENTS

Authentic

548. Sonata a flauto traverso solo e basso. Probably 1735 or earlier (NV 48). W. 134

Ms.: B Bc, 5517

Mod. edn.: K. Walther, Leipzig: Zimmermann, 1958
Lit.: SCHMID/KAMMERMUSIK, 90, 92, 97–98, 101, 167, Anh. 7–8, 18, 20

Incipits from 5517:

549. Solo a oboe col basso. Probably 1735 or earlier (NV 48). W. 135
Ms.: B Bc, 5521 (Michel)
Mod. edns.: K. Walther, Leipzig: Breitkopf & Härtel, [1953]; G. Scheck and H. Ruf, Frankfurt am Main: Deutscher Ricordi, 1954
Lit.: SCHMID/KAMMERMUSIK, 90, 92, 97, 101–02, 167, Anh. 14, 20; FISCHER, 194; SCHULENBERG/INSTRU-MENTAL, 96

Incipits from 5521:

550. Sonata a flauto traverso solo e basso. 1735 (NV 49). W. 123
Ms.: B Bc, 5517
Mod. edn. (with item 551): K. Walther, Kassel: Bärenreiter, 1936, reprinted 1964
Lit.: SCHMID/KAMMERMUSIK, 90, 92, 94–95, 98–99, 101–02, 105–06, 166, Anh. 4, 13, 18, 20; FISCHER, 191, 194, 199, 211; NEWMAN, 419; OTTENBERG, 43, 284, 301

Incipits from 5517:

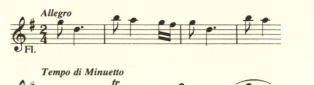

551. Sonata a flauto traverso solo e basso. 1737 (NV 49). W. 124
Ms.: B Bc, 5517
Mod. edn.: See item 550.
Lit.: SCHMID/KAMMERMUSIK, 90, 92, 94, 98, 100–02, 105–06, 166, Anh. 8–10, 13; FISCHER, 191, 194, 199, 214; OTTENBERG, 43, 284, 301; SCHULENBERG/INSTRUMEN-TAL, 10

Incipits from 5517:

552. Sonata a flauto traverso solo e basso. 1738 (NV 49). W. 125
Ms.: B Bc, 5518 (Michel)
Mod. edns.: G. Scheck and H. Ruf, Frankfurt am Main: Deutscher Ricordi, 1954; K. Walther, Leipzig: Zimmermann, 1958
Lit.: SCHMID/KAMMERMUSIK, 90, 92, 95–96, 101, 167, Anh. 19; NEWMAN, 419; OTTENBERG, 284; SCHULEN-BERG/INSTRUMENTAL, 64–65
Vnt. of the 3rd mvt.: 3rd mvt. of item 560

Incipits from 5518:

553. Sonata a flauto traverso solo e basso. 1738 (NV 49).
W. 126
Ms.: B Bc, 5517
Mod. edn.: K. Walther, Leipzig: Zimmermann, 1958
Lit.: SCHMID/KAMMERMUSIK, 90, 92, 95, 100–02, 106–07,
   167, Anh. 4–5, 14, 18, 20; FISCHER, 194; NEWMAN, 419;
   OTTENBERG, 284

Incipits from 5517:

554. Sonata a flauto traverso solo e basso. 1739 (NV 49).
W. 127
Ms.: B Bc, 5517
Mod. edns.: G. Scheck and H. Ruf, Frankfurt am Main:
   Deutscher Ricordi, 1954; K. Walther, Leipzig: Zimmer-
   mann, 1958
Lit.: SCHMID/KAMMERMUSIK, 90, 92, 98, 101, 167, Anh.
   9, 19–20; NEWMAN, 419; OTTENBERG, 284; SCHULEN-
   BERG/INSTRUMENTAL, 44

Incipits from 5517:

555. Sonata a flauto traverso solo e basso. 1740 (NV 49).
W. 128
Ms.: B Bc, 5517
Mod. edn.: K. Walther, Kassel: Bärenreiter, 1940, reprinted
   1960
Lit.: SCHMID/KÁMMERMUSIK, 90, 92, 96–97, 100–01, 106–
   07, 167, Anh. 4, 7, 11, 14, 19; FISCHER, 194; NEWMAN,
   419; OTTENBERG, 87, 284; SCHULENBERG/INSTRU-
   MENTAL, 55

Incipits from 5517:

556. Sonata a flauto traverso solo e basso. 1740 (NV 50).
W. 129
Ms.: B Bc, 5517
Mod. edn.: K. Walther, Leipzig: Zimmermann, 1958
Lit.: SCHMID/KAMMERMUSIK, 90, 92, 96–97, 101, 106,
   167, Anh. 5–6; BEURMANN/KLAVIERSONATEN, 41;
   NEWMAN, 419; OTTENBERG, 284
Vnt. of the 2nd mvt.: 2nd mvt. of item 561

Incipits from 5517:

557. Solo a violoncello col basso. 1740, rev. 1769 (NV 50).
W. 138
Lost
Lit.: SCHMID/KAMMERMUSIK, 168

Incipit from WOTQUENNE/THÉMATIQUE, 1st mvt.:

558. Sonata a viola da gamba solo e basso. 1745 (NV 50).
W. 136
Mss.: B Bc, 5634; D-ddr Bds, Nachlass Klingenberg 6 (mod-
   ern copy)
Mod. edn. (much distorted): P. Klengel, Leipzig: Breitkopf
   & Härtel, 1930
Lit.: SCHMID/KAMMERMUSIK, 90–92, 94, 100–02, 106,

122, 168, Anh. 11, 20; SCHULENBERG/INSTRUMEN-
TAL, 134

NV, 50, lists it as a solo for the flute; no such version has
yet been found.

Incipits from 5634:

559. Solo a viola da gamba e basso. 1746 (NV 50). W. 137
Mss.: B Bc, 5634 (Michel); D-ddr Bds, Nachlass Klingenberg
6 (modern copy)
Mod. edns.: P. Klengel, Leipzig: Breitkopf & Härtel, 1930
(arranged for cello and piano; much distorted); R. van
Leyden, Leipzig: Peters, 1933
Lit.: SCHMID/KAMMERMUSIK, 90–92, 94, 97–98, 102, 106,
122, 168, Anh. 3, 19–20; SCHULENBERG/INSTRUMEN-
TAL, 134

Incipits from 5634:

560. Sonata a flauto traverso solo e basso. 1746 (NV 50).
W. 130
Ms.: B Bc, 5517
Mod. edn.: K. Walther, Leipzig: Zimmermann, 1958
Lit.: SCHMID/KAMMERMUSIK, 90, 92, 97, 101, 106, 167,
Anh. 12–13, 19; NEWMAN, 419; OTTENBERG, 284
Vnt. of the 3rd mvt.: 3rd mvt. of item 552

Incipits from 5517:

561. Sonata a flauto traverso solo e basso. 1747 (NV 50).
W. 131
Mss.: D-brd B, P 893; B Bc, 5517
Mod. edns.: K. Walther, Kassel: Bärenreiter, 1940, reprinted
1960; G. Scheck and H. Ruf, Frankfurt am Main:
Deutscher Ricordi, 1954
Lit.: SCHMID/KAMMERMUSIK, 90, 92, 97, 100–02, 105–06,
167, Anh. 7, 19–20; NEWMAN, 419; OTTENBERG, 284
Vnt. of the 2nd mvt.: 2nd mvt. of item 556

Incipits from 5517:

562. Sonata per il flauto traverso solo senza basso. 1747
(NV 51). W. 132
Early prints: the above title, "In Berlino, 1763, alle spese di
Georgio Ludovico Winter"; MANCHERLEY, 179. Lit.
about MANCHERLEY: See this entry in Bib.
Mod. edns.: A. G. Kurth, Berlin: Raabe & Plothow/Simrock,
[c. 1913]; A. van Leeuwen, Leipzig: Zimmermann, 1925;
K.-A. Methmann, Hannover: Nagel, 1941; M. Wittgen-
stein, New York: Carl Fischer, 1949; L. Siber, Leipzig:
Hofmeister, 1955; G. Scheck and H. Ruf, Frankfurt am
Main: Deutscher Ricordi, 1955; H. U. Niggemann, Leip-
zig: Hofmeister, 1961; L. Moyse, New York: G. Schirmer,
1974; S. Baron, Elkhart, Ind.: Armstrong, [c. 1975]; H.
Teske, Adliswil-Zurich: Amadeus, 1978
Lit. about this work: SCHMID/KAMMERMUSIK, 92, 167,
Anh. 4; NEWMAN, 94; GEIRINGER/CHAMBER, 518

Incipits from the Winter print:

[2 mvts. only]

Possibly Authentic

564.5. Sonata a traversa e continuo. Probably c. 1731 (source of date: DÜRR). BWV 1033
Ms.: D-brd B, St 460 (partly autog.)
Mod. edn.: DÜRR
Despite the title-p. attribution (apparently in CPEB's hand) to J. S. Bach, MARSHALL, based on DÜRR, EPPSTEIN/FLÖTENSONATEN, and EPPSTEIN/STUDIEN, argues that this is largely CPEB's arrangement, amounting to some original composition, of a sonata for unaccompanied flute by J. S. Bach.

Incipits from BWV 1033:

563. Solo für die Harfe. 1762 (NV 51). W. 139
Ms.: B Bc, 13.287 (Michel)
Mod. edns.: H. Neeman, Leipzig: Breitkopf & Härtel, 1940 (order of the 1st 2 mvts. reversed); M. Grandjany, Paris: Durand, 1963 (order of the 1st 2 mvts. reversed); L. Lawrence, New York: Lyra Music, 1963, 1965; H. J. Zingel, Wiesbaden: Breitkopf & Härtel, 1968; J. B. Weidensaul, Teaneck, N.J.: Willow Hall Press, 1979. Only the last of these successfully reconciles the modern harp idiom with the standards of modern scholarship.
Lit.: SCHMID/KAMMERMUSIK, 90, 92, 99–102, 168, Anh. 11–13, 19; D. Berg, "C. P. E. Bach's Harp Sonata," *The American Harp Journal*, vol. 7, No. 4 (Winter 1980), 8–18; SCHULENBERG/INSTRUMENTAL, 6, 60

Incipits from 13.287:

564. Sonata a flauto traverso solo e basso. 1786 (NV 51). W. 133
Ms.: B Bc, 5517
Mod. edns.: H. Ruf, Frankfurt am Main: Deutscher Ricordi, 1955; K. Walther, Mainz: Schott, 1955; H.-P. Schmitz, Kassel: Bärenreiter, 1956
Lit.: SCHMID/KAMMERMUSIK, 91–92, 94, 99, 101–05, 135, 167, Anh. 4, 15–18; GEIRINGER/CHAMBER, 518, 520; SCHULENBERG/INSTRUMENTAL, 102–03

Incipits from 5517:

565. 2 Solo [Sonatas], pour Fletraversier [Flûte traversière] col Basso. 1763 or earlier (source of date: Schaffrath died in 1763.)
Ms.: D-brd B, Mus. ms. 19751/6
Attributed on the cover to "Sigl. Bach & Schaffrath."
Composed jointly with C. Schaffrath, according to the listing in PRIEGER, entry No. 353
Lit.: SCHMID/KAMMERMUSIK, 90, 176

Incipits from Mus. ms. 19751/6:

[Sonata 1]

[Sonata 2]

TRIO SONATAS

Authentic

566. Trio für die Violine, Bratsche und Bass, mit Johann Sebastian Bach gemeinschaftlich verfertigt. Probably 1731 or earlier (source of date: CPEB matriculated at the University of Leipzig in 1731.) NV, 65 (source of the title)
Lost
Also listed in BACH/LEVY. It may be related to item 569 or item 590.5.

567. Sonata a 1 flauto trav., 1 violino e basso. 1731, rev. 1747 (NV 36). W. 143
Mss.: D-brd B, P 357 (autog.); B Bc, 6360 (Michel); US Wc, M412.A2B15
Mod. edn.: R. and M. Ermeler, Frankfurt am Main: Zimmermann, [1932]

Lit.: STEGLICH/HOMILIUS, 60–61; SCHMID/KAMMER-MUSIK, 125–26, 168; OTTENBERG, 33; SCHULENBERG/INSTRUMENTAL, 57–59, 61

Incipits from P 357:

568. Trio a flauto traverso, violino e basso. 1731, rev. 1747 (NV 36). W. 144
Ms.: B Bc, 6360 (Michel)
Mod. edn.: F. Brüggen, Amsterdam: Broekmans en van Poppel, n.d.
Lit.: SCHMID/KAMMERMUSIK, 125, 168; OTTENBERG, 33

Incipits from 6360:

569. Sonata a 1 fl. trav., 1 violino e basso. 1731, rev. 1747 (NV 36). W. 145
Mss.: D-brd B, P 357 (autog.), P (St) 906, Am.B. 53, Am.B. 110; B Bc, 6360 (Michel), 27.905 (keyboard part autog., with this note on the cover in CPEB's hand: "Wenn die Violinstimme dieses Trios aus der Partitur oder von der ausgeschriebenen Violinstimme abgeschrieben wird: so sind 3 Exemplare davon complet da."); US Wc, M362.A2B13.W.145, M412.A2B15
Mod. edn.: A. Dürr, Celle: Moeck, 1963
Lit.: SCHMID/KAMMERMUSIK, 125, 127–28, facing 128, 130, 132, 169, Anh. 28–30, 41–42; OTTENBERG, 33–36, 298–99
BWV 1036, a trio sonata (2 violins and continuo) listed as doubtful among the works of J. S. Bach, is closely related to this work: the 2nd mvt. of BWV 1036 is an a.v. of the

1st mvt. of item 569, and the 3rd mvt. of BWV 1036 is an a.v. of the 2nd mvt. of item 569. Like item 566, item 569 may have been composed jointly by CPEB and his father; or item 569 may be identical to item 566. See also item 590.5.

Incipits from P 357:

570. Sonata a 1 fl. trav., 1 violino e basso. 1731, rev. 1747 (NV 37). W. 146

Mss.: D-brd B, P 357 (autog.); B Bc, 6360 (Michel); US Wc, M412.A2B15

Mod. edn.: A. Dürr, Celle: Moeck, 1963

Lit.: SCHMID/KAMMERMUSIK, 125, 169; OTTENBERG, 33; SCHULENBERG/INSTRUMENTAL, 60–61, 121–23

A.v.: item 542

Incipits from P 357:

571. Sonata [flute, violin, bass]. 1731, rev. 1747 (NV 37). W. 147

Mss.: D-brd B, P 357 (autog.), St 246, Am.B. 109; D-ddr Bds, Mus. ms. theor. 348 (only a keyboard realization of the figured bass); B Bc, 6360 (Michel); US Wc, M362.A2B13.W.147, M412.A2B15

Mod. edn.: H. Ruf, Kassel: Bärenreiter, 1963

Lit.: SCHMID/KAMMERMUSIK, 125–26, 129–31, 133–35, 140, 169, Anh. 31–32, 39, 44–49, 52; OTTENBERG, 33

Incipits from P 357:

572. Sonata a 1 fl. trav., 1 violino e basso. 1735, rev. 1747 (NV 47). W. 148

Mss.: D-brd B, P 357 (autog.), P 367, P 901, St 256 (a.v. for 2 violins and basso), Am.B. 109; B Bc, 6360 (Michel); US Wc, M362.B13.W.148, M412.A2B15; US AA, M322.B12.T48.17--

Mod. edn.: A. Dürr, Celle: Moeck, 1963

Lit.: SCHMID/KAMMERMUSIK, 125, 129, 132, 169, Anh. 30, 42; OTTENBERG, 34, 43, 46, 299, 301

VOSS/MUSICALIEN lists an a.v. for 2 violins and basso; this is probably St 256, which was in the collection of O. von Voss, according to KAST.

Arr.: item 377

Incipits from P 357:

573. Sonata a 1 fl. trav., 1 violino e basso. c. 1745 (NV 37). W. 149

Mss.: D-brd B, P 357 (autog.), P 367, St 569, Am.B. 108; B Bc, 6360 (Westphal); US Wc, M412.A2B15, M362.A2B13.W.149; US AA, M322.B12.T49.17--

Lit.: SCHMID/KAMMERMUSIK, 123, 125–26, facing 126, 129–32, 169, Anh. 33–37, 43

A.v.: item 504

Incipits from P 357:

574. Trio a flauto traverso, violino e basso. 1747 (NV 37). W. 150

Mss.: B Bc, 6360 (Michel); F Pc (autog.); US Wc, M362. A2B13. W. 150; US AA, M322.B12.T5.17--

Lit.: SCHMID/KAMMERMUSIK, 123, 125–26, 169

Incipits from 6360:

575. Sonata a 1 fl. trav., 1 violino e basso. 1747 (NV 38). W. 151

Mss.: D-brd B, P 357 (autog.), P 367, St 247, St 570, Am.B. 109; B Bc, 6360 (Michel); US AA, M322.B12.T5.17--

Mod. edns.: G. Braun, Neuhausen-Stuttgart: Hänssler-Verlag, 1972; K. Walther, New York: Peters, 1977

Lit.: SCHMID/KAMMERMUSIK, 123, 125–26, 130, 132–33, 135, 169, Anh. 37, 43–44, 51–52

A.v.: item 505

Incipits from P 357:

576. Sonata a 3 [2 violins and bass]. 1747 (NV 38). W. 154

Mss.: D-brd B, Am.B. 109 (1st violin part marked "Flaut"), P 229, St 255; B Bc, 6361 (Michel); US Wc, M412.A2B15, M351.A2B14.W.154

Mod. edn. (heavily edited): P. Klengel, Leipzig: Peters, 1933

Lit.: SCHMID/KAMMERMUSIK, 115, 123, 125, 169, Anh. 22–24; SCHULENBERG/INSTRUMENTAL, 122

Listed as falsely ascribed to J. S. Bach in SCHMIEDER, BWV-Anh. 186

Incipits from Am.B. 109:

577. Sonata a 2 violini e basso. 1747 (NV 38). W. 155

Mss.: D-brd B, P 357 (autog.), St 254, Am.B. 107; B Bc, 6361 (Michel); US Wc, M412.A2B15

Lit.: SCHMID/KAMMERMUSIK, 123, 125, 169

Incipits from P 357:

578. Sonata . . . a flauto traverso, violino [or with one of these replaced by keyboard right hand] e basso. 1748 (NV 38). W. 161/2

Mss.: D-brd B, St 245, Am.B. 109; A Wgm, XI 30168 (also contains a modern ms. copy)

Early print: ZWEY TRIO

Mss. probably copied from the early print: D-brd B, P 366; B Bc, 6364

Mod. edns.: J. Lorenz, Leipzig: Zimmermann, [1928]; L. Landshoff, Leipzig: Peters, [1935], reprinted New York: International, 1948

Lit.: BITTER/BRÜDER, I, 59–63; SCHMID/KAMMERMUSIK, 125–26, 171; NEWMAN, 428; OTTENBERG, 83–87, 318

A.v.: D-brd B, St 260, St 572, for flute and obbligato harpsichord (following the recommendation in ZWEY TRIO)

Incipits from ZWEY TRIO:

579. Sonata . . . a 2 violini [or 1 violin] e basso. 1749 (NV 38). W. 161/1

Mss.: D-brd B, St 257; D-ddr SWl

Early print: ZWEY TRIO

Ms. probably copied from the early print: D-brd B, P 366

Mod. edn.: K. Hofmann, Neuhausen-Stuttgart: Hänssler-Verlag, 1980

Lit.: FORKEL/GESCHICHTE, 387–88; BITTER/BRÜDER, I, 59–63; STEGLICH/HOMILIUS, 105–06; MERSMANN; SCHMID/KAMMERMUSIK, 72–73, facing 80, 114–17, 123, 125, 133, 135, 170, Anh. 25–26, 50–51; REESER, 34–36; GEIRINGER/BACH, 361–62; BUSCH, 96, 276; NEWMAN, 24, 141, 422–23, 428; HELM/LITERARY, 291–92; GEIRINGER/CHAMBER, 527–28; COHEN, 12; BERG, 218–19; WADE, 12; OTTENBERG, 83; SCHULENBERG/INSTRUMENTAL, 26, 32–33, 83–84

CPEB's only work provided with a written-out program

Incipits from ZWEY TRIO:

[2 mvts. only]

580. Trio a due flauti e basso. 1749 (NV 38). W. 162

Mss.: D-brd B, St 241; B Bc, 6363 (Westphal)

Mod. edn.: K. Walther, Leipzig: Zimmermann, [1935]

Lit.: SCHMID/KAMMERMUSIK, 111, 123, 124 (read W. 84, not W. 162), 125–26, 171, Anh. 21; SCHULENBERG/INSTRUMENTAL, 6, 75

A.v.: item 506

Incipits from 6363:

581. Trio a flauto traverso, violino e basso. 1754 (NV 38). W. 152

Mss.: D-brd B, St 620 (formerly P 1011, attributed to "Signore Graun"); B Bc, 6360 (Westphal); D-brd LÜh, Mus. H. 359

Lit.: SCHMID/KAMMERMUSIK, 169

A.v.: items 508, 583

Incipits from 6360:

582. Sinfonia a due violini e basso. 1754 (NV 39). W. 156

Mss.: D-brd B, St 251; D-ddr Bds, P 905, P 1219 (finale incomplete); B Bc, 6361 (Michel); A Wn, 18980 (Michel); F Pc, Ms. 13 (autog.?); US Wc, M312.4.A2B13.W.156

Lit.: SCHMID/KAMMERMUSIK, unnumbered p. between pp. 112 and 113, 117–18, 123–27, 135, 170; GEIRINGER/BACH, 362; NEWMAN, 20; SCHULENBERG/INSTRUMENTAL, 91, 131

Incipits from 6361:

Tempo di menuet

Allegro

583. Sonata a 2 violini e basso. 1754 (NV 38). W. 157

Mss.: D-brd B, P 357 (autog.), P 902, St 248, Am.B. 108; B Bc, 6361 (Westphal); an autog. title p. (only) is in an American private collection.

Mod. edns.: A. Fuchs, Leipzig: Brockhaus, [1896] (distorted); H. Riemann, Leipzig: Breitkopf & Härtel, n.d. (heavily edited); B. Hinze-Reinhold, Munich: Leuckart, 1924 (heavily edited)

Lit.: SCHMID/KAMMERMUSIK, 111–12, 123, 125, 170, Anh. 21; NEWMAN, 424; GEIRINGER/CHAMBER, 528

A.v.: items 508, 581

Incipits from P 357:

584. Sonata a II. violini e basso da C. F. E. Bach. 1754 (NV 39). W. 158

Mss.: D-brd B, St 250, St 253 (a.v. for 2 keyboards), St 561, Am.B. 108; D-ddr Bds, M.Th.; D-brd Bch; B Bc, 6361 (Westphal?); A Wgm, IX 3280 (entitled "Divertimento"); GB Lbm, Add. 31680; US Wc, M412.A2B15

Early prints: the above title, "In Berlino, 1763. Alle spese di Giorgio Ludovico Winter"; MANCHERLEY, 159. Lit. about MANCHERLEY: See this entry in Bib.

Mod. edn.: G. Schumann, Munich: Leuckart, 1909, reprinted 1937

Lit. about this work: SCHMID/KAMMERMUSIK, 123, 125, 132, 170, Anh. 43

Incipits from the Winter print:

585. Sinfonia a 3 voc. [2 violins, bass]. Probably c. 1754 (source of date: date of item 507)

Mss.: D-brd B, St 249, St 341 (attributed to JSB), P 900 (ms. set of parts); US Wc, M412.A2B14

Mod. edn: F. Nagel, Wolfenbüttel: Möseler Verlag, 1972

A.v.: item 507

In A Wgm, XI 36265, one of the sources of item 507, "2 Violini" has been corrected to "1 Violino" on the title p. in CPEB's hand. Obviously the trio-sonata version was as well known as the item 507 version. Here, as in item 507, item 114 is an a.v. of the 3rd mvt.

An autog. of item 585, present location unknown, was auctioned among other mss. belonging to M. Pincherle on 8 Nov. 1966, according to PINCHERLE.

Incipits from M412.A2B14:

586. Trio a flauto traverso, violino e basso. 1755 (NV 39). W. 153

Mss.: D-brd B, P 904, St 568; B Bc, 6360 (Westphal); US Wc, M412.A2B15

Lit.: SCHMID/KAMMERMUSIK, 125, 153, 169

A.v.: item 509

Incipits from 6360:

587. Trio a due violini e basso. 1755 (NV 39). W. 159

Mss.: D-brd B, P 903, St 244, St 253; D-ddr Bds, M.Th. 23; B Bc, 6361 (Westphal); US Wc, M312.A2B13.W.159, M412.A2B13; US CA, bMS Mus. 66.3 (copied by S. Hering, donated in mid-20th century to US CA by G. B. Weston)

Lit.: SCHMID/KAMMERMUSIK, 170

A.v.: items 543, 588, 589. Parts are also provided in St 244, St 253, and M412.A2B13 for performance by cembalo obbligato and violin/flute (that is, in the item 543 version).

Item 587 is listed as falsely ascribed to J. S. Bach in SCHMIEDER, BWV-Anh. 187.

Incipits from 6361:

588. Trio a viola, flauto basso [bass recorder, not *Quartflöte*] e cembalo. 1755 (NV 39). W. 163

Mss.: D-brd B, P 357 (autog.); B Bc, 6365 (Michel)

Mod. edns.: H. Brandts-Buys, Mainz: Schott, 1951; G. Piccioli, New York: International, [1955] (arranged for viola, bassoon or cello, and piano)

Lit.: SCHMID/KAMMERMUSIK, 94, 122, 125, 134–35, 171, Anh. 49, 53

A.v.: items 543, 587, 589

Incipits from 6365:

589. Trio a fagotto obligato, flauto basso [bass recorder, not *Quartflöte*] e cembalo. Probably c. 1755 (source of date: date of items 587–588)

Ms.: D-brd B, P 367

A.v.: items 543, 587, 588

Incipits from P 367:

590. Sonata a II violini e basso. 1756 (NV 39). W. 160

Mss.: D-brd B, N. Mus. ms. 10479; B Bc, 6361 (Westphal; vnt.?); a set of ms. parts is in the private collection of E. N. Kulukundis (U.S.).

Early print: MANCHERLEY, 71. Lit. about MANCHERLEY: See this entry in Bib.

Mod. edn. (heavily edited): P. Klengel, Leipzig: Peters, 1933

Lit. about this work: BITTER/BRÜDER, I, 86; SCHMID/KAMMERMUSIK, 117–18, 123–25, 127, 135, 170; GEIRINGER/BACH, 362; OTTENBERG, 87

Vnt.: W. 160, since it apparently comes from the Westphal copy? NV, 39: "ist im Musikalischen Mancherley gedruckt, aber nachher in der lsten Violine etwas verändert worden."

Incipits from MANCHERLEY:

Possibly Authentic

590.5. [Trio sonata for flute, violin, and continuo]. Probably c. 1732–35 (source of date: SIEGELE, 31–46). BWV 1038

Ms.: D-brd Ngm (in the hand of J. S. Bach, though unattributed)

SIEGELE, 31–46, argues that this work, whose continuo is largely borrowed from BWV 1021, is mostly composed by CPEB.

See items 566, 569.

Incipits from BWV 1038:

591. Sonata E♭, 2 violini e basso. Probably before 1768 (source of date: the Berlin provenance of the Itzig ms.)
Mss.: US Wc, M351.A2B14; also in a ms. from the collection of Sara Levy (née Itzig) formerly in the library of the Berlin Singakademie, according to SCHMID/KAMMERMUSIK, 120, 176, Anh. 26. The latter copy is now lost or destroyed.

Incipits from M351.A2B14:

592. Sonata . . . a flauto traverso o violino primo, violino secondo e basso. Probably before 1768 (source of date: same as for item 591)
Ms.: D-brd HVs
Mod. edn.: K. Schneider, Wolfenbüttel: Möseler, 1987
The ms. was formerly in the possession of Isaak Daniel Itzig. Written under CPEB's name on the title p.: "da [C. F. ?] Abel. London." I am indebted to Klaus Schneider, head of the music division of the Stadtbibliothek Hannover, for bringing the ms. of this excellent work to my attention. Discovered in 1945 in the ravaged castle of Ingenheim in Silesia, it was placed in the Hannover library in 1970.

Incipits from the D-brd HVs ms.:

593. Sonata [flute, violin, continuo]. n.d.
In a ms. from the Levy–Singakademie collection mentioned in item 591, according to SCHMID/KAMMERMUSIK, 120, 176, Anh. 26. This ms. is now lost or destroyed.

Incipit of 1st mvt. from SCHMID/KAMMERMUSIK, Anh. 26:

594. Deleted

Doubtful

595. [Sonata for flute, violin, continuo]. 1735 (source of date: BITTER/BRÜDER).
Listed in BITTER/BRÜDER, I, 17; II, 326. ¾ meter, key of G. I have not been able to find such a work.

596. Sonata a 3 strom. [flute, violin, continuo]. Probably c. 1747 (source of date: date of revision of item 503)
Ms.: US Wc, M422.A2B13
A.v. of item 503
An amateurish and apparently hasty copy

Incipits from M422.A2B13:

597. Trio, flauto traverso, violino con cembalo. n.d.
Ms.: US Wc, M362.A2.B135
Ed. as a work of W. F. Bach by H. Brandts-Buys, Amsterdam: Broekmans en van Poppel, n.d., using ms. M.Th. 55 in D-ddr Bds as source. Ed. as a work of Johann Christian Bach by K. Maguerre, Celle: Moeck, 1960, using ms. St 296 in D-brd B. Listed as uncertain among W. F. Bach's works in FALCK, 13, whose source was M.Th. 55; listed as authentic among Johann Christian Bach's works in TERRY, C. S., 332, whose source was St 296. SCHMID/KAMMERMUSIK, 120, 176, Anh. 27, lists the trio as uncertain among CPEB's compositions; his sources were a ms. in the Thulemeir collection of D-ddr Bds (almost certainly M.Th. 55) and a ms. (now lost or destroyed) in the Berlin Singakademie. ROE, 20–21, concludes that the work connot positively be attributed to Johann Christian Bach.

Incipit from M362.A2.B135, 1st mvt.:

OTHER CHAMBER MUSIC

Authentic

598. Duett für eine Flöte und Violine. 1748 (NV 51). W. 140
Early print: VIELERLEY, 67. Lit. about VIELERLEY: See this entry in Bib.
Ms. probably copied from the early print: B Bc, 6366
Mod. edns.: W. Stephan, Hannover: Nagel, 1928; J. Marx, New York: Mercury, 1948
Lit. about this work: SCHMID/KAMMERMUSIK, 168

Incipits from VIELERLEY:

599. Duetto a due Violini. 1752 (NV 51). W. 141
Lost
Lit.: SCHMID/KAMMERMUSIK, 168

Incipit of the 1st mvt. from WOTQUENNE/THÉMATIQUE:

600. Zwölf kleine Stücke mit zwey und drey Stimmen für die Flöte oder Violin und das Clavier. 1758 (NV 40). W. 81
Early prints and lit. about them: See ZWÖLF KLEINE I.
Ms. probably copied from an early print: B Bc, 6372 (Westphal)
Mod. edns.: F. Oberdörffer, Berlin: Vieweg, 1934; K. Walther, Leipzig: Zimmermann, [1971]; WALTHER/DUETTE (Nos. 4, 7, 10)
Lit. about this work: SCHMID/KAMMERMUSIK, 162; WADE, 4
Arr.: of Nos. 1, 4, 11 in item 450; of No. 7 in item 456; of No. 9 in item 480.5; of No. 12 in items 480, 480.5

Incipits from 6372:

No. 1. Menuet

No. 2. Menuet

[No. 1 is repeated after No. 2.]

No. 3. Polonoise

No. 4. Presto

No. 5. Allegro

No. 6. Allegro

No. 7. Presto

No. 8. Allegro

No. 9. Allegretto

No. 10. Allegro assai

No. 11. Andantino

No. 12. Andantino

[No. 11 is repeated after No. 12.]

601. Zwey Menuetten aus C dur für drey Trompeten, Pauken, zwey Quer-Flöten, zwey Fagotts, zwey Geigen und dem Bass. 1762 or earlier (source of date: 1st pub.). W. 192
Early print: MANCHERLEY, 49 (1762). Lit. about MANCH-ERLEY: See this entry in Bib.
Ms. probably copied from the early print: B Bc, 6368 (West-phal)
Lit. about this work: SUCHALLA/ORCHESTERSINFO-NIEN, 277–78
A.v.: item 159

Incipits from 6368:

[The first minuet is repeated after the second.]

602. Menuet mit abwechselnde Trio . . . [2 clarinets, 2 flutes, 2 violins, bass]. Probably 1762–65 (source of date: date of item 165). W. 189/1
Ms.: B Bc, 6371 (Michel)
Lit.: SUCHALLA/ORCHESTERSINFONIEN, 272–75
A.v.: item 165

Incipits from 6371:

[The Menuet is repeated after the Trio.]

603. Menuet mit abwechselnde Trio . . . [2 clarinets, 2 flutes, 2 violins, bass]. Probably 1762–65 (source of date: date of item 167). W. 189/2
Ms.: B Bc, 6371 (Michel)
Lit.: SUCHALLA/ORCHESTERSINFONIEN, 272–75
A.v.: item 167

Incipits from 6371:

[The Menuet is repeated after the Trio.]

604. Polonoise a due clarinetti, due violini e basso. Probably 1762–65 (source of date: date of item 170). W. 190/1
Ms.: B Bc, 6371 (Michel)
Lit.: SUCHALLA/ORCHESTERSINFONIEN, 275–76
A.v.: item 170

Incipit from 6371:

605. Polonoise a due violini e basso. Probably 1762–65 (source of date: date of item 166). W. 190/3
Ms.: B Bc, 6371 (Michel)
Lit.: SUCHALLA/ORCHESTERSINFONIEN, 275–76
A.v.: item 166

Incipit from 6371:

606. Menuet mit abwechselnde Trio . . . [2 clarinets, 2 horns, 2 flutes, 2 violins, bass]. Probably c. 1766 (source of date: date of item 214). W. 189/8
Ms.: B Bc, 6371 (Michel)
Lit.: SUCHALLA/ORCHESTERSINFONIEN, 272–75
A.v.: item 214

Incipits from 6371:

[The Menuet is repeated after the Trio.]

607. Polonoise a due violini e basso. Probably c. 1766 (source of date: date of item 219). W. 190/2
Ms.: B Bc, 6371 (Michel)
Lit.: SUCHALLA/ORCHESTERSINFONIEN, 275–76
A.v.: item 219

Incipit from 6371:

608. Polonoise a due clarinetti, due corni, due violini e basso. Probably 1766 (source of date: date of item 217). W. 190/4
Ms.: B Bc, 6371 (Michel)
Lit.: SUCHALLA/ORCHESTERSINFONIEN, 275–76
A.v.: item 217

Incipit from 6371:

609. Polonoise a due violini e basso. Probably 1766 (source of date: date of item 215). W. 190/5
Ms.: B Bc, 6371 (Michel)
Lit.: SUCHALLA/ORCHESTERSINFONIEN, 275–76
A.v.: item 215

Incipit from 6371:

610. 4 kleine Duetten für 2 Claviere . . . No. 1. Probably after 1767 (source of date of items 610–13: known dates of their a.v.). W. 115/1, Wq n.v. 62
Mss.: D-brd B, P 787 (marked by CPEB?); B Bc, 5870
Mod. edn.: OBERDÖRFFER/DUETTE
Lit.: SCHULENBERG/INSTRUMENTAL, 88–89
A.v.: items 251, 521, 635/2

Incipit from P 787:

611. 4 kleine Duetten für 2 Claviere . . . No. 2. Probably after 1767 (source of date: See item 610). W. 115/2, Wq n.v. 63
Mss.: D-brd B, P 787; B Bc, 5870
Mod. edn.: OBERDÖRFFER/DUETTE
A.v.: items 250, 620/2

Incipit from P 787:

612. 4 kleine Duetten für 2 Claviere . . . No. 3. Probably after 1767 (source of date: See item 610). W. 115/3, Wq n.v. 64
Mss.: D-brd B, P 787; B Bc, 5870
Mod. edn.: OBERDÖRFFER/DUETTE
A.v.: items 324, 620/1, 635/28

Incipit from P 787:

613. 4 kleine Duetten für 2 Claviere . . . No. 4. Probably after 1767 (source of date: See item 610). W. 115/4, Wq n.v. 65
Mss.: D-brd B, P 787; B Bc, 5870
Mod. edn.: OBERDÖRFFER/DUETTE
A.v.: items 254, 255, 518, 614

Incipit from P 787:

614. VI Märche a II corni, II oboi, II clarinetti e fagotto . . . No. 1. After 1767 (source of date of items 614–19: NV, 52, says they were composed in Hamburg). W. 185/1
Ms.: B Bc, 6369 (Michel)
Mod. edns.: OBERDÖRFFER/STÜCKE, LORENZ/MÄRSCHE, SIMON/MARCHES
Lit. on the set (items 614–19): SUCHALLA/ORCHESTER-SINFONIEN, 269–70; OTTENBERG, 315
A.v.: items 254, 255, 518, 613

Incipit from 6369:

615. VI Märche a II corni, II oboi, II clarinetti e fagotto . . . No. 2. After 1767 (source of date: See item 614). W. 185/2
Ms.: B Bc, 6369 (Michel)
Mod. edns.: OBERDÖRFFER/STÜCKE, LORENZ/MÄRSCHE, SIMON/MARCHES
Lit.: See item 614.
A.v.: item 327

Incipit from 6369:

616. VI Märche a II corni, II oboi, II clarinetti e fagotto . . . No. 3. After 1767 (source of date: See item 614). W. 185/3
Ms.: B Bc, 6369 (Michel)
Mod. edns.: OBERDÖRFFER/STÜCKE, LORENZ/MÄRSCHE, SIMON/MARCHES
Lit.: See item 614.
A.v.: items 252, 256

Incipit from 6369:

617. VI Märche a II corni, II oboi, II clarinetti e fagotto . . . No. 4. After 1767 (source of date: See item 614). W. 185/4
Ms.: B Bc, 6369 (Michel)
Mod. edns.: OBERDÖRFFER/STÜCKE, LORENZ/MÄRSCHE, SIMON/MARCHES
Lit.: See item 614.
A.v.: item 328

Incipit from 6369:

618. VI Märche a II corni, II oboi, II clarinetti e fagotto . . . No. 5. After 1767 (source of date: See item 614). W. 185/5
Ms.: B Bc, 6369 (Michel)
Mod. edns.: OBERDÖRFFER/STÜCKE, LORENZ/MÄRSCHE, SIMON/MARCHES
Lit.: See item 614.
A.v.: item 329

Incipit from 6369:

619. VI Märche a II corni, II oboi, II clarinetti e fagotto . . . No. 6. After 1767 (source of date: See item 614). W. 185/6
Ms.: B Bc, 6369 (Michel)
Mod. edns.: OBERDÖRFFER/STÜCKE, LORENZ/MÄRSCHE, SIMON/MARCHES
Lit.: See item 614.
A.v.: item 330

Incipit from 6369:

620. 2 kleine Stücke für 2 Hörner, 2 Clarinetten und Fagott. After 1767 (source of date: composed in Hamburg, says NV, 52). W. 186
Lost
Lit.: SUCHALLA/ORCHESTERSINFONIEN, 270–71
NV, 52, lists a pair of oboes in addition.
A.v. of No. 1: items 324, 612, 635/28. Of No. 2: items 250, 611

Incipits from WOTQUENNE/THÉMATIQUE:

621. Marcia . . . für die Arche, für 3 Trompeten und Paucken. After 1767 (source of date: composed in Hamburg, says NV, 53). W. 188
Ms.: B Bc, 12.465 (Michel)
Mod. edn.: E. Simon, New York: Marks, n.d.
Lit.: SUCHALLA/ORCHESTERSINFONIEN, 272

Incipit from 12.465:

622. Menuet mit abwechselnde Trio . . . [2 horns, 2 flutes, bassoon, 2 violins, bass]. Probably before 1768 (source of date of items 622–26: Items 602, 603 and 622–26 are grouped together in NV, 52, as "8 Menuetten für blasende Instrumente, 2 Violinen und Bass, mit abwechselnde Trii"; they are also grouped together in B Bc, 6371, as "8 Minuetten mit abwechselnde Trios." Items 602 and 603 are a.v. of items 165 and 167, which are dated 1762–65. "Before 1768" [that is, before CPEB's move to his church position in Hamburg] therefore seems a reasonable supposition as a date for items 622–26, despite the fact that the fair copy, B Bc, 6371, was made by CPEB's Hamburg copyist Michel. See item 627). W. 189/3
Ms.: B Bc, 6371 (Michel)
Lit.: SUCHALLA/ORCHESTERSINFONIEN, 272–75
A.v.: item 303

Incipits from 6371:

[The Menuet is repeated after the Trio.]

623. Menuet mit abwechselnde Trio . . . [2 horns, 2 flutes, 2 violins, bass]. Probably before 1768 (source of date: See item 622). W. 189/4
Ms.: B Bc, 6371 (Michel)
Lit.: SUCHALLA/ORCHESTERSINFONIEN, 272–75
A.v.: item 304

Incipits from 6371:

[The Menuet is repeated after the Trio.]

624. Menuet mit abwechselnde Trio . . . [2 horns, 2 flutes, 2 violins, bass]. Probably before 1768 (source of date: See item 622). W. 189/5
Ms.: B Bc, 6371 (Michel)
Lit.: SUCHALLA/ORCHESTERSINFONIEN, 272–75
A.v.: items 305, 635/9

Incipits from 6371:

[The Menuet is repeated after the Trio.]

625. Menuet mit abwechselnde Trio . . . [2 horns, 2 flutes, 2 violins, bass]. Probably before 1768 (source of date: See item 622). W. 189/6
Ms.: B Bc, 6371 (Michel)
Lit.: SUCHALLA/ORCHESTERSINFONIEN, 272–75
A.v.: items 258, 306, 635/12

Incipits from 6371:

[The Menuet is repeated after the Trio.]

626. Menuet mit abwechselnde Trio . . . [2 horns, 2 flutes, 2 violins, bass]. Probably before 1768 (source of date: See item 622). W. 189/7
Ms.: B Bc, 6371 (Michel)
Lit.: SUCHALLA/ORCHESTERSINFONIEN, 272–75
A.v.: item 307

Incipits from 6371:

Vln. 1

[The Menuet is repeated after the Trio.]

627. Polonoise a due violini e basso. Probably before 1768 (source of date: items 604, 605, 607–09, 627 are grouped together in NV, 53, as "6 Polonoisen für blasende Instrumente, 2 Violinen und Bass"; they are also grouped together in B Bc, 6371, as "6 Polonoisen." Items 604, 605 are a.v. of items 170 and 166, which are dated 1762–65; items 607–09 are a.v. of items 219, 217, and 215, which are dated 1766. "Before 1768" therefore seems reasonable as a conjectural date for item 627, if we bear in mind the statement in item 622 about Hamburg and Michel.) W. 190/6
Ms.: B Bc, 6371 (Michel)
Lit.: SUCHALLA/ORCHESTERSINFONIEN, 275–76
A.v.: item 308

Incipit from 6371:

Vln. 1

628. Zwölf zwey- und drey-stimmige kleine Stücke für die Flöte oder Violin und das Clavier. 1769 (NV 41). W. 82
Early print and lit. about it: See ZWÖLF KLEINE II.
Ms. probably copied from the early print: B Bc, 6373 (Westphal)
Mod. edns.: R. Hohenemser, Frankfurt am Main: Breslauer, 1928; K. Johnen and G. Wierzejewski, New York: Peters, n.d.; WALTHER/DUETTE (Nos. II, IV, VIII, X)
Lit. about this work: SCHMID/KAMMERMUSIK, 162; GEIRINGER/BACH, 364; OTTENBERG, 172–74

Incipits from 6373:

Nro. I. *Allegro*

Nro. II. *Allegro*

["Nro. I" is repeated after "Nro. II."]

Nro. III. *Allegro*

Nro. IV. *Allegro*

["Nro. III" is repeated after "Nro. IV."]

Nro. V. *Tempo di minuetto*

Nro. VI. *Tempo di minuetto*

["Nro. V" is repeated after "Nro. VI."]

Nro. VII. *Alla polacca*

Nro. VIII. *Alla polacca*

["Nro. VII" is repeated after "Nro. VIII."]

Nro. IX. *Allegro scherzando*

Nro. X. *Allegro scherzando*

["Nro. IX" is repeated after "Nro. X."]

Nro. XI. *Andante*

Nro. XII. *Andante*

["Nro. XI" is repeated after "Nro. XII."]

629. VI sonate a II corni, II flauti, II clarinetti, fagotto . . .
Sonata I. 1775 (NV 52). W. 184/1
Ms.: B Bc, 6367 (Michel)
Mod. edns.: LORENZ/SONATE, JANETZKY/SONATAS
Lit. on the set (items 629–34): SCHMID/KAMMERMUSIK,
137, 139–40, 171; NEWMAN, 423; SUCHALLA/ORCHES-
TERSINFONIEN, 267–68; GEIRINGER/CHAMBER, 535;
OTTENBERG, 315
A.v. of item 629: item 516

Incipit of item 629 from 6367:

Allegretto
ten.

630. VI sonate a II corni, II flauti, II clarinetti, fagotto . . .
Sonata II. 1775 (NV 52). W. 184/2
Ms.: B Bc, 6367 (Michel)
Mod. edns.: U. Leupold, Braunschweig: Litolff, 1935; OBER-
DÖRFFER/STÜCKE; LORENZ/SONATE; JANETZKY/
SONATAS
Lit.: See item 629.
A.v.: item 520. Arr.: 2nd mvt. of item 299

Incipit from 6367:

Andante

631. VI sonate a II corni, II flauti, II clarinetti, fagotto . . .
Sonata III. 1775 (NV 52). W. 184/3
Ms.: B Bc, 6367 (Michel)
Mod. edns.: U. Leupold, Braunschweig: Litolff, 1935;
LORENZ/SONATE; JANETZKY/SONATAS
Lit.: See item 629.
A.v.: item 519

Incipit from 6367:

Allegro
Fl. 1
Clar. 1

632. VI sonate a II corni, II flauti, II clarinetti, fagotto . . .
Sonata IV. 1775 (NV 52). W. 184/4
Ms.: B Bc, 6367 (Michel)
Mod. edns.: OBERDÖRFFER/STÜCKE, LORENZ/SO-
NATE, JANETZKY/SONATAS
Lit.: See item 629.
A.v.: item 326

Incipit from 6367:

Allegro ma non troppo

633. VI sonate a II corni, II flauti, II clarinetti, fagotto . . .
Sonata V. 1775 (NV 52). W. 184/5
Ms.: B Bc, 6367 (Michel)
Mod. edns.: U. Leupold, Braunschweig: Litolff, 1935; OBER-
DÖRFFER/STÜCKE; LORENZ/SONATE; JANETZKY/
SONATAS
Lit.: See item 629.
A.v.: item 517. Arr.: 1st mvt. of item 299

Incipit from 6367:

634. VI sonate a II corni, II flauti, II clarinetti, fagotto . . .
Sonata VI. 1775 (NV 52). W. 184/6
Ms.: B Bc, 6367 (Michel)
Mod. edns.: LORENZ/SONATE, JANETZKY/SONATAS
Lit.: See item 629.
A.v.: item 331

Incipit from 6367:

Allegretto grazioso

635. Stücke für Spieluhren auch Dreh-orgeln. No. 2 was
probably composed in 1775 or later; the dates of the others
are unknown (source of date of No. 2: date of item 251).
W. 193

Mss.: B Bc, 5886 (Michel, Nos. 1–29); PL Kj, P 745 (autog., No. 30)

Mod. edns.: WALTHER/DUETTE (Nos. 22, 23, 25); WALTHER/STÜCKE (portions); ALTMAN/SUITE (Nos. 1, 4, 9, 18, 23, 24, 27, 28, arranged for organ); ALTMAN/ PIECES (Nos. 2, 11, 17, 22, 26, 29); PIERRE (Nos. 19–21, arranged for flute, viola, and harp); ALTMAN/DUETS (Nos. 19–21, arranged for organ and harp as "Three Duets")

Lit.: SCHMID/KAMMERMUSIK, 168, 171; WALTHER/ FLÖTENUHR; SIMON/MECHANISCHE

A.v.: as noted below the incipits

All these little pieces were probably intended for musical automata; contrary to the impression given by Wotquenne's title, the "flutes" and "clarinets" designated in the ms. are parts of mechanical instruments (musical clocks or barrel organs), though all of the music can be played on traditional instruments (especially one or two keyboard instruments) as well. See item 153.

Incipits from 5886:

[No. 1]

[No. 2]

A.v.: items 251, 521, 610

[No. 3]

[No. 4]

[No. 5. For "Harfen-Uhr"]

A.v.: item 310

[No. 6. For "Harfen-Uhr"]

A.v.: item 311

[No. 7. For "Harfen-Uhr"]

A.v.: item 313

[No. 8. For "Harfen-Uhr"]

A.v.: item 312

[No. 9. For "Harfen-Uhr"]

A.v.: items 305, 624

[No. 10. For "Harfen-Uhr"]

[Menuetto I is repeated after Menuetto II.]

[No. 11]

A.v.: item 314

[No. 12]

A.v.: items 258, 306, 625

[No. 13]

Polonoise I

A.v.: item 315

[No. 14]

Polonoise II

A.v.: item 316

[No. 15]

Polonoise III

A.v.: item 317

[No. 16]

Polonoise IV

A.v.: item 318

[No. 17]

March I

A.v.: items 319, 637/1

[No. 18]

March II

A.v.: items 320, 637/2

[No. 19. For "Flöten" and "Harfe"—i.e., musical clock]

Minuetto I

"Fl." 1

A.v.: item 321

138

[No. 20. For same instrument as in No. 19]

Minuetto II

"Fl." 1

A.v.: item 322

[No. 21. For same instrument as in No. 19]

Polonoise. Gehalten

"Fl." 1

A.v.: item 323

[No. 22. For "2 Flöten"—i.e., flute-clock]

Tempo di menuetto

"Fl." 1

[No. 23. "Für eine Flöten Uhr"]

Allegro

[No. 24. For "2 Flöten"—i.e., flute-clock]

Mässig, geschwind

"Fl." 1

A.v.: item 257

[No. 25]

Polonoise

A.v.: item 636, 1st mvt.

[No. 26. "Duetto für 2 Clarinetten" (i.e., mechanical?)]

Adagio e sostenuto

"Clar." 1

A.v.: item 636, 1st mvt.

[No. 27. Same instrument(s) as in No. 26?]

A.v.: item 636, 2nd mvt.

[No. 28. "Für eine Dreh Orgel"]

A.v.: items 324, 612, 620/1

[No. 29. "Für eine Dreh Orgel"]

A.v.: item 325

Incipit from P 745:

[No. 30. "Presto für eine Spieluhr B"]

A.v.: item 162, 3rd mvt.

636. Duett für 2 Clarinetten. n.d. W. 142
Ms.: B Bc, 5522 (Michel)
Mod. edns.: W. Stephan, Hannover: Nagel, 1928; J. Marx,
   New York: Mercury, 1948
Lit.: SCHMID/KAMMERMUSIK, 168
A.v.: item 635/26, 27

Incipits from 5522:

637. 2 Märsche für 2 Hörner, 2 Hoboen, und Basson. n.d.
W. 187
Ms.: B Bc, 6370 (Michel)
Mod. edn.: J. Lorenz, Berlin: Parrhysius, [1941]

Lit.: SUCHALLA/ORCHESTERSINFONIEN, 271
A.v.: of No. 1, items 319, 635/17; of No. 2, items 320, 635/18

Incipits from 6370:

638. 2 abwechselnde stark besetzte Menuetten mit 3
Trompeten, Pauken, 2 Hörnern, 2 Hoboen, 2 Flöten, 2 Vio-
linen, Bratsche und Bass. n.d. W. 191
Ms.: B Bc, 6371 (Michel)
Lit.: SUCHALLA/ORCHESTERSINFONIEN, 277
A.v.: item 309

Incipits from 6371:

[The first Menuet is repeated after the second.]

Doubtful

639. Fantasia sopra Jesu meines Lebens Leben [Chorale fantasia, 3 parts for unspecified instruments, 1 part for
obbligato oboe; no text]. n.d. Wq n.v. 19
Mss.: D-brd B, P 562, P 778
P 562, not attributed on the ms. except in a modern hand,
   in pencil, is in the hand of an anonymous 19th-century
   copyist; P 778 is in an anonymous hand known to be that
   of many authentic CPEB mss., although the attribution
   to "Em. Bach" seems to be in a different hand. Both mss.
   consist of the same works in the same order: item 639
   and BWV 619. The style of this substantial chorale fantasia
   is that of JSB, not CPEB.

Incipit from P 562:

640. III sonate per il flauto e violino. n.d. TERRY, C. S., 337
Ms.: A Wn, Suppl. Mus. No. 2902 ("Del Signore Bach")
TERRY, C. S., 337, lists this work as possibly by Johann
   Christian Bach.

Incipits of the 1st mvts. from Suppl. Mus. No. 2902:

641. Diverdimento ex D tur, violino, flauto, viola, basso. n.d.
Ms.: PL Wru, Bohn Nachlass, 207, 1 ("Del Sigl. Bach")
Foreign in style and provenance. See item 642.

Incipits from 207, 1:

642. Divertimento ex G♯, flauto traverso, violino, viola e basso. n.d.
Ms.: PL WRu, Bohn Nachlass, 207, 2 ("Del Sigl. P. E. Bach")
Foreign in style and provenance. See item 641.

Incipits from 207, 2:

Spurious

643. Sonata a [glass] harmonica e violoncello. 1753 or later (source of date: date of items 74, 75)
Ms.: CS Pnm, II B 9

Foreign in provenance and medium of performance
The 1st mvt. is an a.v. of the 2nd mvt. of item 75; the 2nd mvt. is an a.v. of the 3rd mvt. of item 74.

Incipits from II B 9:

644. [Three trios for 2 violins and viola]. c. 1765 (source of date: pub. date). TERRY, C. S., 315
Mss.: AM, V.N. 25, V.N. 26, V.N. 27
By Johann Christian Bach. See the list of prints and mss. in TERRY, C. S., 314–16.

Incipits of the 1st mvts., from V.N. 25, V.N. 26, and V.N. 27, respectively:

645. Quintette [for flute, oboe, violin, viola, bass]. c. 1772 (source of date: pub. date). TERRY, C. S., 303
Ms.: CS Bm, IV A 14
By Johann Christian Bach. See the list of prints and mss. in TERRY, C. S., 303–04.

Incipit of the 1st mvt. from IV A 14:

646. Frühlings Erwachen [2 violins, piano]. n.d.
A sentimental parlor piece that appeared in numerous arrangements in the late 19th and early 20th centuries. No trace of it in 18th-century sources. Possibly by Emil Bach, Ole Bull's accompanist

Incipit from an arrangement for violin and piano by E. Kross, Leipzig: Bosworth, 1902:

647. Adagio . . . pour orchestre à cordes. 1904?

"Reconstitué par Francis Casadesus, d'après un document communiqué par Camille St. Saëns en 1904," Paris: Lemoine, 1949. No trace of it in 18th-century sources. Presumably a deliberate falsification by a member of the Casadesus family; see item 497.

Incipit from this publication:

SYMPHONIES

Authentic

648. Sinfonia a due violini, violetta e basso. 1741 (NV 43). W. 173

Mss.: D-brd B, P 969, St 226, St 370; D-ddr Bds, M.Th. 6. Modern ms. score: B Bc, 7228; this score and modern ms. scores of items 649–51, 653–62, in B Bc, 7224, 7226–28, were copied, with many errors, from sets of parts by A. Goeyens in 1899–1900. These scores are signed and dated by Goeyens, typically with the notation "mis en partition d'après les parties separées." The "parties separées" originally bore the library call numbers now assigned to the Goeyens copies. SUCHALLA, 246–47, reports being told by A. Vander Linden, former director of the Brussels Conservatory library, that Alfred Wotquenne (librarian, inspector of studies, and secretary of the conservatory from 1894 to 1918; see pp. xxii–xxiii) had Goeyens make the copies and then sold or auctioned the original sets of parts, whose locations are still unknown. The Stellfeld collection in USAA has copies of the Goeyens scores.

With all their faults, the Goeyens scores originated amid a collection of distinguished provenance (see pp. xxii–xxiii) and may represent CPEB's latest intentions regarding the symphonies they contain.

Mod. edn.: GALLAGHER–HELM/SYMPHONIES

Lit.: SUCHALLA/ORCHESTERSINFONIEN, 18–19, 43–44, 46, 62, 73–74, 95–100, 111–12, 115–16, 121, 246–47

Arr.: item 45

Incipits from St 226:

649. Sinfonia . . . corno 1, corno 2, violino 1, violino 2, viola, basso. 1755 (NV 43; also dated 1755 in CPEB's hand in P 351). W. 174

Mss.: D-brd B, P 351 (autog.), P 899, St 232 (a.v.: the 2 winds are flutes rather than horns), St 580; D-ddr Dlb, Ms. Mus. 3029/N/4. Modern ms. score: B Bc, 7228 (see item 648). This modern score is an a.v. for 2 horns, 2 flutes, strings, continuo.

Mod. edn.: F. Oberdörffer, Berlin: Lienau, 1935, reprinted 1963 (for 2 horns, 2 flutes, strings, continuo)

Lit.: STEGLICH/HOMILIUS, 66–67; SUCHALLA/ORCHESTERSINFONIEN, 19–20, 44–45, 62–63, 74, 112, 114, 116–17, 247–48

Incipits from P 351:

650. Sinfonia a 2 corni, 2 flauti, 2 violini, viola, 2 bassoni e basso. 1755 (NV 43). W. 175

Mss.: D-brd, St 238 (partly autog.; horn and bassoon parts added in CPEB's hand), St 578 (a.v. without wind parts); D-ddr Bds, M.Th. 9 (a.v. without wind parts); D-brd Mbs, Mus. ms. 1159. Modern ms. score: B Bc, 7228 (see item 648)

Mod. edn.: GALLAGHER–HELM/SYMPHONIES

Lit.: FLEULER, 32; VRIESLANDER/BACH, 98–99; SUCHALLA/ORCHESTERSINFONIEN, 11–12, 20–22, 45–46, 63, 83–84, 93, 248–49; SCHULENBERG/INSTRUMENTAL, 130

A.v.: item 104

Incipits from St 238:

651. Sinfonia a 3 trombe, timpani, 2 corni, 2 oboi, 2 flauti, 2 violini, viola e basso. 1755 (NV 43). W. 176

Mss.: D-brd B, St 234 (a.v. without trumpet, timpani, or oboe parts), St 235 (partly autog.), St 375 (a.v. without trumpet, timpani, or oboe parts, though these instruments are indicated on the title p.), St 559 (a.v. without wind parts); F Pc, 1569 a–d (not autog.; a.v. for strings and continuo only, though title p. indicates horns in addition); "Kopenhagen Ms.," according to SUCHALLA/ ORCHESTERSINFONIEN, 250; PL Wn, microfilm archive, microfilm of ms. formerly in Grüssau, "Chori Grissoviensis," Rps 227 (a.v. without trumpet, timpani, oboe, or flute parts). Modern ms. score: B Bc, 7228 (see item 648)

Mod. edn.: GALLAGHER–HELM/SYMPHONIES

Lit.: SUCHALLA/ORCHESTERSINFONIEN, 22–23, 27, 46– 47, 63–64, 74, 87–88, 100–01, 112, 122, 249–50

Incipits from St 235:

652. Sinfonia a II violini, violetta e basso. 1756 (NV 43). W. 177

Mss.: D-ddr Bds, Am.B. 554; CH BEl, ML 212[8] (modern copy); US Wc, M1001.B15.No.5 (modern copy)

Early print: the above title, "alle spese della vedova di Balth. Schmid in Norimberga" [1759]

Ms. probably copied from the original print: B Bc, 7225 (Westphal)

Mod. edn. in K. Geiringer, ed., *Music of the Bach Family: An Anthology,* Cambridge: Harvard University Press, 1955

Lit.: GEIRINGER/BACH, 367–68; SUCHALLA/ORCHES-TERSINFONIEN, 23–27, 47–49, 64, 77, 91–92, 122, 250–52; WELLESZ–STERNFELD/SYMPHONY, 389–90; OTTEN-BERG, 126–28, 236, 281

A.v.: items 115, 653

Incipits from 7225:

653. Sinfonia [2 horns, 2 oboes, 2 flutes, 2 violins, viola, bass]. Probably 1756 (NV 43.). W. 178

Mss.: D-brd B, zu P 351 (Michel?), St 237; "Kopenhagen Ms.," according to SUCHALLA/ORCHESTERSINFO-NIEN, 252. Modern ms. score: B Bc, 7226 (see item 648).

Lit.: GEIRINGER/BACH, 367–68; SUCHALLA/ORCHES-TERSINFONIEN, 24–27, 47–49, 64, 77, 91–92, 106, 112, 122, 250–52; WELLESZ–STERNFELD/SYMPHONY, 389– 90

A.v.: items 115, 652

Incipits from P 351: same as for item 652

654. Sinfonia a 2 corni, 2 violini, 2 oboi, viola e basso. 1757 (NV 43). W. 179

Mss.: D-brd B, St 236 (title p. by CPEB; "2 Corni" and "2 Oboi" inserted into the title by him later; horn and oboe parts also added in CPEB's hand), St 579 (a.v. without wind parts), St 582 (a.v. without wind parts); D-ddr Bds, Am.B. 555 (a.v. without wind parts); A Z, VIII 157. Modern ms. score: B Bc, 7227 (see item 648)

Mod. edns.: A. Wenzinger, Kassel, n.d. (for the full instrumentation plus bassoon; ms. score rentable as Bärenreiter-Ausgabe 3827); GALLAGHER–HELM/SYMPHO-NIES

Lit.: SUCHALLA/ORCHESTERSINFONIEN, 26, 48, 64, 75, 88, 117, 252–53; SCHULENBERG/INSTRUMENTAL, 82– 83, 92–93

Incipits from St 236:

655. Sinfonia a 2 corni, 2 oboi, 2 violini, violetta e basso. 1758 (NV 15, 44). W. 180
Mss.: D-brd B, St 239 (title p. and some corrections by CPEB; "2 Corni" and "2 Oboi" inserted into the title by him later; horn and oboe parts also added in CPEB's hand); D-brd Mbs, Mus. ms. 1160 (vnts. in horn part; adds flutes in Largo). Modern ms. score: B Bc, 7227 (see item 648)
Mod. edn.: GALLAGHER–HELM/SYMPHONIES
Lit.: VRIESLANDER/BACH, 98–99; SUCHALLA/ORCHESTERSINFONIEN, 13, 26–27, 48–49, 65, 75–76, 92–93, 254; SCHULENBERG/INSTRUMENTAL, 7, 67–68
Arr.: item 191

Incipits from St 239:

656. Sinfonia [2 horns, 2 oboes, 2 flutes, 2 violins, viola, bass]. 1762 (NV 44; the incidental mention of a date of 1758 on p. 15 of NV is obviously an error). W. 181
Ms.: D-brd B, P 351 (Michel, with additions by CPEB). Modern ms. score: B Bc, 7227 (see item 648)
Mod. edn.: GALLAGHER–HELM/SYMPHONIES
Lit.: GEIRINGER/BACH, 368; SUCHALLA/ORCHESTERSINFONIEN, 15, 27–28, 49, 65–66, 77, 88, 255
Arr.: item 227

Incipits from P 351:

657. Sinfonia [2 violins, viola, bass]. 1773 (NV 44). W. 182/1
Mss.: D-brd B, St 227, St 371 (title p. and additions in CPEB's hand). Modern ms. score: B Bc, 7224 (see item 648). This

modern score is an a.v. in which 2 oboes and 2 horns are added.
Mod. edns.: H. Riemann, Langensalza: Beyer & Söhne, 1897, reprinted 1916 (ed. as a string quartet); W. Lebermann, Mainz: Schott, 1970; FEDTKE/SINFONIEN
Lit. on the set (items 657–62): AMZ (J. F. Reichardt), XVI (1814), 28–29; BITTER/BRÜDER, I, 242–43; STEGLICH/HOMILIUS, 82, 107–08; BÜCKEN, 168–69; SCHMID/KAMMERMUSIK, 117; GEIRINGER/BACH, 368–69; SUCHALLA/ORCHESTERSINFONIEN, 28–29, 49–50, 122–25, 256–57; WELLESZ–STERNFELD/SYMPHONY, 390–93; WADE, 127; OTTENBERG, 177–84, 236
Lit. on item 657 only: SUCHALLA/ORCHESTERSINFONIEN, 29–30, 50–51, 66, 77–79, 86, 111, 113, 256–57; SCHULENBERG/INSTRUMENTAL, 70–71, 108
Items 657–62 make up, in numerical order, the *Sei Sinfonie a Violino Primo, Violino Secondo, Violetta e Basso* composed for Gottfried van Swieten of Vienna. CPEB no doubt made careful autograph scores of all six symphonies, but the autograph of item 657 has not yet come to light.

Incipits of item 657 from St 371:

658. Sinfonia [2 violins, viola, bass]. 1773 (NV 44). W. 182/2
Mss.: D-brd B, St 373; D-ddr Bds, St 230; B Bc, 25.900 (autog.). Modern ms. score: B Bc, 7224 (see item 648)
Mod. edns.: E. F. Schmid, Hannover: Nagel, [1933], reprinted 1958; FEDTKE/SINFONIEN
Lit.: STEGLICH/HOMILIUS, 115, 121–23; SUCHALLA/ORCHESTERSINFONIEN, 15, 20–32, 51–53, 66, 79–80, 88–89, 100–01, 103–04, 107, 108–10, 118, 257–58; OTTENBERG, 183–84, 284; SCHULENBERG/INSTRUMENTAL, 71, 135–37
See item 657.

Incipits from 25.900:

Presto
Vln. 1

659. Sinfonia [2 violins, viola, bass]. 1773 (NV 44). W. 182/3
Mss.: D-brd B, St 223, St 364 (wrapper title in CPEB's hand); B Bc, 25.901 (autog.). Modern ms. score: B Bc, 7224 (see item 648)
Mod. edns.: E. F. Schmid, Hannover: Nagel, [1931], reprinted 1953; FEDTKE/SINFONIEN
Lit.: SUCHALLA/ORCHESTERSINFONIEN, 32–34, 53–54, 66–67, 80–81, 90, 102–03, 106–08, 109, 258; WELLESZ–STERNFELD/SYMPHONY, 386–88, 392–93; OTTENBERG, 179–83, 284; SCHULENBERG/INSTRUMENTAL, 42
See item 657.
SUCHALLA/ORCHESTERSINFONIEN, 80–81, points out the appearance of "B-A-C-H, E." in the bass at the beginning of the 2nd mvt., emphasized by instrumentation and dynamics: a signature for his admirer Van Swieten. The motive is repeated in transposed form later in the mvt. See items 285, 371.9, 373, 389.6, 484.6, 733/41, 867. See also Irving Godt, "C. P. E. Bach His Mark," *College Music Symposium*, Fall 1979, 154–61.

Incipits from 25.901:

Allegro assai
Vln. 1

Adagio
Vln. 1

Allegretto
Vln. 1

660. Sinfonia [2 violins, viola, bass]. 1773 (NV 45). W. 182/4
Mss.: D-brd B, St 229, St 372 (marked by CPEB); B Bc, 25.902 (autog.). Modern ms. score: B Bc, 7224 (see item 648)
Mod. edns.: H. Riemann, Langensalza: Beyer & Söhne, 1897, reprinted 1916 (ed. as a string quartet); E. Suchalla, Wiesbaden: Breitkopf & Härtel, 1965; W. Lebermann, Mainz: Schott, 1970; FEDTKE/SINFONIEN
Lit.: BÜCKEN, 169; SUCHALLA/ORCHESTERSINFONIEN, 34–35, 54, 67, 82–83, 86, 103, 106–07, 259; WELLESZ–STERNFELD/SYMPHONY, 391–92; OTTENBERG, 284
See item 657.

Incipits from 25.902:

Allegro ma non troppo
Vln. 1

Largo ed innocentemente
Vln. 1

Allegro assai
Vln. 1

661. Sinfonia [2 violins, viola, bass]. 1773 (NV 45). W. 182/5
Mss.: D-brd B, St 231, St 374 (wrapper title and markings in CPEB's hand); B Bc, 25.903 (autog.). Modern ms. score: B Bc, 7224 (see item 648)
Mod. edns.: E. F. Schmid, Hannover: Nagel, 1937; FEDTKE/SINFONIEN
Lit.: SUCHALLA/ORCHESTERSINFONIEN, 12, 35–36, 54–55, 67, 76, 86–87, 106, 260; WELLESZ–STERNFELD/SYMPHONY, 393; OTTENBERG, 284; SCHULENBERG/INSTRUMENTAL, 106–08, 162
See item 657.

Incipits from 25.903:

Allegretto
Vln. 1

Larghetto
Vln. 1

Presto
Vln. 1

662. Sinfonia [2 violins, viola, bass]. 1773 (NV 45). W. 182/6
Mss.: D-brd B, St 224, St 369 (marked by CPEB); F Pc, W 1.1 (autog.). Modern ms. score: B Bc, 7224 (see item 648)
Mod. edn.: FEDTKE/SINFONIEN
Lit.: STEGLICH/HOMILIUS, 94–95, 122; SUCHALLA/ORCHESTERSINFONIEN, 36–37, 56, 68, 83, 90, 108–09, 117, 261; SCHULENBERG/INSTRUMENTAL, 71–72
See item 657.

Incipits from W 1.1:

Allegro di molto
Vln. 1

Poco andante Vln. 1

Allegro spirituoso Vln. 1

663. [Sinfonia for 2 horns, 2 flutes, 2 oboes, 2 violins, viola, cello, bassoon, harpsichord, and violone]. 1775–76 (NV 45; see also below). W. 183/1

Mss.: D-brd B, P 350 (autog.); CS Pk, St 792/32, P 107

Early prints: ORCHESTER-SINFONIEN; Anon., Leipzig: Breitkopf & Härtel, 1801. Lit. on ORCHESTER-SINFONIEN: See this entry in Bib. The known lit. gives no evidence that the (posthumous) Breitkopf & Härtel print had been authorized by CPEB.

Mss. probably copied from an early print (ORCHESTER-SINFONIEN): B Bc, 7223 (Westphal); D-ddr Dlb, Mus. 3029/N/1

Mod. edns.: ANON./SYMPHONIES; A. Horn, Leipzig: Breitkopf & Härtel, 1860 (arranged for piano–4 hands); ESPAGNE; REGER; STEGLICH/SYMPHONIES

Lit. about this work: CPEB/BREITKOPF, 30 Nov. 1778; BITTER/BRÜDER, I, 241–42; D. F. Tovey, *Essays in Musical Analysis*, VI (London, 1939), 8–12 (containing hardly a paragraph that is not misinformed); SUCHALLA/ORCHESTERSINFONIEN, 15, 37–39, 56–57, 68, 81–82, 87, 101–02, 105–06, 108, 111, 113–14, 117–18, 262–64; WELLESZ–STERNFELD/SYMPHONY, 387–88, 393; OTTENBERG, 125, 235–38; SCHULENBERG/INSTRUMENTAL, 75–77, 143

P 350, an autog. score of items 663–66, numbers the four symphonies in CPEB's hand as "Erste," "Zweyte," "Dritte," and "Vierte." At the end of the second symphony of the set, CPEB writes "Ende. d. 11 Nov. 1775"; at the end of the fourth, he writes "Fine. d. 12 J[anuar?] 1776."

Incipits from P 350:

Allegro di molto Vln. 1

Largo Vla.

Presto Vln. 1

664. [Sinfonia for 2 horns, 2 flutes, 2 oboes, 2 violins, viola, cello, bassoon, harpsichord, and violone]. 1775–76 (NV 45; see also item 663). W. 183/2

Mss.: D-brd B, P 350 (autog.); CS Pk, St 793/32 (lacking harpsichord part); US Bp, No. 3 in **M120.18 (19th-century copy)

Early print and lit. about it: See ORCHESTER-SINFONIEN.

Mss. probably copied from the early print: B Bc, 7223 (Westphal); D-ddr Dlb, Mus. 3029/N/1

Mod. edns.: ANON./SYMPHONIES; ESPAGNE; REGER; STEGLICH/SYMPHONIES

Lit. about this work: BITTER/BRÜDER, I, 238–39; SUCHALLA/ORCHESTERSINFONIEN, 15, 39, 57–58, 68–69, 71, 81, 90, 107, 118–19, 265; WELLESZ–STERNFELD/SYMPHONY, 393–94; OTTENBERG, 236; SCHULENBERG/INSTRUMENTAL, 92, 108, 117

Incipits from P 350:

Allegro di molto Vln. 1

Larghetto Vln. 1

Allegretto Vln. 1

665. [Sinfonia for 2 horns, 2 flutes, 2 oboes, 2 violins, viola, cello, bassoon, harpsichord, and violone]. 1775–76 (NV 45; see also item 663). W. 183/3

Ms.: D-brd B, P 350 (autog.)

Early print and lit. about it: See ORCHESTER-SINFONIEN.

Mss. probably copied from the early print: B Bc, 7223 (Westphal); D-ddr Dlb, Mus. 3029/N/1

Mod. edns.: ANON./SYMPHONIES; ESPAGNE; REGER; STEGLICH/SYMPHONIES

Lit. about this work: BITTER/BRÜDER, I, 239–41; SUCHALLA/ORCHESTERSINFONIEN, 40, 58–59, 69–70, 76–77, 87, 104, 107, 110, 114, 117–18, 266

Incipits from P 350:

Allegro di molto Vln. 1

Larghetto Vla.

Presto Vln. 1

666. [Sinfonia for 2 horns, 2 flutes, 2 oboes, 2 violins, viola, cello, bassoon, harpsichord, and violone]. 1775–76 (NV 45; see also item 663). W. 183/4

Ms.: D-brd B, P 350 (autog.)

Early print and lit. about it: See ORCHESTER-SINFONIEN.

Mss. probably copied from the early print: B Bc, 7223 (Westphal); D-ddr Dlb, Mus. 3029/N/1

Mod. edns.: ANON./SYMPHONIES; REGER; STEGLICH/SYMPHONIES

Lit. about this work: BITTER/BRÜDER, I, 242; BÜCKEN, 167; SUCHALLA/ORCHESTERSINFONIEN, 40–41, 59–60, 70, 83, 90–91, 107, 118, 266–67; OTTENBERG, 237

Incipits from P 350:

Possibly Authentic

667. Sinfonia ex G♯ a violino primo, violino secondo, viola e basso. c. 1751? (source of date: a letter of 8 Aug. 1751 from J. W. L. Gleim to J. P. Uz discussing prince Lobkowitz's visit to Berlin and his new association with CPEB; printed in SUCHALLA/ORCHESTERSINFONIEN, 129; SCHMID/KAMMERMUSIK, 41; BUSCH, 45–46). Wq n.v. 69

Ms.: D-brd B, St 228

Lit.: SCHMID/KAMMERMUSIK, 41; SUCHALLA/ORCHESTERSINFONIEN, 280–81

The original title-p. attribution is "de Bach." Next to this another hand has written "de Berlin," and over it in a 3rd hand is "C. P. E."

According to SUCHALLA/ORCHESTERSINFONIEN, 127–34, this is the symphony composed jointly with Prince Ferdinand Philipp von Lobkowitz (1724–84), as listed in both BACH/LEVY (see item 668) and NV, 65. The listing in NV, however, mentions a heavier, though probably optional, instrumentation: "Sinfonie mit dem Fürsten von Lobkowitz, einen Takt um den andern, aus dem Stegreif verfertigt. B[erlin]. Mit Hörnern und Hoboen."

Incipits from St 228:

Spurious

668. Among the large number of other symphonies and "divertimenti" in mss. attributed to CPEB or to "Bach" ("Baach," "Pach," and so forth) in such libraries as B Bc, PL Wn (including its archive of microfilms of symphonies in other Polish libraries), CS Bm, D-ddr LEm, D-brd Rtt, A Gd, A M, and CH E, the bulk are probably by Johann Christian Bach (see TERRY, C. S., 262–83). Not a single addition can be made from any of these sources to the list of genuine symphonies given above. BACH/LEVY lists "18 Symphonien [counting items 652 and 653 as one], wovon 5 gedruckt sind [that is, items 652, 663–66] . . . ," and later, "1 Sinfonie mit dem Fürsten Lobkowitz, aus dem Stegreife, einen Takt um den andern componirt" (item 667?). NV, 43–45, 65, repeats this information.

Vocal

FOR SOLO VOICE(S) (SONGS WITH KEYBOARD ACCOMPANIMENT, UNLESS STATED OTHERWISE)

Authentic

669. [3 Arias for tenor, 2 violins, viola, continuo]. Probably before 1738 (source of date: "in jungen Jahren verfertigt," says NV, 64). W. 211
Ms.: B Bc, 719k (Michel)
Lit.: BITTER/BRÜDER, I, 192–93

Incipits from 719k:

Ed - le   Frei-heit   Göt -ter - glück

Him-mels Toch-ter, Ruh der   See-len

Rei-che bis zum Wol-ken-sit - ze

670. Schäferlied (M. von Ziegler). 1741 (source of date: BUSCH). W. 199/2
Early prints: ODEN; GRÄFE, III, No. 33. Lit. about these prints: See these entries in Bib.
Ms. probably copied from GRÄFE: D-brd B, Mus. ms. 38046
Mod. edn.: FRIEDLÄNDER, Vol. I, Part 2, No. 27
Lit. about this work: GEIRINGER/BACH, 370; BUSCH, 40, 72, 291, 312–14, 334, 369, Anh. 2–3; OTTENBERG, 131
In ODEN the bass is slightly altered at the end, as compared with GRÄFE. Mus. ms. 38046 is a ms. anthology of lieder bound with the print of Speronte's *Singende Muse an der Pleisse* (Leipzig, 1736).

Incipit from ODEN:

Eilt, ihr   Schä -fer, aus   den Grün -den

671. Der Zufriedne (Stahl). 1743 (source of date: BUSCH). W. 199/10
Early prints: ODEN; GRÄFE, IV, No. 19. Lit. about these prints: See these entries in Bib.
Ms. probably copied from GRÄFE: D-brd B, Mus. ms. 30390 (2 separately bound volumes)
Lit. about this work: BUSCH, 72, 314, 323, Anh. 2–3
In ODEN the figures are removed from the bass, a tempo marking is added, the title is omitted, and the text differs slightly, as compared with GRÄFE.

Incipit from ODEN:

Ent - fernt von Gram und   Sor - gen er - wach

672. Die verliebte Verzweifelung (Steinhauer). 1743 (source of date: BUSCH). W. 199/12
Early prints: ODEN; GRÄFE, IV, No. 4. Lit. about these prints: See these entries in Bib.
Lit. about this work: LINDNER, 59; GEIRINGER/BACH, 370; BUSCH, 40, 72, 314, 323, 379, Anh. 2–3
In ODEN the figures are removed from the bass, as compared with GRÄFE.

Incipit from ODEN:

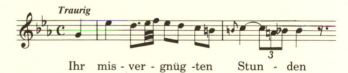

Ihr   mis - ver - gnüg -ten   Stun - den

673. Die Küsse (N. D. Giseke). 1750–53 (source of date: BUSCH). W. 199/4
Early prints: ODEN; RAMLER–KRAUSE I, No. 14; RAMLER–KRAUSE III, I, No. XXXIX. Lit. about these prints: See these entries in Bib.
Lit. about this work: BUSCH, 48, 72, 220, 290, 359, Anh. 2–3

Incipit from ODEN:

Dass ich, bey   mei - ner Lust, durch kei-nen Zwang

674. Trinklied (J. W. L. Gleim). 1750–53 (source of date: BUSCH). W. 199/5

Early prints: ODEN; RAMLER–KRAUSE I, No. 18; RAMLER–KRAUSE III, II, No. LV. Lit. about these prints: See these entries in Bib.

Lit. about this work: BUSCH, 48, 72, 220, 288, 315, 346, 380, Anh. 4–5

Incipit from ODEN:

675. Amint (E. von Kleist). 1750–53 (source of date: BUSCH). W. 199/11

Early prints: ODEN; RAMLER–KRAUSE I, No. 10; RAMLER–KRAUSE III, III, No. II. Lit. about these prints: See these entries in Bib.

Lit. about this work: BUSCH, 47–48, 72, 220, 278, 398, Anh. 2–3

Incipit from ODEN:

676. Die märkische Helene (G. E. Lessing). 1754 (source of date: BUSCH). W. 199/14

Early prints: ODEN; in MARPURG/BEYTRÄGE, I, 1, 88. Lit. about these prints: See these entries in Bib.

Lit. about this work: BUSCH, 51, 72, Anh. 4–5; OTTEN-BERG, 131, 133–34

Incipit from ODEN:

677. Die sächsische Helene (J. W. L. Gleim). 1754 (source of date: BUSCH). W. 199/1

Early prints: ODEN; RAMLER–KRAUSE II, No. 29; RAMLER–KRAUSE III, I, No. LIV. Lit. about these prints: See these entries in Bib.

Lit. about this work: BUSCH, 51–52, 220, 290, Anh. 4–5; OTTENBERG, 142

Incipit from ODEN:

678. Dorinde (J. W. L. Gleim). 1754 or 1755 (source of date: BUSCH). W. 199/7

Early prints: ODEN; RAMLER–KRAUSE II, No. 5; RAMLER–KRAUSE III, I, No. LVIII. Lit. about these prints: See these entries in Bib.

Lit. about this work: BUSCH, 51–52, 220, Anh. 4–5

Incipit from ODEN:

679. Lied eines jungen Mägdchens ("Fräulein von H" [G. E. Lessing?]). 1756 (source of date: BUSCH). W. 199/3

Early prints: ODEN; MARPURG/ODEN I, No. 17. Lit. about these prints: See these entries in Bib.

Lit. about this work: BUSCH, 53, 219, Anh. 4–5

Incipit from ODEN:

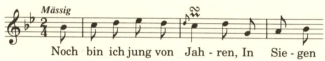

680. Der Morgen (F. von Hagedorn). 1756 (source of date: BUSCH). W. 199/6

Early prints: ODEN; MARPURG/LIEDER, 29. Lit. about these prints: See these entries in Bib.

Lit. about this work: BITTER/ BRÜDER, I, 139–40; LIND-NER, 60; GEIRINGER/BACH, 370; BUSCH, 52, 331, 346, 380, 398, Anh. 4–5

Incipit from ODEN:

681. Die Biene (G. E. Lessing). 1756 (source of date: BUSCH). W. 199/9

Early prints: ODEN; MARPURG/ODEN I, No. 21. Lit. about these prints: See these entries in Bib.

Lit. about this work: LINDNER, 60; BUSCH, 53, 219, 334, Anh. 4–5

Incipit from ODEN:

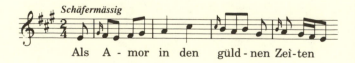

682. Die Küsse (G. E. Lessing). 1756 (source of date:
BUSCH). W. 199/13
Mss.: D-brd B, Mus. ms. 30406, Mus. ms. 40302
Early prints: ODEN; MARPURG/ODEN I, No. 11. Lit. about
these prints: See these entries in Bib.
Lit. about this work: BUSCH, 53, 219, Anh. 4–5

Incipit from ODEN:

Ein Küss-chen, das ein Kind mir schen-ket

683. Der Stoiker (translation from a French original). 1757
(source of date: BUSCH). W. 199/8
Early prints: ODEN; MARPURG/ODEN II, No. 6. Lit. about
these prints: See these entries in Bib.
Lit. about this work: BUSCH, 54, 290, 359, Anh. 4–5

Incipit from ODEN:

Ein fau - ler Feind der Fröh - lich-keit auf Er-den

684. Serin. 1757 (source of date: BUSCH). W. 199/15
Early prints: ODEN; MARPURG/ODEN II, No. 4. Lit. about
these prints: See these entries in Bib.
Lit. about this work: BUSCH, 54, 280, Anh. 4–5

Incipit from ODEN:

Se - rin, der hoch - be - rühm - te Mann

685. La Sophie. Aria. Probably c. 1757 (sources of date: date
of item 125; see also item 685.5)
Mss.: D-brd B, P 743 (autog.); B Bc, 5897 (Westphal)
A.v. of item 125 with a text added to create a substantial
da-capo aria

Incipit from P 743:

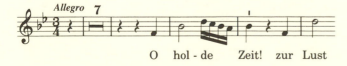

O hol - de Zeit! zur Lust

685.5. Ernestine. Probably c. 1757 (source of date: see
below). W. 199/16
Mss.: D-brd B, Mus. ms. 38050, P 743 (autog.); B Bc, 5897
(Westphal)

Early prints and lit. about them: See ODEN (title changed
to "Auf der Namenstag der Mademoiselle S.").
Lit. about this work: BUSCH, 27, Anh. 12–13
P 743, a 4-p. autograph entitled "Petites Pieces pour le clavecin par C P E Bach," consists of items 123, 685, 685.5,
and 122. Items 122 and 123, says NV, date from 1757;
item 685 is an a.v. of item 125, which is dated 1757 in
NV; all of P 743 appears to have been copied at the same
time.
Unrelated to item 124

Incipit from ODEN:

Das Fest der hol - den Er - ne - sti - nen

686. Herrn Professor Gellerts geistliche Oden und Lieder
mit Melodien (C. F. Gellert). 1757–58 (source of date:
BUSCH). W. 194
Early prints: GELLERT-LIEDER; HILLER/LIEDER (Nos. 15,
36, 38, 40, 55, all with changed texts, on pp. 32, 78, 88,
76, 38, respectively); RHEINECK (Nos. 5, 16, 18, 20, 28,
33, 35, 47, 49, appearing as Nos. 183, 153, 142, 239, 363,
173, 301, 483, 434, respectively; MUSIKALISCHE
BLUMENLESE (No. 1 appearing as No. XVI); MELODIEN
(Nos. 27, 45, both with changed texts, on pp. 54, 195,
respectively); vnt. of No. 27 on p. 53 of the latter collection.
Lit. about these prints: See these entries in Bib.
Mss. probably copied from an early print (GELLERT-
LIEDER): in the private collection of E. N. Kulukundis
(U.S.); D-brd B, N. Mus. ms. 10499 (Nos. 16 and 20 only);
D-ddr Bds, Mus. ms. 30068 (Nos. 8 and 16 only, their 1st
strophes only); US WS (No. 39 only, arranged, 2 copies;
my thanks to Howard Serwer for this notice); US NHu
(No. 13 only, autog.?, mounted in a frame, with an unidentified sketch on the reverse side; gift to US NHu from
the David Opotchinsky family; my thanks to Elias
Kulukundis for notice of this item)
Mod. edns.: BITTER/LIEDER (Nos. 3, 4, 9, 14, 18, 32, 34,
45, 46, 51, 53); FRIEDLÄNDER, Vol. I, Part 2, Friedländer's Nos. 162, 163 (Nos. 9, 13); DITTBERNER (Nos. 4, 9,
10, 12, 18, 21, 26, 32, 34, 45); ROTH (Nos. 7, 9, 14, 15,
30, 32, 34, 39, 44, 46, 48, 49); VRIESLANDER/LIEDER
(Nos. 8, 24, 34, 45, 49, 53)

Lit.: on No.

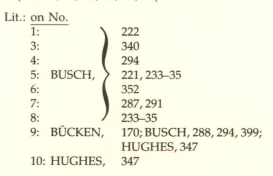

1:		222
3:		340
4:		294
5:	BUSCH,	221, 233–35
6:		352
7:		287, 291
8:		233–35
9:	BÜCKEN,	170; BUSCH, 288, 294, 399; HUGHES, 347
10:	HUGHES,	347

11:            233–35, 294
12:            82, 289–90, 352
13:            290
14:            220–21; HUGHES, 347; CLARK/
              CHORAL, 88–96
16: BUSCH,   221
17:            291
18:            289, 320, 325, 381; HUGHES, 347
19:            402
20:            221, 377
21:            318; CLARK/CHORAL, 88–96
23: HUGHES,   347; CLARK/CHORAL, 88–96
24:            290, 357, 368
25:            357
26:            237, 347
27:            219, 380
28:            221
29:            289, 291
30:            289, 317
31:            332–33, 368
33:            221, 368
34:            289, 325, 381, 399, 402
35: BUSCH,   221, 318
36:            221, 302
37:            237, 289, 294, 318, 402
38:            221
39:            289, 318
40:            221
45:            83, 219, 294, 325
46:            295, 402
47:            221, 289
48:            320, 332, 381
49: VRIESLANDER/BACH, 116; BUSCH, 221, 280,
              318, 331, 333
50: BUSCH, 280, 294, 318
51: BUSCH, 325, 351, 399
53: VRIESLANDER/BACH, 117; BUSCH, 294–95, 318
55: BUSCH, 220, 297

Nos. 24 and 25 are, musically speaking, two separate songs, though No. 25 is textually a continuation of No. 24—the second part of a "Dialogus." See GELLERT/SCHRIFTEN, 215–18.

Arr.: of No. 9, item 826/3; of No. 14, in items 790, 791?, 797?; of No. 21, in item 800; of No. 23, in items 794, 796; of No. 30, item 826/1; of No. 37, item 836; of No. 53, item 826/2

See also item 357.

Incipits from GELLERT-LIEDER:

[No. 1] Abendlied

Für al-le Gu-te sey ge-preist, Gott Va-ter

[No. 2] Zufriedenheit mit seinem Zustande

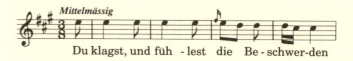

Du klagst, und füh-lest die Be-schwer-den

[No. 3] Das Glück eines guten Gewissens

Be-sitz ich nur Ein ru-hi-ges Ge-wis-sen

[No. 4] Vom Worte Gottes

Gott ist mein Hort! Und auf sein Wort Soll mei-

[No. 5] Weihnachtslied

Auf, schi-cke dich, Recht fey-er-lich Des

[No. 6] Geduld

Ein Herz, o Gott, in Leid und Kreuz ge-dul-dig

[No. 7] Prüfung am Abend

Der Tag ist wie-der hin, und die-sen Theil des

[No. 8] Danklied

Du bists, dem Ruhm und Eh-re ge-büh-ret

[No. 9] Bitten

Gott, dei-ne Gü-te reicht so weit, So

[No. 10] Osterlied

Je - sus lebt, mit ihm auch ich. Tod

[No. 11] Der thätige Glaube

Wer Got - tes Wort nicht hält und spricht: Ich

[No. 12] Der Schutz der Kirche

Wenn Chri-stus sei - ne Kir-che schützt: So mag die

[No. 13] Um Ergebung in den göttlichen Willen

O Herr, mein Gott, durch den ich bin und le-be

[No. 14] Passionslied

Er - for - sche mich, er - fahr mein Herz

[No. 15] Morgengesang

Mein erst Ge - fühl sey Preis und Dank!

[No. 16] Gottes Macht und Vorsehung

Gott ist mein Lied! Er ist der Gott der Stär -ke;

[No. 17] Trost des ewigen Lebens

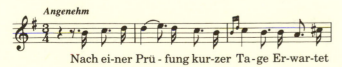

Nach ei-ner Prü - fung kur-zer Ta -ge Er-war-tet

[No. 18] Die Ehre Gottes aus der Natur

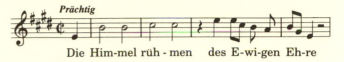

Die Him-mel rüh - men des E-wi-gen Eh-re

[No. 19] Die Liebe des Nächsten

So je-mand spricht: Ich lie - be Gott!

[No. 20] Auf die Himmelfahrt des Erlösers

Jauchzt, ihr Er - lös - ten, dem Herrn! Er

hat sein Werk vol - len - det

[No. 21] Das Gebet

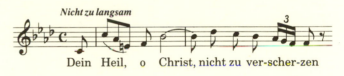

Dein Heil, o Christ, nicht zu ver-scher-zen

[No. 22] Osterlied

Frey - wil - lig hab ichs dar - ge-bracht, Und nie-

[No. 23] Passionslied

Herr, stär - ke mich, dein Lei-den zu be - den-ken

[No. 24] Trost eines schwermüthigen Christen

Du klagst, o Christ,

[No. 25. Untitled]

Zag nicht, o Christ, denn dei - ne Schmer-zen

151

[No. 26] Betrachtung des Todes

Wie si - cher lebt der Mensch, der Staub!

[No. 27] Preis des Schöpfers

Wenn ich, o Schöp-fer, dei - ne Macht, Die Weis-

[No. 28] Von der Quelle der guten Werke

Wenn zur Voll-füh -rung dei - ner Pflicht Dich

[No. 29] Ermunterung die Schrift zu lesen

Soll dein ver-derb-tes Herz zur Hei-li - gung

[No. 30] Trost der Erlösung

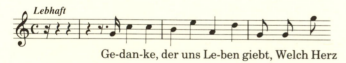

Ge-dan-ke, der uns Le-ben giebt, Welch Herz

[No. 31] Warnung vor der Wollust

Der Wol-lust Reiz zu wi - der - stre-ben

[No. 32] Abendlied

Herr, der du mir das Le - ben, Bis

[No. 33] Das natürliche Verderben des Menschen

Wer bin ich von Na - tur, wenn ich mein

[No. 34] Die Güte Gottes

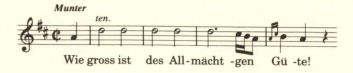

Wie gross ist des All-mächt -gen Gü - te!

[No. 35] Der Weg des Frommen

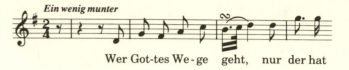

Wer Got-tes We - ge geht, nur der hat

[No. 36] In Krankheit

Ich hab in gu-ten Stun-den Des Le-

[No. 37] Vom Tode

Mei-ne Le-bens-zeit ver - streicht, Stünd -lich

[No. 38] Lied am Geburtstage

Dir dank ich heu - te für mein Le - ben

[No. 39] Versicherung der Gnade Gottes

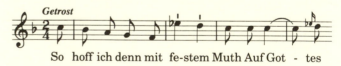

So hoff ich denn mit fe-stem Muth Auf Got - tes

[No. 40] Gelassenheit

Was ists, dass ich mich quä - le? Harr Sei-ner

[No. 41] Allgemeines Gebet

Ich kom-me vor dein An - ge - sicht, Ver-

[No. 42] Osterlied

Er - inn - re dich, mein Geist, er - freut Des

[No. 43] Weihnachtslied

Diess ist der Tag, den Gott ge-

macht; Sein Werd in

[No. 44] Am Communiontage

Ich kom-me Herr, und su - che dich, Müh-

se - lig

[No. 45] Am neuen Jahre

Er ruft der Sonn, und schafft den Mond, Das Jahr

[No. 46] Busslied

An dir al - lein, an dir hab ich ge-sün-digt

[No. 47] Die Liebe der Feinde

Nie will ich dem zu scha - den su-chen

[No. 48] Demuth

Herr, leh - re mich, wenn

ich der Tu-gend die-ne

[No. 49] Wider den Uebermuth

Was ist mein Stand, mein Glück, und

[No. 50] Wider den Aufschub der Bekehrung

Willst du die Bus - se noch, die

Gott ge-beut, ver - schie-ben

[No. 51] Vertraun auf Gottes Vorsehung

Auf Gott, und nicht auf mei - nem

Rath, Will ich mein

[No. 52] Beständige Erinnerung des Todes

Was sorgst du ängst - lich für dein

Le - ben? Es Gott

[No. 53] Der Kampf der Tugend

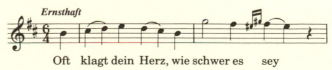

Oft klagt dein Herz, wie schwer es sey

153

[No. 54] Wider den Geiz

Wohl dem, den bess - re Schä -tze   liebt

[No. 55] Die Wachsamkeit

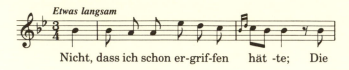

Nicht, dass ich schon er-grif-fen   hät -te;   Die

687. Herausforderungslied vor der Schlacht bey Rossbach (J. W. L. Gleim). 1758 (source of date: BUSCH). W. 199/20
Early prints and lit. about them: See ODEN.
Lit. about this work: LINDNER, 59–60; BUSCH, 54–58, 73, 333, 381, Anh. 12–13; OTTENBERG, 129–30

Incipit from ODEN:

Her-aus aus dei-ner Wol-fes-gruft   Furcht-

688. Freude, du Lust der Götter und Menschen [cantata] (C. M. Wieland). Probably c. 1760 (source of date: 1st pub.). W. 202/A
Early print and lit. about it: See DREY VERSUCHE.
Ms. probably copied from the early print: B Bc, 286 (Westphal)
Lit. about this work: BITTER/BRÜDER, I, 155–59; BUSCH, 68–70
Arr.: item 723

Incipit from DREY VERSUCHE:

Freu-de, du Lust der Göt-ter und Men-schen

689. Deleted

690. Der Traum. 1761 or 1762 (source of date: BUSCH). W. 199/17
Early prints and lit. about them: See ODEN.
Lit. about this work: BUSCH, 72, Anh. 12–13

Incipit from ODEN:

Es war ein Mägd-chen oh - ne Män-gel

691. Die Tugend (A. von Haller). 1761 or 1762 (source of date: BUSCH). W. 199/18
Early prints and lit. about them: See ODEN.
Lit. about this work: BUSCH, 73, Anh. 12–13

Incipit from ODEN:

Freund, die   Tu-gend ist kein lee - rer Na-me

692. Doris (A. von Haller). 1762 or earlier (source of date: BUSCH). W. 199/19
Early prints and lit. about them: See ODEN.
Lit. about this work: BUSCH, 73, 278, Anh. 12–13

Incipit from ODEN:

Des Ta-ges Licht hat sich ver - dun - kelt

693. Das Privilegium (N. D. Giseke). 1762–65 (NV 17). W. 202/B/1 (= 112/6)
Mss.: D-brd B, P 1130 (autog., vnt., without text); D-brd B, Mus. ms. 30048
Early print and lit. about it: See VERSCHIEDEN.
Mss. probably copied from the early print: D-brd B, P 676; B Bc, 286 (Westphal)
Mod. edns.: VRIESLANDER/LIEDER, BERG/FACSIMILE
Lit. about this work: VRIESLANDER/BACH, 125–26; BUSCH, 77, 399, Anh. 14–15
See item 820, then items 190, 842.

Incipit from VERSCHIEDEN:

Ihr Brü-der, zankt nicht mit den Tho-ren

694. Die Landschaft. 1762–65 (NV 17). W. 202/B/2 (= 112/12)
Early print and lit. about it: See VERSCHIEDEN.
Mss. probably copied from the early print: D-brd B, P 676; B Bc, 286 (Westphal)

Mod. edns.: VRIESLANDER/LIEDER, BERG/FACSIMILE
Lit. about this work: VRIESLANDER/BACH, 125–26;
BUSCH, 77, Anh. 14–15

Incipit from VERSCHIEDEN:

Angenehm und mässig

Ge-lieb-tes Feld, dein auf-ge-klär-ter Him-mel

695. Belinde (K. W. Müller). 1762–65 (NV 17). W. 202/B/3
(= 112/14)
Early print and lit. about it: See VERSCHIEDEN.
Mss. probably copied from the early print: D-brd B, P 676;
B Bc, 286 (Westphal)
Mod. edns.: VRIESLANDER/LIEDER, BERG/FACSIMILE
Lit. about this work: BITTER/BRÜDER, I, 141–42; BUSCH,
77, Anh. 14–15

Incipit from VERSCHIEDEN:

Etwas lebhaft

Das Dä-mon nie Be-lin - den rüh-ret

696. Zwölf geistliche Oden und Lieder als ein Anhang zu
Gellerts geistlichen Oden und Liedern mit Melodien (the
poet of No. 4 is L. F. F. Lehr; of Nos. 8, 10, 11, A. L. Karsch).
1764 (source of date: BUSCH). W. 195
Early prints: See GELLERT-ANHANG, 1764; MELODIEN,
p. 188 (vnt. of No. 4). Lit. about these prints: See these
entries in Bib.
Mod. edns.: FRIEDLÄNDER, Vol. I, Part 2, Friedländer's
No. 164 (No. 12); DITTBERNER (Nos. 2, 3); ROTH (Nos.
8, 12); BITTER/LIEDER (No. 11)
Lit.: BUSCH, on No.
        4:      74, 82, 219, 318
        8:      318
        9:      293–94
        10:     319
        11:     291, 366–67
        12:     295, 299, 318, 326, 367, 381

Arr. of No. 12: item 830

Incipits from GELLERT-ANHANG, 1764:

[No. 1] Aufmunterung zur Tugend

Ein wenig langsam

Ins Reich ent-fern-ter E - wig-

[No. 2] Nachahmung der göttlichen Liebe

Angenehm und etwas langsam

Ur-quell der Lie - be! Ew'-ge Gü-te!

[No. 3] Trost-Lied

Gelassen

Ei - le, Herr! mein Herz zu stär-ken, Ma-che

[No. 4] Ermunterung zur Busse

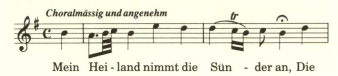

Choralmässig und angenehm

Mein Hei-land nimmt die Sün - der an, Die

[No. 5] Von der Majestät Gottes

Nachdrücklich und etwas langsam

O gro-sse Ma-je - stät, an - be-tens-würd-ges

[No. 6] Die Zufriedenheit in Gott

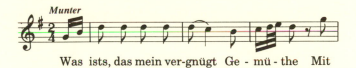

Munter

Was ists, das mein ver-gnügt Ge - mü-the Mit

[No. 7] Der sieben und zwanzigste Psalm

Mässig

Den al - le Him-mel Herr-scher nen-nen, Der

[No. 8] An Gott

Choralmässig und kräftig

Er - heb auf mich dein An - ge-sicht Und lass mich

[No. 9] Der hunderte Psalm

Lebhaft

Ihr Völ - cker jauchzt mit ho - hem Schall

[No. 10] An Gott

Mit Affect und etwas langsam

Wenn ich er-wa-che, denk ich dein! Du Gott

[No. 11] Morgen-Gesang

Etwas munter

Der jun - ge Tag, zu-rück-ge-kom-men

[No. 12] Der acht und achtzigste Psalm

Choralmässig und sehr langsam

Mein Hei-land, mei-ne Zu - ver - sicht! Mein Gott, vor

697. Phillis und Thirsis, eine Cantate in Musik gesetzt von C. P. E. Bach [2 sopranos, 2 flutes, continuo]. 1765 (NV 55). W. 232

Ms.: D-brd B, P 783

Early print: the above title, "Berlin, bey George Ludewig Winter. 1766"

Mod. edns.: G. A. Walther, Leipzig: Breitkopf & Härtel, 1919, reprinted 1928; VRIESLANDER/LIEDER; F. Nagel, Cologne, [c. 1972]

Lit.: HILLER/NACHRICHTEN, 6 Jan. 1767, 218–19; HAM-BURGER CORRESPONDENT, 4 Apr. 1770; BITTER/BRÜDER, I, 159–62; VRIESLANDER/BACH, 123–25; BÜCKEN, 169–70; ENGELKE, 430–32; GEIRINGER/BACH, 370; OTTENBERG, 141–42

Incipits from the Winter print:

Mässig geschwind

Phillis

Thir - sis, willst du mir ge-fal-len

Recitativ

Thirsis

Ach Phill-is! lass mich scherz-en

Angenehm und nicht geschwinde

Thirsis

Der Vo-gel ru - fet oh-ne

698. Bachus und Venus (H. W. von Gerstenberg). 1766 (NV 21). W. 202/D

Early print: VIELERLEY, 117. Lit. about VIELERLEY: See this entry in Bib.

Ms. probably copied from the early print: B Bc, 286 (Westphal)

Lit. about this work: BUSCH, 283, 310, 314, Anh. 18–19

Incipit from VIELERLEY:

Stolz und nicht geschwind

A - mor ist mein Lied! Schön ist er be-kränzt

699. Der Wirth und die Gäste, eine Singode vom Herrn Gleim in Musik gesetzt von Carl Philipp Emanuel Bach [4 solo voices and keyboard] (J. W. L. Gleim). 1766 (source of date: BUSCH). W. 201

Early prints: the above title, "Berlin, bey George Ludewig Winter, 1766"; NOTENBUCH, I, No. 7. Reprint of the 1766 edn. with changes by J. C. F. Rellstab, Berlin, 1790, reprinted 1791 (W. 264). The known lit. gives no evidence that the (posthumous) Rellstab prints had been authorized by CPEB. Lit. about NOTENBUCH: See this entry in Bib.

Mod. edn.: FRIEDLÄNDER, Vol. I, Part 2, No. 77

Lit. about this work: HAMBURGER CORRESPONDENT, 4 Apr. 1770; BITTER/BRÜDER, I, 162–64; STEGLICH/HOMILIUS, 103–04; GEIRINGER/BACH, 370; BUSCH, 77, 222, 310, 315, 361, 368–69, Anh. 16–17

A.v. for 4 solo voices, 2 violins, viola, basso, 2 flutes, 2 horns, keyboard: D-brd B, ms. St 558

Incipit from the Winter print:

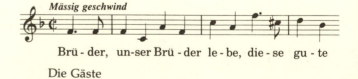

Mässig geschwind

Brü - der, un-ser Brü-der le - be, die-se gu - te

Die Gäste

700. Belise und Thyrsis. Before 1767? (source of date: BUSCH). W. 200/10

Ms.: D-brd B, P 349 (autog.)

Early print: NEUE LIEDER, No. 10. Lit. about NEUE LIEDER: See this entry in Bib.

Lit. about this work: BUSCH, 193, 207–10, 381, Anh. 16–17, 20–21; WIEN-CLAUDI (see below)

A.v.: a transposition and parody ("Allgutiger! gewohnt Gebet zu hören"), poet anon., D-brd B, ms. P 808 (autog.). Added in CPEB's hand: "Auch dieses wünscht von Herzen und in Tönen ein redlicher Vetter/C. P. E. Bach." The ms. was owned and signed by one Ebert, who dates his signature 1819. WIEN-CLAUDI explains at the end of *Zum Liedschaffen:* "Ebert hat das Musikblatt von der Enkelin C. P. E. Bachs, einer in diesem Jahre (1819) verstorbenen Witwe eines Buchdruckergesellen namens Prüfer, erhalten." On the identification of Ebert and Prüfer and on the terms "Vetter" and "Enkelin," see BUSCH, 208–10.

Incipit from NEUE LIEDER:

Be - li - se starb, und sprach im

701. An eine kleine Schöne (G. E. Lessing). Before 1767? (source of date: BUSCH). W. 200/20
Early print: NEUE LIEDER, No. 20. Lit. about NEUE LIEDER: See this entry in Bib.
Lit. about this work: BUSCH, 195, 381, Anh. 16–17

Incipit from NEUE LIEDER:

Klei - ne Schö - ne, küs - se mich, Klei - ne

702. An die Natur (J. H. Röding). 1767 or later (source of date: BUSCH). W. 200/6
Ms.: D-brd B, P 349 (autog.)
Early print: NEUE LIEDER, No. 6. Lit. about NEUE LIEDER: See this entry in Bib.
Lit. about this work: BUSCH, 192, Anh. 40–41

Incipit from NEUE LIEDER:

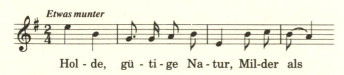

Hol - de, gü - ti - ge Na - tur, Mil - der als

703. An meine Ruhestätte (J. H. Röding). 1767 or later (source of date: BUSCH). W. 200/8
Early print: NEUE LIEDER, No. 8. Lit. about NEUE LIEDER: See this entry in Bib.
Lit. about this work: BUSCH, 193, Anh. 40–41

Incipit from NEUE LIEDER:

Sey mir ge - grüsst, du Ziel von mein-en Sor-gen

704. An den Schlaf (J. H. Röding). 1767 or later (source of date: BUSCH). W. 200/11
Early print: NEUE LIEDER, No. 11. Lit. about NEUE LIEDER: See this entry in Bib.
Lit. about this work: BUSCH, 193, Anh. 40–41

Incipit from NEUE LIEDER:

Komm, sü - sser Freund der Mü - den

705. Die Zufriedenheit (J. H. Röding). 1767 or later (source of date: BUSCH). W. 200/12
Ms.: D-brd B, P 349 (autog.)
Early print: NEUE LIEDER, No. 12. Lit. about NEUE LIEDER: See this entry in Bib.
Lit. about this work: BUSCH, Anh. 40–41

Incipit from NEUE LIEDER:

Im - mer auf der Blu-men-bahn Gold - ne

706. Gartenlied (J. H. Lüttkens). 1767 or later (source of date: BUSCH). W. 200/15
Early print: NEUE LIEDER, No. 15. Lit. about NEUE LIEDER: See this entry in Bib.
Lit. about this work: BUSCH, 194, Anh. 42–43

Incipit from NEUE LIEDER:

Es schallt, o Gott, em - por zu dir

707. Auf den Geburtstag eines Freundes (C. D. Ebeling). 1767 or later (source of date: BUSCH). W. 200/17
Ms.: D-brd B, P 349 (autog.)
Early print: NEUE LIEDER, No. 17. Lit. about NEUE LIEDER: See this entry in Bib.
Lit. about this work: BUSCH, 194, 363, 385, 397, Anh. 42–43

Incipit from NEUE LIEDER:

Hol - de Freu - de, sen - ke dich Von dem

708. [untitled] (J. C. Unzer). 1767 or later (source of date: BUSCH). W. 200/19

Early print: NEUE LIEDER, No. 19. Lit. about NEUE LIEDER: See this entry in Bib.

Lit. about this work: BUSCH, 195, Anh. 42–43

Incipit from NEUE LIEDER:

709. Der Unbeständige ("W . . . "). 1768 or earlier (source of date: BUSCH). W. 202/C/1

Early print: UNTERHALTUNGEN, V, 436

Mss. probably copied from the early print: B Bc, 286 (Westphal); D-brd B, Mus. ms. 40302

Lit.: BUSCH, 99, 382, Anh. 18–19

Incipit from UNTERHALTUNGEN:

710. Phyllis (E. von Kleist). 1768 or earlier (source of date: BUSCH). W. 202/C/2

Early print: UNTERHALTUNGEN, VI, 52

Mss. probably copied from the early print: B Bc, 286 (Westphal); D-brd B, Mus. ms. 40302

Mod. edn.: VRIESLANDER/LIEDER

Lit.: BITTER/BRÜDER, II, 76–77; BUSCH, 99, 360, 382, Anh. 18–19

Incipit from UNTERHALTUNGEN:

711. An die Liebe (F. von Hagedorn). 1768 (source of date: BUSCH). W. 202/C/3

Early print: UNTERHALTUNGEN, VI, 482

Mss. probably copied from the early print: B Bc, 286 (Westphal); D-brd B, Mus. ms. 40302

Lit.: BITTER/BRÜDER, II, 77; BUSCH, 99, 331, 366, 382, Anh. 18–19

Incipit from UNTERHALTUNGEN:

712. Weihnachtslied (D. Schiebeler). 1769 (source of date: BUSCH). W. 202/C/4

Early print: UNTERHALTUNGEN, VII, 262

Mss. probably copied from the early print: B Bc, 286 (Westphal); D-brd B, Mus. ms. 40302

Lit.: BUSCH, 99, Anh. 18–19

Incipit from UNTERHALTUNGEN:

713. Vom Leiden des Erlösers (D. Schiebeler). 1769 (source of date: BUSCH). W. 202/C/5

Early print: UNTERHALTUNGEN, VII, 363

Mss. probably copied from the early print: B Bc, 286 (Westphal); D-brd B, Mus. ms. 40302

Lit.: BUSCH, 99, Anh. 18–19

Incipit from UNTERHALTUNGEN:

714. Klagen einer Schäferinn (D. Schiebeler). 1769 (source of date: BUSCH). W. 202/C/6

Early print: UNTERHALTUNGEN, VII, 459

Mss. probably copied from the early print: B Bc, 286 (Westphal); D-brd B, Mus. ms. 40302

Lit.: BUSCH, 100, Anh. 18–19

Incipit from UNTERHALTUNGEN:

715. Ode auf die Gegenwart sr. kayserlichen Majestät in Rom. 1769 (source of date: BUSCH). W. 202/C/7

Early print: UNTERHALTUNGEN, VII, 539

Mss. probably copied from the early print: B Bc, 286 (Westphal); D-brd B, Mus. ms. 40302

Lit.: BITTER/BRÜDER, II, 77; BUSCH, 100, Anh. 18–19

Incipit from UNTERHALTUNGEN:

Gott und den Kai - ser zu ver - eh - ren

716. Auf die Auferstehung des Erlösers (D. Schiebeler). 1769 (source of date: BUSCH). W. 202/C/8
Early print: UNTERHALTUNGEN, VIII, 262
Mss. probably copied from the early print: B Bc, 286 (Westphal); D-brd B, Mus. ms. 40302
Lit.: BUSCH, 100, Anh. 18–19

Incipit from UNTERHALTUNGEN:

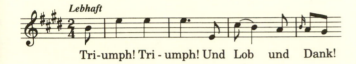

Tri - umph! Tri - umph! Und Lob und Dank!

717. Ode am Communion-Tage (D. Schiebeler). 1769 (source of date: BUSCH). W. 202/C/9
Early print: UNTERHALTUNGEN, VIII, 468
Mss. probably copied from the early print: B Bc, 286 (Westphal); D-brd B, Mus. ms. 40302
Lit.: BUSCH, 100, Anh. 18–19

Incipit from UNTERHALTUNGEN:

Tag, den mir der Herr ge - macht,

718. Loblied (D. Schiebeler). 1770 (source of date: BUSCH). W. 202/C/10
Early print: UNTERHALTUNGEN, IX, 74
Mss. probably copied from the early print: B Bc, 286 (Westphal); D-brd B, Mus. ms. 40302
Lit.: BUSCH, 100, Anh. 18–19

Incipit from UNTERHALTUNGEN:

So lang ich ath - me, Gott! Will ich dein Lob

719. Bey dem Grabe des verstorbenen Mechanicus Hohlfeld (A. L. Karsch). 1770 (source of date: BUSCH). W. 202/C/11
Early print: UNTERHALTUNGEN, IX, 161
Mss. probably copied from the early print: B Bc, 286 (Westphal); D-brd B, Mus. ms. 40302
Lit.: MIESNER/UMWELT, 142–43; BUSCH, 100, Anh. 18–19
See item 280.

Incipit from UNTERHALTUNGEN:

Der du wie duft von Weyh-rauch Koh-len,

720. Schnitterlied (H. W. von Gerstenberg). 1770 (source of date: BUSCH). W. 202/C/12
Early print: UNTERHALTUNGEN, IX, 412
Mss. probably copied from the early print: B Bc, 286 (Westphal); D-brd B, Mus. ms. 40302
Lit.: BUSCH, 101, 331, 382, Anh. 18–19

Incipit from UNTERHALTUNGEN:

Die du dich mit Aeh - ren kränz - est,

Blon - de Ce - res

721. Passionslied (D. P. Scriba). 1770 (source of date: BUSCH). W. 202/C/13
Early print: UNTERHALTUNGEN, IX, 258
Mss. probably copied from the early print: D-brd B, Mus. ms. 40302; B Bc, 286 (Westphal)
Mod. edn.: ROTH
Lit.: BUSCH, 100–01, 283, 352, 399, Anh. 18–19

Incipit from UNTERHALTUNGEN:

Wie? Schön-ster! den mein Her-ze liebt

722. Deleted

723. Der Frühling, eine Tenor-Cantate [tenor, 2 violins, viola, continuo] (C. M. Wieland). 1770–72 (NV 62). W. 237
Ms.: B Bc, 719 l (Michel)
Lit.: BITTER/BRÜDER, I, 159
Arr. of item 688

Incipits from 719 l:

Freu-de, du Lust der Göt-ter und Men-schen

724. Communionlied (D. B. Münter). 1772 or 1773 (source of date: BUSCH). W. 202/E/1

Early print: MÜNTER-LIEDER, No. 19. Lit. about MÜNTER-LIEDER: See this entry in Bib.

Ms. probably copied from the early print: B Bc, 286 (Westphal)

Lit. about this work: BUSCH, 103–04, Anh. 18–19

Incipit from MÜNTER-LIEDER:

725. Freudige Erwartung des Todes (D. B. Münter). 1772 or 1773 (source of date: BUSCH). W. 202/E/2

Early print: MÜNTER-LIEDER, No. 21. Lit. about MÜNTER-LIEDER: See this entry in Bib.

Ms. probably copied from the early print: B Bc, 286 (Westphal)

Lit. about this work: BUSCH, 103–04, Anh. 20–21

Incipit from MÜNTER-LIEDER:

726. Ermunterung zur Beständigkeit (D. B. Münter). 1772 or 1773 (source of date: BUSCH). W. 202/E/3

Early print: MÜNTER-LIEDER, No. 24. Lit. about MÜNTER-LIEDER: See this entry in Bib.

Ms. probably copied from the early print: B Bc, 286 (Westphal)

Lit. about this work: BUSCH, 103–04, Anh. 20–21

Incipit from MÜNTER-LIEDER:

727. Glückseligkeit des Christen (D. B. Münter). 1772 or 1773 (source of date: BUSCH). W. 202/E/4

Early print: MÜNTER-LIEDER, No. 25. Lit. about MÜNTER-LIEDER: See this entry in Bib.

Ms. probably copied from the early print: B Bc, 286 (Westphal)

Lit. about this work: BUSCH, 103–04, Anh. 20–21

Incipit from MÜNTER-LIEDER:

728. Osterlied (D. B. Münter). 1772 or 1773 (source of date: BUSCH). W. 202/E/5

Early print: MÜNTER-LIEDER, No. 44. Lit. about MÜNTER-LIEDER: See this entry in Bib.

Ms. probably copied from the early print: B Bc, 286 (Westphal)

Lit. about this work: BUSCH, 103–04, 314, Anh. 20–21

Incipit from MÜNTER-LIEDER:

729. Des Herrn Wort ist wahrhaftig (D. B. Münter). 1772 or 1773 (source of date: BUSCH). W. 202/E/6

Early print: MÜNTER-LIEDER, No. 49. Lit. about MÜNTER-LIEDER: See this entry in Bib.

Ms. probably copied from the early print: B Bc, 286 (Westphal)

Lit. about this work: BUSCH, 103–04, 289, 314, 382, Anh. 20–21; CLARK/CHORAL, 88–96 (read "MÜNTER, 49" on p. 90)

Arr.: in item 797

Incipit from MÜNTER-LIEDER:

730. Klagelied eines Bauren (Miller). After 1772 (source of date: BUSCH). W. 202/O/2
Ms.: B Bc, 286 (Westphal)
Lit.: BUSCH, 206–07, Anh. 42–43

Incipit from 286:

731. Vaterlandslied (F. G. Klopstock). 1773 (source of date: BUSCH). W. 202/F/1
Ms.: D-brd B, Mus. ms. 30154
Early print: VOSS/1774, 101. Lit. about VOSS/1774: See this entry in Bib.
Ms. probably copied from the early print: B Bc, 286 (Westphal)
Mod. edn.: VRIESLANDER/LIEDER
Lit. about this work: BUSCH, 97, 121, 283, 403, Anh. 20–21; OTTENBERG, 213

Incipit from VOSS/1774:

732. Der Bauer (Miller). 1773 (source of date: BUSCH). W. 202/F/2
Ms.: D-brd Mbs, Mus. ms. 2774, Bd. I (autog.)
Early print: VOSS/1774, 103. Lit. about VOSS/1774: See this entry in Bib.
Ms. probably copied from the early print: B Bc, 286 (Westphal)
Mod. edn.: VRIESLANDER/LIEDER
Lit. about this work: STEGLICH/HOMILIUS, 104; BUSCH, 121–22, 332, 346, 383, Anh. 20–21
The ms. contains this song (with different text, beginning "Der Maienmond lacht in schimmernder Pracht," poet anon.) along with items 736–38, 739.5. Accompanying the ms. are 2 letters (CPEB/VOSS) containing the composer's corrections of and comments on the songs, which he is submitting for inclusion in Voss's 1774 and 1775 anthologies.

Incipit from VOSS/ 1774:

733. Herrn Doctor Cramers übersetzte Psalmen mit Melodien zum singen bey dem Claviere (J. A. Cramer). 1773–74 (source of date: BUSCH). W. 196
Early prints: CRAMER/PSALMEN; SCHIØRRING (No. 19, vnt., appearing as No. 71b, in Danish; see item 843). Lit. about these prints: See these entries in Bib.
Ms. probably copied from an early print (CRAMER/PSALMEN): D-ddr Bds, Mus. ms. 30068 (No. 32 only, its 1st strophe only)
Mod. edns.: BITTER/LIEDER (Nos. 4, 6, 20, 23, 24, 30); ROTH (Nos. 7, 9, 13, 20, 22, 36, 41); DITTBERNER (Nos. 10, 20, 23, 31)
Lit.: on No.

No.		
4:		295, 320, 331, 333, 358–59; CLARK/CHORAL, 173
5:		310
6:	BUSCH,	299, 327
7:		294, 324
8:		327
9:		CLARK/CHORAL, 88–96
10:		310
12:		280–81, 302
13:		327; CLARK/CHORAL, 88–96
14:		299
15:		324
16:		324
18:		376
19:		222, 299, 327, 329
20:		327, 330
22:	BUSCH,	327
23:		281, 315, 333; CLARK/CHORAL, 88–96
24:		328
25:		378
26:		289, 291, 328–29
30:		315, 331; CLARK/CHORAL, 88–96
34:		281
35:		316–17
36:		299
37:		314, 340
41:		115–18, 377

No. 2 is an arr. of item 774.
Arr. of No. 4, item 831; of No. 9, item 832; of No. 13, in item 798; of Nos. 23 and 30, in item 796. The texts of Nos. 9 (verse 2) and 13 (verse 4) are in the P 340 source of item 794, indicating that choral arr. of these 2 psalms made up part of item 794.
BUSCH, 115–18, points out the clearly intentional appearance of "B-A-C-H" four times (counting transpositions and retrogrades) in the first 12 bars of No. 41. See items 285, 371.9, 373, 389.6, 484.6, 659, 867.

Incipits from CRAMER/PSALMEN:

[No. 1] Der erste Psalm

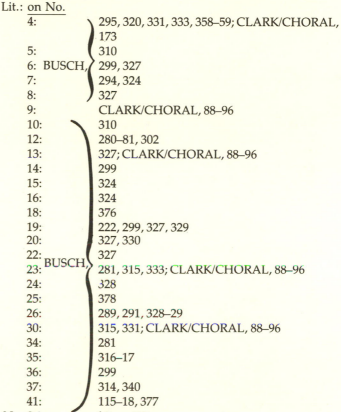

161

[No. 2] Der vierte Psalm

Wenn ich zu dir in mei-nen Aengsten fle-he,

[No. 3] Der sechste Psalm

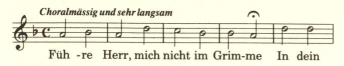

Füh -re Herr, mich nicht im Grim-me In dein

[No. 4] Der achte Psalm

Wer ist so wür -dig als

du, als du, von uns be-wun-dert

[No. 5] Der fünfzehnte Psalm

Wer darf im Zel - te dei - nes Ruh-mes Sein

[No. 6] Der siebenzehnte Psalm

Er-hö - re, Gott, wenn ich dir fle - he

[No. 7] Der neunzehnte Psalm

Die Him-mel ru-fen, je - der eh-ret Die

[No. 8] Der drey und zwanzigste Psalm

Gott ist mein Hirt! Im Schat-ten sei-ner Gü -te

[No. 9] Der fünf und zwanzigste Psalm

Herr, mein ein-zi - ges Ver - lan-gen, Gott, zu dir

[No. 10] Der dreyssigste Psalm

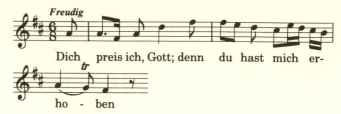

Dich preis ich, Gott; denn du hast mich er-

ho - ben

[No. 11] Der zwey und dreyssigste Psalm

Heil dem, der nicht die Furcht, ge-

straft zu wer - den

[No. 12] Der drey und dreyssigste Psalm

Jauchzt, ihr Ge - rech - ten, dem

Herrn, und las - set, ihn zu

[No. 13] Der acht und dreyssigste Psalm

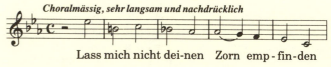

Lass mich nicht dei-nen Zorn emp - fin-den

[No. 14] Der zwey und vierzigste Psalm

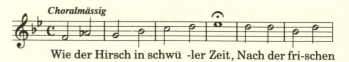

Wie der Hirsch in schwü -ler Zeit, Nach der fri-schen

[No. 15] Der sechs und vierzigste Psalm

Beherzt und lebhaft

Der Herr ist un-sre Macht; ein Schutz in gro - ssen

[No. 16] Der sieben und vierzigste Psalm

Freudig, aber nicht zu geschwind

Froh - lo - cket, ihr Völ - ker, froh-

lo - cket mit Hän - den

[No. 17] Der fünf und sechzigste Psalm

Sanft

Dich, Gott zu Si - on, lobt man in der

[No. 18] Der sieben und sechzigste Psalm

Angenehm und etwas munter

Herr, un - ser Gott, dem wir ver-trau-en

[No. 19] Der sechs und achtzigste Psalm

Choralmässig

Herr, er - hö - re mei - ne Kla - gen! Schau-e

[No. 20] Der acht und achtzigste Psalm

Traurig, sehr langsam, und die Noten gut ausgehalten

Tag und Nacht, du Heil der From-men

[No. 21] Der neunzigste Psalm

Gesetzt, und mässig geschwind

Herr, un-ser Gott, du warst, du bist zu

[No. 22] Der ein und neunzigste Psalm

Choralmässig

Wie se - lig ist, der Gott ver - traut, Der un-

[No. 23] Der drey und neunzigste Psalm

Sehr lebhaft und glänzend

Je - ho - va herrscht, ein Kö - nig ü - ber al-le.

[No. 24] Der sechs und neunzigste Psalm

Er - he - bet Gott durch neu - e Lie-der

[No. 25] Der sieben und neunzigste Psalm

Gesetzt und ein wenig hurtig, nur nicht zu sehr

Je - ho - va re - gie-ret: Es jauch-ze die Er-de

[No. 26] Der neun und neunzigste Psalm

Lebhaft

Der Herr re - giert; die Völ - ker zit-tern;

[No. 27] Der hunderte Psalm

Lebhaft, und nachdrücklich

Es jauch-ze Gott und prei - se Gott al - le

[No. 28] Der hundert und dritte Psalm

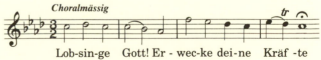

Choralmässig

Lob-sin-ge Gott! Er - wec-ke dei-ne Kräf -te

[No. 29] Der hundert und vierte Psalm

Angenehm und etwas lebhaft

Er - heb, er - heb, o mei - ne See-le

[No. 30] Der hundert und zehnte Psalm

Majestätisch

Je - ho - va sprach zu Gott, dem Soh - ne

[No. 31] Der hundert und eilfte Psalm

Sanft

Ge - lobt sey Gott! Ihm will ich fröh - lich

[No. 32] Der hundert und sechzehnte Psalm

Etwas langsam

Dess freu ich mich, dass Gott zu mei - nen

[No. 33] Der hundert und neunzehnte Psalm

Gelassen

Heil de - nen, wel - che sich un-sträf -lich

[No. 34] Der hundert und ein und zwanzigste Psalm

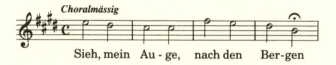

Choralmässig

Sieh, mein Au - ge, nach den Ber-gen

[No. 35] Der hundert und acht und zwanzigste Psalm

Gelassen

Die Gna-de Got - tes sey mit al - len,

[No. 36] Der hundert und dreyssigste Psalm

Choralmässig

Aus der Tie - fe ruf ich dir, Hö -re

[No. 37] Der hundert und neun und dreyssigste Psalm

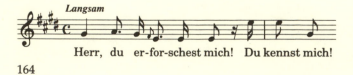

Langsam

Herr, du er-for-schest mich! Du kennst mich!

[No. 38] Der hundert und zwey und vierzigste Psalm

Langsam, und die Noten gut ausgehalten

Gott, es seuf - zet mei - ne Stim - me,

[No. 39] Der hundert und fünf und vierzigste Psalm

Lebhaft

Ich will, mein Gott, du Kö -nig, dir lob-sin-gen,

[No. 40] Der hundert und sechs und vierzigste Psalm

Freudig

Es wer-de Gott von uns er - ho -ben!

[No. 41] Der hundert und acht und vierzigste Psalm

Alla breve

Preis sey dem Got-te Ze - ba -oth!

[No. 42] Der hundert und fünfzigste Psalm

Mässig

Er - hebt, er - he -bet den Herrn,

734. Der Frühling, an Röschen (Miller). 1773–82? (source of date: BUSCH). W. 200/9
Early print: NEUE LIEDER, No. 9. Lit. about NEUE LIEDER: See this entry in Bib.
Lit. about this work: BUSCH, 193, Anh. 36–37

Incipit from NEUE LIEDER:

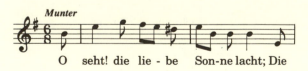

Munter

O seht! die lie - be Son-ne lacht; Die

735. Kantate. Die Grazien (H. W. von Gerstenberg). 1774 (source of date: BUSCH). W. 200/22
Early print: NEUE LIEDER, No. 22. Lit. about NEUE LIEDER: See this entry in Bib.

Mod. edn.: G. A. Walther, Berlin: Stahl, 1942
Lit. about this work: STEGLICH/HOMILIUS, 104; EN-
    GELKE, 433; BUSCH, 195, 397
The text is an excerpt from Gerstenberg's *Tandeleyen* (1759).

Incipit from NEUE LIEDER:

Als an ei-nem Früh-lings-a-ben-de   sich die drey

736. Die Schlummernde (J. H. Voss). 1774 (source of date:
BUSCH). W. 202/G/1
Ms.: D-brd Mbs, Mus. ms. 2774, Bd. I (autog.)
Early print: VOSS/1775, 33. Lit. about VOSS/1775: See this
    entry in Bib.
Mss. probably copied from the early print: B Bc, 286 (West-
    phal); D-brd B, Mus. ms. 30049
Mod. edn.: VRIESLANDER/LIEDER
Lit. about this work: VRIESLANDER/BACH, 125; BUSCH,
    125, 127–28, Anh. 26–27
See item 732.

Incipit from VOSS/1775:

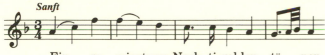

Ein - ge - wiegt von Nach-ti-gal-len - tö - nen

737. Lyda (F. G. Klopstock). 1774 (source of date: BUSCH).
W. 202/G/2
Ms.: D-brd Mbs, Mus. ms. 2774, Bd. I (autog.)
Early print: VOSS/1775, 111. Lit. about VOSS/1775: See this
    entry in Bib.
Mss. probably copied from the early print: B Bc, 286 (West-
    phal); D-brd B, Mus. ms. 30049
Mod. edn.: VRIESLANDER/LIEDER
Lit. about this work: STEGLICH/HOMILIUS, 104; VRIES-
    LANDER/BACH, between 112 and 113, 121–23; BÜCKEN,
    161; BUSCH, 124–27, 283–84, 356, 366, 383, 401, Anh.
    26–27; OTTENBERG, 213, 214–16
One of the letters accompanying the autog. ms. (see item
    732) discusses a change in this song.

Incipit from VOSS/1775:

Dein süs - ses Bild, o Ly - da!

738. Trinklied für Freye (J. H. Voss). 1775 (source of date:
BUSCH). W. 202/I/1
Ms.: D-brd Mbs, Mus. ms. 2774, Bd. I (autog.)
Early prints: VOSS/1776, 107; NOTENBUCH, I, No. 22. Lit.
    about these prints: See these entries in Bib.
Mss. probably copied from an early print (VOSS 1776): B
    Bc, 286 (Westphal); D-brd B, Mus. ms. 30049

Mod. edn.: VRIESLANDER/LIEDER
Lit. about this work: STEGLICH/HOMILIUS, 100; BUSCH,
    130, 222, 288, 383, Anh. 26–27
See item 732.

Incipit from VOSS/1776:

Mit   Ei-chen-laub den   Hut be-kranzt, Wohl-

auf!   Und trinkt den   Wein,

739. Selma [cantata for soprano, 2 flutes, 2 violins, viola,
continuo] (J. H. Voss). 1775? (source of date: BUSCH). W.
236
Mss.: D-brd B, P 349 (autog.); B Bc, 719 d (Michel)
Lit.: GEIRINGER/BACH, 370
A.v.: item 739.5. Not related to item 746
The Westphal–Wotquenne date of 1770 is incorrect; Voss's
    poem is dated 17 Dec. 1774. See BUSCH, 130.

Incipits from P 349:

Sie liebt!   mich

liebt   die Aus - er - wähl -te

Leih mir,   o Blitz,   die Flamm-en-flü -gel,

739.5. Selma [cantata] (J. H. Voss). 1775 (source of date:
BUSCH). W. 202/I/2
Ms.: D-brd Mbs, Mus. ms. 2774, Bd. I (autog.)
Early print: VOSS/1776, 225. Lit. about VOSS/1776: See this
    entry in Bib.
Mss. probably copied from the early print: B Bc, 286 (West-
    phal); D-brd B, Mus. ms. 30049
Mod. edn.: VRIESLANDER/LIEDER
Lit. about this work: BITTER/BRÜDER, II, 82; VRIESLAN-
    DER/BACH, 119–21; ENGELKE, 438–39; GEIRINGER/
    BACH, 370; BUSCH, 130, 290, 295, 314, 321, 325, 340,
    362–63, 377, 383, 397, Anh. 26–27
A.v. of item 739. Not related to item 746. See item 732.

Incipits from VOSS/1776:

Sie liebt!   Mich liebt   die Aus-er-wähl -te!

Leih mir, o Blitz, die Flamm-en-flü - gel,

740. Trinklied (L. C. H. Hölty). 1775–82? (source of date: BUSCH). W. 202/13
Ms.: D-brd B, P 349 (autog.)
Early print: NEUE LIEDER, No. 13. Lit. about NEUE
   LIEDER: See this entry in Bib.
Lit. about this work: BUSCH, 193, 385, Anh. 36–37

Incipit from NEUE LIEDER:

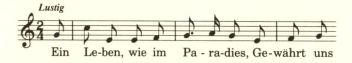

Ein Le-ben, wie im Pa - ra-dies, Ge-währt uns

741. An Doris (A. von Haller). 1775 or 1776 (source of date: BUSCH). W. 200/21
Ms.: D-brd B, P 349 (autog.)
Early print: NEUE LIEDER, No. 21. Lit. about NEUE
   LIEDER: See this entry in Bib.
Lit. about this work: BUSCH, 96, 195, 295, 335, 363, 366,
   371, 383, Anh. 26–27
Incipit from NEUE LIEDER:

Des Ta-ges Licht hat sich ver - dun-kelt, Der

742. Auf den Flügeln des Morgenroths (C. F. Cramer). 1775 or 1776? (source of date: BUSCH). W. 202/O/1
Ms.: B Bc, 286 (Westphal)
Lit.: BUSCH, 206–07, Anh. 26–27

Incipit from 286:

Auf den Flü -geln des Mor-gen - roths

743. Da Schlägt des Abschieds Stunde ("Die Trennung")
(J. J. Eschenburg, after Metastasio). 1775 or 1776? (source of date: BUSCH). W. 202/O/4
Ms.: B Bc, 286 (Westphal)
Mod. edn.: FRIEDLÄNDER, Vol. I, Part 2, No. 79
Lit.: FRIEDLÄNDER/UNGEDRUCKTES; GEIRINGER/
   BACH, 370; BUSCH, 206–07, 366, 378, 383, 403, Anh.
   26–27

Incipit from 286:

Da schlägt des Ab-schieds Stun - de

744. An den Schlaf. 1776 (source of date: BUSCH). W. 202/H
Early print: MUSE, 96. Lit. about MUSE: See this entry in
   Bib.
Ms. probably copied from the early print: B Bc, 286 (West-
   phal)
Lit. about this work: BUSCH, 131, 314, 383, Anh. 26–27;
   WADE, 135

Incipit from MUSE:

Ge-lieb-ter Schlaf, du Freund von mei-nem Her-zen

745. Todtengräberlied (L. C. H. Hölty). 1776–82 (source of date: BUSCH). W. 200/1
Early print: NEUE LIEDER, No. 1. Lit. about NEUE LIEDER:
   See this entry in Bib.
Ms. probably copied from the early print: B Bc, 286 (West-
   phal)
Lit. about this work: BUSCH, 191, 334, 404, Anh. 36–37

Incipit from NEUE LIEDER:

Gra-be, Spa-den, gra - be! Al - les, was ich

746. Selma (J. H. Voss). 1777 (source of date: BUSCH). W. 202/J
Early print: VOSS/1778, 49. Lit. about VOSS/1778: See this
   entry in Bib.
Ms. probably copied from the early print: B Bc, 286 (West-
   phal)
Lit. about this work: BUSCH, 133–34, 294, 401, Anh. 26–27
Not related to item 739 or item 739.5

Incipit from VOSS/1778:

Eil, o May, mit dei-nem Braut - ge-san-ge

747. Aus einer Ode zum neuen Jahr. 1777–82? (source of date: BUSCH). W. 200/14
Ms.: D-brd B, P 349 (autog., in F)
Early prints: NEUE LIEDER, No. 14; VOSS/1778, 203. Lit.
   about these prints: See these entries in Bib.
Lit. about this work: BUSCH, 194, 302, Anh. 36–37

Incipit from NEUE LIEDER:

Der Wei - se blickt zur E-wig-keit hin - ü - ber;

748. An die Grazien und Musen (J. W. L. Gleim). 1778–82? (source of date: BUSCH). W. 200/5
Early print: NEUE LIEDER, No. 5. Lit. about these prints: See these entries in Bib.
Lit. about this work: BUSCH, 192, 288, 346, 348, 385, Anh. 36–37

Incipit from NEUE LIEDER:

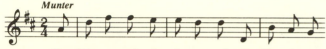

Ihr Mu-sen, seht den A-mor, seht, Ihr Gra-zi - en

749. Herrn Christoph Christian Sturms . . . Geistliche Gesänge mit Melodien zum Singen bey dem Claviere (C. C. Sturm). 1780 (source of date: BUSCH). W. 197
Early prints: See STURM I; Nos. 1 and 12 are printed in a single copy in D-ddr W Riv, title p. and publishing information missing. Lit. about STURM I: See this entry in Bib.
Mod. edns.: BITTER/LIEDER (Nos. 13, 14, 16, 19, 22, 29); DITTBERNER (Nos. 7, 13, 19, 26, 29); ROTH (Nos. 2, 11, 13, 14, 19, 29); VRIESLANDER/LIEDER (Nos. 2, 7, 13, 19, 21, 29)
Lit.: on No.

3:		339; CLARK/CHORAL, 88–96
4:		315
5:		325
6:		356; CLARK/CHORAL, 88–96
7:		235–36, 315, 339
8:	BUSCH,	339
9:		319, 340
10:		384
13:		288, 325, 330; HUGHES, 348; CLARK/CHORAL, 88–96
14:		401
17:		328

19: VRIESLANDER/BACH, 118; BUSCH, 288, 337, 357

20:		340
21:		314–15; CLARK/CHORAL, 88–96
22:	BUSCH,	336
23:		340
24: "		335, 358
25: "		289

29: VRIESLANDER/BACH, 111–112; BÜCKEN, 170; BUSCH, 237, 295, 325, 330, 372, 378, 384; HUGHES, 347–48
30: BUSCH, 289

Arr.: of No. 3, in item 799; of No. 4, item 834; of No. 6, in item 794(?); of No. 9, item 833; of No. 13, in item 795; of No. 21, in item 798
Choral arrangements of Nos. 1, 4–7, 9, 11, 20, 22, and 23, presumably by J. D. Sander, appear in his compilation *Die heilige Cäcilia* (Berlin, 1818–19).

Incipits from STURM I:

[No. 1] Demüthigung vor Gott

Be - tet an vor Gott, ihr Sün -der!

[No. 2] Passionslied

Einst, als dich ihm Ge - rich - te

[No. 3] Loblied für das Seelenleiden Jesu

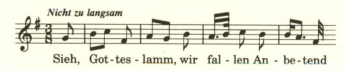

Sieh, Got-tes - lamm, wir fal - len An - be-tend

[No. 4] Osterlied

A-men! Lob und Preis und Stär - ke, Sey dem

[No. 5] Pfingstlied

Sey, Welt ver - söh - ner, sey ge - preist!

[No. 6] Passionslied

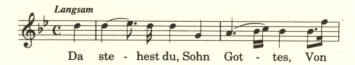

Da ste - hest du, Sohn Got - tes, Von

[No. 7] Gottes Grösse in der Natur

Gross ist der Herr! Von sei - ner Macht

[No. 8] Die Würde des Christen

Mässig

Ich bin ein Christ! Mein Herz ist ru - hig

[No. 9] Todesfreudigkeit

Etwas lebhaft

Gott, dem ich le - be, dess ich bin

[No. 10] Der gestirnte Himmel

Sanft

Mit heil - gem Grau - en blick ich hin

[No. 11] Weihnachtslied

Munter

Vom Grab, an dem wir wal - len, Soll,

[No. 12] Beschleunigung der Busse

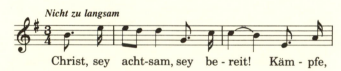

Nicht zu langsam

Christ, sey acht-sam, sey be - reit! Käm - pfe,

[No. 13] Der Tag des Weltgerichts

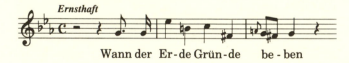

Ernsthaft

Wann der Er - de Grün - de be - ben

[No. 14] Der Frühling

Mässig

Er - wacht zum neu - en Le - ben

[No. 15] Erndtelied

Lebhaft

So weit der Flu - ren Grän - zen blü - hen

[No. 16] Frohe Erinnerung der Wohlthaten Gottes

Sanft, aber nicht zu langsam

Auch mich, o Herr, hast du ge - macht:

[No. 17] Sonntagslied

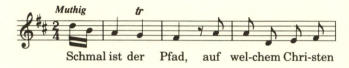

Etwas lebhaft

Dir, Je - su, dir sey die - ser Tag

[No. 18] Der Weg zum Himmel

Muthig

Schmal ist der Pfad, auf wel-chem Chri-sten

[No. 19] Neujahrslied

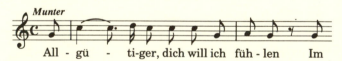

Etwas langsam

Schon wie - der ist von mei - ner Zeit

[No. 20] Sommerlied

Munter

All - gü - ti-ger, dich will ich füh - len Im

[No. 21] Die Fortdauer der Lehre Jesu

Muthig

Um-sonst em-pört die Höl - le sich Mit ih - rem

[No. 22] Dieses und jenes Leben

Etwas langsam

Ein Pil - ger bin ich in der \Welt

[No. 23] Lob des Allgütigen

Mässig und angenehm

All - gü - ti-ger, mein Le - ben - lang

[No. 24] Herbstlied

So weit der We - sen Mil - li - o - nen

[No. 25] Morgenlied

Nun ist es Tag Mit from-men Dank

[No. 26] Abendlied

So flüch - tig, als des Ta - ges Stun - den

[No. 27] Gottes Allgegenwart

Nie bist du, Höch-ster, von uns fern:

[No. 28] Lobgesang

Un-zähl-bar, Herr, sind dei-ne Wer - ke

[No. 29] Über die Finsterniss kurz vor dem Tode Jesu

Nacht und Schatt-en de - cken

[No. 30] Vertrauen auf Gott

Der Herr ist mei - ne Zu-ver-sicht, Mein be-

750. Fischerlied (C. A. Overbeck). 1780 (source of date: BUSCH). W. 202/K/1
Ms.: D-brd B, Mus. ms. 38053

Early prints: VOSS/1781, 161; NOTENBUCH, I, No. 9 (with different text). Lit. about these prints: See these entries in Bib.
Ms. probably copied from an early print (VOSS/1781): B Bc, 286 (Westphal)
Mod. edn.: VRIESLANDER/LIEDER
Lit. about this work: BUSCH, 136–37, 222, 288, 316, 385, Anh. 30–31

Incipit from VOSS/1781:

Wer glei-chet uns freu-di - gen Fi-schern im Kahn?

751. Tischlied (J. H. Voss). 1780 (source of date: BUSCH). W. 202/K/2
Early print: VOSS/1781, 69. Lit. about VOSS/1781: See this entry in Bib.
Ms. probably copied from the early print: B Bc, 286 (Westphal)
Mod. edn.: VRIESLANDER/LIEDER
Lit. about this work: BUSCH, 136–37, 400, Anh. 30–31

Incipit from VOSS/1781:

Ge - sund und fro - hes Mu - tes, Ge-
nie-ssen wir des Gu - tes

752. Herrn Christoph Christian Sturms . . . geistliche Gesänge mit Melodien zum singen bey dem Claviere . . . zweyte Sammlung (C. C. Sturm). 1781 (source of date: BUSCH). W. 198
Early prints and lit. about them: See STURM II in Bib.
Mod. edns.: BITTER/LIEDER (Nos. 18, 29); DITTBERNER (Nos. 6, 18, 19, 29); ROTH (Nos. 6, 29)
Lit.: on No.
  3: BUSCH, 299, 318; CLARK/CHORAL, 88–96
  4: CLARK/CHORAL, 88–96, 174
  6: BUSCH, 299, 318, 328–29, 358, 366, 384; CLARK/CHORAL, 88–96
  9: BUSCH, 328
  11: BUSCH, 142
  14: BUSCH, 335
  15: CLARK/CHORAL, 88–96
  17: BUSCH, 377
  21: CLARK/CHORAL, 88–96
  23: CLARK/CHORAL, 88–96
  26: CLARK/CHORAL, 88–96
  29: BUSCH, 290, 326, 334–35, 384; HUGHES, 347; CLARK/CHORAL, 88–96

Arr.: of No. 3, item 826/4; of No. 4, in item 798 (?); of No. 6, in item 795; of No. 14, in item 807; of No. 15, in item 796; of No. 23, in item 797; of Nos. 26 and 29, in item 795

Incipits from STURM II:

[No. 1] Vertrauen auf Gottes Vorsehung

Entschlossen und etwas langsam

Was sollt ich ängst-lich kla-gen Und

[No. 2] Versicherung der Seligkeit

Mässig

Ich weiss an wen mein Glaub sich hält.

[No. 3] Menschenliebe Jesu

Langsam

Dich bet ich an, Herr Je - su Christ, Du Heil

[No. 4] Die Bestimmung des Christen

Angenehm und etwas langsam

Mein Glück im kur-zem Raum der Zeit

[No. 5] Weihnachtslied

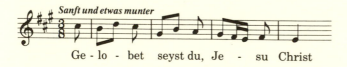

Sanft und etwas munter

Ge - lo - bet seyst du, Je - su Christ

[No. 6] Passionslied

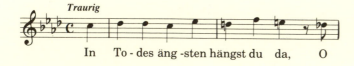

Traurig

In To - des äng -sten hängst du da, O

[No. 7] Osterlied

Hurtig

Er lebt! Des To-des Sie-ger lebt!

[No. 8] Trost der Auferstehung

Getrost und lebhaft

Herr, du bist mei-ne Zu-ver - sicht

[No. 9] Das wohlthätige Leben Jesu

Sanft

Zu dir er-hebt sich mein Ge-mü-the, Du

[No. 10] Fröhlich Erwartung der Auferstehung

Nicht zu hurtig

Einst geh ich oh-ne Be-ben Zu mei-nem

[No. 11] Ermunterung zur Nachfolge Jesu

Etwas langsam

Stär-ke, Je-su, stär-ke mich Wil-lig

[No. 12] Andenken an den Tod

Etwas langsam

Wer weiss, wie nah der Tod mir ist?

[No. 13] Morgenlied

Freudig

Des Mor-gens neu - e Son - ne

[No. 14] Lobgesang auf die Auferstehung Jesu

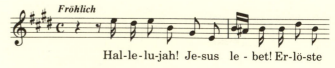

Fröhlich

Hal-le-lu-jah! Je-sus le - bet! Er-lö-ste

[No. 15] Betrachtung des Todes

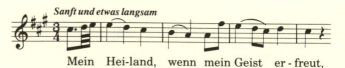

Sanft und etwas langsam

Mein Hei-land, wenn mein Geist er-freut,

[No. 16] Erinnerung an den Tod

Noch bin ich dein Gast, o Er - de

[No. 17] Gott, der Ernährer der Menschen

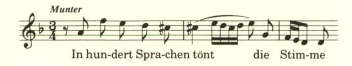

In hun-dert Spra-chen tönt die Stim-me

[No. 18] Empfindungen in der Sommernacht

Der Mond ist auf-ge-gan-gen: Die güld-nen

[No. 19] Gottes Grösse in der Natur

Weit um mich her ist al - les Freu-de!

[No. 20] Nach dem Gewitter

Dir, des Don-ners Schö-pfer dir

[No. 21] Fürbitte des gekreuzigten Jesu für seine Feinde

Um Gna-de für die Sün-der-welt, Flehst du,

[No. 22] Empfindung eines Bussfertigen

Ach, wie viel Bö - ses wohnt in mir!

[No. 23] Lobgesang auf den Tod Jesu

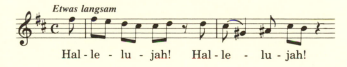

Hal - le - lu - jah! Hal - le - lu - jah!

[No. 24] Bitte um Beystand des heiligen Geistes

Komm, o Geist von Gott ge - ge - ben,

[No. 25] Vorzüge des Menschen

Ihn preist die Sonn am ho - hen Him-mel

[No. 26] Das Reich Jesu

Dir, o du Herr-scher, Je - su Christ

[No. 27] Danklied

Preis sey dem Va - ter! Eh-re sey dem

[No. 28] Ermunterung zur Gelassenheit

Herr, es ge - scheh dein Wil - le!

[No. 29] Jesus in Gethsemane

Schau hin! Dort in Geth-se - ma - ne

[No. 30] Die Sonne

Got - tes Gü - te, Got - tes Macht

753. Lied (F. L. von Stolberg). 1781 (source of date: BUSCH).
W. 202/L/1
Ms.: D-brd B, Mus. ms. 38053
Early print: VOSS/1782, 100. Lit. about VOSS/1782: See this
entry in Bib.

Ms. probably copied from the early print: B Bc, 286 (Westphal)

Mod. edns.: FRIEDLÄNDER, Vol. I, Part 2, No. 166; VRIES-LANDER/LIEDER

Lit. about this work: VRIESLANDER/BACH, 125; GEIRINGER/BACH, 370; BUSCH, 137, Anh. 36–37

Incipit from VOSS/1782:

Ich ging un-ter Er-len am küh-li-gen Bach

754. Das Milchmädchen (J. H. Voss). 1781 (source of date: BUSCH). W. 202/L/2

Ms.: D-brd B, Mus. ms. 38053

Early print: VOSS/1782, 116. Lit. about VOSS/1782: See this entry in Bib.

Ms. probably copied from the early print: B Bc, 286 (Westphal)

Mod. edn.: VRIESLANDER/LIEDER

Lit. about this work: BUSCH, 137, Anh. 36–37

Incipit from VOSS/1782:

Mäd - chen, nehmt die Ei - mer schnell

755. Lied der Schnitterinnen (J. W. L. Gleim). 1782 or earlier? (source of date: BUSCH). W. 200/2

Early print: NEUE LIEDER, No. 2. Lit. about NEUE LIEDER: See this entry in Bib.

Lit. about this work: BUSCH, 191, Anh. 36–37

Incipit from NEUE LIEDER:

Sin - gend gehn wir, fröh - lich sin - gend

756. Nonnelied (anon., "aus dem Canton Schweiz"). 1782 or earlier? (source of date: BUSCH). W. 200/3

Ms.: D-brd B, P 349 (autog.)

Early print: NEUE LIEDER, No. 3. Lit. about NEUE LIEDER: See this entry in Bib.

Mod. edn.: FRIEDLÄNDER, Vol. I, Part 2, No. 78

Lit. about this work: STEGLICH/HOMILIUS, 104; BÜCKEN, 170; GEIRINGER/BACH, 371; BUSCH, 191–92, 330, 360–61, 366, 385, Anh. 36–37

Incipit from NEUE LIEDER:

'S ist kein ver-driess-li-cher Le - be, Als in das

757. Das mitleidige Mädchen (Miller). 1782 or earlier? (source of date: BUSCH). W. 200/4

Early print: NEUE LIEDER, No. 4. Lit. about NEUE LIEDER: See this entry in Bib.

Lit. about this work: BUSCH, 192, 295, Anh. 38–39

Incipit from NEUE LIEDER:

Der from-me Da-mon dau-ert mich Von gan - zen

758. Bevelise und Lysidor ("Der Phönix") (J. A. Schlegel). 1782 or earlier? (source of date: BUSCH). W. 200/7

Ms.: D-brd B, P 349 (autog.)

Early print: NEUE LIEDER, No. 7. Lit. about NEUE LIEDER: See this entry in Bib.

Mod. edns.: in H. Reimann, *Das deutsche Lied*, II (Berlin, 1891–93); FRIEDLÄNDER, Vol. I, Part 2, No. 165

Lit. about this work: BUSCH, 192–93, 385, Anh. 36–37

Incipit from NEUE LIEDER:

Der Mann, der nach den Flit - ter - wo - chen

759. Mittel, freundlich zu werden (J. W. L. Gleim). 1782 or earlier? (source of date: BUSCH). W. 200/16

Early print: NEUE LIEDER, No. 16. Lit. about NEUE LIEDER: See this entry in Bib.

Lit. about this work: BUSCH, 194, 288, 385, Anh. 36–37

Incipit from NEUE LIEDER:

Mein Va - ter küsst die Mut-ter, Die Mut-ter

760. Ich hoff auch Gott mit festem Muth (Elise v.d. Recke). 1785 (source of date: autog.). W. 200/18

Ms.: ALBRECHT lists an autograph dated "Hamburg, den ersten November 1785," owned by Rudolf F. Kallir; presumably this is the same autograph now to be found in a different American private collection.

Early print: NEUE LIEDER, No. 18. Lit. about NEUE LIEDER: See this entry in Bib.

Lit. about this work: BUSCH, 194–96, 363, 368, 370, 384, Anh. 38–39

Incipit from NEUE LIEDER:

Entschlossen und etwas lebhaft

Ich hoff auch Gott mit fe-stem Muth, Er

761. Aria für Diskant, zwei Violinen, Bratsche und Bass . . . "Fursten sind am Lebensziele." 1785 (NV 64). W. 214

Lost

Incipit from WOTQUENNE THÉMATIQUE:

Mit Ausdruck

Für-sten sind am Le - bens-zie - le

762. Freudenlied (auf die Wiederkunft des Herrn Dr. C** aus dem Bade) für 2 Diskante und dem Bass. 1785 (NV 62). W. 231

Ms.: F-Pc, ms. 1563 (autog.?)

The source apparently catalogued by Westphal–Wotquenne is now missing from B Bc.

Lit.: CLARK/CHORAL, 189

Incipit from ms. 1563:

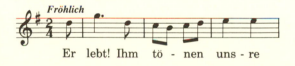

Fröhlich

Er lebt! Ihm tö - nen uns - re

763. Die Alster [?]; Harvstehude (both poems by F. von Hagedorn). Probably near 1788 (source of date: BUSCH)

Lost

Lit.: BUSCH, 211–13, Anh. 52–53

2 "Hagedorn" songs composed "in der letzten Zeit des Lebens" are listed in a letter of August 1791 to Westphal from CPEB's widow (no doubt one of the letters mentioned in note 7 of the introduction to this catalogue), though only "Harvstehude" is mentioned by title. Harvstehude was then an idyllic place just outside the gates of Hamburg on the Alster River. The two titles are associated in a letter from Hagedorn to J. H. Herold.

764. [12 Masonic songs]. 1788 (source of date: BUSCH). W. 202/N/1–12

Early prints: FREYMÄURER-LIEDER, pp. 8, 10, 16, 20, 22, 30, 34, 42, 96, 98, 100, 108, respectively (in the order shown here, not that shown in the incipits in WOTQUENNE/THÉMATIQUE); BOSSLER (No. 10, on p. 23).

Lit. about these prints: See these entries in Bib.

Ms. probably copied from an early print (FREYMÄURER-LIEDER): B Bc, 286 (Westphal)

Lit.: on No. 4, BUSCH, 334, 348; on No. 5, BUSCH, 314, 361; on No. 10, BITTER/BRÜDER, I, 75–76

BUSCH, 181–90, shows that, contrary to MIESNER/HAMBURG, Nachtrag 4, these songs are not by W. F. E. Bach.

Incipits from FREYMÄURER-LIEDER:

[No. 1] Bey Eröffnung der Loge

Munter

Wal - le, sanft, durch Wol-ken, die dich de-cken

[No. 2] Gruss der Versammlungszeit

Etwas lebhaft

Die Son-ne mag im-mer ent - flie - hen

[No. 3] Auf das Fest des heiligen Johannis

Lustig

Bru-der, seyd heu - te recht ver-gnügt

[No. 4] Wechselgesang [for 3 soloists with or without unison chorus]

Mässig

Hier zur Ar - beit an - ge-stellt, Wid-met

[No. 5] Auf das Fest des heiligen Johannis

Lebhaft

Ich kom-me vom Jo - han - nis her, Er

war ein lie - ber Mann

[No. 6] Bruder, unsre Säulen stehen

Mässig

Bru-der, un - sre Säu - len ste-hen

[No. 7] Auf das Vermählungsfest unsers Meisters vom Stuhle

Singt be - gei-stert heu - te, Brü - der

[No. 8] Die ihr im sichern Heiligthum

Die ihr im si - chern Hei - lig - thum

[No. 9] Trinklied bey der Tafel

Trinkt, trinkt, von die - sen fri-schen Wein!

[No. 10] Hoch wie des Adlers kühnster flug

Hoch wie des Ad-lers kühn-ster Flug

[No. 11] Für euch, ihr Schönen

Für euch, ihr Schön-en, Soll er er - tö-nen

[No. 12] Das stille Glück der Maurerey

Last an - dre stolz nach Eh - re dürs-ten

765. Aus den 107ten Cramerschen Psalm (J. A. Cramer). n.d. W. 202/O/3
Ms.: B Bc, 286 (Westphal)
Lit.: BUSCH, 206–07, Anh. 42–43

Incipit from 286:

Kommt, lasst uns sei - ne Huld be - sin-gen

766. [untitled]. n.d. W. 202/O/5
Ms.: B Bc, 286 (Westphal)
Lit.: BUSCH, 206, Anh. 42–43

Incipit from 286:

Die schön-ste soll bey Son-nen-schein

767. Eine italiänische Ariette [soprano, 2 flutes, continuo]. n.d. W. 213
Ms.: F Pc, ms. 1570
The source used by Westphal–Wotquenne (unknown) and ms. 1570 both have the instrumentation shown; but NV, 64, lists it as having parts for an additional 3 violins.

Incipit from ms. 1570:

D'a - mor per te lan - guis-co

Possibly Authentic

768. An den Mond. Sophiens Reise auf der See. n.d. Wq n.v. 11
Ms.: D-brd B, P 1154
Not in HILLER/LIEDER
Not attributed on the ms.; see item 399. See also BUSCH, 220.

Incipit from P 1154:

Ich sah durch Trä - nen - bä - che,

769. Weil Gott uns das Gesicht verleih [?]. n.d. Wq n.v. 12
Ms.: D-brd B, P 912
P 912, in the hands of 2 anonymous copyists of the 2nd half of the 18th century, consists of items 531–34, 769. The copy of item 769 is not attributed on the ms. and is so carelessly written that much of it is illegible.
The keyboard accompaniment is apparently a reduction of instrumental ensemble parts.

Incipit from P 912:

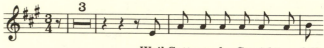

Weil Gott uns das Ge-sicht ver-leih

769.5. Climene. n.d.
Ms.: D-brd B, Mus. ms. 40302
The attribution, "Vom Herrn Bach," is the same and in the same hand as that for authentic works in this ms., which consists partly of CPEB lieder probably copied from UN-TERHALTUNGEN (items 709–21), along with item 682.

Incipit from Mus. ms. 40302:

Die Nach-bar-in Cli - me - ne schrieb

770. Cancionetta. n.d. Wq n.v. 13
Ms.: D-brd B, P 728
See item 353.
On the same page is a keyboard minuet attributed to Kirnberger.

Incipit from P 728:

Se a-mor per le - i t'ac - cen - de

771. Nachahmung einiger Stellen des anderen Psalms, von Kohler (uncertain whether the poet is the "Kohler" in the title). n.d. Wq n.v. 44
Ms.: D-brd B, P 971 ("Von C. P. E. Bach componirt")
Not related to item 733. P 971 contains only this work; it was copied by J. H. Grave (2nd half of the 18th century), copyist of many authentic CPEB works and friend of CPEB.

Incipit from P 971:

Der Herr ist mei - nes Le - bens Kraft.

MAJOR CHORAL WORKS

(**Note:** *Major* means essentially without borrowings from other works, and having wide distribution and high reputation during the composer's lifetime.)

772. Magnificat [SATB chorus, SATB soloists, 2 flutes, 2 oboes, 2 horns, 3 trumpets, timpani, 2 violins, viola, continuo]. 1749, probably also 1780–82 (sources of dates: see below). W. 215
Mss.: D-brd B, P 341 (autog.; on last p.: "Fine. S.D.Gl. Potsdam, d. 25 Aug. 1749."); P 342, P 343 (autog., alternate No. 4 only), P 372, P 994 (alternate No. 4 only), St 191

(partly CPEB and Michel), St 191a (partly CPEB and Michel), Am.B. 170; D-ddr Bds, Mus. ms. 30209 (alternate No. 4 only, annotated and signed by Pölchau)
Early print: G. J. D. Pölchau, ed., *Magnificat a 4 Voci, 3 Trombe e Timpani, 2 Corni, 2 Flauti, 2 Oboi, 2 Violini, Viola e Continuo di Carlo Filippo Emanuele Bach, Maestro di capella de S.A.R.M. la Principessa Amalia di Prussia, Badessa di Quedlinburgo, Direttore de musica della Republica di Hamburgo. Duopo Partitura autografa dell' autore.* Bonna presso N. Simrock [1829, according to PÖLCHAU, 51]. The known lit. gives no evidence that such a (posthumous) print had been authorized by CPEB.
Mod. edns.: C. Deis, New York: G. Schirmer, 1950 (orchestral parts reduced for piano or organ); G. Darvas, London: Eulenburg, 1971; G. Graulich and P. Horn, Neuhausen-Stuttgart: Hänssler-Verlag, 1971
Lit.: HILLER/NACHRICHTEN, 15 Aug. 1768, 51; HAMBURGER CORRESPONDENT, 11 Apr. 1786; AMZ, IX (1806–07), 208, 213; BITTER/BRÜDER, I, 117–31; STEGLICH/HOMILIUS, 90; VRIESLANDER/BACH, 137–40; MIESNER/HAMBURG, 56–58; HADOW, 144–45; GEIRINGER/BACH, 374; OLLESON, 330; OTTENBERG, 76–79, 283, 285; CLARK/CHORAL, 71–72
The trumpet, timpani, and some horn parts were added later by CPEB to St 191, whose cover bears the note "Zahlreiche Stimmen zu meiner Magnificat" in CPEB's hand; this addition is noted in CPEB's hand in the autog., P 341. P 343, owned by Pölchau, contains an alternate "Et misericordia," written, according to Pölchau's annotation, "in Hamburg zwischen 1780–82"; P 994 and Mus. ms. 30209 are copies, annotated by Pölchau, of the alternate "Et misericordia" only. In St 191 there is a figured bass beneath the original canto part; CPEB obviously used this canto-bass combination as a composing score. The "Et misericordia" in this original canto part has an X drawn across each page. In the same set of parts, St 191, there is a separate canto part for the alternate "Et misericordia" (this time without a figured bass added), marked "NB. Canto" in CPEB's hand. The original and alternate "Et misericordia" are similarly treated in the other parts of St 191. Pölchau appended the alternate "Et misericordia" to his 1829 edn. without explanation. This mvt. is missing in the Deis edn.

St 191 also contains the trumpet and timpani parts of item 775, enclosed by mistake.
See items 776, 782, 807, 817, 821a, 821d, 848.

Incipits from P 341:

[No. 1. Chorus]

Canto   Ma - gni - fi - cat a - ni-ma
me - a Do - mi - num

[No. 2. Solo]

[No. 3. Solo]

[No. 4. Chorus]

[No. 5. Solo]

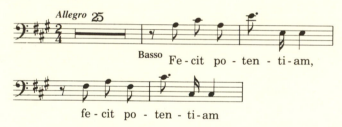

[No. 6. Duet, alto & tenor]

[No. 7. Solo]

[No. 8. Chorus]

[No. 9. Chorus]

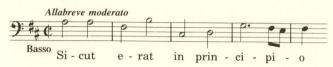

Incipit of the alternate "Et misericordia" from the Pölchau edn.:

773. Der zweyte Psalm, nach der Cramerschen Uebersetzung [SATB chorus] (J. A. Cramer). 1761 or earlier (source of date: 1st pub.). W. 205
Early print: ALLERLEY (1761), 52. Lit. about ALLERLEY: See this entry in Bib.
Mss. probably copied from the early print: B Bc, 286 (Westphal), 6313 (Michel)

Incipit from ALLERLEY:

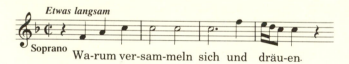

774. Der vierte Psalm, nach der Cramerschen Uebersetzung [soprano, alto, continuo] (J. A. Cramer). 1761 or earlier (source of date: 1st pub.). W. 206
Early print: ALLERLEY (1761), 56. Lit. about ALLERLEY: See this entry in Bib.
Ms. probably copied from the early print: B Bc, 286 (Westphal)
Lit. about this work: BUSCH, 71, 104, Anh. 12–13
Arr.: item 733/2

Incipit from ALLERLEY:

775. Die Israeliten in der Wüste, ein Oratorium [SATB chorus, SSTTB soloists, 2 flutes, 2 oboes, bassoon, 2 horns, 3 trumpets, timpani, 2 violins, viola, continuo] (D. Schiebeler). 1769 (NV 54). W. 238

Mss.: D-brd B, P 956 (2nd violin part only), St 184, St 184a, St 191 (trumpet and timpani parts only, enclosed by mistake with performance parts of item 772; my thanks to Joshua Rifkin for bringing this to my attention); D-ddr Bds, Mus. ms. 30235 (Nos. 14–16 only); D-ddr HER, Mus B 102:2 (score and parts), Mus M 101:1 (parts, incomplete) (my thanks to Howard Serwer for notice of these sources in D-ddr HER); D-ddr ROu (orchestral parts reduced for keyboard); CH E (entitled "Moses"); US Wc, M2000.B12I75; US AA, M2003.B12.I8 (orchestral parts reduced for keyboard); US WS, Herbst Collection, B II; US NHu, Mason collection, MW 10.L95 (Nos. 15–16 only, orchestral parts reduced for keyboard, translated into English)

Early prints: *Die Israeliten in der Wüste, ein Oratorium, in Musik gesetzt von Carl Philipp Emanuel Bach.* Hamburg: Im Verlag des Autors [printed in Leipzig by J. G. I. Breitkopf], 1775; Wien: J. T. v. Trattner, 1777; Paris: Choron, n.d. (orchestral parts reduced for keyboard). The known lit. gives no evidence that the Trattner or Choron prints were authorized by CPEB.

Page proofs of the Breitkopf print, corrected in a hand possibly that of the composer, are in an American private collection.

Mss. probably copied from the 1775 print: B Bc, 1047; a ms. is in the private collection of E. N. Kulukundis (U.S.).

Mod. edns.: H. M. Schletterer, Wolfenbüttel: Holle, 1864 (orchestral parts reduced for keyboard); F. Steffin, Berlin: Bote & Bock, 1955 (orchestral parts reduced for keyboard); G. Darvas, London: Eulenburg, 1976

Lit.: HILLER/NACHRICHTEN, 15 Jan. 1770, 21; HAMBURGER CORRESPONDENT, 28 Oct., 31 Oct. 1769; 14 Sept. 1774, 16 Dec. 1775, 10 Mar. 1779; CPEB/6 Nov. 1769 (account of performance expenses); CPEB/BREITKOPF, 2 June, 24 June 1773; 12 Oct. 1774; 11 Jan., 24 Feb., 15 Apr., 13 June, 11 July, 30 Sept., 10 Nov., 26 Dec. 1775; 17 Jan., 28 Feb. 1776; 3 Feb. 1781; CPEB/FORKEL, 20 Sept. 1775; REICHARDT/BRIEFE, II, 14; AMZ, XX (1818), 73; BITTER/BRÜDER, II, 2–17, 271–78; HASE, 94, 98–101 (the CPEB-to-Breitkopf letter transcribed and discussed by Hase probably dealt with this work, not, as Hase avers, item 779); SCHERING/ORATORIUMS, 343–45; STEGLICH/HOMILIUS, 108, 123; VRIESLANDER/BACH, 140–41; MIESNER/HAMBURG, 23, 73–75; HADOW, 70–73, 145–48; REESER, 42–43; GEIRINGER/BACH, 375; BUSCH, 88, 129, 392; OLLESON, 330–31; BREWER; OTTENBERG, 152, 159, 162–69, 213, 243, 283; CLARK/CHORAL, 186–87

In his edn., in the soprano arias "O bringet uns zu jenen Mauern" and "O selig, wem der Herr gewähret," Steffin adds variations to the da-capo repeat of the vocal part; these variations, he says, are found in CPEB's hand in a copy (not further specified) of the 1775 print and were presumably intended for performance by the soprano Windeme Klopstock, the poet's second wife. The copy is that in D-ddr Bds, 11658, says CLARK.

Incipits from the 1775 print:

[Erster Theil]

[No. 1] Chor der Israeliten

[No. 2] Recit.

[No. 3] Arie

[No. 4] Recit.

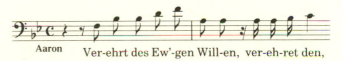

[No. 5] Arie

[No. 6] Recit.

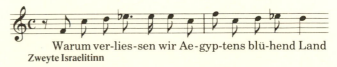

[No. 7] Arie

[No. 8] Recit.

Aaron   Für euch seht Mos-es stets um neu-e Huld

[No. 9] Symphonie

[No. 10] Recit.

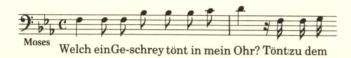

Moses   Welch ein Ge-schrey tönt in mein Ohr? Tönt zu dem

[No. 11] Chor der Israeliten

Discant   Du   bist   der Ur-sprung uns-rer Noth,

[No. 12] Recit.

Moses   Un-dank-bar Volk,   hast du die   Wer-ke voll

[No. 13] Duett [Erste Israelitinn, Zweyte Israelitinn]

Erste Israelitinn   Um-sonst sind uns-re Zah-ren,

[No. 14] Accompagnement

Moses   Gott,   mei-ner Va-ter Gott, was lässest

[No. 15] Arie

Moses   Gott,   Gott,   Gott, sieh dein Volk

[No. 16] Chor der Israeliten

Discant   O Wun-der! O Wun-der! Gott hat

Zweyter Theil

[No. 17] Recit.

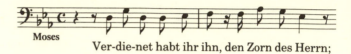

Moses   Ver-die-net habt ihr ihn, den Zorn des Herrn;

[No. 18] Arie; Chor [der Israeliten]

Moses   Gott Is-ra-els,   em-pfan-ge im

[No. 19] Recit.

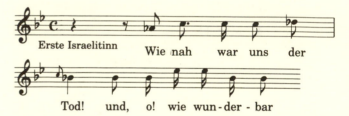

Erste Israelitinn   Wie nah   war uns der

Tod!   und, o! wie wun-der-bar

[No. 20] Arie

Erste Israelitinn   Vor des Mit-tags hei-ssen Strah-len

[No. 21] Accompagnement

Moses   O Freun-de,   Kind-er,   mein Ge-bet hat

[No. 22] Recit.

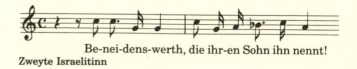

Be-nei-dens-werth, die ihr-en Sohn ihn nennt!
Zweyte Israelitinn

[No. 23] Arie

Zweyte Israelitinn — O se - lig, o se - lig,

[No. 24] Recit.

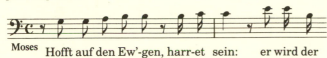

Moses — Hofft auf den Ew'gen, harr-et sein: er wird der

[No. 25] Chor [der Israeliten]

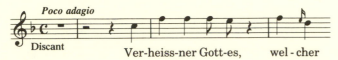

Discant — Ver-heiss-ner Gott-es, wel - cher

[No. 26] Choral

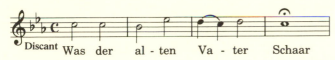

Discant Was der al - ten Va - ter Schaar

[No. 27] Recit.

Tenor O Heil der Welt du bist er-schie-nen,

[No. 28] Chor [der Israeliten]

Discant Lass dein Wort, das uns er-schallt,

776. Passions-Cantate [SATB chorus, SSATB soloists, 2 flutes, 2 oboes, 2 bassoons, 3 horns, timpani, 2 violins, viola, continuo] (Anna Luise Karsch, a pupil of Ramler; also C. D. Ebeling and J. J. Eschenburg, says CLARK, according to PÖLCHAU, 41; A Wn, 0137; and a note [probably in the hand of G. Pölchau] in the textbook accompanying P 337). 1769 (dated in CPEB's hand on P 337). W. 233

Mss.: D-brd B, P 337 (partly Michel? Marked by CPEB, with 2 loose autog. sheets attached, both bearing the same vnt. of No. 8), P 338, P 367 (No. 16 only, vnt., and so identified in WESTPHAL/THÉMATIQUE, p. 53v; Wq n.v. 10; ms. owned by Pölchau), St 192, St 367; D-brd DS, 1331 and 1331 a; D-ddr Bds, Slg. Teschner 219 (cover dated 1807), Am.B. 85 (2 copies, one of which contains an autog. sheet bearing revs. of No. 14 and several other nos.; D-brd

Hs, MA/255 (Chrysander collection); D-brd Mbs, Mus. ms. 1162; D-ddr SWl, 841; D-ddr Dlb, 3029.D.501; D-ddr HER, Mus E 1:4 (keyboard reduction and set of parts, incomplete), Mus G 11.1 (score and parts of No. 2 only) (thanks to Howard Serwer for notice of these sources in D-ddr HER); B Bc, 735 (Westphal); A Wgm, H 27767 (III 8677); A Wn, 0137, 09871; F Pc, D 573/R.45.604; PL Kj, P 756 (No. 16 only, voice parts only); DK Kk, Weyses Samling, MU 6309.1631, MU 6309.1632, MU 6309.1235 (with an autog. sheet attached, bearing a vnt. of No. 8 and a few revs. of No. 14); US Wc, M2000.B12P3; a ms. is in the private collection of E. N. Kulukundis (U.S.).

Early print: ed. by A. J. Steinfeld, Hamburg: Herrmann, 1789 (W. 263). Seriously incomplete, with orchestral parts reduced for keyboard. The known lit. gives no evidence that this (posthumous) print had been authorized by CPEB. In the copy of this print in D-ddr ROu, a letter in manuscript is tipped into the end pages, written by the publisher Herrmann on 6 November 1789 to the Duchess of Mecklenburg/Schwerin; it is a more personal and amplified version of the printed dedication. The title of item 776 is from NV, 56. Wotquenne's title, "Die letzten Leiden des Erlösers," is only one of many, for example, "Das Leiden und Sterben unsers Heilands Jesu Christi," "Der Tod Jesu," "Das vollendete Erlösungswerk Jesu," "Der Sterbende Jesus," "Passions-Oratorium," "Das Leiden Jesu." Textbooks of this work bearing such titles, printed by various publishers in Hamburg, Berlin, Breslau, Colditz/Leissnig, Halberstadt, Göttingen, Schwerin, and Cologne until at least 1780, are to be found, says CLARK, in D-brd B, P 337, Tb 87, Tb 92, Tb 92/1, Tb 93 Nr. 22, Tb 94, T 541 Nr. 28, T 808, T 809, T 810, T 811; D-ddr Bds, Am.B. 85 Bd. I; D-ddr SWl, Mus. 5897 (344 copies); D-brd Ha, A 534/255; D-brd Hs, A/70001 Nr. 7, A/70001 Nr. 20; D-brd Nst, Nor 752 8o; A Wn, 603021-A Musik-5, 4.167-B; A Wgm, 5504'. D-brd B, P 338 contains a separate text in ms.

Mod. edn.: H.-J. Immer, Vaduz, Liechtenstein: Prisca Verlag, 1982 (based on P 337)

Lit.: HAMBURGER CORRESPONDENT, 26 Feb. 1773; 8 Mar. 1774; 11 Mar., 21 Mar. 1775; 5 Mar., 12 Mar. 1776; 1 Mar., 5 Mar. 1777; 7 Mar. 1787; CPEB/FORKEL, 10 Apr., 12 July 1774; REICHARDT/BRIEFE, I, 111; BITTER/BRÜDER, II, 18–44, 279–87, 296, 298; VRIESLANDER/BACH, 141; BÜCKEN, 170–72; MIESNER/HAMBURG, 69–73; HADOW, 145–46; GEIRINGER/BACH, 374–75; BUSCH, 74–76, 293; OTTENBERG, 152, 217, 283; CLARK/CHORAL, 42–78, 98, 220–58; Norbert Bolin, "In rechter Ordnung lerne Jesu Passion: C. Ph. E. Bachs 'Spinnhaus-Passion' (H. 776), Hamburg 1768?" scheduled to appear in 1988 in the *Augsburger Jahrbuch für Musikwissenschaft*

NV, 59, as well as the notice in HAMBURGER CORRESPONDENT, 26 Feb. 1773, says that this work is extracted from the now lost St. Matthew Passion of 1769 (item 782). A textbook of item 782 in D-brd B, T 541, 10, indicates that Nos. 2, 4, 6, 8, 10, 12, 14, 16, part of No. 19, Nos. 20–22, and part of No. 25, all composed by CPEB, are borrowed from item 782. The original source of No. 2 is item 772/4, with different text.

Item 776 is an entirely original work despite its relation to the partly borrowed item 782.

The mss. vary in completeness. P 337 is carefully marked throughout in CPEB's hand. Its title p. bears this note in CPEB's hand: "NB Diese Partitur ist zwar nicht von der Handschrift des Autors, (denn von dieser Cantate in dieser Einrichtung existirt kein Original, weil der Autor hernach Vieles geändert hat) sie ist aber so correct wie möglich und ganz gewiss correkter, als alle übrigen Exemplare, weil sie der Besitzer, nehmlich der Autor sehr oft durchgesehen hat."

My thanks to Howard Serwer and his graduate students, as well as to Stephen L. Clark and Charles C. Gallagher, for their study of the sources of this work.

Incipits from P 337:

[No. 1. Introduction and] Recit.

[No.. 2] Coro

[No. 3] Recit.-Aria

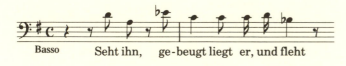

[No. 4] Aria

[No. 5] Recit.

[No. 6] Arioso

[No. 7] Recit.

[No. 8] Arioso

[No. 9] Recit.

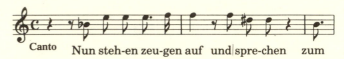

[No. 10] Aria

[No. 11] Recit.

[No. 12. Aria]

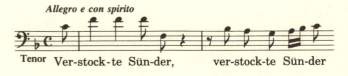

[No. 13] Recit.

[No. 14] Aria

Basso — Donn-re nur ein Wort der Macht, Herr

[No. 15] Recit.

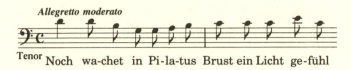

Tenor — Noch wa-chet in Pi-la-tus Brust ein Licht ge-fühl

[No. 16. Duetto: Canto 1, Canto 2]

Canto — Mu-ster der Ge-duld

[No. 17] Recit.

Canto — Die ihr durch des Me-ssias Glauben

[No. 18] Coro

Canto — Las - set uns auf-seh-en

Basso — Auf dass wir der Sün-de

[No. 19] Recit. [accompagnato]

Canto — O du, der Gott mit uns ver-söhnt

[No. 20] Aria

Basso — Der Men-schen Mis - se - that

[No. 21] Coro

Canto — Dann strah-let Licht und Ma-jes - tät

[No. 22] Solo

Basso — Wie froh wird nur der An - blick seyn

[No. 23] Recit.

Alto — Nun sam - melt sich die

grau-en vol - le Macht des bäng-sten

[No. 24] Choral

Canto — Hei - li - ger schöpf - fer Gott!

[No. 25] Recit.

Tenor — Er ruft: es ist voll-bracht, es ist vollbracht

[No. 26] Accomp.

Basso — Die All-macht feyrt den Tod

[No. 27] Coro

Canto — Prei - set ihn er - lös - ste

In St 367, MA 255, and 1162 these three chorales are inserted at the places designated:

Before No. 1 (text from item 686/23):

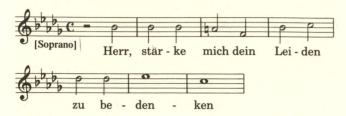

[Soprano]
Herr, stär - ke mich dein Lei - den
zu be - den - ken

Between Nos. 10 and 11:

[Soprano]
Ich füh - le Herr voll Reu und Schmerz

Between Nos. 16 and 17:

[Soprano]
Du schenkst mir tä - glich so viel Schuld

777. Carl Wilhelm Rammlers Auferstehung und Himmelfahrt Jesu [SATB chorus, STB soloists, 2 flutes, 2 oboes, bassoon, 2 horns, 3 trumpets, timpani, 2 violins, viola, continuo] (C. W. Ramler). 1774–80 (sources of date: NV 55; a letter from J. H. Voss to E. T. J. Brückner, 2 Apr. 1774, referring to CPEB's performance of "Ramlers Auferstehung, neu componirt" [the letter is excerpted in BUSCH, 122 and SCHMID/KAMMERMUSIK, 46–47, and printed in VOSS/ BRIEFE, I, 157–62]; the correspondence listed below). W. 240

Mss.: D-brd B, P 336 (autog., No. 1 missing; printed text attached, with its own call no., Hs A/70001, 19), St 178 (autog. and Michel); D-ddr Bds, Slg. Teschner 219 (early 19th century); D-ddr SWl, 858 (the early print with a full set of ms. parts); D-ddr HER, Mus B 102:1, Mus L 104:1 (a score and a set of parts, respectively; my thanks to Howard Serwer for this notice); A Wgm, Q 678-9 (III 14232)

Early print: *Carl Wilhelm Rammlers Auferstehung und Himmelfahrt Jesu, in Musik gesetzt von Karl Philipp Emanuel Bach.* Leipzig: im Breitkopfischen Verlage, 1787

Mod. edns.: H. M. Schletterer, Wolfenbüttel: Holle, 1865 (orchestral parts reduced for keyboard); R. H. Brewer, Delaware Water Gap, Pa.: Shawnee Press, 1970 (abridged; in English translation and with orchestral parts reduced for organ); G. Darvas, Budapest: Editio Musica, 1974

Lit.: CPEB/RAMLER; HAMBURGER CORRESPONDENT, 17 Mar., 4 Apr. 1778; 9 July, 17 Dec. 1784; 12 Jan. 1785; 2 Aug. 1786; 10 Mar. 1787; CPEB/BREITKOPF, 3 Feb. (date received), 14 Feb. 1781; 26 Aug., 19 Oct., 30 Nov. 1785; 29 Feb., 8 June, 28 July, 30 Sept., 26 Oct., 6 Nov., 25 Nov. 1786; 3 Jan., 10 Feb., 30 June, 26 July, 8 Sept., 21 Sept.,

3 Dec. 1787; 3 May 1788; CRAMER/MAGAZIN, II (1784), 256–61; CPEB/WESTPHAL, 2 Jan. 1787; BITTER/BRÜDER, II, 44–60, 288–94; HASE, 102–04; SCHERING/ ORATORIUMS, 372–74; STEGLICH/HOMILIUS, 95; VRIESLANDER/BACH, 141–42; MIESNER/HAMBURG, 74–76; SCHMID/KAMMERMUSIK, 47, 66, 72; REESER, 42–43; GEIRINGER/BACH, 376–77; BUSCH, 86, 233–34, 392; OLLESON, 331; WADE, 2, 28; BREWER; KRAMER; Ludwig Ritter von Köchel et al., *Chronologisch-thematisches Verzeichnis sämtlicher Tonwerke Wolfgang Amadé Mozarts* (Wiesbaden, 1964), K.537d, p. 611; OTTENBERG, 152, 201, 243, 261; CLARK/CHORAL, 168, 190

See items 808, 870.

The place of No. 7 was originally occupied by item 807/6. CLARK observes that in CPEB/RAMLER, 20 Nov. 1780, CPEB requested a new text for No. 7, to which he then composed a new aria; that this is confirmed by the structure and handwriting of P 336 and P 339 (see the note about P 339 in item 807) as well as by the presence of the original text in the textbook attached to P 336; and that in CPEB/RAMLER, 5 Dec. 1781, CPEB says that the *Auferstehung und Himmelfahrt* "ist unter allen meinen Singstücken im Ausdruck und in der Arbeit vorzüglich."

Incipits from the early print:

[*Erster Theil*]

[No. 1] Einleitung

Adagio di molto
Alle Bratschen

[No. 2] Chor

Largo
Discant   Gott, du wirst sei - ne See - le

[No. 3] Recitativ

Adagio
Bass   Ju - dä - a zit - tert!   sei - ne Ber - ge be - ben!

[No. 4] Arie

Allegro
Bass   Mein
Geist, voll Furcht und Freu - - de

[No. 5] Chor

Tri-umph! Tri-umph! Des Herrn

[No. 6] Recitativ

Tenor Die from-men Töch-ter Si-ons gehn nicht oh-ne

[No. 7] Arie

Discant Wie bang hat dich mein Lied be-weint!

[No. 8] Recitativ

Bass Wer ist die Si-o-nit-tinn, die vom Gra-be

[No. 9] Duett [Tenor, Discant]

Tenor Va-ter dei-ner schwa-chen Kin-der,

[No. 10] Recitativ

Tenor Freundin-nen Je-su! sagt, wo-her so oft in die-sen

[No. 11] Arie

Tenor Ich fol-ge dir, ver-klärt-er Held,

[No. 12] Chor

Discant Tod! wo ist dein Sta-chel?

[Fuga]
Allegro

Un-ser ist der Sieg! Dank sey Gott!

Zweyter Theil

[No. 13] Einleitung

Bratsche

[No. 14] Recitativ

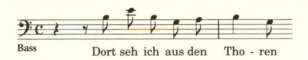

Bass Dort seh ich aus den Tho-ren

[No. 15] Arie

Bass Will-kom-men, Hei-land!

[No. 16] Chor

Discant Tri-umph! Tri-umph! Der Fürst

[No. 17] Recit.

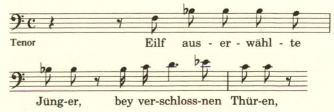

Tenor Eilf aus-er-wähl-te Jüng-er, bey ver-schloss-nen Thür-en,

[No. 18] Arie

[No. 19] Chor

[No. 20] Recitativ

[No. 21] Arie

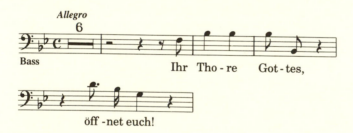

[No. 22] Chor

778. Heilig, mit zwey Chören und einer Ariette zur Einleitung [alto solo, 2 antiphonal SATB choruses, 2 oboes, bassoon, 3 trumpets, timpani, 2 violins, viola, continuo] (Isaiah 6:3, Te Deum Laudamus; trans. Martin Luther). c. 1776 (sources of date: the HAMBURGER CORRESPONDENT 1776 notice listed below; a letter from J. H. Voss to J. W. L. Gleim, 9 Oct., 1776, printed in VOSS/BRIEFE, II, 258–59 and SCHMID/KAMMERMUSIK, 48; BUSCH, 131–32, 136, 234–35). W. 217

Mss.: D-ddr Bds, P 339 (autog., trumpet parts only, 4 bars missing); D-brd B, P 780 (choral parts only, expanded to 3 choirs), St 186, St 583; A Wn, 15517 (autog.); D-ddr HER, Mus L 104.2 (thanks to Howard Serwer for notice of this set of parts)

Early print: *Heilig, mit zwey Chören und einer Ariette zur Einleitung, von Carl Philipp Emanuel Bach.* Hamburg: im Verlage des Autors. Aus der Breitkopfischen Buchdruckerey zu Leipzig. 1779

Mss. probably copied from the early print: D-brd B, St 594; B Bc, 730 (missing)

Mod. edns.: H. M. Schletterer, Wolfenbüttel: Holle, [c. 1865] (orchestral parts reduced for keyboard); K. Geiringer, St. Louis: Concordia, 1956; G. Graulich, Neuhausen-Stuttgart: Hänssler, [c. 1975]

Lit.: CPEB/BREITKOPF, 28 July, 16 Sept., 9 Oct., 13 Nov., 25 Nov., 17 Dec., 19 Dec. 1778; 30 Jan., 20 Feb., 3 Mar., 16 Apr., 20 Apr., 5 June, 12 July, 27 July, 29 July, 20 Sept., 2 Nov., 12 Nov. (and the financial statement accompanying the letter), 1779; 2 Dec. 1780; CPEB/16 Dec. 1779; HAMBURGER CORRESPONDENT, 25 Oct. 1776; 18 Nov. 1778 (by Georg Benda); 31 July, 11 Sept. 1779; 4 Nov. 1783; 17 Oct., 21 Oct. 1785; REICHARDT/KUNSTMAGAZIN, I (1782), 84–85; II (1791), 57; MUSIKALISCHE REALZEITUNG, II. Band (1789), cols. 396, 398; BITTER/BRÜDER, I, 247, 301–06; II, 300, 323; HASE, 94–96; STEGLICH/HOMILIUS, 108; VRIESLANDER/BACH, 143–44; MIESNER/HAMBURG, 73, 75, 93–97; REESER, 42; BUSCH, 131–32, 136, 234–35; GEIRINGER/BACH, 375–76; COHEN, 156; WADE, 53; OTTENBERG, 243–44, 283

C. F. Zelter grossly changed the setting after CPEB's death (as in P 780). Some critical opinion demanded the change, as is illustrated in AMZ XXXI (1829), 830; XXXIV (1832), 447; XXXVI (1834), 818. Zelter enclosed a handwritten rationale in his newly written set of parts; Miesner saw this package (now lost) in the Singakademie library and quoted Zelter's rationale on pp. 95–96 of MIESNER/HAMBURG.

Items 823 and 824 both consist partly of this entire work. See also items 805, 814, 823, 848, 870.

Incipits from the early print:

[No. 1] Einleitung [Ariette]

[No. 2] Chor der Engel . . . Chor der Völker

Cant. Hei - lig

779. Klopstocks Morgengesang am Schöpfungsfeste [SSTB chorus, SS soloists, 2 flutes, 2 violins, 2 violas, cello, continuo; keyboard reduction added] (F. G. Klopstock). 1783 (NV 55]. W. 239

Mss.: D-brd B, St 183; D-brd BNba (with this inscription in Beethoven's hand: "Von meinem teuren Vater geschrieben")

Early prints: *Klopstocks Morgengesang am Schöpfungsfeste, in Partitur und mit beygefügtem Klavierauszuge, componirt von Carl Philipp Emanuel Bach.* Leipzig: im Verlage des Autors [printed by J. G. I. Breitkopf], 1784; Speyer: Bossler, 1785; Wien: Artaria, [1786] (the two latter only with orchestral parts reduced for keyboard). The known lit. gives no evidence that the Speyer print was authorized by CPEB.

Mod. edn.: anon., Leipzig: Breitopf & Härtel, [c. 1926]

Lit.: CPEB/BREITKOPF, 4 Nov., 31 Dec. 1783; 4 Feb., 20 Feb., 18 Apr., 28 Apr., 5 June, 23 June, 17 July, 20 July, 31 July, 18 Aug., 20 Aug., 9 Oct., 8 Dec., 23 Dec. 1784; 13 Apr., 23 July, 14 Sept. 1785; CPEB/ARTARIA, 27 Nov. 1783 (in which CPEB invites Artaria's interest "da Klopstock in Wien geliebt wird"); 19 July, 18 Aug., 3 Sept. 1784; CRAMER/MAGAZIN, 1783, 1115–19; HAMBURGER CORRESPONDENT, 25 Nov., 31 Dec. 1783; 24 Apr., 9 July, 1 Oct., 27 Oct., 17 Dec. 1784; 26 Feb., 20 Dec. 1785; AMZ, XX (1818), 73; BITTER/BRÜDER, II, 82–89, 303, 312–13; HASE, 98–99; STEGLICH/HOMILIUS, 67–68, 82; VRIESLANDER/BACH, 142–43; MIESNER/HAMBURG, 101–02; SCHMID/KAMMERMUSIK, 64; REESER, 43; BUSCH, 97, 143–44, 321; OLLESON, 330–32; WADE, 51; OTTENBERG, 213, 243, 261, 280
See item 775.

Incipits from the 1784 print:

[No. 1, solo-duet: Erster Cant., Zweyter Cant.]

Erster Cant. Noch kommt sie nicht die Son-ne,

[No. 2] Chor

Herr! Herr! Gott! barm - her - zig und
Erster Cant.

[No. 3] Duett [Erster Cant., Zweyter Cant.]

Hal - le - lu ja! Hal - le - lu - ja!
Zweyter Cant.

[No. 4] Accomp.

Erster Cant. O der Son - ne Got-tes! o der

[No. 5] Chor

Hal - le - lu - ja! Hal - le - lu - ja!
Erster Cant.

780. Zwey Litaneyen aus dem Schleswig-Holsteinischen Gesangbuche [i.e., Nos. 790 and 791 from *Vollständige Sammlung der Melodien zu den Gesängen des neuen allgemeinen Schleswig-Holsteinschen Gesangbuchs,* Leipzig, 1785] mit ihrer bekannten Melodie für acht Singstimmen in zwey Chören und dem dazu gehörigen Fundament [i.e., 2 antiphonal SATB choruses with one continuo positioned between them] in Partitur gesetzt, und zum nutzen und vergnügen Lehrbegieriger in der Harmonie bearbeitet von Carl Philipp Emanuel Bach. 1785, possibly 1786 (1786 according to NV, 55; Schiørring's editor's preface is dated "Kopenhagen, den 20 März 1786"; but CPEB's preface is dated "Hamburg, d. 14 März 1785"). W. 204

Mss.: D-brd B, P 344 (mostly autog., the rest Michel), St 179 (No. 1 only, Michel, marked by CPEB), St 368 (No. 2 only, Michel, marked by CPEB)
Early prints: the above title, "Herausgegeben von Niels Schiørring. Kopenhagen, 1786. In Commission bey Chr. Gottl. Proft. Gedruckt bey Aug. Fr. Stein." A Wgm and GB Lbm each have a copy of a print with no publisher named, Wien, 1792; the known lit. gives no evidence that this (posthumous) print had been authorized by CPEB.
Mod. edn.: Nos. 1 and 2 separately in practical score editions with rental parts, J. Leonhardt, Neuhausen-Stuttgart: Hänssler- Verlag, c. 1980; Nos. 1 and 2 together in scholarly edition, J. Leonhardt, ibid.
Ms. probably copied from the Schiørring print: D-ddr Bds, Libr. chor. ms. 80 (dated 1844 on the cover)
Lit.: CRAMER/MAGAZIN, 1784, 121–22; HAMBURGER CORRESPONDENT, 11 Apr., 20 May 1786; REICHARDT/KUNSTMAGAZIN, 1791, 30; BITTER/BRÜDER, I, 306–16; STEGLICH/HOMILIUS, 69; VRIESLANDER/BACH, 65, 129–35; VRIESLANDER/THEORETIKER, 274–75;

MIESNER/HAMBURG, 111; BUSCH, 144–76, 339; WADE, 26, 53

This is a theoretical as well as practical work; see item 871. See also item 802.

Incipits from the Schiørring print:

[No. 1]

E - wi - ger! Er - bar - me dich!
1stes Chor [S]   2tes Chor [S]

[No. 2]

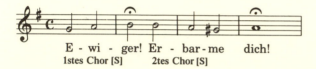

E - wi - ger! Er - bar - me dich!
1stes Chor [S]   2tes Chor [S]

781. Neue Melodien zu einigen Liedern des neuen Hamburgischen Gesangbuchs [i.e., chosen from the *Choralbuch für das neue Hamburgische Gesangbuch,* Hamburg, 1787] nebst einigen Berichtigungen [unison chorus, continuo] (texts of Nos. 1–4, 6–11 by C. F. Gellert; of No. 5, J. A. Freylinghausen; of No. 12, F. G. Klopstock; of No. 13, G. B. Funk; of No. 14, J. A. Cramer). 1787 (NV 55). W. 203

Early prints: the above title, Hamburg, "Im Verlag der Heroldschen Buchhandlung, und gedruckt bey Gottlieb Friedrich Schniebes 1787"; KÜHNAU II (with written-out inner parts); KELLNER

Mss. probably copied from one of these prints: D-brd B, Mus. ms. 38109 (No. 1 only); D-ddr Bds, Mus. ms. 30068 (No. 6 only)

Lit.: HAMBURGER CORRESPONDENT, 28 Aug., 29 Aug. 1787; BITTER/BRÜDER, I, 318–21; VRIESLANDER/BACH, 129; BUSCH, 177–82, 299; WADE, 7

Though all the harmonizations are by CPEB, the melodies of only Nos. 1–4, 6, 7, 9, 12, 13 are unequivocally his; see BUSCH, 177–82.

A.v. of Nos. 3, 6, 13: "3 Choräle aus dem neuen Hamburgischen Gesang Buche mit 3 Trompeten, Pauken, 2 Violinen, Bratsche, Violoncello, Orgel, 4 Singstimme von C. P. E. Bach," ms. M2021.A2B2 in US Wc. Another source of Nos. 3 and 6 in the same a.v., now lost, gave rise to the following entry in WESTPHAL/THÉMATIQUE: "2 Choräle: Gott ist mein Lied. und Gedanke der uns Leben giebt. für 4 Singstimmen, 3 Trompeten, Pauken, Bratsche, und Fundament." WOTQUENNE/THÉMATIQUE, footnote on p. 96, inaccurately transmits Westphal's entry as "4 Choräle . . . ." NV, 64, lists "Choräle, theils mit Trompeten, Pauken und andern Instrumenten . . . ." My thanks to Stephen L. Clark for pointing out this misprint in WOTQUENNE THÉMATIQUE.

Incipits from the Herold print:

[No. 1]

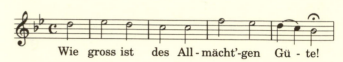

Wie gross ist des All - mächt'-gen Gü - te!

[No. 2]

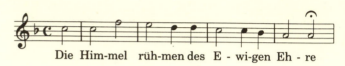

Die Him-mel rüh-men des E - wi-gen Eh - re

[No. 3]

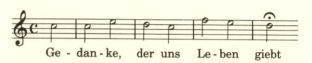

Ge - dan - ke, der uns Le - ben giebt

[No. 4]

Jauchzt, ihr Er - lös'-ten, dem Herrn! Er

[No. 5]

1. Wer ist wohl wie du, Stif - ter

[No. 6]

Gott ist mein Lied! Er ist der Gott

[No. 7]

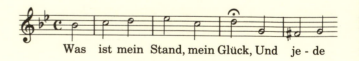

Was ist mein Stand, mein Glück, Und je - de

[No. 8]

Be - sitz ich nur ein ru - hi - ges

[No. 9]

Wohl dem, der bess - re Schät - ze liebt

[No. 10]

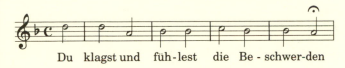

Du klagst und füh - lest die Be - schwer - den

[No. 11]

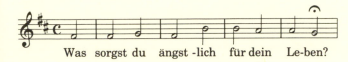

Was sorgst du ängst - lich für dein Le - ben?

[No. 12]

Auf - er - stehn, ja, auf - er - stehn wirst du

[No. 13]

Bald o - der spät des To - des Raub

[No. 14]

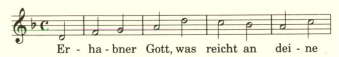

Er - ha - bner Gott, was reicht an dei - ne

CHORAL WORKS FOR SPECIAL OCCASIONS

Note: *For special occasions* means primarily interrelated, often containing borrowings from other C. P. E. Bach works and from other composers, used only in the composer's immediate circle for liturgical or ceremonial occasions. Most of the information given here about wholly or partially lost works comes from MIESNER/HAMBURG; almost all information on extant textbooks comes from CLARK. Virtually all the lost music was in the old Singakademie library; see p. xxiff. CLARK notes these relations among the passions: in the Mark, Luke, and John passions CPEB probably borrowed turba choruses and recitatives—music for the biblical

texts—from Telemann. In the Matthew passions he borrowed turba choruses and chorales from J. S. Bach's *St. Matthew Passion* and composed his own recitatives, except for a few portions borrowed from J. S. Bach. In all the passions, CPEB probably composed his own settings of the nonbiblical texts, exclusive of the above-mentioned chorales.

Passions

782. Passionsmusik nach dem Evangelisten Matthäus [chorus(es), vocal soloists, orchestra with damped timpani, flutes, oboes, horns, bassoons]. 1768–69 and earlier (NV 59; see also below)
Now lost

Lit.: MIESNER/HAMBURG, 58–65, 67–70; HÖRNER, 135; CLARK/CHORAL, 30, 36f., 41–45, 65–78, 98, 102–06, 115–21, 220–58
Borrowed from J. S. Bach: 3 chorales and 10 choruses from the *St. Matthew Passion* (BWV 244); chorales from the *St. John Passion* (BWV 245), *Cantata 153* (BWV 153), and *Cantata 39* (BWV 39); see the note preceding this item and see item 802. Borrowed from Telemann's *St. Matthew Passion* of 1746: one chorus. Borrowed from himself: a chorus from the *Magnificat* (item 772). A textbook of item 782 survives in D-brd B, T 541, 10; if we judge from this textbook, the parts of item 782 actually composed by CPEB comprise the source of most of item 776; that is, item 776 is an entirely original work. See the list of borrowed music in item 776.

Incipit of the opening chorale, from J. S. Bach's *St. John Passion*:

[No. 1. Chorale]

[Soprano] Chri - stus, der uns se - lig macht

783. Passions-Musik nach dem Evangelisten Marcus [chorus, vocal soloists, orchestra with flutes, oboes, bassoon]. 1769–70 and earlier (NV 59; see also below)
Now lost
Lit.: MIESNER/HAMBURG, 65, 67–70; CLARK/CHORAL, 36f., 113–21, 259–86
Recitatives and turba choruses probably borrowed from Telemann; see note preceding item 782. Textbooks: D-brd B, T 541, 11; Tb 93, 2; D-brd Hs, A/70000, 1

Incipit of the opening chorale, from MIESNER/HAMBURG, ex. 15:

[No. 1. Chorale]

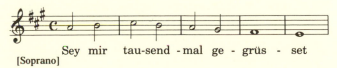

[Soprano] Sey mir tau-send - mal ge - grüs - set

784. Passions-Musik nach dem Evangelisten Lucas [chorus, vocal soloists, orchestra with horns, flutes, bassoons]. 1770–71 and earlier (NV 59; see also below)
Now lost
Lit.: MIESNER/HAMBURG, 65–70; HÖRNER, 135; CLARK/CHORAL, 107–10, 115–21, 287–313
Recitatives and turba choruses probably borrowed from Telemann; see note preceding item 782. Textbooks: D-brd B, T 541, 12; Tb 93, 2; D-brd Hs, A/70000, 2

Incipit of the opening chorus, from MIESNER/HAMBURG, ex. 20:

[No. 1. Chorus]

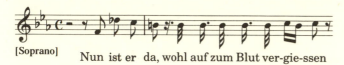

[Soprano]   Nun ist er da, wohl auf zum Blut ver-gie-ssen

785. Passions-Musik nach dem Evangelisten Johannes [chorus, vocal soloists, orchestra with flutes, oboes, bassoons]. 1771–72 and earlier (NV 59; see also below)
Now lost
Lit.: MIESNER/HAMBURG, 66–70; HÖRNER, 135; CLARK/CHORAL, 110–112f., 115–21, 314–39
Recitatives and turba choruses probably borrowed from Telemann; see note preceding item 782. Textbooks: D-brd B, T 541, 13; Tb 93, 3. A ms. copy of J. S. Bach's *St. John Passion* (BWV 245), D-ddr Bds, St 111, contains, in one chorus (No. 39), an alternate text in CPEB's hand. This text, notes CLARK, appears in the textbooks of item 785, which probably means that the J. S. Bach chorus, with the alternate text, was used in item 785. The alternate text is given in Appendix 3 of NBA, II/4, pp. 262–65. See also Mendel's comments in the *Kritischer Bericht* of NBA, II/4, pp. 44–45, 57–59.

Incipit of the opening chorale (not related to item 686/14, though it does use the Gellert text), from MIESNER/HAMBURG, ex. 24, as corrected on Miesner's p. 66, note 4:

[No. 1. Chorale]

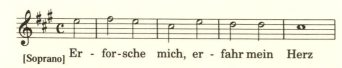

[Soprano]   Er - for-sche mich, er - fahr mein Herz

786. Passions-Musik nach dem Evangelisten Matthäus, "O Hilf, Christe, Gottes Sohn" [first chorus: "Legt eure Harfen hin"] [chorus, vocal soloists, orchestra with flutes, oboes, bassoons]. 1772–73 and earlier (NV 59; see also below)
Now lost
Lit.: MIESNER/HAMBURG, 58–65, 67–70; CLARK/CHORAL, 79–88, 98, 102–06, 115–21, 220–58
Turba choruses and some chorales probably borrowed from J. S. Bach's *St. Matthew Passion* (BWV 244); see note pre-

ceding item 782. Textbooks: D-brd B, T 541, 14; Tb 93, 4; D-brd Hs, A/7000, 3. These textbooks include the texts of items 802/29 and 802/46.

No incipit available

787. Passions-Musik nach dem Evangelisten Marcus [chorus, vocal soloists, orchestra with horns, flutes, oboes]. 1773–74 and earlier (NV 59; see also below)
Now lost
Lit.: MIESNER/HAMBURG, 65, 67–70; CLARK/CHORAL, 113–21, 259–86
Recitatives and turba choruses probably borrowed from Telemann; see note preceding item 782. Textbooks: D-brd B, T 541, 15; Tb 93, 5; D-brd Hs, A/7000, 4

Incipit of the opening chorale, from MIESNER/HAMBURG, ex. 16:

[No. 1. Chorale]

[Soprano] O   Haupt voll Blut und Wun - den

788. Passions-Musik nach dem Evangelisten Lucas [chorus, vocal soloists, orchestra with horns, flutes, oboes, bassoons]. 1774–75 and earlier (NV 59)
Now lost
Lit.: MIESNER/HAMBURG, 60, 65–70; CLARK/CHORAL, 107–110, 115–21, 287–313
Recitatives and turba choruses probably borrowed from Telemann; see note preceding item 782. Textbooks: D-brd B, T 541, 16; D-brd Hs, A/70000, 5

No incipit available

789. Passions-Musik nach dem Evangelisten Johannes [chorus, vocal soloists, orchestra with horns, flutes, oboes, bassoons]. 1775–76 and earlier (NV 60; see also below)
Now lost
Lit.: MIESNER/HAMBURG, 60, 66–70; CLARK/CHORAL, 39, 115–21, 314–39
Turba choruses probably borrowed from Telemann; see note preceding item 782. MIESNER/HAMBURG, 66, mentions "eine besondere Fassung" of the recitatives, presumably meaning that they were newly composed by CPEB. Textbooks: D-brd B, T 541, 17; D-brd Hs, A/70000, 6

Incipit of the opening chorale (without text), from MIESNER/HAMBURG, ex. 25:

[No. 1. Chorale]

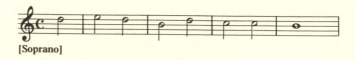

[Soprano]

790. Passions-Musik nach dem Evangelisten Matthäus [chorus, vocal soloists, orchestra with horns, flutes, oboes, bassoon]. 1776–77 and earlier (NV 60; see also below)
Almost entirely lost
Lit.: BITTER/BRÜDER, I, 276–78; MIESNER/HAMBURG, 58–65, 67–70; Alfred Dürr, NBA II, 5, p. 15; CLARK/CHORAL, 79–88, 98, 101–06, 115–21, 220–58
Turba choruses and some chorales probably borrowed from J. S. Bach's *St. Matthew Passion* (BWV 244); see note preceding item 782. D-brd B, P 374 (autog.), entitled "Passio nach dem Mattheo. 1777," contains the opening chorale and 2 other chorales, all composed by CPEB, along with schematic indications as to how the 1777 passion was assembled; these 3 incipits are supplied by CLARK, along with texts coming from the textbook in D-brd B, T 541, 18. The opening chorale is apparently the same one that opens item 798.
D-brd B, P 340, contains the 1st chorus in autog. (source of the 4th incipit quoted here), which is CPEB's arr. of the 1st verse of item 686/14, identified in his hand on the title p. as belonging to this passion. The texts of verses 6 and 5 of item 686/14 are added to P 340 in CPEB's hand below that of verse 1, apparently at a later time; CLARK notes that this corresponds to the use (according to the textbooks) of verse 6 in the 1778 Mark passion (item 791) and verse 5 of the 1784 John Passion (item 797), presumably in the same arr.
Included among the now lost portions described by MIESNER/HAMBURG, 60f., as being in the Singakademie library was an 11-p. autog. score containing verbal indications of how the work was assembled from various sources, along with a completely written-out arioso and aria: "Beschämt flieht Petrus" and "Hier fall ich auch im Staube vor dir nieder." Textbooks: D-brd B, T 541, 18; Tb 93, 6; D-brd Hs, A/70000, 7

Incipits of the 3 CPEB-composed numbers in P 374:

[Opening chorale]

[Soprano] O Lamm Got - tes un - schul - dig

[Chorale]

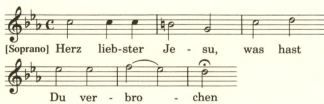

[Soprano] Herz lieb-ster Je - su, was hast
Du ver - bro - chen

[Chorale]

[Soprano] Ach flie - he doch des Teu-fels Strick!

Incipit of the 1st chorus, from P 340:

[No. 2. Chorus]

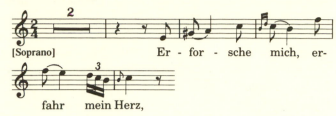

[Soprano] Er - for - sche mich, er-
fahr mein Herz,

791. Passions-Musik nach dem Evangelisten Marcus [chorus, vocal soloists, orchestra with flutes, oboes, bassoons]. 1777–78 and earlier (NV 60; see also below)
Now lost
Lit.: MIESNER/HAMBURG, 65, 67–70; CLARK/CHORAL, 113–21, 259–86
Recitatives and turba choruses probably borrowed from Telemann; see note preceding item 782. Textbooks: D-brd B, T 541, 19; Tb 93, 7; D-brd Hs, A/70000, 8. These show a chorus reusing the text of verse 6 of item 686/14; presumably this is the choral arr. found in D-brd B, P 340 (see item 790).

Incipit of the opening chorale (not related to item 686/23, though it does use the Gellert text), from MIESNER/HAMBURG, ex. 17:

[No. 1. Chorale]

Herr, stär - ke mich, dein Lei - den zu be - den-ken
[Soprano]

792. Passions-Musik nach dem Evangelisten Lucas [chorus, vocal soloists, orchestra with flutes, horns, oboes, bassoons]. 1778–79 and earlier (NV 60; see also below)
Now lost
Lit.: MIESNER/HAMBURG, 65–70; HÖRNER, 135; CLARK/CHORAL, 107–10, 115–21, 287–313
Recitatives and turba choruses probably borrowed from Telemann; see note preceding item 782. Textbooks: D-brd B, T 541, 20; Tb 93, 8; D-brd Hs, A/70000, 9

Incipit of the opening chorus, from MIESNER/HAMBURG, ex. 21:

[No. 1. Chorus]

O Got-tes-lamm, das un-sre Sün-de trä-get
[Soprano]

793. Passions-Musik nach dem Evangelisten Johannes [chorus, vocal soloists, orchestra with horns, oboes, bassoons]. 1779–80 and earlier (NV 60; see also below)
Now lost

Lit.: MIESNER/HAMBURG, 66–70; HÖRNER, 135; CLARK/
CHORAL, 115–21, 314–39

Recitatives and turba choruses probably borrowed from
Telemann; see note preceding item 782. Textbooks: D-brd
B, T 541, 21; Tb 93, 9; D-brd Hs, A/70000, 10

Incipit of the opening chorale, from MIESNER/HAMBURG,
ex. 26:

[No. 1. Chorale]

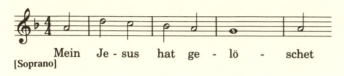

[Soprano] Mein Je - sus hat ge - lö - schet

794. Passions-Musik nach dem Evangelisten Matthäus,
"Jesu, meiner Seelen Licht" [chorus, vocal soloists, orchestra
with flutes and oboes]. 1780–81 and earlier (NV 60; see
also below). Partially Wq n.v. 3
Mostly lost

Lit.: BITTER/BRÜDER, I, 278–81; MIESNER/HAMBURG,
58–65, 67–70; CLARK/CHORAL, 79–88, 98, 102–06, 115–
21, 220–58

Turba choruses and some chorales probably borrowed from
J. S. Bach's *St. Matthew Passion* (BWV 244); see note preceding item 782. D-brd B, P 340, contains (all listed as
Wq n.v. 3, all autog.), in addition to charts showing how
this work was assembled from various sources, the following surviving portions of it, all seconded by the surviving
textbooks, all composed by CPEB, and all given the heading "Passio von 81" in his hand: an accompanied recitative
(1st incipit); an aria, voice part only (2nd incipit); another
accompanied recitative (3rd incipit); a chorus that is
CPEB's arr. of the 1st and 14th verses of item 686/23 (4th
incipit), with the 3rd and 9th verses added apparently
later by CPEB (see below); another aria, voice part only,
and even this part incomplete (5th incipit); and the texts
of items 733/9 (verse 2) and 733/13 (verse 4), indicating
that choral arr. of items 733/9 and 733/13 were part of
item 794. BUSCH, 227–28, says that the music of item 832
was also used in this passion, although the text of item
832 is not present in the textbooks. Textbooks: D-brd B,
T 541, 21a; Tb 93, 10; D-brd Hs, A/70000, 11. These
textbooks contain a chorus text that is the same as the
text for the 4th verse of item 749/6, notes CLARK, indicating that a choral arr. of item 749/6 was probably used in
item 794. As CPEB notes in P 340, the above-mentioned
choral arr. of item 686/23—but with the texts of verses 3
and 9, as they appear in the addition to P 340—was used
again in the 1783 Luke passion (item 796).

Incipits from P 340:

Accomp.

[Bass] Von al - len Him - meln   und von al - len

Arie

[Bass] Nun sterb ich Sün - der

nicht,   der   Va - ter

Accomp.

[Alto] Dein Bey-spiel wird mir Kraft ver-leihn, wenn

Fein - de

Chor

[Soprano] Herr, stär - ke

mich   dein Lei - den

Arie

[Bass] ver - samm - let

euch,   der   Er - de ge - fall - ne

795. Passions-Musik nach dem Evangelisten Marcus
[chorus, vocal soloists, orchestra with oboes]. 1781–82 and
earlier (NV 60; see also below). Partially W. 230
Almost entirely lost

Lit.: MIESNER/HAMBURG, 65, 67–70; CLARK/CHORAL,
113–15, 115–21, 259–86

The source of W. 230, for SATB chorus and strings, is now
missing from B Bc; it is an arr. of item 749/13 (verse 1).
This arr. apparently made up part of item 795. D-brd B,
P 349, contains, in Michel's hand, a different choral arr.
of item 749/13 (verses 1–3); CLARK observes that although
this arr. could not have been used in item 795 as it stands—
since it utilizes the inappropriate instrumentation of trumpets and timpani in combination—an alternate version
minus these instruments, or with damped timpani alone,

might well have been used in item 795. The textbooks indicate that this passion also contained choral arr. (now lost) of item 752, Nos. 6 (verses 1 and 5), 26 (verses 1 and 2), and 29 (verses 1 and 2). The recitatives and turba choruses are probably borrowed from Telemann; see note preceding item 782. Textbooks: D-brd B, T 541, 22; Tb 93, 11; D-brd Hs, A/70000, 12

Incipit of the opening chorale, from MIESNER/HAMBURG, ex. 18:

[No. 1. Chorale]

Incipit of the choral arr. in P 349 (W. 230):

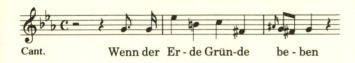

796. Passions-Musik nach dem Evangelisten Lucas [chorus, vocal soloists, orchestra with horns, oboes, flutes, bassoon]. 1782–83 and earlier (NV 60; see also below)
Mostly lost

Lit.: BITTER/BRÜDER, I, 281; MIESNER/HAMBURG, 65–70; CLARK/CHORAL, 107–10, 115–21, 287–313

Recitatives and turba choruses probably borrowed from Telemann; see note preceding item 782. D-brd B, P 340 contains an accompanied recitative and aria (autog., Wq n.v. 2), along with CPEB's choral arr. (autog.) of item 733/23, verses 1 and 4 (not 1 and 2, contrary to CPEB's indication), all marked in CPEB's hand as belonging to this work. Also part of this passion were similar arr. (now lost) of items 733/30 (verses 1 and 3) and 752/15. One chorus is borrowed from item 794: CPEB's autog. choral arr. in P 340 of item 686/23, but this time with the texts of verses 3 and 9; see item 794. Textbooks: D-brd B, T 541, 23; Tb 93, 12.

Incipit of the opening chorale, from MIESNER/HAMBURG, ex. 22:

[No. 1. Chorale]

Incipit of the chorus borrowed from item 794:

Chor

Incipits of the accompanied recitative, aria, and choral arr. from P 340:

Accomp.

Aria

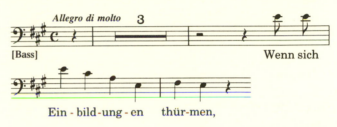

Chor

797. Passions-Musik nach dem Evangelisten Johannes [chorus, vocal soloists, orchestra with oboes]. 1783–84 and earlier (NV 60; see also below)
Mostly lost
Lit.: BITTER/BRÜDER, I, 281–83; MIESNER/HAMBURG, 66–70; HÖRNER, 135; CLARK/CHORAL, 115–21, 314–39
Recitatives and turba choruses probably borrowed from Telemann; see note preceding item 782. D-brd B, P 340 contains the following parts of this work (all autog.) that are identified in CPEB's hand as belonging to this passion: CPEB's choral arr. of item 729, verses 1 and 8; his choral arr. of item 752/23, verses 1, 4, and 5; an accompanied recitative (Wq n.v. 7); an aria (Wq n.v. 9); another aria, voice part only (Wq n.v. 4, preceded by a tipped-in slip

on which is written, in an unknown hand, "Aus der Passion 1784"). P 340 also contains, also in autog., an accompanied recitative and aria (Wq n.v. 8) labeled "No. 3" in CPEB's hand; the extant textbooks indicate that this recitative-aria is also part of item 797. Wq n.v. 8, transposed, is also to be found in an autog. now in a North American private collection, the same ms. containing No. 2 of item 818.5. In both this private source and P 340 the aria is incomplete. Textbooks: D-brd B, T 541, 24; Tb 93, 13. These textbooks show a chorus reusing the text of item 686/14, verse 5; presumably this is the choral arr. that is also part of P 340 (see item 790). The textbooks indicate the following order of surviving incipits; the choral arr. of item 686/14, verse 5, would have its incipit inserted between the 6th and 7th incipits shown here.

Incipit of the opening chorale, from MIESNER/HAMBURG, ex. 27:

[No. 1. Chorale]

[Soprano] Rat, Kraft und Frie - de - fürst und Held

Incipit of the aria, Wq n.v. 4:

[Aria]

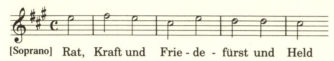

[Bass] Der Gott-mensch geht in Streit als Held,

Incipit of the choral arr. of item 729:

Chor

Cant. Der du selbst die Wahr-heit bist,

Incipits of the accompanied recitative and aria, Wq n.v. 8:

Accomp.

[Bass] Christ, sey Ge-fühl! Gott zürnt! Wer kann ihm

Aria

Die Un-schuld wird ver-folgt, die

Incipit of the accompanied recitative, Wq n.v. 7:

Accomp.

[Soprano] Schon stei-get in Dir Him-mel der Op-fer-flam-me

Incipit of the choral arr. of item 752/23:

Chor

Cant. Hal - le - lu - jah! hal-

le - lu - jah!

Incipit of the aria, Wq n.v. 9:

Aria

[Bass] Wenn ich kei - nen Trost mehr ha-be,

798. Passions-Musik nach dem Evangelisten Matthäus [chorus, vocal soloists, orchestra with horns, flutes, oboes]. 1784–85 and earlier (NV 60; see also below)
Almost entirely lost
Lit.: CPEB/ESCHENBURG (2 letters written months before the Easter 1785 performance, showing CPEB's early and elaborate preparation for passions); BITTER/BRÜDER, I, 283–85; MIESNER/HAMBURG, 58–65, 67–70; BUSCH, 227–28; CLARK/CHORAL, 39–41, 79–88, 98, 102–06, 115–21, 220–58
Turba choruses and some chorales probably borrowed from J. S. Bach's *St. Matthew Passion* (BWV 244); see note preceding item 782. The opening chorale, which was composed by CPEB, is apparently the same as that for item 790. D-brd B, P 349 contains CPEB's choral arr. (autog., W. 224) of item 733/13, 1st verse, which arr. made up part of this passion, as did a similar arr. (now lost) of item 749/21, verses 1 and 5. The source apparently catalogued in WOTQUENNE/THÉMATIQUE is now missing from B Bc. Textbook: D-brd B, Tb 93, 14. This textbook contains a chorus text that is the same as the text for the 2nd verse of item 752/4, notes CLARK, indicating that a choral arr. of item 752/4 was probably used in item 798.

Incipit of the choral arr. from P 349:

1 Coro

Incipits Miesner saw in the Singakademie library, from MIESNER/HAMBURG, ex. 13; the ones after the opening chorale are from an autograph score:

[Opening chorale]

[First chorus]

[Arioso]

[Arioso]

[Aria]

[Aria]

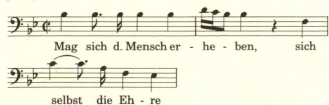

[Aria?]

799. Passions-Musik nach dem Evangelisten Marcus [chorus, vocal soloists, orchestra with flutes, oboes, bassoon]. 1785–86 and earlier (NV 61; see also below)
Almost entirely lost
Lit.: MIESNER/HAMBURG, 65, 67–70; CLARK/CHORAL, 113–21, 259–86
Recitatives and turba choruses probably borrowed from Telemann; see note preceding item 782. A choral arr. of item 752/3, verse 1 (not necessarily item 826/4, notes CLARK), was used in this work, as was a similar arr. (now lost) of item 749/3, verses 1, 3, and 5. Textbooks: D-brd B, T 541, 25; Tb 93, 15; D-brd Hs, A/70000, 13

Incipit of the opening chorale, from MIESNER/HAMBURG, ex. 19:

[No. 1. Chorale]

[Soprano]

800. Passions-Musik nach dem Evangelisten Lucas, "O Lamm Gottes unschuldig" [chorus, vocal soloists, orchestra with flutes, oboes, bassoon]. 1786–87 and earlier (NV 61; see also below). Partially W. 234
Partly lost
Lit.: BITTER/BRÜDER, I, 285–87; MIESNER/HAMBURG, 65–70; HÖRNER, 135; WADE, 26; OTTENBERG, 286; CLARK/CHORAL, 107–10, 115–21, 287–313
D-ddr Bds, P 339 (autog.) contains a partial score (W. 234) marked "Passio secundam Lucam von 87" (WOTQUENNE/THÉMATIQUE incorrectly terms it a St. Matthew passion); verbal indications in the score show how the rest of the passion was to be concocted from various sources. See item 337. The turba choruses and most of the recitatives were probably borrowed from Telemann; see note preceding item 782.
The aria "Dein Heil, O Christ" is CPEB's arr. of item 686/21, 1st verse. As might be surmised by the 4th and 6th incipits, the numbers represented by incipits 4–6 are performed without pause. Textbooks: D-brd B, T 541, 26; Tb 93, 16

Incipit of the opening chorale, from MIESNER/HAMBURG, ex. 23:

193

Incipits of the numbers contained in P 339:

Chor

[Soprano] Mein Er - lö -ser, Got-tes Sohn,

Discant Arie

Dein Heil, o Christ, nicht zu

Bass Arie

Mit-ten un - ter dei - nen Schmer-zen

Accomp.

Thräh-nen bit-trer Reu - e flie-ssen um von

[Bass]

Chor

[Soprano] Dei-nem Freun-de bin ich ähn -lich

Arie

[Tenor] Lob sey dem Mit-tler, Got-tes Soh-ne,

Arie

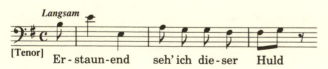

[Tenor] Er-staun-end seh'ich die-ser Huld

Arie

[Bass] Wenn sich zu je - ner

Chor

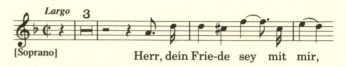

[Soprano] Herr, dein Frie-de sey mit mir,

801. Passions-Musik nach dem Evangelisten Johannes [chorus, vocal soloists, orchestra with flutes, oboes, bassoon]. 1787–88 and earlier (NV 61; see also below).
Now lost
Lit.: MIESNER/HAMBURG, 66–70; HÖRNER, 135; CLARK/ CHORAL, 115–21, 314–39
Recitatives and turba choruses probably borrowed from Telemann; see note preceding item 782. Textbooks: D-brd B, Tb 93, 17; D-brd Hs, A/70000, 14

Incipits of the opening chorale and of the 9 autog. numbers Miesner saw in the Singakademie library, from MIESNER/ HAMBURG, ex. 28:

[No. 1. Chorale]

[Soprano] So gehst du, Je - su, wil - lig hin

[Aria]

[Alto] Dei - ne Men-schen zu be-frei - en

[Aria]

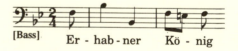

[Bass] Er - hab - ner Kö - nig

[Aria]

[Soprano] Man fleht für

[Chorus]

[Soprano] Seht! welch ein Mensch:

ihr Men-schen seht!

[Aria]

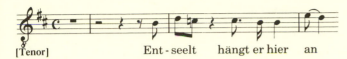

[Tenor] Ent - seelt   hängt er hier   an

[Accompanied recitative]

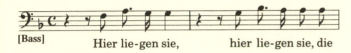

[Bass] Hier lie-gen sie,   hier lie-gen sie, die

[Aria]

[Bass] Wenn ich,   o Mitt-ler   Lie - be

[Chorus]

[Soprano] Singt Lie - der dem Mitt - ler

[Chorale, "Wer ist wohl wie du"]

[Soprano] [Without text]

802. Passions-Musik nach dem Evangelisten Matthäus [SATB chorus, SSTTBBB soloists, 2 flutes, 2 oboes, bassoon, 2 violins, viola, continuo]. 1788 and earlier (for Easter 1789) (NV 61; listed there as CPEB's last work; see also below)
Mss.: D-ddr Bds, P 339 contains a partial score (autog., W. 235, marked "Passion von 89"; WOTQUENNE THÉMATIQUE incorrectly terms it a St. Luke passion); verbal indications and fragments of music in this score show how the rest of the passion was to be assembled from various sources. See items 337, 786. A virtually complete score is in A Wgm, ms. H27768 (III 27038) (Michel, not C. F. G. Schwenke, as surmised in MIESNER/HAMBURG, 60ff.); this source is the only extant one known to me that provides a reliable picture of a passion as produced by CPEB.
Lit.: MIESNER/HAMBURG, 58–65, 67–70; OTTENBERG, 242; CLARK/CHORAL, 97–106, 115–21, 220–58
No. 2 is CPEB's free arr. of item 780/1. No. 1 is borrowed from J. S. Bach's *St. John Passion* (BWV 245; NBA II/4, 15). From CLARK: The same chorales borrowed in item 782 from J. S. Bach's *St. John Passion*, *Cantata 153* (BWV 153) and *Cantata 39* (BWV 39) are borrowed in item 802. Most

of the borrowings are from J. S. Bach's *St. Matthew Passion* (BWV 244); the following is an initial list of such borrowings:
a. Some portions of the music of the recitatives
b. All or part of these chorales and choruses:

CPEB, No.	JSB, NBA II/5	CPEB, No.	JSB, NBA II/5
4	25	38	50b
		40	50d
12	17	44	54
17	37	48	58b
19	38b	50	58d
27	41c	52	61b
32	45a	54	61d
34	45b	55	54

Textbooks: D-brd B, T541, 27; Tb 93, 18; D-brd Hs, A/70000, 15. See item 786.

Incipits from H 27768 (III 27038):

[No. 1] Choral

Canto Je - su, mei-ner See-len Licht, Ur-sprung

[No. 2] Chor

Canto O Je - su Chri - ste, Got-tes Sohn!

[No. 3] Recit.

Tenor Da kam Je - sus mit ih-nen zu ei-nem

[No. 4] Choral

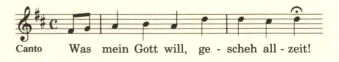

Canto Was mein Gott will, ge - scheh all - zeit!

[No. 5. Recit.]

Tenor Und er kam, und fand sie a - ber schla-fend,

[No. 6] Aria

Andante

Alto Die Bos-heit giebt mit fal - schen Küs-sen

[No. 7] Recit.

Tenor Und al - so bald trat er zu Je - su und sprach:

[No. 8] Accomp.

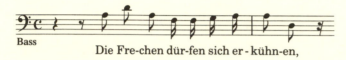

Bass Die Fre-chen dür-fen sich er - kühn-en,

[No. 9] Aria

Larghetto

Bass Du trägst die Fes-seln dei - ner Fein-de,

[No. 10] Choral

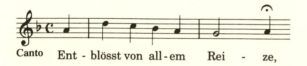

Canto Ent - blösst von all - em Rei - ze,

[No. 11. Recit.]

Tenor Die a - ber Je-sum ge-grif-fen hat-ten,

[No. 12. Duet, Alto & Tenor]

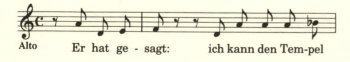

Alto Er hat ge - sagt: ich kann den Tem-pel

[No. 13. Recit.]

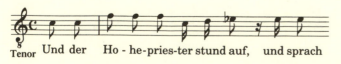

Tenor Und der Ho - he-pries-ter stund auf, und sprach

[No. 14] Coro

Poco allegro

Bass Er ist des To - des schul-dig, er ist des

[No. 15. Recit.]

Tenor Dann spey-e-ten sie aus in sein Au-ge-sicht,

[No. 16] Coro

Allegretto

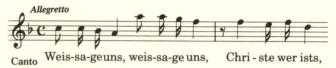

Canto Weis-sa-geuns, weis-sa-ge uns, Chri - ste wer ists,

[No. 17] Choral

Canto Auch ich und mein-e Sün - den, die sich

[No. 18. Recit.]

Tenor Pe-trus a - ber sass drau-ssen im Pa-last,

[No. 19] Coro

Allegro ma non troppo

Canto Wahr-lich, du bist auch ei - ner von de - nen

[No. 20. Recit.]

Tenor Da hub er an sich zu ver - flu-chen und zu

[No. 21] Aria

Adagio

Tenor Im Staub ge - bückt wein ich vor dir,

[No. 22. Recit.]

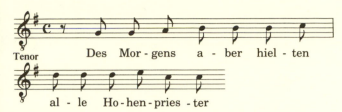

Des Mor - gens a - ber hiel - ten al - le Ho - hen - pries - ter

[No. 23] Coro

Allegro

Canto   Was,   was geh-et uns das an,   was geh-et

[No. 24. Recit.]

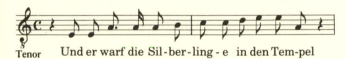

Tenor   Und er warf die Sil-ber-ling - e in den Tem-pel

[No. 25] Choral

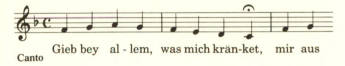

Canto   Gieb bey al - lem, was mich krän-ket, mir aus

[No. 26. Recit.]

Tenor   A - ber die Ho-hen-pries-ter nah-men die

[No. 27. Coro]

Andante

Bass   Es taugt   nicht, es taugt nicht dass wir sie

[No. 28. Recit.]

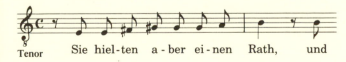

Tenor   Sie hiel-ten a - ber ei - nen Rath,   und

[No. 29] Accomp.

Bass   Die Fein-de rüs-sten sich,   mein Hei-land,

[No. 30. Aria]

Allegro 7

Canto   Er-frecht euch nur, die Un-schuld zu

[No. 31. Recit.]

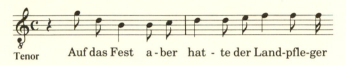

Tenor   Auf das Fest a - ber hat - te der Land-pfle-ger

[No. 32] Coro

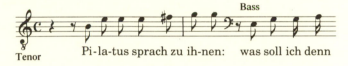

Allegro

Canto   Bar - ra-bam, Bar - ra-bam.

[No. 33. Recit.]

Tenor   Pi-la-tus sprach zu ih-nen: was soll ich denn

[No. 34] Chor

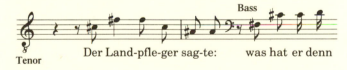

Bass   Lass ihn   creu-

[No. 35. Recit.]

Tenor   Der Land-pfle-ger sag-te: was hat er denn

[No. 36] Choral

Canto   Wie wun-der - bar-lich   ist doch die-se Stra - fe!

[No. 37. Recit.]

Tenor   Sie schrei-en a - ber noch mehr, und spra-chen:

[No. 38] Coro

Lass ihn creu - - -

[No. 39. Recit.]

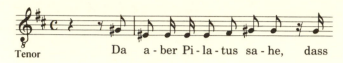

Da a - ber Pi - la - tus sa - he, dass

[No. 40] Coro

Sein Blut kom - men ü - ber uns

[No. 41. Recit.]

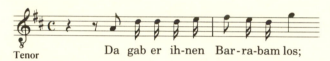

Da gab er ih - nen Bar - ra - bam los;

[No. 42] Coro

Ge - grüs - set seyst du, ge - grüs - set

[No. 43. Recit.]

Und spey - et - en ihn an, und nah - men das

[No. 44] Choral

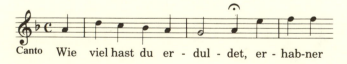

Wie viel hast du er - dul - det, er - hab - ner

[No. 45. Recit.]

Und da sie ihn ver - spot - tet hat - ten,

[No. 46] Aria

Ver - ach - te - te ver - damm - te Sün - der,

[No. 47. Recit.]

Und in dem sie hin - aus gien - gen, fun - den

[No. 48] Coro

Der du den Tem - pel Got - tes zer - bricht und

[No. 49. Recit.]

Des glei - chen auch die Ho - hen - prie - ster spo - tte - ten

[No. 50] Coro

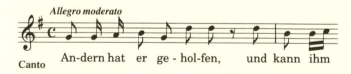

An - dern hat er ge - hol - fen, und kann ihm

[No. 51. Recit.]

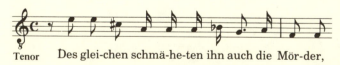

Des glei - chen schmä - he - ten ihn auch die Mör - der,

[No. 52] Coro

Er ru - fet dem E - li - as.

[No. 53. Recit.]

Tenor — Und bald lief ei-ner un-ter ih-nen,

nahm ei-nen

[No. 54] Coro

Allegro

Canto — Halt! Halt! Lass se-hen, ob E-li-as

[No. 2 is repeated here.]

[No. 55] Schluss Choral

Canto — Ich dan-ke dir von Her-zen, O du mein

Easter Cantatas

803. Oster-Cantate [SATB chorus, STB soloists, 3 trumpets, timpani, 2 oboes, 2 violins, viola, continuo] (Cochius). 1756 (source of date: autog.). W. 244

Mss.: D-brd B, P 345 (autog.), P 436, P 779, P 782 (late 19th-century copy, incomplete), P 791, St 182 (marked by CPEB, including performance dates of "69," "76," and "86" in CPEB's hand), St 187, St 598 (incomplete), St 599 (No. 6 only); D-brd Mbs, Mus. ms. 1161; D-ddr Bds, Am.B. 86; B Bc, 724 (Westphal); D-ddr SWl, 837 (2 copies)

Lit.: BITTER/BRÜDER, 131–37; MIESNER/HAMBURG, 76; CLARK/CHORAL, 154–74

Incorrectly dated 1784 in WOTQUENNE/THÉMATIQUE. Title p. of P 345, in CPEB's hand: "Oster-Cantate, wovon die Poesie vom H. Hofprediger Cochius, die Musik von C. P. E. Bachen ist. Beydes ist im Jahr 1756 ververtiget." But No. 7 is by J. S. Bach (BWV 342).

Incipits from P 345:

[No. 1] Coro

Allegro di molto

Canto — Gott, Gott, Gott hat den

[No. 2] Recit.

Basso — So wird mein Hei-land nun er - höht

[No. 3] Aria

Allegro

Basso — Dir sing ich froh, er - stand-ner

[No. 4] Recit.

Tenore — So sei nun See - le sei er-freut

[No. 5] Arioso

Largo

Tenore — Auch ich soll, Je-su, mit dir, mit dir

[No. 6] Aria

Andantino

Canto — Wie freu-dig seh' ich dir ent-

ge - gen

[Note in P 345 after No. 6 in CPEB's hand: "Aus dem Ende: Heut triumpfiert Gottes Sohn, der 3 V."]

[No. 7] Choral

Canto

[Without text. The melody is that of the chorale "Heut triumphieret Gottes Sohn."]

804. Oster Musik [SATB chorus, STB soloists, 3 trumpets, timpani, 2 oboes, 2 solo violins, 2 violins, viola, continuo]. 1778 and earlier (NV 61; see also below.). W. 242
Ms.: B Bc, 723 (Michel)

No. 1 is the first chorus of J. S. Bach's *Christmas Oratorio* (BWV 248). No. 2 has an alternate first phrase, as shown in the incipit, perhaps to reconcile it with the otherwise identical No. 2 of item 805. No. 5 uses the music of item 821g/13.
Lit.: OTTENBERG, 241; CLARK/CHORAL, 154–74

Incipits from 723:

[No. 1] Chor

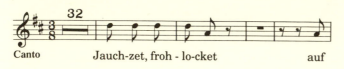

Canto Jauch-zet, froh-lo-cket auf

[No. 2] Accomp.

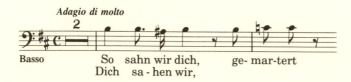

Adagio di molto

Basso So sahn wir dich, ge- mar-tert
Dich sa-hen wir,

[No. 3] Aria

Andante

Tenor So weiss der Herr die Sei-nen aus der

[No. 4] Recit.

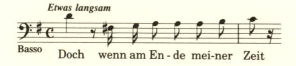

Etwas langsam

Basso Doch wenn am En-de mei-ner Zeit

[No. 5] Aria

Canto Nun freu' ich mich

[No. 6] Choral

Canto Da werd' ich dei-ne Sü-ssigkeit

805. Oster Musik [SATB chorus, STB soloists, 3 trumpets, timpani, 2 oboes, 2 violins, viola, continuo]. 1780 in assembled form (source of date: see below). W. 241

Mss.: D-ddr Bds, Schwenke Aut. 5; B Bc, 722 (Michel)
Incorrectly dated in WOTQUENNE/THÉMATIQUE
Lit.: CLARK/CHORAL, 154–74
A verbal instruction in 722 indicates that item 778 is to be inserted just before the closing chorale. No. 3 is borrowed from item 831. Regarding No. 2, see item 804. According to MIESNER/HAMBURG, 52, 77, item 805 was assembled in 1780 and performed again in 1783.

Incipits from 722:

[No. 1] Choral

Discant Nun dan-ket al-le Gott Mit

[No. 2] Accomp.

Adagio di molto

Bass Dich sa-hen wir, ge-mar-tert

[No. 3] Chor

Prächtig und etwas langsam

Discant Wer ist so wür-dig, als Du,

[No. 4] Recit.

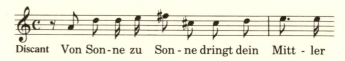

Discant Von Son-ne zu Son-ne dringt dein Mitt-ler

[No. 5] Aria

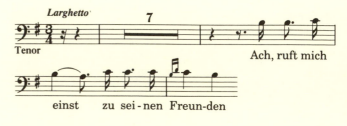

Larghetto

Tenor Ach, ruft mich
einst zu sei-nen Freun-den

[No. 6] Recit.

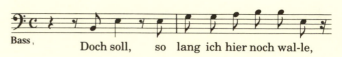

Bass Doch soll, so lang ich hier noch wal-le,

[No. 7 = item 778]

[No. 8] Schluss Choral

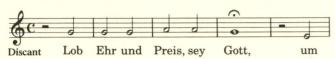

Discant   Lob Ehr und Preis, sey Gott,   um

806. Deleted

807. Osterquartal-Musik [SATB chorus, S (?) ATB soloists, 3 trumpets, timpani, 2 oboes, 2 violins, viola, continuo]. 1784 and earlier (NV 61; see also below.). W. 243

Mss.: D-ddr Bds, P 339 (autog., Part I only, with CPEB's handwriting changing in No. 6); D-ddr Bds, Am.B. 89 (No. 8 only); B Bc, 721 (Michel, Part I only). Part II is lost, though the printed text accompanying P 339 is for both parts.

Lit.: CPEB/5 Mar. 1783 (originally attached to AM.B. 89 and dealing with CPEB's reuse of No. 8); BITTER/BRÜDER, I, 287–92; MIESNER/HAMBURG, 76ff; OTTENBERG, 240; CLARK/CHORAL, 154–74

No. 2 is CPEB's arr. of item 752/14; No. 6 is CPEB's parody of a movement from item 824a (3rd incipit of item 824a); No. 6, says CLARK, originally occupied the place of item 777/7 (which see); No. 8 is CPEB's arr. of No. 9 of item 772. See item 337.

Incipits from P 339:

[No. 1] Chor

Canto   An - be - tung   dem Er - bar - mer!

[No. 2] Chor

Canto   Hal - le - lu - ja Je - sus le - bet!

[No. 3] Accomp.

Bass   wir stan - den wei - nend,   tief in Schmerz ver - loh - ren,

[No. 4] Aria

Bass   Ach! ach! als in   sie - ben - fält' - ge

[No. 5] Accomp.

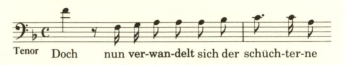

Tenor   Doch   nun ver-wan-delt sich der schüch-ter-ne

[No. 6] Arie

[Soprano?]   Sey ge - grü-sset,   Fürst des

[No. 7] Recit.

Alt   Die ihr ihn fürch - tet,   za-get nicht!

[No. 8] Chor

Bass   Herr! es ist dir kei - ner Gleich

[No. 9] Schlusschoral

Canto   Dank sey dir, o du Frie-de - fürst!

808. [Other Easter Cantatas]
Lit.: MIESNER/HAMBURG, 76ff.

The few fragments of these that were available to Miesner in the Singakademie library before World War II indicated that each was generally used in several Easter seasons, and showed each to be primarily assembled from portions of other works by CPEB and other composers. A textbook of "Oster-Musiken" for 1782, D-brd B, Tb 93, 20, shows that part of the music performed was Nos. 2–7 of item 777.

I have not yet been able to see an "Ostermusik" in the manuscript division of D-brd KNu, part of Ernst Bücken's legacy to that library. An Easter cantata in the Singakademie library, marked with the performance dates "68," "75," "81," says MIESNER/HAMBURG, 76–77, contained this note in CPEB's hand: "Die letzte Arie wird aus den Org. Basse dirig. und ist v. C.P.E. Bach." MIESNER/HAMBURG gives an incipit (of the C. P. E. Bach aria?) from this work in his ex. 32:

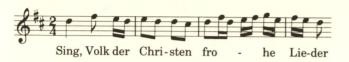

Incipit of the opening chorus of the 1771 "Oster-Musik," from MIESNER/HAMBURG, ex. 33:

[No. 1] Chorus

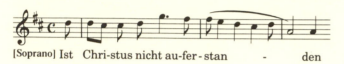

Michaelmas Cantatas

809. Michaelis-Musik [medium of the extant movement: SATB chorus, 2 trumpets, timpani, 2 oboes, 2 violins, viola, continuo]. c. 1769 (source of date: MIESNER/HAMBURG). W. 248

Lit.: CLARK/CHORAL, 154–57, 174–79

D-brd B, P 373 (autog.) contains the chorus (headed "Auf das Michaelis Fest") whose incipit is given here. No other source has been found. According to MIESNER/HAMBURG, 77, the now lost set of parts in the library of the Singakademie was marked "69" as well as "74"; therefore the composition date of 1774 given in WOTQUENNE/THÉMATIQUE seems to be incorrect.

Incipit of the chorus from P 373:

Coro

810. Michaelis-Musik [SATB chorus, vocal soloists, 3 trumpets, timpani, 2 oboes, 2 solo violins, 2 violins, viola, continuo]. c. 1772 (NV 61). W. 245
Ms.: B Bc, 727 (Michel)
Lit.: MIESNER/HAMBURG, 77; CLARK/CHORAL, 154–57, 174–79

Marked on the now lost autog. score in the Singakademie library as having been used in 1772, 1777, 1782, 1786, according to MIESNER/HAMBURG, 77. See item 821c, including the text of the opening chorus.

Incipits from 727:

[No. 1. Chorus]

[No. 2] Aria

[No. 3] Chor [sung with the instrumental portion and some of the text of No. 1]

[No. 4] Recit.

[No. 5] Aria

[No. 6] Recit.

[No. 7] Chor

Canto O Herr, o Herr, es ist kein Gott wie

[No. 8] Chor

Tenor- Hal - le - lu - jah! Heil und Preis Eh-
Bass

re und Kraft

[No. 9] Choral

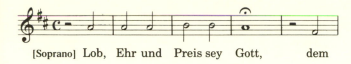

[Soprano] Lob, Ehr und Preis sey Gott, dem

811. [Michaelmas cantata for chorus, vocal soloists, orchestra]. c. 1772 (source of date: MIESNER/HAMBURG)
Now lost
Lit.: MIESNER/HAMBURG, 78; CLARK/CHORAL, 154–57, 174–79
Miesner saw this second 1772 Michaelmas cantata (in the Singakademie library?), which was marked as having been used in 1772, 1778, and 1782 and which may also have been used in a Christmas cantata.

Its incipit from MIESNER/HAMBURG, ex. 37:

[No. 1. Chorus]

[Soprano] Eh - re sei Gott in der Hö-he

812. Michaelis-Musik [SATB chorus, vocal soloists, 3 trumpets, timpani, 2 oboes, 2 violins, viola, continuo]. c. 1775 (NV 61). W. 212, 247
Mss.: D-brd B, Mus. ms. 8170/5 (No. 1 only, soprano part, plus text of the entire cantata), P 349 (Michel, marked by CPEB; No. 6 only [W. 212]); B Bc, 728 (Michel)
Lit.: MIESNER/HAMBURG, 77–78, 80; CLARK/CHORAL, 154–57, 174–79
No. 1 is borrowed from item 821d, No. 4 from item 821e. The first text shown in No. 6 below appears in P 349 in Michel's hand; the second is directly below the first in CPEB's hand. The alternate text appears in the textbook of item 821b.

Incipits from 728:

[No. 1. Chorus]

[Soprano] Sie - he! Sie - he!

Ich be - geh - re

[No. 2. Choral fugue]

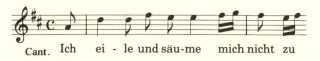

Cant. Ich ei - le und säu-me mich nicht zu

[No. 3] Rec.

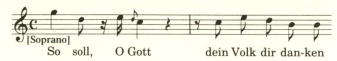

[Soprano] So soll, O Gott dein Volk dir dan-ken

[No. 4] Aria

Bass Noch steht sie zu des Mitt-lers

[No. 5] Recit.

[Bass] Sind mir des grö-ssern Gluck-es Werth?

[No. 6] Aria

Tenor Sing ihm voll Rüh-rung, O Zi - on

[Alternate text:] Sey fromm, mein Sohn, und sanft!

[No. 7] Recit.

Alt Ver-giss nicht dei-nes Got-tes und ha - be

[No. 8] Choral

[Soprano] Das Helf' uns der Herr Je - sus Christ

[Nos. 1 and 2 are repeated here.]

813. Deleted

814. Michaelis-Musik [SATB chorus, TB soloists, 2 trumpets, timpani, 2 oboes, 2 violins, viola, continuo]. 1785 and earlier (NV 62). W. 246
Ms.: B Bc, 726 (Michel; Part I only)
Lit.: MIESNER/HAMBURG, 77–78; CLARK/CHORAL, 154–57, 174–79
WOTQUENNE/THÉMATIQUE incorrectly gives 1772 as the date of composition.
At the end of the portion of this work appearing in 726 is the indication that the "2. Chorigte Heilig mit der Ariette" (that is, item 778) is to be appended. Since, in addition, Nos. 2–4 = Nos. 9–11 of item 821m, item 814 hardly deserves to be called a separate work. Textbook: D-brd B, Tb 83, 20 a

Incipits from 726:

[No. 1] Choral

Canto Der Frev - ler mag die Wahr-heit schmäh'n

[No. 2] Recit.

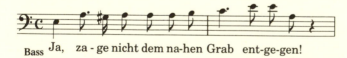

Bass Ja, za - ge nicht dem na-hen Grab ent-ge-gen!

[No. 3] Aria

Bass Schon hör' ich die Po - sau-nen

[No. 4] Choral

Canto Hal - le - lu - ja schal - le dir,

[No. 5] Recit.

Tenor So wer-de dir, so al-ler Men-schen Va-ter

[Item 778 is appended here.]

Christmas Cantatas

815. Weihnachts quartal Stück [SATB chorus, SATB soloists, 3 trumpets, timpani, 2 oboes, 2 flutes, 2 violins, viola, continuo]. 1775 (NV 62). W. 249
Mss.: D-brd B, P 76 (Michel); B Bc, 720 (Michel)
Lit.: CLARK/CHORAL, 155–57, 174–79
According to MIESNER/HAMBURG, 78, this is an excerpt from item 821e. A textbook of item 821e, B Br, Ms. Fétis 4550 B, indicates this.

Incipits from P 76:

[No. 1] Choral

Cant. Auf schi-cke dich recht fey-er - lich

[No. 2] Aria

Allegro pomposo

Bass Gross ist der Herr, gross ist der Herr,

[No. 3] Recit.

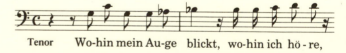

Tenor Wo-hin mein Au-ge blickt, wo-hin ich hö - re,

[No. 4] Aria

Allegro pomposo

Bass Gross ist der Herr, gross ist der Herr,

[No. 5] Chor

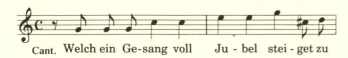

Cant.   Ihr Völ-cker hörts,   und kniet im Stau-be

[No. 6] Recit.

Cant. Welch ein Ge-sang voll   Ju - bel stei - get zu

[No. 7] Duetto [Canto, Alt]

Cant. Al - so   hat Gott die Welt ge - lie-bet

[No. 8] Accomp.

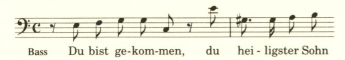

Bass   Du bist ge-kom-men,   du hei - ligster Sohn

[No. 9] Aria

Tenor   Seyd mir ge - seg - net, mei-ne Brü - der!

[No. 10] Chor

Cant. Stets soll mein Herz voll dei-ner Eh - re,

[No. 11: As closing chorale, the 2nd strophe of No. 1 is repeated.]

816. A considerable number of mss. of "Weihnachts-Musik" are lost. See MIESNER/HAMBURG, 52, 78.

Other Church Cantatas

817. Am Pfingstfeste: Herr, lehr' uns thun [vocalists, orchestra with trumpets, timpani, oboes]. 1769 (NV 65) Now lost

Identified in NV, 65, as partly by G. A. Homilius
Lit.: CLARK/CHORAL, 180–81
According to MIESNER/HAMBURG, 77, Nos. 2 and 7 of item 772 were used in this work; these correspond to the 3rd and 6th incipits quoted below. Miesner may have copied the incipit for the opening chorus a fifth too high, but he acknowledged no such mistake, as he did for item 785. Or the seeming discrepancy between the melodic line and the key signature of the first incipit may have resulted from Miesner's omission of the opening four bars.

Incipits from MIESNER/HAMBURG, ex. 35:

[Chorus]

Herr, lehr mich tun nach dei-nem

[Recit.]

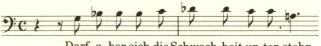

Darf a-ber sich die Schwach-heit un-ter-stehn

[Aria]

Hör'   und ver-schmä - he nicht

[Chorale]

[Accomp.]

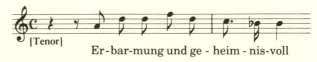

[Tenor]

Er-bar-mung und ge - heim - nis-voll

[Aria]

Wie so - gar   tief   sind dei - ne

[Closing chorale]

818. Am 16. [or 24th] Sonntage nach Trinitatis: Der Gerechte, ob er gleich [vocalists, orchestra with oboes and bassoon]. 1774 [NV 66]
Mss.: D-brd B, P 3 (autog.), St 167
Lit.: CLARK/CHORAL, 180, 182
The opening chorus in its original form was composed in 1676 by Johann Christoph Bach (1642–1703). CPEB added instruments to Johann Christoph's chorus, then completed the work with 2 recitatives, 2 arias, and 1 chorale, repeating the opening chorus at the end. See MIESNER/HAMBURG, 79; GEIRINGER/BACH, 48–50, 373.

Incipits from P 3, except for No. 4, whose music comes from St 167 and whose (partly illegible) text comes from P 3:

[No. 1. Chorus]

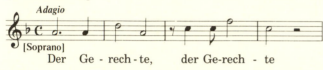

[No. 2] Recit.

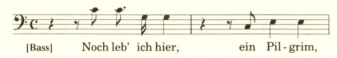

[No. 3] Arie

[No. 4 Chorale]

[No. 5] Rec.

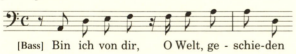

[No. 6] Aria

[No. 1 is repeated here.]

818.5. [Cantata for the 20th Sunday after Trinity] [Chorus, SATB soloists, 2 oboes, 2 horns, 2 violins, viola, continuo]. n.d.
Ms.: D-ddr Bds, Mus. ms. anon. 674 (Michel); ms. of No.

2 only (autog.) in a North American private collection "Aus den Bachschen Auction" (see p. xxiii of this catalogue and AUCTION 1805 in Bib.), says a note on the cover of anon. 674 (in Aloys Fuchs's hand?); "das erste Chor ist vermuthlich, da es oben mit G. H. bezeichnet ist, von Gottfried Homilius. Die beyde *Recitativen* sind Em. Bachs eigner Hand und von ihn corrigiert. Die letzte All. Aria ist nicht in Partitur, sondern nur in Stimmen da."

A set of parts; the only choral part present is for "Canto ripieno"; there are neither autogs. of the two recitatives nor a score. This anomaly is explained by Rachel Wade: Anon. 674 represents CPEB's revision of D-ddr Bds, Mus. ms. autogr. Homilius 1 N, the score of a cantata for the 20th Sunday after Trinity by Gottfried Homilius. CPEB revised bass figures, dynamics, and text in the Homilius autog., crossed out one of Homilius's recitatives and substituted the probably original one indicated in the incipit for No. 2, below, and added Nos. 5 and 6, not present in the Homilius autog. The package CPEB handed to Michel with the instruction to produce a fair copy, anon. 674, consisted of Nos. 1, 3, and 4 of the Homilius score, in the hand of Homilius but with revisions in the hand of CPEB; No. 2, a recitative in the hand of CPEB now in a private collection (see item 797); and Nos. 5 and 6 in a source as yet unknown. Understandably, Michel named no composer. The note added later on the cover shows that at one time all the sources of anon. 674 were shelved together. See WADE/FOUND.

Incipits from Mus. ms. anon. 674:

[No. 1] Chor

[No. 2] Recit.

[No. 3] Aria

[No. 4] Choral

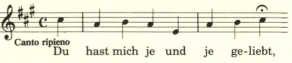

[No. 5] Aria

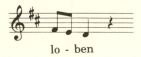

lo - ben

[No. 6] Recit.

Canto Die See - le,   die durch Je - su Blut ge - rei - nigt,

[At end: "Das erste Chor wird wiederholt."]

819. Auf Mariä Heimsuchung: Meine Seele erhebt den Herrn [vocalists, orchestra with horns, oboes, flutes]. n.d. Now lost

Lit.: NV, 65; MIESNER/HAMBURG, 78; CLARK/CHORAL, 180–81

The title page, says MIESNER/HAMBURG, 78 (without naming his source), indicated that part of the work was composed by one Hoffmann (CPEB's bass singer?), with CPEB supplying one chorus (incipit quoted here from MIESNER/HAMBURG, ex. 39; parody of item 772/1?) and one aria (2nd incipit shown here?), and that this pasticcio was used in 1768, 1775, 1776, 1780, and 1786. The remaining incipits are also from MIESNER/HAMBURG, ex. 39.

[Chorus]

[Soprano] Mei - ne See - le er - hebt den Herrn

[Aria]

[Soprano] Ich will mich dir mit al - lem

[Accomp.]

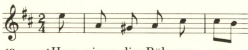

[Soprano] Herr, nimm dies Rüh-men an

[Aria]

[Bass] Mein Herz ver - senkt sich in das

820. A considerable number of cantata mss. are lost.
Lit.: MIESNER/HAMBURG, 79; CLARK/CHORAL, 183
D-ddr Bds, P 339 (autog.), 61, contains the schematic plan only of a "Sonntagsmusik" for the 18th Sunday after Trinity. See items 830, 832, 834.

D-brd B, P 1130 (autog.) arranges a fragment of item 190 to be used, apparently, with a cantata. This arrangement is entitled in J. S. Bach's hand "Dominica 6 post Trinit., Concerto a 4 Voci e 4 Stromenti"; it bears the note in CPEB's hand that the Concerto [?] "ward am 3 Adv. 73 wieder gemacht," along with CPEB's further notes on how part of an unidentified cantata is to be performed. P 1130 also contains, also in autog., items 693 (vnt.), 842/9 (vnt. with partial text), and 842/10 (with partial text), along with 3 instrumental sketches (the 3rd one arr. from the 3rd mvt. of item 190), all presumably for use in the same cantata.

The Commerzbibliothek of Hamburg contains, in vol. VII of a collection of *Trauergedichte*, call no. S/281, the text of a funeral cantata for the Hamburg burgomaster Frans Doormann, "aufgeführt von" CPEB. At the places in RECHNUNGSBUCH where the cost accounts for this and other such performances are given (with ritual acknowledgment to the widow that "Das Honorarium . . . wird der Generosité der Fr[au] Burgom[eister] überlasten"), CPEB notes that his honorarium is not only for "Bemühung" but also for "Composition." No doubt there are other such "compositions," mentioned and unmentioned in RECHNUNGSBUCH, that will never come to light. My thanks to Walter Stephani, through Stephen L. Clark, for notice of this text.

Inauguration Cantatas

821. Seventeen *Einführungsmusiken*, or inauguration cantatas honoring new pastors in Hamburg and neighboring churches, are listed with dates and names of pastors in NV, 57–58, as having been composed by CPEB. Item 821c is listed in NV, 65–66, as having been composed partly by CPEB. NV does not list an inauguration cantata composed by CPEB for Pastor Eberwein in 1772, but RECH-NUNGSBUCH, p. 101, contains the cost account for this performance in CPEB's hand, including an entry "für die Composition und Direction," and textbooks of this cantata are extant in B Br, 4550 B and D-brd Ha, A 534/7. These textbooks share several texts with the textbooks of item 821j, the 1780 Rambach inauguration cantata (textbooks in D-brd Ha, A 767/6 and D-brd SAAmi, P VIII, 14), and the texts of the two cantatas are metrically similar as well, which indicates that the 1780 Rambach cantata is probably a parody of the 1772 Eberwein. This, notes CLARK, is probably why the 1772 Eberwein cantata is not listed in NV. Thus there are about 18 *Einführungsmusiken* attributed wholly to CPEB, and one attributed partly to him. I am much indebted to Stephen L. Clark not only for much new information about these works—especially their textbooks—but also for persuading me that they constitute a solid body of original composition by CPEB (contrary to the judgment of Miesner and others) which is to be distinguished from approximately 21 other inauguration cantatas produced by, but not primarily composed by, CPEB. RECHNUNGSBUCH contains the cost accounts and dates of most of these cantatas, whether composed by CPEB or not, usually signed by CPEB or his wife; in these accounts the costs for "composition" and "direction" are clearly indicated. AUCTION 1805 lists occasions and dates.

The music of CPEB's predecessor Telemann was most often used when the work was not by CPEB. According to MIESNER/HAMBURG, 86, 88, in virtually all these works, whether composed by CPEB or another, Part II was begun with a "Veni, Sancte Spiritus." NV, 63, lists two "Veni" settings as having been composed by CPEB. Of the two "Veni" settings seen by Miesner, one, item 825, is undisputed; the other, item 855, was composed by Telemann, according to MIESNER/HAMBURG, 86. CLARK wonders whether item 855 too might not have been composed by CPEB, in view of the importance of the "Veni" in the inauguration cantatas; he also points out that the consistent appearance of the "Veni" text in the extant textbooks of these works might have indicated other "Veni" settings by Telemann (who composed ten settings of the Latin text and four settings of its German counterpart, "Komm heiliger Geist"). The texts of the inauguration cantatas were often written by the Hamburg clergy, and occasionally by the new pastor himself. Textbooks of inauguration cantatas either composed or produced by CPEB survive in these quantities and in these libraries: for 19 cantatas, in B Br, Ms. Fétis 4550 B; for 5 cantatas, in D-brd B, P 346, P 348, Mus T 99, 6, Mus T 99, 9, and Mus Tb 95; for 7 cantatas, in D-brd Ha, A 534/7, A 767/6, Ministerialarchiv III B Fasc. 1, Kirche zu Moorfleth I 1 and I 2; for 11 cantatas, in D-brd SAAmi, P VIII, 14. As indicated in individual items below, an occasional newspaper announcement of an inauguration cantata survives.

A collation of these original sources, along with information from MIESNER/HAMBURG (pp. 82–89, 128–32), CLARK/CHORAL (pp. 11–13, 39, 122–51), and AUCTION 1805, supplies the following list of inauguration cantatas *produced* by CPEB during his Hamburg years; works also *composed* by CPEB, along with item 821c, are marked with asterisks:

1768	Brandes	1776	Greve
1769	Heidritter	*1776	Wächter
*1769	Palm	*1777	Gerling
1771	Flügge	*1778	Sturm
*1771	Klefeker	*1780	Rambach
1771	Schuldze	1781	Steen
*1771	Schuchmacher	1781	Lampe
1772	Klug	*1782	Jänisch
*1772	Eberwein	1783	Lüttkens
*1772	Haeseler	1784	Som
*1772	Hornbostel	*1785	Gasie
*1773	Winkler	1785	Goeze
1773	Behrmann	1785	Emke
*1773	Von Döhren	*1785	Schäffer
1773	Wichmann	1785	Bracke
*1773	Müller and	1786	Cropp
	Schetelig	1786	Wessel
1775	Fulda	1786	Müller
*1775	Michaelsen	*1787	Berkhahn

*1775	Friderici	*1787	Willerding
1776	Schultze		

The items marked with asterisks are, then, the basic list of CPEB's inauguration cantatas. Of these works the following music or information has been found.

821a. Herrn Pastors Palm Einführungsmusik [chorus, vocal soloists, orchestra with trumpets, timpani, oboes, bassoon] (D. Schiebeler). 1769 (source of date: discussion in item 821) Now lost

Lit.: HAMBURGER CORRESPONDENT, 30 June, 1 July (presenting the texts of 2 recitatives and 2 arias), 5 July, 11 July 1769

Part I of the score that MIESNER/HAMBURG, 87, describes as having been in the Singakademie library was autog.; Part II was in the hand of a copyist. One duet in this work, says ibid., was arr. from No. 5 of item 772. Textbook: D-brd SAAmi, P VIII, 14, 9 (incomplete)

Incipit of the opening chorus, from MIESNER/HAMBURG, ex. 44:

[No. 1. Chorus]

[Soprano] Herr, ich will dir dan-ken   un - ter den

821b. Herrn Past. Klefeker Einführungsmusik [chorus, vocal soloists, orchestra with trumpets, timpani, oboes, flutes] (Ahlers), 1771 (source of date: discussion in item 821) Now lost

Lit.: HAMBURGER CORRESPONDENT, 2 Apr. 1771; CLARK/CHORAL, 177

From MIESNER/HAMBURG, 87: The score he saw in the Singakademie library was autog. One aria was arr., with different text, from the W. 212 portion (No. 6) of item 812. This is also indicated in a textbook, D-brd Ha, Kirche zu Moorfleth I 1, No. 139.

Incipit of the opening chorus, from MIESNER/HAMBURG, ex. 45:

[No. 1. Chorus]

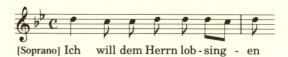

[Soprano] Ich   will dem Herrn lob - sing - en

821c. Bey Einführung Herrn Past. Schuchmachers vor der Predigt [SATB chorus, STB soloists, 3 trumpets, 2 oboes, 2 violins, viola, continuo] (C. D. Ebeling). 1771 (source of date: discussion in item 821)

Ms.: D-brd B, P 348 (Part I only, though the accompanying printed text is for the entire work)

Lit.: CPEB/SCHUCHMACHER; HAMBURGER CORRESPONDENT, 12 Nov. 1771 (presenting part of the text, and identifying Ebeling as the poet); BITTER/BRÜDER, I, 262–64

Spelled "Schuchmacher" in the printed text accompanying P 348 and "Schuhmacher" in NV, 65–66. Incorrectly termed a "1775 version" of W. 245 by KAST, 24; see item 810. A note on the first p. of the score says that Nos. 1–4 are by CPEB, Nos. 5–9 are "von mir (Syndicus Schuback in Hamburg)," and No. 10 is by CPEB; the composer of the final chorale setting is not identified.

Incipits of Part I from P 348:

[No. 1] Coro

[No. 2] Recit.

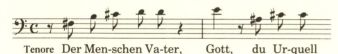

[No. 3] Arioso

[No. 4] Aria

[No. 5] Recit.

[No. 6. Accompanied recitative]

[No. 7. Aria]

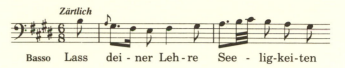

[No. 8] Arie

[No. 9] Choral

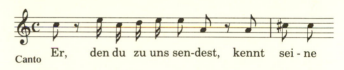

[No. 10] Recit.

[No. 11] Choral

[No. 1 is repeated here.]

821d. Herrn Pastors Haeseler Einführungsmusik [SATB chorus, STB soloists, 3 trumpets, timpani, 2 oboes, 2 bassoons, 2 violins, viola, bass, continuo]. 1772 (source of date: discussion in item 821)

Ms.: D-brd B, P 346 (autog., incomplete; includes complete printed text)

Lit.: BITTER/BRÜDER, I, 264–65; WADE, 13

Incorrectly identified as W. 247 in KAST; see item 812.

The printed text in P 346 indicates that Nos. 6–12 are, respectively, a recitative, "Du predigst Gottes Heil der Welt"; an aria, "Ich sehe dich auf Golgotha"; a recitative, "Heil und Gerechtigkeit"; an aria, "Ich zittre; hilf mir"; a chorale, "Tritt du mir zu"; a "Veni, Sancte Spiritus" as standard beginning of Part II (see discussion in item 821 above); the chorus "Gott! ich hebe" as No. 12, which survives in P 346 and whose incipit is given below; and, as the closing number, a repeat of No. 1. No. 3 is borrowed from item 772/3.

209

Incipits of the music that survives in P 346:

Erster Theil

[No. 1] Chor

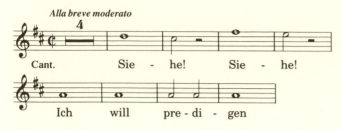

[No. 2] Accomp.

[No. 3] Aria

[No. 4] Recit.

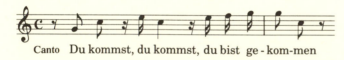

[No. 5] Choral

Zweyter Theil [A chorus, "Veni Sancte Spiritus," is inserted as No. 11; see discussion in item 821.]

[No. 12] Chor [with soloists]

[According to the text, No. 1 is repeated here.]

821e. Herrn Pastors Hornbostel Einführungsmusik [vocalists, orchestra with trumpets, timpani, oboes, flutes]. 1772 (source of date: discussion in item 821)

Now lost. See items 812, 815.

Miesner presumably saw a ms. in the Singakademie library.
    Textbooks: B Br, Ms. Fétis 4550 B; D-brd SAAmi, P VIII, 14, 11

Two incipits from MIESNER/HAMBURG, ex. 48:

[Chorus]

[Aria]

821f. Einführungs Musik (für Pastor Winkler) [SATB chorus, SATB soloists, 3 trumpets, timpani, 2 oboes, 2 violins, viola, continuo]. 1773 (source of date: discussion in item 821). W. 252

Mss.: D-brd B, P 340 (autog., incomplete), P 347 (Michel)

Lit.: BITTER/BRÜDER, I, 265–66

MIESNER/HAMBURG, 87, states that the now lost set of parts he saw in the Singakademie library bore CPEB's notations that this cantata was used also for the Steen and Emke inaugurations, and that its Part II became Part II of the Bracke inauguration cantata. A textbook in D-brd Ha, A 534/7, indicates such reuse for the Steen and Bracke inaugurations, says CLARK.

Incipits from P 347:

Erster Theil

[No. 1] Chor

[No. 2] Duetto [Canto, Tenor]

[No. 3] Recit.

Tenor   Im in-ner-sten er-schütt-er-te die See-le,

[No. 4] Choral

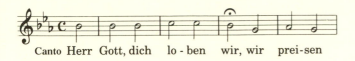

Canto Herr Gott, dich lo-ben wir, wir prei-sen

[No. 5] Accomp.

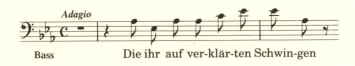

Bass   Die ihr auf ver-klär-ten Schwin-gen

[No. 6] Aria

Bass   Hoch wie Got-tes Wun-der

steht er-bau-et

[No. 7. Recitative]

Alt   Er ruft euch, nicht mit sei-nes Don-ners Stim-me,

[No. 8] Chor

Canto   Heil uns, heil uns, sein Frie-den ist er-

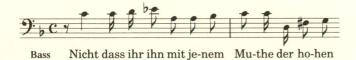

schie-nen

[No. 9] Recit.

Bass   Nicht dass ihr ihn mit je-nem Mu-the der ho-hen

[No. 10] Chor

Canto   O Herr, o Herr, wir die-nen dir

[No. 11] Aria

Tenor   Kei-ne Reu-e

soll den Vor-satz uns

[No. 12] Choral

Canto Herr, dein Ge-bot ist Heil, dein Weg ist

Zweyter Theil [A chorus, "Veni, Sancte Spiritus," is inserted as No. 13; see discussion in item 821.]

[No. 14] Aria

Alto   Der Geist des Herrn

sey mit uns e-wig-lich,

[No. 15. Recitative]

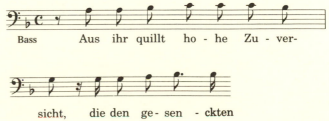

Bass   Aus ihr quillt ho-he Zu-ver-

sicht,   die den ge-sen-ckten

[No. 16] Aria

Canto ... Gott krönt das

En - de der

[No. 17] Accomp.

Basso Du bist es, Theu-rer, dem er sei-ne ver-waiss-te

[No. 18] Coro

Cant. solo Hei - lig,

821g. Einführungs-Music [for Pastor Friderici] [SATB chorus, SATB soloists, 3 trumpets, timpani, 2 flutes, 2 oboes, 2 horns, 2 violins, viola, continuo]. 1775 (source of date: discussion in item 821). W. 251

Ms.: D-brd B, P 347 (Michel)

Lit.: BITTER/BRÜDER, I, 271–72

D-brd B, P 347 (Michel) consists of three inauguration cantatas, labeled only "Einführungsmusik" without further identification. Other sources show that two of these cantatas are items 821f and 821 m. CLARK offers the following evidence that the third, whose incipits are given here, was for the inauguration of Pastor Friderici in 1775: It is one of the four inauguration cantatas by CPEB for which no textbook has been found: 1773 Von Döhren, 1775 Friderici, 1775 Michaelsen, and 1787 Willerding. The surviving incipits from Part II of the 1787 Willerding (see item 821o) have nothing in common with those of part II of item 821g. The instrumentation of item 821g corresponds to that of 1775 Friderici but not to that of either 1773 Von Döhren or 1775 Michaelsen, as these 3 instrumentations are listed in NV, 57.

The text of Part II is virtually identical to the text of the Som inauguration cantata of 1784 (textbook in B Br, 4550 B). The music of No. 13 is borrowed in item 804/5.

Incipits from P 347:

Erster Theil

[No. 1] Chor

Cant. Der Herr le - bet und ge-

lo - bet sey mein Hort

[No. 2. Recitative]

Tenor Von dei-nen Wun-dern rings um-ge-ben, ist un-ser

[No. 3. Aria]

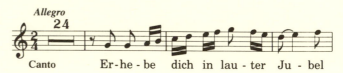

Canto Er-he - be dich in lau - ter Ju - bel

[No. 4. Recitative]

Tenor Al-lein, was wärst du, was wä - re dein

gröss - tes

[No. 5] Aria

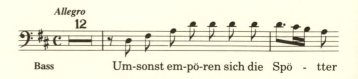

Bass Um-sonst em-pö-ren sich die Spö - tter

[No. 6. Recitative]

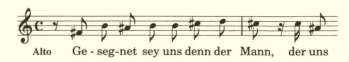

Alto Ge - seg-net sey uns denn der Mann, der uns

[No. 7] Aria

Tenor　Ru - he sanft, ver - klähr - ter

[No. 8. Recitative]

Canto　Dann wol-len wir,　ver-eint mit dir, das Lob des

[No. 9] Choral

Canto　Hei - lig ist un-ser Gott,　hei - lig ist

[No. 10. Recitative]

Bass　Die fro-he Hoff-nung hem-me dei-ne Kla-ge,

[No. 11] Choral

Canto　Es dan - ke Gott und lo - be　dich,

Zweyter Theil [A chorus, "Veni, Sancte Spiritus," is inserted as No. 12; see discussion in item 821.]

[No. 13] Aria

Canto　　Dein Wort, o Herr, ist

[No. 14. Recitative]

Tenor Wer　die-ses hel - le Licht ver - kennt, und

[No. 15] Aria

Bass　　Das Wort des höch-sten

stärkt auch un - ter

[No. 16] Choral

Canto Herr,　un - ser Hort! lass　uns dies Wort;

[No. 17] Recit.

Bass　Lass uns dies Wort — so wün-schet un-sre See-le,

[No. 18] Aria

Alto　　Nun so　tritt mit hei - term Sinn,

[No. 19] Choral

Cant.　Lob, Ehr' und　Preis sey　Gott, dem　Va - ter

[No. 20] Choral

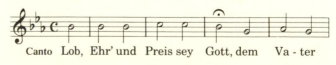

Canto　Lob, Ehr' und　Preis sey　Gott, dem　Va - ter

[A note at the end of the score indicates that No. 1 is repeated after the benediction.]

821h. Herrn Pastors Gerling Einführungsmusik [vocalists, orchestra, including trumpets, timpani, oboes, bassoons]. 1777 (source of date: discussion in item 821)
Now lost

213

MIESNER/HAMBURG, 88, reports having seen the autog. score and parts in the Singakademie library. This cantata, says ibid., was used also for the Lüttkens inauguration; this is corroborated in AUCTION 1805. Textbooks: B Br, Ms. Fétis 4550 B; D-brd B, Mus T 99, 9; Mus Tb 95

Incipits of 3 arias, from MIESNER/HAMBURG, ex. 50:

[Aria]

[Tenor] Wie herr-lich ist dies Wort er - füllt

[Aria]

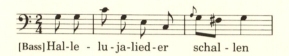

[Bass] Hal-le - lu-ja-lied-er schal - len

[Aria]

[Bass] Ber - ge wei-chen Hü - gel fal - len

821i. Herrn Pastors Sturm Einführungsmusik [vocalists, orchestra, including trumpets, timpani, horns, flutes, oboes]. 1778 (source of date: discussion in item 821)
Now lost
MIESNER/HAMBURG, 85–86, discusses this work on the basis of the score he saw in the Singakademie library; in item 21 of his "Nachträge" he notes that it was used also for the Bracke inauguration. But textbooks for both the Sturm and Bracke inauguration cantatas in B Br, Ms. Fétis 4550 B, indicate that it was used only for Part I of the Bracke inauguration.

Incipits from MIESNER/HAMBURG, ex. 43 (voice ranges not designated):

[No. 1. Chorus]

Neh - met das Wort an mit

[No. 2. Aria]

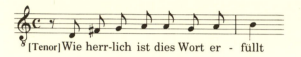

Was dei - ner Bo-ten Zun - ge

[No. 3. Recitative]

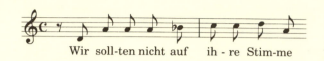

Wir soll-ten nicht auf ih - re Stim-me

[No. 4. Chorale]

Wohl dem, der mit Lust und Freu - de

[No. 5. Recitative]

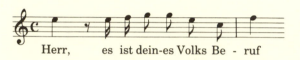

Herr, es ist dein-es Volks Be - ruf

[No. 6. Aria]

Wer wagts, zu dir em - por zu

[No. 7. Recitative]

Ach, oh-ne Ret-tung lä-gen wir

[No. 8. Chorale]

Zi - on, Gott ist nicht dein Rä - cher

[No. 9. Accompanied recitative]

O du, für un-sre Sün-den am

[No. 10. Aria]

Lass auf dei - nen Ruf

[No. 11. Chorale]

Ich bin mein Heil, ver - bun - den

[Part II. A chorus, "Veni, Sancte Spiritus," is inserted as No. 12; see discussion in item 821.]

[No. 13. Recitative]

Ge - hor-chet eu - ren Leh - rern

[No. 14. Aria]

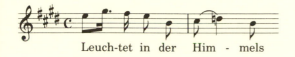

Leuch-tet in der Him - mels

[No. 15. Accompanied recitative]

Sei uns ge-seg-net, sei will-komm-en

[No. 16. Aria]

Da stehst du an des Al - tars

[No. 17. Chorale]

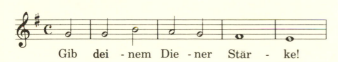

Gib dei - nem Die - ner Stär - ke!

[The textbook indicates that the opening chorus is repeated here.]

821j. Herrn Pastors Rambach Einführungsmusik [vocalists, orchestra, including trumpets, timpani, oboes, bassoons]. 1780 (source of date: discussion in item 821)
Now lost. No report of it in MIESNER/HAMBURG. Textbooks: D-brd Ha, A 767/6; D-brd SAAmi, P VIII, 14, 17. See discussion in item 821 regarding the relation of this cantata to the one performed in 1772 in honor of Pastor Eberwein.

821k. Herrn Pastors Jänisch Einführungsmusik [vocalists, orchestra, including trumpets, timpani, flutes, oboes]. 1782 (source of date: discussion in item 821)
Now lost
MIESNER/HAMBURG, 88, reports having seen the autog. (score?) in the Singakademie library. He notes that this cantata was used also for the Cropp inauguration; this is corroborated in AUCTION 1805 and in the textbook for the Cropp inauguration, B Br, 4550 B.

Incipit of the opening chorus, from MIESNER/HAMBURG, ex. 51:

[Chorus]

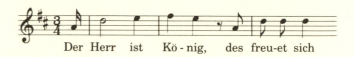

Der Herr ist Kö - nig, des freu-et sich

821l. Zur Einführung des H. P. Gasie [SATB chorus, SATB soloists, 3 trumpets, timpani, 2 oboes, 2 violins, viola, continuo]. 1785 (source of date: discussion in item 821). W. 250
Ms.: D-brd B, P 346 (autog.), including a printed textbook
Lit.: BITTER/BRÜDER, I, 272–73. Other textbooks: B Br, Ms. Fétis 4550 B; D-brd SAAmi, P VIII, 14, 19. Page 112 of RECHNUNGSBUCH, detached from that volume and in F Pn, gives a cost account of this performance.

Incipits from P 346:

Erster Theil

[No. 1] Chor

Gnä-dig und barm-her - zig ist der Herr, Ge - dul - dig

[No. 2.] Recit.

So weit der Him-mel geht, geht sei - ne

[No. 3] Aria

Bass Wenn Men-schen dein ver-ges-sen, O Christ!

[No. 4] Recit.

[Soprano?] Drum sor-get nicht: was wird was klei-den,

[No. 5] Arie

Allegretto
Cant.   O seht,   wie so harm-los der

[No. 6] Recit.

Tenor Blickt auf die Flu-ren hin!   Wie präch - tig

[No. 7] Arie

Andante
Tenor   Ab   ge - härm - ter   Wan - gen

[No. 8] Chor

Mässig
Cant.   Trach - tet am   er - sten
nach dem   Rei   che

[No. 9] Accomp.

Langsam
Bass   Lag-ert sich um dei-ne Pfa-de grau - en-vol-les

[No. 10] Choral

Ich   will mit   dein - em   Will   -   en

Zweyter Theil [A chorus, "Veni, Sancte Spiritus," is inserted as No. 11; see discussion in item 821.]

[No. 12] Recit.

Etwas langsam
Bass   Liebst du mich?   Liebst du mich? — wei-de mei-ne

[No. 13] Arioso

Larghetto
Tenor   Herr,   du wei-ssest al - le   Din-ge,

[No. 14] Recit.

Tenor   Freu dich des Herrn,   der dir den neu-en Hir-ten

[No. 15] Accomp.

Langsam
Bass   Hier   ru - het er dem Gar-ben-tag ent-ge-gen,

[No. 16] Arioso

Langsam
Alt   Da geht er schon   zur heil - gen Stä-te,

[No. 17] Schlusschoral

Cant.   Dir,   Gott, Me - ssi -as,   sin - gen   wir

[The textbooks indicate that No. 8 is repeated here.]

821m. Herrn Pastors Schäffer Einführungsmusik [SATB chorus, SATB soloists, 3 trumpets, timpani, 2 oboes, 2 violins, viola, continuo]. 1785 (source of date: discussion in item 821). W. 253

Ms.: D-brd B, P 347 (Michel)
Lit.: BITTER/BRÜDER, I, 266–70
In P 347 the work is entitled merely "Einführungsmusik";
but MIESNER/HAMBURG, 83, says that the now lost
Singakademie library ms. identified it as the inauguration
music for Schäffer. This is confirmed by textbooks in B
Br, Ms. Fétis 4550 B; D-brd SAAmi, P VIII, 14, 20. See
item 814.

Incipits from P 347:

Erster Theil

[No. 1] Chor

[No. 2] Recit.

[No. 3] Arie

[No. 4] Recit.

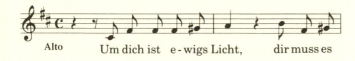

[No. 5] Chor

[No. 6] Recit.

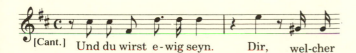

[No. 7] Arie

[No. 8] Choral

[No. 9] Recit.

[No. 10] Arie

[No. 11] Choral

Zweyter Theil [A chorus, "Veni, Sancte Spiritus," is inserted as No. 12; see discussion in item 821.]

[No. 13] Accomp.

[No. 14] Arie

217

[No. 15] Accomp.

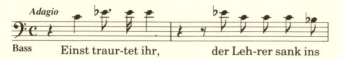

Bass   Einst trau-tet ihr,   der Leh-rer sank ins

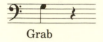

Grab

[No. 16] Arie

Tenor   Zei-ge dich, der Heer-de blick-en,

[No. 17] Schluss Choral

Canto Gott, der du dei-nes Volcks ge-den-ckest,

[The textbooks indicate a repeat of No. 1 here.]

821n. Herrn Pastors Berkhahn Einführungsmusik [vocalists, orchestra, including trumpets, timpani, flutes, oboes]. 1787 (source of date: discussion in item 821)
Now lost
MIESNER/HAMBURG, 88, reports having seen the autog. score of Part I and the parts for Part II in the Singakademie library. Textbooks: B Br, Ms. Fétis 4550 B; D-brd B, Mus T 99, 6; D-brd SAami, P VIII, 14, 21

Incipits of the accompanied recitative that begins this work (voice range undesignated) and of the aria that begins Part II, from MIESNER/HAMBURG, ex. 53:

[No. 1. Accompanied recitative]

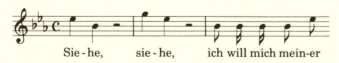

Sie-he,   sie-he,   ich will mich mein-er

[Aria]

Sei ge-grüsst an dem Al-ta-re

[Tenor]

821o. Herrn Pastors Willerding Einführungsmusik [vocalists, orchestra, including trumpets, timpani, flutes, oboes, bassoons]. 1787 (source of date: discussion in item 821)
Now lost

218

MIESNER/HAMBURG, 86, 88, reports having seen the autog. score in the Singakademie library; he says that a chorale replaced the customary "Veni" (see discussion in item 821) at the beginning of Part II.

Incipits of the accompanied recitative that begins the work, and of 2 mvts. of Part II, from MIESNER/HAMBURG, ex. 54:

[No. 1. Accompanied recitative]

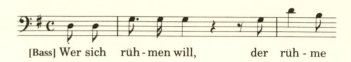

[Bass] Wer sich rüh-men will,   der rüh-me

[Chorale]

[Soprano] Mit Ehr-furcht wer-fen wir uns nie-der

[Arioso]

[Bass] Wer mich hö-ret, der hö-ret

Other Congratulatory Cantatas, Part A

822a. Oratorium zur Feier des Ehrenmahls der Herrn Bürger-Capitains [captain of the local militia] in Hamburg [SATB chorus, SSAATTBB soloists, 2 trumpets, timpani, 2 horns, 2 flutes, 2 oboes, bassoon, 2 violins, 2 violas, continuo] (C. W. Alers). 1780 (NV 56)

Ms.: A Wgm, H 23559 (III 8678) (Michel, bearing the pencil marking "Aus Westphals Bibl.!" on the cover)
Lit.: RECHNUNGSBUCH, Sept. 1780; HAMBURGER CORRESPONDENT, 13 Oct. 1780; MIESNER/HAMBURG, 102–09; CLARK/CHORAL, 191–94

See item 823. Textbook: D-brd Hs, A/70014, 2

Incipits from H 23559 (III 8678):

[No. 1] Chor

Diskant   Hebt an ihr

Chö-re der Freu-den

[No. 2] Recit.

Hammona
Heil mir! Ich hö-re mei-ner Söh-ne

[No. 3] Aria

Hammona
Du Schöp-fer mei - ner

[No. 4] Recit. [and chorus]

Die Dankbarkeit Ich seg-ne dich, Ham-mon-a!

[No. 5] Aria

Allegro
Die Dankbarkeit
Ent-fleuch, ent-fleuch in dein-es Ab-grunds

[No. 6] Recit.

Der Patriotismus
Nein, nein, Ham-mo-na! zwei-fle nicht;

[No. 7] Aria

Allegro
Der Patriotismus
Wir soll - ten, kalt und hoch

[No. 8] Choral

Diskant Sollt ich mein-em Gott nicht sin-gen?

[No. 9] Recit.

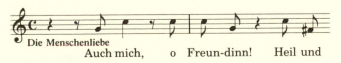

Die Menschenliebe
Auch mich, o Freun-dinn! Heil und

[No. 10] Chor

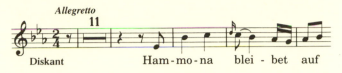

Allegretto
Diskant Ham-mo-na blei - bet auf

[No. 11] Recit.

Die Menschenliebe
Ich seh's, du liebst mich noch, und eh-rest

[No. 12] Arioso

Etwas langsam
Singstimme
Hör - e von der wäl - le höhn

[No. 13] Recit.

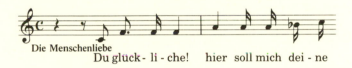

Die Menschenliebe
Du glück- li-che! hier soll mich dei - ne

[No. 14] Duetto [Hammona-Die Menschenliebe]

Etwas langsam
Hammona
Zur trüm-mer-te Städ-te wer

[No. 15] Recit.

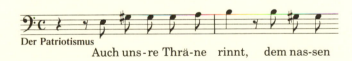

Der Patriotismus
Auch uns-re Thrä-ne rinnt, dem nas-sen

[No. 16] Choral

Diskant Du Gott der Stär-ke! Ham-burgs Gott

822b. Serenata zu demselben Endzweck [i.e., another cere-
mony honoring the Bürger-Capitain] [SATB chorus, SATB
soloists, trumpet, timpani, drum, fife, 2 flutes, 2 violins,
viola, continuo] (C. W. Alers). 1780 (NV 56)

Ms.: A Wgm, H 27769 (III 29337) (Michel, bearing the pencil
  marking "Aus Westphals Bibl.!" on the cover)
Lit.: RECHNUNGSBUCH, Sept. 1780; MIESNER/HAM-
  BURG, 102–09; CLARK/CHORAL, 191–94
Textbook: D-brd Ha, A 534/227

Incipits from H 27769 (III 29337):

[No. 1] Chor

[No. 2] Recit.

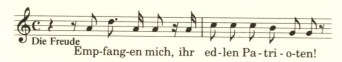

[No. 3] Terzett [Diskant, Tenor, Bass]

[No. 4] Recit.

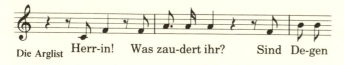

[No. 5] Arioso, ma poco presto

[No. 6] Recit.

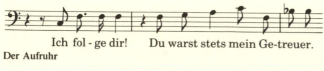

[No. 7] Aria

[No. 8] Recit.

[No. 9] Chor

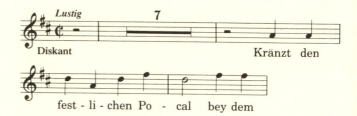

822c. Oratorium zu demselben Endzweck [see item 822b]
[vocalists, orchestra, including trumpets, timpani, flute,
oboes, bassoon] (C. W. Alers). 1783 (NV 56)
Lost
Lit.: MIESNER/HAMBURG, 102–09; CLARK/CHORAL,
  191–94
Textbooks: D-brd Hs, Scrin 37 and A/70014, 3

822d. Serenata zu demselben Endzweck [see item 822b]
[SATB chorus, ATBB soloists, 2 trumpets, timpani, drum,
fife, 2 oboes, bassoon, 2 violins, viola, continuo] (C. W.
Alers). 1783 (NV 56)
Ms.: D-brd Hs, Scrin 37 (Michel), including printed text.
  Another textbook is in D-brd Hs, A/70014,3.
Lit.: MIESNER/HAMBURG, 102–09; CLARK/CHORAL,
  191–94

Incipits from Scrin 37:

[No. 1] Chor

[No. 2. Recitative]

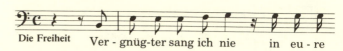

[No. 3] Arioso

[Die Freiheit]
Strömt dan-kend hin zu Jo-sephs

[No. 4] Recit.

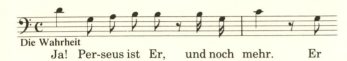

Die Wahrheit
Ja! Per-seus ist Er, und noch mehr. Er

[No. 5] Duetto. Die Freiheit und die Wahrheit

Die Wahrheit
Ge - rächt ist un - sers Na - mens

[No. 6] Recit.

Der Nachruhm
Ihr seid ge-rächt, und seid es werth, zu seyn

[No. 7] Arioso

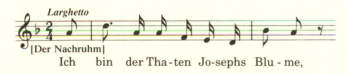

[Der Nachruhm]
Ich bin der Tha-ten Jo-sephs Blu - me,

[No. 8] Accomp.

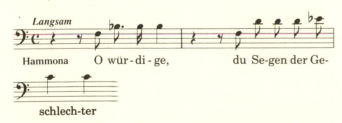

Hammona O wür-di-ge, du Se-gen der Ge-

schlech-ter

[No. 9] Chor

Cant.
Lasst uns sing-en: Jo-seph

le - be! Ham-burgs

823. Musik am Dankfeste wegen des fertigen Michaelis-Thurms [celebrating the completion of the tower of St. Michael's Church in Hamburg] [vocalists, orchestra, including trumpets, timpani, oboes, bassoon] (J. L. Gericke, according to the textbook). 1786 [source of date: see below]. NV 57

Lost

RECHNUNGSBUCH contains an account of expenses for a "Feyerlichkeit" at St. Michael's in Oct. 1786, probably referring to this occasion; this account is printed in MIESNER/HAMBURG, 128. Other lit.: HAMBURGER CORRESPONDENT, 8 Mar. 1780

Lit.: CLARK/CHORAL, 186–88

Miesner, who presumably saw a ms. of this cantata in the Singakademie library, notes (MIESNER/HAMBURG, 92) that it borrowed from items 778, 822a, and 824e; the incipit of the latter borrowing, a parody, is the 2nd shown here. The 1st 3 incipits are quoted from MIESNER/HAMBURG, ex. 57. MIESNER/HAMBURG, 92ff., also quotes, in full, an accompanied recitative depicting thunder and lightning (4th incipit shown here). Textbook: D-brd Ha, A 640/71

[No. 1. Chorus]

[Soprano] Ver - sam - melt euch dem Herrn zu

[Chorus]

Sie - he da! sie - he

[Aria]

Er - de, hö - re! Him - mel, hö - ret

[Accompanied recitative]

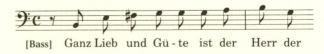

[Bass] Ganz Lieb und Gü - te ist der Herr der

Other Congratulatory Cantatas, Part B

824a. Cantate auf die Vermählung des Hen. von G. und der Fräul. von H. [vocalists, orchestra]. 1763 (source of date: see below). NV 56

Apparently lost. According to MIESNER/HAMBURG, 53, 90, a ms. of this work existed in USSR KA; but regarding this library, see item 192. Miesner says that the date comes from the ms. and that a note by E. F. Schmid attached to the ms. identifies "Hen. von G." as Ewald von Grotthus (see item 272).

Called "Trauungs-Cantate" in NV, 56
Lit.: CLARK/CHORAL, 189–90
The movement corresponding to the 3rd incipit was parodied in No. 6 of item 807. See item 777/7.

Some incipits from MIESNER/HAMBURG, ex. 55:

[Aria]

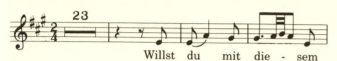

Willst du mit die - sem

[Aria]

So tre - tet her-bei, ver-

lo - be - te

[Aria]

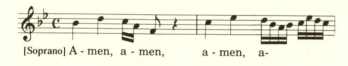

[Soprano] A - men, a - men, a - men, a-

[Arioso]

Ge - trost, der Gott, der Gott, der uns

[Aria]

Lob, Preis und Eh - re

824b. Geburtstags-Cantate [vocalists, orchestra, including trumpets, timpani, flutes]. 1769 (NV 56)
Lost. See item 824f.
Lit.: MIESNER/HAMBURG, 91; CLARK/CHORAL, 189

824c. Herrn Dr. Hoeck Jubelmusik [vocalists, orchestra, including trumpets, timpani, oboes]. 1775 (NV 58)
Lost

Lit.: CLARK/CHORAL, 188–89
AUCTION 1805 and textbook comparison show that Part I was also used for the Som inauguration in 1784 (see textbook: D-brd Hs, A/70016, 27).

824d. Herrn Syndicus Klefeker Jubelmusik [vocalists, orchestra, including trumpets, timpani, horns, oboes]. 1775 (NV 59)
Lost
Textbook: D-brd Hs, A/70016, 29
Lit.: HAMBURGER CORRESPONDENT, 1775, Nr. 108; CLARK/CHORAL, 188–89
Not related to item 821b

824e. Dank-Hymne der Freundschaft, ein Geburtstags-Stück [vocalists, orchestra, including trumpets, timpani, flutes, oboes, horns, bassoon]. 1785 (NV 57)
Now lost
Lit.: CLARK/CHORAL, 189–90
From MIESNER/HAMBURG, 91: He saw Part I only, in autog., in the Singakademie library. A chorale is arr. from (no. 16 of?) item 822a. Item 778 also makes up part of this work.
See item 823.

Incipits from MIESNER/HAMBURG, ex. 56:

[Chorus]

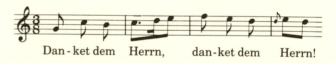

Dan - ket dem Herrn, dan-ket dem Herrn!

[Aria]

Wie soll dir Erd und A - sche

[Aria]

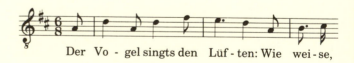

Der Vo - gel singts den Lüf - ten: Wie wei - se,

[Aria]

O Va-ter, bei dies - en Ge - dan - ken

[Chorus]

Lo- bet den Herrn in sein- em Heil- ig- tum

824f. Jubelmusik auf den Geburtstag der Madame Stresow [performance medium unknown]. n.d.
Lost
Lit.: CLARK/CHORAL, 191
Listed in AUCTION 1805 and mentioned without source attribution in the "Nachträge" of MIESNER/HAMBURG. It may be the same work as item 824b, notes CLARK, since both NV and AUCTION 1805 list only one birthday cantata.

Individual Choruses

Note: Even where the relations have not been traceable, many of these are no doubt portions of the incomplete choral works already listed.

825. Motetto. Veni sancte spiritus [S, S, B, continuo]. After 1767 (source of date: composed in Hamburg, says NV, 63). W. 207
Ms.: B Bc, 85 (Michel)
Lit.: MIESNER/HAMBURG, 81
See item 855.

Incipit from 85:

Soprano I Ve - ni, ve - ni san - cte spi-ri-tus

826. 4 Mottetten von 3 Gellertschen Liedern und 1 Stürmschen Liede [SAB, SATB, SA, SATB, respectively, all with continuo]. Nos. 1–3 after 1767 (source of date: composed in Hamburg, says NV, 63–64); No. 4, 1781 or later (source of date: pub. date of item 753). W. 208
Mss.: D-brd B, P 349 (autog.), P 781 (No. 3 only; Michel), St 188 (Michel, some CPEB); B Bc, 725 (Michel)
Early print: No. 3 pub. by N. Simrock, Bonn, c. 1823. The known lit. gives no evidence that such a (posthumous) print had been authorized by CPEB.
Lit.: BITTER/BRÜDER, I, 300
Nos. 1–3 are arr. of item 686, Nos. 30, 53, and 9, respectively; No. 4, an arr. of item 752/3, was used in item 799. See also item 357.

Incipits from 725:

[No. 1] Trost der Erlösung

Cant.
Ge-dan-ke, der uns Le - ben

[No. 2] Der Kampf der Tugend

Cant. Oft klagt dein Herz wie schwer es sey

[No. 3] Bitten

Cant. Gott, dei - ne Gü - te reicht so weit

[No. 4] Menschenliebe Jesu

Cant. Dich bet ich an, Herr Je - su Christ,

827. Einchöriges Heilig [SATBB chorus, 3 trumpets, timpani, 2 oboes, 2 violins, viola, continuo]. CPEB's introduction composed after 1767 (source of date: the introduction was composed in Hamburg, says NV, 62). W. 218
Mss.: D-brd B, P 3 (autog.), St 185 (wrapper marked by CPEB?); B Bc, 730 (missing)
Lit.: MIESNER/HAMBURG, 98; GEIRINGER/BACH, 373
An arrangement of the chorus "Sicut locutus est" from J. S. Bach's *Magnificat* (BWV 243), with the addition of a 15-bar introduction by CPEB

Incipit from P 3:

Cantus Hei - lig, Hei - lig

828. Sanctus [SATB chorus, 3 trumpets, timpani, 2 oboes, 2 violins, viola, continuo]. After 1767 (source of date: composed in Hamburg, says NV, 63). W. 219
Ms.: B Bc, 87 (modern copy)
Lit.: MIESNER/HAMBURG, 98

Incipit from 87:

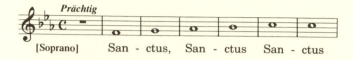

Incipit from P 340:

829. Spiega, ammonia fortunata [SSTB chorus, 3 trumpets, timpani, 2 horns, 2 flutes, 2 oboes, 2 violins, viola, continuo]. 1770 (NV 56). W. 216
Ms.: B Bc, 3708 (Westphal)
For the 1770 visit of the Swedish crown prince to Hamburg
Lit.: OTTENBERG, 151–52

Incipit from 3708:

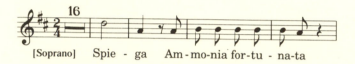

830. Mein Heiland, meine Zuversicht [SATB chorus, 2 oboes, 2 violins, viola, continuo]. 1771 (NV 62). W. 221
Mss.: D-brd B, P 349 (Michel), P 431; B Bc, 719 a (Michel)
Lit.: WADE, 127; CLARK/CHORAL, 180–81
Arr. of item 696/12
MIESNER/HAMBURG, 79, reports seeing a now lost fragment of text in the Singakademie library in which this chorus is identified as the introduction to a "Sonntagsmusik" for the 10th Sunday after Trinity, which may be "Herr, deine Augen sehen nach dem Glauben," the same cantata listed in NV, 65, as being partly composed by J. S. Bach (possibly BWV 102, according to SCHULZE, 491). A fragment of a JSB cantata of this title is in D-ddr Bds, St 41, notes CLARK/CHORAL; the cover indicates performances in 1776, 1777, 1781, and 1786 and bears the note in CPEB's daughter's hand, "Von J. S. B. u. 1 Chor von C. P. E. B."

Incipit from P 349:

831. Der 8. Psalm. Wer ist so würdig als du [SATB chorus, 3 trumpets, timpani, 2 oboes, 2 violins, viola, continuo]. 1774 (NV 62). W. 222
Mss.: D-brd B, P 340 (autog., including printed text), P 928, St 189 (partly Michel?, marked by CPEB); B Bc, 719 c (Michel); D-ddr Dlb, 3029/D/8
Lit.: BITTER/BRÜDER, I, 298–300
Arr. of item 733/4. Used in item 805. See item 834.

832. Zeige du mir deine Wege [SATB chorus, 2 violins, viola, continuo]. 1777 (NV 62). W. 223
Ms.: B Bc, 719 b (Michel)
Arr. of item 733/9, verse 3. Probably part of a 1777 "Sonntagsmusik" for the 8th Sunday after Trinity, says MIESNER/HAMBURG, 80.
See item 794.

Incipit from 719 b:

833. Gott, dem ich lebe [SATB chorus, 3 trumpets, timpani, 2 oboes, 2 bassoons, 2 violins, viola, continuo]. 1780 (NV 63). W. 225
Mss.: B Bc, 719 e (Michel, containing instructions for a different arr.); A Wgm, Q 2388 (V 14330) (2 trumpets rather than 3)
Arr. of item 749/9. Attached to item 856 in a 1781 performance of funeral music, according to MIESNER/HAMBURG, 100
The 719 e copy is strophic like its model, with all strophes chosen for arr. (4, in this case) set to the same music, while in Q 2388 (V 14330) (same copyist as for Q 2391 [V 14347] in item 836) all 4 strophes are written out, each with different orchestration. Since the latter plan was more usual in such arr. by CPEB, Q 2388 (V 14330) might seem to be the more reliable source; yet 719 e is a ms. of much more familiar provenance.

Incipit from 719 e:

834. Amen, amen, Lob und Preis [SATB chorus, 3 trumpets, timpani, 2 oboes, 2 violins, viola, continuo]. 1783 (NV 63). W. 226
Mss.: D-brd B, P 340 (autog., including printed text), St 190 (Michel, marked by CPEB); B Bc, 719 f (Michel)
Arr. of item 749/4.

Part of a "Sonntagsmusik" for Quasimodogeniti, 1783, says BITTER/BRÜDER, I, 298, no doubt because the printed texts of items 831 and 834 in P 340 are part of a "Text zur Musik am Sonntage Quasimodogeniti, 1783 . . . "

Incipit from P 340:

835. Leite mich nach deinem Willen [SATB chorus, 2 horns, 2 oboes, 2 violins, viola, continuo]. 1783 (NV 63). W. 227
Mss.: D-brd B, St 180 (mostly Michel and CPEB); D-ddr Bds, Am.B. 89 (marked by CPEB); B Bc, 719 g (Michel); US Wc, M2020.B14L3. The handwritten card catalogue of mss. in D-ddr Bds lists a ms. in Pölchau's hand whose call no. is "T"; this ms. cannot be located at present.
Early print: the above title, ed. G. Pölchau, Wien: Steiner, [1820, according to PÖLCHAU]
Ms. probably copied from the early print: A Wgm, V 14331(?)
Lit.: CPEB/5 MAR. 1783; VRIESLANDER/BACH, 129
Conceived as an independent work, yet undoubtedly part of a larger work as well, as is shown by the indications "recit. tacet" and "Choral" in CPEB's hand in the set of parts comprising St 180

Incipit from 719 g:

836. Meine Lebenszeit verstreicht [SATB chorus, 3 trumpets, timpani, 2 oboes, 2 violins, viola, continuo]. 1783 (NV 63). W. 228
Mss.: D-brd B, P 340 (Michel); B Bc, 719 h (Michel); A Wgm, Q 2391 (V 14347) (2 trumpets rather than 3)
Lit.: BITTER/BRÜDER, I, 299
Arr. of item 686/37. Part of the funeral music for Bürgermeister Scheele in 1783, according to MIESNER/HAMBURG, 101; the printed text accompanying P 340 shows that this movement fits between two chorales in a larger work.
The P 340 arr. is strophic like the song on which it is modeled, with both strophes chosen for arr. set to the same music, whereas in Q 2391 (V 14347) (same copyist as for Q 2388 [V 14330] in item 833), both strophes are written out, each with different orchestration. For the reason pointed out in item 833, Q 2391 (V 14347) might seem the more reliable source; but the P 340 source was copied by Michel himself.

Incipit from P 340:

837. Meinen Leib wird man begraben [SATB chorus, 3 trumpets, timpani, 2 violins, viola, continuo]. 1788 or earlier (sources of date: NV 63 and MIESNER/HAMBURG [see below]). W. 229
Ms.: B Bc, 719 i (Michel)
The complete text of this work is among those in the collection of printed texts in B Br, Fétis 4550 B.
Part of the funeral music for Bürgermeister Luis in 1788, according to MIESNER/HAMBURG, 101

Incipit from 719 i:

838. Merckt und Seht [SATB chorus, 2 trumpets, 2 oboes, 2 violins, viola, continuo]. n.d. Wq n.v. 1
Ms.: D-brd B, P 896 (autog., incomplete)
A partly indecipherable note added in an unfamiliar hand connects it with a "Bachischen Passion nach dem Lucas."

Incipit from P 896:

839. Antiphona für 4 Singstimmen. N.d. W. 209; NV, 64
Lost

Incipit from WOTQUENNE/THÉMATIQUE:

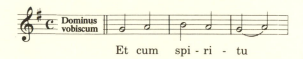

840. Amen für 4 Singstimmen. N.d. W. 210; NV, 64
Lost

Incipit from WOTQUENNE/THÉMATIQUE:

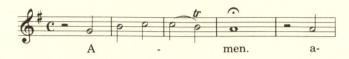

A - men. a-

841. Wirf dein anliegen auf. N.d. NV, 65
Lost

An anonymous motet arr. by CPEB. MIESNER/HAMBURG,
81, says that D-ddr SWl (Sign. 26) and D-brd B (D-ddr
Bds?) both have an anonymous motet of this title but that
neither ms. bears a reference to CPEB.

No incipit available

Chorale Settings

(Note: See also "chorale" in the Index of Genres.)

842. 10 Choräle zur Liedern des Grafen von Wernigerode
[SATB]. 1767 or earlier (source of date: 1st pub.). W., foot-
note on p. 96; NV, 64
Mss.: D-brd B, P 1130 (autog., Nos. 9 and 10 only; No. 9 is
a vnt. with partial text, No. 10 has partial text); PL Wru,
Va 1 bb (autog., without title)
Early print (vnts., without attribution to the composer):
MELODIEN (presently inaccessible for page citations).
Lit. about MELODIEN: See this entry in Bib.
Lit. about this work: BUSCH, 78–85, Anh. 56
See item 820 for its connections with items 190, 693, 842/9,
10.

Incipits from Va 1 bb:

[No. 1]

[Soprano]Be - freyt von Schuld und Sor - gen, er - blick ich

[No. 2]

[Soprano]Den-noch bleib ich stets an dir, ob-gleich

[No. 3]

[Soprano] Die All-macht siegt, wann sie die Lie-be

[No. 4]

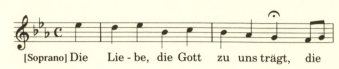

[Soprano] Die Lie - be, die Gott zu uns trägt, die

[No. 5]

[Soprano] Die Zeit geht hin, mein ar - mer Geist und Sinn

[No. 6]

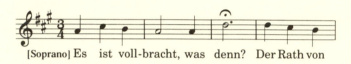

[Soprano] Es ist voll-bracht, was denn? Der Rath von

[No. 7]

[Soprano]
Dem e - wig wah - ren Glü - cke das
Fleisch und Blut nicht

[No. 8]

[Soprano Des Glau-bens Geist steht un - be - we-get,

[No. 9]

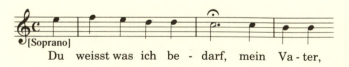

[Soprano]
Du weisst was ich be - darf, mein Va - ter,

[No. 10]

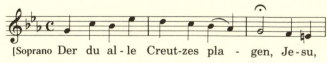

[Soprano Der du al - le Creut-zes pla - gen, Je-su,

843. Naglet til et Kors paa Jorden [unison chorus, keyboard] (B. G. Sporon). 1781 or earlier (source of date: 1st pub.)
Early print: SCHIØRRING, No. 71 b. Lit. about SCHIØR-RING: See this entry in Bib.
Lit. about this work: BUSCH, 154–76, 222, 299, 384–85, Anh. 32–33; OTTENBERG, 217
Identified as vnt. of item 733/19 by BUSCH, 154–59, 222, and printed by her (first strophe only), Anh., ex. 3a

Incipit from BUSCH:

[Soprano] Nag - let til et Kors paa jor - den,

844. [3 Chorales for S, continuo] (J. A. Cramer, Klopstock, anon., respectively). 1785 or earlier (source of date: 1st pub.)
Early print: ZINCK, nos. 52, 76, 113. Lit. about ZINCK: See this entry in Bib.
Identified as CPEB's by BUSCH, 151–74, and printed there (1st strophe only in each case), Anh., ex. 3a, with the warning that Zinck might have made editorial changes in the chorales that CPEB submitted to him.

Incipits from BUSCH:

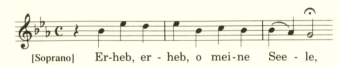

[Soprano] Er-heb, er - heb, o mei-ne See - le,

[Soprano] Des E - wig-en und der Ster-bli-chen Sohn,

[Soprano] Von gan-zem Her-zen rüh-men wir,

845. [4-Part chorale]. 1786 or earlier (source of date: 1st pub.)
Early print(?): KÜHNAU I
According to BUSCH, 176–77, Anh. 38–39, CPEB was apparently the anonymous composer of one of the chorales in KÜHNAU I; the specific chorale cannot be identified.

846. Deleted

Other Individual Movements
of Choral Works; Fragments

847. [Trumpet and timpani parts added to C. H. Graun's *Te Deum*]. 1756 or later (source of date: Graun finished the *Te Deum* in 1756). NV, 66
Ms.: D-brd B, Mus. ms. 8170/5 (autog. score, owned by Pölchau)

Title on the cover in CPEB's hand: "3 Trompeten und Pauken zum Graunischen Te Deum."

Incipit of 1st trumpet part, 1st mvt.:

[1st trumpet]

848. [Instrumental introduction to the "Credo" of J. S. Bach's *B Minor Mass*, BWV 232]. c. 1786 (source of date: a notice in HAMBURGER CORRESPONDENT, 1 Apr. 1786). NV, 66
Mss.: D-brd B, P 22 (Michel), St 118
The printed program accompanying P 22, undated, shows that the introduction (properly identified) and Credo were parts of a "Konzert für das medizinische Armeninstitut" in Hamburg, also including parts of Handel's *Messiah* and a "Sinfonie" by CPEB, along with items 772 and 778.

Incipit from P 22:

Einleitung zum Credo

Viol. 1

849. Deleted

850. [2 Recitatives]. n.d. NV, 89
Lost
One recitative by CPEB in each of 2 cantatas by C. F. C. Fasch for the 2nd Sunday after Epiphany and the 16th Sunday after Trinity

851–53. Deleted

854. [Various accompanied recitatives, chorales, etc. added to church works of other composers]. NV, 66, 82, 89
Almost entirely lost. A "Feria 1 Nativ. Christi [added to title in CPEB's hand:] von H. Capellmeister [K. H.] Graun," Mus. ms. 8182 in D-brd B, contains, in addition to the usual emendations in CPEB's hand (see pp. xxi–xxii), a recitative in CPEB's hand that resets Graun's recitative "O süsses Blick, o angenehmstes Glück!" plus a substitute chorale in CPEB's hand, "Jesu kommt uns, lasst uns laufen." Mus. ms. 7918 in D-brd B, a "Festo Johannis Baptiste Concerto" attributed to J. G. Goldberg, contains, in CPEB's hand, a textless recitative (partially crossed out) and a setting of a chorale, "Johannes ging vor Jesu her." Other such changes made in his personal and family collection of church music, in order to satisfy the demands of his Hamburg position, will no doubt appear in the future.

A *Michaelis Quartalstück 78/84* for chorus, vocal soloists, and orchestra, c. 1778 (source of date: dated title p. in CPEB's hand), ms. in D-brd B, St 266, is composed jointly with J. C. F. Bach.

Lit. on the *Michaelis Quartalstück 78/84:* MIESNER/HAMBURG, 81; GEIRINGER/BACH, 402; CLARK/CHORAL, 184–86

Title p. of the *Michaelis Quartalstück 78/84:* " . . . von J.C.F.B.C.P.E. Das Bass-accomp. von C.P.E.B." CPEB's only part of it is the "Bass-accomp.," along with the verbal indication that a "Heilig," probably item 778, is to be appended.

GEIRINGER/BACH, 402, suggests that item 827, a much less important "Heilig," was the work appended; but since item 778 is the all-purpose addition in so many other works, and since item 827 is not all by CPEB, it seems more logical that item 778 was the one meant here. GEIRINGER/BACH confuses item 813 with W. 246 (item 814).

Incipit from St 266:

[Accompanied recitative]

[Bass]   Was seh' ich dort?   Wie schreckt

Doubtful

855. [Chorus,] Veni, sancte spiritus a 2 violini, violetta, violoncello, 2 oboi, 2 corni, con 3 trombe e timpani ad libitum; canto, alto, tenore, basso ed organo. 1760 (source of date: MIESNER/HAMBURG). W. 220
Now lost

By Telemann, according to MIESNER/HAMBURG, 85–86; but see discussion in item 821. Possibly one of the two "Veni" settings listed on p. 63 of NV as having been composed by CPEB. The other is item 825.

Incipit from WOTQUENNE/THÉMATIQUE:

Ve - ni   sanc - te   Spi - ri - tus

856. [Motet,] Selig sind die Todten [SATB chorus, 3 trombones, 2 horns, 2 oboes, 2 violins, viola, continuo]. Probably before 1781 (source of date: MIESNER/HAMBURG, and CPEB's 1781 use of the work)
Ms.: A Wn, Suppl. Mus. 22883 (modern copy)
Probably by Telemann

Apparently different, after the opening chorus, from a now lost ms. of the same title formerly in the Singakademie library; see MIESNER/HAMBURG, 98–101. According to MIESNER/HAMBURG, CPEB used it for the funeral music of Bürgermeister Rumpf in 1781, augmenting it on this occasion with item 833.

Incipit of the opening chorus from Suppl. Mus. 22883:

Vln. 1

857. [Choral fragment,] Ecce cui iniquitatibus. n.d. Wq n.v. 5
Ms.: D-brd B, P 349

Although P 349 was owned by Pölchau and is largely in the hands of CPEB and Michel, this fragment and item 858 seem to have been added to its blank staves by an amateur after the completion of the ms.

Incipit from P 349:

[Soprano] Ec - ce   cui   in   i - ni-qui-ta-ti - bus

858. [Choral fragment,] Miserere mei. n.d. Wq n.v. 6
Ms.: D-brd B, P 349
See item 857.

Incipit from P 349:

[Soprano]   Mi - se - re - re   me - i

859. Aria, Sey mir gesegnet [S, violino principale, violino primo, viola]. n.d. Wq n.v. 22
Ms.: D-ddr Bds, St 548

On the cover in a hand different from that of the copyist: "C. P. E. Bach (?)." On an added sheet inside the cover (in the same hand?): "C. P. E. Bach. Autograph." The shaky handwriting (the same as that for a few authentic CPEB works, according to KAST) is probably the reason why this ms. was identified as an autog.; but the hand is not CPEB's.

Incipit from St 548:

[Soprano]   Sey mir ge-

seg - net,   du die   Woh-nung

Spurious

860. [4-Voice chorale] Hilf dass ich Folge. c. 1725 (source of date: date of the J. S. Bach work). Wq n.v. 16
Ms.: D-brd B, P 349 (autog.)
Lit.: MIESNER/HAMBURG, 110
Transposition, with new text, of the J. S. Bach chorale "Was mein Gott will, gescheh allzeit" from *Cantata 144* (BWV 144)

Incipit from P 349:

861. Missa [SATB chorus, 2 trumpets, timpani, 2 trombones, 2 horns, 2 oboes, 2 violins, viola, continuo]. n.d.
Ms.: A Wgm, I 7445
Of unusual provenance, unmentioned in any primary source, stylistically unlike CPEB, considered dubious in MIESNER/HAMBURG (111–13) and a forgery in SCHMID/MGG (col. 934)
Among the masses in score format listed in NV, 87 as by other composers are 14 scores by Bernhardi, Schmidt, Zelenka, Hasse, Wilderer, Bassani, and G. Benda; perhaps one of these was the composer.

Incipit of the 1st mvt. from I 7445:

862. Die Pilgrime auf Golgatha . . . Oratorium [SATB chorus, vocal soloists, 2 horns, 2 flutes, 2 oboes, 2 violins, viola, continuo] (F. W. Zachariae). n.d.
Ms.: D-brd Mbs, Mus. ms. 1568
Of unusual provenance, stylistically unlike CPEB, unmentioned in any work dealing with CPEB. Not the same text as that of J. C. F. Bach's lost oratorio *Die Fremdling auf Golgotha* of 1776, text by Herder. The score was purchased at auction by D-brd Mbs in 1865 among a group of works by Telemann; perhaps he is the composer.

Incipit of the 1st mvt. from Mus. ms. 1568:

[No. 1] Recitat. Der erste Pilgrim

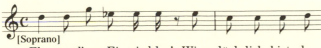

863. Passions-Cantate [St. Mark Passion] [SATB chorus, vocal soloists, 2 horns, 2 oboes, 2 violins, viola, continuo]. n.d.
Ms.: D-brd KNu, 5 P 208 (incorrectly catalogued in D-brd KNu and in PRIEGER as a St. Matthew Passion)
Not related to BWV 198. The ms. is dated 1753. Formerly in the collection of Erich Prieger (see PRIEGER, p. 20), it is of somewhat unusual provenance, stylistically unlike CPEB, unmentioned in any primary source. By Telemann?

Incipit of the 1st mvt. from 5 P 208:

[No. 1. Aria]

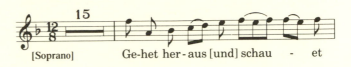

864. [Cantata,] [chorus, vocal soloists, orchestra?], Esto mihi. n.d.
Incorrectly attributed to CPEB in EITNER. MIESNER/HAMBURG, 53, reports that he saw a ms. (in USSR KA?) whose first page identifies the composer as Johann Ernst Bach (1722–77), though the wrapper attributes the work to CPEB.

Incipit not available

865. Motetta [SATB chorus]. Kommt, lasst uns anbeten. n.d.
Mss.: PL Wu, 6997; US WS, Herbst Collection, A219; US BETm, 85.2
Early print, with text translated into English: C. I. Latrobe, ed. and compiler, *Selection of Sacred Music*, 6 vols. (London, 1806–26)
In 6997 CPEB's name is written in pencil, obviously later than the date of the ms.; the provenance is foreign (despite the prestige of the Latrobe anthology) and the work is not mentioned in any 18th-century work dealing with CPEB.

Incipit from 6997:

866. [11 Motets] [SATB chorus]. n.d.
Ms.: D-ddr ARk (uncatalogued), in a single-volume ms.
    collection of motets
Not attributed in the ms.; foreign in style and provenance,
    unmentioned in any primary source. By J. E. Bach (1722–
    77)?

Incipit of the 1st motet:

866.5. Aria, der Todt Jesu [SS soloists, orchestra]. n.d.
Ms.: D-brd RH, ms. 1251
From a larger work (not C. H. Graun's *Tod Jesu*). Foreign
    in style and provenance, unmentioned in any primary
    source

Incipit from 1251:

Theoretical

Authinct

867. Miscellanea musica. Probably written throughout CPEB's career. W. 121

Ms.: B Bc, 5895 (mostly Michel); D-ddr Bds, Mus. ms. theor. 60 (?)

Lit.: WADE, 65–66, 71

A compilation of CPEB's exercises in figured bass, modulation and chord-progression schemes, canon and counterpoint; sketches for items 300 and 536; fragmentary themes and "Einfälle"; fughetta on C-F-E-B-A-C-H (see item 285); 16-bar "Bauerntanz"; etc. One canon that appears in both realized and unrealized form in 5895 is copied with acknowledgment of CPEB's authorship in "26 Canoni aperti dei varii Autori," D-ddr Bds, Mus. ms. autogr. Albrechtsberger 2; a label on the cover of the "26 Canoni" reads, "Originale von Joh. Georg Albrechtsberger/Domkapellmeister bei St. Stephan in Wien/(1736 - + 1809.)/(Canoni diversi/ Æ [Aloys Fuchs?]. 1828."

868. Versuch über die wahre Art das Clavier zu spielen, mit Exempeln und achtzehn Probe-Stücken in sechs Sonaten erläutert von Carl Philipp Emanuel Bach, königl. preuss. Cammer-Musikus [part I]. 1753 and earlier (source of date: 1st pub.). W. 254

Early prints: the above title, "Berlin, in Verlegung des Auctoris. Gedruckt bey dem Königl. Hof-Buchdrucker Christian Friedrich Henning. 1753"; reprinted Berlin, "in Verlegung des Auctoris" (printed by G. L. Winter), 1759; reprinted by E. B. Schwickert, Leipzig, 1780 (the 1780 reprint issued with a reprint of Part II); 2nd edn. Leipzig: E. B. Schwickert, 1787 (not a 3rd edn., contrary to the title p.; issued with the same reprint of Part II).

Part II of the Versuch is item 870. The Probestücken are items 70–75. The 1787 edn. was accompanied by the Sechs neuen Clavier-Stücken (items 292–97). For the complex publishing history of the two groups of pieces and their relation to the Versuch, see PROBESTÜCKE.

Mod. edns.: Both parts of the Versuch, condensed and misinterpreted, ed. G. Schilling, Herzberg, 1852, reprinted Berlin, 1856; both parts, abridged, ed. W. Niemann, Leipzig, 1906, reprinted 1917, 1920, 1925; both parts trans. and ed. as Essay on the True Art of Playing Keyboard Instruments by W. J. Mitchell, New York: Norton, 1949 (incorporating nearly all printed revisions made by CPEB [see item 870]; editor's introduction also appears in MITCHELL/INTRODUCTION); facsimile edn. of the 1st edns. of both parts, with appendix incorporating changes of the 1787 and 1797 edns., by L. Hoffmann-Erbrecht, Leipzig: Breitkopf & Härtel, 1957. None of the modern edns. includes the Probestücke or the Sechs neuen Clavier-Stücken.

Lit.: CPEB/11 JAN. 1773; CPEB/10 APR. 1780; CPEB/BREITKOPF, 8 FEB. 1785; BITTER/BRÜDER, I, 91–97, 106–12;

SCHENKER/BEITRAG; VRIESLANDER/BACH, 145–57; VRIESLANDER/THEORETIKER, 235–79; ENGELKE, 436–40; SCHMID/MGG, col. 934; GEIRINGER/BACH, 356–57; MÜLLER, 56–58, 60; MITCHELL/MODULATION; COHEN; BERG, 54–55, 77–84, 173–80, 210, 223–26; WADE, 63–65, 73–74, 81, 88, 92, 96; ELDER; ROE, 12, 14, 15, 110; OTTENBERG, 100–01, 144, 170–01, 253, 267, 273. See also H. M. Brown and J. W. McKinnon, "Performing Practice," The New Grove Dictionary of Music and Musicians (London, 1980), especially the bibliography of this article.

A copy of Part I of the 1787 edn. containing alterations and corrections in CPEB's hand along with a 23-p. ms. supplement (not clear whether the supplement was also autog.) was auctioned by Sotheby in London, 19–21 June 1922, and by N. Charavay in Paris, 3 April 1925, according to SCHMID/MGG, col. 934.

Ms. Fétis 2971 in B Br (item 873), entitled "Von der Fingersetzung," is labeled (by Fétis?) as an autograph containing changes destined for a new edn. of the Versuch; this note is repeated in WOTQUENNE/THÉMATIQUE (W. 256). HUYS describes the contents of Ms. Fétis 2971 as partially appearing in the 1759 and 1762 edns. of the Versuch, with other parts being never published but only inserted in ms. in a copy of the 1787–97 edn. owned by B Br. On the contrary, "Von der Fingersetzung" is not autog. but is in the hand of Westphal; it is merely a copy of parts of the examples accompanying Part I of the Versuch (perhaps borrowing from Rellstab's condensation of the same material in the "Einleitung" of his edn. of C. P. E. Bachs Anfangsstücke mit einer Anleitung . . . , Berlin: Rellstab, 3 printings from 1788 to 1790 [W. 259]; see KURZE I). The ms. examples inserted into the B Br copy of the 1787–97 edn. are simply the universally known musical examples of the Versuch, containing about half a dozen alternate fingerings (which may have been added by anyone) not shown in any edn. of the treatise. Neither of these B Br sources, then, promises any legitimate addition to the Versuch as it is presented in the Mitchell edn.

869. Einfall, einen doppelten Contrapunct in der Octave von 6 Tacten zu machen, ohne die Regeln davon zu wissen. c. 1757 (source of date: 1st pub.). W. 257

Early print: in MARPURG/BEYTRÄGE, III (1757), 167–81, with commentary by Marpurg. Lit. about BEYTRÄGE: See this entry in Bib.

Ms. copied from the early print: B Br, Fétis II 4171 (Westphal; Westphal also copied Marpurg's commentary but added a few observations of his own.)

Mod. edn.: Translation and discussion in HELM/EINFALL

Lit.: BITTER/BRÜDER, I, 112–14

A permutational scheme in which the random choosing of

6 successive numbers between 1 and 9 can be repeated to produce nearly 3 billion different "compositions" by following charts, or twice that number if the 2 contrapuntal parts are inverted. See items 7–12, 216, 875.

870. Carl Philipp Emanuel Bachs Versuch über die wahre Art das Clavier zu spielen, zweyter Theil, in welchem die Lehre von dem Accompagnement und der freyen Fantasie abgehandelt wird. Nebst einer Kupfertafel. 1762 and earlier (source of date: 1st pub.). W. 255

Early prints: the above title, "In Verlegung des Auctoris. Berlin, 1762. Gedruckt bey George Ludewig Winter"; reprinted Leipzig: E. B. Schwickert, 1780 (issued with a reprint of Part I); reprinted Leipzig: E. B. Schwickert, 1787 (issued with the 2nd edn. of Part I); 2nd edn., Leipzig: E. B. Schwickert, 1797 (containing additions undoubtedly by CPEB, not in the Mitchell translation but present in the appendix of the Hoffmann-Erbrecht facsimile edition listed in item 868)

Mod. edns.: See item 868.

Lit.: HILLER/NACHRICHTEN, 18 July, 25 July 1768; CPEB/ 11 JAN. 1773; CPEB/10 APR. 1780; BITTER/BRÜDER, 97–112; HASE, 88; VRIESLANDER/BACH, 145–57; SCHENKER/IMPROVISATION; VRIESLANDER/THEORETIKER, 235–79; MITCHELL/MODULATION; COHEN; WADE, 63–65, 73–74, 81, 88, 92, 96; ELDER; KRAMER. See also "Lit." in item 868.

See items 160, 868.

The most important of the 1797 additions is a paragraph at the end of the appendix of the Hoffmann-Erbrecht edition. ELDER, 1–2, 7–8, 15–20, 23–27, using this paragraph and CPEB/FORKEL, 10 Feb. 1775, shows that the fantasias in KENNER IV, KENNER V, AND KENNER VI (items 277–79, 284, 289, 291) were intended by CPEB as further illustrations for the chapter on improvisation that closes Part II of the Versuch; that is, these fantasias function as the "supplements" promised by CPEB in the foreword of Part II (p. 171 of the Mitchell translation).

KRAMER locates and discusses the three harmonically daring movements cited vaguely by CPEB in the above-mentioned paragraph: the passage referred to without example as "in einem Duett aus meiner Auferstehung Jesu" is measures 9–20 of the duet "Vater deiner schwachen Kinder" of item 777; the examples cited under (a), "aus einem meiner Rondos," are from measures 45–46, 69–71, and 105–07 of item 260, being harmonically "conciliated" (Kramer's term) in measures 121–28 of that same mvt.; and the examples cited under (b), "aus meinem Heilig," are from measures 46–47, 53–54, 68–69, and 69–70 of item 778. Schwickert made 2 printing errors in the examples cited under (a) and (b), says KRAMER: there should be a double bar after the 4th note under (a), and a flat rather than a 6 over the 5th note under (b).

871. Zwey Litaneyen aus dem Schleswig-Holsteinischen Gesangbuch . . . 1785, possibly 1786 (source of date: see item 780). W. 204

These 2 choral litanies, listed more fully as item 780, fulfill the requirement that litanies be repetitious, and in so doing they amount to a theoretical work. They consist of nearly 100 different harmonizations (different according to the expression of the text) of a single short motive and are represented by the composer as an exercise in variation of harmony.

Possibly Authentic

872. Gedanken eines Liebhabers der Tonkunst über Herrn Nichelmanns Tractat von der Melodie. Probably 1755 (source of date: pub. date)

Early print: the above title, Nordhausen, 1755

Lit.: DÖLLMANN, 14–15, 26–28; D. A. Lee, "The Instrumental Works of Christoph Nichelmann," Ph.D. dissertation, University of Michigan, 1968, 44–46; WADE, 2; T. Christensen, "Nichelmann Contra C. P. E. Bach: Issues of Harmonic Theory in the *Empfindsamer Stil*," paper read at the national meeting of the American Musicological Society, New Orleans, October 1987

Pamphlet of 16 pp. A critical response to C. Nichelmann's *Die Melodie nach ihrem Wesen sowohl, als nach ihren Eigenschaften* (Danzig, 1755), which uses CPEB's music unfavorably in some examples. Christensen says that the polemic ensuing after 1755 had its culmination in CPEB's 1762 publication of the 2nd part of the *Versuch*, some chapters of which can be read as a rebuttal to Nichelmann.

Spurious

873. Von der Fingersetzung. n.d. W. 256.
See item 868.

874. Kurze Anweisung zum Generalbass. N.d. W. 258
Ms.: B Br, Ms. Fétis 6487 (Westphal), incorrectly labeled (in the hand of Fétis?) an autograph, and so termed also in WOTQUENNE/THÉMATIQUE. Apparently unrelated to either CPEB's *Versuch* or J. M. Bach's *Kurze und systematische Anleitung zum General-Bass* (Cassel, 1780)

875. Anleitung, so viel Walzer man will mit Würfeln zu componieren. n.d.
Early print: the above title, Berlin: Rellstab, n.d.
Lit.: DEUTSCH; HELM/EINFALL
Apparently an adaptation of J. P. Kirnberger's *Allzeit fertige Menuetten- und Polonoisenkomponist* (Berlin, 1757); also attributed to Haydn and Mozart, among other composers
See items 7–12, 216, 869.

Guide to Early Prints Entirely by C. P. E. Bach, in Order of First Publication

How to use: Where no item number is given, see the Bibliography; where an item number is given, see that item in the main body of the catalogue. In both places, full bibliographical information is listed: for example, W. number(s) where applicable, first editions, other early prints, prints apparently unauthorized, and literature about prints.

Lifetime

1731
  Menuet pour le clavessin
  (item 1.5)
1742 or 1743
  Prussian Sonatas
1744
  Württemberg Sonatas
1745
  Concerto (item 414)
1751
  Zwey Trio
1752
  Concerto (item 429)
1753
  Versuch I (item 868)
  Probestücke
c. 1753
  Concertos I
1757
  Einfall (item 869)
1758
  Zwölf kleine I
  Gellert-Lieder
1759
  Sinfonia (item 652)
1760
  Reprisen-Sonaten
  Concerto III (item 417)
c. 1760
  Concertos II
1761
  Fortsetzung
1762
  Versuch II (item 870)
  Oden

1763
  Zweyte Fortsetzung
  Sonata (item 562)
  Sonata (item 584)
1764
  Gellert-Anhang
  Sonatina I (item 458)
1764 or 1765
  Sonatina II (item 461)
1765
  Verschieden
1766
  Leichte
  Kurze I
  Sonatina III (item 462)
  Phillis und Thirsis (item 697)
  Der Wirth und die Gäste (item 699)
Before 1768
  Huberty
1768
  Kurze II
1770
  Damensonaten
  Zwölf Kleine II
c.1770
  A favourite concerto (item 190)
1772
  Sei concerti
1774
  Cramer Psalmen
1775
  Die Israeliten in der Wüste (item 775)
1776
  Accompanied Sonatas I
  Accompanied Sonatas II

1777
  Accompanied Sonatas III

1779
  Heilig (item 778)
  Kenner I

1780
  Sturm I
  Kenner II
  Orchester-Sinfonien

1781
  Kenner III
  Sturm II
  Canzonette (item 275)

1783
  Kenner IV

1784
  Morgengesang am Schöpfungsfeste (item 779)

1785
  Kenner V
  Una sonata (item 209)

1786
  Zwey Litaneyen (item 780)

1787
  Auferstehung und Himmelfahrt Jesu (item 777)
  Neue Melodien
  Kenner VI
  Sechs Neuen

Posthumous

1789
  Neue Lieder
  Passions-Cantate (item 776)
1790
  Preludio
1791
  Trois rondeaux
1792
  Trois sonates
1801
  Sinfonia (item 663)
c. 1802
  Grande sonate (item 51)
1803
  Menuet de Locatelli (item 14)
  Folie d'Espagne (item 263)
c. 1823
  Bitten (item 826/3)
1829
  Magnificat (item 772)

Undated

  Six fugues
  Canzonetta (item 69)
  Sonate (item 173)
  A favorite sonata (item 186)
  Solfeggio . . . Berlin (item 220)
  Solfeggio . . . Stockholm (item 220)
  Concerto (item 404)

Guide to Early Prints
Containing Music of C. P. E. Bach
with Music of Other Composers,
in Order of First Publication

Titles refer to the Bibliography, where full information is given on facts of publication, contents by item number in this catalogue, W. number(s) where applicable, literature about printed collections, apparently unauthorized inclusions in printed collections, and so forth.

Not listed here: early prints not mentioned in any primary or secondary literature about C. P. E. Bach except for their listing in RISM, Vol. B II

Lifetime

1737–43
Gräfe
1753
Ramler–Krause I
1753–54
Marpurg/Abhandlung
1754–78
Marpurg/Beyträge
1755
Marpurg/Anleitung
Ramler–Krause II
1755–65
Oeuvres
1756
Marpurg/Lieder
Marpurg/Oden I
1756–57
Marpurg/Raccolta
1758
Marpurg/Fugen
1759
Marpurg/Oden II
1759–64
Marpurg/Briefe
1760
Drey Versuche
c. 1760
Collection I
1761
Hiller/Sinfonien
1761–62
Marpurg/Sinfonie
Collection II

1761–63
Allerley
1762
Tonstücke
Nebenstunden
1762–63
Marpurg/practisch
Mancherley
c. 1762–66
Kleine
1766–70
Unterhaltungen
1767
Melodien
1767–68
Ramler–Krause III
1770
Vielerley
1773
Münter-Lieder
1774–82
Voss
1776
Muse
1779
Hiller/Lieder
1780
Rheineck
1781
Schiørring
1783–96
Notenbuch
1785
Zinck

1786
  Kühnau I
  Blumenlese
1788
  Bossler
  Freymäurer-Lieder

Posthumous
1790
  Kühnau II
1796
  Kellner

Undated
  Winterschmidt

Works Not Listed in
Wotquenne's Thematic Catalogue
(Wotquenne/Thématique)

Rachel W. Wade

Following is a list of works mentioned in this thematic catalogue but not (except for items 336 and 842) in WOTQUENNE/THÉMATIQUE. Some are authentic works of C. P. E. Bach, some are possibly by C. P. E. Bach, and some are in the doubtful or spurious categories.

Item No.	Work

For Keyboard Instrument Alone: Authentic

1	[2 Marches, 2 polonaises, in D, g, G, g]. 1730-31
242	Concerto per il cembalo solo [in F]. 1770
255	[untitled, in D]. Probably 1775
256	[untitled, in F]. Probably 1775
257	[untitled, in D]. Probably 1775
258	Menuet [in F]. Probably 1775
285	[untitled fughetta on the name "C. Filippo E. Bach" (C-F-E-B-A-C-H) in F]. 1784
333	La Juliane [in F]. n.d.
334	[untitled, in a]. n.d.
336	5 Choräle mit ausgesetzten Mittelstimmen [in b, F, b, a, G]. n.d. Wq n. v. 21, 20 (the 4th and 5th chorales) [WOTQUENNE/THÉMATIQUE, footnote, p. 96]
337	Choral [Wo Gott zum Haus nicht gibt; in F]. n.d.

For Keyboard Instrument Alone: Possibly Authentic

339	Sonata per il cembalo solo [in e]. 1762 or earlier
340	Polonoise [in G]. Probably 1768 or later
341	Sonata [in C]. n.d.
342	Sonata [in c]. n.d.
343	Sonata per il cembalo solo [in D]. n.d.
344	Sonata. cembalo solo [in E–flat]. n.d.
345	Solo [in F]. n.d.
346	Sonata per il chembalo solo [in c]. n.d.
347	Sonata per il cembalo solo [in B–flat]. n.d.
348	Fantasia [in E–flat]. n.d.
349	Fantasia e fuga [in d]. n.d.
350	Fuga per il organo [in C]. n.d.
351	Arioso con variazioni [in A]. n.d.
352	Adagio per il organo A 2 clavire e pedal [in d]. n.d.
353	Polonoise [in D]. n.d.
354	Polonoise [in D]. n.d.
355	Polonoise [in A]. n.d.
356	[untitled, in G]. n.d.
357	[Choral-Vorspiel in G]. n.d.

For Keyboard Instrument Alone: Doubtful

358	[Sonata for keyboard in C]. 1732
359	Garten-Sonata [in D]. 1762 or earlier
360	Fuga [in B–flat]. 1764?
361	A favourite overture of Sig. Bach of Berlin [for unaccompanied piano in D]. c. 1785
362	Sonata [in C]. n.d.
363	Sonata [in e]. n.d.
364	Sonata [in F]. n.d.
365	Sonata [in G]. n.d.
366	Sonata [in G]. n.d.
367	Sonata [in B–flat]. n.d.
368	Sonata [in F]. n.d.
369	Sonata [in A or G?]. n.d.
370	Sonata [Suite] a clavicembalo solo [in B–flat]. n.d.
371	Sinfonia per il clavicembalo [in B–flat]. n.d.
371.5	Andante, Allabreve [in F, a]. n.d.
371.6	Andante [in c]. n.d.
371.7	Arietta con variationes [in D]. n.d.
371.8	Fantasia [in e]. n.d.
371.9	Sonata di Preludio e Fuga [on B–A–C–H] [in F, d]. n.d.
372	Fuga [in d]. n.d.
373	Fuga (sopra il nome de Bach) [in C]. n.d.
373.5	Fuga ex D moll, Fugetta in D moll, Fugetta in D dur. n.d.
374	La Walhauer [in A]. n.d.
375	Menuetto mit v Variazionen [in E–flat]. n.d.
375.5	Menuetto, Trio, Menuetto [with variations] [in F, F, F]. n.d.

For Keyboard Instrument Alone: Spurious

376	Ach Gott und Herr [in B–flat]. c. 1732
377	[Sonata in a minor]. c. 1735 or c. 1747
377.5	Contrapunctus: 4 Fugen [in d, d, d, d]. c. 1745–50
378	VI Sonate [in B–flat, G, d, F, B–flat, D]. 1757 or earlier
379	Sonata [in F]. c. 1763

380   Polonoise [in E–flat]. c. 1765
381   Clavier-Sonate [in C]. 1770 or earlier
382   5., 4., 6. Sonate . . . [in E and c]. c. 1770
383   Sonata. Concerto [in A]. c. 1771
384   A favourite concerto for the harpsichord or piano
        forte [unaccompanied, in A]. c. 1771?
385   Due sonate per il cembalo solo del sigl. Daniele Turck,
        la troisi- la quartiem mons. P. E. Bach [in B–flat and
        D]. 1776 or earlier
387   Sonata [in a]. n.d.
388   Fuga [in C]. n.d.
389   Fuga [in c]. n.d.
389.5 Fuga, Praeludium [in B–flat, d]. n.d.
389.6 [Two fugue expositions on B–A–C–H]. n.d.
390   Parthia [in C]. n.d.
390.5 Gigue [in B–flat]. n.d.
391   And.te ed allegro [in G]. n.d.
392   Le travagant [in G]. n.d.
392.1 Le caressant-le contente [in C]. n.d.
392.2 Le petit maître [in F]. n.d.
392.3 Le flegmatique-en colère [in B–flat]. n.d.
392.4 Le moribant [in d]. n.d.
392.5 Il est vive [in D]. n.d.
393   Allein Gott in der Höh [in G]. n.d.
394   Vater unser im Himmelreich [in d]. n.d.
395   Giga con variazioni [in F]. n.d.
396   Alla pol [acca] con variatio [in G]. n.d.
397   Minuetto [I–II, in D]. n.d.
398   Menueten zum tantzen: Menuet 1 [in D]. n.d.
399   Tempo di men [uetto]-variation [in A]. n.d.
400   [untitled, in A]. n.d.
401   [untitled, in a]. n.d.
402   [untitled, in a]. n.d.

Concertos and Sonatinas: Authentic
        None

Concertos and Sonatinas: Possibly Authentic
480   Sonatina III, cembalo concertato, violino primo,
        violino secondo, due flauti, violetta E basso [in D].
        Probably c. 1762
480.5 Sonatina a [cembalo concertato,] 2 flauti, 2 violini,
        viola e basso [in D]. Probably c. 1762
481   Concerto cembalo, violino primo, violino secondo,
        viola e basso [in g]. n.d.
481.5 Concerto cembalo, violino primo, violino secondo,
        viola e basso [in e]. n.d.
482   [11 flute concertos]. n.d.
483   [Concertos for harpsichord and orchestra]

Concertos and Sonatinas: Doubtful
484   Cembalo [con]certato, due violini, viola e cont. [in d].
        c. 1732–34
484.1 Concerto per il flauto traverso con due violini, viola e
        basso [in d]. Probably c. 1747
484.2 Concert für clavier . . . [harpsichord, 2 violins, viola,
        bass, in f]. Probably c. 1753
484.3 Concerto . . . cembalo obligato, violino primo,
        violino secondo, viola e violono [in E–flat]. n.d.

484.4 Concerto a cembalo concertato, 2 violini, viola, basso
        [in B–flat]. n.d.
484.5 Concerto . . . [harpsichord, 2 horns, 2 flutes, 2
        oboes, 2 violins, viola, bass, in D]. n.d.
484.6 Concerto a 5 pp: cembalo concertato, violino primo,
        violino secondo, viola e basso [in B–flat]. n.d.
484.7 Concerto per il clavicembalo con due violini, violetta,
        e basso [in D]. n.d.
484.8 Concerto per il cembalo [in G]. n.d.
484.9 Ex c. moll cembalo certato. violin: 1, violin: 2, viola e
        basso [in c]. n.d.
485   Concerto . . . [harpsichord, 2 violins, viola, bass, in
        F]. n.d.
486   Concerto . . . [harpsichord, 2 violins, viola, bass,
        in c]. n.d.

Concertos and Sonatinas: Spurious
487   Concerto cembalo concertato, violino 1mo, violino
        2do, viola, basso [in d]. c. 1759
488   Concerto . . . [harpsichord, 2 violins, bass, in B–flat].
        1763 or earlier
489   Concerto . . . [harpsichord, 2 violins, bass, in G].
        1763 or earlier
490   [Concerto for harpsichord and orchestra, in A]. 1768
        or earlier
491   Sonatina a harmonica [glass harmonica], 2 violini e
        violoncello [in C]. 1775 or later
492   Concerto per il clavi cembalo, violino primo, violino
        secondo, viola e basso [in C]. 1777 or earlier
493   Sonatina a harmonica [glass harmonica], 2 violini,
        viola e basso [in C]. 1777 or later
494   Concerto . . . [harpsichord, 2 violins, viola, bass,
        in E–flat]. 1780 or earlier?
495   Concerto per il cembalo concert. con due violini e
        basso del Sigr. Bach [in F]. 1780 or earlier?
496   Concerto di cembalo . . . accompagnato di due
        violini e vioncello [in B–flat]. 1780 or earlier
497   Concerto for violin or viola with piano or orchestra
        accompaniment [in D; also arranged as a concerto
        for orchestra, concerto for 4 viols, etc.] c. 1905
498   Concerto . . . [harpsichord, 2 violins, viola, bass, in
        B–flat]. n.d.
499   Concerto . . . [harpsichord, 2 violins, viola, bass, in
        f]. n.d.
500   [Harpsichord concerto, in D]. n.d.
501   [Harpsichord concerto, in B–flat]. n.d.

Chamber Music with a Leading Keyboard Part: Authentic
540   [Sonata fragment for keyboard and melody instru-
        ment(s), in E]. n.d.
541   [Sonata for keyboard and viola, in F]. n.d.

Chamber Music with a Leading Keyboard Part: Possibly Authentic
542   Sonata per il cembalo e violino [in A]. Probably c.
        1731 or 1747
542.5 Sonata, cembalo obligato con violino [in g]. c. 1734 or
        earlier
543   Trio a cembalo obligato e violino [in B–flat]. Probably
        c. 1755

544 Sonata ex E♯ a cembalo e violino [in E]. n.d.

Chamber Music with a Leading Keyboard Part: Spurious
545 Es d[ur] Trio fürs obligate Clavier u. die Flöte. Mid-18th century
546 Sonate pour le clavecin, le violon et la basse [in C]. c. 1775
547 Sonate pour le clavecin, le violon et la basse [in G]. c. 1775

Solo Sonatas for Wind or String Instruments: Authentic
None

Solo Sonatas for Wind or String Instruments: Possibly Authentic
564.5 Sonata a traversa e continuo [in a]. Probably c. 1731
565 [Two sonatas for flute and continuo, in G and b]. 1763 or earlier

Trio Sonatas: Authentic
566 Trio für die Violine, Bratsche und Bass, mit Johann Sebastian Bach gemeinschaftlich verfertigt [key unknown]. Probably 1731 or earlier
585 Sinfonia a 3 voc. [2 violins, bass, in D]. Probably c. 1754
589 Trio a fagotto obligato, flauto basso [bass recorder, not quartflöte] e cembalo [in F]. Probably c. 1755

Trio Sonatas: Possibly Authentic
590.5 [Trio sonata for flute, violin, and continuo, in G]. Probably c. 1732–35
591 Sonata E♯, 2 violini e basso. Probably before 1768
592 Sonata . . . a flauto traverso o violino primo, violino secondo e basso [in c]. Probably before 1768
593 Sonata [flute, violin, continuo, in E–flat]. n.d.

Trio Sonatas: Doubtful
595 Sonata for flute, violin, continuo, in G]. 1735
596 Sonata a 3 strom. [flute, violin, continuo, in d]. Probably c. 1747
597 Trio, flauto traverso, violino con cembalo [in F]. n.d.

Other Chamber Music: Authentic
None

Other Chamber Music: Doubtful
639 Fantasia sopra Jesu meines lebens Leben [chorale fantasia, 3 parts for unspecified instruments, 1 part for obligato oboe: no text, in a]. n.d.
640 III sonate per il flauto e violino [in D, G, C]. n.d.
641 Diverdimento ex D tur, violino, flauto, viola, basso. n.d.
642 Divertimento ex G♯, flauto traverso, violino, viola e basso. n.d.

Other Chamber Music: Spurious
643 Sonata a [glass] harmonica e violoncello [in C]. 1753 or later
644 [Three trios for 2 violins and viola, in D, E–flat, G]. c. 1765
645 Quintette [for flute, oboe, violin, viola, bass, in C]. c. 1772

646 Frühlings Erwachen [2 violins, piano, in C]. n.d.
647 Adagio . . . pour orchestre à cordes [in b]. 1904?

Symphonies: Authentic
None

Symphonies: Possibly Authentic
667 Sinfonia ex G♯ a violino primo, violino secondo, viola e basso. c. 1751?

Symphonies: Spurious
668 [Note about authenticity of various symphonies attributed to C. P. E. Bach]

For Solo Voice(s): Authentic
685 La Sophie. aria [in B–flat]. Probably c. 1757
763 Die Alster [?] and Harvstehude [key unknown]. Probably near 1788

For Solo Voice(s): Possibly Authentic
768 An den Mond. Sophiens Reise auf der See [in E–flat]. n.d.
769 Weil Gott uns das Gesicht Verleih [? in A]. n.d.
769.5 Climene [in G]. n.d.
770 Cancionetta [in G]. n.d.
771 Nachahmung einiger Stellen des anderen Psalms, von Kohler [in C]. n.d.

Major Choral Works
None

Choral Works for Special Occasions
782 Passionsmusik nach dem Evangelisten Matthäus [key unknown]. 1768–69 and earlier
783 Passions-Musik nach dem Evangelisten Marcus [in A]. 1769–70 and earlier
784 Passions-Musik nach dem Evangelisten Lucas [in c]. 1770–71 and earlier
785 Passions-Musik nach dem Evangelisten Johannes [in E]. 1771–72 and earlier
786 Passions-Musik nach dem Evangelisten Matthäus, "O Hilf, Christe, Gottes Sohn" [key unknown]. 1772–73 and earlier
787 Passions-Musik nach dem Evangelisten Marcus [in F]. 1773–74 and earlier
788 Passions-Musik nach dem Evangelisten Lucas [key unknown]. 1774–75 and earlier
789 Passions-Musik nach dem Evangelisten Johannes [in G?]. 1775–76 and earlier
790 Passions-Musik nach dem Evangelisten Matthäus [in A]. 1776–77 and earlier
791 Passions-Musik nach dem Evangelisten Marcus [in a]. 1777–78 and earlier
792 Passions-Musik nach dem Evangelisten Lucas [in a]. 1778–79 and earlier
793 Passions-Musik nach dem Evangelisten Johannes [in F]. 1779–80 and earlier
794 Passions-Musik nach dem Evangelisten Matthäus, "Jesu, meiner Seelen Licht" [in d]. 1780–81 and earlier

795 Passions-Musik nach dem Evangelisten Marcus [in A]. 1781–82 and earlier

796 Passions-Musik nach dem Evangelisten Lucas [in a]. 1782–83 and earlier

797 Passions-Musik nach dem Evangelisten Johannes [in A]. 1783–84 and earlier

798 Passions-Musik nach dem Evangelisten Matthäus, [in A]. 1784–85 and earlier

799 Passions-Musik nach dem Evangelisten Marcus [in a]. 1785–86 and earlier

800 Passions-Musik nach dem Evangelisten Lucas, "O Lamm Gottes unschuldig" [in F]. 1786–87 and earlier

801 Passions-Musik nach dem Evangelisten Johannes [in A]. 1787–88 and earlier

802 Passions-Musik nach dem Evangelisten Matthäus [in d?]. 1788 and earlier

Easter Cantatas
808 [Other Easter cantatas]

Michaelmas Cantatas
811 [Michaelmas cantata, in D]. c. 1772

Christmas Cantatas
816 [Lost Christmas cantatas]

Other Church Cantatas
817 Am Pfingsfeste: Herr, Lehr' uns Thun [in E–flat]. 1769

818 Am 16. [or 24th] Sonntage nach Trinitatis: Der Gerechte, ob er gleich [in d]. 1774

818.5 [Cantata for the 20th Sunday after Trinity, in D]. n.d.

819 Auf Mariä Heimsuchung: Meine Seele erhebt den Herrn [in D]. n.d.

820 [Lost church cantatas]

821 Einführungsmusik:
   a. Palm 1769
   b. Klefeker 1771
   c. Schuchmacher 1771
   d. Haeseler 1772
   e. Hornbostel 1772
   h. Gerling 1777
   i. Sturm 1778
   j. Rambach 1780
   k. Jänisch 1782
   n. Berkhan 1787
   o. Willerding 1787

Other Congratulatory Cantatas, Part A
822a Oratorium zur Feyer des Ehrenmahls der Herrn Bürger-Capitains in Hamburg [in E–flat]. 1780

822b Serenata zu demselben Endzweck [in D]. 1780

822c Oratorium zu demselben Endzweck [key unknown]. 1783

822d Serenata zu demselben Endzweck [in D]. 1783

823 Musik am Dankfeste wegen des fertigen Michaelis-Thurms [in C]. 1786

Other Congratulatory Cantatas, Part B
824a Cantate auf die Vermählung des Hen. von G. und der Fräul. von H. [in A]. 1763

824b Geburtstags-Cantate [key unknown]. 1769

824c Herrn Dr. Hoeck Jubelmusik [key unknown]. 1775

824d Herrn Syndicus Klefeker Jubelmusik [key unknown]. 1775

824e Dank-Hymne der Freundschaft, ein Geburtstags-Stück [in C]. 1785

824f Jubelmusik auf den Geburtstag der Madame Stresow [key unknown]. n.d.

Individual Choruses
838 Merckt und seht [in C]. n.d.
841 Wirf dein Anliegen auf [key unknown]. n.d.

Chorale Settings
842 10 Choräle zur Liedern des Grafen von Wernigerode [in C, G, G, E–flat, d, A, C, B–flat, C, E–flat] [mentioned in WOTQUENNE/THÉMATIQUE, footnote, p. 96]. 1767 or earlier

843 Naglet til et Kors paa Jorden [in g]. 1781 or earlier

844 [3 Chorales, for S, continuo in E–flat, A, D]. 1785 or earlier

845 [4-Part chorale; key unknown]. 1786 or earlier

Other Individual Movements of Choral Works; Fragments
847 [Trumpet and timpani parts added to C. H. Graun's *Te Deum*; key unknown]. 1756 or later

848 [Instrumental introduction to the "Credo" of J. S. Bach's *B Minor Mass*]. c. 1786

850 [2 Recitatives for cantatas by C. F. C. Fasch; key unknown]. n.d.

854 [Various accompanied recitatives added to church works of other composers]

Choral Works: Doubtful
856 [Motet] Selig sind die Todten [in E–flat]. Probably before 1781

857 [Choral fragment] Ecce cui iniquitatibus [in G]. n.d.

858 [Choral fragment] Miserere mei [in a]. n.d.

859 Aria, sey mir gesegnet [in D]. n.d.

Choral Works: Spurious
860 [4-Voice chorale] Hilf dass ich folge [in C]. c. 1725

861 Missa [in E–flat]. n.d.

862 Die Pilgrime auf Golgatha . . . Oratorium [in B–flat?] n.d.

863 Passions-Cantate [St. Mark Passion] [in F]. n.d.

864 [Cantata] Esto mihi [key unknown]. n.d.

865 Motetta. Kommt, lasst uns anbeten [in a]. n.d.

866 [11 Motets] [key of the 1st motet is g]. n.d.

866.5 Aria, der Todt Jesu [in G]. n.d.

Theoretical: Authentic
None

Theoretical: Possibly Authentic

872   Gedanken eines Liebhabers der Tonkunst über Herrn
      Nichelmanns Tractat von der Melodie. Probably
      1755

Theoretical: Spurious

875   Anleitung, so viel Walzer man will mit Würfeln zu
      componieren. n.d.

Index of Names of Persons
in Special References

Rachel W. Wade

(Figures in italics are page numbers; figures in roman type are item numbers. See Bibliography for names of persons in another context.)

Abel, [C. F. ?], 592
Agricola, [J. F.], 155
Ahlers, 821b
Albrecht, O. E., 760
Albrechtsberger, J. G., 867
Alers, C. W., 822a–d
Altnickol, J. C., 484.2
Anna Amalia of Prussia, *xxiv*, 345, 772
Artaria, 779
Bach, Anna Carolina Philippina, *xix–xx, xxiii*, 830
Bach, Anna Magdalena, 1, 16
Bach, C. E., 386
Bach, Carl Philipp Emanuel
as cataloguer, *xix–xxiii*
as editor, 381
as engraver, 1.5
as reviewer, 75

letters by, *xix, xiii*, 33, 209, 267, 277–9, 284–5, 289, 291–2, 349, 386, 461, 542.5, 663, 732, 775–9, 798, 835, 868, 870; *see also* Bibliography (p. *255*), passim, but especially ACCOMPANIED SONATAS, BITTER BRÜDER, CPEB, CRAMER/PSALMEN, DIDEROT, ENGELKE, GELLERT-LIEDER, HASE, HELM/LITERARY, KENNER, LEICHTE, ORCHESTER-SINFONIEN, REPRISEN-SONATEN, SEI CONCERTI, STEGLICH/HOMILIUS.

mss., autograph, 1, 4, 6, 16, 17, 32.5, 36, 44, 46, 49, 57, 60, 62, 82, 84, 87, 96–8, 106–7, 116, 122–3, 125, 127–8, 136–8, 141, 151–4, 158, 162–4, 177, 189–90, 211–13, 226, 242, 248–58, 260, 267, 269, 272, 275, 289–90, 298–301, 333–4, 337, 348, 376, 403–5, 408–12, 414–15, 418, 420–3, 427, 429, 432–3, 440–9, 453–4, 458–60, 465–6, 468–9, 476–9, 484, 506, 510–14, 522–36, 540, 564.5, 567, 569–75, 577, 582–3, 588, 635, 649—51, 654–5, 658–66, 685, 689, 693, 700, 702, 705, 707, 732, 736–41, 747, 756, 758, 760, 762, 772, 777–8, 780, 790, 794, 796–8, 800, 802–3, 807, 809, 818, 820, 821a–821b, 821d, 821f, 821h, 821k, 821l, 821n, 821o, 824e, 826–7, 831, 834–5, 838, 842, 860, 868

mss., initial page marked by, 9–10, 12, 21, 47, 51

mss., marked by, 4, 43, 46, 51, 61, 84–6, 106, 131, 406, 408, 410, 443, 446, 448, 502, 506, 512, 656–7, 660–2, 776, 780, 785, 790, 796, 803, 808, 812, 831, 834, 835

mss., revised by, xxi–xxii, xxvii, 5, 11, 13, 15, 19–20, 22–3, 36, 52–3, 68, 106, 135, 176, 192, 211, 213, 444, 655, 868

mss., title pages marked by, 8, 32.5, 143, 175, 440, 447–54, 503, 510, 513, 536, 569, 661, 776, 827

mss., titles or title pages written by, 18, 56, 107, 121, 156, 177, 442, 505, 507–8, 511, 545, 654–5, 657, 659, 661, 854

Bach, Emil, 646
Bach, Johann Bernhard, *xx–xxii*
Bach, Johann Christian, *xx–xxi*, 69, 70–5, 345, 351, 361, 379, 382–4, 386–7, 484.2, 484.6, 488–90, 492, 494–6, 546–7, 597, 640, 644–5, 668
Bach, Johann Christoph (1642–1703), 818
Bach, Johann Christoph Friedrich, *xx–xxi*, 381, 414, 854, 862
Bach, Johann Ernst, 341, 368, 864, 866
Bach, Johann Michael, 484.6, 500.2, 874
Bach, Johann Sebastian (1685–1750), *xi, xx–xxi, xxiii–xxv*, 1, 16, 190, 334, 350, 370, 373, 373.5, 376, 377.5, 388–9, 390.5, 403, 483–4, 484.6, 507, 542.5, 545, 564.5, 566, 569, 576, 585, 587, 590.5, 639, 782, 785–6, 790, 794, 798, 802–4, 820, 827, 830, 848, 860, 863

works by or attributed to, as listed in SCHMIEDER:
BWV 39: 782, 802
BWV 48: 376
BWV 96, 98, 100: 373.5
BWV 102: 830
BWV 144: 860
BWV 153: 782, 802
BWV 198: 863
BWV 232: *xx*, 848
BWV 243: *xx*, 827
BWV 244: *xx, xxiv*, 782, 786, 790, 794, 798, 802
BWV 245: 782, 785, 802
BWV 248: *xx*, 782, 802, 804
BWV 342: 803
BWV 575: 389
BWV 772–801: *xx*
BWV 846: 390.5

BWV 1007:12: *xx*
BWV 1020: 542.5
BWV 1021: 590.5
BWV 1031: 542.5, 545
BWV 1033: 564.5
BWV 1036: 569
BWV 1038: 590.5
BWV 1052a: 484
BWV 1080: *xx*, 377.5
BWV Anh. 40: 16
BWV Anh. 90: 388
BWV Anh. 108: 373
BWV Anh. 122–5: 1
BWV Anh. 129: 16
BWV Anh. 185: 507
BWV Anh. 186: 576
BWV Anh. 187: 587
BWV Anh. 188: 16
BWV Anh. 189: 403

Bach, Johann Sebastian (1748–1778), *xxi*
Bach, Johanna Maria, *xix–xxiv*, 21, 566, 667–8, 763, 821
Bach, Wilhelm Friedemann, *xx*, 16, 341, 363, 380, 389, 422, 484.2, 486, 597
Bach, Wilhelm Friedrich Ernst, 764
Bassani, 861
Beethoven, L. van, *xxiv*, 779
Behrmann, 821
Benda, F., 484.1
Benda, G., *xxi–xxii*, 275, 378, 499, 778, 861
Berg, D., *xi, xxiv–xxvi*, 7–12, 16–17, 19–21, 23, 133, 135, 211, 213, 387
Beringer, 0., 389
Berkhahn, 821, 821n
Bernhardi, 861
Beurmann, E., *xi, xix, xxvii*, 8, 11, 24, 70–5, 106, 126, 162, 173, 192, 362
Bitter, C. H., *xi, xxii–xxiii*, 525, 542.5, 595, 834
Blechschmidt, E.-R., *xi, xxiv–xxvi*
Bode, J. J. C., *xix*
Borsch, J. S., 350
Bracke, 821, 821f, 821i
Brahms, J., *xxv*, 512, 514
Brandes, 821
Brandts-Buys, 597
Breig, W., 484
Breitkopf, J. G. I., *xix–xx,xxv*, 267, 461, 499, 501, 542.5, 663, 775, 777–9, 868
Bruckner, A., *xxiv*
Brückner, E. T. J., 777
Buck, C., 419, 428, 483
Bücken, E., 483, 490, 808
Burney, C., *xix*
Busch, G., *xi*, 676–84, 686–7, 689–92, 696, 699–721, 723–59, 763–4, 768, 781, 794, 843–5
Casadesus family, 497, 647
Clark, S., *xi, xxi*, 775–7, 781, 785, 790, 794–5, 798–9, 802, 807, 820–1, 821f, 821g, 824f, 830
Cochius, 803

Cramer, C. F., *xix*, 75, 275, 742
Cramer, J. A. 733, 765, 773–4, 781, 844
Cropp, 821, 821j
Dadelsen, G. von, *xi, xxiii, xxv*, 1, 859
Davis, S., *xi*
Deis, C., 772
De Vuyst, J., *xi*
Diderot, D., 83
Duckles, V., 483
Dürr, A., 542.5, 545, 564.5
Dunoyer, C., *xi*
Ebeling, C.D., 707, 776, 821c
Ebert, 700
Eberwein, 821, 821j
Eitner, R., *xxv*, 863
Elder, E., *xi*, 870
Elvers, R., *xi,*
Emke, 821, 821f
Engelhardt, R., 399, 402
Eppstein, H., 564.5
Erk, L. C., *xxiv*
Eschenburg, J. J., 743, 776, 798
Falck, M., 16, 363, 380, 597
Fasch, C. F. C., 155, 850
Fedtke, T., 102, 133, 372
Fétis, F-J., *xxii–xxiii*, 868, 874
Fillion, M., *xi*
Fischer, K. von, 484
Fischof, J., 373
Flügge, 821
Forkel, J.N., *xxiii,* 33, 75, 284, 289, 291, 525, 542.5, 775–6, 870
Fox, P., *xi*
Frager, M., *xxiv*
Friderici, 821, 821g
Fuchs, A., 583
Fuchs, Aloys, 341
Funk, G. B., 781
Gallagher, C. C., 776
Gasie, 821, 821l
Gaus, 0., 372
Geiringer, K., 818, 854
Gellert, C. F., 686, 781, 785, 791, 826
Gerber, E. L., *xix, xx*, 483, 490
Gericke, J. L., 823
Gerling, 821, 821h
Gerstenberg, H. W. von, 75, 698, 720, 735
Giseke, N. D., 673, 693
Gleim, J. W. L., 667, 674, 677–8, 687, 699, 748, 755, 759, 778
Godt, I., 659
Goeyens, A., 648
Goeze, 821
Golde, 275
Goldhan, W., *xi*
Gotha, Herzogin von [Luise Dorothea], 275
Grandjany, M., 563
Grasberger, F., *xi*
Grasnick, F. A., 388, 393–4

Graun, 386, 581
Graun, C. H., 847, 866.5
Grave, [J. H.], 484.2, 484.7, 542, 771
Grell, A. E., 360, 408, 481.5
Greve, 821
Grotthus, D. E. von, 272, 824a
Grützmacher, F., 510
Haeseler, 821, 821d
Hagedorn, F. von, 680, 711, 763
Haller, A. von, 691–2, 741
Handel, G. F., 848
Hase, H. von, 775
Hasse, 861
Hauser, F., *xxiv*
Haydn, J., 875
Heidritter, 821
Helm, S., *xi*
Herder, J. G. von, 862
Hering, S., 480.5
Herold, J. H., 763
Herrmann, 776
Hill, G., *xi*
Hill, R. S., *xxiv*
Hinze-Reinhold, B., 583
Hoboken, A. van, *xxv*, 373
Hoeck, 824c
Hoffmann, 819
Hoffmann-Erbrecht, L., 868, 870
Hohfeld, J., 280, 719
Hölty, L. C. H., 740, 745
Homilius, G. A., 817, 818.5
Hornbostel, 821, 821e
Hortschansky, K., 370
Hummel, Hummell, 69, 484.6
Huys, B., *xi*, 868
Itzig, I. D., xxiii–xxiv, 592
Jacobi, E., *xx*, 479
Jaenecke, J., *xi*, *xxv*
Jänisch, 821, 821j
Janitsch, 69
Jones, R. D., 171
Kallir, R. F., 760
Karsch, A. L. 696, 719, 776
Kast, P., *xi*, *xxiv–xxvi*, 16, 348, 353, 360, 514, 542, 572, 821c, 821d, 859
Kellner, J. P., 388
Kirnberger, J. P., xxiv, 69, 353, 375.5, 389.5, 399–402, 770, 875
Klefeker, 821, 821b, 824d
Kleist, E. von, 675, 710
Klengel, P., 558–9, 576, 590
Klopstock, F. G., 731, 737, 779, 781, 844
Klopstock, W., 775
Klug, 821
Kobayashi, Y., 348, 542.5
Kohler, 771
Köhler, K.-H., *xi*
Koldofsky, A., 483
Koldofsky, G., 483
Koussevitzky, S., 497

Kramer, R., 188, 870
Krause, P., 334
Kreutz, A., 272
Kulukundis, E. N., 32, 47, 55, 69, 75, 84, 100, 126, 134, 136–40, 184–5, 204–7, 216, 225, 277–8, 411, 423, 430, 434, 441, 484.7, 590, 686, 775–6
Lampe, 821
Landowska, W., 483, 490
Lange, M., *xxiv*
Larsen, J.P., *xi*
Lasocki, D., 445
Latrobe, C. I., 865
Lauschmann, R., 466
Lawrence, L., 563
Lebermann, W., 497
Ledebur, C. F. von, *xxii*
Lee, D. A., 348, 487, 498
Lehr, L. F. F., 696
Leopold, G., 872
Lessing, G. E., 676, 679, 681–2, 701
Levy, S., *xx*, xxiii–xxiv, 344, 566, 591, 593, 667–8
Lewis, N,. *xxiv*
Lobkowitz, Prince Ferdinand Philipp von, 667
Locatelli, P., 14
Luis, 837
[Luise Dorothea], Herzogin von Gotha, 275
Luther, M., 778
Lüttkens, J. H, 706, 821, 821h
Maguerre, K., 597
Maria Theresa, xxv
Marpurg, F. W., 69, 75.5, 76, 338, 869
Marshall, R. L., 542.5, 545, 564.5
Martell, P., *xxii*
Martiny, A., *xi*
McCorkle, D. M., *xi*
McCorkle, M. L., *xi*, 290
Mekota, B. A., 377
Mendel, A., 785
Mendelssohn, A. (1776-1835), *xxiv*, 344
Mendelssohn, F., xxiii–xxiv
Metastasio, 743
Michaelsen, 821, 821g
Michel, xxii–xxiii, xxv–xxvi
  as copyist, 1.5, 3–13, 15–19, 21, 23, 32.5, 36, 42–8, 51–2, 54, 56–7, 60–2, 64–5, 68, 78, 83–4, 97–8, 106–7, 114, 116, 121, 127–8, 133–8, 141, 143, 151–8, 162–4, 171, 174–8, 189, 192, 211–13, 227, 248–9, 263–4, 272, 275, 280, 292–302, 336, 340, 403, 405–10, 413, 416, 419, 422–5, 427, 430–9, 441, 445, 447–57, 459, 463–70, 477–8, 504–5, 507–12, 514–15, 534–9, 542.5, 549, 552, 559, 563, 567–72, 574–7, 582, 588, 602–9, 614–19, 621–7, 629–38, 653, 656, 669, 723, 772–3, 776–7, 780, 795, 802, 804–5, 807, 810, 812, 814–15, 821f, 821g, 821m, 822a, 822b, 822d, 825–6, 830–7, 848, 867
Miesner, H., *xi*, *xxi*, 275, 280, 764, 778, 783, 789–93, 796–802, 805, 808–11, 815–19, 821, 821a, 821b, 821e, 821f, 821h, 821i, 821j, 821m, 821n, 821o, 823, 824a, 824e, 824f, 830, 832–3, 836–7, 841, 855–6, 861, 864
Miller, 730, 732, 734, 757
Mitchell, W. J., 280, 868, 870

Mitringer, H., *xi*
Mozart, W. A., *xxiv*, 81, 875
Müller, 821
Müller, K. W., 695
Müller, W., 192
Münter, D. B., 724–9, 849
Müthel, J. G., 350
Naegeli, H., 501
Neeman, H., 563
Nemetz-Fiedler, K., 123
Newman, W. S., *xi*, 417, 435, 461
Nichelmann, C., 348, 484.2, 487, 498, 872
Niemann, W., 868
Opotchinsky, D., 686
Oppel, J. E., 484.3
Ottenberg, H.-J., 143
Overbeck, C. A., 750
Palm, 821, 821a
Penzel, C. F., 545
Pincherle, M., 585
Plamenac, D., 292
Plath, W., *xxiv*
Pölchau, G., *xxii–xxiii*, *xxv*, 389.5, 484, 772, 776, 835, 847
Poelitz, [K. H. L.], 371
Pollain, F., 439
Porter, C. H., *xi*
Pretlack, Franz Freiherr von, *xxv*
Pretlack, Ludwig Freiherr von, *xxv*
Prieger, E., 483, 490, 541, 565
Primrose, W., 510
Prüfer, 700
Rambach, 821, 821j
Ramge, H., *xi*
Ramler, C. W., 776–7
Raspé, P., *xi*
Recke, Elise v.d., 760
Reichardt, J. F., 389.5
Rellstab, J. C. F., 699
Restout, D., 483
Riedel, F. W., *xxv*
Riegel, J., 388
Riemann, H., 583
Rifkin, J., 775
Röding, J. H., 702–5
Roe, S., 69, 104, 351, 377, 379, 597
Roskam, 188
Ruf, H., 504
Rumpf, 857
Sander, J. D., 749, 833
Sasse, D., *xxiv*
Schäffer, 821, 821m
Schaffrath, C., 565
Scheele, 836
Scheffler, 360
Scheidler, 275
Scherlitz, 275
Schetelig, 821
Schicht, J. G., 542.5
Schiebeler, D., 712–14, 716–18, 775, 821a

Schilling, G., 868
Schiørring, N., 780
Schlegel, J.A., 758
Schmid, B., 435
Schmid, E. F., *xi*, *xx*, 21, 416, 482, 537–41, 565, 591, 593, 597, 824a, 861
Schmid, L., *xx*
Schmid, M., *xx*
Schmidt, 861
Schmieder, W., 1, 16, 373, 388–9, 542.5, 576, 587
Schnapper, E. B., 69
Schniebes, G. F., *xx–xxi*
Schneider, K., 592
Schuback, 821c
Schubert, F., *xxiv*
Schuchmacher, Schuhmacher, 821, 821c
Schulenberg, D., *xi*
Schuldze, 821
Schultze, 821
Schulze, H.-J., *xxiii*, 481.5, 484.2, 484.6, 830
Schwartz, H., 479
Schweitzer, A., 275
Schwenke, C. F. G., *xxiii*, 802
Schwickert, E. B., 292, 870
Scriba, D. P., 721
Seifert, J. G., 500
Selinger-Barber, R., 75.5, 348–9, 370
Serwer, H., *xi*, 686, 775–8
Siegele, U., 484, 590.5
Simon, J., 373
Sitt, H., 512, 514
Smigelski, W., 484.2
Smith, C., *xxiv*, 96–8
Som, 821
Sperontes (J. S. Scholze), 16, 670
Sporon, B. G., 843
Stahl, 671
Steen, 821, 821f
Steffan, 155
Steffin, F., 775
Steglich, R., 1
Steinberg, M., 497
Steinfeld, A. J., 776
Steinhauer, 672
Stephani, W., 820
Stevens, J., *xi*
Stolberg, F. L. von, 753
Stresow, 824f
Sturm, C. C., 749, 752, 821, 821i, 826
Suchalla, E., *xi*, *xix*, *xxii–xxv*, 484.1, 487, 498, 648, 651, 653, 659, 667
Swieten, G. van, 657–62
Szarvady, W., 484.2
Tartini, G., 399
Telemann, G. F., *xxi–xxii*, 782–5, 787–9, 791–3, 795–7, 799–801, 821, 855–6, 862–3
Terry, C. S., 70–75, 382, 387, 546–7, 597, 640, 644–5, 668
Terry, M., *xi*, *xix*, *xxii*, 267, 392
Thulemeier, F. W. von, *xxiv*

Timbrell, C., *xi*
Tischer, J. N., 501
Tovey, D. F., 663
Troth, E.W., *xi*
Türk (Turck), D. G., 385
Uldall, H., 445, 484.2, 484.3, 498–501
Unzer, J. C., 708
Uz, J. P., 667
Vander Linden, A., *xi, xxii*, 648
Von Döhren, 821, 821g
Voss, J. H. von, 572, 732, 736–739.5, 746, 751, 754, 777–8
Voss, O. von, 484.4, 572
Voss-Buch, Count von, *xxiv*
Vrieslander, O., 272, 376
Wächter, 821
Wade, R., *xi, xix–xx, xxv–xxvi*, 192, 383–4, 419, 428, 480.5, 481, 481.5, 482–90, 492, 494–501, 818.5
Wagener, R., *xxii*
Webster, J., *xi*
Weidensaul, J. B., 563
Welcker, 69
Welter, F., *xxi*
Wenzinger, A., 654
Wernigerode, Grafen von, 842
Wessel, 821
Wessely, K. B., *xx*
Weston, G. B., 408
Westphal, J. C., *xix*, 28
Westphal, J. J. H.
as cataloguer or source of information, *xix–xxii, xxv–xxvii*, 155, 338, 349, 386, 445, 484.6, 525, 739, 762–3, 767, 776, 781

as collector of C. P. E. Bach's music, *xix–xxiii, xxv–xxvii*, 7-8, 10–12, 21, 23, 42–3, 47–8, 52, 56–7, 61, 64, 349, 777, 822a, 822b

as copyist, *xix, xxiii, xxv–xxvii*, 2, 14, 38–41, 44, 54–5, 58–9, 63, 65–7, 69, 75.5, 76–7, 79–82, 84–7, 89–102, 105, 107–14, 116–18, 120, 122–5, 131–4, 144–9, 153–5, 159, 165–72, 179, 195, 210, 214–26, 234, 240–1, 249–54, 259, 263, 275, 285, 293–4, 301–31, 336, 338, 349, 404, 442–3, 573, 580–1, 583–4, 586–7, 590, 600–1, 628, 652, 663–6, 685, 688–9, 693–5, 698, 709–21, 724–32, 736–8, 739.5, 742–6, 750–1, 753–4, 764–6, 773–4, 776, 803, 829, 868–9, 874
Whitehead, P. J. P., *xxiv*
Wichmann, 821
Wieland, C. M., 688, 723
Wilderer, 861
Willerding, 821, 821g, 821o
Winkler, 821, 821f
Wolf, J., *xxiv*
Wolf, J. K., 500
Wotquenne, A., *xix, xxii–xxvii*, 37, 442, 460, 463–4, 635, 648, 739, 761–2, 764, 767, 781, 798, 800, 802–3, 805, 809, 814, 840, 868, 874
Zachariae, F. W., 862
Zelenka, J. D., 861
Zelter, C. F., *xxiii–xxiv*, 778
Zhitomirskaia, S. V., 192
Ziegler, M. von, 670
Zinck, B. F., 844

Corrections of Work-List
in The New Grove Dictionary
of Music and Musicians *(1980)*

Change all headings of "probably authentic" to "possibly authentic." Also note in this catalogue that the *Grove* category "doubtful or spurious" has been split into two categories, "doubtful" and "spurious," as indicated in individual corrections below.

H. No. in Grove	H.No. in This Catalogue, If Different	Other Corrections
1	1.5	
35	32.5	
		H.44 = W.118/3
		H.51–2 = W.65/20 [266, 268]; 65/21
88	101.5	H.101.5 = W.112/19 [119/5]
		H.116–20 = W.62/16–20
		H.136–40: Add: 138, cf H.334
		H.159–60 = W.116/15; 117/14; i.e., Minuet, C, by ?1762 [*601]; Fantasia, D, by 1762, pubd in *Versuch*, ii [cf 870]
		H.161 = W.52/5; i.e., Sonata, E, 1762 (1763)
		H.162 = W.53/1; i.e., Sonata, C, 1762 (1766²)
		H.163–5 = W.53/5; 68; 112/3 [116/9]; i.e., Sonata, C, 1762 (1766²); Veränderungen und Auszierungen über einige meiner Sonaten, completed 1762 or later, autograph *D-bds*; Minuet, D, 1762–5 (1765) [*602]; 165 ed. in HL
		H.166 = 112/5 [116/10]; i.e., Alla polacca, a, 1762–5 (1765) [*605]; ed. in VK
		H.167–72 = W.112/9, 11, 16–17 [116/11–14]; 116/1–2; i.e., Minuet, D; Alla polacca, g [*603, *154]; Minuet, A; Alla polacca, D [*604]: 1762–5 (1765); Minuet, Polonoise, E♭, by 1763 [1762]; 168, 170 ed. in in VK, 169 ed. in HL. Note: *Musikalisches Mancherley* was pubd in 1762–3; read [1763] wherever *Grove* identifies it as [1762].
103	75.5	
239	340	(moved to "possibly authentic" category)
		H.243–7: In 2nd line, change (1770) to (1779)

H. No. in Grove	H.No. in This Catalogue, If Different	Other Corrections
		H.248 = W.65/47; i.e., Sonata, C, 1775
		H.249–54 = W.116/23–8; i.e., Sechs leichte Clavier-Stückgen, C, F, D, G, B♭, D, 1775, B (autograph), *B-Bc*, intended as a set [259, 493, 518, 521, 534, 610–11, 613–14, 616, 620, 635: all *; 255–6, variants]; cf 259
		H.255–8: change 3rd line to read: [*613–14, *616, *625, *635; 252, 254, 306, variants]
		H.259: Change end of 3rd line to read: cf 493
		H.285: Change end of 3rd line to read: cf 867
		H.292–7: In 2nd line, change 869 to 868
		H.332: Deleted; found to be vnt. of H. 9, 11
		H.334: Change to read: Variations, C, late variant of 3rd movt of H.138
335	352	(moved to "possibly authentic" category)
339	348	
340	359	(moved to "doubtful" category)
341	339	
342	371	(moved to "doubtful" category)
343–5	341–2, 368	(368 moved to "doubtful" category)
346	343	
347	344	
348	345	
349–50	346–7	
351		Deleted
352	370	(moved to "doubtful" category)
353–8	362, 364–6, 387, 367	(387 moved to "spurious" category; the others moved to "doubtful" category)
359	349	
360	350	

H. No. in Grove	H. No. in This Catalogue, If Different	Other Corrections
361	351	
362–4	395–7	(moved to "spurious" category)
365–8	400–02,	(moved to "spurious" category)
	398	Change to read: 2 untitled, A, a; frag, a; Menuetten zum tantzen, D, frag
369	353–6	Change to read: Polonoise, D; Polonoise, D; Polonoise, A; Larghetto, G
370	374	(moved to "doubtful" category)
371	376	(now in "spurious" category)
372	378	(now in "spurious" category)
373	379	Change to read: Sonata, F, *c* 1763, *B*, kbd part only of sonata by J. C. Bach
374	360	(now in "doubtful" category)
375	380	(now in "spurious" category)
376	381	(now in "spurious" category)
377	382	(now in "spurious" category)
378	383	(now in "spurious" category)
379	384	(now in "spurious" category)
380	385	(now in "spurious" category)
381	386	(now in "spurious" category)
382	361	(now in "doubtful" category)
383	363	(now in "doubtful" category)
384	390	(now in "spurious" category)
385–90	392–392.5	(now in "spurious" category)
392	388	(now in "spurious" category)
393	389	(now in "spurious" category)
394	373	(now in "doubtful" category)
395–6	393–4	(now in "spurious" category)
397	407	Change to read: Allegro, c, *B*; kbd arr. of 3rd movt of H.407
398	375	(now in "doubtful" category)
399–401	399–402	(now in "spurious" category) Change to read: Tempo di men[uetto]-variation, A; untitled, A; untitled, a; untitled, a, *B* [399, 402 by Kirnberger; 400–01 ? by Kirnberger] H.402: Delete entire line
408–9	409–10	
410	408	
426	484.1	(moved to "doubtful" category) H.480: Change to read: Sonatina III, D, hpd, 2 fl, str, *c* 1762, *LEm*; combination of 80, 82, 453, 480.5, 600/12
481	480.5	Change to read: Sonatina, D, hpd, 2 fl, str, *c* 1762, *D-B*; combination of 80, 82, 453, 480, 600/9, 600/12
483	484.4	(now in "doubtful" category)
484–5	481, 481.5	
486	484.2	(now in "doubtful" category)
490	491	(now in "spurious" category)
491	492	(now in "spurious" category)
492	493	(now in "spurious" category)
493–4	494–6	(now in "spurious" category) Change to read: 3 concs., E♭, F, B♭, hpd, insts, by 1780, 494–5, *D-GOl*, 496, *WRtl* [all by J. C. Bach]
495	484.3	(now in "doubtful" category)
496	499	(now in "spurious" category)
497	498	(now in "spurious" category)
498	486	(now in "doubtful" category) Change to read: Conc., C, hpd, insts, *CS-Bm* ["del Sig. Bach"]
499	484.5	(now in "doubtful" category) Change to read: Conc., b, hpd, insts, *CS-Bm* ["del Sig. Bach"], *D-Ds* ["Carlo Bach"]
500	485	(now in "doubtful" category) Change to read: Conc., F, hpd, insts, *CS-Bm* ["del Sig. Emen. Pach"]
501	497	(now in "spurious" category) Change to read: Conc., D, vn/va/4 viols, pf/orch; [by Henri Casadesus, *c* 1905]
503		Change to read: Sonata, d, hpd, vn, 1731, rev. 1747 [*596]
504		Change to read: Sonata, C, hpd, vn, 1745 [*573]
506		Change to read: Trio, E, hpd, fl, ?1749 or later [*580]
508–9		Change to read: 2 sonatas, G, hpd, fl, 1754–5 [*581, *583, *586]
516–21		Change to read: Sei Sonate, E♭, E♭, E♭, B♭, E♭, B♭, hpd, cl, bn, after 1767 [*251, *254–5, *299, *610, *613–14, *629–31, *633, *635]
522–4		Change to read: [3] claviersonaten, i, a, G, C, hpd, vn, vc, 1775 (Leipzig, 1776); [†491]
536		Change "sketches in 868" to "sketches in 867"
545		(now in "spurious" category)
546–7		(now in "spurious" category)
572–5		Change to read: 4 sonatas, a, C, G, D, fl, vn, bc, 572 1735, rev. 1747 [+377], 573 1745 [*504], 574 1747, 575 1747 [*505]
578–9		H. nos. omitted in *Grove*; H.578–9 = W.161/2, 1. In 2nd line, change E♭ to c
587–9		In "W" column, read: 159; 163
590		Change "sonata, F" to "sonata, d"
593		Change beginning to read: Sonata, E♭, fl, vn, bc . . .
594		Deleted
595		(now in "doubtful" category)
596		(now in "doubtful" category)
597		(now in "doubtful" category) Change 1st line to read: Trio, F, fl, vn, hpd, attrib . . .
601		[*159], not [*161]
602–3		[*165, *167], not [*167, *169]
604–5		[*170, *166], not [*168, *172]
610–13		Substitute between brackets: *250–51, *254–5, *324, *518, *521, *614, *620, *635

H. No. in Grove	H. No. in This Catalogue, If Different	Other Corrections
614–19		Substitute between brackets: *252, 254–6, *327–330, *518, *613
635		Change beginning to read: [30] Stücke für Spieluhren . . . . Add between brackets: [*162]
639		(now in "doubtful" category) Change 2nd line to read: ob, 3 insts, *D-B*
640	643	(now in "spurious" category)
641	644	(now in "spurious" category) Change beginning to read: 3 trios, D, E♭, G . . .
642	645	(now in "spurious" category)
643	640	(now in "doubtful" category)
644–5	641–2	(now in "doubtful" category)
646		(now in "spurious" category)
647		(now in "spurious" category)
667		(moved to "possibly authentic" category)
685		Between brackets, change "125" to "*125"
686		Add between brackets: ?*791, ?*797, *796
697		Change "Rosbach" to "Rossbach"
689		Change H. No. to 685.5, change date to "probably c. 1757"
696		On line 4, change "Karschin" to Karsch"
699		On line 1, change "Bleim" to "Gleim"
700–1		On line 1, change "Thrysis" to "Thyrsis"
702–8		On line 1, change "Lütkens" to "Lüttkens"
718–21		On line 1, change "Karschin" to "Karsch"
722		Deleted (see 739)
723		Change to read: Der Frühling, cantata (Wieland), T, str, bc, 1770–72 [*688]
736–7		Change 200/G/1–2 to 202/G/1–2
738		= W.202/I/1. Change to read: Trinklied für Freye (Voss), 1775, in *Musen-Almanach*, ed. J. H. Voss (Hamburg, 1776); cf 732

H. No. in Grove	H. No. in This Catalogue, If Different	Other Corrections
739		= W.236. Change to read: Selma (Voss), cantata, S, 2fl, 2 vn, va, bc, ?1775
	739.5	= W.202/I/2. Alternative version of 739, 1775, in *Musen-Almanach*, ed. J. H. Voss (Hamburg, 1776); cf 732
749		Add between brackets: ?*794
752		Add between brackets: ?*798
755–60		Change last 2 lines to read: Muth (E. von der Recke): 755–9 by ?1782, 760 1785, all (1789)
776		Change beginning to read: Passions-Cantate (L. Karsch), solo vv, . . .
791		Read "791–3."
797		On line 2, change "†724" to "†729."
806		Deleted
813		Deleted
821–4		Change "c50" to "c30."
846		Deleted
848		Deleted
849	848	
	849	Deleted
851–2		Deleted
853	859	
855	860	(now in "spurious" category)
856	855	(now in "doubtful" category)
857	856	(now in "doubtful" category)
858	861	(now in "spurious" category)
859	862	(now in "spurious" category)
860	863	(now in "spurious" category)
861	864	(now in "spurious" category)
862–3	857–8	(now in "doubtful" category)
864	865	(now in "spurious" category)
865	866	(now in "spurious" category)
866	866.5	(now in "spurious" category)
869	868	
872		(now in "doubtful" category)
873		(now in "spurious" category)
874		(now in "spurious" category)
875		(now in "spurious" category)

Concordance of Wotquenne Numbers (W.)
with Item Numbers
in This Catalogue (H.)

W.	H.	W.	H.	W.	H.	W.	H.
1	403	43/3	473	54/1	204	62/1	2
2	404	43/4	474	54/2	205	62/2	20
3	405	43/5	475	54/3	184	62/3	22
4	406	43/6	476	54/4	206	62/4	38
5	407	44	477	54/5	185	62/5	39
6	409	45	478	54/6	207	62/6	40
7	410	46	408	55/1	244	62/7	41
8	411	47	479	55/2	130	62/8	55
9	412	48/1	24	55/3	245	62/9	58
10	413	48/2	25	55/4	186	62/10	59
11	414	48/3	26	55/5	243	62/11	63
12	415	48/4	27	55/6	187	62/12	66
13	416	48/5	28	56/1	260	62/13	67
14	417	48/6	29	56/2	246	62/14	77
15	418	49/1	30	56/3	261	62/15	105
16	419	49/2	31	56/4	269	62/16	116
17	420	49/3	33	56/5	262	62/17	117
18	421	49/4	32	56/6	270	62/18	118
19	422	49/5	34	57/1	265	62/19	119
20	423	49/6	36	57/2	247	62/20	120
21	424	50/1	136	57/3	271	62/21	131
22	425	50/2	137	57/4	208	62/22	132
23	427	50/3	138	57/5	266	62/23	210
24	428	50/4	139	57/6	173	62/24	240
25	429	50/5	126	58/1	276	63/1	70
26	430	50/6	140	58/2	273	63/2	71
27	433	51/1	150	58/3	274	63/3	72
28	434	51/2	151	58/4	188	63/4	73
29	437	51/3	127	58/5	267	63/5	74
30	440	51/4	128	58/6	277	63/6	75
31	441	51/5	141	58/7	278	63/7	292
32	442	51/6	62	59/1	281	63/8	293
33	443	52/1	50	59/2	268	63/9	294
34	444	52/2	142	59/3	282	63/10	295
35	446	52/3	158	59/4	283	63/11	296
36	447	52/4	37	59/5	279	63/12	297
37	448	52/5	161	59/6	284	64/1	7
38	454	52/6	129	60	209	64/2	8
39	465	53/1	162	61/1	288	64/3	9
40	467	53/2	180	61/2	286	64/4	10
41	469	53/3	181	61/3	289	64/5	11
42	470	53/4	182	61/4	290	64/6	12
43/1	471	53/5	163	61/5	287	65/1	3
43/2	472	53/6	183	61/6	291	65/2	4

W.	H.	W.	H.	W.	H.	W.	H.
65/3	5	70/5	86	109	453	116/9	165
65/4	6	70/6	87	110	459	116/10	166
65/5	13	70/7	107	111	1.5	116/11	167
65/6	15	71	502	112/1	190	116/12	168
65/7	16	72	503	112/2	144	116/13	169
65/8	17	73	504	112/3	165	116/14	170
65/9	18	74	507	112/4	145	116/15	159
65/10	19	75	511	112/5	166	116/16	338
65/11	21	76	512	112/6	693	116/17	338
65/12	23	77	513	112/7	179	116/18	108
65/13	32.5	78	514	112/8	146	116/19	301
65/14	42	79	535	112/9	167	116/20	302
65/15	43	80	536	112/10	147	116/21	153
65/16	46	81	600	112/11	168	116/22	154
65/17	47	82	628	112/12	694	116/23	249
65/18	48	83	505	112/13	191	116/24	250
65/19	49	84	506	112/14	695	116/25	251
65/20	51	85	508	112/15	148	116/26	252
65/21	52	86	509	112/16	169	116/27	253
65/22	56	87	515	112/17	170	116/28	254
65/23	57	88	510	112/18	149	116/29	303
65/24	60	89/1	525	112/19	101.5	116/30	304
65/25	61	89/2	526	113/1	193	116/31	305
65/26	62	89/3	527	113/2	194	116/32	306
65/27	68	89/4	528	113/3	195	116/33	307
65/28	78	89/5	529	113/4	196	116/34	308
65/29	83	89/6	530	113/5	197	116/35	309
65/30	106	90/1	522	113/6	198	116/36	310
65/31	121	90/2	523	113/7	199	116/37	311
65/32	135	90/3	524	113/8	200	116/38	312
65/33	143	91/1	531	113/9	201	116/39	313
65/34	152	91/2	532	113/10	202	116/40	314
65/35	156	91/3	533	113/11	203	116/41	315
65/36	157	91/4	534	114/1	228	116/42	316
65/37	174	92/1	516	114/2	229	116/43	317
65/38	175	92/2	517	114/3	230	116/44	318
65/39	176	92/3	518	114/4	231	116/45	319
65/40	177	92/4	519	114/5	232	116/46	320
65/41	178	92/5	520	114/6	233	116/47	321
65/42	189	92/6	521	114/7	234	116/48	322
65/43	192	93	537	114/8	235	116/49	323
65/44	211	94	538	114/9	236	116/50	324
65/45	212	95	539	114/10	237	116/51	325
65/46	213	96	449	114/11	238	116/52	326
65/47	248	97	450	115/1	610	116/53	327
65/48	280	98	451	115/2	611	116/54	328
65/49	298	99	452	115/3	612	116/55	329
65/50	299	100	455	115/4	613	116/56	330
66	272	101	460	116/1	171	116/57	331
67	300	102	456	116/2	172	117/1	241
68	164	103	457	116/3	214	117/2	220
69	53	104	463	116/4	215	117/3	221
70/1	133	105	464	116/5	216	117/4	222
70/2	134	106	458	116/6	217	117/5	145
70/3	84	107	461	116/7	218	117/6	147
70/4	85	108	462	116/8	219	117/7	149

W.	H.	W.	H.	W.	H.	W.	H.
117/8	144	122/5	227	178	653	199/6	680
117/9	146	123	550	179	654	199/7	678
117/10	148	124	551	180	655	199/8	683
117/11	223	125	552	181	656	199/9	681
117/12	224	126	553	182/1	657	199/10	671
117/13	225	127	554	182/2	658	199/11	675
117/14	160	128	555	182/3	659	199/12	672
117/15	195	129	556	182/4	660	199/13	682
117/16	234	130	560	182/5	661	199/14	676
117/17	79	131	561	182/6	662	199/15	684
117/18	80	132	562	183/1	663	199/16	689
117/19	89	133	564	183/2	664	199/17	690
117/20	90	134	548	183/3	665	199/18	691
117/21	91	135	549	183/4	666	199/19	692
117/22	122	136	558	184/1	629	199/20	687
117/23	92	137	559	184/2	630	200/1	745
117/24	93	138	557	184/3	631	200/2	755
117/25	94	139	563	184/4	632	200/3	756
117/26	81	140	598	184/5	633	200/4	757
117/27	95	141	599	184/6	634	200/5	748
117/28	109	142	636	185/1	614	200/6	702
117/29	123	143	567	185/2	615	200/7	758
117/30	110	144	568	185/3	616	200/8	703
117/31	111	145	569	185/4	617	200/9	734
117/32	112	146	570	185/5	618	200/10	700
117/33	113	147	571	185/6	619	200/11	704
117/34	96	148	572	186	620	200/12	705
117/35	97	149	573	187	637	200/13	740
117/36	114	150	574	188	621	200/14	747
117/37	82	151	575	189/1	602	200/15	706
117/38	124	152	581	189/2	603	200/16	759
117/39	98	153	586	189/3	622	200/17	707
117/40	125	154	576	189/4	623	200/18	760
118/1	69	155	577	189/5	624	200/19	708
118/2	155	156	582	189/6	625	200/20	701
118/3	44	157	583	189/7	626	200/21	741
118/4	54	158	584	189/8	606	200/22	735
118/5	65	159	587	190/1	604	201	699
118/6	226	160	590	190/2	607	202/A	688
118/7	14	161	578–9	190/3	605	202/B/1	693
118/8	275	162	580	190/4	608	202/B/2	694
118/9	263	163	588	190/5	609	202/B/3	695
118/10	259	164	466	190/6	627	202/C/1	709
119/1	76	165	468	191	638	202/C/2	710
119/2	99	166	431	192	601	202/C/3	711
119/3	100	167	435	193	635	202/C/4	712
119/4	101	168	438	194	686	202/C/5	713
119/5	101.5	169	445	195	696	202/C/6	714
119/6	102	170	432	196	733	202/C/7	715
119/7	75.5	171	436	197	749	202/C/8	716
120	264	172	439	198	752	202/C/9	717
121	867	173	648	199/1	677	202/C/10	718
122/1	45	174	649	199/2	670	202/C/11	719
122/2	104	175	650	199/3	679	202/C/12	720
122/3	115	176	651	199/4	673	202/C/13	721
122/4	191	177	652	199/5	674	202/D	698

W.	H.	W.	H.	W.	H.	W.	H.
202/E/1	724	203	781	228	836	253	821m
202/E/2	725	204	780, 871	229	837	254	868
202/E/3	726	205	773	230	795	255	870
202/E/4	727	206	774	231	762	256	868, 873
202/E/5	728	207	825	232	697	257	869
202/E/6	729	208	826	233	776	258	874
202/F/1	731	209	839	234	800	259	See KURZE I.
202/F/2	732	210	840	235	802	260	Regarding W.
202/G/1	736	211	669	236	739	261	259, see also
202/G/2	737	212	812	237	723	262	H. 868.
202/H	744	213	767	238	775	263	776
202/I/1	738	214	761	239	779	264	699
202/I/2	739.5	215	772	240	777	265	See PRELUDIO.
202/J	746	216	829	241	805	266	See TROIS SONATES.
202/K/1	750	217	778	242	804	267	See KURZE I.
202/K/2	751	218	827	243	807	268	51
202/L/1	753	219	828	244	803	269	14
202/L/2	754	220	855	245	810	270	263
202/M	See H. 75.	221	830	246	814	271	220
202/N	764	222	831	247	812	272	386
202/O/1	742	223	832	248	809		
202/O/2	730	224	798	249	815		
202/O/3	765	225	833	250	821l		
202/O/4	743	226	834	251	821g		
202/O/5	766	227	835	252	821f		

W. 273–8 lists portraits of the composer, not dealt with in H.
W. 279 is the NACHLASS-VERZEICHNIS.

Concordance of Numbers in Kast,
Die Bach-Handschriften (Wq n.v.)
with Item Numbers in This Catalogue (H.)

Wq n.v.	H.		Wq n.v.	H.
1	838		36	498
2	796		37	256
3	794		38	257
4	797		39	258
5	857		40	407
6	858		41	390
7	797		42	391
8	797		43	391
9	797		44	771
10	776		45	399
11	768		46	400
12	769		47	401
13	770		48	402
14	376		49	398
15	393		50	353
16	860		51	354
17	394		52	355
18	337		53	171
19	639		54	340
20	336		55	356
21	336		56	392
22	859		57	392.1
23	341		58	392.2
24	342		59	392.3
25	343		60	392.4
26	344		61	392.5
27	339		62	610
28	345		63	611
29	368		64	612
30	379		65	613
31	7		66	352
32	9, 11		67	484.4
33	487		68	484.3
34	360		69	667
35	350		70	535

Bibliography

Not listed here:

1. Early and modern prints of single compositions. See the individual items in the main body of the catalogue for these. Early prints of single compositions may be located by consulting the Guide to Early Prints Entirely by C. P. E. Bach.
2. Literature about single compositions. Again, see the individual items in the main body of the catalogue. "Lit." usually means discussion, not merely a listing or a mention.
3. Early printed collections not mentioned in any primary or secondary literature about C. P. E. Bach except for their listing in RISM, vol. B II.

Within this bibliography, abbreviations for early published music collections are underlined. If such a collection consists entirely of music by CPEB, its abbreviation is also marked below with an asterisk. A third distinction of such a published music collection might be that its individual items were composed in different years and are thus scattered in the main body of the present catalogue; in such a case the individual items are listed below not in numerical order but according to their order in the collection. For *chronological* surveys of the early prints of CPEB's music, see Guide to Early Prints Entirely by C. P. E. Bach and Guide to Early Prints Containing Music of C.P.E. Bach with Music of Other Composers.

Abhandlung von der Fuge: See MARPURG/ABHANDLUNG.

ACCOMPANIED SONATAS I. Carl Philipp Emanuel Bachs Claviersonaten mit einer Violine und einem Violoncell zur Begleitung. Erster Sammlung. Leipzig: im Verlage des Autors [printed by Bernhard Christoph Breitkopf & Sohn], 1776 (items 522-24; W. 90). Lit.: CPEB/FORKEL, 20 Sept. 1775; CPEB/BREITKOPF, 2 Apr., 2 May, 18 June, 19 July, 31 July, 6 Aug., 7 Aug., 23 Aug. 1776; HAMBURGER CORRESPONDENT, 6 Sept. 1776, 22 Feb. 1777; FORKEL/BIBLIOTHEK, II (1778), 275-300; ROCHLITZ/FREUNDE, IV (1832), 301; BITTER/BRÜDER, I, 208-11; HASE, 94-95; STEGLICH/HOMILIUS, 108; VRIESLANDER/BACH, 96; SCHMID/KAMMERMUSIK, 72, 79-80, 136 (facing page), 163; GEIRINGER/BACH, 362-63; NEWMAN, 29, 102-03; GEIRINGER/CHAMBER, 535; WADE, 40-41

ACCOMPANIED SONATAS II. Six Sonatas for the Harpsichord or Piano-Forte [accompanied by violin and cello] composed by C. P. E. Bach, Director of the music at Hamburgh. London, printed and sold by Robert Bremner, 1776 (items 525-30; W. 89). Another edn.: *Six Sonates pour le Clavecin ou Piano Forte Accompagnées d'un Violon & Violoncelle Composées par C. P. E. Bach, Maître de Chapelle et Directeur de Musique à Hambourg. Oeuvre Second.* Chez Jean Julien Hummel à Berlin avec Privilège du Roi, à Amsterdam au Grand Magazin de Musique et aux Addresses ordinaires, [1778]. Lit.: CPEB/FORKEL, 20 Sept. 1775; HAMBURGER CORRESPONDENT, 1777, No. 61 (Bremner edn.); ROCHLITZ, IV (1832), 301 (Hummel edn.); BITTER/BRÜDER, I, 211-12; SCHMID/KAMMERMUSIK, 81-82, 150, 163; GEIRINGER/BACH, 362-63; GEIRINGER/CHAMBER, 535; COHEN, 111

ACCOMPANIED SONATAS III. Carl Philipp Emanuel Bachs Claviersonaten mit einer Violine und einem Violoncell zur Begleitung. Zweyte Sammlung. Leipzig: im Verlage des Autors [printed by Johann Gottlob Immanuel Breitkopf], 1777 (items 531-34; W. 91). Lit.: CPEB/BREITKOPF, 20 Nov., 30 Dec. 1776; 28 Jan., 4 Apr., 19 June, 13 July, 23 July, 9 Aug,. 27 Sept., 4 Oct., 26 Nov., 10 Dec. 1777; 3 Jan., 21 Feb. 1778; FORKEL/BIBLIOTHEK, II (1778), 275-300; BITTER/BRÜDER, I, 210-11; HASE, 95; STEGLICH/HOMILIUS, 108; VRIESLANDER/BACH, 96; SCHMID/KAMMERMUSIK, 72, 79-80, 149-50, 164; GEIRINGER/BACH, 362-63; NEWMAN, 29, 102-03; GEIRINGER/CHAMBER, 535; WADE, 40-41

ALBRECHT. O. E. Albrecht, *A Census of Autograph Music Manuscripts of European Composers in American Libraries* (Philadelphia, 1953)

ALLERLEY. *Musikalisches Allerley von verschiedenen Tonkünstlern,* 9 vols. Berlin: F. W. Birnstiel, 1761-63 (items 2, 40, 63, 66, 69, 109-13, 123, 155, 773-74. Lit.: HILLER/NACHRICHTEN, 12 Feb. 1770, 56; BITTER/BRÜDER, I, 79-83; BUSCH, 71, 104; WADE, 56; OTTENBERG, 140-41. *Musikalisches Allerley, Musikalisches Mancherley,* and *Musikalisches Vielerley* (see MANCHERLEY and VIELERLEY in this bibliography) are anthologies of music aimed frankly at the amateur market. The appearance of ALLERLEY in 1761-63 no doubt stimulated the production of MAN-

CHERLEY in 1762–63 and VIELERLEY in 1770. The first two anthologies were issued serially, a few pages each week (with an occasional sonata or set of keyboard variations continued from one issue to the next); the third was published as a single volume. All three contain a potpourri of pieces designed for middle-class tastes: little marches, polonaises, minuets, fantasias, solfeggios, character pieces, and sets of variations for keyboard; easy duets and sonatas for wind and string instruments; simple strophic odes and lieder for voice and keyboard; and so on. Sometimes the level is more challenging, as in arias or cantatas for solo voice with keyboard accompaniment, or full-fledged sonatas for keyboard or winds or strings. ALLERLEY and MANCHERLEY mention no editor and are obviously the productions of their respective publishers, each of whom supplied a short preface. MANCHERLEY omits many names of composers. VIELERLEY names CPEB as editor (though CPEB did not provide a preface) and is superior to its two predecessors in quality of appearance, quality of music, and (probably) accuracy of attribution. The composers named in the three anthologies are mostly from Berlin (CPEB, Kirnberger, K. H. Graun, Quantz, Marpurg, Janitsch, Agricola, Seyfarth, C. F. Fasch, and others) or other parts of north Germany (J. C. F. Bach, C. F. Cramer, C. Höckh, J. F. Gräfe, etc.).

ALTMAN DUETS. L. Altman, ed., *Three Duets*. Dayton, Ohio: Sacred Music Press, [c. 1976] (item 635, Nos. 19–21, arr. for organ and harp)

ALTMAN PIECES. _____, ed., *Six pieces for a Musical Clock Mechanism*. Cincinnati: World Library of Sacred Music, [c. 1971] (item 635, Nos. 2, 11, 17, 22, 26, 29)

ALTMAN SUITE. _____, ed., *Suite for an Organ Clock*. Boston: McLaughlin & Reilly, 1964 (item 635, Nos. 1, 4, 9, 18, 23–24, 27–28, arranged for organ)

AMZ. *Allgemeine musikalische Zeitung* (Leipzig, 1798–1849)

Anleitung zur Clavierspielen: See MARPURG/ANLEITUNG.

ANON./SYMPHONIES. [Anon. ed., four symphonies.] Leipzig: Peters, n.d. (an early edn.?) (*ORCHESTER- SINFONIEN)

AUCTION 1805. *Verzeichniss von auserlesenen . . . meistens Neuen Büchern und Kostbaren Werken . . . welche nebst den Musikalien aus dem Nachlass des seel. Kapellmeisters C.P.E. Bach . . . Montags, den 4ten März 1805 in Hamburg . . . offentlich verkauft werden sollen.* Hamburg: Conrad Müller, 1805. A copy is in D-ddr Bds, Mus. Db 313.

AUERBACH. C. Auerbach, *Die deutsche Clavichordkunst des 18. Jahrhunderts,*, 3rd edn. (Kassel, 1959)

Bach, C. P. E., correspondence in general: See "Bach, Carl Philipp Emanuel, letters by," in Index of Names of Persons in Special References.

BACH/LEVY. Johanna Maria Bach (CPEB's widow), letter of 5 Sept. 1789 to Sara Levy (née Itzig) of Berlin. The letter is now in the Bach-Haus in Eisenach and is printed in the appendix of Vol. II of BITTER/BRÜDER.

BALASSA. G. Balassa, ed,. *Six Sonatas.* Budapest: Editio Musica, 1965 (items 516–21)

BARFORD/AFTERTHOUGHTS. P. Barford, "Some Afterthoughts by C. P. E. Bach," *Monthly Musical Record*, 90 (May–June, 1960), 94–98

BARFORD/FANTASIA. _____, "A Fantasia by C. P. E. Bach," *Monthly Musical Record*, 85 (July–Aug., 1955), 144–50

BARFORD/KEYBOARD. _____, *The Keyboard Music of C. P. E. Bach* (London, 1965)

BAUMGART. E. F. Baumgart, ed., . . . *Clavier-Sonaten, Rondos, und freie Phantasien für Kenner und Liebhaber.* Breslau: Leuckart, 1863 (*KENNER I–VI). Good edns., unlike those of Bülow and other contemporaries of Baumgart; valuable preface. Regarding this edn., see SCHENKER/BEITRAG, 7.

BERG. D. Berg, "The Keyboard Sonatas of C. P. E. Bach: An Expression of the Mannerist Principle." Ph.D. dissertation, State University of New York at Buffalo, 1975

BERG/EDITIONS. _____, editions of CPEB's keyboard sonatas in 3 vols. for Henle Verlag, Munich, in progress (Vol. I, published in 1986 as *Klaviersonaten: Auswahl, Band I*, contains items 23, 32.5, 36–37, 40–41, 47, 50, 53, 56–57; Vol. II is scheduled to contain items 59, 78, 83, 106, 116, 118–19, 121, 129, 131–32, 133 [and its revision, 135]; Vol. III is scheduled to contain items 150, 156–57, 174, 177–78, 189, 211, 240, 248, 280.)

BERG/FACSIMILE. _____, compiler, *The Collected Works for Solo Keyboard by Carl Philipp Emanuel Bach, 1714–1788*, 6 vols. New York: Garland, 1985 (Vol. I, items 24–29, 70–75, 184–85, 188, 193–207, 228–38, 267, 273–74, 276–78, 292–97; Vol. II, items 30–34, 36–37, 50, 62, 101.5, 126–30, 136–42, 144–51, 158, 161–63, 165–70, 173, 179–83, 186–87, 190–91, 208, 243–47, 260–62, 265–66, 268–71, 279, 281–84, 286–91, 693–95; Vol. III, items 2–5, 7–13, 15–19, 21, 23, 32.5, 40, 42–43, 46–48, 51, 53, 59, 63, 66, 77, 104, 118–20, 210, 227, 240; Vol. IV, items 6, 45, 52, 56–57, 60–61, 64, 68, 78, 83–87, 106–07, 133–34, 143, 152, 156–57, 174–78, 189, 192, 211–13, 242, 248, 280, 298–99; Vol. V, items 1.5, 44, 54, 65, 69, 75.5, 76, 81, 92–99, 108–14, 123–25, 153–55, 158–60, 171–72, 214–26, 241, 249–55, 256–59, 263, 272, 275, 301–31, 338, plus the parts of item 164 that pertain to items 62, 128, 136–38, 141, 151, 158, 162; Vol. VI, items 1, 14, 20, 22, 38–39, 41, 49, 55, 58, 67, 79–80, 82, 89–91, 100–01, 102, 105, 116–17, 121–22, 131–32, 135, 209, 300, plus the parts of item 164 that pertain to items 36, 116, 127, 163). Photographic reproductions of early mss. and prints, with introductions and critical notes

BERG/JAMS. _____, "Towards a Catalogue of the Sonatas of C. P. E. Bach, "*Journal of the American Musicological Society*, XXXII (Summer 1979), 276–303

BERG/NOTES. Various communications from Darrell Berg,

especially concerning changes in CPEB's keyboard works

BERG/VARIATIONS. D. Berg, "C. P. E. Bach's 'Variations' and 'Embellishments' for His Keyboard Sonatas," *Journal of Musicology*, II (1983), 151–73. To be published in *Bach-Jahrbuch*, 1988, as "Revision in C. P. E. Bachs Klaviersonaten"

Berlinische Oden und Lieder: See MARPURG/ODEN I, MARPURG/ODEN II

BEURMANN/KLAVIERSONATEN. E. Beurmann, "Die Klaviersonaten Carl Philipp Emanuel Bachs." Ph.D. dissertation, Georg-August-Universität, Göttingen, 1952

BEURMANN/REPRISENSONATEN. _____, "Die Reprisensonaten Carl Philipp Emanuel Bachs," *Archiv für Musikwissenschaft*, 13 (1956), 168–79

BITTER/BRÜDER. K. H. Bitter, *Carl Philipp Emanuel und Wilhelm Friedemann Bach und deren Brüder* (Berlin, 1868, reprinted Kassel, 1973 and Leipzig, 1973)

BITTER/LIEDER. _____, ed., *Geistliche Lieder* . . . . Berlin, Simrock, [1867] (item 686, Nos. 3–4, 9, 14, 18, 32, 34, 45–46, 51, 53; item 696, No. 11; item 733, Nos. 4, 6, 20, 23–24, 30; item 749, Nos. 13–14, 16, 19, 22, 29; item 752, Nos. 18, 29). Overedited

BLECHSCHMIDT. E. R. Blechschmidt, *Die Amalienbibliothek* (Berlin, 1965)

BOSSLER. H. P. K. Bossler, ed., *Musikalische Anthologie für Kenner und Liebhaber. Erster Band*. Speyer, 1788 (item 764/10). Lit.: BUSCH, 223. The known lit. gives no evidence that CPEB authorized the appearance of this work in this collection.

BRANDTS-BUYS. H. Brandts-Buys, ed., *Praeludium and Six Sonatas*. Hilversum, Netherlands: Harmonia-Uitgave, n.d. (items 53, 84–87, 108, 134)

BREIG. W. Breig, "Bachs Violinkonzert d-Moll. Studien zu seiner Gestalt und seiner Entstehungsgeschichte," *Bach-Jahrbuch*, LXII (1976), 7–34

BREITKOPF. J. G. I. Breitkopf, *Catalogo IV de' Soli, Duetti, Trii . . . che se trovano in Manoscritto . . .* (Leipzig, 1763) (in Brook, B. S., listed below)

BREWER. R. H. Brewer, "C. P. E. Bach and His Oratorios," *The Choral Journal* (Jan. 1981), 34–40

Brook, B. S., ed,. *The Breitkopf Thematic Catalogue: The Six Parts and Sixteen Supplements, 1762–1787* (New York, 1966)

_____, *Thematic Catalogues in Music, an Annotated Bibliography* (Hillsdale, N.Y., 1972)

BUCK. C. H. Buck III, "Revisions in Early Clavier Concertos of C. P. E. Bach: Revelations from a New Source," *Journal of the American Musicological Society*, XXIX (Spring 1976), 127–32

BÜCKEN. E. Bücken, *Musik des Rokokos und der Klassik* (Potsdam, 1927)

BÜLOW. H. von Bülow, ed., *Sechs Sonaten*. Leipzig: Peters, 1862, reprinted 1928, 1945 (the latter by International) (items 31, 173, 186–87, 208, 247). Falsified, primarily through additions to the harmony; see SCHENKER/BEITRAG, 4–6; STEGLICH/HOMILIUS, 100–03.

BURNEY/STATE. C. Burney, *The Present State of Music in Germany, the Netherlands, and United Provinces . . .* (London, 1773), included in Vol. II of P. A. Scholes, ed., *Dr. Burney's Musical Tours in Europe*, 2 vols. (London, 1959)

BUSCH. G. Busch, *C. Ph. E. Bach und seine Lieder* (Regensburg, 1957). Not always cited in the present catalogue are examples in the Busch "Anhang," which may be found by consulting the pages cited from Busch's main text.

CALAND. E. Caland, ed., *Neues C. Ph. E. Bach-Album*. Münster: Bisping, 1929 (items 74, 142, 151, 188, 278, 283–84, 296; single mvts. from *ZWEYTE FORTSETZUNG and *KENNER IV)

CALAND-GOEBELS. E. Caland and F. P. Goebels, eds., *Sieben Hauptwerke aus dem Klavierschhaffen* . . . . Wilhelmshaven: Heinrichshofen, 1975 (items 94, 110, 128, 141, 261, 274, 276)

Catalogue de la Bibliothèque de F.J. Fétis acquis par l'etat Belge (Paris, 1877)

CHRYSANDER. F. Chrysander, "Eine Klavier-Phantasie von Karl Philipp Emanuel Bach mit nachträglich von Gerstenberg eingefügten Gesangsmelodien zu zwei verschiedenen Texten," *Vierteljahrsschrift für Musikwissenschaft*, 7 (1891), 1–25

CLARK. S. L. Clark, various communications to the author on sources of, functions of, and original documents relating to CPEB's choral music

CLARK/CHORAL. _____, "The Occasional Choral Works of C. P. E. Bach." Ph.D. dissertation, Princeton University, 1984

Clavierstücke verschiedener Art: See *VERSCHIEDEN.

CLERCX. S. Clercx, "La forme du rondo chez Carl Philipp Emanuel Bach," *Revue de musicologie*, 19 (Aug. 1935), 148–67

COHEN. P. Cohen, *Theorie und Praxis der Clavierästhetik Carl Philipp Emanuel Bachs* (Hamburg, 1974)

COLE. M. S. Cole, "Rondos, Proper and Improper," *Music & Letters*, 51 (Oct. 1970), 388–99

COLLECTION I. *Collection récréative contenant VI sonates pour le clavecin . . . Oeuvre 1*. Nuremberg: J. U. Haffner, [1761– 62] (item 132)

COLLECTION II. *Collection récréative contenant VI sonates*

pour le clavecin . . . Oeuvre IIème. Nuremberg: J. U. Haffner, [1761–62] (item 41)

*CONCERTOS I. *Concertos for the Harpsicord, or Organ. With Accompanyments for Violins etc.* . . . London: John Walsh, [c. 1753] (items 414, 429, 417). In this edn. the keyboard parts include arrangements of the tuttis to allow the option of unaccompanied performance. The known lit. gives no evidence that this print was authorized by CPEB.

*CONCERTOS II. *A Second Sett of Three Concertos for the Organ or Harpsicord with Instrumental Parts.* London: Longman, Lukey & Co., [c.1760] (items 421, 444, 428). This edn. treats the keyboard parts as in *CONCERTOS I. The known lit. gives no evidence that this print was authorized by CPEB.

CPEB/6 NOV. 1769. C. P. E. Bach, "Specification der Kosten wegen der Einweyhungs Music der neuen Lazareth Kirche . . . Hamburg, d. 6 Nov. 1769," autog. ms. in D-brd Hs, 1929/594. CLARK notes that this is p. 66 of the RECHNUNGSBUCH, detached from that volume.

CPEB 1770. An "Eigenhändiges thematisches Verzeichnis von Menuetten und Polonoisen" made by CPEB about 1770 is listed in Leo Liepmannssohn's *Lagerkatalog* No. 174 (Berlin, 22 Oct. 1910), along with a "Thematisches Verzeichnis einer musikalischen Bibliothek" supposedly in CPEB's hand (see SCHMID/MGG, col. 935). However, the copy of this *Lagerkatalog* owned by Albi Rosenthal, proprietor of the Otto Haas firm of London (successor to the Liepmannssohn firm), bears the comment "Zweifelhaft" written in the hand of Otto Haas over both these entries, and no buyer's name appears in the margin, which indicates that the manuscripts were probably withdrawn from the auction. I am indebted to Mr. Rosenthal for this information, and to Rachel W. Wade for putting me in touch with him. It seems likely that ms. 5898 in B Bc, entirely in the hand of Westphal and making up W. 116 ("Sammlung von Menuetten, Polonoisen und andern Handstücken . . ."; see the Concordance of Wotquenne Numbers), was copied in accordance with an orderly thematic catalogue of such pieces.

CPEB/11 JAN. 1773. C. P. E. Bach, open letter in HAMBURGER CORRESPONDENT, No. 7 (1773)

CPEB/16 DEC. 1779. _____, letter to J. P. Kirnberger in Berlin, printed in appendix of Vol. II of BITTER/BRÜDER

CPEB/10 APR. 1780. _____, letter to E. B. Schwickert in Leipzig, printed in NOHL, 68

CPEB/5 MAR. 1783. _____, letter to Princess Amalia, printed in BITTER/BRÜDER, II, 302

CPEB/28 APR. 1784. _____, Letter to Advocaten Grave in Greifswald, printed in appendix of Vol. II of BITTER/BRÜDER

CPEB/ARTARIA. Letters from CPEB to the publisher Artaria in Vienna, mss. I.IV. 68558, 68560–61, 68563–66, 68568–70 in A Wst

CPEB/AUTOBIOGRAPHY. C. P. E. Bach, autobiographical sketch published as an insertion in Vol. III of J. J. C. Bode's and C. D. Ebeling's translation of BURNEY/STATE: *Carl Burney's der Musik Doctors Tagebuch seiner musikalischen Reisen . . .* (Hamburg, 1773), facsimile edn., ed. R. Schaal (Kassel, 1959), 198–209. The autobiographical sketch is translated with commentary by W. S. Newman as "Emanuel Bach's Autobiography," *The Musical Quarterly*, LI (April 1965), 363–72, and is published in facsimile edition with annotations by Newman as *Carl Philipp Emanuel Bach's Autobiography*, Facsimiles of Early Biographies, IV (Hilversum, Netherlands, 1967).

CPEB/BREITKOPF. _____, *Briefe von Carl Philipp Emanuel Bach an Johann Gottlob Immanuel Breitkopf und Johann Nicolaus Forkel*, ed. with commentary by E. Suchalla. Mainzer Studien zur Musikwissenschaft, herausgegeben von Helmut Federhofer, Bd. 19 (Tutzing, 1985). The largest single collection of CPEB's letters

CPEB/ESCHENBURG. _____, letters to J. J. Eschenburg, 2 Oct., 1 Dec. 1784; reprinted in NOHL, 2nd edn.

CPEB/FORKEL. _____, letters to the music historian J. N. Forkel in Göttingen, printed in the appendixes of both vols. of BITTER/BRÜDER

CPEB/LISTE VON LIEDERN. _____, untitled autograph ms. in D-brd Hs, 1913/8997. the siglum given here is the title assigned by the library.

CPEB/RAMLER. _____, 2 letters to K. W. Ramler, 5 May 1778 and 20 Nov. 1780, printed in F. Wilhelm, compiler, "Briefe an Karl Wilhelm Ramler," *Vierteljahrsschrift für Litteraturgeschichte*, IV (1891), 254 (No. 29), 256–57 (No. 31); 2 letters to Ramler, 5 Dec. 1781 and 21 Jan. 1785, D-ddr WRgm

CPEB/SCHUCHMACHER. C. P. E. and J. M. Bach, "Unkosten wegen der Einführungs-Musik Sr. Wohlerwürden, des Herrn Pastors Schuchmacher zu St. Jacobi . . . Hamburg, d. 12 Nov. 1771," ms. in A Wgm in the hand of Johanna Maria Bach with additions in the hand of CPEB. CLARK notes that this is p. 89 of the RECHNUNGSBUCH, detached from that volume.

CPEB/VOSS. C. P. E. Bach, 2 letters to J. H. Voss, 5 Aug. and 9 Sept. 1774, accompanying Mus. ms. 2774 , Bd. I (autog.) in D-brd Mbs; the 9 Sept. letter partly reprinted in BUSCH, 126, and in partial facsimile between pp. 112 and 113 of VRIESLANDER/BACH; the entire 9 Sept. letter printed ibid., 122

CPEB/WESTPHAL. _____, letters to the organist J. J. Westphal in Schwerin, four of which, part of Fétis's purchase from the Westphal estate, are printed in BITTER/BRÜDER, appendix of Vol. II, eight others in E. R. Jacobi, "Five Hitherto Unknown Letters from C. P. E. Bach to J. J. H. Westphal" and "Three Additional Letters from C. P. E. Bach to J. J. H. Westphal," *Journal of the American Musicological Society*, XXIII (Spring 1970), 119–27, and XXVII (Spring 1974), 119–25

CRAMER/FLORA. C. F. Cramer, ed., *Flora, erste Sammlung* (Hamburg, 1787)

CRAMER/MAGAZIN. _____, ed., *Magazin der Musik* (Kiel and Hamburg, 1783–89)

*CRAMER/PSALMEN. *Herrn Doctor Cramers übersetzte Psalmen mit Melodien zum Singen bey dem Claviere von Carl Philipp Emanuel Bach.* Leipzig: im Verlage des Autors [printed by Bernhard Christoph Breitkopf & Sohn], 1774 (item 773; W. 196). Lit.: CPEB/BREITKOPF, 24 June, 4 Oct., 9 Oct., 21 Oct., 3 Dec., 21 Dec. 1773; 6 Feb., 9 Feb., 7 Apr., 21 Apr., 16 May, 27 May, 18 July, 12 Oct. 1774; 24 Feb. 1775; HAMBURGER CORRESPONDENT, 20 Oct. 1773, 15 July 1774; CPEB/FORKEL, 4 Mar., 12 July, 5 Aug. 1774; BITTER/BRÜDER, II, 61–70, 295, 297–99; HASE, 93–94; STEGLICH/HOMILIUS, 103; BÜCKEN, 170; GEIRINGER/BACH, 372; BUSCH, 90, 104–18, 270–74, 280–82, 291, 297–99, 302, 310, 317–20, 327–33, 356, 375–76, 382, 389, Anh. 20–27; WADE, 49; OTTENBERG, 213, 217, 280

CRANZ. Anon. ed. [partly ed. by Brahms, according to WADE, 451], *Sechs Concerte für das Pianoforte.* Leipzig: A. Cranz, [1862] (*SEI CONCERTI). The engraver's model for Brahms's edn. of No. 4 of *SEI CONCERTI, partly in Brahms's hand, is in an American private collection.

CRICKMORE. L. Crickmore, "C. P. E. Bach's Harpsichord Concertos," *Music & Letters*, 39 (July 1958), 227–41

CUDWORTH. C. Cudworth, "Ye Olde Spuriosity Shoppe, or Put It in the Anhang," *Music Library Association Notes*, XII (1954–55), 25–40, 533–53

Czach, R., "Thematisches Verzeichnis der Instrumentalkompositionen F. W. Rusts, " in his *Friedrich Wilhelm Rust* (Essen, 1927)

DADELSEN. G. von Dadelsen, *Bemerkungen zur Handschrift Johann Sebastian Bachs, seiner Familie und seines Kreises* (Trossingen, 1957)

DADELSEN/NBA. See NBA.

*DAMENSONATEN. *Six sonates pour le clavecin, à l'usage des dames, composées par Charles Philippe Emanuel Bach, Maître de Chapelle de S. A. R. Madame la Princesse Amélie de Prusse, Abbesse de Quedlinbourg, Directeur des Musiques de la Ville Impériale de Hambourg. Oeuvre premier.* A Amsterdam, chez J. J. Hummel, Marchand et Imprimeur de Musique [1770] (items 204–5, 184, 206, 185, 207; W. 54). Another edn.: *Sei Sonate per il Clavicembalo solo all' uso delle Donne . . . .* Riga: J. F. Hartknoch [printed in Leipzig by Breitkopf], 1773, reprinted 1786. Lit.: BITTER/BRÜDER, I, 205; HASE, 93–4; VRIESLANDER/BACH, 170; REESER, 40; NEWMAN, 45, 260, 423; BARFORD/KEYBOARD, 19, 139–41; RADCLIFFE, 588; see also Critical Notes in BERG/FACSIMILE.

DARBELLAY. E. Darbellay, ed., *Sechs Sonaten mit veränderten Reprisen für Klavier.* Winterthur, Switzerland: Amadeus (Peters), 1976 (*REPRISEN-SONATEN)

Dennerlein, H., "Thematisches Verzeichnis der Instrumentalwerke von J. F. Reichardt," in his *Johann Friedrich Reichardt und seine Klavierwerke* (Münster, 1930)

DEUTSCH. O. E. Deutsch, "Mit Würfeln komponieren," *Zeitschrift für Musikwissenschaft*, XII (1929–30), 595ff.

DIDEROT/CPEB. D. Diderot, 2 letters of 8 Apr. 1774 and shortly thereafter to CPEB, printed in HAMBURGER CORRESPONDENT, 1774, No. 57; in *Neuen gelehrten Mercur*, Altona, 1774, 2. Band, 14. Stück, 105 f.; and in SCHMID/KAMMERMUSIK, 45–46

DITTBERNER. J. Dittberner, ed., *Fünfundzwanzig ausgewählte geistliche Lieder.* Leipzig: Kahnt, 1917 (item 686, Nos. 4, 9–10, 12, 18, 21, 26, 32, 34, 45; item 696, Nos. 2–3; item 733, Nos. 10, 20, 23, 31; Item 749, Nos. 7, 13, 19, 26, 29; item 752, Nos. 6, 18–19, 29). Overedited

DÖLLMANN. H. Döllmann, *Christoph Nichelmann (1717–1762), ein Musiker am Hofe Friedrichs des Grossen* (Löningen, 1938)

DOFLEIN. E. Doflein, ed., *Sechs Sonaten.* Mainz: Schott, 1935 (*PROBESTÜCKE)

DREY VERSUCHE. *Drey verschiedene Versuche eines einfachen Gesanges für den Hexameter.* Berlin: G. L. Winter, 1760 (item 688). Lit.: BITTER/BRÜDER, I, 155–59; LINDNER, 71–73; BUSCH, 68–70

DRUMMOND. P. Drummond, *The German Concerto: Five Eighteenth-Century Studies* (Oxford, 1980)

DÜRR. A. Dürr, ed., *Sonate C-dur für Flöte und Basso continuo BWV 1033, Sonaten Es-dur, g-moll für Flöte und obligates Cembalo BWV 1031, 1020 überliefert als Werke Johann Sebastian Bachs.* Kassel: Bärenreiter, 1975 (items 542.5, 545, 564.5)

Egli: See MUSIKALISCHE BLUMENLESE.

EITNER. R. Eitner, *Biographisch-bibliographisches Quellen-Lexikon der Musiker und Musikgelehrten der christlichen Zeitrechnung bis zur Mitte des 19. Jahrhunderts . . .* (Leipzig, 1898–1904)

ELDER. E. G. Elder, "Carl Philipp Emanuel Bach's Concept of the Free Fantasia," M. A. thesis, Eastman School of Music, 1980

ENGELKE. B. Engelke, "Gerstenberg und die Musik seiner Zeit," *Zeitschrift der Gesellschaft für Schleswig-Holsteinische Geschichte*, LV (1927), 417–48

EPPSTEIN/FLÖTENSONATEN. H. Eppstein, "Über J.S. Bachs Flötensonaten mit Generalbass," *Bach-Jahrbuch*, LVIII (1972), 12–23

EPPSTEIN/STUDIEN. _____, *Studien über J.S. Bachs Sonaten für ein Melodieinstrument und obligates Cembalo* (Uppsala, 1966)

ESPAGNE. F. Espagne, ed., *4 Orchester-Sinfonien.* Leipzig: Peters, 1860 (items 663–65—only the first 3 of *OR-CHESTER-SINFONIEN—despite the title)

"Essay" Sonatas: See *PROBESTÜCKE.

Exempel nebst 18 Probestücken: See *PROBESTÜCKE.

FALCK.   M. Falck, "Thematisches Verzeichnis der Werke von Wilhelm Friedemann Bach," in his *Wilhelm Friedemann Bach* (Leipzig, 1913, 2nd edn. 1919)

FARRENC.   L. Farrenc and A. Farrenc, eds., *Le trésor des pianistes*, 20 vols. Paris: A. and L. Farrenc, 1861–74 (reprinted New York, 1977), Vols. XII and XIII as bound in the US Wc copy of the 1st edn.; other copies are bound and numbered differently (items 2, 5, 15, 21, 24–34, 36, 38–41, 47, 51, 55, 58–60, 66, 68, 71–75, 78, 84, 105, 116–19, 121, 130–32, 173–74, 176–79, 186–87, 189, 192, 208, 211–13, 244, 246–47, 267, 269, 274, 276, 280, 282–83, 298). Remarkably good edns. for their time, in that they generally avoid arbitrary editorial changes.

FEDTKE/ORGELWERKE.   T. Fedtke, ed., *Orgelwerke*, 2 vols. Frankfurt am Main: Litolff (Peters), 1968 (items 75.5, 84–87, 102, 107, 133–34, 352, 372)

FEDTKE/SINFONIEN.   _____, ed., [*Sechs Sinfonien*]. New York: C. F. Peters, 1975–76 (items 657–62)

FÉTIS/BIOGRAPHIE.   F.-J. Fétis, *Biographie universelle des musiciens et bibliographie générale de la musique*, 2nd edn. (Paris, 1860–65, 1878–81)

FISCHER.   K. von Fischer, "C. Ph. E. Bachs Variationen-werke," *Revue Belge de Musicologie*, VI (1952), 190–218

FISCHER/NBA. See NBA.

FLEULER.   M. Fleuler, *Die norddeutsche Symphonie zur Zeit Friedrichs des Grossen, und besonders die Werke P. E. Bachs* (Berlin, 1908)

Flora: See CRAMER/FLORA.

FORKEL/ALMANACH.   J. N. Forkel, ed., *Musikalischer Almanach für Deutschland* (Leipzig, 1782–84, 1789)

FORKEL/BIBLIOTHEK.   _____, *Musikalisch-kritische Bibliothek*, 3 vols. (Gotha, 1778–79)

FORKEL/GESCHICHTE.   _____, *Allgemeine Geschichte der Musik* (Leipzig, 1788)

FORTSETZUNG. Fortsetzung von Sechs Sonaten fürs Clavier. Berlin: gedruckt und zu finden bey George Ludewig Winter, 1761 (items 150–51, 127–28, 141, 62; W. 51). Some copies of the same edn. have the title *Suite de Sonates pour le Clavecin par Charl. Phil. Eman. Bach.* HASHIMOTO notes a considerable number of differences among individual examplars of this print. Other edns.: London: John Walsh, n.d.; Leipzig: Johann Gottlob Immanuel Breitkopf, 1785. See *REPRISEN-SONATEN. Lit.: HAMBURGER CORRES-PONDENT, 4 Apr. 1770; BITTER/BRÜDER, I, 77–78; VRIESLANDER/BACH, 170; BEURMANN/KLAVIER-

SONATEN, 93–117; RADCLIFFE, 587. The known lit. gives no evidence that the Walsh print was authorized by CPEB.

FOX.   P. R. Fox, "Melodic Nonconstancy in the Keyboard Sonatas of C. P. E. Bach." Ph. D. dissertation, University of Cincinnati, 1983

FREYMÄURER-LIEDER. *Freymäurer-Lieder mit ganz neuen Melodien von den Herren Capellmeistern Bach, Naumann und Schulz.* København und Leipzig: G. G. Proft [printed by Breitkopf in Leipzig], 1788 (item 764). The same edn. is also found under these titles: *Allgemeines Liederbuch für Freymäurer, Dritter Band, mit ganz neuen Melodien von Bach, Naumann und Schulz; Vollständiges Liederbuch der Freymäurer Dritter Theil, mit ganz neuen Melodien von den Herren Capellmeistern Bach, Naumann und Schulz.* Lit: HASE, 104; BUSCH, 181–90, 283, 294, 311, 315, 386, Anh. 38–41

FRIEDHEIM.   P. Friedheim, ed., *Six Sonatas for Keyboard.* New York: Galaxy, 1967 (items 18, 46, 57, 119, 142, 182)

FRIEDLÄNDER.   M. Friedländer, *Das deutsche Lied im 18. Jahrhundert* (Stuttgart, 1902) (uses items 670, 686/9, 686/13, 696/12, 699, 743, 753, 756, 758 as examples)

FRIEDLÄNDER/UNGEDRUCKTES.   _____, "Ein unge-drucktes Lied von Ph. E. Bach," *Jahrbuch der Musikbibliothek Peters*, 6 (1899), 65–67

Fünfzig und sechs neue Melodien: See RHEINECK.

GALLAGHER–HELM/SYMPHONIES.   C. C. Gallagher and E. E. Helm, eds., *Carl Philipp Emanuel Bach: Six Symphonies*, Series C, Vol. VIII of *The Symphony, 1720–1840*, ed. Barry S. Brook and Barbara B. Heyman (New York: Garland, 1979–), 1982 (items 648, 650–51, 654–56)

GÁT.   J. Gát, ed., *Four Fantasias for Piano.* Budapest: Zenemükiadó, n.d. (items 277–78, 284, 291)

GEIRINGER/BACH.   K. Geiringer, *The Bach Family* (New York, 1954)

GEIRINGER/CHAMBER.   _____, "The Rise of Chamber Music," Vol. VII of *The New Oxford History of Music*, ed. E. Wellesz and F. W. Sternfeld (London, 1973), 515–73

GELLERT-ANHANG. Zwölf geistliche Oden und Lieder als ein Anhang zu Gellerts geistlichen Oden und Liedern mit Melo-dien von Carl Philipp Emanuel Bach. Berlin, 1764. Gedruckt und zu finden bey George Ludewig Winter. Reprinted 1771; reprinted with *GELLERT-LIEDER, Leipzig: J. G. I. Breitkopf, 1784; facsimile reprint of this combination in Hildesheim: G. Olms, 1973 (item 696; W. 195). Lit.: HAM-BURGER CORRESPONDENT, 4 Apr. 1770; BITTER/BRÜDER, I, 153–55; BÜCKEN, 170; BUSCH, 73–76, 310, 381, Anh. 14–15; HUGHES, 347

GELLERT-LIEDER. Herrn Professor Gellerts geistliche Oden und Lieder mit Melodien von Carl Philipp Emanuel Bach. Berlin, 1758. Gedruckt und zu finden bey George Ludewig Winter. Reprinted 1759, 1764, 1771; reprinted with *GELLERT-

ANHANG, Leipzig: J. G. I. Breitkopf, 1784; facsimile reprint of this combination in Hildesheim: G. Olms, 1973 (item 686; W. 194). Lit.: HAMBURGER CORRESPONDENT, 4 Apr. 1770, 20 Oct. 1773, 15 July 1774; REICHARDT/KUNSTMAGAZIN, I (1782), 172; CPEB/BREITKOPF, 3 Sept. 1783; BITTER/BRÜDER, I, 142–53; STEGLICH/HOMILIUS, 103; BÜCKEN, 169–70; BUSCH, 58–68, 270–74, 278–80, 283, 297–98, 301–02, 305–13, 317, 352, 356, 370, 374, 380, 382, 389–90, 399–406, Anh. 6–13; AUERBACH, 81–83; BARFORD/KEYBOARD, 143–44; HUGHES, 347; WADE, 1, 6; OTTENBERG, 131, 134–37

GELLERT/SCHRIFTEN. C. F. Gellert, *C. F. Gellerts sämmtliche Schriften. Zweyter Theil* . . . (Reutlingen, 1774)

GERBER. E. L. Gerber, *Historisch-biographisches Lexikon der Tonkünstler* . . . , 2 vols. (Leipzig, 1790–92), Vol. II, "Anhang"

Gesammlete Nachrichten: See WESTPHAL/NACHRICHTEN.

Göttinger Musen-Almanach: See VOSS/1774 etc.

GRÄFE. J. F. Gräfe, ed., *Sammlung verschiedener und auserlesener Oden* . . . , 4 vols. Halle, 1737–43 (items 670–72). Lit.: BUSCH, 39–41, 379

HAAG. C. R. Haag, "The Keyboard Concertos of Karl Philipp Emanuel Bach." Ph.D. dissertation, University of California at Los Angeles, 1956

HADOW. W. H. Hadow, *The Vienna Period*, Vol. V of *The Oxford History of Music* (London, 1931), reprinted 1939

HAMBURGER CORRESPONDENT. *Staats- und gelehrte Zeitung des Hamburgischen unpartheyischen Correspondenten* (Hamburg, 1767–89)

Hamburger Gesang-Melodien: See *NEUE MELODIEN.

HASE. H. von Hase, "Carl Philipp Emanuel Bach und Joh. Gottl. Im. Breitkopf," *Bach-Jahrbuch*, VIII (1911), 86–104

HASHIMOTO. Communication from Eiji Hashimoto, March 6, 1982, regarding CPEB's keyboard works

HASHIMOTO/FORTSETZUNG. E. Hashimoto, ed., *Fortsetzung von Sechs Sonaten fürs Clavier*. Tokyo, Zen-On Music Co., 1984 (*FORTSETZUNG)

HASHIMOTO/REPRISEN. _____, ed., *Sechs Sonaten fürs Clavier mit veränderten Reprisen*. Tokyo, Zen-On Music Co., 1984 (*REPRISEN-SONATEN)

HASHIMOTO/ZWEYTE FORTSETZUNG. _____, ed., *Zweyte Fortsetzung von Sechs Sonaten fürs Clavier*. Tokyo, Zen-On Music Co., 1984 (*ZWEYTE FORTSETZUNG)

Helm, E. E., "Bach, Carl Philipp Emanuel," *The New Grove Dictionary of Music and Musicians* (London, 1980). Some of the "H." numbers in the works-list of this article have had to be changed in the light of research since 1980; see, in this catalogue, Corrections of Work-List in *The New Grove Dictionary of Music and Musicians* (1980).

HELM/EINFALL. E. E. Helm, "Six Random Measures of C. P. E. Bach," *Journal of Music Theory*, X (Spring, 1966), 139–50

HELM/LITERARY. _____, "The 'Hamlet' Fantasy and the Literary Element in C. P. E. Bach's Music," *The Musical Quarterly*, LVIII (April 1972), 277–96

HERRMANN/LEICHTE. K. Herrmann, ed., *Leichte Tänze und Stücke für Klavier*. Hamburg: Sikorski, 1949 (items 65, 91–92, 96–98, 122, 145, 147, 165, 169, 310, 320, 325)

HERRMANN/SONATEN. K. Herrmann, ed., *Sonaten und Stücke*. Leipzig: Peters, 1938 (items 94, 126–28, 153, 158, 263, 280, 288, 311, 338)

Herrn Christoph Christian Sturms . . . geistliche Gesänge: See *STURM I, *STURM II.

Herrn Doctor Cramers übersetzte Psalmen: See *CRAMER/PSALMEN.

Herrn Professor Gellerts Geistliche Oden und Lieder: See *GELLERT-LIEDER.

HILL. R. S. Hill, "The Former Prussian State Library," *Music Library Association Notes*, III (September 1946), 327–50

HILLER/LIEDER. J. A. Hiller, ed., *Lieder und Arien aus Sophiens Reise* . . . . Leipzig: J. F. Junius [printed by J. G. I. Breitkopf], 1779 (item 686, Nos. 15, 36, 38, 40, 55). Lit.: BUSCH, 220–21

HILLER/NACHRICHTEN. _____, ed., *Wöchentliche Nachrichten und Anmerkungen die Musik betreffend* (Leipzig, 1766–70)

HILLER/SINFONIE. _____, ed., *Raccolta delle megliore Sinfonie di più celebri Compositori di nostro tempo, accommodate all' Clavicembalo*. Leipzig: J. G. I. Breitkopf, 1761 (item 45)

Historisch-kritische Beyträge: See MARPURG/BEYTRÄGE.

HÖRNER. H. Hörner, *Gg. Ph. Telemanns Passionsmusiken* (Leipzig, 1933)

HOFFMANN-ERBRECHT/HAFFNER. L. Hoffmann-Erbrecht, "Der Nürnberger Musikverleger Johann Ulrich Haffner" and "Nachträge," *Acta Musicologica*, XXVI (1954), 114–26; XXVII (1955), 141–42

HOFFMANN-ERBRECHT/PROBESTÜCKE. _____, ed., *18 Probestücke in sechs Sonaten nebst "Sechs neuen Sonatinen" zum Versuch* . . . . Leipzig: Breitkopf & Härtel, 1957 (*PROBESTÜCKE, *SECHS NEUEN)

*HUBERTY. *Six sonates pour le Clavecin . . . Oeuvre I*. Paris: Huberty, [before 1768] (items 55, 19, 56, 67, 18, 48, and item 54 as an addition not indicated in the title. Regarding this addition of item 54, see the notes in items 48 and 54 on P 673. Some copies of the same edn. have this title and imprint: *Six sonates pour le clavecin . . . oeuvre 1er. à Paris: Chès l'Editeur rue du Chantre; Lyon, les frères le Goux; Rouen, les marchands de musique (gravées par Ceron). The known lit. gives no evidence that this print was authorized by CPEB.

HUGHES. R. Hughes, "Solo Song," Vol. VII of *The New Oxford History of Music*, ed. E. Wellesz and F. W. Sternfeld (London, 1973), 336–65

HUYS. B. Huys, *De Gregoire le Grand à Stockhausen* (Brussels, 1966)

JACOBI/CONCERTO. E. R. Jacobi, "Das Autograph von C. P. E. Bachs Doppelkonzert in Es-dur für Cembalo, Fortepiano und Orchester (Wq. 47), Hamburg 1788," *Die Musikforschung*, XII (1959), 488–89. Also enclosed as a *Sonderdruck* in some copies of Jacobi's edn. of this concerto (item 479)

JACOBS. R. Jacobs and R. Eitner, *Thematischer Katalog der von Thulemeir'schen Musikalien-Sammlung in der Bibliothek des Joachimsthal'schen Gymnasiums zu Berlin* (Leipzig, 1899; Beilage zu den *Monatshefte für Musikgeschichte*, XXX–XXXI, 1898–99)

JAENECKE. J. Jaenecke, *Die Musikbibliothek des Ludwig Freiherrn von Pretlack (1716–1781)* (Wiesbaden, 1973)

JANETZKY/SONATAS. K. Janetzky, ed., *6 Sonatas*. London: Musica Rara, 1958 (items 629–34)

Jenkins, N., and B. Churgin, *Thematic Catalogue of the Works of Giovanni Battista Sammartini* (Cambridge, Mass., 1976)

JOHNEN/SONATEN. K. Johnen, ed., *Sechs Sonaten für das Klavier*. Leipzig: Mitteldeutscher Verlag/Peters, 1950 (*DAMENSONATEN*)

JOHNEN/SONATINEN. _____, ed., *Sechs Sonatinen für Klavier*. Leipzig: Mitteldeutscher Verlag/Peters, 1952 (items 7–12)

JONAS. O. Jonas, ed., *Kurze und leichte Klavierstücke* . . . . Vienna: Universal Edition, 1962 (*KURZE I–II*)

JONES/NBA. See NBA.

KAST. P. Kast, *Die Bach-Handschriften der Berliner Staatsbibliothek* (Trossingen, 1958)

KELLNER. D. Kellner, *Treulicher Unterricht im Generalbass* . . ., 7th edn. Hamburg: J. G. Herold, 1796 (item 781; the known lit. gives no evidence that CPEB had authorized the [posthumous] appearance of this work in this collection)

*KENNER I. *Sechs Clavier-Sonaten für Kenner und Liebhaber, der Madam Zernitz, gebohrne Deeling in Warschau, aus besonderer Hochachtung und Freundschaft gewidmet und componirt von Carl Philipp Emanuel Bach. Erste Sammlung*. Leipzig, im Verlage des Autors [printed by J. G. I. Breitkopf], 1779 (items 244, 130, 245, 186, 243, 187; W. 55). Lit.: CPEB/BREITKOPF, 21 Feb., 1 May, 28 July, 16 Sept., 9 Oct., 13 Nov., 25 Nov., 2 Dec., 19 Dec. 1778; 3 Mar., 8 Apr., 16 Apr., 20 Apr., 5 June, 12 July, 27 July, 29 July (including Breitkopf's "Auslieffer. Liste"), 20 Sept., 2 Nov., 12 Nov. (and the financial statement accompanying the letter), 1779; 3 May 1788; HAMBURGER CORRESPONDENT, 24 Aug., 25 Sept. 1778; 31 July 1779; BITTER/BRÜDER, I, 212–14;

HASE, 96; VRIESLANDER/BACH, 170–73; ENGELKE, 436–40; SCHMID/KAMMERMUSIK, 80–81, 144; REESER, 39–41; GEIRINGER/BACH, 58–59; NEWMAN, 45, 77, 86; BARFORD/KEYBOARD, 18–19, 105–07; WADE, 55; ELDER; see also Critical Notes in BERG/FACSIMILE.

*KENNER II. *Clavier-Sonaten nebst einigen Rondos fürs Forte-Piano für Kenner und Liebhaber, Sr. Koenigl. Hoheit Friedrich Heinrich, Marggrafen zu Schwed unterthaenig gewidmet und componirt von Carl Philipp Emanuel Bach. Zweyte Sammlung*. Leipzig: im Verlage des Autors [printed by J. G. I. Breitkopf], 1780 (items 260, 246, 261, 269, 262, 270; W. 56). Lit.: CPEB/BREITKOPF, 10 Dec., 29 Dec. 1779; 15 Jan., 25 Jan., 13 Mar., 21 Mar., 29 Apr., 19 Mar., 4 July, 26 Aug. (and the list of *Praenumeranten* accompanying the letter), 15 Sept., 6 Oct., 27 Oct. 1780; 3 May 1788; CPEB/ARTARIA, 8 Feb. 1780; HAMBURGER CORRESPONDENT, 11 Aug., 13 Oct. 1780; BITTER/BRÜDER, I, 214–16; HASE, 96; VRIESLANDER/BACH, 170–73; SCHMID/KAMMERMUSIK, 80–81, 144; REESER, 39–41; GEIRINGER/BACH, 58–59; BEURMANN/REPRISENSONATEN, 169; NEWMAN, 45, 77, 84, 86; BARFORD/KEYBOARD, 18–19, 105–07; COLE, 392; WADE, 53, 55; ELDER; see also Critical Notes in BERG/FACSIMILE.

*KENNER III. *Clavier-Sonaten nebst einigen Rondos fürs Forte-Piano für Kenner und Liebhaber, Sr. Excellenz dem Freyherrn von Swieten unterthaenig zugeeignet und componirt von Carl Philipp Emanuel Bach. Dritte Sammlung*. Leipzig: im Verlage des Autors [printed by J. G. I. Breitkopf], 1781 (items 265, 247, 271, 208, 266, 173; W. 57). Lit.: HAMBURGER CORRESPONDENT, 9 Mar., 16 Nov. 1781; CPEB/BREITKOPF, 9 Apr., 1 May, 15 July (?), 24 July (?), 19 Sept., 9 Nov., 21 Nov. 1781; 14 Sept. 1785; 3 May 1788; CPEB/ARTARIA, 26 Sept. 1781; REICHARDT/KUNSTMAGAZIN, 1782, 87; FORKEL/ALMANACH, III (1784), 22–38; BITTER/BRÜDER, I, 217–21; HASE, 96; VRIESLANDER/BACH, 170–73; SCHMID/KAMMERMUSIK, 80–81, 144; REESER, 39–41; GEIRINGER/BACH, 58–59; NEWMAN, 28–29, 45, 77, 86; BARFORD/KEYBOARD, 18–19, 105–07; COLE, 392; WADE, 53, 55; ELDER; see also Critical Notes in BERG/FACSIMILE.

*KENNER IV. *Clavier-Sonaten und freye Fantasien nebst einigen Rondos fürs Fortepiano für Kenner und Liebhaber, componirt von Carl Philipp Emanuel Bach. Vierte Sammlung*. Leipzig: im Verlage des Autors [printed by J. G. I. Breitkopf], 1783 (items 276, 273–74, 188, 267, 277–78; W. 58). Lit.: CPEB/BREITKOPF, 17 Aug., 10 Sept., 15 Oct., 9 Nov., 30 Nov., 28 Dec. 1782; 26 Apr., 25 June, 23 July, 3 Sept., 4 Nov. 1783; 14 Sept. 1785; 3 May 1788; CPEB/ARTARIA, 15 Oct. 1782; HAMBURGER CORRESPONDENT, 15 Oct. 1782; 2 Sept., 19 Sept. 1783; CRAMER/MAGAZIN, I (1783), 1238–55; BITTER/BRÜDER, I, 221–25; HASE, 96–97; VRIESLANDER/BACH, 170–73; SCHMID/KAMMERMUSIK, 116, 144; CLERCX, 148–49; REESER, 39–41; GEIRINGER/BACH, 58–59; BEURMANN/REPRISENSONATEN, 169; AUERBACH, 77; NEWMAN, 45, 77, 86, 88; BARFORD/KEYBOARD, 18–19, 105–07; COLE, 391–92, 399; BERG, 57–58; WADE, 55; ELDER; See also Critical Notes in BERG/FACSIMILE.

*KENNER V. *Clavier-Sonaten und freye Fantasien nebst einigen Rondos fürs Fortepiano für Kenner und Liebhaber, Sr. Herzoglichen Durchl. Peter Friedrich Ludewig, Herzogen zu Holstein und Fürst-Bischofen zu Lübeck unterthänigst gewidmet und componirt von Carl Philipp Emanuel Bach. Fünfte Sammlung.* Leipzig: im Verlage des Autors [printed by J. G. I. Breitkopf], 1785 (items 281, 268, 282–83, 279, 284; W. 59). Lit.: CPEB/ARTARIA, 27 Jan., 4 Oct. 1785; CPEB/BREITKOPF, 15 Apr., 15 June, 8 July, 23 July, 26 Aug., 19 Oct. 1785; 3 May 1788; HAMBURGER CORRESPONDENT, 3 Dec., 20 Dec. 1785; CRAMER/MAGAZIN, Jg. 4 (1786), 869–72; BITTER/BRÜDER, I, 225–27; HASE, 97; VRIESLANDER/BACH, 170–73; SCHMID/KAMMERMUSIK, 144; REESER, 39–41; GEIRINGER/BACH, 58—59; NEWMAN, 45, 77, 86; BARFORD/KEYBOARD, 18–19, 105–07; COLE, 392; WADE, 7, 53; ELDER

*KENNER VI. *Clavier-Sonaten und freye Fantasien nebst einigen Rondos fürs Fortepiano für Kenner und Liebhaber Ihro Hochgräflichen Gnaden Maria Theresia, Reich-Gräfin zu Leiningen-Westerburg unterthänig gewidmet und componirt von Carl Philipp Emanuel Bach. Sechste Sammlung.* Leipzig: im Verlage des Autors [printed by J. G. I. Breitkopf], 1787 (items 288, 286, 289–90, 287, 291; W. 61). Lit.: CPEB/BREITKOPF, 30 Sept., 26 Oct. 1786; 3 Jan., 5 May, 12 May, 19 May, 30 June, 26 July, 21 Sept. 1787; 3 May 1788; HAMBURGER CORRESPONDENT, 11 Oct., 21 Oct. 1786; 3 July 1787; CPEB/ARTARIA, 5 Mar. 1787; BITTER/BRÜDER, I, 227–30; HASE, 97; VRIESLANDER/BACH, 170–73; SCHMID/KAMMERMUSIK, 144; REESER, 39–41; GEIRINGER/BACH, 58–59; BEURMANN/REPRISENSONATEN, 169; NEWMAN, 45, 77, 86; BARFORD/KEYBOARD, 18–19, 105–07; COLE, 392; ELDER; see also Critical Notes in BERG/FACSIMILE.

Kirke-Melodierne: See SCHIØRRING.

KLEINE. *Kleine Sing- und Spielstücke fürs Clavier von verschiedenen Meistern,* 3 vols. Berlin: F. W. Birnstiel, [c. 1762–66] (item 108)

KNÖDT. H. Knödt, "Zur Entwicklungsgeschichte der Kadenzen im Instrumentalkonzert," *Sammelbände der Internationalen Musikgesellschaft,* XV (1913–14), 375–419

KOBAYASHI. Y. Kobayashi, "Neuerkenntnisse zu einigen Bach-Quellen an Hand schriftlicher Untersuchung," *Bach-Jahrbuch,* LXIV (1978), 43–60

KOLLMANN. A. F. C. Kollmann, *An Essay on Practical Musical Composition* (London, 1799)

KRAMER. R. Kramer, "The 'New' Concept of Modulation in the 1770s and 1780s: C.P.E. Bach in Theory, Criticism, and Practice," paper read at the annual meeting of the American Musicological Society, Denver, November 1980, pub. with revisions and additions as "The New Modulation of the 1770s: C. P. E. Bach in Theory, Criticism, and Practice," *Journal of the American Musicological Society,* XXXVIII (Fall 1985), 551–92

KREBS. C. Krebs, ed., *Die Sechs Sammlungen von Sonaten, freien Fantasien und Rondos für Kenner und Liebhaber.* Leipzig: Breitkopf & Härtel, 1895, rev. by L. Hoffmann-Erbrecht, 2nd edn. 1953. The original Krebs edn. reprinted New York: Kalmus, n.d. (*KENNER I–VI). All good edns.

Kritische Briefe: See MARPURG/BRIEFE.

KÜHNAU I. J. C. Kühnau, ed., *Vierstimmige alte und neue Choralgesänge . . . Erster Theil.* Berlin: Verlag des Autors, 1786 (item 845; the known lit. gives no evidence that CPEB authorized the appearance of this work in this collection).

KÜHNAU II. _____, ed., *Vierstimmige alte und neue Choralgesänge . . . Zweiter Theil.* Berlin: Verlag des Autors, 1790 (item 781; the known lit. gives no evidence that CPEB authorized the [posthumous] appearance of this work in this collection).

Küntzel, G., "Thematisches Verzeichnis der Konzerte von Johann Friedrich Fasch," in his *Die Instrumentalkonzerte von Johann Friedrich Fasch* (Tutzing, 1965)

*KURZE I. *Kurze und leichte Clavierstücke mit veränderten Reprisen und beygefügter Fingersetzung für Anfänger von C.P.E. Bach.* Berlin: bey George Ludewig Winter. 1766. Reprinted 1780 (items 193–203; W. 113). A 1786 reprint of the Winter edn., but under the name of Breitkopf as publisher, is reported in HASE, p. 101, but has not been found. Other edns. containing various portions of this collection (the known lit. gives no evidence that any of them were authorized by CPEB): *C.P.E. Bachs Anfangsstücke mit einer Anleitung . . .*, Berlin: C. F. Rellstab, 3 printings from 1788 to 1790 (W. 259; the "Anleitung" consists of rules of fingering extracted from the *Versuch* [see item 868] and the movements are dismembered by presenting the varied repeats as separate pieces); *Fünf kurze und leichte Clavierstücke . . .*, Berlin: F. W. Birnstiel, 1790 (W. 261); *Fünf kurze und leichte Clavierstücke . . .* ,Linz: Akadem. Buchhandlung, 1795 (W. 262); *Kleine leichte Klavierstücke . . . Erste Sammlung*, Wien, Musikalisch-Typographische Verlagsgesellschaft, 1799 (W. 267); *Kleine leichte Klavierstücke, Zweyte Sammlung*, Wien, K. F. Täubel, 1799; *Neue Sammlung kleiner leichter Clavierstücke . . .* , Wien, J. G. Binz, 1799. Lit.: HILLER/NACHRICHTEN, 12 Aug. 1766, 52–53; HAMBURGER CORRESPONDENT, 4 Apr. 1770; BITTER/BRÜDER, I, 89; VRIESLANDER/BACH, 173–74; JONAS, editor's preface; BARFORD/KEYBOARD, 21–22, 137–39; WADE, 32, 129; see also Critical Notes in BERG/FACSIMILE.

*KURZE II. *Kurze und leichte Clavierstücke mit veränderten Reprisen und beygefügter Fingersetzung für Anfänger von C. P. E. Bach. Zweyte Sammlung.* Berlin: bey George Ludewig Winter, 1768 (items 228–38; W. 114). A 1786 reprint of the Winter edn., but under the name of Breitkopf as publisher, is reported in HASE, p. 101, but has not been found. Portions contained in *C.P.E. Bachs Anfangsstücke mit einer Anleitung . . .*, Berlin: C. F. Rellstab, 3 printings from 1788 to 1790 (W. 259; see the comment on this edn. under *KURZE I). Lit: HAMBURGER CORRESPONDENT, 4 Apr.

1770; BITTER/BRÜDER, I, 89; VRIESLANDER/BACH, 173–74; JONAS, editor's preface; BARFORD/KEYBOARD, 21–22; WADE, 32; see also Critical Notes in BERG/FACSIMILE.

LANDOWSKA. W. Landowska, *Landowska on Music* (New York, 1964), trans. and ed. by D. Restout, assisted by R. Hawkins

LANGLAIS. J. Langlais, ed., *Six Sonatas for Organ.* Chicago: FitzSimons, 1957 (*PRELUDIO). Heavily edited

LEDEBUR. C. F. von Ledebur, *Tonkünstler-Lexicon Berlin's von den ältesten Zeiten bis auf die Gegenwart* (Berlin, 1861)

LEE. D. A. Lee, *The Works of Christoph Nichelmann: A Thematic Index* (Detroit, 1971)

*LEICHTE. *Sechs leichte Clavier-Sonaten von Carl Philipp Emanuel Bach. 1766.* Leipzig: bey Bernhard Christoph Breitkopf & Sohn, 1766 (items 162, 180–82, 163, 183; W. 53). Another edn.: *Six Sonatas for the Piano-Forte or Harpsicord.* London: Longman, Lukey & Co., 177?. The known lit. gives no evidence that the Longman, Lukey & Co. print was authorized by CPEB. Lit.: HILLER/NACHRICHTEN, 21 Oct. 1766, 132; CPEB/BREITKOPF, 8 Feb. 1785; BITTER/BRÜDER, I, 89; HASE, 88; VRIESLANDER/BACH, 170; NEWMAN, 423; RADCLIFFE, 588; BERG, 56–57; see also Critical Notes in BERG/FACSIMILE.

LEWIS. N. Lewis, "The Great Music Find," London *Times*, April 3, 1977, p. 17

Lieder der Deutschen: See RAMLER–KRAUSE III.

Lieder und Arien aus Sophiens Reise: See HILLER/LIEDER.

LINDNER. E. O. Lindner, *Geschichte des deutschen Liedes im 18. Jahrhundert* (Leipzig, 1871), reprinted Wiesbaden, 1968

LORENZ/MÄRSCHE. J. Lorenz, ed., *Sechs kleine Märsche.* Berlin, Parrhysius, [1941] (items 614–19)

LORENZ/SONATE. _____, ed., *Sei Sonate.* Milan: Ricordi, 1939 (items 629–34)

MANCHERLEY. *Musikalisches Mancherley.* Berlin: G. L. Winter, 1762–63 (items 59, 77, 81, 92–95, 118–20, 171–72, 339, 359, 562, 584, 590, 601). Lit.: HILLER/NACHRICHTEN, 12 Feb. 1770, 56; BITTER/BRÜDER, I, 83–87; BERG, 226–27; OTTENBERG, 141. See the general description under ALLERLEY in this bibliography.

MARPURG/ABHANDLUNG. F. W. Marpurg, ed., *Abhandlung von der Fuge . . . .* Berlin: A. Haude und J. C. Spener, 1753–54 (items 75.5, 76)

MARPURG/ANLEITUNG. _____, ed., *Anleitung zum Clavierspielen . . . .* Berlin: A. Haude und J. C. Spener, 1755 (item 338)

MARPURG/BEYTRÄGE. _____, ed., *Historisch-kritische Beyträge zur Aufnahme der Musik.* Berlin: G. A. Lange, 1754–78, reprinted Hildesheim, New York: G. Olms, 1970 (items 676, 869). Lit.: BUSCH, 51

MARPURG/BRIEFE. _____, ed., *Kritische Briefe über die Tonkunst . . . ,* 3 vols. Berlin: F. W. Birnstiel, 1759–64 (item 108)

MARPURG/FUGEN. _____, ed., *Friedr. Wilh. Marpurgs Fugen-Sammlung. Erster Theil.* Berlin: G. A. Lange [printed in Leipzig by Breitkopf], 1758 (item 99). Lit.: HASE, 87

MARPURG/LIEDER. _____, ed., *Neue Lieder zum Singen beym Claviere . . . .* Berlin: G. A. Lange, 1756 (item 680). Lit.: BUSCH, 52

MARPURG/ODEN I. [_____, ed.,] *Berlinische Oden und Lieder.* Leipzig: J. G. I. Breitkopf, 1756 (items 679, 681–82). Lit.: BUSCH, 53; HASE, 86

MARPURG/ODEN II. [_____, ed.,] *Berlinische Oden und Lieder. Zweyter Theil.* Leipzig: J. G. I. Breitkopf, 1759 (items 683–84). Lit.: BUSCH, 53–54; HASE, 86

MARPURG/PRACTISCH. _____, ed., *Marpurgs Clavierstücke mit einem practischen Unterricht für Anfänger und Geübtere,* 3 vols. Berlin: A. Haude und J. C. Spener, 1762–63 (items 22, 101–02)

MARPURG/RACCOLTA 1756/7. _____, ed., *Raccolta delle più nouve Composizioni di Clavicembalo di differenti Maestri ed Autori per l'anno 1756.* Leipzig: J. G. I. Breitkopf, 1756 (items 67, 79–80, 89–90). Ibid., *per l'anno 1757.* Leipzig: J. G. I. Breitkopf, 1757 (items 91, 101, 105, 122). In both these collections Marpurg combines single movements to make larger "compositions." Lit.: HASE, 86–87

MARPURG/SINFONIE. _____, ed., *Raccolta delle megliore Sinfonie . . . accommodato all' Clavicembalo.* Lipsia, J. G. I. Breitkopf, 1761–62 (item 104)

MARSHALL. R. L. Marshall, "J.S. Bach's Compositions for Solo Flute: A Reconsideration of their Authenticity and Chronology," *Journal of the American Musicological Society,* XXXII (Fall, 1979) 463–98

MARTELL. P. Martell, "Die Musik-Sammlung der Staatsbibliothek zu Berlin," *Allgemeine Musik-Zeitung,* LVII (1930), 325–29

MELODIEN. *Melodien zu der Wernigerödischen Neuen Sammlung geistlicher Lieder.* Halle: im Verlag des Waisenhauses, 1767 (item 686, Nos. 27, 45; item 696, No. 4; item 842). Lit.: BUSCH, 78–85

MERSMANN. H. Mersmann, "Ein Programmtrio Karl Philipp Emanuel Bachs," *Bach-Jahrbuch,* XIV (1919–20), 137–70

Michelitsch, H., "Thematischer Katalog," in her *Das Klavierwerk von Georg Christoph Wagenseil* (Vienna: 1966)

MIES. P. Mies, ed., *Sonaten und Charakterstücke.* Augsburg: Böhm (formerly Volksvereinsverlag Mönchen-Gladbach), 1928 (items 25, 40, 109, 110, 113)

MIESNER/HAMBURG. H. Miesner, *Philipp Emanuel Bach in Hamburg* (Leipzig, 1929, reprinted Wiesbaden, 1969)

MIESNER/STAHL. _____, "Beziehungen zwischen den Familien Stahl und Bach," *Bach-Jahrbuch*, XXX (1933), 71–76

MIESNER/UMWELT. _____, "Aus der Umwelt Philipp Emanuel Bachs," *Bach-Jahrbuch*, XXXIV (1937), 132–43

MITCHELL/INTRODUCTION. W. J. Mitchell, "C.P.E. Bach's 'Essay': An Introduction," *The Musical Quarterly*, XXXIII (1947), 460–80

MITCHELL/MODULATION. _____, "Modulation in C.P.E. Bach's *Versuch*," in *Studies in Eighteenth Century Music* (Festschrift for K. Geiringer), ed. H. C. Robbins Landon (London, 1970)

MÜLLER/SCHÄTZE. W. Müller, *Die musikalischen Schätze der Bibliothek Königsberg* (Königsberg, 1870)

MÜNTER-LIEDER. *D. Balthasar Münters . . . erste Sammlung geistlicher Lieder mit Melodien von verschiedenen Singkomponisten.* Leipzig, in der Dyckischen Buchhandlung [printed by Breitkopf], 1773 (items 724–29). Lit.: HASE, 93; BUSCH, 102–04, 310, 315, 374, 382

MUSE. *Die Muse. Erster Theil.* Leipzig, in J. C. Müllers Buch- und Kunsthandlung, 1776 (item 744). Lit.: BUSCH, 131, 315

Musen-Almanach: See VOSS/1774 etc.

Musikalische Anthologie: See BOSSLER.

MUSIKALISCHE BLUMENLESE. J. H. Egli, ed., *Musikalische Blumenlese . . . .* Zürich, 1786 (item 686/1; the known lit. gives no evidence that CPEB authorized the appearance of this work in this collection)

Musikalischer Almanach: See FORKEL/ALMANACH.

MUSIKALISCHE REAL-ZEITUNG. *Musikalische Real-Zeitung* (Speier, 1789)

Musikalisch-kritische Bibliothek: See FORKEL/BIBLIOTHEK.

NACHLASS-VERZEICHNIS (NV). J. M. Bach [CPEB's widow], C. P. E. Bach, et al., *Verzeichniss des musikalischen Nachlasses des verstorbenen Capellmeisters Carl Philipp Emanuel Bach . . .* (Hamburg, 1790). Based on earlier lists made by CPEB and Johanna Maria Bach, and probably by J. J. H. Westphal, J. G. I. Breitkopf and others. Reprinted with notes by H. Miesner as "Philipp Emanuel Bachs musikalischer Nachlass," *Bach-Jahrbuch*, XXXV–XXXVII (1938, 1939, 1940–48). Reprinted in facsimile, with annotations and a preface by Rachel W. Wade, as *The Catalog of Carl Philipp Emanuel Bach's Estate: A Facsimile of the Edition by Schniebes, Hamburg, 1790* (New York, 1981)

NBA. J. S. Bach, *Neue Ausgabe sämtlicher Werke*, ed. by Johann-Sebastian-Bach Institut Göttingen and Bach-Archiv Leipzig (Kassel, 1954–), especially *Kritische Berichte*: Ser. II, Bd. 5 (1974) by Alfred Dürr; Ser. V, Bd. 1 (1978) by R.D. Jones; Ser. V, Bd. 4 (1957) by G. von Dadelsen; Ser. VII, Bd. 7 (1971) by W. Fischer

NEBENSTUNDEN. *Nebenstunden der Berlinischen Musen . . . Erste Sammlung.* Berlin, F.W. Birnstiel, 1762 (item 20)

NEUE LIEDER. Neue Lieder-Melodien nebst einer Kantate zum Singen beym Klavier componirt von Karl Philipp Emanuel Bach. Lübeck, 1789 [but see note below], bey Christian Gottfried Donatius [printed in Leipzig by C. G. Täubel] (items 745, 755–57, 748, 702, 758, 703, 734, 700, 704, 705, 740, 747, 706, 759, 707, 760, 708, 701, 741, 735; W. 200). CPEB/LISTE VON LIEDERN shows that even though this collection was published posthumously, it had been assembled for publication by the composer himself, since the LISTE contains nearly all the titles of *NEUE LIEDER and no others. Lit.: HAMBURGER CORRESPONDENT, 19 Nov. 1788 (an announcement that the collection is already available, despite the printed publication date of 1789); BITTER/BRÜDER, II, 78–82; LINDNER, 60; GEIRINGER/BACH, 371; BUSCH, 75, 190–205, 287–88, 294, 316, 381, 385

Neue Lieder zum Singen beym Claviere: See MARPURG/LIEDER.

NEUE MELODIEN. Neue Melodien zu einigen Liedern des neuen Hamburgischen Gesangbuchs, nebst einigen Berichtigungen von Carl Philipp Emanuel Bach, des Hamburgischen Musik-Chors Director. Im Verlag der Heroldschen Buchhandlung, und gedruckt bey Gottlieb Friedrich Schniebes, 1787 (item 781; W. 203). Lit.: MIESNER/HAMBURG, 110–11; BUSCH, 177–82, 282, 291, 299, 385, Anh. 38–39

NEWMAN. W. S. Newman, *The Sonata in the Classic Era* (Chapel Hill, N.C., 1963)

NOHL. L. Nohl, compiler, *Musiker-Briefe* (Leipzig, 1867; 2nd edn. 1873)

NOTENBUCH. *Notenbuch zu des akademischen Liederbuches erstem Bändchen . . . ,* 2 vols. Altona: J. D. A. Eckhardt, 1783–96 (items 699, 738, 750). Title of 2nd vol.: *Melodien zu den Gesellschaftlichen Liederbuche . . . .* Lit.: BUSCH, 222

OBERDÖRFFER/DUETTE. F. Oberdörffer, ed., *Vier Duette für zwei Klaviere.* Kassel: Bärenreiter, 1944 (items 610–13)

OBERDÖRFFER/SONATEN. _____, ed., *Sechs kleine Sonaten.* Kassel: Bärenreiter, 1944 (items 516–21)

OBERDÖRFFER/STÜCKE. _____, ed., *Kleinere Stücke.* Berlin: Lienau, c. 1935 (items 614–19, 630, 632–33)

ODEN. Oden mit Melodien vom Herrn Carl Philipp Emanuel Bach. Berlin: bey Arnold Wever, gedruckt bey Johann Gottlob Immanuel Breitkopf in Leipzig, 1762. Reprinted 1774. (items 677, 670, 679, 673–74, 680, 678, 683, 681, 671, 675, 672, 682, 676, 674, 689–92, 687; W. 199). Lit.: MARPURG/BRIEFE, I, 243; BITTER/BRÜDER, I, 139–41; LINDNER, 58–60; HASE, 88; GEIRINGER/BACH, 369–70; BUSCH, 71–73, 379

Oden mit Melodien: See also RAMLER–KRAUSE I, RAMLER–KRAUSE II.

OEUVRES. *Oeuvres mêlées contenant VI sonates pour le clavecin de tant de plus célèbres compositeurs rangés en ordre alphabetique,* 12 vols. Nuremberg: J. U. Haffner, 1755–65 (items 38, 39, 58, 116–17, 131, 133, 368)

Oeuvres posthumes . . .: See *TROIS SONATES.

OLLESON.   E. Olleson, "Church Music and Oratorio," Vol. VII of *The New Oxford History of Music*, ed. E. Wellesz and F. W. Sternfeld (London, 1973), 288–335

*ORCHESTER-SINFONIEN. *Orchester-Sinfonien mit zwölf obligaten Stimmen: 2 Hörnern, 2 Flöten, 2 Hoboen, 2 Violinen, Bratsche, Violoncell, Fagott, Flügel und Violon. Seiner königlichen Hoheit, Friedrich Wilhelm, Prinzen von Preussen, unterthänigst gewidmet von Carl Philipp Emanuel Bach, Capellmeister und Musikdirektor in Hamburg.* Leipzig: im Schwickertschen Verlage [printed by J. G. I. Breitkopf], 1780 (items 663–66; W. 183). Lit.: CPEB/BREITKOPF, 30 Nov. 1778; 25 Jan., 24 Feb. 1780; HAMBURGER CORRESPONDENT, 1 Sept., 29 Dec. 1780; 17 Dec. 1783; BITTER/BRÜDER, I, 237–43; HASE, 97; VRIESLANDER/BACH, 97–102; BÜCKEN, 168–69; SUCHALLA/ORCHESTERSINFONIEN, 13, 123–24, 261–62; WELLESZ–STERNFELD/SYMPHONY, 393–94; BERG, 1

OTTENBERG.   H.-G. Ottenberg, *Carl Philipp Emanuel Bach* (Leipzig, 1982)

PIERRE.   F. Pierre, ed., *Deux menuets et un polonaise*. Paris: Editions musicales transatlantiques, [c. 1975] (item 635, Nos. 19–21, arranged for flute, viola, and harp)

PINCHERLE.   M. Pincherle, auction catalogue *Cent raretés musicales* (Paris: Etienne Ader, 1966)

PLAMENAC.   D. Plamenac, "New Light on the Last Years of Carl Philipp Emanuel Bach," *The Musical Quarterly*, XXXV (1949), 565–87

PÖLCHAU.   G. Pölchau (1773–1836), [4-volume catalogue of his music collection], D-ddr Bds, Mus. ma. theor. Kat. 61, 56, 51, 41

Poetische Blumenlese: See VOSS/1774 etc.

*PRELUDIO. *Preludio e sei Sonate pel Organo composto del Signor Carlo Filippo Emanuele Bach, il Maestro di Capella in Hamburg.* Berlino, alle spese et colle lettere di Rellstab, [1790] (items 107, 86–87, 134, 84, 53, 85, most with changes; W. 265). Lit.: VRIESLANDER/BACH, 97; GEIRINGER/BACH, 97. The known lit. gives no evidence that this (posthumous) print had been authorized by CPEB.

PRIEGER.   G. Kinsky, *Musik-Sammlung aus dem Nachlasse Dr. Erich Prieger — Bonn, nebst einigen Beiträgen aus anderem Besitz. III. Teil. Musikerbriefe, Handschriften, Musikalien* (Cologne: Lempertz, 1924) [Catalogue of auction in Cologne, 15 July 1924]

*PROBESTÜCKE. *Exempel nebst 18 Probestücken in 6 Sonaten zu C.P.E. Bachs Versuch über die wahre Art das Clavier zu spielen auf XXVI Kupfer-Tafeln* [that is, a separately issued volume meant to accompany Part I of the *Versuch*, consisting of various short musical examples along with six 3-movement sonatas (or 18 "Probestücken") illustrating this part of the *Versuch*]. Berlin, im Verlage des Autors [printed by C. F. Henning], 1753, reprinted Berlin: G. L. Winter, 1759–62; 2nd edn. Leipzig: E. B. Schwickert, 1780, reprinted by Schwickert as "dritte" edn. in the same year and again in 1787. The 1787 edn. is *. . . mit sechs neuen Clavier-Stücken vermehrt auf XXXI Kupfer-Tafeln* [that is, augmented with six new single movements, otherwise known as the *Sechs neuen Sonatinen* or *VI Sonatine nuove*]. RISM, Vol. A/I/1, gives 1780 as the date of two exemplars in NL DHgm of an edn. containing these six new single movements. This is obviously an error (Schwickert's?), since the new works were not composed until 1786; see PLAMENAC, 566–68. The *Probestücke* are items 70–75 (part of W. 63), the *Sechs neuen Clavier-Stücken* are items 292–97 (the rest of W. 63), the *Versuch* is items 868, 870 (W. 254–55).

ROE, 409, lists two editions in which the *Probestücke* are printed with incorrect attributions: "Methode ou Recueil de Connoissances Elémentaires pour le Forte-Piano ou Clavecin . . . Composé . . . par J.C. Bach et F.P. Ricci" (Paris: Le Duc, c. 1785) and "Six Progressive Lessons for the Harpsichord or Piano Forte . . . . Composed by Mr. Bach, Master to the Celebrated Mr. Schroeter . . . ." (London: Forster, c. 1784). See also commentary in item 70.

Lit. on the *Probestücke*: BITTER/BRÜDER, I, 96; VRIESLANDER/BACH, 165–67; SCHMID/KAMMERMUSIK, 144; GEIRINGER/BACH, 357; NEWMAN, 419, 424, 791–92; BARFORD/KEYBOARD, 18, 94–95; RADCLIFFE, 585–86; COHEN, 115; BERG, 102; ELDER, 2–3; ROE, 111, 114–17, 409; see also Critical Notes in BERG/FACSIMILE.

Lit. on the *Sechs neuen Clavier-Stücken*: REESER, 40; GEIRINGER/BACH, 359; NEWMAN, 76, 419, 423; RADCLIFFE, 592; COHEN, 115; ELDER, 12–15

PROD'HOMME.   J. G. Prod'homme, "Diderot et la musique," *Zeitschrift der Internationalen Musikgesellschaft*, XV (1913–14), 156ff., 177ff.

*PRUSSIAN SONATAS. *Sei Sonate per Cembalo che all' Augusta Maestà di Federico II Ré di Prussia D.D.D. l'Autore Carlo Filippo Emanuele Bach, Musico di Camera di S.M. Alle spese di Balth. Schmid in Norimberga.* [1742 or 1743] (items 24–29; W. 48). Lit.: BITTER/BRÜDER, I, 51–53; SHEDLOCK, 87–91; STEGLICH, 64–65; VRIESLANDER/BACH, 161–63; SCHMID/KAMMERMUSIK, 80–81; BEURMANN/KLAVIERSONATEN, 33; GEIRINGER/BACH, 354–55; NEWMAN, 14, 372, 377–78; BARFORD/KEYBOARD, 17; RADCLIFFE, 584; COHEN, 111; BERG, 47, 96, 144, 240; WADE, 30–31; ROE, 111; OTTENBERG, 280

Raccolta delle megliore Sinfonie: See HILLER/SINFONIE, MARPURG/SINFONIE.

Raccolta delle . . . Composizioni: See MARPURG/RACCOLTA.

RADCLIFFE.   P. Radcliffe, "Keyboard Music," Vol. VII of *The New Oxford History of Music*, ed. E. Wellesz and F. W. Sternfeld (London, 1973), 574–610

RAMLER-KRAUSE I.   [C. W. Ramler and C. G. Krause, eds.,] *Oden mit Melodien. Erster Theil.* Berlin: F. W. Birnstiel, 1753 (items 673–75). Lit.: BITTER/BRÜDER, I, 138–39; BUSCH, 42–50

RAMLER–KRAUSE II. C. W. Ramler and C. G. Krause, eds., *Oden mit Melodien. Zweyter Theil.* Berlin: F. W. Birnstiel, 1755 (items 677–78). Lit.: BITTER/BRÜDER, I, 139; BUSCH, 51–52

RAMLER–KRAUSE III. C. W. Ramler and C. G. Krause, eds., *Lieder der Deutschen mit Melodien,* 4 vols. Berlin: G. L. Winter, 1767–68 (items 673–74, 677–78). Lit.: BUSCH, 75, 220

RECHNUNGSBUCH. *Rechnungsbuch der Kirchen-Musiken,* ms. in D-brd Ha, 2432, CCCCLXII (462), partly in the hands of CPEB and his wife, Johanna Maria. Excerpts printed in MIESNER/HAMBURG, 125–26. See CPEB/6 NOV. 1769, CPEB/SCHUCHMACHER, and item 821m.

REESER. E. Reeser, *The Sons of Bach* (Stockholm, 1949)

REGER. M. Reger, ed., [four symphonies]. Leipzig: Peters, [1910] (*ORCHESTER-SINFONIEN; free arrangement, amounting to distortion, for piano-4 hands)

REICHARDT/BRIEFE. J. F. Reichardt, *Briefe eines aufmerksamen Reisenden die Musik betreffend,* 2 vols. (Frankfurt am Main, Leipzig: 1774–76)

REICHARDT/KUNSTMAGAZIN. _____, ed., *Musikalisches Kunstmagazin,* 2 vols. (Berlin, 1782, 1791; reprinted Hildesheim, 1969)

*REPRISEN-SONATEN. *Sechs Sonaten fürs Clavier mit veränderten Reprisen Ihro Königlichen Hoheit der Prinzessin Amalia von Preussen unterthänigst zugeeignet, und verfertiget von Carl Philipp Emanuel Bach.* Berlin, 1760, gedruckt und zu finden bey George Ludewig Winter (items 136–39, 126, 140; W. 50). Some copies of the same edn. have the title *VI. Sonates pour le clavecin avec des reprises variées.* Other edns.: Leipzig: Johann Gottlob Immanuel Breitkopf, 1785; Berlin: Johann Karl Friedrich Rellstab, [1786]; London: John Walsh, [1763]; London: William Randall, [177?]. According to NV, p. 53, a copy of the first print contains alterations in the hand of CPEB. Just such a copy is in GB Lbm, K.10.a.28. Copies also marked by CPEB are reported in BARFORD/KEYBOARD, 18, 101–04, to be in F Pc (with marking dated 1788) and "Brussels." These and other sources are taken into account in DARBELLAY and HASHIMOTO/REPRISEN. The two sets published as continuations, *FORTSETZUNG and *ZWEYTE FORTSETZUNG, are neither dedicated to Princess Amalia nor characterized by "veränderten Reprisen." Other lit.: HAMBURGER CORRESPONDENT, 4 Apr. 1770, 22 July 1786; CPEB/BREITKOPF, 23 July, 26 Aug., 14 Sept., 20 Sept., 19 Oct., 30 Nov. 1785; BITTER/BRÜDER, 66–72; SHEDLOCK, 94–100; HASE, 101; STEGLICH/HOMILIUS, 85; VRIESLANDER/BACH, 167–69; BÜCKEN, 166–67; SCHMID/KAMMERMUSIK, 144, 152–53; CLERCX, 161–62; BEURMANN/KLAVIERSONATEN, 93–117; GEIRINGER/BACH, 358; BEURMANN/REPRISENSONATEN; BARFORD/AFTERTHOUGHTS, 94–98; NEWMAN, 30, 424–26, 587; RADCLIFFE, 586–87, 610; WELLESZ–STERNFELD/SYMPHONY, 387; COHEN, 111; BERG, 55, 75–77; WADE, 3,

28, 31, 86, 97; ROE, 114–15; see also Critical Notes in BERG/FACSIMILE. The known lit. gives no evidence that the Rellstab, Walsh, or Randall prints were authorized by CPEB.

RHEINECK. C. Rheineck, ed., *Fünfzig und sechs neue Melodien . . . .* Memmingen: J. C. Diesel [printed in Augsburg by J. J. Lotter], 1780 (item 686, Nos. 5, 16, 18, 20, 28, 33, 35, 47, 49). Lit.: BUSCH, 221. The known lit. gives no evidence that CPEB authorized the appearance of these works in this collection.

RIEMANN. H. Riemann, ed., *Ausgewählte Kompositionen.* Leipzig: Steingräber, n.d. (items 29, 37, 51, 75, 89–90, 94–95, 173, 220, 234, 265, 291). Grotesquely overedited

RISM. *Répertoire international des sources musicales* (International Inventory of Musical Sources), pub. by the International Musicological Society and the International Association of Music Libraries, Vol. A/I/1 (Kassel: Bärenreiter, 1971) and Vol. B II (Munich, Duisburg: Henle, 1964)

ROCHLITZ/FREUNDE. J. F. Rochlitz, ed., *Für Freunde der Tonkunst,* 4 vols. (Leipzig, 1824–32)

ROE. S. W. Roe, "The Keyboard Music of J.C. Bach." Ph.D. dissertation, Oxford, 1981

ROSE. J. M. Rose, ed., *Six Sonatas for Clavier.* Bryn Mawr, Pa.: Theodore Presser, 1973 (*FORTSETZUNG)

ROTH. H. Roth, ed., *30 Geistliche Lieder.* Leipzig: Peters, 1922 (item 686, Nos. 7, 9, 14–15, 30, 32, 34, 39, 44, 46, 48–49; item 696, Nos. 8, 12; item 721; item 733, Nos. 7, 9, 13, 20, 22, 36, 41; item 749, Nos. 2, 11, 13–14, 19, 29; item 752, Nos. 6, 29)

Sammlung verschiedener . . . Oden: See GRÄFE.

SASSE. D. Sasse, "Berlin," *Die Musik in Geschichte und Gegenwart,* I (Kassel, 1949–51)

Schaefer-Schmuck, K., "Thematisches Verzeichnis der Klavierwerke G. P. Telemanns," in her *Georg Philipp Telemann als Klavierkomponist* (Borna-Leipzig, 1934)

SCHENKER/BEITRAG. H. Schenker, *Ein Beitrag zur Ornamentik als Einführung zu Ph. E. Bachs Klavierwerken,* 2nd edn. (Vienna, 1908). Trans. Hedi Siegel and Carl Parrish in *The Music Forum,* IV (1976). See note for SCHENKER/KLAVIERWERKE.

SCHENKER/IMPROVISATION. _____, "Die Kunst der Improvisation," *Das Meisterwerk in der Musik,* Vol. I (Munich, 1925)

SCHENKER/KLAVIERWERKE. _____, ed., *Klavierwerke,* 2 vols. Vienna: Universal Edition, 1902 (items 130, 173, 186–187, 188 [incomplete], 208, 243–44, 245 [incomplete], 246–47, 268, 282 [incomplete]. A companion volume to SCHENKER/BEITRAG, which draws on it for examples—a fact that the reader of SCHENKER/BEITRAG must discover for himself

SCHERING/ORATORIUMS. A. Schering, *Geschichte des Oratoriums* (Leipzig, 1911), reprinted Hildesheim, 1966

SCHERING/REDENDE. _____, "C. Ph. E. Bach und das redende Prinzip in der Musik," *Jahrbuch der Musikbibliothek Peters*, XLV (1938), 13–29; also included in Schering's *Vom musikalischen Kunstwerk*, ed. F. Blume (Leipzig, 1949)

SCHIØRRING. N. Schiørring, ed., *Kirke-Melodierne til den 1778 udgangne Psalmebog*. Kiøbenhavn: N. Schiørring, 1781 (items 733/19, 843). Lit.: BUSCH, 222, 291

Schleswig-Holsteinischen Gesangbuch: See ZINCK.

SCHLEUNING. P. Schleuning, "Die Fantasie," *Das Musikwerk*, Vols. 42, 43, trans. A. C. Howie (Cologne, 1971) (uses items 225, 234, 300 as examples)

SCHMID/KAMMERMUSIK. E. F. Schmid, *Carl Philipp Emanuel Bach und seine Kammermusik* (Kassel, 1931)

SCHMID/MGG. _____, "C. Ph. E. Bach," *Die Musik in Geschichte und Gegenwart*, I (Kassel, 1949–51)

SCHMID/TRIOS. _____, ed., *Sechs Trios*. Kassel: Bärenreiter, 1952 (*ACCOMPANIED SONATAS II)

SCHMIEDER. W. Schmieder, *Thematisch-Systematisches Verzeichnis der Werke Johann Sebastian Bachs* (Leipzig, 1950)

SCHNAPPER. E. B. Schnapper, ed., *The British Union-Catalogue of Early Music Printed before the Year 1801* (London, 1957)

Schneider, C. A., "Thematischer Katalog der Instrumental-Sonaten von J. F. Fasch," in his *Johann Friedrich Fasch als Sonatenkomponist* (Cologne, 1936)

Schneider, M., "Thematisches Verzeichnis der musikalischen Werke der Familie Bach" [that is, only Heinrich, Johann Michael, and Johann Christoph Bach], *Bach-Jahrbuch*, IV (Leipzig, 1907), 103–77

SCHÜNEMANN. G. Schünemann, "Thematisches Verzeichnis" of J. C. F. Bach's works, *Denkmäler deutscher Tonkunst*, LVI (Leipzig, 1917)

SCHULENBERG. D. Schulenberg, communications to the author on CPEB's keyboard works

SCHULENBERG/INSTRUMENTAL. _____, *The Instrumental Music of Carl Philipp Emanuel Bach* (Ann Arbor, 1984)

SCHULZE. H.-J. Schulze, ed., *Bach-Documente*, III (Kassel, 1972). Supplement to *Johann Sebastian Bach Neue Ausgabe sämtlicher Werke*

SCHULZE/SCHREIBER. _____, "Der Schreiber 'Anonymous 400'—ein Schüler Johann Sebastian Bachs," *Bach-Jahrbuch* (1972), 104–17

SCHULZE/WADE. _____, review of *The Keyboard Concertos of Carl Philipp Emanuel Bach* by Rachel W. Wade, *Bach-Jahrbuch* (1984), 181–83

Sechs leichte Clavier-Sonaten: See *LEICHTE.

*SECHS NEUEN (= *Sechs neuen Sonatinen = Sechs neuen Clavier-Stücken = VI Sonatine nuove*): See *PROBESTÜCKE.

Sechs Sonaten, etc.: See *Sei Sonate*, etc.

*SEI CONCERTI. *Sei Concerti per il Cembalo concertato accompagnato da due Violini, Violetta e Basso, con due Corni e due Flauti per rinforza; dedicati all' Altezza Serenissima di Pietro, Duca regnante di Curlandia &c. &c., e composti da Carlo Filippo Emanuele Bach, Maestro di Capella di S.A.R.M. la Principessa Amalia de Prussia, Badessa di Quedlinburgo, e Direttore di Musica della Republica di Hamburgo. In Hamburgo, alle spese dell' Autore* [printing begun by G. L. Winter in Berlin and completed by J. G. I. Breitkopf in Leipzig]. 1772 (items 471–76; W. 43.). Lit.: HAMBURGER CORRESPONDENT, 30 Apr. 1771; 25 Apr., 12 Sept. 1772; CPEB/BREITKOPF, 14 Nov. 1772; BURNEY/STATE, 220; BITTER/BRÜDER, I, 205–08; HASE, 93; STEGLICH/HOMILIUS, 108; ULDALL, 47–48; GEIRINGER/BACH, 366; HAAG, 199–201; CRICKMORE, 228–30, 235–37, 239; STEVENS, 250–76; SUCHALLA/ORCHESTERSINFONIEN, 208–09; BERG, 1; WADE, 38, 49–50, 57–58, 123, 140, 149, 151

Sei Sonate, Six Sonatas, Six Sonates, Sechs Sonaten, etc. (early prints): See *ACCOMPANIED SONATAS II, *DAMENSONATEN, HUBERTY, *KENNER I, *LEICHTE, *PRUSSIAN SONATAS, *REPRISEN-SONATEN, *PROBESTÜCKE, *WÜRTTEMBERG SONATAS.

VI [Sei] *Sonatine nuove*: See *PROBESTÜCKE.

SELINGER-BARBER. R. Selinger-Barber, "Die Klavier-Fantasien Carl Philipp Emanuel Bachs." M. A. thesis, University of Hamburg, 1984

SERBIN. M. Serbin, "A C. P. E. Bach Mystery Story," *American Record Guide*, XXIV (September 1957), 7f.

SHEDLOCK. J. S. Shedlock, *The Pianoforte Sonata: Its Origin and Development* (London, 1885), reprinted with foreword by W. S. Newman (New York, 1964)

SIEGELE. U. Siegele, *Kompositionsweise und Bearbeitungstechnik in der Instrumentalmusik Johann Sebastian Bachs* (Stuttgart, 1975)

SIMON/B-A-C-H. J. Simon, "B-A-C-H," *Die Musik*, IX (Nov. 1909), 226–32

SIMON/MARCHES. E. Simon, ed., *6 Marches*. New York: E. B. Marks, 1948 (items 614–19; percussion added)

SIMON/MECHANISCHE. _____, *Mechanische Musikinstrumente früherer Zeiten und ihre Musik* (Wiesbaden, 1960)

SIMON/SONATAS. _____, ed., [six sonatas]. San Antonio: Southern, 1972 (items 516–21)

*SIX FUGUES. *Six fugues pour le piano-forte*. Bonn, Cologne: N. Simrock, n.d. (2nd mvt. of item 75.5, items 99–101, 101.5, 102). The known lit. gives no evidence that this print was authorized by CPEB.

Six Sonates . . . à l'usage des Dames: See *DAMENSONATEN.

SMITH 1968. C. Smith, "Music Manuscripts Lost during World War II," *The Book Collector*, XVII (Spring, 1968), 26–36

SMITH 1975. _____, "Tracking Down Original Scores Missing in the War," *Smithsonian*, VI (Dec. 1975), 86–93

Sonaten mit veränderten Reprisen: See *REPRISEN-SONATEN.

Staats- und gelehrte Zeitung: See HAMBURGER CORRESPONDENT.

STEGLICH/HOMILIUS. R. Steglich, "Karl Philipp Emanuel Bach und der Dresdner Kreuzkantor Gottfried August Homilius im Musikleben ihrer Zeit," *Bach-Jahrbuch*, XII (1915), 39–145

STEGLICH/PREUSSISCHE. _____, ed., *Preussische Sonaten*. Hannover: Nagel, 1927–28, reprinted New York: Kalmus, n.d. (*PRUSSIAN SONATAS)

STEGLICH/SYMPHONIES. _____, ed., *Vier Orchestersinfonien*. Leipzig: Breitkopf & Härtel, 1942, reprinted 1966 (*ORCHESTER-SINFONIEN; *Das Erbe deutscher Musik, Reichsdenkmale*, Band 18)

STEGLICH/WÜRTTEMBERGISCHE. _____, ed., *Württembergische Sonaten*. Hannover: Nagel, 1927–28, reprinted New York: Kalmus, n.d. (*WÜRTTEMBERG SONATAS)

STEVENS. J. R. Stevens, "The Keyboard Concertos of Carl Philipp Emanuel Bach." Ph.D. dissertation, Yale University, 1965

Stilz, E., *Die Berliner Klaviersonate zur Zeit Friedrichs des Grossen* (Saarbrücken, 1930)

*STURM I. *Herrn Christoph Christian Sturms, Hauptpastors an der Hauptkirche St. Petri und Scholarchen in Hamburg, geistliche Gesänge mit Melodien zum Singen bey dem Claviere vom Herrn Kapellmeister Carl Philipp Emanuel Bach, Musikdirektor in Hamburg.* Hamburg, bey Johann Henrich Herold [printed in Leipzig by J. G. I. Breitkopf], 1780. Reprinted 1781, 1782. (item 749; W. 197). Lit.: HAMBURGER CORRESPONDENT, 25 Apr., 22 Aug., 1 Sept., 1780; 30 Sept. 1786; BITTER/BRÜDER, II, 71–74; HASE, 97–98; BÜCKEN, 170; GEIRINGER/BACH, 372; BUSCH, 88, 138–45, 294, 296–98, 302, 310, 317–19, 331–32, 374, 384, 396, Anh. 26–31; OTTENBERG, 213

*STURM II. *Herrn Christoph Christian Sturms, Hauptpastors an der Hauptkirche St. Petri und Scholarchen in Hamburg, geistliche Gesänge mit Melodien zum Singen bey dem Claviere vom Herrn Kapellmeister Carl Philipp Emanuel Bach, Musikdirektor in Hamburg. Zweyte Sammlung.* Hamburg, bey Johann Henrich Herold [printed in Leipzig by J. G. I. Breitkopf], 1781. Reprinted 1792. (item 752; W. 198). Lit.: HAMBURGER CORRESPONDENT, 29 June 1781; 29 Nov., 7 Dec. 1782; BÜCKEN, 170; GEIRINGER/BACH, 372; BUSCH, 138–45, 294, 296–98, 302, 310, 317–19, 331–32, 374, 384, Anh. 32–37; WADE, 53; OTTENBERG, 213

SUCHALLA/ORCHESTERSINFONIEN. E. Suchalla, *Die Orchestersinfonien Carl Philipp Emanuel Bachs nebst einem thematischen Verzeichnis seiner Orchesterwerke* (Augsburg, 1968)

SUCHALLA/RISM. _____, "Bach, Carl Philipp Emanuel," *International Inventory of Musical Sources* (RISM), Vol. A/I/1: *Einzeldrucke vor 1800* (Kassel, 1971)

TERRY, C. S. C. S. Terry, *John Christian Bach* (London, 1929), including a thematic catalogue of J. C. Bach's works. Reprinted with additions by H. C. Robbins Landon (London, 1967)

TERRY, M. M. Terry, "C. P. E. Bach and J. J. H. Westphal—A Clarification," *Journal of the American Musicological Society*, XXII (Spring, 1969), 106–15

Thieme, G. E. H., "Werkverzeichnis" in her *Daniel Gottlob Türk (1750–1813)* (Borna, Leipzig, 1936)

TONSTÜCKE. *Tonstücke für das Clavier vom Herrn C.P.E. Bach und andern classischen Musikern.* Berlin: Wever, 1762 (taken over by J. G. I. Breitkopf in Leipzig). 2nd edn. 1774 under the title *C.P.E. Bach, Nichelmann und Händels Sonaten und Fugen fürs Clavier. Zweyte Auflage* (items 55, 100). Lit.: HASE, 88

*TROIS RONDEAUX. *Trois Rondeaux pour le Clavecin ou Pianoforte . . . .* Vienne, Magazin de Musique, [c. 1791] (items 288, 283, 290). The known lit. gives no evidence that this (posthumous) print had been authorized by CPEB.

*TROIS SONATES. *Oeuvres posthumes de C.P.E. Bach. Trois Sonates pour le Clavecin ou le Piano-Forte.* A Berlin, de l'imprimerie et dans le magasin de musique de Rellstab [1792] (items 121, 51, 21; W. 266). The known lit. gives no evidence that this print had been authorized by CPEB.

III [Trois] Sonates pour le Clavecin: See WINTERSCHMIDT.

ULDALL. H. Uldall, *Das Klavierkonzert der Berliner Schule* (Leipzig, 1928)

UNTERHALTUNGEN. *Unterhaltungen*, 10 vols. Hamburg: M. C. Bock, 1766–70 (items 709–21)

*VERSCHIEDEN. *Clavierstücke verschiedener Art von Carl Philipp Emanuel Bach. Erste Sammlung.* Berlin, 1765 bey George Ludewig Winter (items 190, 144, 165, 145, 166, 693, 179, 146, 167, 147, 168, 694, 191, 695, 148, 169–70, 149, 101.5; W. 112). Lit.: HAMBURGER CORRESPONDENT, 4 Apr. 1770; BITTER/BRÜDER, I, 88–89; VRIESLANDER/BACH, 169–70; BUSCH, 76–77; see also Critical Notes in BERG/FACSIMILE.

Verzeichnis von den Musicalien . . . Voss: See VOSS/MUSICALIEN.

VIELERLEY. C. P. E. Bach, ed., *Musikalisches Vielerley*. Hamburg: M. C. Bock, 1770 (items 69, 155, 210, 214–25, 227, 240–41, 381, 598, 698). Lit.: HAMBURGER CORRESPONDENT, 10 Feb., 4 Apr. 1770; *Hamburger Unterhaltungen*, 10 (1770), 73; HILLER/NACHRICHTEN, 1770, 5,

56; BITTER/BRÜDER, I, 202–05; BUSCH, 101–02, 315, 382; WADE, 28, 39; ROE, 411; OTTENBERG, 170. See the general description under <u>ALLERLEY</u> in this bibliography.

Vierstimmige . . . Choralgesänge: See <u>KÜHNAU I, KÜHNAU II</u>.

Vollständige Sammlung der Melodien: See <u>ZINCK</u>.

<u>VOSS/1774/1775/1776/1778/1781/1782</u>. [J. H. von Voss, ed.,] *Göttinger Musen-Almanach fürs Jahr 1774*, Göttingen: J. C. Diederich, 1774 (items 731–32); [idem], *Göttinger Musen-Almanach fürs Jahr 1775* [another title of the same work: *Poetische Blumenlese auf das Jahr 1775*], Göttingen, Gotha: J. C. Diederich, 1775 (items 736–37); *Musen-Almanach, herausgegeben von Voss*, Hamburg: Berenberg, 1776 (items 738, 739.5); ibid., Hamburg, C. E. Bohn, 1778 (items 746–47); ibid., Hamburg: C. E. Bohn, 1781 (items 750–51); ibid., Hamburg: C. E. Bohn, 1782 (items 753–54). Lit. on these Voss edns. in general: SCHMID/KAMMERMUSIK, 47–48; BUSCH, 287–88, 294, 310, 316, 385, 399–400. Lit. on the 1774 edn.: BUSCH, 188–24. On the 1775 edn.: BUSCH, 123–29. On the 1776 edn.: HAMBURGER CORRESPONDENT, 7 Nov. 1775; BUSCH, 129–30. On the 1778 edn.: BUSCH, 132–35. On the 1781 edn.: HAMBURGER CORRESPONDENT, 4 Oct. 1780; BUSCH, 135–37. On the 1782 edn.: HAMBURGER CORRESPONDENT, 1 Sept. 1781; BUSCH, 135, 137–38

VOSS/BRIEFE. J. H. von Voss, *Briefe von Johann Heinrich Voss nebst erläuternden Beilagen*, ed. A. Voss (Halberstadt, 1829–33)

Voss, J. H. Von, *Musik-Catalog. Entheilt: Die Thema's der Partituren zur Vocal- auch Vocal mit Instrumental-Musik. nach alphabetische Ordnung*, ms. in D-ddr Bds

VOSS/MUSICALIEN. *Verzeichnis von den Musicalien des Koenigl. Würkl. Geheimen Etats . . . Kriegs . . . und dirigenten Ministre, Herrn Freiheren von Voss, Excellenz*, ms. in D-ddr Bds

VRIESLANDER/BACH. O. Vrieslander, *Philipp Emanuel Bach* (Munich: 1923)

VRIESLANDER/KLEINE. _____, ed., *Kleine Stücke für Klavier*. Hannover: Nagel, 1930, reprinted New York: International, 1947 (items 54, 144, 146, 148–49, 166, 168, 170, 214–16, 218, 220–24, 241, 292–97)

VRIESLANDER/KURZE. _____, ed., *Kurze und leichte Klavierstücke*. Vienna: Universal Edition, 1914 (*<u>KURZE I, II</u>)

VRIESLANDER/LEICHTE. _____, ed., *Vier leichte Sonaten*. Hannover: Nagel, 1932, reprinted Kassel: Bärenreiter, 1959 (items 21, 42, 56, 143)

VRIESLANDER/LIEDER. _____, ed., *Lieder und Gesänge*. Munich: Dreimaskenverlag, 1922 (item 686, Nos. 8, 24, 34, 45, 49, 53; items 693–95, 697, 710, 731–32, 736–38, 739.5; item 749, Nos. 2, 7, 13, 19, 21, 29; items 750–51, 753–54). Valuable introduction

VRIESLANDER/THEORETIKER. _____, "Philipp Emanuel Bach als Theoretiker," in *Von neuer Musik*, ed. H. Grues (Cologne: 1925), I, 222–79

WADE. R. W. Wade, *The Keyboard Concertos of Carl Philipp Emanuel Bach* (Ann Arbor, 1981)

WADE/AMS. _____, "Determining the Authenticity of Works Attributed to Carl Philipp Emanuel Bach," paper read at the annual meeting of the American Musicological Society, Minneapolis, October 1978

WADE/FOUND. _____, "Newly Found Works of Carl Philipp Emanuel Bach," *Early Music* (in press)

WADE/JAMS. _____, communciation in *Journal of the American Musicological Society*, XXX (Spring 1977), 162–64

WALTHER/DUETTE. K. Walther, ed., *Zehn leichte Duette für zwei Flöten*. Frankfurt am Main: Zimmermann, 1971 (item 600, Nos. 4, 7, 10; item 628, Nos. II, IV, VIII, X; item 635, Nos. 22–23, 25)

WALTHER/FLÖTENUHR. _____, "C. Ph. E. Bachs Kleine Stücke für die Flötenuhr," *Zeitschrift für Schulmusik*, 6 (1933), Nos. 6–7

WALTHER/SONATEN. _____, ed., *Vier Sonaten für Flöte und Klavier*. Leipzig: Breitkopf & Härtel, 1955 (items 505–06, 508–09)

WALTHER/STÜCKE. _____, ed., *Kleine Stücke für die Flötenuhr*. Wolfenbüttel: Kallmeyer, n.d. (portions of item 635)

WELLESZ–STERNFELD/CONCERTO. E. Wellesz and F. W. Sternfeld (using material provided by J. LaRue), "The Concerto," Vol. VII of *The New Oxford History of Music*, ed. E. Wellesz and F. W. Sternfeld (London, 1973), 434–502

WELLESZ–STERNFELD/SYMPHONY. E. Wellesz and F. W. Sternfeld (using material provided by J. LaRue), "The Early Symphony," Vol. VII of *The New Oxford History of Music*, ed. E. Wellesz and F. W. Sternfeld (London, 1973), 366–433

WELTER. F. Welter, "Die Musikbibliothek der Sing-Akademie zu Berlin," *Sing-Akademie zu Berlin: Festschrift zum 175jährigen Bestehen*, herausgegeben von Werner Bollert (Berlin, 1966), 33–47

Wernigerödischen Lieder: See <u>MELODIEN</u>.

WESTPHAL/NACHRICHTEN. J. J. H. Westphal, compiler, *Gesammlete Nachrichten von dem Leben und den Werken des Herrn Carl Philipp Emanuel Bach . . . nebst einer Sammlung verschiedener Recensionen und Beurteilungen seiner herausgegebenen Werke*, ms. Fétis 4779 in B Br

WESTPHAL/THÉMATIQUE. J. J. H. Westphal, *Catalogue thématique des oeuvres de Ch. Ph. Emm. Bach*, ms. Fétis 5218 in B Br

WHITEHEAD. P. J. P. Whitehead, "The Lost Berlin Manuscripts," *Music Library Association Notes*, XXXIII (Sept. 1976), 7–15; idem, "The Berlin Manuscripts Recovered," XXXVI (March 1980), 773–76

WIEN-CLAUDI. H. Wien-Claudi, *Zum Liedschaffen Carl Philipp Emanuel Bachs* (Reichenberg, 1928)

WINTERSCHMIDT. *III Sonates pour le Clavecin, composées par Mrs. C.P.E. Bach, C. S. Binder et C. Fasch*. Nuremberg: Winterschmidt, n.d. (item 134)

Wöchentliche Nachrichten: See HILLER/NACHRICHTEN.

WOLF. J. Wolf, *Zur Geschichte der Musikabteilung der [Berliner] Staatsbibliothek* (Berlin, 1930)

WOLFF. C. Wolff et al., "Johann Sebastian Bach," *The New Grove Dictionary of Music and Musicians*, ed. Stanley Sadie (London, 1980)

WOTQUENNE/CONSERVATOIRE. A. Wotquenne, *Catalogue de la Bibliothèque du Conservatoire Royal de Musique de Bruxelles*, 5 vols. (Brussels, 1889–1914)

WOTQUENNE/THÉMATIQUE. _____, *Catalogue thématique des oeuvres de Charles Philippe Emmanuel Bach (1714–1788)* (Leipzig, 1905); some copies entitled *Thematisches Verzeichnis der Werke von Carl Philipp Emanuel Bach (1714–1788)*. Reprinted under the later title (Wiesbaden, 1964, reprinted 1972)

WÜRTTEMBERG SONATAS. Sei Sonate per Cembalo dedicate all' Altezza Serenissima de Carlo Eugenio Duca di Wirtemberg e Teckh . . . Composto da Carlo Filippo Emanuele Bach, Musico di Camera de S.M. il Rè di Prussia, Ec. Ec. Opera II^{da}. Alle Spese di Giovanni Ulrico Haffner, Intagliatore in rame e Virtuoso di Liuto in Norimberga [1744] (items 30–31, 33, 32, 34, 36; W. 49). Other early edns. of the set: Nürnberg: Johann Wilhelm Windter, n.d. [possibly early than the Haffner edn.; see HOFFMANN-ERBRECHT/HAFFNER]; Wien und Pesth, Bureau des arts et d'industrie, n.d.; Berlin, Amsterdam: Johann Julius Hummel, n.d. Other lit.: AMZ, XII (1809), 193–96; BITTER/BRÜDER, I, 54–57; STEGLICH/HOMILIUS, 64–65; SCHMID/KAMMERMUSIK, 144; BEURMANN/KLAVIERSONATEN, 33; GEIRINGER/BACH, 355; BARFORD/KEYBOARD, 17; RADCLIFFE, 585; COHEN, 111; BERG, 47, 67, 96, 144; WADE, 59–60; ROE, 111; see also Critical Notes in BERG/FACSIMILE. The known lit. gives no evidence that the Bureau des arts or Hummel prints were authorized by CPEB.

ZINCK. B. F. Zinck, ed., *Vollständige Sammlung der Melodien . . . des neuen allgemeinen Schleswig-Holsteinischen Gesangbuchs*. Leipzig: im Verlag der mit dem Gesangsbuchs-Privilegio begnadigten Piorum Corporum, 1785 (item 844). Lit.: BUSCH, 282, 384–85

ZWEY TRIO. Zwey Trio, das erste für zwo Violinen und Bass, das zweyte für 1. Querflöte, 1. Violine und Bass; bey welchen beyden aber die eine von den Oberstimmen auch auf dem Flügel gespielet werden kan: verfertiget und Sr. Erlaucht dem Hochgebohrnen Grafen und Herrn, Herrn Wilhelm des heiligen Römischen Reichs . . . in Unterthänigkeit zugeeignet von Carl Philipp Emanuel Bach, König. Preussischen Camer Musicus. Nürnberg in Verlegung Balth. Schmids seel. Wittib. [1751] (items 578–79; W. 161). Lit.: WADE, 96

ZWEYTE FORTSETZUNG. Zweyte Fortsetzung von Sechs Sonaten fürs Clavier. Berlin, gedruckt und zu finden bey George Ludewig Winter, 1763 (items 50, 142, 158, 37, 161, 129; W. 52). Another edn.: London: William Randall, n.d. See *REPRISEN-SONATEN. Lit.: HAMBURGER CORRESPONDENT, 4 Apr. 1770; BITTER/BRÜDER, I, 78–79; VRIESLANDER/BACH, 170; RADCLIFFE, 587–88. The known lit. gives no evidence that the Randall print was authorized by CPEB.

Zwölf geistliche Oden und Lieder als ein Anhang: See *GELLERT-ANHANG.

ZWÖLF KLEINE I. Zwölf kleine Stücke mit zwey und drey Stimmen für die Flöte oder Violin und das Clavier, von Carl Philipp Emanuel Bach. Berlin, 1758. Gedruckt und zu finden bey George Ludewig Winter. Reprinted 1759. (item 600; W. 81) Another early edn.: Berlin: C. F. Rellstab, 1792. Lit.: HAMBURGER CORRESPONDENT, 4 Apr. 1770. The known lit. gives no evidence that the Rellstab print was authorized by CPEB.

ZWÖLF KLEINE II. Zwölf zwey- und dreystimmige kleine Stücke für die Flöte oder Violine und das Clavier vom Herrn Capellmeister Bach in Hamburg. Im Verlag bei Friedrich Schönemann, Kupferstecher in Hamburg [1770] (item 628; W. 82). Lit.: GEIRINGER/CHAMBER, 535